We Are Not Animals

"Rizzo-Martinez confines his study to Mission Santa Cruz, but his story has broader relevance.... His effort to identify Native voices and motives in colonial sources is not only fitting for a book on the history of Native people but also imperative for understanding a colonial institution where Native people were always in the majority. Beyond its contributions to mission historiography, in its emphasis on internally dynamic and adaptive Native politics, Rizzo-Martinez's work bridges the era of Spanish colonization with the later nineteenth century and offers a useful interpretive model for future scholarship on Native survival into the twentieth century."

—Khal Schneider, *Native American and Indigenous Studies*

"Deeply researched and fresh in conception, methodology, and breadth, *We Are Not Animals* is a major contribution to the study of Native California and the missions.... In a singular and exceptional way among historians, Martin Rizzo-Martinez identifies Native people by name, family, and tribe [as] he follows the survivors of the Amah Mutsun nation through the American genocide of the late nineteenth century."

—Lisbeth Haas, professor emeritus of history at
the University of California, Santa Cruz

"Rizzo-Martinez unearths Native voices from the archive to provide an overdue historical account of the Indigenous experience in Santa Cruz and surrounding region. By decentering colonial institutions like the missions and non-Native voices, Rizzo-Martinez effectively places Indigenous space and knowledge at the center of this study, a valuable model for future scholars of the Native experience in California."

—Yve Chavez (Tongva), coeditor of *Visualizing Genocide:
Indigenous Interventions in Art, Archives, and Museums*

"Both heartbreaking and inspiring, *We Are Not Animals* is a history of destruction as well as of California Indian survival against great odds. Rizzo-Martinez has written a deeply researched study of Indigenous peoples in Santa Cruz and surrounding areas that improves our understanding of Native American experiences in California as a whole."

—Benjamin Madley, author of *An American Genocide: The United
States and the California Indian Catastrophe, 1846–1873*

"*We Are Not Animals* is an important book in California mission studies, deploying established sources and a significant, frequently overlooked one—confirmation records—to reveal Indian community building inside the mission to which Franciscans were oblivious. Rizzo-Martinez effectively demonstrates how Indians exploited the mission system for their own ends and carries the story through early California statehood, challenging previous interpretations that missionization had extinguished Indian culture. *We Are Not Animals* marks the arrival of a sophisticated scholar to the conversations about early California history."

—James A. Sandos, Farquhar Professor of the American Southwest, Emeritus, University of Redlands

We Are Not Animals

Indigenous Politics of Survival, Rebellion, and Reconstitution in Nineteenth-Century California

MARTIN RIZZO-MARTINEZ

Foreword by
Amah Mutsun Tribal Chair
Valentin Lopez

University of Nebraska Press | Lincoln

© 2022 by the Board of Regents of the University of Nebraska

All rights reserved
The University of Nebraska Press is part of a land-grant institution with campuses and programs on the past, present, and future homelands of the Pawnee, Ponca, Otoe-Missouria, Omaha, Dakota, Lakota, Kaw, Cheyenne, and Arapaho Peoples, as well as those of the relocated Ho-Chunk, Sac and Fox, and Iowa Peoples. ∞

First Nebraska paperback printing: 2024
Library of Congress Cataloging-in-Publication Data
Names: Rizzo-Martinez, Martin, author.
Title: We are not animals: indigenous politics of survival, rebellion, and reconstitution in nineteenth-century California / Martin Rizzo-Martinez.
Description: Lincoln: University of Nebraska Press, 2022. | Includes bibliographical references and index.
Identifiers: LCCN 2021015301
ISBN 9781496219626 (hardback)
ISBN 9781496238757 (paperback)
ISBN 9781496230324 (epub)
ISBN 9781496230331 (pdf)
Subjects: LCSH: Santa Cruz Mission—History. | Ohlone Indians—History. | Ohlone Indians—Missions—California—Santa Cruz—History. | Yokuts Indians—History. | Indians, Treatment of—California—Santa Cruz. | Santa Cruz (Calif.)—History—19th century. | Santa Cruz County (Calif.)—Genealogy. | BISAC: SOCIAL SCIENCE / Ethnic Studies / American / Native American Studies | HISTORY / United States / State & Local / West (AK, CA, CO, HI, ID, MT, NV, UT, WY)
Classification: LCC E99.C8744 R59 2022 | DDC 979.4/01—dc23

LC record available at https://lccn.loc.gov/2021015301

Set in Monotype Bulmer by Laura Buis.

This book is dedicated to the memory of the tens of thousands of Indigenous individuals and families who perished in the California missions and as a result of successive colonial invasions; to the survivors who persevered thanks to their ingenuity and tenacity; and to their many descendants who are still here today because their ancestors gave everything to survive against impossible odds. It is my hope that this book contributes to a better understanding of the history of the people who called these lands home for thousands of years prior to colonization.

A story also grows. It never remains the same. Though one wants to tell it the same as one heard it, one always puts in a word more or less. And there are many people in this world who are great gossips, they fix up a story very nice, even if they don't know it. And still more so if it is a story of a religion, they always want to make the people believe more. And with time it changes more, so that when a story has passed through the lives of many people surely it is already impossible to tell what story it is, for it is already changed fundamentally, and it is not recognized as the same story that it was earlier. And when the story is written or made into a book, it still is a story and nothing more, they only took the story which was growing, more or less, or took the turns that very various people had given it and gathered them together pruning them off to make a single book. They say that when the story is written it is different, but to me it is the same, it is still a story.

> —Maria Ascención Solórsano de Cervantes
> to John P. Harrington, 1929

Contents

List of Illustrations	xi
Foreword by Valentin Lopez	xiii
Acknowledgments	xvii
Introduction	1
1. First Were Taken the Children, and Then the Parents Followed	23
2. The Diverse Nations within the Mission	69
3. The Mission of Padre Killers	109
4. Chief Malimin (Coleto) and the Rise of the Yokuts	143
5. Not Finding Anything Else to Appropriate	175
6. Genocide and American Fantasies of Ancient Indians	203
7. They Won't Try to Kill You If They Think You're Already Dead	227
Conclusion	255
Notes	269
Bibliography	433
Index	467

Illustrations

CHARTS

1. Age at death of mission-born people, 1791–1831 — 112
2. Population in 1812 at Mission Santa Cruz, by language — 113
3. Incoming Yokuts, by gender — 168
4. Burials by gender at Mission Santa Cruz, 1813–34 — 168
5. Marriages between Awaswas, Mutsun, and Yokuts at Mission Santa Cruz — 169

FIGURES
Following page 174

1. Modified ceramic gaming pieces from Central California missions
2. Drawing of Indigenous people gaming at Mission Dolores (San Francisco)
3. Macedonio Lorenzana and Jose Joaquin Juarez
4. Justiniano Roxas, likely named Yrachis
5. Justiniano Roxas
6. Justiniano Roxas, from Elliot's *Illustrations of Santa Cruz County*
7. Jose "Cache" Lend
8. Rafael "Tahoe" Castro
9. Drawing of the Ruins of the Old Mission Church of Santa Cruz, 1859
10. Possibly Maria Filomena, taken in the early 1900s
11. Native American participants in Zayante Indian Conference, 1907

MAPS

1. Indigenous landscape of Po Pe Lo Ut Chom
2. Tribal territories
3. Indigenous tribes impacted by Mission Santa Cruz
4. Approximate locations of Yokuts villages
5. Westside Santa Cruz, ca. 1840

TABLES

1. Number of baptisms, by tribe
2. Livestock reported near Mission Santa Cruz, 1791–97
3. Agricultural yields at Mission Santa Cruz, 1791–97
4. 1796 Mission Santa Cruz baptisms, by month
5. Baptisms, births, burials, and populations of Indigenous Christianized Indians
6. Mission Santa Cruz baptisms before 1797, by tribe
7. Percentage of Awaswas speakers among overall Mission Santa Cruz population
8. Agricultural crops planted at Mission Santa Cruz
9. Livestock count in Mission Santa Cruz pastures, 1791–1810
10. Missionaries assigned to Mission Santa Cruz
11. Fugitive deaths by 1810, by region
12. Indigenous alcaldes, 1796–1811
13. Indigenous regidores, 1797–99
14. Mission Santa Cruz population totals, 1791–1812
15. Conspirators arrested in connection with assassination
16. Percentage of Awaswas tribal members still alive in 1812
17. Change in percentage of Awaswas-speaking tribes, 1799 vs. 1812
18. Most frequent Indigenous padrinos at Mission Santa Cruz
19. Conspirators arrested and sentenced, with burial dates and locations
20. Population of Santa Cruz County, 1791–1860
21. Mission Santa Cruz demographics, 1813–34
22. Identification of Yokuts baptisms, 1813–34
23. Alcaldes elected, 1796–1831
24. Occupations of men and women in 1825
25. Indigenous individuals' jobs, 1834 census
26. Indigenous overseers, 1834 census
27. Distribution of Indigenous people
28. 1841 Census of Indigenous communities
29. Overall populations, including "Indians"
30. Family of Meregildo and Maria Agueda

Foreword

VALENTIN LOPEZ

My name is Valentin Lopez, and I am the chair of the Amah Mutsun Tribal Band. Our tribe is composed of the descendants of the Indigenous peoples taken to Missions San Juan Bautista and Santa Cruz in Central California.

The true history of California missions has never been told. In 1820 the last *padre presidente* of the California mission system, Friar Mariano Payeras, wrote to his superiors in Mexico City that Alta California had been "deserted and depopulated of Indians within a century of its discovery and conquest by the Spaniards." In his words the missionary priests had "baptized them, administered the sacraments to them and buried them." Payeras sought a better explanation that the Franciscans could use as an alibi to "shelter us from slander and sarcasm," when the terrible impacts of the missions in Alta California were looked back upon.[1]

To this day, in elementary schools and mission museums throughout California, you will be told that the Indians came to the missions voluntarily—the Indians came to find a better life, the Indians came to learn agriculture, or the Indians came to find God. These are all lies.

Growing up, I learned from our tribal elders that Mission Santa Cruz was the most brutal of all twenty-one California missions and that the life expectancy after arriving at the mission was less than two years. I heard stories of a sadistic priest who enjoyed whipping and torturing the Indians, oftentimes bringing the Indians to near death. I learned later that his name was Friar Andrés Quintana. As a youth, I heard that the Indians strangled and killed this priest, crushing his testicles in the process. We believed there was a very specific payback message in this act.

The Spanish and Franciscans believed Indian culture and spirituality had nothing of value to offer. They acted as if Indians did not have souls and therefore were not human beings. Because of this, when the Indians were enslaved, whipped, raped, and killed, it wasn't a sin. Approximately thirty tribes were taken to Mission Santa Cruz, and to my knowledge my lineage is the only one that has survived to the present day.

As our tribe continues a process of truth telling, we uncover lost details of our family histories and stories. Recently, I learned that although I have ancestors who lived at Mission Santa Cruz and another ancestor is recognized as the last speaker of the Awaswas language, they do not descend from Awaswas territory (the traditional territory of the Indians who lived in the vicinity of Santa Cruz). Upon learning that our tribe may not have direct ties to Awaswas territory, we have made great effort to be transparent about this new information.

Not only has the true history of the California mission period never been told; the true history of the Mexican and American periods in California has never been told either. All three periods of brutal colonization included efforts to destroy and dominate California Indian culture, spirituality, environments, and humanity. In 1900 the population of California Indians had decreased by over 96 percent from the time of first contact.[2] Many tribes completely disappeared.

Often when I'm speaking to the public about our tribe, I'll ask: "How were our ancestors supposed to teach their children to be happy, to know how to love, to have confidence and optimism? How could our ancestors teach their children to fulfill their sacred obligation to take care of Mother Earth and all living things? How could they learn their ceremonies, learn how to take care of their food, medicine, and basketry plants when every day was a struggle for their survival?"

During mission times our ancestors couldn't teach these sacred and self-esteem-building qualities to their children. Parents were often forcibly separated from their children and threatened with violence, restricting important intergenerational relationships. These conditions continued for over one hundred years and through many generations. As a consequence, our people have suffered from historic trauma, which has resulted in addiction, suicide, depression, poverty, and incarceration.

In 2011 our tribe began holding bimonthly wellness meetings to address this trauma. We have learned at our meetings that to heal from historic trauma, it's important that the truth of our tragic history be told. For this reason our tribe is immensely grateful to Dr. Martin Rizzo-Martinez for his research on Mission Santa Cruz, his doctoral work, and this book, *We Are Not Animals*. We appreciate that Martin worked closely with our tribal historian, Ed Ketchum, to incorporate key additional information from our tribal oral histories into this text.

Martin shows how historians can play an important role in telling truthful history, supporting Native communities, and contributing to the healing process of a tribe that has suffered generations of historic trauma.

Our tribe is appalled by the way the State of California and the Catholic Church ignore true history, glorifying and honoring devastating falsehoods while promoting the missions as idyllic tourist destinations for economic gain. Today many restaurants, hotels, museums, and other enterprises in California benefit from these harmful narratives.

Throughout California there are many symbols that are intended to celebrate the mission period, such as the ubiquitous El Camino Real mission bell markers and statues of Junípero Serra, the founder of the California mission system. To our tribal citizens these symbols are constant reminders of the near-total extermination of our ancestors in an attempt to erase our Native culture, spirituality, and environments. As our tribe speaks out against these symbols of destruction, domination, and genocide and advocates for their removal from public displays, Martin has stood alongside us in support.

Over the strong objections of numerous California tribes, including ours, the Catholic Church canonized Junípero Serra in 2015. By granting sainthood to Serra, the church effectively declared that the actions Serra took to destroy and dominate Indigenous culture, spirituality, and environments were saintly and worthy of emulation by those who want entry into heaven. As the accounts in this book clearly demonstrate, the behavior and ideology of those who founded and presided over the missions was anything but saintly.

Ascención Solórsano, an important leader of our tribe who passed away in 1929, had a saying that went, "A lie is a lie until the truth arrives." It is time for the truth of mission history to be told.

Acknowledgments

This book has benefited greatly from the contributions, critiques, and suggestions offered generously by mentors, friends, and colleagues. Many conversations and collaborations have contributed to the conception and writing of the histories contained herein, although all mistakes, errors, and misunderstandings are of my own doing.

I have been extremely fortunate to have many wonderful advisors and mentors along the way. This book would not have been written without the help of each of them. First and foremost, I'm grateful for the feedback and guidance of my mentor and good friend Beth Haas. Her guidance, constructive criticisms, and enthusiasm have greatly shaped my own growth and work over the years. I have also been fortunate to work closely with Cliff Trafzer, who inspires me with his commitment to making academic study relevant today through his work with contemporary Native communities. Amy Lonetree, who I've been fortunate to have as a mentor for many years, has always encouraged me to write about the hard truths of colonialism. Matthew O'Hara has challenged me to investigate the larger colonial context of my project. Ben Madley offered incredibly thoughtful feedback through his unofficial "postdoc." Mark Hylkema generously offered his many insights and deep knowledge, helping me to gain a better sense of these lands and histories. I am excited to work together on our forthcoming book project about the Quiroste. A special thank you to the late great Randy Milliken, who generously shared his research and insights and patiently responded to my many questions. I am especially grateful for my teacher, mentor, and dear friend Stan Rushworth, whose early encouragement helped me to have the confidence to pursue these questions and ultimately to write this book.

I am greatly indebted to Indigenous Californian friends and colleagues who have helped me to understand Indigenous perspectives while challenging my colonial assumptions. I'm grateful for all that I continue to learn from my friend and Amah Mutsun tribal chair Val Lopez. Amah Mutsun tribal historian Ed Ketchum took the time to read through, offer critique, and share his insights and deep knowledge of this history, generously responding to my many inquiries. I am inspired by the exciting work of Amah Mutsun scholars Julissa Lopez and Alexii Segona. I continue to learn from the teachings of friends and colleagues within the Bay Area Indigenous community: Gregg Castro, Corrina Gould, Patrick Orozco, Anne Marie Sayers, and Kanyon Sayers-Roods. A special thank-you to Caroline Ward and Kagen Holland for their inspiration and friendship. I learned so much from their courage and perseverance and am grateful to them for inviting me to be a part of their Walk for the Ancestors. I have learned a lot from activists like Cat Wilder and Malia Valentine and the Santa Cruz Indigenous Solidarity group, who continue to do great work.

I have also benefited and been inspired by the work and feedback of many scholars at the University of California, Santa Cruz (UCSC), including Pedro Castillo, Jon Daehnke, Greg O'Malley, and Eric Porter. I am also grateful for the colleagues I worked with through UCSC, many of whom offered important feedback and critiques along the way, including Natalie Baloy, Nick Barron, Samantha Williams, and Dustin Wright. I have been fortunate to work with and participate in conference panels with colleagues Katie Keliiaa, Andrew Shaler, and Amanda Wixon, all of whose work I greatly admire. I have learned much from my friend Rick Flores, who helped me to better understand Indigenous plants and traditional ecological knowledge (TEK). I am grateful to Melanie Mayer, who so frequently helped to alert me to many documents and insights along the way. A special thank-you to Rebecca Hernandez and Tsim Schneider for their friendship and insights, both from whom I continue to learn so much.

I am grateful for the support from my publishers at the University of Nebraska Press, including Heather Stauffer, Ann Baker, and copyeditor Elizabeth Gratch, and especially to Matt Bokovoy, who generously offered extremely insightful feedback and support from day one. I am indebted to Stella D'Oro, who has generously and patiently helped to make the maps, charts, and figures found throughout this book, and to Wyatt Young for his help with the book index. I have learned much from the engaging writing style of Boyd Cothran and am grateful for his support and friendship.

Thank you to Anastasiia Cherygova and Erica Jomphe for generously helping with French translations. This book has benefited from the friendship and feedback from Santa Cruz historians Traci Bliss, Aaron Brick, Sangye Hawke, and Dean Silvers.

I have been fortunate to receive financial support generously offered by numerous institutions along the way, without which this book would not be possible. Thank you to those that have believed in my work and supported my research. Thank you to the University of California Chancellor's Postdoctoral Fellowship and to Kimberly Adkinson and Mark Lawson. Thank you to the folks involved in the Critical Mission Studies Grant, including Charlene Villasenor Black, Ross Frank, Jennifer Hughes, and Renya Ramirez.

My research has taken me to numerous archives, and my work has been made possible by the assistance of many wonderful archivists. Luisa Haddad, Nicolas Meriwether, and Elisabeth Remak-Honnef at the McHenry Special Collections aided me greatly with their knowledge of the extensive collections at UCSC. Monica Orozco helped me on my numerous visits to the collections at the Santa Bárbara Mission Archive-Library. Thank you to Theresa Salazar and the Bancroft Collections and to Jeffrey Burns and the collections at the San Francisco Archdiocese. Father Carl Faria kindly directed me to countless resources held within the archives of the Monterey Archdiocese and generously responded to my many inquiries. Thank you to Marla Novo for help with the archives at the Santa Cruz Museum of Art and History. A special thank-you to Charlene Duval, Rob Edwards, and the Edna Kimbro Archives. In many ways my work follows in the steps taken years ago by Kimbro; reading through her notes was confirmation that I was on the right path. Thank you to the folks in the California wing of the Archivo General de la Nación. I am grateful for the help from my landlord, translator, and guide during my research in Mexico City, Herzonia Yáñez.

Many dear friends and family have also helped to support me in my work, either directly or indirectly. A very special thank-you to my copyeditor Denise Leto, who improved upon my writing tremendously. I've been blessed to share ideas with and hear feedback from friends Kathy Bisbee, Jon Bodnar, Homayun Etemadi, Sandino Gomez, Marc-Éddy Loriston, Daniel Stonebloom, Phoenix Toews, and Tiffany Wong. I've been blessed with the support of wonderful family—the Hovises, Martinezes, and Rizzos—and am especially inspired by my nieces and nephew. A special thank-you to my dad for sharing your love of history and inspiring me with our family stories of early colonial New Mexico. A very special thank-you to my mom for teaching me through example to see the world through a lens of compassion, kindness, and generosity. Thank you to my little Olive and Mouse, who've been by my side or on my lap through much of the writing, editing, and rewriting process. And most of all, to the love of my life, Lisa, who constantly inspires me by her strength, courage, and great capacity for love. You bring such love and joy into my life. I am forever grateful.

We Are Not Animals

Introduction

**How They Killed a Serpent That Lived
in the Santa Cruz Mountains**

There was a snake in the Santa Cruz Mountains, and there was a redwood tree, and it already had the tree smooth, smooth from climbing up that tree so much to get sight of people. That snake did not eat people a few at a time but he got them all in a bunch. Ah, but the Indians were smart to make their defenses, you will see. It used to climb up and it just stayed there spying, and when it saw many people there far away in the plains occupied with their harvests of seeds and acorns or whatever they could find, it gave a very loud whistle and down at once it came and it went dragging itself quick as the devil to where they were, and it surrounded them and caught them all in the loop, and squeezed them and ate them up.

That animal lived in the sea. And there it was for many years just killing, killing the people and they could not do anything to it, and it already was finishing them off.

Now just see, the story is not going to be long. The people got to thinking how to escape and how they might kill it (the snake). Then they set the women to making baskets, large enough to cover up a hole which would hold a man. And that animal that used to come forth had its time to come forth, I do not remember but think it was in the morning when it used to come out. And then the men were removing the trees and clearing the ground, so that it would be like a clear and smooth plain, and the women making the baskets, and the men clearing the ground, and when they had already cleared away everything well, they started making holes that they could get into and not be seen. And when they had already finished the baskets and the holes, then the men went to get into the holes, and every one carried his basket and placed it beside the hole. And others of the men went to hide themselves in the woods around about there. They knew at what time the snake would come out. And when he ascended the tree he gave a whistle, and down he came thither he went where the people were. The men were standing beside the holes, so that the snake would see them, waiting for it to come to eat them up. And the rest of the men were hidden in the woods, behind the trees, ready to help those that were standing by the holes and baskets. And those that were standing there beside the holes had their weapons and those [who] were in the woods also had their weapons. And when the snake came and surrounded them, the men who were beside the holes all got into the holes, and covered themselves over with the baskets and the snake came and surrounded them, and crushed all the baskets to pieces, and the men who were in the woods came jumping out with their bows and knives and they all attacked it, and those who were inside the holes were also stabbing it from below, and some of them brought strong tobacco and they were throwing handfuls of tobacco into its mouth when it would open its mouth. Well, they killed it.

Well, when they killed that snake, when the Indians came gathering together from everywhere, for they were afraid that that snake would resuscitate the same as One Leg resuscitated. And they cut it all to pieces, and all of them ate it, they ate it up among themselves, they did not give it to the ants, and thus it was that the Indians of Santa Cruz put an end to that snake. And it did not come to life again.[1]

When I first read "How They Killed a Serpent That Lived in the Santa Cruz Mountains," I interpreted the story as a possible reference to Indigenous collaboration against the threat of Spanish colonialism and disruption. After sharing my doctoral work with Amah Mutsun tribal historian Ed Ketchum, the great-grandson of Solórsano, he was quick to point out that this story predated Spanish colonial occupation and more likely spoke to a conflict from long ago, a "conflict between the snake clan and other clans that dominated the Santa Cruz Mountain area."[2] Of course, this makes much more sense and speaks to the existing Indigenous politics and histories that long predate the colonial histories of the eighteenth and nineteenth centuries. My initial reading of this story made the common mistake of centering the story with the Spanish, interpreting the story to be a response to colonial powers. I was seeing Indigenous histories as a reaction to others, instead of recognizing that Indigenous people's actions, responses, and motivations were informed by their own histories and politics, which stretch back over millennia. With his critique and shared perspective on this story, Ketchum helped to point out my misinterpretation and to remind me of the larger focus of this study.

This is a book about Indigenous politics. It is about the politics of survival, resistance, rebellion, and perseverance through the nineteenth century, focusing on the stories and perspectives of Indigenous tribes, families, and individuals from the region that is today called Santa Cruz County. While the Indigenous people discussed in these chapters clearly struggled with the steady onslaught of disruption, relocation, and at times genocidal colonial policies that included militaristic engagement by Spanish, Mexican, and U.S. soldiers, they persevered and made decisions informed by their own histories, values, and cultural perspectives.[3] This book aims to tell this history from Indigenous perspectives, privileging the voices of Indigenous people, found in oral histories along with other sources, rather than those of the colonists who for far too long have held center stage in historical studies of California.[4] In doing so, the chapters of this book examine this history with an emphasis on stories of rebellion, resistance, and, ultimately, survival, all of which meant different things for a diversity of Indigenous tribes, families, and perspectives.

The key to writing this book has been listening. The stories that I am writing about in this book are not my own stories or that of my family. As I am a historian who does not trace his lineage back to the Indigenous people of this study, it is absolutely imperative that I listen and learn from local descendants.[5] Listening to contemporary Native people like Ketchum, Amah Mutsun tribal chair Valentin Lopez, and others helps me better understand the importance of this history today and how these historical issues and struggles continue to inform ongoing battles to protect sacred spaces and advocate for the tribe.[6] This listening includes centering the oral histories of Mission Santa Cruz survivor Lorenzo Asisara, who gave three interviews in the 1870s and 1880s.[7] Asisara's stories are among the very few Indigenous voices recorded from someone who lived in a California mission, and his stories convey traumas but emphasize moments of rebellion and resistance.[8] This book draws on the interviews of Maria Ascención Solórsano, recorded by John P. Harrington in 1930.[9] Solórsano's stories are used throughout this book to give insight into historical events and dynamics. The multigenerational oral histories of Asisara, Ketchum, Lopez, and Solórsano are all crucial sources that inform this study, and I put these stories in dialogue with archival sources to shed light on Indigenous perspectives of this history and to counterbalance the colonial archives. These oral histories focus on stories of trauma and disruption and yet highlight Indigenous responses and rebellions, acts of resistance and perseverance. Following the lead of these stories, this book does the same.

My methodology also includes listening critically to non-Native sources. The most important of these are the thousands of baptismal, godparentage, marriage, confirmation, and burial records that were written and kept by the Franciscan missionaries but heavily informed by Native peoples.[10] I argue that these chancery records indeed constitute an Indigenous archive: the information contained within them illuminates important values like kinship and family ties and reveals clues about larger dynamics and inner workings. While the Franciscan missionaries technically may have physically written these documents, the individual records were informed by the Indigenous peoples who supplied the padres with the information to record. For this study I built my own database to include thousands of records relating to Indigenous people from Santa Cruz and neighboring communities, enabling me to follow patterns of movement, kinship, and tribal relations that transcend mission boundaries.[11]

Drawing on my database of these records, I have been able to make connections between individuals, families, kinship networks, and tribes.[12] These stories challenge the narratives left by the settler colonial societies that have predominantly written the histories of California.[13] By interconnecting the data from these records with stories and information given in the Spanish, Mexican, and U.S. archives, along with the previously mentioned oral histories, I have been able to reconstruct stories and to recognize connections across mission communities. The Franciscan sacramental records are crucial to any study of Indigenous California. This book helps to explore the boundaries of these records, as throughout I suggest new ways of reading them. There is still much more that can be done with these records, new stories and connections that will be illuminated by historians in the coming years.[14]

By centering on the perspectives of local Indigenous people, this book seeks to explore how they understood these times.[15] I grapple with questions such as: How did they make sense of their circumstances and situations? How did they understand the changing world around them? How did their long histories and knowledge inform their decisions and choices? To answer these questions, I followed the lead of scholars, many of them Indigenous, calling for decolonizing methodologies.[16] This endeavor includes the privileging of Indigenous voices, focusing on Indigenous categories and epistemologies, as well as understanding the fundamental differences in worldview and culture between local Indigenous people and the colonizing occupying society.[17] Such an approach requires recognizing that Indigenous oral histories describe a different world altogether than the one experienced by the colonizers who wrote the vast majority of the early accounts of this period.[18] While both colonizers and Indigenous peoples inhabited the same physical space, the colonizing perspective, informed by the long Spanish history of colonial relations throughout the hemisphere, failed to recognize the existing Indigenous landscape. To write a history that does not repeat the same colonial projections requires a constant diligence in questioning and challenging colonial assumptions, much in the way that Ketchum offered in his ongoing and generous critique and feedback. This approach results in a retelling of the California mission myth, this time from the perspective of Indigenous peoples, although the scope of this book extends well beyond the mission era.[19] In order to accomplish this retelling, my methodological approach also draws on insights from disciplines that are better equipped to address these categories, including archaeology, anthropology, ecology, and psychology.

My research is informed by works of ecologists who have focused on understanding Native land-management practices, often referred to as Traditional Ecological Knowledge (TEK), arguing for a deeper understanding of the impact of geographic and ecological reorganization on Native networks of knowledge.[20] Similarly, important questions about historical and transgenerational trauma help lend understanding to the impact of colonial violence and disruption.[21] Colonial occupation of California involved a process of corporal and psychological violence perpetrated against Indigenous people. Contemporary studies suggest that these kinds of traumas literally reshape the body and brain, causing disruptions that often pass to subsequent generations and help explain incidences of addiction, depression, detachment, violence, and other coping mechanisms.[22] Disciplines such as archaeology and anthropology can allow for a closer understanding of Indigenous practices and culture than historical sources may afford.[23] Right now is an exciting time in the field, as a new wave of archaeologists have been articulating a more dynamic understanding of mission communities.[24] My work is in dialogue with many of the exciting new studies in archaeology, such as the work of Tsim Schneider and Lee Panich, studies that have focused on the "archaeology of persistence."[25] These scholars argue for a more fluid and plural understanding of ethnicity and culture, one that recognizes that ethnicity is "dynamic and continually in transformation in relation to ever-changing social conditions."[26] These types of studies help us approach the archives with a sensitivity to the Indigenous world inhabited at the time of Spanish colonization and occupation.

Building on Studies of Indigenous California

The study of California Indians began in earnest in the mid-twentieth century, when Sherburne F. Cook and others wrote about the terrible attrition and death rates.[27] The emphasis on demographic collapse was understandable, given the terrible rates of death, disease, and loss within the missions, and provided an important counterpoint to Franciscan historians who celebrated the California missions and missionaries.[28] This important intervention brought the emphasis to the great losses experienced by Native Californians but otherwise reinforced harmful notions of Native Californian extinction and the "vanishing Indian."[29] Studies such as that of Native Californian scholars Rupert Costo and his wife, Jeannette Henry Costo, called out the genocidal nature of the California missions, identifying this huge demographic collapse brought on by a combination of disease, abusive treatment, and warfare.[30] By focusing on the very real and important death and brutality, these studies omitted the history of survival and perseverance that testifies to the strength, ingenuity, and resourcefulness of Indigenous Californians. The next wave of historians, influenced by the larger trends toward social and cultural histories, found ways to read patterns of demographic change to understand the impact of disease, death, and hardship on Native Californians.[31] Studies like those of Deborah A. Miranda and Cutcha Risling Baldy have shifted the emphasis from extinction to survival while applying a gendered analysis of courtship, marriage, sexuality, and family life to examine experiences of Indigenous Californian women.[32] These demographic studies worked closely with the data to illustrate population decline, disease, and other important patterns within Spanish California.[33] Robert H. Jackson, in particular, produced broad demographic studies focused on Mission Santa Cruz, where he documented patterns of death and disease in the midst of various waves of diverse tribal peoples.[34]

More recently, a few historians have pushed beyond these demographic studies to reveal that we can indeed learn more about life within the missions.[35] The work of James A. Sandos examines the limits and meaning of Indigenous "conversion" to Catholicism, along with the role of prominent Indigenous musicians within the missions.[36] Steven W. Hackel examined Spanish-Indian relations in Monterey, explored political and social development within mission communities, and worked to present Indigenous accounts of rebellion.[37] He does an excellent job of tracing out Spanish-Indian dynamics in the realms of religious induction, marriage and sexuality, politics and leadership, labor and economy, and crime and punishment.[38] However, his emphasis on the binary of Spanish-Indian relations results in a failure to identify the complexities of ongoing Indigenous politics.[39] Furthermore, as other scholars have noted, his work oversimplifies Indigenous motivations and "ignores the key role that the violence and brutality of the missionaries played in recruitment of Indian peoples into the mission system."[40]

My book is in dialogue with these works as well as a variety of historical and anthropological works that recognize the nuanced and complicated Indigenous politics that formed within mission communities.[41] Studies like those of Lisbeth Haas and Yve B. Chavez have prioritized Indigenous voices and perspectives, examining Indigenous religious and political leaders, dancers, painters, sculptors, and translators within the mission to reveal Indigenous power.[42] Haas argues that despite the physical dislocation, death, and severe limitations in Spanish and Mexican society, "within the missions, native translators, artisans, traditional, and new leaders used Indigenous forms of authority, knowledge, and power to seek redress and to sustain the community."[43] Haas, Hackel, Sandos, and others have pushed the boundaries of our understanding of Indigenous life within the missions, helping to expand beyond broad demographic studies that offer limited arguments of death, loss, and destruction.[44] My work builds on these studies, offering specific examples of Indigenous power and politics in the Indigenous population of the Santa Cruz region.[45]

This book extends its scope beyond the Spanish colonial era, along the lines of other comparative studies like those of historian Benjamin Madley and anthropologist Kent Lightfoot.[46] Historical studies of California Indians after U.S. statehood in 1850 have traditionally been conducted in relative isolation from studies of the Spanish and Mexican eras. Early scholarship on California Indian history during the era of United States occupation focused on violence, removal, and warfare.[47] More recently, studies of genocide and brutality in the U.S. era have expanded these studies to demonstrate thoroughly the level of state-sponsored violence during this period.[48] Some of these studies have challenged the exclusion of Native Californians from historical studies of labor and historical narrative.[49] Other scholars have looked at the ways that historical memory and official records viewed this history, critiquing the whitewashing of violence and the preservation of "American innocence."[50] My book extends beyond the Spanish and Mexican eras into U.S. statehood, attempting to bridge these distinct historical studies.

This study is in conversation with other important studies of Native Californian communities, including other mission-surviving peoples, such as the Acjachemen, Chumash, Kumeyaay, Luiseño, Miwok, Tataviam, and Tongva peoples.[51] Their communities continue to persevere today, and their histories can teach us about how Indigenous Californians found ways to survive and rebuild community. While the Indigenous communities at each mission site differed, there were some distinct differences that could be traced along geographic lines. For example, the missions from the Chumash territory of the Santa Barbara region southward tended to have larger numbers of people united by linguistic and cultural similarities, whereas the northern Bay Area missions became home to a greater diversity of linguistically and culturally distinct tribes. The aforementioned studies help illuminate the limitations of the missions and the ways in which Indigenous politics, trade, and interrelations persisted while shedding light on the distinct histories of different regions.[52] These studies, the scholars who have produced them, and contemporary Indigenous leaders have been collaborating to retell these histories in new ways that recognize the continued presence of Native Californian communities.[53] The stories of other California tribes and peoples intersect with the stories of Bay Area Indigenous peoples, while the specific historical struggles and circumstances show both commonalities and differences. Together these studies go far beyond the limiting binaries of colonizer and colonized to contribute to a dynamic emerging field that recognizes tribal and ethnic difference.

Indigenous political, social, economic, spiritual, and kinship networks extended well beyond the missions, across neighboring mission communities, and with those who remained in their home villages or otherwise lived outside of Spanish settlement. Mission Santa Cruz figures prominently in these stories as a central space of Indigenous production, ingenuity, and politics.[54] Yet this history extends beyond the Spanish Franciscan missions both geographically and temporally. Mission Santa Cruz, like the other California missions, became a space of Indigenous politics in which economic, social, political, and spiritual ties and relations persisted and changed over time. The mission was a space where many Native families witnessed births and deaths, built new alliances and rivalries, and often experienced great losses. But there is much to explore beyond the physical and geographic boundaries of the missions, reaching into what has been called the "hinterlands." Significantly, recent archaeological scholarship, like that of Tsim Schneider, has pushed back on the reading of Indigenous Californian history centered on missions, rightfully broadening colonial landscapes and our understanding of Indigenous experiences.[55] My work seeks to help extend this narrative beyond the mission walls by providing evidence of enduring lives and relationships outside the mission boundaries, between mission and fugitive communities. This study seeks to examine the ways in which colonial violence and disruption impacted many tribes and villages outside the immediate vicinity of Mission Santa Cruz, along with Indigenous responses.[56]

Local tribes understood themselves in terms of tribes, villages, families, kin, moiety, and spiritual affiliations. These complex identity politics continued to inform decisions and relations. This book similarly emphasizes these categories, despite the multiple colonially imposed labels or categories. Spanish colonizers introduced and imposed the social category of "Indian" across linguistic and culturally distinct peoples.[57] As a result, there are many Indians in nineteenth-century Santa Cruz. Spanish society relied on a complicated *sistema de castas* (caste system), which relied on genealogy and purity of lineage and drew lines between *gente de razón* (people of reason) and *gente sin razón* (people without reason), the latter being the domain of the "barbarous" Indigenous people.[58] The complicated status of Indigenous people has produced problematic archives and documents.[59] Franciscan missionaries imposed an additional category of distinction based upon Catholic baptism—*neofito* or *gentile*.[60] For many colonists during the Spanish colonial era, the move north represented a chance to transcend similar racial distinctions in their homelands, an opportunity for upward social mobility.[61] Later, under the Mexican national regime, the category of Indian was officially abolished. In the U.S. era the category collapsed further with the imposition of racial understandings, as those identified as Indians held no rights and became targeted by policies of extermination.[62] Instead of relying on these colonial categories, I center Indigenous categories of identity to reveal a complex web of networks connecting individuals and families across the greater region.

Indigenous Santa Cruz

In 1793 a pan-tribal Indigenous group attacked newly founded Mission Santa Cruz. Nearly twenty years later, an Indigenous woman named Yaquenonsat (Fausta) helped strategize and lead the assassination of an abusive padre.[63] Rebellions, assassinations, fugitive flights, and poisonings—Santa Cruz Indigenous communities resisted and challenged colonial violence throughout the nineteenth century. Indigenous people gathered, sang their songs, prayed their prayers, held their sweat lodge ceremonies, and built community with other survivors. A diverse group of Indigenous tribes and families adapted to and expressed themselves politically and culturally through three distinct types of colonial encounters involving Spain, Mexico, and the United States. They formed new alliances and expanded kinship networks and relied upon traditional knowledge and practices to help ensure their survival and make sense of their rapidly changing world. This is a story of Indigenous resistance and leadership, revealing a dynamic world of Indigenous politics and negotiations. These diverse tribes, kinship networks, and families devised a variety of tactics to survive through this "time of little choice."[64] This is a history of the many tribes brought together by colonial disruption, a history of individuals and families who persevered through a time of incredible upheaval and loss.

At the time of initial Spanish colonial settlement in 1791, around 1,400 Indigenous people from seven independent tribes called the region known today as Santa Cruz County home. Over the next century this area became home to people from over thirty autonomous tribes from throughout the larger Bay Area, tribes such as the Uypi, Aptos, Sayanta, Chaloctaca, Tomoi, Sumus, Ausaima, Tejey, and Huocom, among others. These diverse tribes spoke one of three distinct languages—Awaswas Ohlone, Mutsun Ohlone, or Yokuts.[65] By the time Mexican officials closed Mission Santa Cruz, in 1834, the total surviving Indigenous population numbered just over 200, a small fraction of the 2,289 Indigenous people baptized at the mission.[66] Furthermore, many of those who died were children or infants. Of the 471 babies born at Mission Santa Cruz between 1791 and 1831, 359 died before reaching their fifth birthday, which is over 75 percent of all babies born, while just over 80 percent did not survive to turn fifteen.[67] In stark contrast, multiple archaeological studies have shown that in precontact San Francisco Bay Area Indigenous society, somewhere around 75 percent of Native children survived into adulthood (past the age of sixteen or seventeen), meaning that life at the missions meant a Native baby's odds of survival into adulthood went from about a 75 percent chance to a 20 percent chance by moving to Mission Santa Cruz.[68]

But the numbers alone fail to tell the depths of loss, devastation, and trauma experienced by Indigenous people during their years at the mission. A close look at the families living within the mission shows that men and women regularly and unceasingly were forced to bury their spouses, their children, and their relatives. Around thirty-five distinct tribes entered

Mission Santa Cruz, and the survivors watched their kin die in rapid succession. By the time the mission secularized, the vast majority of these tribes had lost all or nearly all of their members. And yet demographic analysis reveals a relatively consistent mission population, but this is a facade. The numbers remain consistent only because Spanish soldiers increasingly targeted new tribes and territories to locate and capture new "recruits" to augment the mission population.[69] In the era of U.S. occupation the situation for Indigenous people became even more dire, as U.S. policies targeted Indigenous people for extermination.[70] In addition to over a century of colonially imposed violence, the local Indigenous community also faced tremendous loss from epidemics of smallpox, syphilis, malaria, and diphtheria. Still, between 100 and 200 people survived well into the latter half of the nineteenth century, testifying to their strength and ingenuity in developing new strategies for survival. In a situation of overwhelming death and loss, survival itself was a revolutionary act. This is the story of their perseverance and survival.

Each California mission's history is unique, shaped by the local ecology and resources, proximity to other Spanish settlements, the temperament of the Franciscan missionaries stationed there, and most important, by the specific histories and cultural realities of local Indigenous peoples.[71] Further confirming the stories of Chairman Lopez, my research finds that Mission Santa Cruz did indeed become home to some of the most abusive padres. But the Indigenous community frequently challenged their authority. At times some padres referred to Mission Santa Cruz as the "mission of padre killers."[72] The missionaries regularly requested removal, complaining about the weather, isolation, and the unruly population. But did the mission live up to its notorious reputation? Some Native converts did act as "padre killers," but Indigenous responses to the missionaries were complicated and diverse. Others worked closely with padres, catching fugitives or protecting the mission from foreign threats. Indigenous people employed a variety of strategies for survival.

Santa Cruz is an ideal site for this study for multiple reasons. First, Mission Santa Cruz remained relatively small in population. Owing in part to its relative isolation, the mission population never reached much higher than five hundred people. Santa Cruz is bounded by a redwood-filled mountain range, making the beachfront plateaus tough to reach by land. After initially avoiding the coastal marshland passages, the Franciscans eventually established Mission Santa Cruz in order to reach the various mountain and coastal tribal people who had resisted relocation to Mission Santa Clara. The relatively small population compared to sites such as Mission Santa Clara, which regularly had over one thousand Native people, allows for this case study to encompass a more complete and nuanced reading of the histories of individuals and families. This is especially helpful in tracing the kinship and family networks into the years after U.S. statehood.

Second, as mentioned earlier, Santa Cruz was a site of constant challenge and rebellion. Even though Indigenous families at other California missions resisted and challenged Spanish authorities, Mission Santa Cruz stands out for its very visible and documented history of resistance. Out of all the Northern California missions, Santa Cruz was the only one to face a direct attack during the Spanish colonial era and the only one where a padre was successfully assassinated.[73] It was a site of attempted poisonings and subsequent arrests, ongoing flights of fugitives, and other examples of uprising and confrontation—of an active negotiation of Indigenous politics. In the years after the mission closed, Santa Cruz continued to be a place where Indigenous peoples advocated and fought for their rights and lands. This rich history of resistance and rebellion offers plenty of examples of Indigenous agency worthy of examination.

Third, the padres at Mission Santa Cruz kept excellent records. The Franciscan missionaries of California generally kept detailed records of all ecclesiastical events, including baptisms, burials, marriages, and confirmations. At some missions, such as Mission Santa Clara, the padres were less concerned with documenting the families and tribal identities of incoming Indigenous people, instead renaming villages and tribes with the names of Catholic saints. Other missions, such as Mission San Luis Rey and Soledad, are missing critical books and records. For the most part, with notable exceptions, the padres at Mission Santa Cruz kept diligent records. This relative accuracy greatly aids this study, as analysis of these copious records allows for a nuanced reading of patterns of movement, relocation, intermarriage, and godparentage.

Fourth, this is the first study to focus on this history in the Santa Cruz area. While early Franciscan historians such as Zephryn Engelhardt, Maynard Geiger, and Florian Guest focused on documenting the histories of each mission, few recent studies have followed this approach, despite the potential for applying new analyses.[74] This book revisits this case study approach by focusing on a specific mission community while offering my methodological approach of de-centering the mission institution and instead centering Indigenous experiences, politics, and defiance. This case study microhistory focuses on the specific histories found in Santa Cruz while at the same time illuminating statewide trends and patterns found with Indigenous defiance throughout the larger region.

The first chapter of this book examines the initial movement of local Indigenous people into Mission Santa Cruz. By first tracing out the Indigenous landscape of the region, I found that preexisting alliances and rivalries helped to inform reasons for relocation to Mission Santa Cruz. I argue that in this time of little choice, a diversity of Native peoples made decisions of vital importance for themselves, their families, and their kin. Indigenous families and leaders responded to Spanish colonialism in diverse ways. Leaders from the rival Aptos and Uypi tribes vied for power and standing within the mission community, while the northern-lying Quiroste, the largest and strongest of the local tribes, offered shelter and formed alliances with fugitives. This pan-tribal group, led by leaders such as Ochole and Charquin, attacked the mission two years after its founding. This Quiroste-led rebellion was one of very few direct attacks on a mission during this period. Indigenous leaders made their choices based on preexisting political dynamics. Chapter 1 ends in 1798, the last year of significant baptism of local Awaswas speakers. In response to the Quiroste-led attack, new padres arrived with harsher, more aggressive methods of conversion. Within a few years padres and soldiers had relocated the vast majority of local tribes to the mission.

Chapter 2 reveals the formation of hybrid political, social, gender, and economic roles within the expanding and diversifying mission community between 1798 and 1810. In these years Spanish soldiers extended their colonial campaign by inducting Mutsun-speaking Ohlone tribes from farther east. These tribes felt the impact of ecological, economic, and political disruption by Spanish colonial settlements and responded to these changes in a variety of ways. The Ausaima actively challenged the Spanish and the Native youth who came of age during these years, many of whom became leaders within the mission and worked in collaboration with the missionaries. This was a period of increasing conflict, as many of these villagers challenged Spanish relocations, engaging in small-scale warfare, raids on cattle and livestock, and other acts of resistance. Those who joined the mission blended Spanish and Indigenous economic, spiritual, social, and political practices. They became *sacristans* (sextons), *pajes* (pages), and *padrinos* (godparents); through godparentage they built and expanded kinship relations. Some became musicians, weavers, masons, carpenters, laborers, farmers, shoemakers, tailors, or cooks. Indigenous leaders continued to exert influence, often through elected mission *alcaldes* (mayors). This chapter ends in 1810, when the last of the large groups of Mutsun people came to the mission.

The 1812 assassination of Padre Andrés Quintana, the only successful assassination of a padre in the Northern California missions, is the subject of chapter 3. My research reveals that this incident was much more than an isolated moment of rebellion. At the center of this story is an Indigenous woman, Yaquenonsat, a spiritual and political leader from Mutsun territory. She brought with her the strategy she had learned from inland tribes. Through marriage she joined herself and her Sumus people with a kinship group of Awaswas-speaking Ohlone, which included some of the first families that had arrived in the earliest days of the mission. The assassination was a response to the specific cruelties of Padre Quintana. This close examination of the families and tribes involved reveals the persistence of female leadership and patterns of interconnection between Indigenous communities both within neighboring missions and outside. Overall, this chapter reveals how local Indigenous people developed and communicated strategies of resistance across the greater Bay Area.

Newly arrived Yokuts leaders filled the vacuum left after the arrest of the assassination conspirators. This transition and the impact of these Yokuts tribal people is the focus of chapter 4. This chapter covers the years between 1810 and 1834, a time of Indigenous fugitives, horse thieves, cattle raiders, and military recovery excursions into Yokuts territories. California transitioned politically to Mexican governance during this time, which led to consequences for the mission and Indigenous people.[75] Arriving Yokuts joined Awaswas- and Mutsun-speaking Ohlone but carved out their own political and social roles within the mission. Some of these Yokuts, such as Chief Malimin (Coleto) and his sons, worked closely with the padres, tracking down fugitives and supervising others. Indigenous people made choices regarding their interactions with the padres. And yet they made these choices within a larger context of social, psychological, and corporal domination by the padres, as the succession of abusive padres continued. Furthermore, while some of these incoming men received a degree of power within the mission community, women continued to be abused by certain padres.

Secularization and emancipation, which began in the early 1830s, is the focus of chapter 5. In Santa Cruz, despite Mexican policies abolishing racial categories and establishing Indigenous citizenship, rights for Indigenous people were slow in coming.[76] It wasn't until 1839 that a few Indigenous members of the mission received small plots of land. Following emancipation, two distinct communities formed in lands adjacent to the mission. The political shifts discussed in chapter 4 helped shape the formation of these two Indigenous communities, as the Yokuts leaders and their kin received the Potrero—the lands behind the mission that would in later years become known as the local reservation. The Sayanta man Geronimo Chugiut and his Awaswas-speaking kin lived in the resource-rich Westside of Santa Cruz, the second community that emerged. The 1840s were a decade when some former mission residents gained small parcels of land, a limited degree of citizenship, and partial entry into the larger economic and social world of the local Californios.

Indigenous survival through the early years of U.S. statehood is the focus of chapters 6 and 7. As California became a U.S. state, in 1850, Indigenous people first became a minority of the overall local population. As Santa Cruz grew into an industrial city, more and more people moved into the area, eclipsing the couple hundred Indigenous survivors. Under American political rule, the social category of Indian collapsed to envelop Californios and Indigenous people in one singular underclass, excluded from legal and human rights and targeted by lynching and persecution. Chapter 6 focuses on the changing status of Indians in the era of U.S. occupation and the contrast between genocidal policies and the fascination of early ethnographers in celebrating the so-called vanishing Indian. Chapter 7 looks at the Potrero, the last remaining "reservation" on former mission lands. The Potrero remained an Indigenous space until the early 1880s, and this chapter traces the stories of families that survived through this era and moved into places like Watsonville to survive beyond the occupation of Potrero lands by incoming colonizers. In Santa Cruz, Native families responded to these threats with a variety of survival strategies—including passing as Mexican, relocation, arson, searching out nearby Native communities, and continuing to draw on traditional spiritual songs, dances, and sweat lodges for healing and strength.

Ultimately, this book offers new methodological approaches to the study of Native California, innovations that could similarly speak to studies of colonization, early nationalism, borderlands studies, and Indigenous studies. My research reveals a dynamic Indigenous world that existed beyond the gaze or understanding of the missionaries, soldiers, and explorers who settled and colonized the region. Indigenous leaders and families negotiated new alliances and kinship networks, engaged in disputes or conflicts based on long-standing rivalries, and otherwise learned about, shared with, and engaged with other Indigenous peoples. This dynamic world of Indigenous politics and negotiation helped shape the history and development of Santa Cruz as it grew into a city. Despite the complex web of Indigenous politics that helped shape this history, today it remains barely visible, most notably commemorated in town and street names such as Aptos, Soquel, and Zayante. Meanwhile, contemporary descendants of these Indigenous families remain on the peripheries of U.S. society. My book seeks to challenge this erasure by revealing their rich and important Indigenous history, overlooked for far too long. This is a story of the strength and resiliency of these families, who persevered and innovated in order to survive and carry on their traditions.

"We Are Not Animals"

A story, from which I take the title of this book, helps illustrate my methodology and the considerations that I use here. In 1812, twenty years after the establishment of Mission Santa Cruz, a group of Indigenous men and women gathered in response to the sadistic brutality of an abusive padre. Padre Andrés Quintana had recently procured a whip fitted with iron tips and had beaten two young men nearly to death. According to Asisara, who related this story some sixty-plus years after the events, mission members discussed their options. Asisara claimed that Lino, an eighteen-year-old man who served as Quintana's personal assistant, had argued:

> The first thing we need to do is to keep the Padre from having the desire to punish people in such a manner, for *we are not animals*. He tells us in his sermon that God does not command this [type of punishment] in his example or doctrine.
>
> Tell me, then, what are we to do with the Padre? Run him off, we cannot do, nor can we take him before a judge since we do not know who commands him to do what he does to us.
>
> It will be better if we kill the Padre, without anyone knowing about it, not even the pages nor anyone else, only those that are here present.[77]

In this story Lino recognizes that Quintana has overstepped his boundaries and has failed to follow his own preachings. Lino also grasps that the mission system does not allow for them to "take him before a judge"—as there is no protection built in for Indigenous people. They are left with only one option if they are to challenge Quintana's abuses. But to analyze the implications of the phrasing used by Lino in this story ("we are not animals"), it is important to address an ongoing discussion in California historiography. This discussion revolves around ways of understanding the role of the institution of the California missions. Historian Madley recently argued that the California missions were the first mass incarceration institutions in California, finding comparison to the prisons that are found all through Central California today.[78] But despite similarities in the harsh treatment and control imposed over Native lives and bodies within the missions, there remains room to appreciate the extent to which Native people fully engaged with these institutions, finding ways to subvert and challenge their hegemonic control.

The basis for the comparison of missions to the mass incarceration system rests on the reliance of colonial settlements on Indigenous labor at the missions. Indigenous laborers produced all the food and clothing and built the shelters for incoming colonizers. Spanish Franciscan missionaries relied on Indigenous labor to support and build their colonial settlement project; however, while Madley's mass incarceration model recognizes a limited degree of Indigenous resilience and persistence, I argue that active rebellion and defiance were a defining feature of Indigenous experience at the missions, not relegated to isolated incidents.

This book aims to take this analysis of defiance deeper, not simply in this case study but by demonstrating a new methodological approach to a fine-grain analysis of Indigenous agency during this era of Californian history and recognizing the centrality of Indigenous power within colonial spaces.[79] As scholars Lee Panich and brothers Tsim and Khal Schneider collectively responded to Madley, "By neglecting California Indians' efforts to resist, evade, and escape the missions, scholars overlook explanations for Indian persistence and risk an ironic return to historical interpretations of colonization that take only Spanish aims and action seriously."[80] Furthermore, the comparison of historical missions to contemporary institutions such as the mass incarceration system problematically projects modern institutions onto historical ones. I believe that it is far more relevant to try to understand the missions by centering on the ways in which Indigenous peoples historically understood their own situations, engagement with, and treatment by the missionaries and Spanish colonizers.

I propose that Indigenous people saw that the Spanish treated Native people much as they treated their livestock. The Spanish colonization of California involved a process of dehumanization. Indigenous people at the missions perceived this clearly, as witnessed in the statements made by Lino—"we are not animals." As they did with the livestock, Spanish missionaries and soldiers used excessive corporal punishment as a means of "instruction" and behavioral modification. Missionaries taught Indians to use goads and yokes to control the livestock, while using whips and stocks to control Indigenous people themselves. Preoccupied with keeping the labor of Indigenous people at the missions continual and productive, Spanish authorities fixated on Indigenous procreation and fertility, drawing on methods similar to those used in animal husbandry practices. The missionaries kept the youth corralled and separated in enclosures like the *monjeríos* and *jayuntes*, girls' and boys' dormitories, and made sure that Native people were fed just enough to give them the strength to plow the fields, shear the sheep, weave the clothing, and build the adobe buildings needed to spur on the colonial project.

When Lino asserted that "we are not animals," his statement was a complicated one, especially when considering the ways that Indigenous peoples related with local animals. Indigenous people throughout the region we today call California lived in interrelationship with animals and their environment. They had very different relationships to animals than did the Spanish colonizers. Indigenous peoples communicated with local animals through their dreams, prayers, and songs. They often named their villages and homelands in correspondence to local animals. Families and tribal communities kept special ties with certain animals and sought their strength in their prayers and medicine. They recognized animals as spiritual beings and held dances and ceremonies to honor them and sought to learn from their wisdom and medicine.

So, when Lino said, "No somos animales"—we are not animals or, as another translator has put it, "They treated us as animals"—he likely meant that they were not animals in the way that the Spanish saw and treated them.[81] Lino and the others would have been charged with taking care and overseeing the mission livestock on a daily basis. They would have been taught by the missionaries to use whips, goads, yokes, and corporal punishment as a regular means of controlling the cattle, sheep, and swine held in the mission pastures. They clearly saw the similarities in style of Spanish oversight and control. And they certainly would have understood the differences between Indigenous and Spanish relationships with animals.

Consider this story from Solórsano: "Some mothers used to keep the baby's navel cord and others did not, and others used to throw them into the fire. The cow when she gives birth, later eats up the afterbirth, it is a very curious thing, it must be their religion."[82] Well into the twentieth century, Solórsano articulates an Indigenous understanding of animals. She observes the behavior of the Spanish imported cows and seeks to learn from it, to gain understanding of the spirituality of the cows. A very different approach than that of the Spanish. Then consider a note that the infamous Padre Junípero Serra recorded about the Rumsen people of Monterey Bay: "As regards the soldiers and the Fathers, after carefully looking them over, they had come to the conclusion that they were the sons of the mules on which they rode."[83] There is a similar approach here, as in both accounts Indigenous people attempted to understand the interrelationships, knowledge, and powers of the new animals. So, when Lino proclaimed, "We are not animals," it was not a critique of the state of being an animal or a declaration of difference between animals and humans but, instead, a deeper critique and rejection of the way in which the Spaniards treated both their animals and Indigenous people at the missions.

One final consideration before beginning this study. In addition to the question of *how* people survived, it is critical to remember the *why* as well. The emphasis here is on survival but much more than survival. It is stories of Indigenous politics and families, and the survival of these families is a testament to the strength, resiliency, and ingenuity of these ancestors. Furthermore, these families not only survived against terrible odds, but they maintained their humanity in doing so. Through building new kinship ties with other survivors, they shared stories, songs, ceremonies, rituals, and laughter, whenever possible. To these ends, I'll now wrap up this introduction with two short stories shared by Solórsano that illustrate this point. While her interviews with Harrington served a crucial role in sharing linguistic, cultural, and historical information for her descendants and the Amah Mutsun today and in the future, her stories also reveal her great sense of humor and the enormous value she placed on building community.

How One Burro Was Missing

When people talk about losing something and have it all the time, like I do, who go around hunting my glasses and have them put up on top of my head, I always recall a story which my deceased mother used to tell me about a man who would always count his burros and never took account of the burro on which he was sitting, and he felt very unhappy and used to think that one of his burros was missing, and there he was sitting on the one that was missing. That indeed can happen.

How the Relatives Used to Celebrate in My House at Gilroy

Sometimes there used to be a day at my house that was quiet all day long and then some of my relatives and friends would come and one of them would go fetch a gallon of wine and at once they got started and brought more. And straightaway they would get out the guitar and begin to sing and they kept singing and drinking wine all night. My son, Rosalillo, was the one that played the guitar and the accordion also. And Don Tiburcio Guerrero sang different songs almost all night for he knew many.[84]

The Indigenous tribes, families, and individuals who inhabited the space of Santa Cruz throughout the nineteenth century persevered despite enormous odds and obstacles. They did so through a diversity of tactics but most importantly by maintaining community and rebuilding new ties with fellow survivors. This is their story of survival, perseverance, and the ingenuity that they used to make it through these times.

1

First Were Taken the Children, and Then the Parents Followed

On the night of December 14, 1793, a party of Indigenous people from a variety of local tribes joined together to launch an attack on the recently established Mission Santa Cruz. The assailants burned down several Spanish buildings and shot arrows at Spanish soldiers, wounding one. This group included Indigenous fugitives from neighboring Spanish-controlled missions, along with Native villagers who had thus far avoided entry into the missions. The fugitives had been gathering in lands north of Mission Santa Cruz in the years leading up to the attack. They had found refuge in the village of Mitenne, in the traditional territories of the Quiroste, the largest and most economically and politically powerful of the Santa Cruz mountain tribes. A Quiroste man named Ochole (Formerio) led the attack, which was a response to the relocation of several Quiroste women to Mission Santa Cruz, including two of Ochole's daughters.[1] Franciscan missionaries had overseen the marriages of two of these women to recently baptized Indigenous men from different villages, disrupting traditional marriage arrangements. While the attack was in part a response to Spanish occupation and colonial disruption, it also coincided with long-standing patterns of Indigenous political boundary disputes in connection to the movement of women across tribal territorial boundaries. As the buildings burned in the night sky, the Spaniards were reminded that they were on Indigenous lands, that they were the foreigners in this local Indigenous society with its own long history, customs, and practices.

The intertribal group of fugitives and villagers had gathered at Mitenne as a response to Spanish colonialism, and while the attack took place just over two years after the founding of Mission Santa Cruz, it had been over twenty years since the Spanish first established permanent settlements in the region. The fact that the attackers burned down Spanish buildings is especially significant given the huge role that fire played as a tool for Californian Indigenous communities. Although dramatic, this was not exceptional. At various times Indigenous rebels used flaming arrows and fire to attack and burn structures at Missions San Diego, San Luis Obispo, and Santa Barbara. The attacks on San Luis Obispo in the 1770s led directly to the ubiquitous use of the iconic red tile roofs throughout the California missions.[2] The use of fire as a tool of resistance is not surprising, considering that fire was a key component of Indigenous land management practices, today referred to as traditional ecological knowledge (TEK). Controlled fires were central to these complex and highly sophisticated practices, which helped create and maintain landscape diversity.[3] For millennia Indigenous Californians had used controlled fires to transform the environment, converting unproductive shrubland into resource-rich grasslands.[4] For Spanish explorers and colonizers the presence of smoke or fires signified the proximity of Indigenous settlements. The Spanish Franciscan colonial strategy was to control and dominate Indigenous culture and practices, and just six months before the attack, Spanish authorities outlawed the use of fires by Indigenous people in California.[5]

The attack reveals the underlying presence of Indigenous politics, both in the motivations and in the methods involved. Indigenous people of the region met Spanish colonization of Alta California with constant challenge and resistance, drawing on the strength of cultural practices, community networks, and ingenuity. To understand the history of Indigenous survival and resistance, it is important first to understand the complex and interwoven social, cultural, political, economic, and spiritual world of Indigenous California. Spanish colonizers, and later their Mexican and American counterparts, drastically underestimated and misinterpreted the depth of complexity and sophistication of Indigenous Californian societies. This chapter first examines the Indigenous society of the region now known as Santa Cruz County and then proceeds to trace the early stages of social, political, environmental, and psychological disruption with the imposition of Spanish colonization, from settlement in 1770 up until 1797.

For Indigenous peoples this was a time of difficult decisions in an increasingly chaotic and devastatingly disruptive world, or, as Randall Milliken characterized it, "a time of little choice."[6] The Quiroste had welcomed and fed Spanish explorers back in 1769; less than twenty-five years later, members of the same village led this intertribal attack. By 1797 the vast majority of tribal members from the local mountains had been baptized and relocated to lands surrounding the mission.[7] A combination of circumstances led to relocation to the missions and the ensuing social and political reorganization. These included Spanish enticement and gifting, Indigenous peoples vying for newly forming political powers, hunger caused by environmental reorganization and the impact of new livestock and crops, and aggressive proselytizing by the Franciscans. Yet Indigenous response to these changes varied: some challenged Spanish imposition in ways ranging from subtle resistance to outright rebellion, while others adapted and learned to navigate this new social order.

Indigenous Societies

When this world was finished (by creator), the Eagle, Hummingbird, and Coyote were standing on top of a high mountain in Monterey county. The world was being flooded, and when the water rose to their feet, Eagle carried Hummingbird and Coyote and flew away to a still higher mountain. There the three stood until the water went down. Then Eagle sent Coyote down the mountain to see if the world was dry. Coyote came back and said, "The whole world is dry." Eagle said: "Go and look in the river. See what there is there." Coyote did so and came back saying, "There is a beautiful girl." Eagle then said, "She will be your wife, in order that people may be raised again." Eagle gave Coyote a trowel of abalone shell and a stick to dig with. Coyote married the girl. Coyote's children went out over the world and became the forefathers of the different tribes.[8]

Some Indigenous tribes in the area knew the Santa Cruz Mountains by the name Mak-Sah-Re-Jah (see map 1).[9] The tallest peak in Mak-Sah-Re-Jah (the Santa Cruz Mountains) is that of Mount Umunhum, which translates to mean "place of Hummingbird."[10] The Uypi called their homeland Aulintak, which translates to "place of Red Abalone," and is known today as the city of Santa Cruz.[11] The mountainous coastal territories south of the San Francisco Peninsula were home to various Indigenous tribes. These lands had their own names and histories and were understood in terms of regional boundaries defined by hunting grounds, carefully tended grasslands and resources, village sites, and sacred places. These were all Indigenous territories onto which Spanish colonizers would later impose their own names and labels.[12]

The tribes of the San Francisco Bay Area, though divided into smaller independent polities, were united by common languages and through economic, social, political, and spiritual interrelations. While both colonizers and Indigenous peoples inhabited the same physical space, the colonizing perspective, informed by the long Spanish history of colonial relations throughout the hemisphere, failed to recognize the existing Indigenous landscape. The Spanish referred to the up to fifty autonomous tribes collectively as Costanoan, a label encompassing a diversity of peoples who inhabited the area from the northern tip of the San Francisco Peninsula down to Big Sur and from the Diablo range south to the edge of the San Joaquin Valley on the eastern side. Today they are more commonly known collectively as the Ohlone, though even that name contributes to an overgeneralization and is in dispute by some contemporary tribes.[13] For example, the largest group of descendants of the people examined in this book, who survived Missions Santa Cruz and San Juan Bautista, today prefer to go by their current name: the Amah Mutsun Tribal Band.[14]

Six distinct tribes lived within the Mak-Sah-Re-Jah region (moving southeast to northwest): the Aptos, Uypi, Cotoni, Sayanta, Chaloctaca, and Quiroste (see map 2).[15] The coastal mountain range stretches from south of the San Francisco Peninsula southward to the Pajaro Valley and is bounded on the east by the Santa Clara Valley. These redwood forest mountains created a situation of relative geographic isolation from the inland tribes of the various valleys. The mountain tribes were united linguistically, as they spoke a language called Awaswas, a branch of the larger Ohlonean language family.[16] Though they spoke the Awaswas language, they inhabited multilingual regions interconnected through shared symbols and rituals as well as monetary, trade, and complex kinship relationships.[17]

This shared cultural world connected with a larger Indigenous California, where long-distance trade relations and communication characterized linguistically diverse societies that shared a variety of resources and practices, spiritual and physical, tracing back over thousands of years. It is only in the last forty-plus years that archaeologists have focused on the unique world of the people of Mak-Sah-Re-Jah.[18] New movements in archaeology have approached their studies from a perspective of persistence, recognizing that individuals and families have drawn upon dynamic cultural values to navigate times of disruption and change.[19] Some archaeologists have begun working collaboratively with tribal members and Native archaeologists to ensure that research is undertaken respectfully and that information gained can help restore Indigenous knowledge and be of service to contemporary tribal members.[20]

The tribes of the San Francisco Bay Area have called these lands home for millennia, as settlement in the area stretches back at least thirteen thousand years.[21] Evidence of widespread trade relations throughout and beyond California goes back thousands of years. Abalone and Olivella snail shells, which grew in abundance, were valuable export resources and were used as monetary units for commerce throughout Indigenous California.[22] Coastal tribes exchanged these rich resources for goods such as obsidian from inland tribes. A major cultural shift appears in the archaeological record beginning around 1000 CE, with the arrival of new technologies such as notched line sinkers and circular shell fishhooks, bows and arrows, flanged steatite pipes, stone "flower-pot" mortars, new Olivella shell bead types, and "banjo" effigy ornaments signifying the development of the Kuksui secret society.[23]

The long history of the people of this region bespeaks deep ancestral roots and the resulting knowledge and intimacy with the local environs. Local people shaped cultural practices around the environment and the availability of resources. The mountain region consists of a mix of ecological zones: coastal terraces that rise upward into the heavily forested mountain range, river drainages and narrow river valleys with steep slopes and ridges, along with upland meadows on open flats along mountain slopes and crests. The coast had a mix of beachheads alongside river drainages as well as a number of tule-filled marshes and wetland estuaries. Tule, or wood when tule was not available, was used for homes and village structures, shelters, and mats.[24] Extended-family tribal units rotated seasonally between semipermanent village sites, following seasonal availability of resources. These seasonal patterns often involved groups spreading out throughout a broader territory in spring and fall, then coming together in a central location during winter and summer.[25] Grass-covered terraces provided a large variety of plants and resources for food, basketry, and clothing, while the dense forests of redwoods, oaks, and Douglas fir provided hunting grounds and acorns, which were an essential part of the regional diet. The temperate weather allowed for minimal clothing; Ohlone men tended to go without clothing, while women wore plaited grass or tule skirts and sometimes wore buckskin aprons. Some chiefs wore rabbit skin capes to signify status. Unlike Ohlone tribes in the Santa Clara and San Francisco Bay Area who lived in larger, flat plains that allowed for greater stability and permanent village sites, mountain and coastal tribes along this region developed their own mix of foraging and collecting strategies, adjusted to best utilize available resources.[26]

The Indigenous peoples of this area used complex strategies of land management that had been developed, refined, and perfected over thousands of years.[27] Land management techniques enhanced the productivity of their ecosystems, actively modifying and constructing the local environment. While these densely forested lands, with their proximity to the coast, were rich in natural resources, this abundance was not the by-product of luck and circumstance. Spanish, and later American, colonizers failed to recognize the importance and value of Indigenous traditional ecological knowledge in maximizing the productivity of these lands. Native peoples carefully managed the lands and local fauna through a process of tillage, seed harvesting, pruning, seed broadcasting, transplanting, mulching/fertilizing, weeding, coppicing, irrigation, and, most important, prescribed burning.[28]

Fire was central to Indigenous Californian land management practices, as local people used controlled fires to transform the landscape from shrublands into highly productive, resource-rich grasslands.[29] Through periodic burns, tribes cleared brush under trees and expanded meadows and fields. The use of fires in seasonal rotations to manage the landscape is a central feature that distinguished Indigenous Californians from other advanced agrarian societies. This practice led to great diversification and range of foods and resources and helped maintain flexibility as tribes created resource-rich landscapes and options for seasonal relocation.[30] Many plants, such as the California hazelnut, needed burning in order to flourish, requiring the high heat of fires to break open seeds in order to germinate.[31] The clearings formed by these burns in turn attracted larger animals, such as the black-tailed deer, which locals hunted regularly.[32] Burning broke down dry vegetation and increased nutrients in the soil, helping provide grazing options for deer, elk, and antelope, while burning under oak trees eliminated insects and infestations of acorns.[33] Repeated burning of chaparral greatly increased the annual flow from watersheds, leading to more access to water.[34] Chaparral was the favored habitat for grizzly bears, so its removal had the added benefit of reducing grizzly habitat.[35] Fire was also used for hunting, as Ohlone tribes used fire to drive rabbits into traps and nets, where they could then kill them with clubs.[36]

Indigenous Californians are known for making some of the most complex and beautiful baskets in the world. They carefully groomed grasses, sedges, rushes, and forbs not only for crucial seeds and foodstuffs but also as materials for basketmaking. Baskets were central to life, as they were used for winnowing, cooking, and serving food; for carrying berries, acorns, and other resources; and for leaching, seed beating, and making cradles, hats, and water bottles.[37] Oak woodlands in particular provided thermal cover, escape, dens, nests, and foraging spots to a large number of animals and birds. Native Californians regularly hunted animals such as jackrabbit, cottontail, kangaroo rat, ground squirrel, deer, antelope, quail, and badger, along with waterfowl such as the canvasback duck, common merganser, and blue-winged teal. They were also known to eat dog, wildcat, skunk, raccoon, tree squirrel, mole, hawk, dove, mud hen, snake, lizard, and tortoise.[38] Also sharing the terrain were grizzly bears, coyotes, and mountain lions.

Coastal tribes had access to important resources that they used in trade. Shells from mussels, barnacles, limpets, chitons, abalone, and clams could be used for ceremonial purposes and traded to inland tribes; they have been found in archaeological digs throughout the greater Bay Area. They also gathered offshore vegetal resources such as kelp, seaweed, and sea palm, which were either roasted for immediate consumption or dried and stored.[39] Harbor seals, northern elephant seals, sea lions, and numerous fish provided sources of protein and fat. They caught fish by day—and by bonfire at night—using spear points and even poison from soaproot or doveweed.[40]

San Francisco Bay Area Ohlone tribes belonged to a social network connected through kinship, trade, warfare, and ceremony.[41] Within the tribes themselves, independent extended-family networks existed as interconnected villages. Ohlone peoples, like many Indigenous Americans, understood their own conceptions of family and social relations, commonly referred to by anthropologists as kinship networks. The concept of kinship involved a network of familial ties that bound together smaller groups within larger intertribal networks. Neighboring tribes were bound together through intermarriages, shared spiritual practices, and trade. In later years, after the imposition of the Spanish missions, the creation of new kinship ties and interconnections would become instrumental in aiding survival.

Warfare between neighbors was common; they typically fought over boundaries, resources, or marriage partners, which included a pattern of "wife stealing."[42] Archaeological records suggest that some precontact warfare, likely over territorial boundaries, could involve violent confrontations and even slaughter.[43] Tribes rich in resources, such as the Quiroste of Año Nuevo, who had access to shells used as currency as well as cliff rock used for arrows, likely needed their larger numbers to defend these resources. Cinnabar mines along the east side of Mak-Sah-Re-Jah provided red paint used ceremonially throughout the area, and stories of confrontations over these mines persisted into the 1840s.[44]

Long-standing traditions of exogamous marriage (marrying outside of one's group), which the Spanish interpreted as wife stealing, was connected to histories of regional warfare and may well be tied to motivations for the Quiroste-led attack in 1793, as will be discussed later. A large number of local Indigenous "marriages" took place between members of neighboring tribes, extending familial connections across these lines. While San Francisco Bay Area Indigenous society was patrilineal, it was not patriarchal, as women held a variety of positions of power.[45] Women often served as healers or spiritual leaders. Chiefdom was hereditary, typically handed down to sons, though if no son was available, then sisters or daughters could become chiefs. Women led important dances and rituals.[46] Relationships were fluid, as emphasis was on the rearing of children rather than the preservation of a monogamous relationship.[47] Polygamy was common, especially among elites, as prominent figures, male and female, often had multiple partners.[48] As scholar Deborah A. Miranda, herself Indigenous to the Monterey Bay Area and a member of the Ohlone-Costanoan Esselen Nation, has effectively demonstrated, Indigenous notions of gender were nuanced and fluid and included the existence of third-gender roles, as Ohlone society, like many others in Native North America, allowed for individuals to take gender roles that did not correspond to biological sex.[49]

Ohlone society tended toward a relative egalitarianism within tribal communities; while labor was divided along gendered lines, social status was not strictly divided. Chiefs exercised power during warfare but were otherwise limited. In times of change, new chiefs required community approval. The role of the chief involved obligations to the community, as the chief was expected to provide food for visitors and those who were without food as well as providing property for ceremonies and giving approval for these ceremonies. Chiefs were not the only ones who enjoyed social prestige; Ohlone tribes had orators, who carried out important duties. These orators were likely multilingual, serving as diplomats negotiating trade and commerce with neighboring tribes as well as greeting incoming foreigners.[50]

Ohlone people lived in a rich spiritual world within an ideology and cosmology that was embodied in the lands they called home. Individuals belonged to, and drew meaning from, the specific places in which they lived.[51] While each independent tribe had its own narratives, the Ohlone collectively espoused a type of animism, a spiritual system that prevailed throughout the Indigenous Americas. As such, they understood that all animate and inanimate objects have spirits that could be malevolent or benevolent, and thus people were careful to make gifts in places of power.[52] Spanish explorers frequently encountered religious shrines throughout the land. Feathered objects, poles, and food were left as offerings.[53] Dreams were an important avenue for connecting with the spirit world. One could connect with dream helpers, who offered songs and talismans for protection or warning.[54] Dream helpers could teach people ways of healing or offer other important insights and knowledge.[55]

Oral traditions instructed local communities on the right way to live in relationship with their environment and in community with their neighbors.[56] There are stories of creation, navigation of space, and cultural practice revolving around local geographical markers and influences.[57] While few narratives from the people of Mak-Sah-Re-Jah persist in the public domain, those that do show much in common with other California tribes.[58] These narratives center around animal spirits—Coyote, Snake, Bear, Eagle, or others—and teach lessons about morality and history as rooted in geographic space.

Spiritual practices were plural, not exclusive, as numerous traditions were practiced, including the Kuksui (sometimes recorded as Kuksu or Cocosuy), tradition. Kuksui ceremonies involved gatherings of healers and elders from a variety of neighboring tribes at sacred sites. The Kuksui ceremony involved an elaborate production of songs and dance, with some dancers dressing with Big Head regalia signifying the Kuksui and other spirits.[59] Sometimes Kuksui dances were used for healing, as related in a story by Mutsun elder Barbara Sierra de Solórsano:

> How they used to make Cocosuy dances for curing the sick: When my mother and father were young they used to go to see the medicine man doings there. . . . They just had a captain who did not talk to anybody, he just lived there inside the sweathouse. He was the same as a priest. They used to carry his food to him. The captain of the Rancheria took care of him. And if a person took sick, one went to talk with the captain of the Rancheria to see if they could save him. And then the captain went over and consulted with four men, with just four men. . . . And then the captain and the four went over to talk with the man of the sweathouse, and that medicine man would tell them: "Let us make a dance for finding his life, to see where he will find his life, to see if he is going to have a long life or short, let us see in the dance."
>
> And then the four men and two women and one speechmaker (there was always one of those) would drink a little of that water and that little quantity of water would not come to an end, it remained as full as it was at first. Then the captain would say to the mournful ones: "Do not ye cry any longer, because he is already of life, he is going to resuscitate," and they beheld the dead person breathing. And they would bring him back until they would be giving him nourishment. My father and mother got to see this.[60]

As related in this story, Ohlone tribes also had members who served as doctors, healers, sorcerers, or medicine people.[61] They used herbs and medicine, controlled the rain and weather, foretold the future, mediated between the human and spirit worlds, and brought people back to life. The Rattlesnake Doctor could cure or prevent rattlesnake bites and could sense if somebody nearby had killed a rattlesnake.[62] In addition to healing and foretelling the future, their duties often included finding lost objects, removing contamination, and sharing games. As mediators between the human and spirit worlds, they could design and distribute amulets or charm stones to placate spirits. Storytelling and the preservation of tribal knowledge and history could be performed by an orator, storyteller, or doctor. Illness was diagnosed and healed through song or dance or through herbs. Unsuccessful sorcerers could be killed for failing to heal.[63] Ohlone commonly utilized sweat lodges to purify and heal as well as for religious ceremony.[64]

Bear Doctors were of particular importance and held special powers, and Santa Cruz was known for having many of them, possibly in connection with the large number of bears in the mountains. Some of these doctors wore bearskin and used bear claws or teeth to evoke bear medicine, but others did something more.[65] Maria Ascención Solórsano spoke about them at length:

> In the dance is where they form themselves into bears, with fur and snout and all. The medicine man has to talk to the bears in the dance and thus one turns into a bear. Kaan yete 'oreypu, I am going to turn into a bear. . . . I heard say that there at Santa Cruz was where there were more of these bear doctors, that there were many of them there. . . .
>
> A man that used to turn bear they called "ooreema" and "ooreemakwa" when there were several. Don't you see, the word mentions the "ores"—the bear. . . .
>
> No, they did not put on bear skins, the bear doctors did not. Do you know how they used to turn into bears here? It was in the very fire itself that they used to turn into bears. A great blaze was made out doors in the evening and the people gathered together and the bear doctors used to dance beside the fire, making their witchcraft, and thereupon they would throw themselves on all fours in the fire,

and they were burning, and there were explosive sounds, and the face was formed first, and then the fur, and at last they would turn out, panting, panting, just like a bear. Hiccepunak'oreese, he turned bear. And as soon as they finished doing this, they would take to the country in order to kill animals or for doing damage. . . . There is a head of those bear doctors, a man who is the leader of them. It is there with him that they hold their meeting, and then when they already make themselves animals with him, each of them takes his road already turned into an animal.[66]

Animals were a central part of Ohlone cosmology, as family units were typically aligned with specific animals, forming hereditary clans.[67] Animals served as dream helpers, totem animals, and teachers from stories and shared narratives as well as distinguishing clans and moieties.[68] Creation narratives involved Coyote, Eagle, and Hummingbird. Many local Ohlone tribes have creation stories that recall flooding and survival atop sacred mountains. For Ohlone with territories from modern Santa Cruz to the south, Mount Umunhum was the sacred mountain, while northern Ohlone spoke of Tuyshtak (Mount Diablo).[69] Tools and ceremonial regalia were made from animal remains or fashioned into shapes or representations of animals. Ohlone prayed to animals in their ceremonial dances and in preparation for hunting.[70] Local narratives reflected the distinctive coastal and redwood makeup of this region, embedding stories and knowledge formed over thousands of years through an intimate understanding of landscape and territory.[71]

Tribal names reflected names for the geographic region, while families or kinship groups sometimes identified by village site.[72] Identity was understood on multiple levels, as a plurality. These larger kinship networks divided tribal identification into clans, which identified hereditarily with specific animals as totems, such as deer, fox, bear, crow, rabbit, skunk, owl, or elk.[73] These totem affiliations reflected social, economic, and ritual status and entailed ritual responsibilities for clan members, who led ceremonies associated with their animal.[74] These clan affiliations were ritual relationships to spiritual beings (connected with their specific animal).

Another identity distinction that bound people together was the moiety.[75] Moiety affiliations associated extended kinship networks with certain animals, animal families, or natural elements. In the larger San Francisco Bay Area, moieties appear to have been tied to the animals that lived in particular landscapes, and village and community names often reflected these affiliations. Different moiety affiliations bound families and neighboring tribes together through ties of reciprocity. For example, some moieties were in charge of ensuring proper ritual burial and funereal ceremonies for those of other moieties.[76] Amah Mutsun tribal historian Ed Ketchum theorized that these different moiety affiliations were associated with villages and regions, which makes sense considering that village name sites tend to correspond to these categories. From Ketchum, describing village names in the Mutsun territories (see map 2):

> The moieties [sic] normally include deer, bear, coyote, reptiles, predatory birds, other birds, water and earth. Looking at the map, elk/deer Tiuvta [Place of the Elk] is found on the west, to the north is Matalan—coyote/wolf, to the east is Orestac and Orestimba—bear, to the south and west are Guacharon/Chalon—Condor, predator birds, and in the center are fish people—Unijaima, snakes—Ippitak (rattle snake) and kotretak (gopher snake) and salamanders—Welelismo. I doubt this was coincidental. I wish I knew the meaning of Tamarox. If it were Hawk it would be great as the Condor story would have a place in the landscape. The Mutsun dictionary did not include a definition for Tamarox. [The village of] Tamarox is in the Spanish land grant [under the title] Quien Sabe—*Who Knows*. I have been told there are a lot of cliffs which would be ideal for hawk nests, but again I have found no definition for Tamarox.[77]

Games were another important element of social life—tribes would gather, play, and compete against each other. Games included one called "gome," a ball race in which participants would race while kicking a wooden ball along long distances, often spanning tribal boundaries.[78] Onlookers would bet on the victor. Stickball games and a number of bone-and-shell guessing games were also played. "Dice" games were played with eight-inch-long wooden sticks painted black and white on the sides. Six of these sticks were thrown, and players scored when they landed all black or white. Archery contests were organized for sport as well as training for hunting.[79]

The reverberations of European colonization likely impacted local peoples long before any direct physical encounter took place.[80] Archaeologists have noted a demographic decline in the area after 1600. Some have theorized that this decline occurred as a result of catastrophic contact with European diseases.[81] I estimate the Indigenous population among all of the people of Mak-Sah-Re-Jah before arrival of the Spanish at around fourteen hundred (see table 1).[82] Awareness of Spanish existence and exploration probably reached Ohlone lands before actual contact. Word of encounters with northern tribes such as the Miwok, from visitors such as Sir Francis Drake, and, later, of missionary settlements in the early 1700s down in Baja likely would have arrived through trade channels.[83] The passage of Spanish ships along the coastline, like those of Juan Rodriguez Cabrillo, Sebastian Rodriguez Cermeño, and Sebastián Vizcaíno, would have likely been observed from shore.[84] The presence of multiple networks of trade and communication suggest knowledge of these foreign expeditions, and this is reflected in repeated stories told by Native people of armed men in attire similar to that of the Spanish explorers.[85] In any case, permanent Spanish colonization and settlement began in 1769, and direct encounter with the Spanish resulted in immense change for local peoples over a relatively short time.

Indigenous Landscape at the Time of Spanish Arrival

At the time of Spanish arrival and settlement, the tribes of the coastal lands of the Mak-Sah-Re-Jah lived in territories marked by watersheds with ridgelines as boundaries (see figs. 1 and 2, map 3). Long-standing interrelations built around trade, diplomacy, and intermarriage would have informed a complex society with its own history and politics that have largely not been recorded. However, some signs in the archives give us a sense of some of these political and geographical boundaries. In addition, we can triangulate the relative proximity of these tribes based on patterns of intermarriage as well as an analysis of archaeological records.[86]

At the southern edge of this area was the territory of the Aptos (see map 2).[87] The chief of the Aptos during this time was Molegnis (Baltasar

Dieguez), who would have been around thirty years old when the Spanish founded the first of their local missions in 1770.[88] The Aptos tribe was one of the larger groups of the region. Aptos Creek bounded the western edge of Aptos lands, which included the shores of Monterey Bay from modern-day Aptos eastward about halfway to the Pajaro River.[89] To the south of the Aptos lay the Calenda-ruc region (*calen* meaning "ocean," *ruc* meaning "house"), which was along the coast on both sides of the Pajaro River.[90] Aptos intermarriages show that they had connections to the Uypi and Calenda-ruc tribes with territories to the north and south, respectively, and a large number of intermarriages with the Cajastaca or Cajastac, which was almost certainly the name of one of the village sites for one of the two large groups of Aptos.[91] One hundred and seventeen people were identified as Aptos in the baptismal records between 1791 and 1797 and another sixty-eight baptized as being from the Cajastaca village between 1795 and 1802.

The Uypi were just north of the Aptos, likely with Arana Gulch serving as boundary between Uypi and Aptos lands.[92] Oral histories imply that the two tribes may have had a bit of a rivalry.[93] The Uypi homeland was along the mouth of the San Lorenzo River, the site of modern Santa Cruz.[94] The chief of the Uypi was Soquel (Hermenegildo); his wife was Rosuem (Josefa).[95] Uypi villages included Aulintak (place of the Red Abalone), near the mouth of the San Lorenzo; Chalamü, approximately one mile northwest of Aulintak; and Hottrochtac, one mile farther northwest.[96] The Uypi were the first group baptized in large numbers at Mission Santa Cruz—104 Uypi people were baptized between 1791 and 1795—the first group completely absorbed into the mission. Uypi individuals intermarried with neighboring Aptos, Cajastaca, Chaloctaca, Chitactac, Cotoni, Pitac, and Sayanta—many of the same groups that make up the estimated Awaswas Ohlone linguistic speakers.[97] These tribal intermarriages helped to solidify alliances and interconnections between neighboring groups. The coastal homeland of the Uypi was rich in meadowlands and coastal terraces, the meadowlands rich in mixed hardwood and evergreen forests adjacent to highly productive marine habitats. The Spanish identified it as ideal for permanent settlement, and it eventually became the lands upon which they built Mission Santa Cruz.

The Cotoni were the next people who lived northwesterly up the coast from the Uypi, the boundary between the two territories most likely between

Baldwin and Major's Creeks. The Cotoni had coastal villages near modern Davenport and Scott's Creek. Their homelands likely included the inland ridge in the Bonny Doon area and the UC Santa Cruz meadows and oaks as well. Ninety-three Cotoni were baptized between 1792 and 1800. Further information is found in the interviews of Lorenzo Asisara, the son of the Cotoni man named Llencó (Venancio).[98] Asisara claimed that his "father's tribe was Jlli, and he belonged to the tribe that lived up the coast. They lived upon shellfish, which they took from the seacoast, and carried them to the hills, where their rancherias were. The remains of the shells are there now, and can be seen in numerous places."[99] In another interview Asisara reported that his father was from the coastal village named Asar.[100] Asisara's recollections reaffirm the importance of the abundant ocean resources for these coastal tribes.

The baptismal books and existing studies present the Cotoni and the Achistaca as two distinct groups, but it seems more likely that the two were the same people, with the Achistaca being the inland village of the coastal Cotoni.[101] Villagers from Achistaca were designated as such despite the clear ties with the Cotoni.[102] The village of Achistaca most likely refers to the various village sites in the Saddle Mountain area, nearby what is today called Little Basin. In fact, Achistaca may very well refer to all the upland Cotoni village sites in a more plural sense, including the village sites up from Little Basin toward Buzzard's Roost.[103] It seems likely that the names we have for villages refer to something more of a broad area where villages rotate, rather than a fixed dot on a map, as we conceive cities today. Between 1791 and 1795 the Spanish at Mission Santa Cruz baptized eighty-five Achistaca villagers. Prominent Achistaca included Upejen (Serafina Josefa), who was connected through kinship with a Sayanta man, Roiesic (Pascual Antonio Arenaza), and his two partners, Tuicam (Margarita de Cortona) and Chitemis (Rafaela Gazetas).[104] These intermarriages helped bind together neighboring tribes and villages, facilitating social cohesion throughout the region.

The village sites of the Chaloctaca and Sayanta are along neighboring watersheds and ridges, and patterns of intermarriages and families traveling together on diplomatic visits to Mission Santa Clara suggest that the Cotoni (Achistaca), Chaloctaca, Sayanta, and Uypi all had strong ties, probably reinforced through kinship and intermarriage.[105] Archaeologist Mark Hylkema related the following with regard to these villages: "I think that the Chaloctaca occupied Lexington Reservoir basin where there are a large number of sites and many bedrock mortars. That reservoir includes upper Los Gatos Creek and wraps around the base of Mount Umunhum. Sayant[a] was likely centered at Quail Hollow, and Scotts Valley, Rancho Sayantaca (Zayante Road and town of Zayante). No villages on ridge tops except Ben Lomond Mountain where Cotoni and Achistac were, and deep middens abound."[106]

The majority of recorded Chaloctaca are interrelated through one large extended kinship family, headed by Gelelis (Gabriel Cañizares) and Ypasin (Juana Eudovigis Pinedo).[107] This large family was interconnected through kinship to the Sayanta.[108] Their second-oldest son, Ules (Andres Cañizares), and his wife, Lluillin (Maria de la Purificacion de Landa), became central figures in the mission community, the former a particularly rebellious figure whom the padres labeled "incorrigible" for continually challenging their authority.[109] Only thirty-eight people were baptized at Mission Santa Cruz as Chaloctaca between 1792 and 1795, though it appears that quite a few had already been baptized at Mission Santa Clara.[110] This is likely due to their proximity to Mission Santa Clara, as their homeland region near the present-day Lexington Reservoir would have been just southwest of the mission and likely the closest source of redwoods for the missionaries. The Chaloctaca had intermarriages with Achistaca, Cotoni, Partacsi of the Santa Clara Valley, Sayanta, and Somontoc. The large number of intermarriages with Sayanta in particular suggests that there was substantial overlap between the two villages.

The Sayanta village was a smaller village that was in the mountains around the Zayante Creek drainage, near modern Zayante and Quail Hollow Ranch.[111] Sixty-nine Sayanta were baptized at Mission Santa Cruz between 1791 and 1795. A number of Sayanta, often in small groups along with Achistaca, Chaloctaca, and Uypi, visited Mission Santa Clara, where their children received baptism before the founding of Mission Santa Cruz. These visitations suggest a high degree of intertribal collaboration, intermarriage and alliance networks among the mountain tribes. The Sayanta were baptized after the Uypi and had pre-mission intermarriages with Achistaca and Chaloctaca villagers. The alliances between these neighboring tribes persisted through the mission years and would grow to include more tribes and families in the following years.

The Somontoc are one of the most difficult mountain villages to pinpoint, as many of them were among the earliest to receive baptism at Mission Santa Clara.[112] They represent one group that was greatly divided between mission communities and might be connected to a group known as the Matalan, whose members mostly received baptism at Mission Santa Clara. It is possible that Somontoc was a village site of the Matalan people, given the *-toc* suffix (place of) in Somontoc. It appears that Somontoc was located along the upper Guadalupe River in New Almaden Valley, up through Los Capitancillos Creek, below Mount Umhunhum.[113] Members of the Somontoc village were generally listed by the padres at Mission Santa Clara as "San Carlos," indicating that they were part of the San Carlos district. Only seventeen were eventually baptized at Mission Santa Cruz, though some of those who had their children baptized at Mission Santa Clara eventually moved to Santa Cruz.[114] Oral histories from the American era report that rivalries existed between "Santa Clara Indians" and those from Santa Cruz, references to fighting over cinnabar resources used to make red paint (vermillion), which would make sense considering the proximity of the cinnabar mines in the Somontoc territory of New Almaden.[115] It is possible that this is a reference to the Somontoc, as Santa Cruz missionaries referred to them as Santa Clara Indians. The first Somontoc to receive baptism at Mission Santa Cruz was Euxexi (Ambrosio), who was tied through kinship to Achistaca, Chaloctaca, and Sayanta families.[116]

Situated at the central coast of the San Francisco Peninsula, the largest and most politically powerful of these tribes was the Quiroste.[117] The Quiroste lived to the north of the Cotoni, their territory ranging on the Pacific Coast from Waddell Creek on the southern side up to Pescadero and inland to the ridge up at Skyline Boulevard. The Quiroste controlled the production of two major coastal exports—the tough rocks along the cliffs that could be located along the beach at low tide, known as Monterey chert, which were used as the raw materials for chipped stone tools such as spears, knives, scrapers, drills, darts, and arrowheads throughout the larger Bay Area, and Olivella snail shell beads, which served as currency throughout Indigenous California. Quiroste people appear among the early San Francisco Peninsula coastal groups baptized at Mission San Francisco. A few of the village names are recorded in the Spanish baptismal records.

Sujute (Gregoria), wife of an Oljon (the tribe just north of the Quiroste), was "from Churmutcé, farther south than the Oljons."[118] This would be a village site in a place now known as the town of Pescadero and was likely the largest Quiroste village site. Uégcém (Maria Bona), wife of a Cotegen (the tribe just north of the Oljon), was from "the family of the Quirogtes of the village of Mitine [sic] to the west of Chipletac."[119] The site of Mitenne is understood to be in what is now known as Quiroste Valley and is the location of one of the more famous early encounters with the Spanish.

Early Colonial Encounters

It was the people of the large Quiroste village of Mitenne that had fed and lent scouts to the expedition led by Don Gaspar de Portolá in 1769, the first direct interaction between the San Francisco Bay Area tribes and Spanish explorers.[120] Before their arrival at Mitenne, Portolá's party had their first experience with local tribal members farther south. Many of the men were sick from malnutrition, and eleven men had to be carried by stretcher at this point in the journey. They were hoping to encounter one of two ships that carried reserve provisions and had planned to meet the others at their intended destination of Monterey. With so many of the men sick and weary, a small group of baptized Indigenous Baja Californian scouts, led by Sergeant Don José Francisco Ortega, traveled ahead of the recuperating expedition members and encountered what was most likely the Tiuvta village of the Guacharron people, inhabited by nearly five hundred villagers alongside a large river. The scouts described a chaotic encounter, first with women grieving, followed by signs that they interpreted as peaceful, as warriors placed arrowheads into the ground. The Tiuvta villagers fed the scouts, who then returned to the larger group. By the time Portolá's men arrived a few days later, they found the village deserted, surrounded by burned grasslands, with a large bird stuffed with grass on a wooden pole. They interpreted the empty village and burned grasses to mean that the villagers had fled out of fear of the approaching party. The expedition then named the river Pajaro (bird) because of the incident, which it remains today. The travelers were disappointed, as they badly needed food and hoped to ask the villagers for scouts to help them traverse these unknown lands.[121]

The reality behind the vacated village almost certainly had less to do with a reaction to the Spanish and much more to do with traditional practices of the Guacharron people. The burned grasslands were likely part of the seasonal burning, practiced throughout Indigenous California. Ketchum suggests that these events involved the condor ceremony, an important ceremony of mourning, when the condor doctors carried messages to and from the deceased. This theory would explain the presence of crying women whom the scouts first encountered. According to Ketchum, the Guacharron likely journeyed south to the coastal Moss Landing area to have ceremony with the condor doctor during this time as, in local tradition, the dead traveled westward into the ocean, and the Moss Landing site would have allowed for this communication. Indeed, Portolá's men would run into the same villagers on their way back southward, supporting this theory.[122] Ketchum explains that the condor ceremony was celebrated when Mars is hidden from view by (or conjunct with) the sun. Condor, with its red head, is associated with the red planet, Mars. At the time the Portolá expedition arrived in early October, Mars would have been conjunct with the sun. The presence of the stuffed condor and the vacated village site certainly supports Ketchum's theory of the condor ceremony.[123]

After passing the vacated Tiuvta village, the Portolá party continued northward, not directly encountering any more people until they eventually arrived at the village of Mitenne. The expedition had passed through these coastal mountain lands in the fall—the timing also coinciding with when these tribes left their coastal terrace village sites for their winter homes in the forests to hunt and gather acorns. While it is certainly possible that some villagers spotted the Spanish explorers, the Spanish only reported seeing burned plains and evidence of evacuated village sites.[124] They also passed well-worn trails, recognizing that many people lived in the area.[125] Again, it was the scouting party, led by Ortega with the baptized Indigenous people from Baja, that preceded the larger group and arrived on October 22 at the Quiroste village of Mitenne, near present-day Año Nuevo. The Quiroste villagers welcomed the expedition, exchanging food for Spanish glass beads and cloth.[126] The rest of the men arrived the following day, sick from malnutrition.

The Mitenne villagers were generous to Portolá's men. Cartographer Miguel Costansó wrote that the villagers "received us with a great deal of affability and kindness, nor failed to make the usual present of seeds kneaded into thick dough-balls; they offered us also some bits of honeycomb with a certain syrup which some said was wasp-honey. . . . In the midst of the village was a great house of spherical shape, very roomy; while the other little houses, which were of pyramidal construction and very small-sized, were built of pine splints. And because the big house [Casa Grande] stood out so from the rest, the village was so named."[127] Costansó and the other diarists named the village Casa Grande and noted that it had about two hundred people. The Quiroste villagers seemed to indicate that the expedition would find the ship carrying extra provisions by traveling north for three days and offered food for Portolá's people.[128] The next day the Quiroste lent guides to help them navigate their way northward. The Portolá party made its way to San Francisco, then returned southward to Monterey. As the Portolá party traveled southward and back through the Casa Grande village site on November 18, they found it deserted.[129] Shortly after their return to Monterey, permanent Spanish settlement began in the region, with the founding of Mission San Carlos on the Monterey Peninsula on June 3, 1770.

The founding of Mission San Carlos began a process of Indigenous baptism and relocation in the Monterey Bay area to the south of Santa Cruz.[130] The tribes living in the Pajaro Valley had the most direct contact with the Spanish in the early years, as recruiting expeditions and Spanish overland movement utilized the Pajaro Valley basin for travel northward to the San Francisco Peninsula.[131] Mission San Carlos also baptized the Esselen people south of Monterey.[132] The number of baptisms in the first few years was low: only 31 Indigenous people had been baptized by the end of 1772.[133] This number increased slowly, as 435 total baptisms of Indigenous peoples had taken place by the time Mission Santa Clara was founded in June 1777, a relatively low number compared to those in the years that followed.[134]

The responses of the local Indigenous communities played a key role in shaping the establishment and growth of each mission, along with factors such as the temperament of the priests involved and local environment. Due to the comparatively small number of Spanish soldiers, protocol dictated that they avoid outright conflict. At the same time, however, Spanish protocol authorized retaliation against Natives who challenged Spanish authorities. By the spring of 1777 Spanish soldiers had killed three Tamyen Ohlone men of the San Francisco Peninsula for butchering mules, thereby establishing boundaries and rules around Spanish livestock.[135] Following the founding of Mission Santa Clara in the densely populated Santa Clara Valley, local baptism and relocation to the mission continued at a slow pace.

The overwhelming pattern of baptisms at the various local missions shows that Indigenous children received baptism before their parents, likely the result of a combination of factors. These include deliberate conversion strategy on the part of the missionaries as well as an Indigenous strategy for information gathering, as suggested by Ketchum, who theorizes that Indigenous communities sent some of these youth into the missions as spies.[136] All but one of the first sixty-six baptisms performed in the first six months, from June to December 1777, were children under the age of ten.[137] The Spanish strategy was to offer baptisms along with gifts of beads and wool clothes.[138] Families came in groups with their children to receive these gifts.[139] Once children (or adults) received baptism, they were considered charges of the missionaries. The missionaries believed they had responsibility for their souls as well. Baptized children remained with their parents, at least until age ten, at which point they worked closely with the friars, who taught them Spanish and the Catholic religion.[140]

These youth played complicated roles, walking between the Catholic world presented by the friars and the Indigenous worlds of their kin. They were in a position both to inform their communities about the ways of the new colonizers and to help the missionaries recruit their family and kin. By the end of December 1777, groups of teenagers began to receive baptism, along with some of their parents. From the missionaries' perspective, these youth became instrumental to future recruitment, as they received passports (*paseos*) and were encouraged to retrieve friends and family members. These young people learned to navigate the newly forming political and social world that took shape under the control of the padres.

The Spanish imposed a new distinction on Indigenous peoples, referring to the newly baptized as *neofitos*, or "newly Christianized Indians," and to the unbaptized as *pagans* or, more frequently, *gentiles*.[141] Some of these newly baptized young men gained the trust of the missionaries and played instrumental roles in bringing in new Indigenous people. One of the early "Christianized Indians" was ten-year-old Pablo.[142] The son of

Guachismic (Rudesindo) and Toppi (Lucia Maria), Pablo followed his brother in getting baptized, along with his parents.[143] The family's tribal identity is listed as "San Francisco Solano," which refers to the contemporary city of Alviso. Pablo was an important member within the baptized Native community at Santa Clara, earning a role as mission interpreter and teacher, translating Catholic teachings for incoming baptized Native people. Through the years he served as godparent in 160 baptisms at Mission Santa Clara as well as a few at neighboring missions Dolores and San Juan Bautista, where he visited and assisted with Catholic instruction for newly baptized Native people.[144]

Pablo appears to have earned a high level of trust with the Franciscans, as he enjoyed a level of mobility, accompanying soldiers on their travels, serving as interpreter and assistant.[145] Pablo eventually spent time helping in the early years at Mission Santa Cruz, where he was in charge of teaching the catechism.[146] While there, he performed a baptism on a dying seventy-year-old Cajastaca man, Ulléug (Jose Manuel).[147] The teaching of confirmation and performance of baptism reflect the prominent position that Pablo had achieved within Spanish society and suggest that a generation of young converts began to fill crucial roles as translators and performers of Catholic practices. With the help they provided, these youth made it possible for the padres to run the missions in the early years of colonization.

Small groups of tribal members from Mak-Sah-Re-Jah traveled to Mission Santa Clara beginning in the late 1770s. Most of these groups consisted of Chaloctaca, Sayanta, Somontoc, and Uypi couples and families tied through kinship.[148] These groups illustrate that there was a large degree of intertribal coordination and cooperation. On these visits children received baptism, while parents likely received beads, cloth, and trade goods from the Spanish, which they then integrated into existing Indigenous economic systems. By the end of 1790 nearly one hundred children from throughout Mak-Sah-Re-Jah had been baptized at Mission Santa Clara, laying the groundwork for Spanish expansion into the area.

Even with the baptism of these children, the vast majority of Mak-Sah-Re-Jah people remained outside the influence of the missions, a situation that caused concern for the Spaniards. By 1791 the Spanish had made plans to establish two more missions—Missions Santa Cruz and Soledad.[149] In the months leading up to the founding of Mission Santa Cruz, contact and negotiations took place between the Spanish missionaries at Mission Santa Clara and a number of people from tribes in Mak-Sah-Re-Jah, while visitations by Spanish friars helped solidify plans to build in the region.[150] A group of Mak-Sah-Re-Jah people, including a number of prominent tribal leaders from the southwestern mountains, visited Mission Santa Clara in May 1791. This group included Chief Soquel and his wife, Rosuem, the leaders of the Uypi tribe who lived at the mouth of the San Lorenzo River.[151] The couple's two daughters received baptism, and discussions were held with the padres regarding the founding of a mission on their lands.[152] Soquel and Rosuem had traveled to Mission Santa Clara along with a number of other prominent neighbors and allies, including Chaloctaca, Sayanta, and Somontoc, possibly as part of a diplomatic party visiting the settlement.[153]

Establishment of Mission Santa Cruz

For Indigenous families that had thus far resisted missionization and baptism, aided by the relative geographic isolation provided by the mountain range, circumstances changed rapidly following permanent Spanish settlement in the region. The establishment of a mission site and the subsequent relocation of local peoples resulted in new colonial relations with the Franciscan padres, who sought to impose their cultural traditions and intervened in local families and society in several distinct areas, including practices for labor, child-rearing, marriage, and courtship.

On September 10, 1791, a group of seven children of Mak-Sah-Re-Jah parents received baptism at Mission Santa Clara.[154] The presiding priests included Friars Baldomero Lopez and Isidro Salazar, who had recently arrived from Mexico City. Nearly two weeks later, on September 22, Second Lieutenant Hermenegildo Sal set out from Mission Santa Clara with two padres, one corporal, and two soldiers to found Mission Santa Cruz.[155] Following behind them were seven servants carrying provisions that would be used for the establishment of the mission, two mounted soldiers, and forty head of cattle. Upon arrival on September 25, the Spanish found a coastal terrace, where they could look down upon the merging of willow- and tule-filled marshes that met with the lush redwood, Douglas fir, black oak, and laurel forests that characterized the coastline.[156] The Spanish viewed the dense forests of these homelands as rich resources for the building of their colonial settlements. They settled on flats near the San Lorenzo River after encountering six baptized Indians from Mission Santa Clara, who appear to have been sent ahead of the founding party, and promptly sent them to find Chief Soquel and his people.[157]

As was a common dynamic, labor of young Indigenous converts played a central role in the settlement of Mission Santa Cruz and the expansion of Catholic and Spanish occupation. Sal ordered these youth to cut wood to build a ramada for the padres, then set them to work clearing a field for the purpose of planting wheat. Sal commented that these youth were "very pleasant" and industrious, while he reported reservations about Soquel.[158] He also reported frustration at having to wait for the Indigenous children in Soquel's company to stop playing and talking before he could discuss business, reflecting Spanish and Indigenous differences in child-rearing.

The padres were dismissive of the Ohlone parents, noting that they taught their children to hunt and to fish and that "they merely recount to them the fables which they heard in their pagan state," disparaging the types of knowledge being taught, though they admitted that "they esteem their wives, love their children, but these latter receive their education from the missionary fathers."[159] Indigenous child-rearing, which included instruction in hunting, gathering, and the various cultural practices, stood in stark contrast to the instruction given by the padres, which focused on the spiritual practices of Catholicism and denigrated the traditional practices of their parents as sinful and evil. Furthermore, by instructing baptized youth in reorganizing traditional fields into agricultural fields for Spanish crops, Spanish authorities continued a larger regional pattern of directing Indigenous labor.[160]

Soquel was given two birds and two cows, likely a gift for the founding of the mission on his homelands. The Spanish informed the Uypi that they were welcome to come work at the mission as long as they followed the rules that they were given. Given the approach of the rainy fall season and the Spanish gifts of cows and birds, along with the planting of Spanish crops, it seems likely that Soquel negotiated food for his people in exchange for the founding of Mission Santa Cruz. An exchange would seem to reflect a concern over the availability of food, due perhaps to either the growing impact of Spanish regional settlement on animal populations or the impact of a series of particularly harsh winters.[161] No records suggest that cattle were given to anyone other than Soquel, despite the group of locals who accompanied the chief and his family on their trips to Mission Santa Clara. By negotiating an exchange of animals for recognition of the Spanish settlement, Soquel shows one response to the rapidly changing world in which he found himself. Despite Lieutenant Sal's reluctance to trust Soquel, he promised to make him the first baptism at the new mission and served as godparent in his baptism.[162]

Sal established a set of standing orders for the guards at Mission Santa Cruz, orders that reflected the sense of vulnerability the Spanish felt regarding the locals:

> Item 8. Whenever Indians come in you are to go out to meet them. If they bring weapons you will order them to give them up before allowing them to enter the mission.
> Item 9. You will treat the Indian population well, adopting measures to regale the headmen and to make them see that the soldiers and the missionaries will not interfere with them nor cause them any harm, so long as they make no provocation.
> Item 10. Never deprecate any kind of notice that the Indians bring regarding rumor of insurrection. If they take up arms in a surprise attack, you will be ready with yours. And at the first suggestion that they want peace, you will immediately suspend fighting and promptly inform me as briefly as possible, so that I can pass it along to the Chief [governor], and await his orders.
> Item 11. Soldiers are not permitted to go roving about the countryside, to become familiar with local villagers, even less to attempt any kind of extortion against the natives. If any soldier contravenes this order he will receive from me punishment as deserved, according to the severity of the offense.[163]

These orders reflect an ongoing concern about Indigenous aggression as well as Spanish protocol in the early stages of colonial occupation. Item 11 is indicative of a larger concern throughout Alta California of soldiers abusing villagers.

Throughout colonial California, missionaries reported threats of sexual abuse of Indigenous women by soldiers, colonizers, and friars. Franciscan missionary complaints of Spanish soldiers raping Indigenous women had been commonplace since the earliest days of Spanish colonization, and rules were typically put in place to try to prevent this crime.[164] Many Spanish restrictions attempted to address the threat. Since the vast majority of colonizers were men, conversations about marriage frequently took place, which resulted in rules regarding intermarriage between Spanish soldiers and an expanding social class of "Indian."[165] This classification included not only Indigenous people of the area but also a broader group of Indigenous peoples upended by the colonial process. The diverse settling community was made up of people arriving on the central coast from faraway locations such as Alaska, Baja California, mainland Mexico, Siberia, and others, including the Nuu-chah-nulth, who were indigenous to Vancouver Island in the Pacific Northwest.[166] Approval by Franciscan padres was considered sufficient, though the approval of Spanish civil officials was generally sought.[167] One such marriage took place without documented license at Mission Santa Cruz in May 1794 between soldier Jose Azebes and a fourteen-year-old Uypi girl, Ojoc (Feliciana Ormachea).[168]

Indigenous responses to the newly established mission varied. The majority of local peoples held off baptism, while others brought their children or chose to receive baptism themselves. The Santa Cruz Mission–born Lorenzo Asisara explained: "First were taken the children, and then the parents followed. The padres would erect a hut, and light the candles to say mass, and the Indians, attracted by the light—thinking they were stars—would approach, and soon be taken. These would bring in others, such as their relatives."[169] Asisara, whose father was one of the earliest baptized Cotoni men, would have likely heard these stories from his father and others at the mission. This story suggests that the baptism of children was used as a strategy for later enticing their families into the mission. Indeed, at Mission Santa Cruz, children made up most of the early baptized people. By the end of 1791 the newly forming community numbered eighty-nine, including only thirteen adults.[170] The mention of lighted candles suggests curiosity about the new technologies and customs of the settling Spanish. The first baptisms followed a pattern in which one child (in the first year primarily Achistaca, Aptos, Sayanta, and Uypi) received baptism, followed shortly by his or her family and relatives, who would often show up in small groups. Some of the parents of these children avoided baptism for up to five years, while other parents followed their children more quickly into the mission.[171] Proximity to and distance from the mission heavily shaped these patterns, with those closer to the mission entering earlier.

Once baptized, Indigenous people became wards of the Franciscan missionaries. Given the baptized Natives' status as dependents, the missionaries felt little compunction about tracking them down by military force if they left the community without permission.[172] After baptism they were instructed to relocate to the lands surrounding the new mission and build traditional tule houses with their families on these lands. As diverse tribal communities relocated to the mission, on Uypi lands, they organized their homes according to kinship, familial, and tribal networks.[173] Soquel, along with his daughter and three local children, received teachings and Catholic confirmation at Mission Santa Clara in February 1792.[174] The aforementioned Pablo of Mission Santa Clara first appeared as a confirmation teacher and translator in May 1793.[175] It seems that either the padres sent Soquel due to a lack of qualified teachers at Mission Santa Cruz at this early stage, or it may have been a political ploy by the Spanish to distance a leader they clearly disliked from his own people. The first confirmations did not take place at Mission Santa Cruz until May 1793, with the arrival of Pablo, so Soquel and the others may have been sent to start this process of Catholic training and teaching early.[176]

Why tribal members would choose to receive baptism knowing that this would mean relocation is a complicated issue, which often involved political consequences within existing Indigenous political hierarchies. The lure of creating new political alliances and power played a factor for some. Molegnis, the leader of the Aptos, who lived just south of the Uypi, challenged the leadership of Soquel and Rosuem. Molegnis received baptism shortly after the Uypi leader and, at fifty years of age, was by far the oldest to receive baptism in the first few months of the mission.[177] He and his twenty-five-year-old wife, Solue (Ana de la Relde), were the first to receive confirmation, a symbol of status within the mission community.[178] This previously mentioned contention between Soquel and Molegnis might have influenced Molegnis's decision to enter the mission, as he may have wanted to preserve his own political standing within the tribal communities that were rapidly relocating to the mission.

The case of Molegnis's baptism and his subsequent Catholic wedding highlight another way that the missionaries sought to reorganize tribal life—through the disruption of marriage and partnerships. Catholic marriages were an important tool for the missionaries to impose their sexual ethics on polygamous peoples.[179] The padres arranged the men and women in separate lines, while interpreters explained the Catholic view of marriage. The missionaries asked the men a series of questions, including whether they wished to be married and whether they had previously engaged in sexual relations with any of the women present. If they admitted to having prior relations, they were required to marry the individual. If they said they had not, they were free to choose a woman to marry; however, if the selected woman showed unwillingness, they were asked to choose another.[180] Prior to the establishment of the mission, Molegnis had had two children with different partners.[181] After his baptism he was paired with the young Aptos woman Solue, and the two partook in a Catholic marriage ceremony along with three other couples shortly thereafter.[182]

The records show that Native people exercised a degree of control over when to receive baptism, taking into account the imposition of Catholic marriage and monogamy. Some parents resisted baptism to avoid having to make a decision among their numerous partners. In one Chaloctaca-Sayanta family, Cholmos (Acisclo), fifty-year-old son of Chaloctaca elders Gelelis and Ypasin, had children with two women: three with a Chaloctaca woman named Nisipen (Maria Guadalupe Cruz) and two with Ullegen (Aciscla), a Sayanta woman.[183] The first of his children to receive baptism was the two-year-old son of Ullegen, Panuncio, who was among the seven children baptized at Mission Santa Clara two weeks before the founding of Mission Santa Cruz.[184] About a year later the first large group of Chaloctaca, including elders and grandparents Gelelis and Ypasin as well as Cholmos's eldest son, twenty-nine-year-old Tunegees (Bernardo Hablitas Jauregui), received baptism. This group included Nisipen and two of her children, a two-year-old son and a seven-year-old daughter.[185] Within a few years of their joining the community, grandfather Gelelis, seven-year-old Tipan (Maria del Carmen Hablitas), and her mother, Nisipen, had all died.[186] Cholmos and Ullegen remained outside the mission community with their young son, Tanca (Pantaleon), until February 1795, four months after the death of Nisipen.[187] Reasons aren't recorded in the baptismal records, so why Cholmos and Ullegen came in after Nisipen's death remains an open question. Nisipen never married during her time at the mission, and given the overlapping birthdates of the children, it is likely that Cholmos did not want to conform to Catholic monogamy and chose to come in only after the passing of his first wife.[188]

By spring of 1792 smaller groups of young adults began to join the mission community, some perhaps in hopes of finding new avenues to political, economic, and social mobility or status in this newly emerging community. One such example is found with Lacah (Julián Apodaca).[189] The twenty-six-year-old was a Chaloctaca from a different family than the predominant clan of Gelelis. Instead, he came from a village noted as "Sucheseu" and arrived by himself in June 1792.[190] Lacah became one of the first two elected alcaldes, or mayors, in 1796.[191] Though technically elected by Native people, these alcaldes were handpicked by the missionaries to become the "voice of the padres," and failure to follow instructions could result in corporal punishment.[192] Lacah was one of a number of younger converts who gained the favor of the padres.[193]

Others visited the missions when traditional medicines failed to provide a cure for new illnesses. The Spanish brought a host of viruses and disease that traditional healers were unequipped to deal with.[194] The Franciscan missionaries required baptized Native people to be clothed in Spanish wool, to signify new status within the mission. Wool clothing, when unwashed or unchanged, harbors disease-carrying parasites such as fleas and lice.[195] Some received baptism on the verge of death, as is the case with Llaggen (Angela), who died four days after receiving baptism in December 1791.[196] She likely came to Mission Santa Cruz seeking refuge, hoping that the padres' promise of medicine and spiritual powers could provide relief where traditional healers could not. While the friars may have interpreted these late-life conversions as proof of acceptance of Catholicism, it is more likely that people hoped that the new spiritual leaders brought with them the knowledge and ceremony needed to cure new ailments.[197]

Infant mortality rates were abysmal at the mission, but children who survived played important roles in communicating new Catholic rituals.

By the end of 1797 forty-six children had been born at the mission. Of these, thirty-five did not live to age ten, twenty-eight of them dying in infancy.[198] Of the eleven who did survive, we know for certain that five lived beyond twenty years and became key assistants to the missionaries. Among them is Lino, son of Chaloctaca couple Ules and Lluillin.[199] Lino was the fourth child born within the mission and the first to live to fifteen years. In his teenage years he served as a godfather and marriage witness and as the personal page of Padre Quintana.[200] The padres kept close guard over the young children, teaching them Spanish and Catholic customs at an early age.[201]

One way that the padres instituted tight social control was by the construction of the boys' and girls' dormitory in 1793.[202] These dormitories, referred to in Spanish as *monjeríos* (girls' dormitories or, literally, nunneries) and *jayuntes* (boys dormitories), were locked at night to keep people from leaving and signified a major shift in family organization.[203] The separation of young men and women reflected a huge departure from life before Spanish arrival, while the separation of young women from elder married women would have also impacted the transmission of important teachings.[204] Unmarried women, girls age ten and older, and widows were held in the monjeríos, with unmarried and adolescent men held in the jayuntes. Both structures separated unmarried youth from their families, while married couples were permitted to live in homes surrounding the mission. The padres used these buildings, in essence, to impose abstinence and sexual control over Native women.[205]

The isolation of women in these monjeríos sometimes led to terrible abuses, as related in one story of padres repeatedly entering the monjerío to select women they wished to violate.[206] Scholars such as Charles Sepulveda have examined the institution of the monjeríos and patterns of violence toward Indigenous women, drawing connections between violence toward Native women and violence toward the environment, ultimately arguing that Western understandings of separation between humans and nature produced the heteropatriarchal system that the Spanish brought to California.[207] The monjeríos were notorious for their poor upkeep.[208] As one visitor commented, they "were so abominably infested with every kind of filth and nastiness, as to be rendered not less offensive than degrading of the human species."[209] Another visitor to

Mission Santa Clara observed the lack of windows and lone locked door of the monjerío, comparing it to "a prison for state-criminals." This visitor went on to note that "these dungeons are opened two or three times a-day, but only to allow the prisoners to pass to and from the church. I have occasionally seen the poor girls rushing out eagerly to breathe the fresh air, and driven immediately into the church like a flock of sheep, by an old ragged Spaniard armed with a stick. After mass, they are in the same manner hurried back to their prisons."[210] Governor Diego de Borica described the monjeríos in 1797 as "small, poorly ventilated, and infested."[211] And yet the padres focused their derision on the women themselves, not their oppressive circumstances, obsessing about what they viewed as a lack of chastity or virtue, complaining, "Unchastity is the vice most dominant among them."[212]

At some point, though it isn't recorded, Native workers built the jayuntes. Some years later Asisara described the ways that the dormitories were used to control and monitor the Native youth, recalling that "one night [Fr. Ramón Olbes] took in his own hands the key of the jayunte to lock up the single men. . . . He had a list of all those who were inside the jayunte, in order to know if some were absent and who it was."[213] Children under the age of ten lived with their parents after baptism, with the proviso that they partake in Catholic teachings. Once they reached the age of ten, boys and girls were separated from their families and required to live in the locked dormitories with the rest of the baptized single adult men and women.

Spanish power in the region grew slowly over time, and in these early years of the mission formation, Spanish control and influence were kept in check by the heavily populated Native villages and territories. Spanish presence at the missions typically consisted of two missionaries, two to five soldiers, a handful of converted Baja California Natives, and the occasional visit by governmental officials or other emissaries. Direct Spanish control was limited, including the ability of the missionaries to offer Catholic instruction and teachings.[214] Furthermore, even as mission lands extended to transform a wider range of pasturelands and agricultural fields, the mountains and grasslands offered plenty of alternatives for people who had intimate knowledge of them. Many tribal elders and families chose to avoid baptism, staying outside the reach of the missionaries. Others became fugitives of the missions, fleeing to live in the forests or their former homelands.[215] But regardless of how far outside Spanish influence some chose to remain, the maintenance and growth of mission pasture and agricultural lands extended beyond the immediate environment.

Environmental Impact of Livestock

For local tribes the forests represented ancient homelands, filled with sacred places and traditional hunting grounds, a geography inscribed with deep history and meaning shaped over thousands of years. For the Spanish colonizers these landscapes represented untapped material resources with no spiritual or cultural value. The large number of terraced fields became targets for environmental reorganization. The Spanish failed to recognize the extent of Indigenous labor involved in the carefully tended grassland resources, instead seeing fallow, wild fields in need of cultivation. Young, newly baptized peoples were put to work reorganizing traditional resources into Spanish agricultural fields or pasturelands. The environmental disruption and transformation that followed Spanish settlement resulted in a loss of available grasslands for traditional foraging and ecological practices for Indigenous peoples throughout the larger San Francisco Bay Area.[216] The combination of livestock expansion and three consecutive years of regional drought between 1793 and 1796 led to food shortages.[217] Early conflicts between Spanish and Indigenous peoples revolved around cattle, resource management, and the transformation of grasslands into pasturelands.[218] The Spanish brought along large numbers of cattle, sheep, horses, pigs, and mules, all of which required extensive pasturelands (see tables 2 and 3). Additionally, Spanish agricultural practices were imposed on the lands surrounding the missions, as padres instructed newly christened youth to transform existing lands and resources into agricultural fields of wheat, barley, corn, kidney beans, chickpeas, lentils, peas, pinto beans, and fava beans.

The transformation of these cultivated grasslands into livestock grazing lands and agricultural fields quickly led to a reduction of available foodstuffs for those who chose to stay on their traditional lands, as hunger led to an increase in the number of baptisms. The vast majority of new arrivals received baptisms during the winter months, suggesting that the transformed fields reduced grazing lands for deer, elk, and other animals that locals hunted during the colder months (see table 4). The number of livestock rose dramatically in the first six years of the mission, particularly sheep and cattle, which alone numbered nearly two thousand animals by the end of 1796 (see table 2). Furthermore, the dominant agricultural products at Mission Santa Cruz included wheat and corn, which required more grazing pastures.

While these new Spanish food products altered diets, traditional foods continued to form a large part of Native American diets.[219] An incident at Mission San Carlos (Monterey) highlights the continued prominence of coastal resources as well as growing opportunities and access for Ohlone peoples. In 1790 a group of eighty to one hundred men from villages in Santa Clara went to help erect buildings near Mission San Carlos, in exchange for gifts of glass beads, shirts, blankets, and shells. Spanish soldiers were careful to disarm the men of their bows and arrows and offered provisions. But most of the Indigenous workers had brought with them seeds, rabbit, fish, wild fruit, and other foods from their homes. This was supplemented with beef and a cornmeal mush with beans, provided by the Spanish soldiers. Governor Pedro Fages recounted giving the workers blankets and glass beads and authorizing them to go down to the beach and gather abalone shells, which they loaded onto mules to carry back. The governor noted that they valued these shells for working them into coinage that they and their wives spent.[220] This event illustrates the continued value of traditional foods and practices as well as the availability of new opportunities for inland peoples to access rich coastal resources that had previously been harvested and traded by coastal tribes.

It is important to consider the impact of Spanish livestock on Indigenous spiritual practices and understandings. The introduction of new animals brought up by the colonizers would have carried important implications for people in whose cosmology animals held such importance. Moreover, Spanish usage of livestock animals differed considerably from Indigenous relationships with animals, with whom they viewed themselves to be in relations of obligatory ceremony.[221] The horse, in particular, seems to have been quickly integrated into Indigenous spiritual practices.[222] Spanish authorities feared that if Indigenous people gained access to firearms and horses, they could become an imposing military threat, while the use of horses symbolized higher status within Spanish society. Spanish officials attempted to restrict access to both firearms and horses, with mixed results. The constant dearth of firearms among the Spanish soldiers made it easier to prevent their trade, but the need for skilled equestrians for mission livestock management resulted in many skilled Indigenous horse riders.[223] Padre Junípero Serra noted that at Mission San Carlos some Indigenous "had come to the conclusion that [the Spaniards] were the sons of the mules on which they rode."[224] Years later, in 1827, American trapper Jedediah Smith described a similar reaction to his horses in the northern Sacramento Valley, observing that "many Indians came as near the camp as I would permit and sat down. I gave them some presents. . . . They were under the impression that the horses could understand them and when they were passing they talked to them and made signs as to the men."[225] People who understood themselves as living in multiple ways in connection and communication with local animals—horses and other animals—did not hold to the Catholic belief in humans' dominion over animals. While horses certainly became important elements of the new social and spiritual world, one wonders what Indigenous people thought of the livestock that shared their lands. Soquel received cow and fowl for the use of his lands. Was this for hunger, or did these exotic animals hold a certain spiritual intrigue for local peoples?[226]

The transformation of the environment impacted local animals, further disrupting spiritual foundations of local Indigenous people. Diminishing grasslands deprived deer and elk of grazing lands. The loss of deer, elk, and other animals that thrived in the tended grasslands, in turn, had an effect not only on Indigenous hunters but also on predators such as wolves and bears. These predators were drawn to the easy prey of the sedentary livestock, which lured them closer to the mission grazing lands, possibly to supplement diminishing deer and elk populations.[227] Spanish guards and missionaries did not see the local wildlife with the same reverence as the locals. They were recorded to have shot bears for target practice and eventually captured bears for entertainment purposes, pitting them against cattle in bear-and-bull fights.[228] Ketchum has pointed out that these fights served symbolic purpose, with the Spanish identifying themselves with the bull and the Natives with the bear.[229] The subjugation of sacred animals such as Bear would certainly have added to the psychological and spiritual turmoil of Indigenous locals.

The Quiroste-Led Challenge

Many Indigenous people found relocation to the missions an unacceptable prospect, and they instead chose to fight back. By the beginning of 1793 an intertribal resistance movement formed in the mountains south of San Francisco, in the homeland of the Quiroste. This movement eventually led to an outright attack on Mission Santa Cruz, the first recorded physical attack on a mission north of Monterey. The attack was precipitated, in part, by the disruption of traditional marriage practices, in some ways continuing the preexisting patterns of regional warfare that tended to ignite over the stealing of women across regional boundaries. Governor Fages described patterns of intertribal aggression in 1775, stating that these attacks involved "setting fire to this or that village of the adversary, sacking it, and bringing away some of the women either married or single."[230] The attack on Mission Santa Cruz follows this pattern. This short-lived resistance movement also demonstrated the limits of Spanish hegemony, as both baptized and unbaptized Native people collaborated in challenging Spanish authority.

Charquin (Mateo), chief of the powerful Quiroste tribe of the Point Año Nuevo area, was the leader of this movement.[231] Charquin was about sixty years old when he was baptized, in November 1791, at the San Pedro outstation along with a mixed group of Oljon and Quiroste people.[232] His two daughters, Cuc chítí (Ninfa) and Puchute (Marina), were baptized the week before he and his wife, Yaccham (Emerenciana), received baptism.[233] The day after their baptism, Charquin and Yaccham were married according to Catholic custom as well.[234] It is possible that the imposition of marriage interfered with Charquin's traditionally more fluid polygamous standing as chief, though the records do not show whether he had more than one partner before baptism. Hermenegildo Sal recalled that Charquin stayed less than eight days before returning to his village of Mitenne. Though around twenty Quiroste had received baptism at Mission San Francisco beginning in 1787, the majority of them were young children who were vastly outnumbered by other tribal members within this newly forming community of recently baptized.²³⁵ They were greatly outnumbered by their neighbors, the Oljon. In the years prior to Spanish colonization, the Quiroste were the largest and most powerful of the local tribes, but here Charquin would have found himself an outsider, bereft of previous political influence. He actively resisted attempts to bring him back to the mission and took up arms against the Christianized Indians who were sent after him.

In the year following Charquin's baptism, a number of Quiroste continued to bring their children in for baptism. Thirteen Quiroste received baptism at Mission San Francisco, three at the San Pedro outstation. Ten of the thirteen were children under the age of ten. Another thirteen received baptism at Mission Santa Clara, twelve of them children. Though the documents make it clear that Charquin resisted all enticements to return, it is unclear whether his whole family was with him during this time. His daughter Puchute, who would have been around four years old at the time, died in November 1792 and was buried at Mission San Francisco.²³⁶ As no mention is made in her burial record about her body being recovered in the mountains, it is probable that she stayed with the mission community after Charquin left. Did the missionaries insist on her staying behind when her father left, or did he agree to leave her there? It is unclear what impact this had on Charquin. The allure and promise of these new communities divided the tribal world, forcing them to face tough choices.

In January 1793 Diego Olbera, a servant at Mission San Francisco who had served as godparent for Charquin's baptism, made a trip to the mountains to locate the missing Quiroste, most likely attempting to bring Charquin and his people back to the community.²³⁷ At the same time, Charquin's village of Mitenne, nestled in the hard-to-reach mountains, was becoming a refuge for runaways.²³⁸ Fugitives from different tribes throughout the region sought refuge with the Quiroste, perhaps out of appreciation for the political and economic power of the tribe. By early 1793 Friar Baldomero Lopez reported that Charquin was harboring around twenty runaways from Mission San Francisco.

In February 1793 an incident took place that escalated the growing tension between the Spanish at Mission Santa Cruz and the resisting fugitive community. Two young couples left Mitenne to receive baptism at Mission Santa Cruz, the first Quiroste to make the trip south to the new mission. The couples, Uetex (Secundino Maldonado) and Tuiguimemis (Manuela Yrien) and Uayas (Bartolome Lopez) and Miscamis (Bonifacia Ubartondo), received baptism, quickly followed by Catholic marriages.[239] Lieutenant Sal reported that when the couples returned to Mitenne with licenses to visit, Charquin threatened to kill the men and take their wives. Thus, they were forced to choose between joining the mission community or staying in their village.[240] The men fled and returned by night in an attempt to recover their wives. When Charquin found them, he took their weapons, leaving them to return to the mission alone. Both Sal and Friar Lopez called upon the Spanish governor to provide soldiers to deal with the Charquin situation. Shortly after this incident, most of the baptized Natives at the San Pedro outstation were moved up to San Francisco, possibly as a response to concern about Charquin.

While there is no record of response from the governor, there is indirect evidence that he sent troops and that Charquin was captured.[241] In early May the bodies of two young baptized Quiroste runaways were found in the mountains, indicating that an expedition of some sort had been moving through the area.[242] In the following days forty Quiroste received baptism at Mission San Francisco, including ten couples, a dramatic rise over the previous months.[243] It is unknown whether Spanish soldiers captured and brought them in or whether they came of their own free will, as the records do not indicate one way or the other, though the sudden increase seems to suggest evidence of military intervention. References to Charquin's capture appear in letters in July and September, including a mention by Governor José Joaquín de Arrillaga that he was considering giving him a pardon.[244]

Despite the capture of Charquin, the Quiroste community continued to harbor both runaways and resistance fighters. But Quiroste response was complicated and not unified. While some were motivated to resist the Spanish, others continued to join mission communities in both San Francisco and Santa Clara. In November 1793 another expedition into the mountains reported seven dead fugitives, including Charquin's wife, Yaccham, who had apparently avoided capture up to this point.[245] Also in November, a young girl, Chuchigite (Maria Francisca), was baptized at Mission Santa Cruz.[246] Chuchigite was the sister of Tuiguimemis, one of the two baptized women who had been held by Charquin. At some point, either around the time of the baptism of her younger sister or when Charquin was captured, Tuiguimemis, along with Miscamis, returned to Mission Santa Cruz. It is likely a combination of Chuchigite's move into the mission and the return of Tuiguimemis or Miscamis that led to the attack on Mission Santa Cruz.

On the night of December 14 a group of both baptized and unbaptized peoples from the northwest made an attack on Mission Santa Cruz, wounding two soldiers and setting fire to the roof of the corral and old guardhouse. The corporal returned fire, but nobody was killed in the encounter. Father Fermín Francisco de Lasuén, who served as president of the Alta California padres from 1785 until his death in 1803, recounted what had sparked the attack: "The motive they have given is this, that the soldiers had taken away to San Francisco various Christian Indians belonging to that place who had been fugitives from there for some time, and that they had taken a Christian Indian woman away from a pagan man, and it was he who was the principal instigator and leader of the disorder."[247]

The attack was connected with the recent return to the mission of the Quiroste women. One of the leaders of the attack was Ochole, father of Tuiguimemis and Chuchigite. Curiously, a three-year-old Quiroste girl, Juanchita (Maria Expectacion), was baptized the day after the attack, only to die eleven days later.[248] No other note is made of this, but one wonders whether she was injured and left behind during this encounter. Nonetheless, Fray Baldomero Lopez and Hermenegildo Sal alerted Spanish authorities, who in turn sent soldiers from both Monterey and San Francisco. Governor Arrillaga sent word that Second Lieutenant Pablo Cota had been dispatched from Monterey, while San Francisco sent Sergeant Pedro Amador to catch Ochole and the rebels.[249] By January 18 word had been received that nine baptized Native scouts sent to catch them had not found them.[250] On February 1 they returned with eight prisoners, including one named Pella, who was indicated as the ringleader.[251] The letter reporting the capture of Pella included mention of hostile Indians making arrows and preparing for further fighting.[252] In the months and years following the Quiroste attack, Spanish officials responded by expanding their military presence.

In the aftermath of the Quiroste attack, San Francisco Bay Area Native people continued to aggravate Spanish authorities while attempting to replace diminishing traditional game such as elk and deer by raiding Spanish livestock. A month after the Quiroste attack, Indians were sighted eating cows belonging to Mission Santa Clara.[253] The last Quiroste baptisms at Mission Santa Cruz took place on February 23, when two adult women, Quisuam (Gregoria) and Mañem (Eufemia), received baptism.[254] They moved shortly thereafter to Mission Santa Clara, most likely to join their families, or perhaps the padres of Santa Cruz no longer wished to deal with the Quiroste women.[255]

The surviving resistance movement persevered outside the reach of Spanish control, but by the end of 1794 the last remaining large groups of Quiroste had relocated to mission communities. These migrations signaled the end of this movement. In July 1794 Charquin's brother, Meve, who was nicknamed *El Calvo* (Baldy), arrived at Mission Santa Clara, asking Spanish authorities for forgiveness and asylum.[256] Governor Arrillaga gave him neither, citing that "his was not a crime that is given ecclesiastical immunity."[257] Instead, Meve was arrested and exiled to the presidio in San Diego, while Charquin was sent to the presidio in Santa Barbara.[258] It is not entirely clear why Meve decided to turn himself in. It seems that the defeat of the rebellion, along with ongoing relocation to mission sites, is indicative of larger turmoil and disruption, a psychological crisis at a time when the majority of Quiroste people began relocating to mission communities.[259]

Others involved with the resistance movement joined the mission community as well. Ochole was baptized along with sixty-two others at Santa Clara that fall, as the Spaniards rounded up the remaining Quiroste.[260] The tribe found themselves split among mission communities at San Francisco, Santa Clara, and to a lesser extent Santa Cruz. This is an example of the Spanish tactic of dividing troublesome tribal peoples among disparate geographies, a strategy that would be used with later tribes as well.[261] The decision to divide the Quiroste among various missions was informed by a number of factors—the geographic proximity of the Quiroste to the northern missions as well as concern over further unrest at Mission Santa Cruz that could potentially be fomented by the presence of members of this once powerful and influential tribe.

Overall, this Quiroste-led rebellion pointed to the limits of Spanish hegemony, as numerous reports of collaboration between gentiles and *neofitos*—categories that the Spanish used to distinguish classes of Indians—revealed that these lines were not as rigid as the Spanish believed.[262] Charquin was not one for confinement, as he continued to baffle Spanish authorities and fled the presidio at Santa Barbara.[263] Charquin was then recaptured and sent along with Ochole and another unrelated man down to San Diego.[264] Fear and anxiety over Indigenous aggression and resistance at Mission Santa Cruz continued through March 1796, as soldiers prepared for a possible attack. For his part the governor gave orders to tone down the approach with the gentiles.[265] Charquin and Ochole eventually died while in prison, Charquin in November 1796, Ochole in July 1797.[266]

The Cruel Methods of Padre Manuel Fernández

Another factor that influenced the relocation of Indigenous people into the missions was the temperament and evangelical approach of the missionaries. In the first three years and four months after the founding of Mission Santa Cruz, the two priests assigned to the mission, Fathers Baldomero Lopez and Isidro Salazar, followed the larger San Francisco Bay Area pattern of initially baptizing infants and youth. Both Lopez and Salazar, who appeared to have spent much time quarreling about how to run the mission, were unhappy with their workload and frequently petitioned to return to Mexico.[267] In the summer of 1794 Father Manuel Fernández, a new padre, arrived at Mission Santa Clara. Unlike Spanish soldiers, who were well aware of the military prowess and large numbers of local peoples and followed strict rules to avoid confrontation whenever possible, some incoming friars had no such knowledge.[268]

Friar Fernández arrived at Mission Santa Clara with a reputation for making complaints and not getting along with other padres.[269] Within three months of his arrival, Fernández created a tense situation at the mission that required recently promoted First Lieutenant Hermenegildo Sal to travel down with a few soldiers from the San Francisco Presidio. The commissioner of the new pueblo of San José, Gabriel Moraga, related that Father Fernández had threatened those who refused to be baptized. Fernández had a reputation for threatening to burn down villages that did not submit to baptism, but on this day he had gone beyond threats and horsewhipped a man who had not responded immediately to his call. Shortly after, a man the Spanish called El Mocho (The Cripple) complained of the padre visiting his village. Fernández accused El Mocho of dissuading his relatives from baptism, ordered him to be tied up, and demanded the administration of several lashes. El Mocho arrived unable to stand, covered in welts and wounds. In response, local villagers abandoned their homes for the hills to the east, while a young Indigenous man armed and painted for war was caught either planning an insurrection or attempting to work sorcery against the Spanish. A Spanish soldier, Ygnacio Soto, apprehended the man, who warned him that the local villagers were preparing to attack Pueblo San José. When Sal and a few of his soldiers arrived, they met with local chiefs. Sal assured them that Fernández had spoken out of line, calmed the locals, and forestalled further conflict.[270]

This event resulted in conflict between Fernández and the local soldiers. The soldiers knew that the colonizers at the Pueblo were badly outnumbered by local villagers and therefore sought to avoid the overly aggressive type of proselytizing favored by Fernández. The response of the soldiers and military reflected the growing tensions between the Spanish civil government and the church. Further, it indicates an acknowledgment of the tenuous position of the colonizers as well as the power and numbers of local Indigenous peoples. The civilian settlement of San José, founded just seventeen years earlier, on November 29, 1777, as El Pueblo de San José de Guadalupe, was the first attempt at a civilian settlement in the northern part of Alta California.[271] Three months after the incident involving Fernández, he was sent to work at Mission Santa Cruz, where he appears to have continued his aggressive approach.[272]

Fernández quickly became involved in further controversy, threatening to incite more Indigenous retaliation within three months after his arrival in May 1795. Both Salazar and Lopez were allowed to leave Mission Santa Cruz within a short period after Fernández arrived, and a transition took place, with Fernández becoming the padre in charge of the mission.[273] Under Fernández's oversight the number of livestock pastures and agricultural fields, all created by Indigenous labor, rose dramatically beginning in 1795 (see tables 2 and 3). Fernández continued his aggressive proselytizing tactics, chasing down runaways, entering villages to the south of Mission Santa Cruz, and threatening to punish those who did not relocate to the mission. Reports during this time point to increasing threats from local peoples, as soldiers assigned to the mission cited threats of hostility in their requests for military support.[274] Fernández's behavior prompted scolding from his superior, Fray Lasuén, who reprimanded him for an incident in which Fernández chased down a runaway and attempted to take him by force. Fernández, accompanied by a soldier and a number of Christianized Indians, spent three days visiting local villages. He took arms from the unbaptized and created rifts between the baptized and unbaptized by giving the confiscated weapons to the baptized Natives.[275]

In spite of the official disapproval of his methods, Fernández's tactics proved effective in increasing conversions. In the first three years after the establishment of Mission Santa Cruz, the number of baptisms held steady at around eighty per year. In 1794 the number rose to an average of just over ten a month. In 1795, the year Fernández arrived and began to supervise baptisms, the number increased dramatically, almost doubling that of the previous year (see table 5). The total of 258 baptisms in 1795 would be the highest number for any given year in the existence of Mission Santa Cruz. It was at this point that a number of parents of children who had been baptized early finally received their own baptism at Mission Santa Cruz, which Fernández noted with delight.[276] His aggressive tactics came with consequences, however, as the number of deaths around the mission also increased after Fernández's arrival, nearly tripling in the first year. While causes of death aren't clearly marked in the registries, the unusually high number can be attributed to a combination of harsh winters, poor sanitation, and severe treatment. For recent converts these staggering figures reflected a time of extreme loss, but for Spanish missionaries the increasing number of converts signified successful work.

Transformation of the Indigenous World

By 1796 the majority of tribal peoples living throughout Mak-Sah-Re-Jah had relocated to mission communities. Some local people, mostly elders, continued to take refuge in traditional homelands in the forests.[277] A convergence of environmental, psychological, social, and political changes, coupled with threats of violence and aggressive proselytizing, resulted in this massive reorganization. Those who relocated to Mission Santa Cruz began to accept and create new social, political, and gender roles. By the same token, Natives negotiated the imposed Spanish categories in terms of Indigenous values, with a sensibility informed by their own traditional values and histories.

Spanish hegemony and authority had limits, as this relocated community continued to perform dances and ceremonies outside of Spanish control and observation.[278] Trade networks and the production of shell money persisted through this time and began to incorporate Spanish glass beads into the system.[279] Indigenous peoples continued to hunt and to gather foods and herbal medicines, often preferring their traditional foods to the crops that they produced for Spanish society.[280] And yet Spanish authorities sought to undermine Indigenous values by waging a psychological campaign of shame and subservience.[281] Father Francisco Palóu, who had served closely under Father Serra and had briefly served as interim president of the Alta California padres before Father Lasuén took over in 1785, observed the process with pride: "Before baptism, they had no sense at all of shame, these feelings are immediately dominant in them as soon as baptism is received, so that if it is necessary to change the clothing because they have outgrown them, they hide themselves nor will they show themselves naked before any one, and much less before the Fathers."[282]

Missionization involved a process of imposing new values, overwriting Indigenous knowledge and practices with those of the Spanish Catholic. Local peoples navigated these changes with respect to their traditional ways, but it is impossible to deny the psychological, environmental, physical, and spiritual costs of the colonial process.

There is considerable debate about the extent of forced conversions and the centrality of military and forceful intimidation of Indigenous people to accept the baptismal process.[283] Evidence suggests that while Franciscan and Spanish authorities certainly imposed their own notions of right and wrong, resulting in a system of imprisonment, corporal punishment, public shaming, and other means of behavioral control, incidents of forced relocation to mission sites in these early years were minimal.[284] Spanish soldiers and military officials were aware of both the local peoples' skills with archery and warfare and recognized that they did not have enough soldiers to sustain a militaristic takeover and therefore attempted to minimize outright confrontation in these early years. Missionaries targeted Indigenous youth and tempted villagers with Spanish material trade goods such as blankets and glass beads. These enticements combined with additional driving factors such as changes in the environment, availability of food resources, and the loss of trade partners and kin networks resulting from the large numbers of relocating villagers.

But this predominately peaceful approach to drawing in new Indigenous villagers changed in the years following the Quiroste-led attack. The threat of this uprising had been the impetus for Spanish authorities to increase calls for military support. In the years that followed, Spanish occupation and settlement continued to expand, and this increasing military presence emboldened the colonizers to take more aggressive steps to control local peoples with threats. The threat of another attack by the Mak-Sah-Re-Jah peoples justified, in the minds of Spanish authorities, a call for bolstering the local military presence.

By the end of 1796 life had changed dramatically for local peoples. Many important leaders had died shortly after relocating to the new mission, including Soquel, his wife, Rosuem, and Gelelis.[285] The relative stability of the overall population numbers is misleading. Baptized Natives were dying at high rates, but the overall population numbers were maintained by a steady stream of new arrivals (see tables 5 and 6). By 1797 the Spanish missionaries had begun seeking new Native converts from outside the immediate vicinity, extending the reach of Spanish incursion, while the growing population experienced an increasing influx of foreign-born tribes and peoples. In the coming years the growing mission-based communities adapted to these changes by developing new economic, social, political, and gender roles, even as they drew on traditional practices to navigate this rapidly changing world.

2

The Diverse Nations within the Mission

For local Native people, games played important roles in social life, before and after the arrival of Spanish colonizers (see figs. 1 and 2). Games and competition had long been a way for local Native people to negotiate difference and build and strengthen new alliances with neighbors.[1] Maria Ascención Solórsano described one example:

> The game of *gome* was a race in which each runner had his ball that he went kicking all along the way, and the ball hampered him much from arriving promptly, and they could not touch it with their hands, and if it went into a hole or a bad place, it gave them much trouble to get it out using nothing but their feet. Sometimes it was arranged that one go on horseback accompanying each runner, they went like their umpires to see that each one played well, for the races are very long and sometimes the players scattered out much.[2]

Here Solórsano was referring to the traditional game of *gome*, which underwent slight changes, in this example, as a response to the arrival of the horse. In addition to building community and navigating differences between the growing number of tribal communities relocating to the mission, Indigenous peoples living at Mission Santa Cruz frequently evaded the padres' watch to gamble, drink, and fraternize with the settling community across the San Lorenzo River at the Villa de Branciforte. Games and gambling were a form of building and navigating social cohesion, and members of the Indigenous community at Mission Santa Cruz quickly learned and excelled at the card games that the Spanish colonizers brought with them, despite the ongoing concerns of the padres, who saw the inhabitants at the Villa as a corrupting influence.[3] In addition to the games played with the settlers at the Villa de Branciforte, archaeological evidence and oral histories both show that these games continued within the mission community throughout its duration.[4] President of the California Franciscan missions Fermín de Francisco Lasuén observed that Indigenous people picked up the nuances of card playing quickly and that both baptized and unbaptized people learned to beat their teachers regularly.[5] In playing these games, Indigenous communities made sense of their changing realities by drawing on familiar values that must have offered some comfort by tracing back to traditional practices.

In modifying the game of gome to take advantage of changing circumstances with the availability of horses, the increasingly diversifying Indigenous community adjusted, adapted, and navigated this rapidly changing world by drawing on familiar values and practices. The colonial world that emerged in the Santa Cruz region in the early 1800s was made up of a diaspora of Indigenous people, which included colonizers from throughout Mexico and the Pacific Rim, along with Mutsun-speaking Indigenous communities from farther inland. Despite the imposition by the missionaries of binaries such as Indian and Spaniard, or *neofito* and *gentil*, this world was much more complex, and the alliances and networks that formed at the time reflect this diversity. The influx of new peoples along with the extreme mortality rates necessitated the formation of new kinship ties and interconnections. Gambling and games within the confines of the mission and across the river at the neighboring villa was an important avenue for navigating these changes.

In the years between 1798 and 1810, large groups of Indigenous families from Native villages along the eastern and northern sides of Mak-Sah-Re-Jah arrived at Mission Santa Cruz. These people spoke Mutsun, an Ohlone dialect distinct from that spoken by the local Awaswas speakers. The expanding mission-based population navigated not only the diverse linguistic and cultural worlds of these numerous tribes but also the colonial imposition of Spanish and Franciscan values and practices. These incoming people engaged in their own Indigenous politics, using a variety of strategies to persevere through their changing situations. Some tribal members actively challenged Spanish soldiers, while others assisted the soldiers and missionaries in their expeditions in exchange for status and favors. Spanish occupation, which grew increasingly militant during these years, expanded to include new missions and civilian settlements. These new settlements impacted Indigenous trade networks and competed for access to inland resources. Indigenous resistance characterized these times, reflected in the frequent flights of fugitives and the theft of Spanish livestock, which was a response to growing competition for natural resources.[6] Mission Santa Cruz became a hub of Indigenous networks, supplementing and altering traditional trade and interrelations by building new connections with incoming strangers.

This chapter examines the emerging social world within the mission community and at the diversity of Indigenous responses to these new circumstances. Those who remained at the mission faced harsh treatment and exposure to disease that led to demographic collapse. Survivors took on new spiritual, political, economic, and social roles that helped them navigate Spanish society. New leaders emerged, some from existing political networks and others from new alliances formed between tribes that had previously been separated by great distances. The ecological impact of Spanish colonization reduced the availability of traditional resources, reinforcing the need to learn new skills and labor practices such as farming, weaving, livestock management, metalworking, and building construction.

This was a time when local peoples, in the face of tremendous loss and change, renegotiated political and social boundaries by drawing on Indigenous values and practices. This period has been historically viewed as a moment of forced assimilation, in which Indigenous peoples learned Spanish culture and traditions at the cost of their own histories and cultures.[7] Despite the undeniable demographic collapse and constant challenges, a diversity of Indigenous peoples used a variety of strategies to survive. Indigenous people within and outside of the missions relied on traditional practices and values to adapt and persevere through this time of perpetual change and adversity.

The diversity of relations within the mission community is best understood by examining the persistence of tribal identities, illuminating new social and political roles that were formed out of traditional relations.[8] The complex social worlds found within the California mission communities have only recently been the focus of academic study.[9] The forming mission communities became home to a diverse Indigenous world in which traditional allies and enemies at times exploited these differences in negotiating new rights within and outside of mission communities. The oceanfront territories around Mission Santa Cruz became home to a greater number of peoples from traditional homelands to the east. By 1810 these new arrivals greatly outnumbered Indigenous peoples from the nearby mountains and local territories.

Indigenous resistance and challenges to Spanish occupation continued long after the Quiroste rebellion in late 1793. In addition to ongoing concerns about growing discontent and challenges from in the people of Mak-Sah-Re-Jah, a confrontation took place farther north.[10] In April 1795 a group of baptized Indigenous peoples engaged in battle with Indigenous villagers north of San Francisco while attempting to bring back runaways who had fled Mission Dolores (San Francisco).[11] This group had fled because of a combination of factors, including an outbreak of an unknown epidemic in March, poor sanitary conditions, food shortages, overwork, and harsh corporal punishment at the hands of missionaries and soldiers.[12] By summer the flights had escalated, as hundreds fled Mission Dolores for their traditional homelands. Meanwhile, ongoing Indigenous attacks on Spanish livestock continued in the lands between Missions Santa Cruz and Santa Clara, spurred by a combination of three consecutive years of drought and growing hostility toward the colonizers.[13] Spanish authorities responded by strengthening their military presence and expanding civilian settlements in an attempt to bolster their control over the region.

Tribes farther to the east increasingly had to deal with Spanish colonial expansion. Concern over English and Russian Pacific expansion, and particularly English naval prowess, motivated Spanish officials to increase the Spanish population and hegemony in Alta California.[14] These plans resulted in the founding of three new settlements, all in the year 1797: (in order of construction) Mission San José, Villa de Branciforte, and Mission San Juan Bautista. The civilian settlement Villa de Branciforte was built just across the San Lorenzo River from Mission Santa Cruz.[15] These three sites intensified the overall Spanish impact on the lives of Indigenous communities throughout the region in a variety of ways. The tribes living in the vicinity of the new Mission San Juan Bautista, which was built midway between Missions San Carlos (Monterey) and Santa Cruz, had their own long histories of contact and engagement with Spanish explorers. With the creation of the new mission, Spanish military parties began a process of relocating tribal members, often splitting communities between mission sites. Spanish authorities sought to redefine and redraw existing tribal territories and boundaries into "recruiting" zones between Missions Santa Cruz, Santa Clara, and San Juan Bautista.

Colonial Impact on Mutsun-Speaking Tribes

For local Awaswas-speaking tribes, which had already relocated most of their peoples to Mission Santa Cruz lands by 1797, the ensuing years provided a number of challenges in terms of simple survival.[16] Disease and poor sanitary and work conditions combined to make mission life difficult. In 1798 Awaswas-speaking tribal members made up nearly 60 percent of the total mission population. By 1810 local tribes made up just over 25 percent of the mission population (see table 7). As more tribes relocated to mission lands, people from the local mountain tribes represented a decreasing percentage of the overall mission population. Newly arriving tribal members—who spoke one of the distinct Ohlone languages, Mutsun or (less frequently) Tamyen—had to learn to live alongside local tribes. Mission Santa Cruz became a hub of Indigenous networks of diverse tribes.[17]

One of the main reasons for this demographic loss was disease. Epidemics swept through the community, as local peoples had little immunity to pathogens brought northward by Spanish colonizers. These pathogens spread through a variety of ways. Pathogens such as measles ravaged mission populations, often passing between mission communities. Meanwhile, chronic endemic diseases such as dysentery, tuberculosis, and pneumonia spread as a result of poor sanitation, exposure to fecal matter, and parasites that lived in the wool clothing worn by those at the mission.[18] The impact of these new diseases and the inability of traditional healing methods to affect them would have had an additional impact on survivors. Infected fugitives, who may have fled to interior lands in hopes of healing, might have unwittingly spread disease among Native villages.[19] In 1802 an unknown disease passed through missions from San Luis Rey to San Carlos and San Juan Bautista, though it does not appear to have reached Santa Cruz.[20]

In 1806 measles broke out in February or March and lasted until June.[21] Within a mere four months, seventy-eight people had died: sixty adults and eighteen children. Within the mission community tribal members tended to live among their kin, resulting in a degree of self-segregation within the larger community. Aptos tribal members were hit hardest by the disease, as twenty-seven of the burials were Aptos people or their children, including eight from the Aptos village of Cajastaca alone.[22] Reports of various diseases passing through the mission population in San Francisco in December 1805 suggest that this outbreak also passed through to the north.[23]

Mutsun-speaking tribes from the east had felt the impact of the missions in economic, ecological, and militaristic ways. Tribes traditionally relied upon long-standing trade networks connecting neighboring territories. Coastal Awaswas speakers and inland Mutsun speakers traded ocean resources, red paint from cinnabar deposits on the eastern side of Mak-Sah-Re-Jah, salt gathered from saline rivers and lakes flowing through the southern Santa Clara Valley, and tar from near the Pitac village.[24] The people from the village of Orestac (Bear Place), on the east side of the mountains, had a quarry from which they extracted material to form mortars and pestles.[25] Inland tribes relied on coastal goods such as mussels and shellfish, marine mammals, sea salt, Monterey chert (for making arrowheads), abalone shells, and Olivella shells (used for commerce and ornamentation) and exported pine nuts and obsidian from eastern Yokuts territories. While trade continued through the mission years and later, limited access to resources as well as the diminishment of these resources due to ecological impact, would have affected trade relations far inland.[26] These traditional trade relations weakened as newly baptized peoples shifted from traditional labor practices to tending livestock and agricultural fields. Archaeological findings suggest that while certain traditional practices maintained their importance, such as the consumption of mussels to supplement their diets, other practices, such as harvesting traditional plant resources and hunting birds and wild animals, diminished.[27] The relocation of peoples to mission lands often included official restrictions on traditional harvesting practices.[28]

This disruption of traditional trade networks would have impacted inland tribes, which was likely partly responsible for the hostility of Mutsun villagers toward Spanish soldiers in eastern lands. The impact of this hostility is reflected in Spanish anxieties and their reluctance to pursue runaways who traveled toward what the Spanish called the *tulares*, the swampy, tule-filled lands of the San Joaquin Valley.[29] Spanish authorities feared confrontation with members of eastern villages after having encountered aggression.[30] While the Spanish characterized the inland tribes as more warlike and confrontational, it is more likely that the aggression the Spanish witnessed was a response to three things: growing awareness of and frustration with Spanish expansion and occupation, ecologic and economic disruption of resources and trade goods by Spanish livestock and agricultural projects, and collaboration with an increasing number of fugitives from the mission sites.[31]

The growth and expansion of agricultural production and livestock pasturelands surrounding Spanish settlements greatly impacted the availability of Indigenous grasses and traditional resources (see tables 8 and 9). The relative isolation of Mission Santa Cruz made it difficult to import provisions during winter months, which spurred aggressive agricultural development.[32] Pasturelands also increased to accommodate growing numbers of livestock, especially cattle, horses, and sheep, the latter of which grew to over two thousand head by 1800. The horse population grew to such an extreme by 1806 that it threatened to overtake pasturelands for cattle; the issue was widespread enough throughout local missions that padres called for the systematic slaughter of over twenty thousand horses.[33] At Mission Santa Cruz the number of horses fell from thirty-two hundred in 1806 to one thousand in 1809 (see table 9). The introduction of livestock also led to an increase in predators, such as bears and wolves, which in turn would have impacted populations of local animals such as elk and deer. This ecological reorganization greatly diminished availability of traditional plants and animals around the mission, and this ecological transformation extended beyond the immediate sphere of Spanish settlements.

The introduction of swine to the Santa Cruz and neighboring regions by 1797 had an especially harmful impact. Recently arrived pigs would have targeted foods such as underground vegetation along with acorns, carefully tended resources that formed an important part of diets for local peoples. Wild pigs would have eaten through Indigenous fields and gardens at a rapid rate, taking advantage of the rich resources in the carefully tended fields while depriving local tribes of important foods.[34] By the end of Mission Santa Cruz's first year, missionaries counted twenty-eight pigs on mission lands, yet none appear in the records a mere six years later (see table 9). Flooding during the first winter had caused a relocation of the initial mission site, and it is likely that some of the pigs escaped and became feral. It is also possible that missionaries were negligent in their accounting of swine, as evidenced by the omission of chickens from their reports, despite letters discussing the faulty construction of chicken coops near the mission.[35]

At times local tribes responded aggressively to Spanish encroachment on resources, prompting Spanish officials to expand their military presence. This is exemplified in a conflict over access to salt deposits. The Ausaima (Salt People) fought back, in response to Spanish and mission-based Native people taking salt from local deposits.[36] It is likely that baptized Native people took advantage of the Spanish disruptions of traditional territorial boundaries to access resources that previously had been out of reach, within the territories of neighboring tribes.[37] The aggressive response of the Ausaima, which was itself a response to Spanish encroachment on Indigenous resources and territories, prompted further military advancement by the Spanish.

The Arrival of Mutsun Ohlone People

The individuals and families that relocated to Mission Santa Cruz over the ensuing years came from tribes and villages that had their own histories of interactions with Spanish colonizers dating back over twenty years, to the early days of Spanish regional occupation. As missionaries sought to increase the spiritual conquest of the region, they targeted territories to the east and north. Spanish overland expeditions had passed through these lands as early as 1770 while charting overland routes connecting Monterey and San Francisco through the series of inland valleys. The expeditions led by Gaspar de Portolá and Juan Bautista de Anza encountered numerous eastern valley tribal villages, likely homelands of the Unijaima (Fish People) and Ausaima.[38] By 1792, shortly after the founding of Mission Santa Cruz, these eastern valley tribes had taken to robbing Spanish and baptized Native convoys and shipments that passed through their lands.[39] These attacks came from the same groups, likely Ausaima, Mutsun, and Unijaima, that repeatedly attacked cattle and livestock in pastures south of Mission Santa Clara and the civilian pueblo San José.[40] In 1796 the same people, along with others who bordered the Pajaro River, such as the Guacharron (Condor People), had to deal with the incendiary proselytizing of Friar Manuel Fernández.[41]

Most Indigenous people who relocated to Mission Santa Cruz in the years following 1798 came from two directions. A smaller percentage came from lands to the north, in the direction of Santa Clara, where the two missions worked to complete the removal of the tribes living along the northern edges of Mak-Sah-Re-Jah (see map 3). The northern groups included people from the Partacsi, Ritocsi, and Somontoc villages. The majority of incoming people came from eastern tribes, from the eastern side of Mak-Sah-Re-Jah, down along the Coyote Reservoir, upper Pacheco Creek drainage, and the inland Pajaro River, in what is now southeastern Santa Clara Valley. The largest of these tribes included the Ausaima, Mutsun, Pagsin, and Unijaima, people. Ausaima people came from villages such as Chipuctac (Mallard Duck Place) and Poitoquix, while Unijaima people came from villages such as Chitactac, Pitac (Tick Place), and Thithirii.[42] Following the establishment of Mission San Juan Bautista on Mutsun lands a mere forty miles from Mission Santa Cruz, many of these peoples became divided between neighboring missions. Around 1806 missionaries began to bring in people from even farther east, along the outer border of Ohlone-speaking territories, namely the Sumus and Tomoi.

Indigenous names, tribal or village affiliation, kinship ties, and other information was kept by the baptismal, marriage, burial, and confirmation records of the Franciscan missionaries at each mission. Each new baptism was given a specific baptismal number, which was used to keep track of each member of the mission. The specificity of the information varied depending on the missionaries who kept the records. Incoming missionaries typically arrived with little regional knowledge or experience and relied on their predecessors for instruction (see table 10). In the early years at Mission Santa Cruz, Friars Baldomero Lopez and Isidro Salazar kept careful notation of tribal affiliation. Following the arrival of Friar Manuel Fernández, whose antipathy toward the locals is well documented, missionary record keepers shifted their focus.[43] Fernández began to implement a more generalized assignment of ethnic or tribal identity, less attuned to Indigenous categories and much more in line with that found in the records at Mission Santa Clara, where Fernández had served before his arrival at Mission Santa Cruz.[44] By 1798 Friars Francisco Gonzales and

Domingo Carranza had arrived, and Fernández would have been the one to introduce them to the record-keeping protocols.[45] Ambiguities and contradictions characterize the records of Fernández and those who came after him, reflecting either a lack of interest in tribal identities, confusion over political and social boundaries, or both.[46]

Beginning in 1795, missionaries assigned large groups of incoming people one of two general designations—from "el paraje de San Juan" or from San Francisco Xavier.[47] The groups classified as San Juan referred to tribes that lay to the east of Mission Santa Cruz, in the direction of the newly established Mission San Juan Bautista. San Juan–designated peoples included members of the villages of Chitactac and Pitac (Unijaima), Chipuctac and Poitoquix (Ausaima), Cajastaca (Aptos), Auxentaca, Uculi, Achachipe, Tomoi, and even members of the first Yokuts tribe to arrive, the Locobo—basically any of the eastern tribes. People designated as San Francisco Xavier included Uculi and Tomoi, along with villagers from places like Chitactac, Orestac, and Acastaca. While the San Francisco Xavier groups appear to come from farther east in Ohlone territory, members of the same tribes crossed between these two designations, making tribal affiliation difficult to discern.

Understanding tribal identity is further complicated by the complex identity politics of local peoples. While the missionary records reflect a simple inclusion of region or tribal name, often individuals appear to have identified themselves in a more plural, complex manner. Tribal names reflected the names of specific territories, but individuals often referred to themselves based on village or large kinship network identities. Neighboring tribes intermarried frequently, reflecting fluid identity politics; some individuals identified as members of different groups in marriage, burial, and census records. Nonetheless, an examination of patterns of intermarriage and multiple tribal identities allows for a general understanding of regional polities.

The northern tribes included people from the villages Partacsi and Ritocsi, both of which had a history of tribal members being baptized at Mission Santa Clara. In fact, Ritocsi village children were among the very first baptisms there. The Ritocsi village was situated along upper Stevens Creek watersheds. In those initial baptisms, the missionaries noted the Ritocsi villagers as being from the "arroyo de San José de Cupertino," a label that persists with the contemporary city of Cupertino. The majority of Ritocsi people had received baptism and relocated to Mission Santa Clara, listed as "San Juan Bautista" or as "San José de Cupertino."[48] Ritocsi people arrived at Mission Santa Cruz as early as 1793 and up until 1801. Fourteen people from Ritocsi received baptism at Mission Santa Cruz under the designation of "San Jose," "San Josef," "Xitocsi," or "Ritoci."[49] Despite the large Ritocsi village being one of the first to baptize and relocate to Mission Santa Clara and elsewhere, archaeological evidence suggests that in the post mission years, some mission-surviving families returned to the former village site along Stevens Creek.[50]

Partacsi traditional lands included the Saratoga Creek and Saratoga Gap, in the high mountains and valleys a little southeast of the upper Pescadero Creek, on the eastern slope of the Santa Cruz Mountains. About thirty members received baptism at Mission Santa Cruz, mostly under the name "San Bernardo."[51] The Padres at Mission Santa Clara had relocated the majority of Partacsi villagers, many listed as being "Nuestra Patron de San Francisco," though some were listed as being part of the "San Bernardino" district, between 1787 and 1801. There appear to be about four other nearby villages named in the Santa Clara records—Lamaytu, Muyson, Pornen, and Solchequis.[52]

While small numbers of people came from the northern tribes, the majority came from the east. The first to arrive were from the Chitactac (Unijaima) village from the Uvas Creek region of the eastern side of Mak-Sah-Re-Jah; they arrived as early as 1795 and continued to arrive until around 1802. The village site is now known as Chitactac-Adams County Park, near Gilroy. Petroglyphs and grinding stones that line the rock formations alongside Uvas Creek can still be seen today. Scholars have noted that these "cup-and-ring" petroglyphs appear throughout the world and often are associated with rainmaking, fertility enhancement, puberty rites, or shamanic ritual.[53] The Chitactac villagers were the largest group and the primary group that was listed by padres as being from "el paraje de San Juan." Parents of some of the children baptized under this name later identified themselves as from the village of Pitac, showing interconnections between the two Unijaima villages. Members identified as Pitac received baptism later than the Chitactac, suggesting that Pitac was located farther from Mission Santa Cruz. Around ninety

Chitactac and seventy Pitac people entered Mission Santa Cruz beginning in 1795.

Many tribes ended up with members split between different missions, possibly as a strategy by the missionaries to destabilize or otherwise reduce the power and influence of the tribes within the mission communities. This split could also reflect differing motivations or strategies among the tribal members. For example, three Unijaima tribal members from unidentified villages came to Mission Santa Cruz, with many others designated as Unijaima who ended up at Mission San Carlos.

Auxentaca, likely a village site, was the name ascribed to a large number of people relocated to Mission Santa Cruz. The village is estimated to have been along Coyote Creek in the hills to the east of Morgan Hill, in the area of Gilroy Hot Springs and Henry Coe State Park. Overall, around forty Auxentaca entered Mission Santa Cruz, mostly around 1800. Many more received baptism at Mission Santa Clara under the name of "San Carlos" between 1802 and 1805. They entered with villagers from places named Maynucsi, Murcuig, Quemate, "San Antonio," and Sojues. It is likely that the small number listed under the tribal names of Achachipe, Muistac, and Taratac at Mission Santa Cruz came from the larger Auxentaca group. The name Churistac, which possibly refers to either the village Juristac or another site where the Kuksui ceremony was practiced, was listed for eight Auxentaca people on marriage, death, or census documents.[54] Other village sites listed include Muistac and Taui.

One of the largest and most powerful of the tribes of this region, the Ausaima, was split between Mission Santa Cruz and the newly founded Mission San Juan Bautista. It is likely that the Ausaima, who numbered well over three hundred individuals, included the two large villages Chipuctac and Poitoquix.[55] The majority of Ausaima people relocated to Mission Santa Cruz came from Chipuctac, while those from Poitoquix mostly ended up at Mission San Juan Bautista. Some of these tribal members had brought their children to be baptized at Mission Santa Clara, though they later received their own baptism at Mission Santa Cruz.[56] Around twenty Ausaima were among the early baptisms at Mission San Carlos, in the early 1790s. Ausaima territory bordered Mutsun lands, and while few of the Mutsun are recorded as having arrived at Mission Santa Cruz, this large tribe made up the majority of people at Mission San Juan Bautista, while some also lived at Mission San Carlos. The few Mutsun who ended up at Mission Santa Cruz were those listed as "Churistac," which could potentially denote Juristac (Big Head Place).[57] At Mission San Juan Bautista, Mutsun people from the Juristac village were listed as either Juristac or Xisca (Risca), which is likely short for Juristac.[58]

From 1806 to 1808 the Tomoi were the largest group to come to Mission Santa Cruz. The Tomoi traditionally lived around and controlled Pacheco Pass.[59] People baptized who were recorded as being from village sites Acastaca, Puchenta, Sitectac, or Uculi were likely part of the larger Tomoi tribe.[60] It is likely that these are names of specific village sites within the larger Tomoi territory. Along with the Tomoi came another group, the Sumus. The Sumus (alternatively listed as Sumu or "de la sierra de la Sumus") lived along the central and eastern coast ranges southeast of the Santa Clara Valley.[61] Some Sumus had familial connections to a group listed as Tayssen at Mission Santa Clara.[62]

The Ausaima tribe, which held lands with the rich salt deposits that the Spanish and other tribes coveted, resisted relocation the longest and with the most direct conflict.[63] Around 40 people identified as Chipuctac received baptism at Mission Santa Cruz, while 278 Ausaima received baptism at Mission San Juan Bautista.[64] The Ausaima appear to have both aided and challenged Spanish colonizers, engaging with them in different ways over time.[65]

In an incident in late 1798, Ausaima members aided the Spanish in retaliating against a common enemy—from an unidentified Indigenous village. That November, members of this unidentified village killed six Christianized Indigenous men and captured two Ausaima women. The previous year members of the same unnamed village had killed a baptized person from Mission Santa Clara. In response to the recent capture of the two Ausaima women, a party of ten Spanish soldiers, eight baptized Natives, and twenty-four unbaptized Ausaima people joined together to track down the "evildoers." A battle ensued, in which Spanish soldiers and their allies killed the chief of the villagers, recorded with the name Fatilloste, and a few others. The Spanish and Ausaima party arrested two of these villagers and brought them to Mission San Carlos to be taught Spanish, in the hopes that they would become translators.[66]

By 1799 Ausaima villages began to harbor fugitives from the missions, reflected in the letter from Governor Diego de Borica articulating rules for engagement with the Ausaima villagers. That April members of an Ausaima village killed a baptized Native while traveling between Missions San Carlos and Santa Clara. By June the same village harbored fugitives from Missions San Carlos, Santa Clara, Santa Cruz, and the newly erected San Juan Bautista. This pattern of fugitive flight and shelter in Indigenous villages had begun locally with the Quiroste movement of the early 1790s and continued throughout the mission era. In response to the gathering group of fugitives in this Ausaima village, Borica gave specific instructions to utilize the help of a baptized man from Santa Cruz. This unidentified man claimed the Ausaima had been his traditional enemies and offered to help track down the fugitives. The ensuing search party included fourteen Spanish soldiers, ten baptized Natives from San Carlos and San Juan Bautista, and ten more baptized men, likely Ausaima, who could help navigate and act as interpreters. Spanish authorities instructed the party to arrest the individuals responsible for killing the baptized man two months earlier, imposing Spanish legal practice on these villagers.[67] Conflicts with the unbaptized Ausaima villagers continued. In 1802 Spanish authorities sent Sergeant Gabriel Moraga with troops to "visit" the Ausaima village.[68] Likely wearied by the ongoing militaristic engagements, the Ausaima villagers did not hold out much longer. By 1805 the majority of them lived at Mission San Juan Bautista, with smaller numbers at Mission Santa Cruz.[69]

Fugitives

Russian navy captain Otto von Kotzebue, who led an expedition to the area in 1816, noted that

> twice in the year they [Native peoples living at the missions] receive permission to return to their native homes. This short time is the happiest period of their existence; and I myself have seen them going home in crowds, with loud rejoicings. The sick, who cannot undertake the journey, at least accompany their happy countrymen to the shore where they embark, and there sit for days together, mournfully gazing on the distant summits of the mountains which surround their homes; they often sit in this situation for several days, without

taking food, so much does the sight of their home affect these new Christians. Every time some of those who have the permission, run away; and they would probably all do it, were they not deterred by their fears of the soldiers, who catch them, and bring them back to the Missions as criminals; this fear is so great, that seven or eight dragoons are sufficient to overpower several hundred Indians.[70]

Throughout colonial California, Indigenous people found ways to resist through regular flights from the mission or from simply not returning after visitations to relatives and homelands.[71] The conflict between the Ausaima and the Spanish colonials exemplifies the growing numbers of fugitives who were fleeing the surrounding missions. In 1930 Maria Ascención Solórsano recounted to John P. Harrington: "The Chauchilas fought much to escape from the Spanish, and they went very far into the Great Mountain Range to hide away. You should have seen how they got them and brought them here, how sad they were. The Indians had signals there in the high mountains for notifying the other Indians if the Spanish were coming."[72] Her recollection speaks to how the fight to remain outside the missions was remembered vividly in the oral histories. Similarly, the documentation showing ongoing flights of fugitives attest to the importance of a return to these homelands. Throughout the 1790s and 1800s, baptized Natives increasingly challenged Franciscan control by leaving mission communities, returning to homelands, or joining with other villages.[73] Furthermore, archaeological evidence of things like hopper mortars (shallow mortars for grinding, presumably in transitory residence sites) demonstrates technologies that fugitive communities developed to facilitate the mobility they needed to remain outside the sphere of Spanish control.[74] The prevalence of these fugitive flights casts doubt on the accuracy of the population figures reported by missionaries. As the missions expanded their encroachment and sought to relocate a larger geography of peoples, large groups fled. The missionaries granted seasonal *paseos* (passes) to individuals and families, realizing that they needed to grant them access to traditional homelands or lose them altogether.[75] Frequently, individuals or families refused to return from seasonal paseos, but the practice continued. Padre Lasuén recognized that these paseos were crucial to keeping the peace, reporting:

The greatest hindrance in civilizing the Indians lay in the allowing them to go to their beaches and mountains. . . . And they are right, because by enjoying once more their old freedom the Indians remain attached to it, and so they lose in a few weeks the progress in knowledge and civilization gained in many months . . . . In that case they are slower to return, for their pagan relatives keep on inviting and entertaining them; and if they notice that they do not come, or that they are slow in doing so, and they are told as an excuse that the Father does not like to give permission, they hesitate very much about becoming Christians. We must remember that the majority of our *neofitos* are so attached to the mountains that if there were an unqualified prohibition against going there, there would be danger of a riot.[76]

One of the earliest of these movements was the aforementioned flight of at least 280 people from Mission Dolores in 1795. As discussed in the first chapter, the reasons for entering the mission included a mix of environmental factors (scarcity of resources), political and social disruption from the loss of large numbers of villagers, and aggressive proselytizing. And yet, despite the uncertainties of the changing world outside of the missions, the situation at Mission Dolores was in such turmoil that this large flight resulted from a confluence of overcrowding, poor sanitary conditions, disease (likely typhus), heavy-handed corporal punishment, and a lack of warm food during the harsh winter of 1795. A group of newly baptized Saclan people left Mission Dolores on a sanctioned vacation but decided not to return by late April. Spanish authorities sent a baptized man in pursuit, resulting in a confrontation between runaways and their pursuer. The common factor in the majority of fugitive flights was the runaways' recent arrival to the missions. This suggests that those who had not bought in to the Spanish Catholic system or those who still had strong connections with family or relatives living in traditional lands were less likely to remain and endure poor conditions and treatment.[77]

The recovery of fugitives became a key motivation for colonial expeditions eastward. In 1796 Governor Borica commented on the flight of two men from Mission San Carlos into the eastern swamp-filled tulares of the San Joaquin Valley. His letter reflected a growing apprehension by the Spanish toward the people of the tulares—the Yokuts tribes, who remained hostile toward Spanish invading expeditions.⁷⁸ His concerns about dealing with the Yokuts prompted renewed discussions about the extent of military accompaniment with Franciscan expeditions. Back in 1788, Friar Lasuén had suggested that expeditions to recover or recapture fugitives rely on Native scouts, although in some cases they could include military assistance.⁷⁹

By 1796 reports of runaways had become so frequent that the governor set guidelines for when missionaries could request military assistance in their pursuits. Borica stated that the military could only be used in this capacity when runaways were considered dangerous or when they escaped to difficult lands with hostile villages. While these open stipulations left room for Franciscan interpretation, Borica emphasized the established practice of sending Indigenous *auxiliaries* (assistants) to find nonthreatening fugitives.⁸⁰ Borica made it clear that he did not want the padres calling on soldiers for every incident of escape, attesting to the frequency of these occurrences.⁸¹

At Mission Santa Cruz reports of runaways were first recorded in 1797, coinciding with the arrival of new converts from eastern lands.⁸² Yearly burial records first appear with reports of runaways who had died while away from the mission at the end of 1796.⁸³ At the end of most ensuing years, burial records listed the confirmed deaths of fugitives who had received baptism at Mission Santa Cruz, presumably incorporating reports and accounts from various expeditions that had taken place throughout the year. By 1810 there had been seventy deaths recorded for fugitives. Of those, only ten of these reported deaths were of members of Awaswas-speaking tribes or villages, while forty-six were of Mutsun-speaking people, and the other four were people from the eastern Yokuts-speaking tribes (see table 11).

The rising number of fugitive flights in 1798 from Missions Santa Cruz, San Carlos, and San Juan Bautista reflects resistance to increasing Spanish expansion and incursion into eastern lands. Missionaries at the newly established Mission San Juan Bautista reported runaways fleeing westward into Calenda-ruc territories near Monterey.⁸⁴ Meanwhile at Mission Santa Cruz, Friar Manuel Fernández reported a large group of 138 fugitives who had gone missing.⁸⁵ By the end of April, Joaquin Mesa, a Spanish soldier celebrated for his recapturing of fugitives, returned 52 of the runaways back to the mission.⁸⁶ Burial records at the end of 1798 report 15 dead afar of

Diverse Nations within the Mission

the mission ("fallecido en la gentilidad"); presumably, these deaths had been confirmed by Mesa or other soldiers.[87] The reports do not list the cause of death, though it is certainly possible that the soldiers themselves had killed some of the fugitives.

These ongoing flights meant that the actual number of people living at the mission was typically lower than the annual reported figures. While some have estimated that across California missions, between 5 and 10 percent of the Indigenous populations could be fugitive at any given time, my research suggests that the actual percentage of escapees could be quite a bit higher.[88] For example, while the year-end census of 1797 reported 509 individuals living at the mission, taking into account the 138 who had fled, the total population was effectively 371 (over 27% fugitive). Governor Borica observed this over-reportage and used the discrepancy to challenge the missionaries' concerns about the potential encroachment on mission lands by the foundation of the Villa de Branciforte and the incoming colonial settlers.[89] These erroneous population figures suggest that overall numbers were inflated to justify continued funding and land claims, not only in 1798 but in other years as well. These inaccuracies also show that Spanish control over Indigenous peoples was not as complete as missionaries would have liked Spanish officials to believe. Missionaries responded to tensions over land usage between the church and civic authorities by overstating the needs and numbers of the Indigenous population.

The reasons for flight were numerous. Maria Ascención Solórsano recalled the labor conditions and motivations for flight for Native individuals living at the missions: "The new Indians were very wild but they did not show it. After they were getting them tame already they would put some of them to work at the houses of the [Spanish] Californians. It was not only the men that used to run away, women and children would also run away. It was the children that were the most wanted, for they would grow up in the Mission or at the houses of the native Californians. All that was given them for their work was the poor clothes and food that they received."[90] Food shortages were common and explain why mission-based Indigenous communities continued to supplement their diets with traditional foods, which was one motivation for flight.[91] But clearly, one of the most compelling reasons that people fled was to return to their ancestral lands and kin. At Mission Santa Cruz the majority of fugitives originally came from villages and tribes distant from the mission. However, despite the emphasis on meticulous record keeping by the missionaries, nine individuals from local tribes disappeared from the records, without burial information or other documents accounting for them.[92] This absence suggests that they left the mission community, either joining with other runaways, meeting up with kin who lived outside the mission, or living on their own in ancestral territories. A document in 1799 reported that recovered fugitives explained that they were returning to their old haunts ("antiguas querencias").[93] On some occasions it appears that certain villages harbored fugitives. Reports indicate that the Ausaima, for example, consistently welcomed runaways.[94] Farther east, in 1799, a report listed the Pagsin or Tamarox village of Orestac as antagonistic to Spanish expeditions.[95]

Other times intertribal relations predating Spanish arrival motivated movement and flight. While Spanish expeditions to recapture runaways explored inland regions to inform future expansion, these forays delved into lands and territories that had their own histories and interrelations with coastal peoples. At times Spanish officials exploited traditional conflicts to convince Christianized Natives to aid them to pursue and capture fugitives. Governor Borica urged Santa Cruz missionaries to accept help in finding fugitives from one unidentified baptized Native. Borica noted the Native's familiarity with the lands surrounding Mission San Juan Bautista, where he believed the fugitives to have run, as well as his antipathy toward the runaways, who he claimed were his traditional enemies.[96] To what extent this individual may have also used the Spanish soldiers to his own ends in enacting revenge is unknown, as the history of animosity between these people was not further commented upon.

While these preexisting conflicts may have motivated some, records show that other Indigenous individuals within the mission community worked to help fugitives escape. Motivation for these collaborations remains unknown, but it is possible that kinship, tribal alliances, and frustration with Spanish conquest may all have played a part. Historians have noted that fugitives shared knowledge and insight from Spanish society, including skills such as horse riding and care.[97] An undated report mentions Ules, head of the most prominent family of Achistaca, as having become a particular problem.[98] This undated letter, which must have been written shortly after 1798, referred to Ules as "incorrigible," with a reputation for consistently disrupting and challenging Franciscan control.[99] The padres also mentioned his involvement in assisting newly baptized people to flee the mission and cited a concern about the small numbers of women as motivation for flight. The Franciscans claimed that the Indigenous men were frustrated with their inability to give in to their desires. Indigenous testimonies, such as those from the Mission Dolores fugitives, suggest that flight was motivated by a combination of hardships, abuses, and lack of resources. It is certainly possible that the lack of women played into dissatisfaction, but this interpretation was more likely linked to rejection of Spanish Catholic marriage impositions than simple desire. The missionaries' emphasis on Indigenous desire was often a projection of Catholic sexual anxieties. It is more likely that many struggled with the imposition of Catholic marriage requirements of lifelong monogamy, which must have been difficult for a people who traditionally practiced a relative fluidity in partnerships.[100]

Some Indigenous fugitives fled with their families to avoid the imposition of Franciscan rules regarding child-rearing and education, as some of these flights appear to have been motivated by a desire to protect Indigenous children from Catholic indoctrination.[101] Missionaries administered daily instruction to children five years and older, teaching them Christian doctrine and, undoubtedly, instructing them on the evils of their parents' "pagan" culture.[102] Missionaries often remarked on the targeting of the young as a strategy for spiritual conversion and to break them of their traditional practices and culture. Friar Lasuén noted that spiritual training was least effective with the elders: "With these young people this instruction is quite effective; with those of middle age it is fairly satisfactory; but with the very old the bare essentials alone can be taught, and this with much difficulty."[103] The 1798 report by Friar Fernández shows that of the 138 fugitives, 58 were children.[104] These families may have wanted to preserve traditional parental relationships rather than lose them to the missionaries.

A large family with ties to the Chipuctac, Chitactac, and Pitac villages illustrates the ways Indigenous families found to subvert the imposition of Spanish Franciscan ideals of marriage and child-rearing.[105] The family, who began to arrive in 1796, consisted of the father, Toyup (Niceforo); his twelve children; and their four or five different mothers.[106] Toyup appears to have found ways to maintain his ties to multiple wives, as only one of his partners entered the mission initially, while his frequent fugitive flights gave him time to maintain his connection with the others.[107] Toyup appears to have brought his children with him when going fugitive from the mission; seven of his children's burial records show that they died while fugitive.[108] These seven were between the ages of four and fifteen at their reported deaths, within the ages that would have been required to receive Catholic instruction.[109] The records of Toyup and his family indicate that fugitivism was a way to maintain ties with kin outside of the mission as well as to keep children away from complete immersion in Catholicism.

For newly arriving people, fleeing the mission was a common strategy. A letter written in 1809 lists a large group of forty-one runaways who fled Mission Santa Cruz, illustrating the degree of difficulty the missionaries had in keeping these newly baptized people on mission lands.[110] This group was entirely composed of people from eastern lands, a mix of Auxentaca, Chitactac, Sumus, and Tomoi. Among them are seven children as well as a distinct list of five women (and one child) who left without their husbands, a list headed by Yaquenonsat (Fausta), a Sumus leader.[111] The letter listed six more fugitives from the plains ("de los llanos"), Locobo people from Yokuts lands to the east.

As was the pattern throughout the California missions, recaptured fugitives were treated with a strict system of punishment and consequences by the missionaries and Spanish civic authorities.[112] Oral histories support the documents' reports of the frequent flights of Indigenous women, as Solórsano described: "When the Indian girls used to run away they hid themselves in the hollows of trees and in the caves of the mountains. It was a dangerous thing to take food to them. What sufferings they experienced; many of them never came back."[113] In one documented case Spanish authorities gave twenty-five lashes to three recaptured Native women at Mission San Carlos.[114] These authorities called on Indian *auxiliaries* to help track and capture the fugitives. In some instances they sent auxiliaries with messages and proposals to offer the fugitives. In May 1809, for example, the padres instructed auxiliaries to travel east to tell fugitives that they could avoid punishment by returning in a timely manner.[115] By creating these distinct roles, the padres elevated the status of these auxiliaries, who gained favors and privileges, creating social stratification within the growing Indigenous community at the mission.[116]

Spanish Notions of Crime and Punishment

> The Spanish Padres were very cruel toward the Indians. They abused them very much, they had them eat badly, dress badly, and they made them work like slaves. I also was subjected to that cruel life. The Padres did not practice what they preached in the pulpit.[117]

The Spanish imposed much more than notions of gender and family on Indigenous inhabitants at the missions; they also imposed new social hierarchies and social systems, including a system of justice and punishment. Indigenous tribes had their own long-standing systems of justice and punishment, and this undermining of traditional Indigenous culture and values psychologically destabilized Indigenous people, forcing them to adjust and learn new social rules. Within the missions the padres policed Indigenous behavior and imposed Spanish Franciscan concepts of crime, right and wrong, and consequences as an integral part of their instructions.[118] Spanish officials took steps to ensure the implementation of punishments, including floggings, the use of shackles, forced labor, and public displays meant to make examples out of rule breakers.[119] Punishments were so strongly associated with Spanish settlements, and the presidios in particular, that the very names of the Spanish establishments became associated with punishment. As Solórsano described in the oral histories from the 1930s, "*Pirisiryo* is all that the Indians used to call Monterrey [sic], because that was where they used to hang people."[120] Acquisition of instruments of punishment and control were a part of the establishment of a mission. Alferez Hermenegildo Sal ordered a pair of shackles and chains to be brought along with the initial supplies for Mission Santa Cruz, "for when the need to punish arises."[121] Punishment and acceptable behavior was culturally based, and mission authorities frequently punished Natives for failure to adhere to Franciscan and Spanish practices.

Corporal punishment was tied to parental instruction, or at least a critique of Indigenous parenting styles. Governor Borica argued that corporal punishment was meant to correct for a lack of parental guidance.[122] Yet Borica also cautioned the missionaries at Santa Cruz that even "when they wanted to castigate an Indian in a stronger way than can be applied [by the rules] of the mission, to follow [Spanish] instructions," a directive that illuminates a pattern of friars overstepping rules for punishment.[123]

The missionaries used stocks to make examples out of those who broke their laws. This type of punishment put the transgressor into a vulnerable and painful position in front of the mission community to serve as a deterrent for others. This punishment had lasting impact, as many years later Solórsano recalled: "I saw at the Mission stocks which they used to use for punishing the Indians. They used to put an Indian with his neck between two pieces of wood and kept him there as long as the sentence had been pronounced to be, sometimes for days. Sometimes some of them died."[124]

Mission San Juan Bautista quickly imposed systems of punishment for the crime of eating cattle, despite the increasing encroachment of pastures and livestock on traditionally tended grasslands. Prescribed punishments for this breach included imprisonment and twenty lashes every fifteen days over two months.[125] A young Esselen man named Gonzalo served time in the presidio in Monterey, where he was put in shackles for theft of cattle, the shackles likely serving as a public display to discourage theft.[126] Gonzalo was cited for this theft as well as for being "incorrigible," reflecting his lifelong conflict with Spanish soldiers—as his father was killed by Spanish soldiers when he was five years old. The infamous Gonzalo continued to challenge Spanish authority throughout his life, escaping from the presidio in San Diego and making it back to the mountains between Santa Clara, Santa Cruz, and San Francisco. Spanish soldiers reportedly found his body a few months after his escape in 1823.[127]

Indians, Mestizos, and the Villa de Branciforte

The population in the region grew not only through the influx of Indigenous people from the east but also through new colonial settlements, populated by people from diverse backgrounds, including Indigenous peoples from throughout the hemisphere. While it is impossible to say whether there were any local Indigenous people who continued to live in the dense forests outside of the scope of Spanish control, the last recorded baptism of local tribal members took place in 1802.[128] A report in 1805 claimed that Mission Santa Cruz had "concluded its conquest, baptized all of the gentiles that occupied the immediate area between there and Missions Santa

Clara and San Juan Bautista, for all around to the north from Monterey and through the hills are no gentiles to be found."[129]

Identity politics for Indigenous peoples revolved around tribal, linguistic, territorial, familial, and kinship connections and relations. After the arrival of Spanish colonizers, Indigenous people became enmeshed in identity politics that had been shaped by the long history of Spanish colonial relations.[130] The Spanish colonial world involved a complex set of identity politics, in which society was split between the *gente de razon* (people of reason) and *gente sin razon* (people without reason)—a dichotomy that worked along the lines of civilized or uncivilized.[131] Those considered "sin razon" fell under the social category of "Indian," a category that was applied to a diversity of people. Spanish-born Marqués de Branciforte, for example, referred to a group of mixed-raced peoples as "Indios."[132] Spanish society classified a diversity of peoples as Indian. In Alta California the category could be applied to colonists with Indigenous roots, local Indigenous peoples, or others relocated to the region through colonialism—such as the Aleutians, whom the Russians had brought southward to hunt sea mammals along the coast.

These Aleutians, referred to by the Spanish as "Russian Indians," began to interact with local peoples through the early 1800s and spent time hunting seal just north of Santa Cruz, along the San Mateo coastline, in the fall of 1810.[133] This coastline was traditional land of the Cotoni, Oljon, and Quiroste, known for its abundance of sea mammals. The removal of these seafaring tribes would have contributed to greater numbers of these mammals, benefiting the Aleutians.[134] By spring of 1811 this group had moved southward, where they were sighted in Santa Cruz.[135] A month later Russian Indians complained of a stolen boat, leading to suspicion that the Uypi might be responsible.[136]

Spanish racial categories (*sistema de castas*) suggested a hierarchy organized around gradients of racial mixture, ranging from the top categories of "pure" Spanish blood to various mixtures of European, Indigenous American, and African.[137] For Spanish citizens the movement northward into the new territories became an opportunity to transcend restrictive social and racial categories by becoming gente de razon, by virtue of being among the colonists.[138] And on top of that, as discussed earlier, Franciscan friars further divided local Indigenous peoples into two categories—baptized (*neofiitos*) and unbaptized (*gentiles* or pagans). These distinctions and categories existed in the Franciscan imaginaries but had real-life impact, as missionaries viewed baptized villagers as their charges. After baptism, missionaries required newly baptized people to live on mission lands, under the guidance and oversight of the missionaries.

In an attempt to reinforce Spanish occupation and claim to the region, Spanish authorities worked to expand their settlements. This expansion went hand in hand with an escalation of military presence, ostensibly to prepare for potential conflict with the English or Russians but additionally to help secure Spanish settlements against potential Indigenous military challenges.[139] Viceroy in charge of Alta California at the time, the Marques de Branciforte intended the Villa de Branciforte to address both the civilian and military expansion goals by providing homes for retired soldiers.[140] The plan was to grant lands in the new villa to soldiers upon the completion of their service. Governor Borica and engineer extraordinaire Alberto de Córdoba chose the site from three potential destinations: the Alameda, the Arroyo del Pajaro, and the area surrounding Mission Santa Cruz.[141] Ultimately, they chose the lands near Mission Santa Cruz in order to fortify the coast, adding potential naval support to the San Francisco and Monterey settlements.[142] They also noted the abundance of resources—woods, water, fields to convert to pasturelands, stone, lime, and the right kind of soil for adobes, brick, and tile. Branciforte and other Spanish officials implemented a plan to build Villa de Branciforte across the San Lorenzo River from Mission Santa Cruz by December 1796.

Plans for the Villa de Branciforte included the construction of dwellings for chiefs of neighboring Indian villages. Officially, the plans instructed, "between the officers' houses are to be incorporated sites in order that chieftains of *rancherías* may be invited to live among Spaniards and thus assure the loyalty of their subjects."[143] The intention was to facilitate cultural adjustment by placing the Indian community alongside the Spanish colonists. Spanish authorities additionally wrote rules prohibiting bows and arrows in the villa. None of these aspects of the plan were put into practice, as the local Christianized community remained solely on mission lands. The intention and ultimate rejection of these plans highlight the ideological gulf between the religious orders and the secular Spanish government and military. While religious leaders continued to view Indigenous peoples through a paternalistic and condescending lens, in need of instruction and close oversight, some within the Spanish government advocated for a quicker route to Indigenous citizenship.[144]

The Franciscan missionaries complained about the villa when they first learned of the plans, which was merely two weeks before settlement was to begin.[145] Though no records confirm this, the short timeline of notification suggests that the governmental officials anticipated a critical Franciscan reception. President of the California Franciscan missions Padre Lasuén complained that the villa was "the greatest misfortune that has ever befallen mission lands . . . this is a flagrant violation of all law. If any remedy can be found, it would be wrong not to apply it."[146] The violation that Lasuén referred to was of rules governing the proximity of towns to missions. Concerns over encroachment on mission lands formed the basis of complaints from throughout the Franciscan order.[147] Lasuén also complained about the potential negative influence on the recently baptized.[148]

Governor Borica responded with three counterarguments. First, he noted the overreporting of the Indigenous population, mentioned earlier. Second, the lack of local unbaptized Native peoples in the surrounding lands meant that the mission population was unlikely to grow. Third, he felt that the high death rates reduced the need for expanding mission lands. The reports of resource abundance left the governor confident that there would be little infringement by the settlers on the mission needs and lands. He further contended that the villa would provide a market for excess agricultural products made by Indigenous laborers.[149] The missionaries filed complaints but to no avail. Once the settlement had been founded, these complaints increased. At the heart of the objections were the padres' concerns that the villa would encroach on the mission pasturelands.

Conflicts between the villa and the nearby Franciscans revolved principally around issues of land usage and control. While the government delineated the San Lorenzo River as the natural boundary, missionaries complained that the lands to the east, under control of the villa, consisted of the ideal pasturelands. By 1807 Friars Quintana and Carranza petitioned for control of Rancho Corralitos, which lay across the river and beyond the neighboring villa—a site that remained contested between the two communities for a few years.[150] Meanwhile, residents of the villa complained that the ideal agricultural lands lay on the west side of the San Lorenzo, under control of the mission. The situation left each side complaining about their lack of access.

Governor Borica suggested that the population of the villa be augmented by colonizers from throughout New Spain. Spanish officials sent word to recruit volunteers throughout Guadalajara, Guanajuato, Potosí, Valladolid, and Zacatecas, but finding families to volunteer to settle the remote northern reaches proved difficult, despite the promise of land. Spanish officials organized two principal groups. The first, from Guadalajara, consisted of eight men condemned for crimes including theft, rape, drunkenness, vagrancy, and refusal to pay taxes.[151] Of these eight men Spanish officials recorded three as full-blood Indians.[152] The inclusion of convicts at the villa prompted concern from locals—padres, soldiers, and civilians. A couple of these convicts had attempted to kill Spanish authorities such as Governor Borica and Commander Sal. Missionaries continually filed concerns about the newly arrived civilian colonizers corrupting the Christian and pagan Indians.[153] A second group of colonizers, which included sixteen men, women, and children, arrived from Guanajuato. This group included a number of trained artisans—including a carpenter, tailors, farmers, miners, and a saddler.[154]

By the end of 1797 the Villa de Branciforte consisted of forty inhabitants, the majority with mixed Indigenous and Spanish heritage. Of these only one identified as "Indian," while nine identified as "mestizo." The discrepancy between the three Indios of the Guadalajara group and the one girl identified as Indio in the local census suggests a difference in self-identification after arrival. The move north into Alta California allowed for the construction of new identities, enabling some people to shed their stigmatized Indian status. And yet many colonizers carried with them their Indigenous histories and ties, leading one oral history to note that "a bunch of Aztec Indians from Mexico were living" at San Juan Bautista.[155] The mixed-blood status of the majority of Villa de Branciforte settlers is reflected in the inclusion of only four under the status of "Pale colored."

Two brothers who arrived in 1798, Jose Antonio and Felipe Hernandez, are listed as Indios from Guadalajara. Yet despite their secondary social and racial status, the two became full citizens at Villa de Branciforte. In 1805 Felipe Hernandez served as the villa's commissioner. Jose Antonio

Diverse Nations within the Mission 95

Hernandez served as marriage witness in twelve marriages in 1817, alongside two Indigenous men from the neighboring mission.[156] Their acceptance as part of the settling gente de razon reflects the shifting racial status of settlers in Alta California, transcending the limitations of the Indio status conferred upon their arrival.

The complicated racial identities of the settlers resulted in a society of many Indians. Villa de Branciforte combined with Mission Santa Cruz to create a local population that included many who might be considered to fall within the social category of Indian. The settlers of the villa included couples like Marcos Villela and his wife, María Bibiana, a young Rumsen woman from the village of Achasta, the land where the city of Monterey was built.[157] Another couple in the area were Francisco Tapia and his wife, Maria de Nutka, who had been kidnapped and brought to the region from her homeland on the northern Nootka Sound.[158] As early as 1809, the three children of infamous Southern Californian Indigenous revolutionary Toypurina (Regina Josefa) moved to the villa along with their father, Spanish soldier Miguel Montero.[159] The couple's two daughters, Juana de Dios Montero and Clementina Montero, became fixtures in the community despite their ongoing feuds with the local missionaries.[160]

Interactions between the settlers of Branciforte and the Indigenous people at Mission Santa Cruz suggest that these two communities shared some cultural values, at least more so than with the missionaries. As discussed at the beginning of this chapter, Branciforte residents and the mission community got together to play cards and other games. Gaming between the villa and mission communities forged bonds outside the Franciscans' influence and understanding. It is likely that the predominately mestizo settling community found greater connection with Indigenous locals than with the Spanish-born missionaries. In addition to concerns about sharing lands with the incoming colonizers, many of the critiques leveled by the missionaries against the Villa de Branciforte residents revolved around fears that they would corrupt the Indigenous locals.[161] The mission-based community made sense of their changing circumstance by relying on traditional ways to form bonds and connections, through games and competition.

Labor and Gender within the Mission

And when they would give blouses and skirts to the women, oh how they cried, and later they would throw away all that had been given them, they threw them away out in the country. Oh what hardships those poor Indians passed through when they took them into the Mission.[162]

For the growing mission-based community, traditional economic relations continued to inform labor and trade, even as the missionaries imposed new labor practices. Traditional labor involved the careful management of grasses, roots, seeds, and other plant resources. Indigenous communities divided labor roles along gendered lines in different ways than the Franciscans. Indigenous women tended the grasses and plants, including the gathering of acorns and other nuts, berries, tubers, and resources, while Indigenous men hunted and gathered food.[163] Trade relations between tribes had revolved around available resources within given territories. Coastal tribes were rich in valued resources such as seashells, sea salt, and raw materials for arrowheads, as found in the Quiroste lands around Año Nuevo. Drastic ecological changes in the region altered and impacted trade and resource access, but Indigenous peoples continued to utilize traditional resources, often supplementing new material customs within the missions.

Missionaries imposed strict gendered rules, insisting on divisions between men and women along patriarchal lines found in Spanish Catholic society. These stood in stark contrast to the local, relatively egalitarian Indigenous society, in which women could hold positions of power. While Indigenous society had divided labor along gendered lines, Catholic practice insisted on a greater degree of separation, especially between young men and women. Ultimately this imposition resulted in separate living quarters for unmarried women. Furthermore, as Deborah Miranda has demonstrated, missionaries imposed strict gender identities, failing to recognize third-gendered (or two-spirited) peoples in local Indigenous communities while demanding that they identify along biological lines, corresponding to deep-seated Spanish and Catholic sexual rules.[164]

Indigenous people, both baptized and unbaptized, negotiated with Spanish authorities, offering their labor in exchange for goods, such as cloth, grains, beads, or food.[165] In the case of unbaptized villagers, the Spanish negotiated with local chiefs, who provided laborers for projects. Sometimes Natives contracted labor in exchange for access to new resources that may not have otherwise been available in their home territories.[166] In some cases the availability of goods from labor exchanges reduced interest in relocating to mission lands, suggesting that access to Spanish goods provided one major incentive for receiving baptism.[167] At times working for Spanish settlers appears to have caused problems between tribes. In 1797 a group of unbaptized Indigenous villagers were working on construction projects in the pueblo of San José when a different Indigenous group targeted and threatened to attack them.[168] The reason for the friction was never stated explicitly. It may have been a response to the one group engaging in labor for the Spanish, but it also could have been related to preexisting tensions and completely unrelated to the Spanish. In any case, compared to Spanish laborers, those Indigenous laborers who received payment were paid a flat rate comparable to the bottom of the Spanish pay scale.[169]

As the majority of Indigenous people received baptism and relocated to mission lands, they lost the power to negotiate labor terms. As a result, their labor became compelled instead of contracted, and they faced tougher working conditions. In 1799 Governor Borica instructed Santa Cruz missionaries to avoid working Natives excessively in the construction of Mission structures.[170] Borica would not have spoken out if there were not a pattern of compelled labor. Following relocation, labor was negotiated between the church missionaries and Spanish government officials or local civilians, resulting in a de facto system of compelled Indigenous labor. Mission authorities administered punishments for refusing to follow directions and complete labor tasks.[171] Furthermore, presidios often used convicts for public works projects.[172] The use of terms such as *labor* is problematic in this situation. And yet the missionaries justified the imposition of labor, seeing the teaching of Spanish labor skills, housing, and daily meals as an exchange for services rendered.

The building of Spanish settlements required specialized artisan craftsmen including blacksmiths, carpenters, and masons. Over time baptized

Natives gained access to training in these fields.[173] The construction of Spanish settlements required many skilled artisans, so Spanish authorities agreed to train Indigenous workers. The first four craftsmen recruited from Mexico City specifically to teach these skills to baptized Natives arrived at Monterey in March 1791.[174] Disputes over payment of the artisan instructors resulted in Father Lasuén reluctantly agreeing to have local missions, including Mission Santa Cruz, send four men to the presidios to learn a craft.[175]

While the documents do not reveal the names of those trained at the presidios, census documents from the 1830s show that some continued to utilize their specialized training. The use of skills such as masonry and carpentry would have been instrumental in the many labor projects engaged in by Indigenous people during the mission era. This training was reserved for young males between the ages of seven and thirteen. Four men, each of whom would have been within this age range in the late 1790s, are listed in the 1834 census as artisans.[176] In that census Chugiut (Geronimo Miguel), a young Sayanta who was baptized as a ten-year-old in early 1793, is listed as a mason.[177] The Aptos man Chalelis (Roque Guerrero), who had been an infant when baptized in the early months after the mission's establishment, is later listed as a smith.[178] The other two, the Cotoni man Chomor (Daniel) and the Partacsi man Gemos (Sebastian Aparicio), worked as carpenters.[179] The coastal Cotoni used tule boats. Perhaps young Chomor incorporated experience with traditional boat building into his later woodworking and carpentry.

Indigenous labor practices included work in construction and building, albeit in different forms and materials than Spanish styles. Despite the insistence by Spanish officials that local Natives were unskilled, it is likely that traditional Indigenous construction practices continued to hold value for locals. In 1794 laborers built a structure to house single women and widows near Mission Santa Cruz.[180] Families continued to live in tule-style houses on lands behind the mission, while the first buildings in the area were made of a rough palisade plastered over with mud and roofed with local tules and earth, a construction style similar to the Indigenous style known as *jacal*.[181] Complaints made after a visitation to Villa de Branciforte in 1806 suggest that despite grand construction plans, the settlers similarly lived in small houses of mud and timber, with roofs thatched with tule.[182]

While the Spanish administrators saw this as a sign of laziness and avarice on the part of the settlers, it is possible that the traditional tule-thatched housing of the Indigenous peoples living in lands behind the mission worked well for the unfamiliar environment of Santa Cruz.

Native trade networks persisted, as archaeological findings at Mission Santa Cruz show that shell money and Spanish glass beads, long incorporated into existing Indigenous economic systems, continued to be used throughout the mission period.[183] Goods produced at the mission became incorporated into existing trade networks, according to a report by Father Lasuén. The padre reported that Indigenous people used goods produced at the mission in exchange for beads or seeds, establishing their own rates of exchange.[184] In the 1814 questionnaire Mission Santa Cruz padres responded that while Indigenous families continued to eat salmon, codfish, seals, and lamprey, which they caught in the nearby rivers and ocean, they also maintained their own cornfields, aside from the mission fields.[185] In this way it appears that the mission-based Native community integrated the production from their labor at the mission as well as the products of their traditional practices into existing trade networks, altering but not destroying long-established economic relations with easterly tribes.

Indian Alcaldes—New Political Hierarchies

> There was a man there whom they called the alcalde, in the language they called him Kalti, whose duty was just to see that all knelt.[186]

Indigenous communities throughout the Spanish Americas were permitted by Spanish authorities to have limited political infrastructure, even in the California missions.[187] Established in the early years of Spanish conquest, Indian councils and self-government preserved or reinterpreted Indigenous politics into newly created positions of self-government.[188] In Alta California laws required that each mission hold elections, beginning five years after establishment. The governor instructed missionaries to oversee these yearly elections and to pick three candidates, then allow the remaining baptized Natives to elect two alcaldes and two regidores, or councilmen.[189] The padres often bestowed the alcaldes with large wooden "staff of leadership" to symbolize their authority.[190] The oversight of the candidates was a concession following concerns by missionaries that the elected men would hold too much control within their communities.[191] At some of the missions the padres chose former tribal leaders to serve as alcaldes. In some cases these alcaldes actively worked against the padres and advocated for their communities.[192] The newly elected served as mouthpieces for the missionaries, upholding and communicating mission rules for the residents. While the majority of people spoke their own diverse Indigenous languages, these alcaldes would have worked as translators and intermediaries, communicating between the padres and the tribes. Although official letters did not stipulate that only men could hold these positions, the conspicuous absence of any elected women demonstrates the patriarchal views of the missionaries.[193]

Despite the appearance of political powers for elected alcaldes, Franciscan missionaries continued to exercise the majority of control. Missionaries reserved the right to subject these alcaldes to corporal punishment while prohibiting them from bringing charges against the Franciscans.[194] The latter prohibition differed importantly from Indian political and legal rights in central Mexico, where appeals of excessive labor demands, charges of mistreatment, or manipulated elections offered opportunities to seek protection through legal channels. In northern New Spain, Indians were left without legal protection.[195] But these alcaldes' main responsibility lay in conveying news and instructions from the padres, becoming especially proficient in Spanish as well as in Catholic teachings.[196] It is likely that these elected alcaldes exercised a degree of their own control over the friars' messages. Linguistic fluency may have afforded them social and political power within their own communities.

At Mission Santa Cruz the first of these elections was held at the end of 1796, resulting in the election of Geturux (Canuto) and Lacah (Julian).[197] In the 1814 questionnaire Mission Santa Cruz padres reported that elected alcaldes and regidores oversaw laborers and administered punishments to those they deemed lazy or negligent (see tables 12 and 13).[198] Only sporadic records of the alcalde elections remain today, but what we do know still shows certain patterns. At Mission Santa Cruz traditional chiefs did not dominate alcalde elections. The chief of the Uypi, Soquel, died earlier in the year 1796, before the first elections, so it is possible that he would have been elected. Molegnis, chief of the Aptos, and his children survived another decade beyond these elections, but none of his family served as alcalde. Perhaps the missionaries deliberately promoted representatives from outside existing power structures. Or, alternatively, maybe Molegnis was not interested in the position.

Certain patterns appear among the alcaldes. They tended to be mature adults in their thirties or forties, among the earliest individuals to arrive at the mission, and all men (table 12). The selection of alcaldes would have likely prioritized those who had best learned Catholic practices and the Spanish language, as the padres would have picked those who best exemplified new Christian cultural practices. Each alcalde came from a different tribe, likely to influence a larger breadth of baptized people. While the earliest alcaldes came from local tribes, by 1799 a man from the Chitactac village east of the mountains took on that role, presumably helping to spread Catholic instruction to his people. Only Lacah shows up as serving more than once. Few records survive regarding the regidores, but similar patterns of gender and age appear among them as well (see table 14).

At Mission Santa Cruz alcaldes appear to have had some control over the gendered division of young men and women. The padres at Mission Santa Cruz recognized certain men with the designation of *alcalde de mujeres* (mayor of the women), suggesting that these designees held the keys to the *monjeríos* or otherwise supervised the women. No other mission recorded these gendered designations among the alcaldes.[199] Other than translation and communication, the Franciscans never specified the roles of the alcaldes in formal documents, but given the use of separate locked dormitories for men and women, it is likely that the alcaldes were responsible for locking up the young and elder single men and women.[200] Franciscans required that young men and women, as well as widows and singles, stay in separate dormitories at night.

Despite their absence from official political structures, it is clear that hereditary leaders and elders continued to influence the community. Mission Santa Cruz padres reported that traditional chiefs and spiritual leaders continued to hold great sway and that they performed ceremonial songs and dances in the forests and fields through the night.[201] At Mission San

Carlos the question about Indian leadership prompted an admission from one padre: "Even today they show more respect and submission to their chiefs than to the alcaldes who have been placed over them for their advancement as citizens."²⁰² New political designations such as alcalde entered Indigenous politics alongside traditional leaders, not replacing them as the missionaries had intended. Furthermore, collaboration between elected alcaldes and traditional political leaders in the coming years would testify to the persistence of Indigenous political leadership.²⁰³

Spiritual and Kinship Connections through Godparentage

Baptized Indigenous people found ways to preserve traditional spiritual and kinship ties through Catholic ceremony and customs.²⁰⁴ Catholic baptism required the selection of a *padrino* (godfather) or *madrina* (godmother) at the time of baptism. For Franciscans, padrino responsibilities served as a mix of symbolic prestige and responsibility for spiritual (and potentially material) guidance for baptized infants or children in the case of parental loss.²⁰⁵ In the early years after the founding of Mission Santa Cruz, the settling gente de razon often performed this role.²⁰⁶ This group included a mix of Spanish soldiers, artisans, visiting officials, and servants, typically baptized individuals from the Baja California missions. In these early years the role of godparent was typically divided by gender, as men or boys received a padrino and women or girls received a madrina. The gendered use of godparents changed as Indigenous community members began to serve as padrinos in later baptisms, as kinship relations and linguistic fluency became more central to the padrino role.

Beginning in 1794, three Indigenous women began to fulfill the role of madrina. One of them, Maria Rafaela, was an Indigenous woman from the San Diego area who had moved northward with her Spanish husband.²⁰⁷ The other two, young Uypi women Oyoc (Feliciana Savedra) and Uychilli (Columba), received baptism locally and married Spanish soldiers, Jose Azebes and Jose de la Cruz, respectively, on the same day in 1794.²⁰⁸ In these early years it appears that only the Indigenous wives of respected Spanish citizens performed this important role, likely reflecting a trust by Franciscan missionaries that these women were well versed in Spanish and Catholic culture by virtue of their marriages.

By late 1796 and early 1797 Indigenous people began to serve as padrinos, reflecting a slow shift of responsibilities to members of the mission community. The transition to Indigenous participation in godparentage could also indicate the potential integration of these roles into traditional understandings of Indigenous kinship and relational politics. A thirteen-year-old Uypi girl, Chaitin (Agueda), was the first Indigenous woman not married to a Spaniard to serve as madrina.[209] The baptized child, Joaquin, was tied to Chaitin through family as her half-brother, sharing the same Uypi father, Maguen (Thomas).[210] While not all of the padrinos reflect clear kinship ties, the majority of these early Indigenous godparents were of the same tribe as at least one of the parents. The sixth child to receive an Indigenous godparent demonstrates the complexity of many of these ties, as a young Cotoni infant received his father's stepmother as madrina.[211]

The overall use of local Indigenous people as padrinos increased dramatically in 1806, when 36 of the overall 113 baptisms included Indigenous godparents.[212] This shift toward local Indigenous padrinos corresponds to the changing of the guard among the missionaries. Notably, the malcontent Friar Manuel Fernández never utilized local Indigenous padrinos in the baptisms that he oversaw. The use of local Indigenous padrinos corresponds to the baptisms performed by José de la Cruz Espi and Francisco Gonzalez through 1800. By 1807 58 of the total 66 padrinos involved in baptisms were local Indigenous people. Many of them included newly arrived Locobo, Sumus, and Tomoi. While the number dropped to only 18 out of the total 54 over the next two years, in 1810, when large numbers of Yokuts arrived, Indigenous community members served as the vast majority of all padrinos.

For women, excluded from formal political participation by the friars, the role of madrina was one of few roles of prominence offered within the missions.[213] Although women performed just under 16 percent of the padrinos roles allocated to Indigenous community members between 1796 and 1810, some women served as madrina repeatedly, such as Samórim (Fabiana Arraez) and Yuñan (Serafina).[214] A young Achistaca woman, Samórim entered the mission as a five-year-old in 1791, while the Cajastaca-born Yuñan entered the mission in early 1795 as a six-year-old. Samórim served as madrina fifty-one times and Yuñan thirty-seven times, more than any other men or women who served as padrinos.

Along with the role of padrino, Indigenous youth could perform other important ecclesiastical roles, including that of *paje* or *acólito* (page or acolyte) as well as the sacristan, or sexton.²¹⁵ Those holding these roles frequently served as marriage witnesses, as they would have been assisting with the ceremonies. The paje was typically a young boy who served to assist the friar with Catholic ritual. At Mission Santa Cruz missionaries selected pajes from among the children and likely kept them close to ensure Catholic instruction and limit traditional influences as a strategy for indoctrination, which the friars considered "instruction." Those born within the mission or those with parents who had received baptism seem to have received special attention. This special status is reflected in the case of young Lino, eldest of the mission-born children and son of Ules, the Achistaca upstart previously noted for his reputation for challenging the friars. In one baptism for which Lino served as padrino, he is noted as "paje de Padre Quintana," the only note of a personal paje made in all Santa Cruz mission records.²¹⁶

The sacristan—a role that was first identified in marriage records beginning in early 1816—according to Franciscan Catholic tradition, was the person in charge of setting up and maintaining rituals and the various books, oils, candles, chalices, and other tools of Catholic ritual including the ringing of bells or digging of graves.²¹⁷ At Mission Santa Cruz this role was assigned to men who had lived within the mission for a considerable time, such as Acogüen (Urbano), an Aptos man who, as one of the earliest to arrive as a young boy, had lived at the mission for almost thirty years by the time he became sacristan in 1816.²¹⁸ Serafin, a mission-born Sumus man, rose from paje to sacristan, earning the promotion as a young man of fourteen in 1816.²¹⁹

Another important role within the mission community was that of interpreter. Spanish colonialism depended greatly upon Indigenous translators, and local missionaries recognized the need to utilize existing linguistic skills of mission residents to communicate with incoming peoples.²²⁰ Local tribes had members who served as orators—likely multilingual people who helped facilitate trade, commerce, and diplomatic relations.²²¹ It was these orators who often greeted early Spanish expeditions, and the job of interpreter likely fell to them. Within the new mission communities, interpreters would have served multiple functions—as cultural mediators teaching newly baptized people to navigate Spanish and Franciscan cultural worlds.[222] Governor Borica recognized the existing linguistic skills of some locals as well as the need to single out and teach Spanish to those with linguistic skills, even recent captives.[223] Additionally, interpreters acted as guides for Spanish expeditions; for example, an unidentified person at Mission Santa Cruz acted as interpreter and guide in a Spanish military pursuit of runaways in 1799.[224] The motivations of these guides are difficult to pinpoint, but in some cases preexisting rivalries and conflicts inspired some to assist in capturing fugitives.[225]

At Mission Santa Cruz at least three different Indigenous individuals worked as interpreters. The first among them was Aror (Juan Francisco), a young Uypi boy who arrived at the mission as a five-year-old in 1791 and was among the first wave of baptisms.[226] Aror appears in the documents as a padrino in 1807, shortly after serving as marriage witness.[227] A young Cotoni man, Chachoix (Silvestre), also served as interpreter for the mission.[228] Chachoix, who entered the mission in 1794 as a ten-year-old, first appeared as a padrino in August 1800.[229] While both Chachoix and Aror appear to have helped interpret the diverse Ohlone dialects within the mission, the addition of Yokuts speakers beginning in 1806 required greater linguistic range, which fell to two other men from tribes farther east than the coastal Cotoni and Uypi.

A twenty-eight-year-old Tomoi named Putiltec (Macario) arrived at the mission in early 1807.[230] As the Tomoi tribe lived along the border of the Yokuts-speaking territories to the east, Putiltec quickly became the chief translator for the incoming Yokuts. A study of a Yokuts-language catechism entitled "Lengua de los Llanos," written shortly after his arrival, concluded that Putiltec wrote this catechism by translating from his Native Ohlone dialect into a Yokuts dialect.[231] His role as interpreter led to him serving as "interpreter of the Tulareños [Yokuts]" and padrino thirty times at Mission Santa Cruz, beginning in 1817.[232] Putiltec's elevated status as interpreter may have eventually helped him gain mobility, as he appears to have worked in San Francisco in a similar role.[233] The last man identified by the records as an interpreter at Mission Santa Cruz, Huilgen (Juan Bautista), was originally baptized by officials from Mission San Carlos (Monterey) on a military expedition into Yokuts territory.[234] He lived at Mission Santa Cruz and helped to interpret for the incoming Yokuts.

Following the induction of the majority of local Indigenous people to Mission Santa Cruz by 1798, a new wave of Mutsun-speaking Ohlone began to arrive. The disruption of economic, ecological, political, and social relations between Indigenous polities during this time impacted tribes and villages to the east. It was a time characterized by increasing Spanish colonial settlement and military presence in the area, with the building of new pueblos and missions throughout the greater region. Meanwhile, the growing Indigenous population learned new labor practices and participated in the political and spiritual hierarchies of the mission. They took on these new roles by incorporating their own traditional practices and values. These Indigenous translators, builders, laborers, and Christians were fundamental to the expansion of Spanish colonial settlement.

Along with the need to adapt to rapidly changing circumstances, the reality of new disease and demographic collapse began to take its toll on the mission-based community. And yet, perhaps partly in reaction to this harsh reality, Indigenous people did not passively enter the mission community, as many chose to resist and fight against this rapid Spanish expansion. Frequent flights of fugitives attest to regular rejection of these new conditions. Eastern villages harbored these runaways, forging bonds and learning from each other. Fugitives offered unique insights into Spanish colonial practices and perspectives, information that aided resistant communities. Baptized and unbaptized Indigenous people sometimes collaborated in resisting missionization. At times they competed for resources or otherwise sought to undermine traditional enemies. They participated in an Indigenous politics of negotiations, alliances, and conflicts, charting a diversity of pathways in this quickly changing colonial world.

3

The Mission of Padre Killers

In October 1812 a group of Indigenous men and women, pushed to their limits by an abusive padre, responded through the extraordinary act of assassinating this cruel and sadistic figure—Padre Andrés Quintana. Since the founding of Mission Santa Cruz just over twenty years earlier, the expanding Indigenous mission community had consistently found ways to challenge authority, but this situation called for something more than fugitivism, work stoppage, or subtle resistance. And while Indigenous peoples throughout Alta California had previously targeted padres for retribution, this incident stands out in part for the way in which the Indigenous community was able to trick Spanish officials into thinking that Quintana had died of natural causes.[1] The assassination and the subsequent concealing of the deed required a great deal of coordination and an understanding of the consequences by the growing Indigenous community. Previous scholarship has characterized the assassination as a moment of Indigenous resistance, a rebellion against the cruel sadism of Padre Quintana.[2] While this explanation is accurate in a broad sense, a close analysis of the conspirators and events reveals a much more nuanced story of Indigenous politics. At the center of this story was a woman of significant power and influence who drew upon her experiences and networks outside of the mission to help take out this padre who targeted the young members of this community with his sadism. In what was a truly collaborative undertaking, the conspirators drew on tactics formulated by Chocheño-speaking Ohlone of the East Bay, imported through Mutsun-speaking Ohlone from the east, and carried out by Awaswas-speaking Ohlone at Mission Santa Cruz. This exchange of tactics and ideas across geographic and political lines resulted from new alliances forged within the mission community. In order to understand the circumstances leading up to the assassination, it is important to consider the larger context of loss, death, and devastation facing the Indigenous community that formed at Mission Santa Cruz.

From a distance the overall Indigenous population at the mission might appear to fluctuate only slightly, but this relative stability belies the harsh reality of drastic demographic collapse (see table 14). The appearance of stability was a result of the constant influx of new tribal members from farther and farther away from the mission. Burials consistently outnumbered births, and in many years deaths outnumbered both births and baptisms of incoming villagers. Between 1795 and 1811 an average of just fewer than 60 burials of Indigenous people took place per year at Mission Santa Cruz, an average of 5 a month (see table 14). Over the same period the total population averaged of 475 people, meaning that around 12.6 percent of the population died each year.[3]

While the demographic impact and statistical analysis offers a devastating view of this loss, it is important to consider the lived personal experiences of Indigenous people within the missions. An up-close view of individuals and families reveals the immense loss and resulting trauma Indigenous survivors undoubtedly experienced. In case after case, individuals lost multiple spouses, siblings, and children in dizzying succession. It is one thing to read about this or to trace the data in the documents, but it is hard to imagine how survivors navigated these harsh realities of life at the mission. How did this loss impact their worlds? How did losing child after child affect their worldviews, their attempts to have optimism or to have hope for their future? Extended kinship and tribal units that, prior to Spanish colonization, had formed long-standing communities fell apart quickly, with the vast majority of tribal members dying within a few years. It is crucial to recognize this larger context of loss and trauma facing Indigenous peoples during these years in order to better understand the stakes and larger struggle for survival.

Given the frequency of burials, funereal and mourning rituals would have certainly played a crucial role in building community among survivors.[4] For Bay Area Indigenous communities mourning rituals consisted of a variety of practices, including the cutting of one's hair, the use of red and black paints, and wailing. While wailing and crying in Catholic society often signified grief and affection for the departed, Indigenous Bay Area people practiced wailing as a means of helping to send the spirit of the departed along its way and to protect the living.[5] Oral histories speak of the wailing of the community after learning of the death of Padre Quintana, though it seems likely, considering his abusive ways, that the community wailed to protect themselves from his spirit.[6] Nonetheless, the missions were undeniably places of deep mourning and loss, and the dire circumstances facing the Indigenous community explain why they were pushed to such extreme actions.

It was a time of incredible suffering and bereavement, and with the extremely high infant mortality rates, this would have been especially true for young mothers.[7] Mortality rates of children born within the missions were abysmal. Overall, children born at Mission Santa Cruz rarely survived into adulthood. In fact, over 75 percent died before reaching the age of five, with over half dying before their first birthday, a dire situation in which less than 20 percent of the mission-born Indigenous children survived into adulthood.[8] These statistics reflect a combination of terrible conditions, as poor living and work conditions intersected with diseases that became endemic to the mission communities. They also call to mind stories of infanticide. These stories persist among descendants of mission survivors, signaling a situation in which conditions were so horrific that some parents grappled with the unimaginable decision whether to abort or kill their children rather than subject them to life within the missions.[9] Padres at neighboring Missions Santa Clara, Santa Cruz, and San José all complained about abortion as one of the most common vices among Native women, with the San José padres complaining that "the women are addicted to the practice of abortion which is the principal reason of the small number of births."[10] Whether the appalling infant mortality numbers reflect poor living conditions, endemic disease, deliberate infanticide, or some combination thereof, there is no denying the dreadful situation facing parents and families at the missions.

The conspirators involved in the assassination of Padre Quintana were almost all local Awaswas-speaking tribal members, people who had been at the mission since the early days. As such, they were intimately aware of the harsh conditions for Indigenous community members and the abusive behavior of Quintana. They were also very aware of the dismal survival rates for newborn children at the mission. By the time of the assassination, in October 1812, only 35 of the 234 newborn Indigenous children baptized

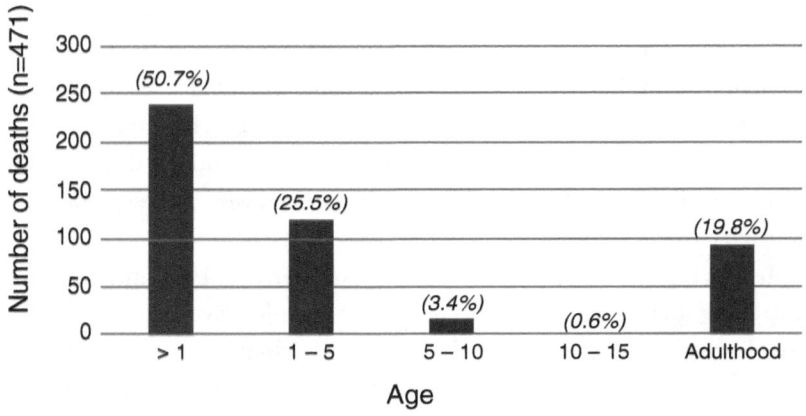

Chart 1. Age at death of mission-born people, 1791–1831

in Santa Cruz since the founding of the mission were still alive (see figure 6). Between 1810 and 1811 20 children were born.[11] Of these 20, only 3 were still alive by the time of the assassination.[12] As long-standing members of the Mission Santa Cruz community, many were expected to be community leaders, and some of them served as godparents to the children born in these years.[13] Furthermore, these local Awaswas speakers were quickly finding themselves outnumbered by incoming groups of culturally and linguistically distinct strangers.

Demographic Shift with the Arrival of the Yokuts

To maintain the steady workforce despite the large number of deaths, the missionaries and soldiers sought to induct Indigenous villagers from farther inland. In its first twenty years of existence, there were three waves of arrivals of distinct ethnic and linguistic groups at Mission Santa Cruz. The first two waves consisted of people from a diversity of Ohlone-speaking tribes of increasingly larger geographic range, relatively local Awaswas speakers, and Mutsun speakers from the inland side of the Mak-Sah-Re-Jah mountain range. The second wave of Mutsun speakers arrived in large numbers over a period of about a decade, beginning approximately in 1797. The third wave was made up of tribal members from the Northern Valley Yokuts villages that lay farther east. The Yokuts

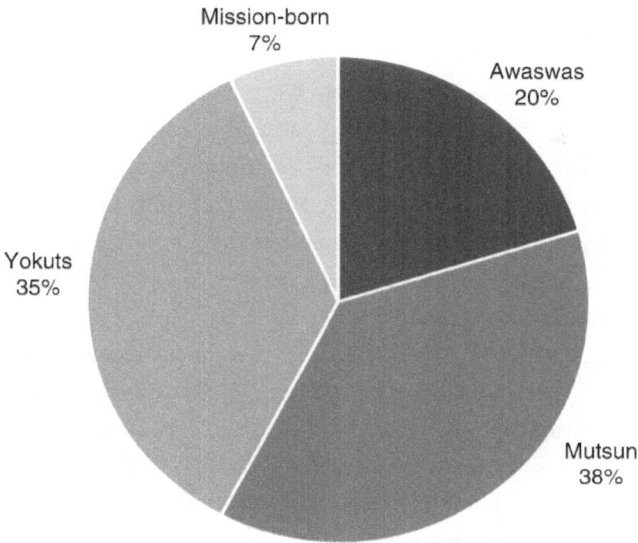

Awaswas (n=101)
Local tribes from Mak-Sa-Re-Jah

Mutsun (n=186)
8 Auxentaca, 22 Chipuctac, 24 Chitactac, 8 Partocsi, 15 Pitac, 7 Sitectac, 83 Sumus/Tomoi, and 19 from various villages including Unijaima and San Francisco Xavier

Yokuts (n=175)
45 Locobo, 42 Chaneche, 64 Tejey, 10 Uculi, and 14 from various villages

Mission-born (n=35)
Children born to parents baptized and living at Mission Santa Cruz

Chart 2. Population in 1812 at Mission Santa Cruz, by language

people, whose lands bordered those of the Mutsun-speaking Ohlone tribes, were linguistically distinct from the Ohlone tribes of the greater Bay Area. Increasingly hostile Spanish military expeditions into Yokuts territories to capture fugitives resulted in an influx of Yokuts villagers into the mission community.

In the years leading up to the assassination, the influx of large numbers of Northern Valley Yokuts villagers began to change the overall ethnic and cultural dynamics within the mission community.[14] By the time of the assassination in 1812, Awaswas-speaking tribal members made up about 20 percent of the total mission population; they were vastly outnumbered by the combination of Mutsun-speaking Ohlone and Yokuts (see tables 16 and 17, fig. 6).[15] The overall population at the mission remained relatively stable, but this stability was a result of the constant introduction of newly baptized Indigenous people, who offset the high numbers of deaths (see table 14).[16] In order for local tribal members to maintain power and influence, it was necessary for Awaswas-speaking leaders to expand their kinship networks. Drastic loss and demographic collapse characterized the Indigenous world surrounding Mission Santa Cruz, and survivors formed new alliances in a rapidly changing social world.[17]

In the spring of 1810, 119 Yokuts arrived at the mission, a mix of people identified as Tejey and Chaneche (see map 3).[18] They joined families from the Locobo tribe, who had been the first Yokuts speakers to join Mission Santa Cruz, with 60 arriving between February 1806 and June 1808.[19] Chief (*capitan*) Malimin (Coleto) and his family led the newly arrived Tejey people.[20] The homeland of the Tejey is near present-day Gustine, on the eastern side of the hills of Henry W. Coe State Park. These tribes lived to the east of the homelands of the Sumus and Tomoi, and members of the Tomoi played roles in assisting their transition to the mission.[21] Collectively, Yokuts tribal members made up a little over one-third of the overall population within just a few years of arrival (see fig. 7). The Yokuts and various Ohlone groups within the mission were linguistically distinct but were tied together through cultural, spiritual, and economic interrelations. As relative neighbors, the Yokuts and southeastern Ohlone (Mutsun speakers) had long-standing trade relations. They now found themselves building new connections and relations within the growing, diverse community forming around the mission.

Despite the changing demographics within the mission, the conspirators involved in the assassination did not include members from these newly arrived Yokuts villages. The men and women involved were connected through long-standing kinship networks between members of local Awaswas-speaking peoples of the region, with one crucial exception—the woman were credited with developing and ensuring the success of the plot. These local leaders engaged in their own direct political action to protect their growing mission community against a padre who failed to fulfill his social and spiritual obligations. Moreover, these leaders held positions of authority within the mission, and they used their standing and access to protect their community.[22]

The Assassination

Knowledge of the Quintana murder is handed down through a variety of sources, including official correspondence and reports by Spanish authorities as well as the account given by Lorenzo Asisara in an 1877 interview.[23] Asisara was born in 1820, eight years after the assassination. His Cotoni father was one of the conspirators, and Asisara's account of the assassination provides a rare perspective of the oral history as remembered by the Indigenous community. Asisara is one of very few Indigenous people who lived in the missions and was able to share his stories in the later years of his life.[24] Asisara himself is a complicated individual who lived through much change, surviving at least into the 1890s. He spent time in the Spanish military in the 1840s, a job that eventually played a key role in his story being recorded.[25] His narrative, although it provides many details and Spanish names, at times contributes to the erasure and marginalization of Indigenous women that is commonly found in the Spanish and U.S. archives. His account relates how the story itself has been remembered within the community, naming individuals involved and offering details not found in the official Spanish accounts.[26]

At some point in the fall of 1812 Padre Quintana beat two men nearly to death. Spanish government correspondences confirm Asisara's narrative, relating that the assassins targeted Padre Quintana over his excessive reliance on corporal punishment, via lashings from his whip, which was likely a cat-o'-nine tails.[27] The timing of the assassination corresponded to inside knowledge of the planned unveiling of a newly fashioned whip, the tips of which Quintana had had specially fitted with metal.[28] The assassination plan was put into motion following the beating of two people nearly to death.[29] The use of corporal punishment and even torture as a means of social control is well documented in mission correspondence and testimony from various Indian rebellions and trials, which frequently cited excessive physical abuse as the primary motivating factor for justified violent retaliation.[30] Many years later Maria Ascención Solórsano would describe an example of the punishment and lashings of Indigenous men and woman at Mission San Juan Bautista:

> You know what they used for lashing the people at the mission was a quince-tree switch, which is the limberest there is. It did not go to pieces even if they gave ten lashes with it, and they also used a whip. When they lashed the Indians of the Mission, what they gave most commonly was fifty lashes. They always took the shirt and pants off the Indian that they were going to lash and made him lie face down on the ground. And sometimes they left the blouses on the women and merely raised their skirts up over their backs so that their haunches would be well exposed and then they hit them good on their pure haunches, and sometimes they made them take off their blouses and skirts so that they were as bare as the men. . . . The man who was doing the whipping first gave a swing to the whip and then hit with full force right on the haunches and on the back too, or wherever he wanted to, and it din't [sic] matter to him what part of the body. And there was he who was being whipped, groaning and crying and twisting around also from the pain. When they were finished whipping him they threw a bucket of cold water with salt in it over the punished person, and his body remained all cut up from the lashes. The Padres ordered the people whipped for having disobeyed them in any manner, and the men because they did not do their work, or because they quarreled with their women, and for their drunken spells, and for any other disobedience. They remained still and sore for various days afterward.[31]

While this description was not directly connected to Mission Santa Cruz, the practice of lashings and punishment was practiced throughout the California missions. Quintana's penchant for corporal punishment and his fashioning of this "special" whip to inflict deeper wounds played a key role in motivating the conspirators to take matters into their own hands. The severe beating of these two young men prompted a meeting of conspirators who eventually planned the assassination.

The assassination was planned collectively and secretly by a coalition of Indigenous people, who afterward, along with many men and women of the mission community, successfully concealed the assassination from the Spanish priests and soldiers for up to two years. According to Asisara, a group of fourteen men and women gathered at the home of the mission gardener, Lacah (Julián), and his wife, Yaquenonsat (Fausta), in response to Quintana having beaten two young men nearly to death.[32] The group gathered at the behest of Yachacxi (Donato), one of the two young men who had received this brutal beating, so "that they could discuss how to prevent the further cruel punishment that Padre Quintana inflicted on them."[33]

At the center of the story was a father and his son—the Chaloctaca men Ules (Andrés) and Lino.[34] Ules and Lino were central in the planning as well as the actual confrontation with Padre Quintana. It was Lino who took the lead in the conversation about what to do with the Padre, as Asisara recounted:

> [Lino] said: "Tell me, then, what are we to do with the padre? Run him off, we cannot do, nor can we take him before a judge since we do not know who commands him to do what he does to us."
>
> To this, Andrés [Ules] who was the father of the page Lino, responded: "It will be better if we kill the Padre, without anyone knowing about it, not even the pages nor anyone else, only those that are here present."[35]

It was Yaquenonsat who formulated and proposed the plan that they would eventually use to kill Quintana. This plan called for Yaquenonsat to ask Quintana to administer last rites to her husband, as she told her husband and the group, "You [Lacah], who is always sick, this is the only way, think if this is not the best way."[36] Because of her husband's duties as a mission gardener, their home sat in the middle of the mission plaza. When Quintana walked toward Lacah's home, the young men would then surround and ambush him.

In the evening following the planning meeting, Yaquenonsat summoned Quintana, but the young men failed to carry out their end of the plan. Yaquenonsat again asked Quintana to come administer last rites to Lacah, and a second time the young men failed to execute the plan. It was at this point that Yaquenonsat threatened the young men, telling them that "if they do not fulfill what they have promised, [she] will accuse them."[37] Asisara described the third attempt and confrontation with Padre Quintana:

> Lino told him these words, "Stop here, Father, take a moment to talk."
>
> Then the other two pages who carried the lamps turned and when they saw all the people gathered to attack the Padre, then took off running with their lanterns.
>
> The Padre said to Lino, "Ay son, what are you going to do?"
> Lino replied, "Those that want to kill you will tell you."
> "What have I done, children, that you will kill me?"
> "Because you have made a whip of iron," replied Andrés [Ules].
> And so, the Padre replied, "Ay children! Leave me now for I am going to go now."
> Andrés [Ules] asked him why he made the iron whip.
> Quintana said that it was only for the bad ones.
> And then many cried, "As you are in the hands of the bad ones now, remember God!"[38]

After committing the deed, the conspirators placed Quintana's dead body back in his quarters, making it appear as if he had died in his sleep. According to Asisara's story, the assassins then proceeded to unlock the single men's and women's dormitories, letting everyone out to enjoy a night of celebration.[39] Before dawn they returned to their quarters, preventing the Spanish officials and soldiers from discovering what had transpired.

The assassination remained hidden from the Spanish soldiers and padres for around two years.[40] The death of Padre Quintana was officially declared to be a result of his lingering illness.[41] Some questions remained, as a coroner was brought in to exhume the body, though his report supported a conclusion of death by natural causes.[42] The cover-up of the assassination of Padre Quintana continued undetected by Spanish officials until, as the oral history tells, about two years after the assassination a soldier overheard two seamstresses gossiping and bickering about the deed. The soldier, who understood enough of what was being said to arouse his suspicions, alerted the authorities, who rounded up sixteen men, tied them by their thumbs, and marched them to San Francisco for trial.[43]

Spanish authorities convicted and sentenced nine of the sixteen men. Yaquenonsat did not appear to have been apprehended or identified by Spanish authorities, as it seems that the Spaniards, with their patriarchal perspectives, failed to conceive of a woman playing a central role in the assassination. Spanish soldiers held the arrested men at the San Francisco Presidio until there was a trial, where they testified regarding the assassination. Confirmation of their conviction and sentences was sent from Mexico City in 1816, though specific dates aren't given in the records (see table 19). After hearing their testimonies, the Spanish government handed down sentences for these nine men.

The First Mission-Born Generation

One of the principal figures in the assassination is the young man Lino. Despite the staggering infant mortality figures within the mission, some did survive into adulthood (see fig. 6). As the first generation growing up within the mission system, these youth worked closely with the friars, taking on important duties within the spiritual practices and daily rituals. This first generation of children fortunate enough to survive were frequently given special standing within the mission community. Missionaries placed particular importance on children, recognizing that the success of their spiritual conquest rested in the ability to teach these children the ways of Catholicism and indoctrinate them in Spanish Catholic Franciscan ways of life. As a result, children born to parents living within the mission community frequently became cultural translators and community leaders, individuals who, through their proximity to the padres and soldiers, learned to straddle the conflicting social and spiritual worlds within the mission.[44] In addition to serving as *padrinos* (godparents) or marriage witnesses, these children often played special roles within the church, such as *pajes* (pages) or *sacristans* (sextons). In these roles the children could interpret Franciscan Catholicism and Spanish society for their families and communities, as we see in the case of Lino.

Lino was born in September 1793, the fourth child born within the mission. By the age of fourteen, in 1807, Lino was the oldest living child born in the mission.⁴⁵ As the oldest surviving youth within the mission community, Lino served as the personal paje of Padre Quintana in the years leading up to the assassination.⁴⁶ By the time of the assassination in 1812, Lino was nineteen years old and had served as witness in thirty-three marriages as well as padrino for two baptisms.⁴⁷ The role of marriage witness often reflected kinship ties and interconnections. This is reflected in Lino's story and kinship ties with those involved in the assassination. He served as padrino for the child of the Sumus chief, Chitecsme (Mateo), and his wife, Yachename (Matea), both Sumus kin of Yaquenonsat.⁴⁸ He served as marriage witness for two of the men who were also directly involved in the assassination. One of these marriages involved a man who would soon be convicted as a fellow conspirator in the assassination, Quihueimen (Quirico), and his wife, Chesente (Maria Concepcion).⁴⁹ The other was the marriage of the man who initially called the conspirators together, Yachacxi, and his wife, Yuñan (Serafina).⁵⁰

The oral histories of Asisara fondly recall Lino as a man of particular skill and vitality. Asisara describes Lino as having "more skill and ability than the others" and says that "Lino was pure Indian, but as white as any Spaniard, and a naturally good looking man."⁵¹ Given the racial ideologies prevalent at the time of his interview, in 1877, it seems likely that Asisara reflected an internalization of Spanish, Mexican, and American racial categories. Here he venerated Lino, who had died a few years prior to Asisara's birth, by identifying him in the positive racial terms of the time.⁵² In any case, Asisara's story reflects that the mission community remembered Lino as an able leader and protector of his people.

Lino came from one of the largest and earliest families to be baptized at Mission Santa Cruz, a prominent Chaloctaca family. Lino's parents, Ules and Lluillin, were the first Chaloctaca couple baptized at the mission, in early 1792.⁵³ The couple had close ties with the local Uypi chief, Soquel, and his wife Rosuem, as they had joined them in visiting Mission Santa Clara shortly before the founding of Mission Santa Cruz. One of Ules and Lluillin's sons, Cucufate, had been baptized along with the daughters of the Uypi chief.⁵⁴ Cucufate was also the first child to die after the founding of Mission Santa Cruz.⁵⁵ The family was part of the Chaloctaca tribe, a small group associated through marriage patterns and baptisms to the larger Sayanta, located north of Mission Santa Cruz, in the mountains between Missions Santa Cruz and Santa Clara (see map 1).[56] Ules's parents were baptized shortly after he and Lluillin received their baptisms.[57] The first five Chaloctaca, who were all part of the same family, were given the surname Cañizares in their baptismal records. The vast majority of Indigenous baptisms did not note surnames, so the inclusion of a surname typically denoted special standing. It is also probable that Lino's grandparents were the leaders of the Chaloctaca people. Overall, forty Chaloctaca were baptized at Mission Santa Cruz between 1792 and 1796, while around seventy Sayanta received baptism during the same time. Just under 15 percent of the original Sayanta and Chaloctaca peoples at Mission Santa Cruz survived to the time of the assassination (see table 16).[58]

Ules appears to have had ongoing conflict with the padres—he is the person described in a letter from the late 1890s as "incorrigible" and "unbearable" in disrupting the mission community.[59] Perhaps the loss of his son shortly after the founding of Mission Santa Cruz had led Ules to distrust the missionaries. Spanish authorities would eventually arrest three members of the Cañizares family for their roles in the Quintana assassination: Ules, his brother Sirinte (Fulgencio), and his son Lino.[60] Furthermore, the other conspirators were closely tied to this family through kinship, revealing the extended kinship network at the center of this story.

It is tempting to interpret the assassination as a refutation of Franciscan Catholicism, but statements attributed to Lino suggest otherwise.[61] Lino decried Padre Quintana's brutality and hypocrisy, stating that "the first thing that we need to do is to keep the Father from fulfilling his desires to punish people in this way, for we are not animals; he says in his sermons that God does not command this [type of punishment], in his examples and doctrine."[62] Lino recognized Quintana's actions as outside the bounds of correct behavior described in his sermons and teachings—Quintana failed to fulfill his spiritual obligations to Lino's community. After years of serving as his personal paje, aiding Quintana in his rituals, Lino was uniquely qualified to observe and interpret Quintana's actions and sermons. The assassination itself was neither a rejection of Catholicism nor an anticolonial rebellion. It was a direct response to Quintana's sadism. In fact, Lino articulated a sophisticated understanding of Quintana's teachings and found him guilty of hypocrisy.

Ohlone spiritual practices allowed for a plurality of traditions, and there is reason to believe that Lino and the others understood their assassination within both Catholic and Indigenous measures of justice.[63] While they took part in Catholic ceremony and attended sermons by the missionaries, they also continued to practice their songs and dances and use their earthen sweat lodges.[64] In the 1930s ethnographer John P. Harrington collected information from Ohlone peoples throughout the Bay Area. In his notes he recorded that Ohlone traditions called for the execution of spiritual leaders who failed to fulfill their responsibilities, suggesting a basis for understanding Indigenous practices of dealing with hypocritical spiritual leadership.[65] The assassins, as remembered by Asisara, articulated a sense of justice and of hypocrisy informed by traditional practices yet interpreted through the new teachings of Franciscan Catholicism.

Lino's proximity to Quintana gave him access that eventually facilitated the assassination and subsequent cover-up, but it also meant that he suffered frequently at the hands of the padre. Spanish reports of the incident consistently single out Lino as the object of frequent punishment by Quintana. Governor Solá, who defended Quintana's character and his use of corporal punishment by stating that the padre had "great love for his Indians," himself admitted after hearing the defenses of the conspirators that Quintana had targeted Lino for "frequent punishment."[66]

Although it is not easy to find direct evidence of sexual abuse in historical documents, the circumstances surrounding Quintana's assassination make it clear that Quintana's cruel behavior likely involved some degree of sexual abuse.[67] Multiple accounts claim that the assassins mutilated Quintana's genitalia, though the various reports disagree about the exact nature of this disfigurement, some saying that he was castrated and others claiming that his testicles had been crushed.[68] Neither genital mutilation nor castration is a widespread Indigenous practice in the region, so the use of this very specific type of punishment suggests some degree of retribution.

One possibility is that Quintana had sexually abused Lino. If not Lino, then it is possible that Quintana had sexually abused someone else close to the assassination. The involvement of Ules and Sirinte, Lino's father and uncle, respectively, in the assassination suggests that Lino's family was at the very least extremely concerned with the way that Quintana had treated him (see table 15). It is not difficult to imagine that sexual abuse could have been an important factor in motivating the conspirators, even if it is not directly stated in the archives. Furthermore, persistent rumors recorded in the 1840s claim that Quintana's murder was a case of revenge for Quintana's rape of a young woman, the partner of one of the assassins.[69] Taking this story into consideration, perhaps the victim of Quintana's sexual predation was Lino's wife, Humiliana.[70] Yet another possibility is that Quintana may have targeted Yuñan, the wife of Yachacxi. Yuñan and Yachacxi married in July 1812, a few months before Yachacxi suffered the beating that set the assassination in motion.[71] Could Yachacxi's beating have been precipitated by Quintana's rape of Yuñan? While it is impossible to know the details of Quintana's abusive behavior, ample evidence suggests that sexual abuse was involved, one way or another.

Lino and Humiliana were united in their ferocious sense of survival in a world in which children rarely lived to adulthood, the fourth and fifth children born to parents within the mission; by the time of the assassination, they were the two oldest mission-born youth. Humiliana, whose parents identified as Aptos, was three months younger than Lino. Lino and Humiliana married in May 1813, six months after Quintana's assassination.[72] Humiliana served as *madrina* six times; the first took place three months after her marriage, while she was pregnant with her and Lino's daughter, Petra Nicanor.[73] Their daughter was born in January 1814, while her father was being held in San Francisco, awaiting his sentence for the assassination. It is unlikely that Petra Nicanor ever met her father, though before her death, in 1851, she eventually owned a piece of mission land during the Mexican era with her husband, Chuyucu (Victoriano), and their children.[74] Remarkably, Petra Nicanor's burial record mentions her father, some thirty years after his passing, a reflection of Lino's legacy and importance in the mission community.[75]

As mentioned earlier, the cover-up of the assassination of Padre Quintana continued undetected by Spanish officials until, as the oral history tells, sometime around two years after the assassination a soldier overheard two seamstresses gossiping and bickering about the deed. Humiliana is remembered as one of these women, along with Shomam (Maria Tata).[76] Here Asisara's account and that of retired soldier José Eusebio Galindo intersect, as they both tell of two women being overheard.[77] The story is remembered by Asisara and Galindo as an example of jealous bickering, although other sources suggest that the women were talking about "serving another padre in the same way."[78] We will never know what exactly was overheard to alert the soldier, but whatever was said was enough to raise the suspicions and raise the alarm for the Spanish authorities.[79]

The soldier who overheard the women discussing the assassination, identified as Carlos Castro, understood enough of the Awaswas language to suspect that they were talking about foul play. He was the one who alerted the authorities, who then arrested the sixteen men and marched them to San Francisco for trial in either late 1814 or early 1815. Spanish authorities held Lino and the eight other convicts at the San Francisco Presidio until confirmation of their punishments was received from Mexico City in 1816. By that time Ules and three others had died at the presidio in San Francisco (see table 19).[80] Lino received a sentence of two hundred lashings and ten years at the presidio in Santa Barbara, while his uncle Sirinte was given two hundred lashes and six years at the same presidio.[81] Neither Lino nor Sirinte survived their time in Santa Barbara. Lino died in April 1817, while Sirinte died two years later, in May 1819.[82] Humiliana married a Tomoi man named Marichimas (Wenceslao) about six months after news of Lino's death was reported back to Mission Santa Cruz.[83] She had five children with Marichimas, in addition to Petra Nicanor, and eventually died in 1829.[84]

While Lino was the lead paje involved in the assassination, Asisara mentions the participation of two other young pajes in the planning and assassination itself. Asisara recounts that the young pajes timidly assisted, following the orders of the older and more seasoned Lino. These two pajes are identified as Miguel Antonio, the son of the aforementioned Yachacxi, and Vicente, a mission-born Aptos boy.[85] Vicente was only eleven years old at the time of the assassination, and Miguel Antonio was ten. By 1812 Vicente had lost his mother and his younger brother and survived along with his father, Zuem (Agapito de Albiz). Zuem was the eleventh Aptos to be baptized at Mission Santa Cruz, within the first three months of the founding, by late 1791.[86] Vicente maintained a relatively low-key existence within the mission community, as he never married or had children and did not serve as padrino or witness for any services. Miguel Antonio married and had two children in the 1820s, one of which, Nicanor, lived until at least the 1840s; he served as padrino for two baptisms in the early

1830s.[87] Neither Vicente nor Miguel Antonio was convicted in the Quintana assassination, and both lived into the 1830s.[88]

Kinship Ties with Mission Santa Clara

A careful analysis of the conspirators involved in the assassination brings to light another important facet of Indigenous Bay Area mission life: movement and interconnections between mission communities. While biannual reports from the missionaries often mentioned the existence of Indigenous individuals who had received their initial baptism at a different mission living at Mission Santa Cruz, these reports did not give any explanation about how or why they had relocated.[89] Movement and relocation of individuals, marriage partners, and families were not typically documented with specificity, leaving historians to believe that the missions acted as closed systems. And yet the reports and mission records, such as the Book of Marriages, show that some individuals relocated and married across mission communities. If the missions were truly closed systems, then one wonders how individuals could meet and marry across these lines. Clearly, kinship ties and long-standing interrelations continued across communities separated by missions. The persistence of these kinship ties and interrelations is supported by archaeological research, which has documented that individuals and families continued to engage in exchange and economic relations and to connect with kin across mission boundaries and homelands alike.[90] The presence of two brothers involved in the Quintana assassination helps reveal this ongoing pattern of relocation and the persistence of kinship ties.

Prior to the founding of Mission Santa Cruz, in 1791, local peoples interacted with soldiers and missionaries from San Carlos (Monterey region) and Santa Clara. Mission Santa Clara was the closest site where mountain tribal people from Mak-Sah-Re-Jah, including members of the group located in present-day downtown Santa Cruz, the Uypi, could go to receive baptism (see map 1).[91] Interrelations and connections between peoples throughout the region continued during the mission years: sacramental registries show marriages and other interrelations between residents at Missions San Carlos, San Juan Bautista, Santa Clara, and Santa Cruz, while census records show individuals baptized at these missions holding residence at neighboring missions.[92] Often these marriages and movement followed tribal or familial lines. Asisara mentions that three Indians from Mission Santa Clara participated in the assassination. We know for certain that two brothers, Leto Antonio and Secundino Antonio, both baptized at Mission Santa Clara, were among those found guilty of the assassination and held in San Francisco.[93]

The presence of these brothers at Mission Santa Cruz is surely due to their kinship ties with local polities and peoples, as Spanish missionaries had baptized both brothers four years before the founding of Mission Santa Cruz (see table 15). Their half-sister, Chacualis (Toquato), from the same father, was baptized at Mission Santa Clara on May 21, 1791, which is the same day that the chief of the Uypi, Soquel, and his wife, Rosuem, brought their young daughter, Clara de la Cruz, for baptism.[94] The two are the only baptisms recorded that day, though they precede another group of baptisms of children with parents from the Santa Cruz region by a week.[95] The proximity of these baptisms suggests that Secundino Antonio and Leto Antonio, along with their other three brothers and sister, were Uypi or another neighboring tribe with strong kinship ties to the Uypi leader. Their connections with the Uypi people would explain their continued ties to Mission Santa Cruz as well as their investment in protecting the community against the abuses of Quintana.[96] Leto Antonio, the older of the two brothers, played a leadership role at Mission Santa Clara, as he served as paje, padrino for baptisms, and marriage witness between 1799 and 1806.[97] The brothers must have relocated to Mission Santa Cruz sometime after 1806, possibly as a reward for their service at Mission Santa Clara. Their relocation and eventual participation in the assassination helps illustrate ways in which baptized Indigenous peoples might have used their privilege to gain mobility to connect with kin across mission boundaries.

Women and Erasure

The California missions have been remembered as quietly masculinized places, with women's lives and contributions often hidden from historical study.[98] Within Indigenous Californian communities, women had long held positions of political, social, and spiritual power, at times playing key roles in Indigenous rebellions.[99] That power followed them into the missions and was known by Indigenous communities, which continue to recognize the importance of female leadership today.[100] And while it is not surprising that Spanish archives have rendered Indigenous female leadership as invisible, considering the patriarchal emphasis of Spanish society, Asisara's account contributes to this erasure.

At the center of this assassination story is Yaquenonsat, who is credited with initially developing the strategy, summoning the abusive padre, and ultimately ensuring his execution. And yet, in his recounting of the assassination story, Asisara never directly identified Yaquenonsat by name; he only calls her "la muger [sic] de Julían" (the wife of Julían), part of a larger pattern of Asisara's neglecting or failing to recognize women and their concerns.[101] But despite the omission of women in the archives, it is clear that women continued to play prominent roles within the mission communities, and in this situation two women were heavily involved in the assassination and surrounding events—Yaquenonsat and the Aptos woman Yuñan.[102]

Along with their mutual involvement in these events, the two women share a special designation, as they both are listed as being *monjas* (nuns) in baptismal records, having served as madrinas.[103] Among all the Santa Cruz records, these are the only two times that anyone received these special monja notations. In fact, among all existing baptismal records throughout all twenty-one California missions, Yuñan and Yaquenonsat are the only madrinas listed as monjas.[104] These designations seem to suggest that they held special status or standing within their community. While the traditional role of the monja within Spanish colonial society was very specific to Catholicism, the lives of these two women suggest that this designation may have meant something distinctly related to their own community. Historians have demonstrated that Indigenous men were often able to maintain power within the missions through taking on the role of alcalde, but women have heretofore been considered to have been without parallel avenues to power.[105] Perhaps roles such as monjas or madrinas offered opportunities for women to exercise political or social status and standing to some degree. A closer examination of the lives of Yaquenonsat and Yuñan will help to shed light on who they were and what their monja status meant within their community.

Yaquenonsat arrived at Mission Santa Cruz in early 1807, part of a large group of nearly fifty Sumus and Tomoi, tribes from the second wave of Ohlone speakers from farther inland (see map 1). Yaquenonsat was the oldest female Sumus in this group of baptisms, identified as thirty-eight years of age. Tribal standing and hierarchies were frequently reflected in the baptismal ordering, and the fact that Yaquenonsat was listed fifth in this large group, directly after the family of the chief and before the rest of the men and women, which was atypical, is another clue suggesting that she enjoyed an elevated status. Her special status could indicate her role as spiritual or political leader of the tribe, or perhaps it reflects that she is a former wife of the chief.

Eight months after her arrival, Yaquenonsat married Lacah, a former alcalde and a mission gardener.[106] Her marriage to an existing political leader at her age suggests a political pairing, likely building new kinship connections between the Sumus and the Chaloctaca.[107] As will be discussed in later chapters, the Sumus did indeed appear to build strong ties with the Awaswas Ohlone local tribes. As mission gardener, Lacah had a house that sat in the middle of the mission plaza, near the padres. Perhaps Yaquenonsat strategically married Lacah, knowing that this would allow her to keep an eye on Padre Quintana.

Within two years of her arrival, Yaquenonsat led a group of women fugitives, though records show that she returned to the mission soon after.[108] A clue to understanding the nature of Yaquenonsat's power and standing might be found in the group of fugitives with whom she was listed in 1809. Among the group of women was one young boy named Siboo (Canuto), a Sumus child from a family connected with Yaquenonsat's tribe.[109] Though his father remained at the mission, the boy and his mother joined Yaquenonsat's group of fugitive women. Maria Ascención Solórsano, a member of the Amah Mutsun and last fluent Mutsun speaker, spoke of this same Siboo many years later.[110] Solórsano had known Siboo in her childhood and mentioned that by the 1870s he was living in Watsonville. Siboo, as Solórsano related, had bear medicine: he would turn into a bear to scare away cowboys. As related in the first chapter, she had also told Harrington that there were many bear doctors in Santa Cruz. Siboo, who was raised at Mission Santa Cruz since early childhood, with the exception of his time spent as a fugitive, would have learned his powers from people at the mission. Could it have been Yaquenonsat who taught him? Solórsano also explained that "women also used to turn bear, and they were worse ones than the men."¹¹¹ It is certainly possible that Yaquenonsat taught children like Siboo important spiritual practices such as bear medicine, which could be one explanation for his presence in the group of fugitives.

As a Sumus woman from the eastern hills over the Mak-Sah-Re-Jah mountains, Yaquenonsat was the only identified member of the conspirators not from the lands within the immediate vicinity of the mission. In forming the plan to kill Quintana, Yaquenonsat drew on her experiences and insight gained from events near her homelands before her initial entry into Mission Santa Cruz in 1807.¹¹² Two years prior to her arrival, an incident took place forty to fifty miles north of Sumus territory. In January 1805 Padre Pedro de la Cueva, recently arrived at Mission San José from Mexico City, was summoned to an Asirin village to administer last rites and hear the confessions of a few sick fugitive baptized Natives, presumably to prepare them for death in the Catholic tradition. Accompanied by two soldiers and a small group of baptized Native guides, de la Cueva and his party encountered dense fog. Either because of the fog or misdirection by one of the guides (as de la Cueva later claimed), the party walked into an ambush by a hostile Luecha village. The attackers killed three of the Native guides and one of the soldiers, the mayordomo of Mission San José, Ygnacio Higuera. Padre de la Cueva was shot in the eye with an arrow during the encounter, though he survived.¹¹³ This ambush marked the first time a Spaniard was killed by tribal people in the San Francisco Bay Area as well as the first wounding of a Franciscan priest.¹¹⁴

While it is not possible to know if this attack was premeditated, the evidence suggests that de la Cueva may have made his share of enemies. Padre de la Cueva, who spent less than two years total in Alta California, had a reputation for extreme cruelty and indolence. On several occasions he pulled a dagger on his companions during his trip into Alta California.¹¹⁵ When the Russian exploratory expedition under Count Nikolai Petrovich Rezanov visited the Bay Area in 1806, diarist Georg von Langsdorff described his encounter with the friar. Padre de la Cueva invited the Russian party to visit Mission San José, where he "promised to entertain [them] with a dance of the Indians, if they would come and visit."¹¹⁶ De la Cueva "announced that they were to have a holiday from their work, that they might dress themselves in their very best attire, and prepare for a dance," and then he "distributed a number of ornaments among the best dancers, who immediately withdrew with them to make the necessary preparations."[117] De la Cueva apparently not only controlled their work schedule but also their access to ceremonial ornaments, exercising a great deal of social control over the baptized Native people under his charge.[118]

After de la Cueva's return to Mexico City in 1806, his abusive behavior continued. He reportedly so frightened the other friars by his acts of drunken violence that they locked themselves in their rooms to keep safe.[119] The drunken, hostile, and controlling behavior of de la Cueva may have prompted this ambush by the Luecha villagers.[120] Certainly, the details of this successful ambush would have made their way down to Sumus territory and would have been fresh in Yaquenonsat's memory when the need came to deal with a similarly cruel padre. Her importation of strategy into Mission Santa Cruz would demonstrate the exchange of tactics and ideas between Indigenous peoples inside and outside the missions.

The similarities between the attacks on de la Cueva and Quintana extend beyond the padres' shared propensity for cruelty. Padre de la Cueva was tactically exposed to the ambush because of his insistence on imposing Catholic funerary rituals, the same tactic later proposed by Yaquenonsat and used in the plot to assassinate Padre Quintana. Whether the de la Cueva attack consciously used funereal rites as a pretense to call the padre or not, the success of the attack and de la Cueva's insistence on responding to the call demonstrated the Catholic attachment to these impositions. Yaquenonsat appeared to have learned to manipulate this insistence on Catholic rites, using it to surprise Quintana.

The Ohlone had their own long-standing funereal and mortuary practices, traditions that helped reinforce kinship and community interrelations.[121] Mourning and funereal rituals involved obligations built around moieties and animal clan identities, rituals of social cohesion that helped foster interconnectivity. According to Ketchum, "Eagle or Condor People could handle the dead," suggesting that certain groups were tasked with caring for the deceased.[122] Franciscan missionaries interpreted these practices as "heathen" while imposing Catholic rites. Considering the atrocious frequency of death among the Indigenous community at the missions, funereal and mourning rituals would have certainly continued to play a crucial role in building community among survivors.[123] Was Yaquenonsat's use of this tactic a subtle challenge or critique of the imposition of new rituals and the restriction of long-standing practices? It certainly seems possible.

While Asisara's story credits Yaquenonsat with playing key roles in ensuring the success of the assassination, her husband, the gardener Lacah, was also vital to the plot. The conspirators met at the home of Yaquenonsat and Lacah, and it was Lacah who feigned illness in order to create the pretense for summoning Quintana.[124] Lacah had a history of prominence at Mission Santa Cruz, as he was one of the first two men elected as alcalde there, about fifteen years prior to the assassination.[125] While alcaldes officially served as the "voice of the padres" in relating the missionaries' instructions back to the others, they sometimes played key roles in rebellions and resistance movements within the missions.[126] Documents do not indicate how long Lacah held office, but he appears to have shifted from the role of alcalde to that of gardener, another important role.

Like so many others, Lacah's story is also one of great loss, reflecting the incredibly difficult conditions of mission life. Lacah entered Mission Santa Cruz by himself, a few months after Ules (Lino's father) and his family, in June 1792. Records indicate that Lacah was a member of the Sucheseu rancheria, which is most likely named for one of the Chaloctaca villages. He is the only one identified from this particular rancheria.[127] He entered the mission as an adult of twenty-six years, at a time when most of those baptized were children. Overall, he married five times and had two children, though both children died in their youth, and his first four wives had all died by 1807, when he married Yaquenonsat.[128] For his role in the assassination, Lacah was convicted and sentenced to two hundred lashes and six years at Santa Barbara Presidio.[129] He died before completing his sentence, on December 2, 1820.[130]

The story of another conspirator, Euxexi, reflects not only loss but the persistence of kinship relations from pre-mission times. Euxexi was also convicted for Quintana's murder, but he did not survive long enough in the harsh conditions of the San Francisco Presidio to complete his sentence (see table 15).[131] In late 1793 Euxexi had been the first of his people, the Somontoc, to enter Mission Santa Cruz. The Somontoc had a much longer history of interaction with other missions, as five Somontoc children had been baptized at Mission Santa Clara in the two years before the founding of Mission Santa Cruz.[132] The latest of these had been the baptism of Euxexi's daughter, Clementina, which had been performed two weeks before Mission Santa Cruz was established.[133] Overall, only fifteen Somontoc were baptized at Mission Santa Cruz, with another eleven baptized at Mission Santa Clara, suggesting that the Somontoc existed as a smaller subgroup of a larger polity or that other Somontoc people had been baptized into another mission under a different name. Of the fifteen baptized in Santa Cruz, only three, including Euxexi, survived to 1812. Euxexi's previous partner, Ocot (Nicolasa), died nine months after her own baptism at Mission Santa Cruz.[134]

In the years that followed, Euxexi married five times; each of his wives died shortly after marriage.[135] Euxexi became stepfather to three children in 1812, when he married his fifth wife, Sajuero (Nila), a Pitac.[136] Euxexi's connection to the conspirators occurred through multiple links and illustrates the complexity of the kinship ties that bound the community together. Ocot, Euxexi's first partner and the mother of his daughter, was a member of the prominent Chaloctaca Cañizares family and Lino's aunt. He was also connected through his relationship with his brother-in-law Llencó, the father of Lorenzo Asisara, the one who would tell the story so many years later.[137] Llencó was connected to Euxexi through his first wife, who was Euxexi's sister, Tuquion (Maria Rafaela).[138]

While he was not arrested for the assassination, we know through the story related by his son, Asisara, that Llencó was one of the sixteen men marched to San Francisco by Spanish soldiers. Baptized at the age of twenty, in mid-1793, he is the lone Cotoni involved in the conspiracy. Llencó came from the Cotoni rancheria of Jlli or Asar, both of which lay north of Mission Santa Cruz, somewhere near present-day Davenport (see map 1).[139] By the beginning of 1812, only twelve of the original ninety-three baptized Cotoni survived, about 13 percent (see table 16). At some point after the assassination, Llencó became a mission gardener, possibly replacing Lacah after his arrest.[140] Llencó married three times; his first wife, who died in 1800, was Euxexi's sister.[141] His third wife, Lihutsatme (Manuela), gave birth to Asisara in 1820.[142] Llencó continued to hold influence within the mission community, serving as witness to three marriages, all in 1817, a few years after his return to the mission following the trial.[143] Llencó survived until 1838, when he died of smallpox in the epidemic that swept through the surviving community.[144]

Along with Yaquenonsat, the other woman identified as a monja was Yuñan. She and her husband, Yachacxi, were also central conspirators. The young couple married about three months prior to the assassination. Lino was one of the witnesses to this marriage.[145] At some point shortly after their wedding, Yachacxi received a particularly harsh beating at the hands of Quintana, which was the abuse that inspired him to call together the group of conspirators in order to plan the assassination.[146] The abuse of twenty-three-year-old Yachacxi and eighteen-year-old Lino shows that Quintana frequently targeted the youth for punishment. Considering the high mortality rate for Indigenous youth, it seems likely that Ules and some of the older conspirators were motivated in part by a desire to protect the young men and women at the mission. It is somewhat surprising that Yachacxi was not one of the men convicted of the assassination, considering the key role that he played in initiating the meeting of conspirators. Though it is not stated directly, it seems likely that, ironically, the severity of his beating may have saved his life: His injuries might very well have rendered him unable to participate directly in the assassination.

At the time of the assassination, twenty-three-year-old Yachacxi served as "Alcalde de Mugeres [*sic*]," or "Mayor of the Women," within the mission.[147] Unlike other California missions, Mission Santa Cruz appears unique in splitting alcaldes' duties between overseeing men and overseeing women, as none of the other missions record similar designations. However, at Mission Santa Cruz this role was available only to men, as no women served in this capacity or in any role as alcalde. Given the emphasis on the locking and holding of keys to the dormitories, Yachacxi's responsibilities must have included overseeing and locking the *monjeríos*. In the years following the assassination, Yachacxi retained a position of social standing within the mission community, continuing to serve as padrino in the years following the convictions, before his eventual death in 1833.[148]

Yachacxi had entered Mission Santa Cruz as a five-year-old in 1794, among a large group of Cotoni from the Achistaca village region. This group of baptisms included Yachacxi's father, Lleguix (Angel), as well as the Aptos woman who would become his first wife, Sauten (Antonia Ynés).[149] Yachacxi and Sauten had three children together, of which two, along with Sauten, had died by 1812.[150] Their one surviving child, Miguel Antonio, was one of the three pajes, along with Lino and Vicente, who helped plan and carry out the Quintana assassination. Yachacxi remarried in 1812, this time to Yuñan, a woman from the Cajastaca village baptized about a year before Yachacxi. By 1812 about 15 percent of the baptized Achistaca population at the mission was still alive, with slightly more than 20 percent of Yuñan's people, the Aptos and Cajastaca, still living in the mission as well (see table 16).

Yuñan had six children, five with Yachacxi.[151] Yuñan played a prominent role in the mission community, and her story demonstrates the ways in which some women were able to exercise influence and power by navigating within the Catholic mission community. Yuñan was baptized along with the first group of Cajastac in 1795, at the age of six. Something about young Yuñan must have stood out even at an early age, as she appears at the top of the list of young women receiving confirmation.[152]

Yuñan's special status within the mission community is most visible through her role as madrina in numerous baptisms. She served as madrina thirty-seven times between 1808 and 1830, the first time when she was eighteen or nineteen (see table 18).[153] Within Catholic practices, godparents had responsibility for the spiritual upbringing of the child. For Indigenous community members, however, this role may have held additional meaning drawing on Indigenous practices, such as establishing kinship between diverse tribes and families. Out of the thirty-seven times Yuñan served as madrina, thirteen were to newborn or very young children, many of whom were siblings.[154] She also served as madrina for newly arrived adult women, suggesting that she was responsible for helping them adjust to Catholic life at the mission. For example, in 1826 Yuñan served as madrina for a group of seventeen Yokuts girls and women between the age of ten and twenty-four from a variety of villages.[155]

So, what did it mean for Yuñan and Yaquenonsat to carry the designation of monja? Women became nuns for many reasons in Spanish Franciscan Catholic society. For some women it was an avenue to authority, to knowledge and power within the church. It did not necessarily mean that they believed in Catholicism, as we cannot know what their beliefs were without more information. In the case of Yaquenonsat, considering her standing with Indigenous spiritual power and possibly Bear Medicine, it seems likely that the monja title was given by an Indigenous translator who described her to the padre who wrote it. The word monja was likely the closest Spanish equivalent to signifying her spiritual standing within their community.

For Yuñan her designation as a monja was clearly not intended to signify the traditional Catholic celibate world of the nun, as she was a married woman with multiple children. So, what did it mean for Yuñan to be listed as a monja? Indigenous women at the mission clearly performed important roles in healing and childbirth as midwives, *curanderas* (healers), and herbalists.[156] And yet Yuñan was madrina for newly arrived adults more frequently than for newborn children, which makes the role of midwife less likely. Her role seemed to be more of advisor, possibly on spiritual or cultural matters, helping children and adults adjust to expectations and practices within the mission while building new kinship relations between certain families and tribal groups.

For Yuñan this role may have reflected her facility with Catholicism, or it may have signified a broader sense of power and authority within her community. For Yaquenonsat it seemed to suggest that she held power and influence, most likely having little to do with Catholicism. The role of monja had to do with the colonial church and avenues of authority and power accessible to women.[157] With Yaquenonsat and Yuñan the designation of monja points toward the presence of women who held particular power and influence within the Mission Santa Cruz Indigenous community, women whose lives and circles intersected with the extraordinary act of assassinating an abusive missionary.

The Survivors

While the majority of those convicted of the assassination died within a few years of receiving their sentences, two managed to survive their convictions and lived into the 1830s: Ètop (Antonio Alberto) and Quihueimen. Ètop was baptized in 1797 as part of a second wave of Cajastaca villagers to receive baptism at Mission Santa Cruz. The missionaries renamed Ètop after engineer extraordinaire Alberto Cordoba, who helped build the neighboring Villa de Branciforte and served as padrino for four baptisms while he was in the area, including that of Ètop.[158] Ètop is unique among the convicts in that he was able to appeal and testify his way out of bondage.[159] Ètop, like the other conspirators, played important roles in the mission, serving as witness for two marriages in 1801 and as padrino for the birth of Rustico, the son of fellow conspirator and his good friend Quihueimen, in 1811.[160]

Ètop is mentioned in Asisara's account as one of the mission cooks.[161] Ètop's wife, Najam (Victoriana), entered the mission seven months after Ètop. She and Ètop had two children together, Sostenes and Fidel, born in 1799 and 1803, respectively.[162] The role of cook within the mission community is one worthy of closer examination. In a visit by Padre Estévan Tapis in 1818, special effort was made to address rumors about the attempted poisonings of two former padres.[163] Tapis, who had served as *padre presidente* between 1803 and 1812, advised the missionary authorities to ignore the rumors, pointing out that the reason cooks from Mission San Juan Bautista had been used at Mission Santa Cruz lay with the lack of trained cooks in Santa Cruz, as, he noted, the three Mission Santa Cruz cooks accused of poisonings were serving time in prison.[164] Cooks had special access and reveal a vulnerability of which padres and soldiers were very conscious, as numerous poisonings occurred or were suspected to have occurred throughout the California missions.[165]

Ètop was convicted for his involvement in Quintana's assassination and had been sentenced to two hundred lashes and six years in the presidio.[166] For some unknown reason Ètop was able to plead his case in November 1820, after having served four years of his sentence.[167] Ètop explained in his testimony that he "was imprisoned because the Indian Quirico [Quihueimen] invited him to help kill the padre," that Quihueimen "had come by [his] house to say prayers," and that the two men had passed through the garden on their way to Quihueimen's house, as Ètop claimed, "to steal pears."[168] Ètop claimed that it was on the way to the garden that Quihueimen told him of the plan to kill Quintana and that when they entered the garden, they encountered the rest of the men. According to Ètop, he heard Ules talking about killing Quintana, at which point Ètop claimed he left the group, learning of Quintana's death the following day. He further testified that he had fled to the mountains after he heard about the assassination.[169] He continued to testify that he eventually came down from the mountains at the request of his son, Sostenes, who had been sent by Padre Marcelino.[170] In his testimony he admitted to being guilty of not alerting the soldiers and overseers of the plot to murder Quintana but not of participating directly in the assassination.[171] His testimony stands at odds with the account by Asisara, which places the cook Ètop at the initial meeting, suggesting that either Asisara was wrong about his initial collaboration or that Ètop was able to navigate the Spanish legal system successfully to get himself an early release.

Ètop's response to learning about the assassination, according to his testimony, was to run to the mountains to get away from the mission, which is significant when considering Ètop's story after his release. When asked why he fled to the mountains if he was innocent, he replied that "while he had been working his son had alerted him that they [presumably the soldiers] had been bothering others," asking around, which led him to flee to the hills.[172] He looked to the mountains for refuge from the soldiers, possibly somewhere in Mak-Sah-Re-Jah near his home village of Cajastaca, a flight that prefigures Ètop's return to the mountains later in life.

After his release from imprisonment, Ètop did not show up in any of the Mission Santa Cruz documents or census rolls, instead appearing in the records of Mission San Carlos, to the south, neighboring the Presidio of Monterey. His presence in the archives is minimal, noted only in three more records. In 1824 he was recorded as marrying Unijunis (Catarina), the daughter of one of the earliest baptized families of Mission San Carlos listed as being Calenda-ruc.[173] The Calenda-ruc region lay just south of Ètop's home village of Cajastaca, so it is possible that Ètop was already familiar with Catarina or her people before his imprisonment (see map 2). After his harsh treatment by Spanish authorities, it would make sense for Ètop to keep distance from the missions by resettling with familiar neighbors. Four years later, in 1826, they had a daughter, Maria de la Concepcion.[174] Her baptismal record lists her place of birth as "in the mountains, where her parents ordinarily spend their time."[175]

It appears that Ètop returned to the hills after his release, as he did in response to the Quintana assassination. Did he return to his homelands near Cajastaca? His proximity to Mission San Carlos in later years suggests that he relocated to the mountains closer to Monterey, possibly in the hills near modern Big Sur, a relatively undeveloped region that archaeological studies have shown became a refuge for fugitives through the mid-nineteenth century.[176] Perhaps refugees such as Ètop and his family gathered in unoccupied forests, in a way similar to the Quiroste-led group from the 1790s. Ètop died in 1832.[177]

Quihueimen is the only other convicted conspirator to survive his sentence. Quihueimen was Uypi, from the region directly surrounding Mission Santa Cruz, and entered the mission as a seven-year-old. The thirty-third Uypi baptized at Mission Santa Cruz, he received baptism merely one and a half months after the mission's founding. Quihueimen's first marriage, to Monguis (Liberata) in October 1798, was brief, as her burial records appear with the report on fugitives found dead outside of the mission at the end of 1799.[178] Like so many others within the missions, Quihueimen lost multiple spouses. It was Quihueimen's third marriage, to Chesente, which took place in 1808, that finally lasted.[179] His friend Ètop served as padrino to their son Rustico.[180]

Chesente was baptized at Mission Santa Clara and had moved to Santa Cruz by 1800, when she married Tuliám (Prudencio).[181] Chesente's baptismal record indicates her tribal identity as being "San Carlos," which likely meant that she was from the Mak-Sah-Re-Jah range, tied to people from Mission Santa Cruz through tribe and kinship. Chesente's marriage to Tuliám was the third marriage recorded between men from Mission Santa Cruz and women from Mission Santa Clara. By 1812 there were eight marriages between women from Santa Clara and men from Santa Cruz.[182] The marriages and relations between members of the varying local mission populations are part of a pattern of mobility and movement between these Indigenous communities.[183] As was the case with Chesente, many of these marriages followed traditional patterns, solidifying kinship ties.[184]

Before serving time for his participation in the assassination, Quihueimen performed important functions within the mission community. He served as padrino for eight baptisms between 1808 and 1810 and as witness in four marriages in 1810.[185] Quihueimen was sentenced to two hundred lashes and six years, serving his time at the presidio at Santa Barbara along with Lacah, Sirinte, and Lino (see table 19).[186] Unlike the others, Quihueimen survived his sentence and returned to Mission Santa Cruz.[187] His wife,

Chesente, died in 1815, while Quihueimen was still awaiting his sentence in the presidio in San Francisco.[188]

A few years after his release, Quihueimen married Ulalixmi (Coleta), a Yokuts woman who arrived in the 1820s, with whom he had a third child.[189] Quihueimen eventually died in a smallpox epidemic, in 1838, though his numerous grandchildren survived into the American statehood years, and it is possible that his descendants continue to live today.[190] Quihueimen continued to serve as padrino in his later years, after his return to Mission Santa Cruz.[191] Among the people for whom he served as padrino was Catarina, the daughter of Xuclan (José Ricardo), the mission song leader and good friend of Asisara.[192] Xuclan was born shortly before the assassination, the son of a Sumus couple who entered the mission about eight months prior to Yaquenonsat.[193]

Mission of Padre Killers

The assassination of Padre Quintana was an important moment for the Indigenous community of Mission Santa Cruz and a challenge to the Spanish authorities that reflected the fears and anxieties of the padres and soldiers. The assassination emboldened the Native community and elevated the status of the conspirators and their descendants. In 1818 Padre Estévan Tapis visited Mission Santa Cruz, reporting back to the concerned Californio community about the "mission of friar killers," reassuring them that rumors of an unruly neophyte population had been overstated and that talk of attempted poisonings was not to be believed.[194] Tapis continued by reaffirming that he "was very content in [his position at Mission] San Juan," making it clear that he was not interested in relocating.[195] The fears and concerns of the Spanish soldiers and missionaries stemmed from the bold actions of this group of Indigenous leaders six years earlier, who defended their growing community from the punishments of an overreaching padre. Indigenous oral histories speak of a community willing to challenge unjust treatment by the padres. The prominent standing of the descendants of the conspirators, reflected in land ownership by descendants of Lino and Quihueimen, points toward ongoing appreciation for those who gave their lives to kill this abusive padre.

So, what does this analysis of the individuals involved in the Quintana assassination tell us about life at Mission Santa Cruz? The involvement of an extensive kinship network made up of alliances between Awaswas-speaking people with long-standing ties to the region show that some families were able to maintain power and influence within the mission community for long periods of time, over twenty years in this case. The involvement of Yaquenonsat reveals that some women were able to maintain power and influence within the mission community while also showing the expansion of kinship ties to include newly arriving tribal leaders. This point is an important one, given the ongoing demographic collapse facing the mission community. Against this backdrop of immense loss and constant mourning, ritual and kinship ties helped to build community and alliances between survivors.

Immense loss, trauma, and abuse characterized this difficult time of change and disruption and informed decisions of great consequence. The assassination itself was an assertion of Indigenous politics—the rejection of a particularly abusive padre who overstepped his authority in committing excessive physical and, very likely, sexual abuses. The conspirators turned to Indigenous conceptions of justice and punishment, combining Catholic and traditional spiritual values in determining how to deal with this abusive spiritual leader.

The conspirators, most of whom paid for their participation with their lives, are remembered with reverence for their roles in protecting their community. The continued prominence of the conspirators who survived—and the descendants of those who did not—along with the persistence of oral histories celebrating their actions, reveals a level of heroification and veneration. Some of these conspirators or their children eventually owned, even if briefly, some portion of former mission lands, including Lino's daughter Petra Nicanor and her family, Quihueimen's son Rustico and his family, and song leader Xuclan, who shared his home with his friend Lorenzo Asisara.[196] The depth of knowledge and detail that we have about this assassination is itself a result of the privilege and access that Llencó's son, Asisara, attained through his navigation of racial and social status. It is because of Asisara's racial and social transcendence and his relationship with soldiers such as José María Amador—privileges not afforded to the majority of Indigenous survivors—that the rich detail of this story has reached a greater audience. Like Lino and the conspirators before him, Asisara and others holding special status within the mission utilized their proximity to the padres to move between worlds, to bring knowledge of the Spanish and Catholic social and spiritual worlds back to their communities.

In a rapidly changing world that had undergone environmental, social, political, and psychological upheaval, these leaders demonstrate an ability to navigate and survive this time of diminishing options by committing to big decisions, choosing extreme actions with dire consequences. Lino, as a young leader in the mission community, asserted an awareness of right and wrong; he, Yaquenonsat, and the other leaders chose to uphold the social order on their own as a part of this new world, protecting not only their own people but the incoming Yokuts as well.

And yet, despite the expansion of kinship ties and alliances, the arrest and exportation of the conspirators created a political void at Mission Santa Cruz. This void opened up new avenues to ascendant power for newly arrived Yokuts leaders, which would soon be filled by members of the Tejey. These new leaders found ways to ingratiate themselves with the missionaries, to wrest power from the local tribes, and to gain special access and rights. And yet the reputation of Mission Santa Cruz as a site where Indigenous people challenged Franciscan and Spanish control would persist. Large-scale flights of fugitives increased, along with challenges, direct and subtle. In the coming years the Spanish colonizers found themselves facing independence movements across the Americas, while the Franciscan padres faced cries for emancipation from within and outside of the mission community.

4

Chief Malimin (Coleto) and the Rise of the Yokuts

In May 1817, amid fears about a potential attack by French Argentine pirate Hippolyte Bouchard, Padre Jayme Escude turned to the one man he could trust to help arm and defend Mission Santa Cruz: the Tejey Yokuts chief Coleto Malimin. Escude ordered that Malimin and twenty-five of his men be armed with their bows and arrows to prepare in case Bouchard's ships were sighted along the coast.[1] Though Bouchard never did attack Mission Santa Cruz, Escude's order shed light on the ascendancy to power of Chief Malimin and his men, who rose to fill the vacuum in political leadership left following the arrest of the Quintana assassination conspirators. A year before Bouchard's threat, Malimin had won a position of trust for himself, his sons, and his people by helping track down a large group of fugitives. Malimin and his people, relatively recent arrivals at Mission Santa Cruz, immersed themselves in the existing Indigenous politics at the mission, navigating their way into positions of power and influence by working closely with the missionaries. Their stories reveal one way in which Indigenous peoples at the missions in a time of devastating change struggled to achieve the ultimate goal: survival.

Large numbers of Northern Valley Yokuts from the San Joaquin Valley entered the missions during the 1810s and 1820s.[2] Some of these Yokuts people, like Malimin, found ways to attain social and political status and power by working closely with Spanish or Mexican soldiers and missionaries to track down fugitives.[3] Others actively challenged Franciscan control by supporting fugitives from the mission, working with unincorporated villages to thwart and challenge Spanish military incursion into their riparian homelands. And despite the elevation of some Yokuts men, Yokuts women continued to endure many missionaries' abusive and dehumanizing fixation on reproduction and sexuality, often leading to psychological torment, rape, and the transmission of venereal disease.

Indigenous peoples of Mission Santa Cruz built multiple communities formed around extended kinship networks and shaped by linguistic and tribal differences. In the decades that followed the Quintana assassination, local Awaswas speakers and Mutsun Ohlone speakers from the east side of the Mak-Sah-Re-Jah mountain range became increasingly outnumbered by large groups of Yokuts-speaking tribes from the eastern San Joaquin Valley. Ethnic, linguistic, and cultural differences played a role in shaping political and social hierarchies within the mission. The building of new alliances and the extension of kinship networks proved necessary in the face of continued death and loss, in some cases challenging preexisting rivalries.

Malimin and his men, a group that included his own sons, exemplify the emergence of new political leadership within the mission community and the rise in power for some newly arrived Yokuts. The 1810s and 1820s were a time when Spanish colonial settlements operated within the larger context of a movement toward Mexican independence, when conversations about Indigenous rights and citizenship shaped a larger dynamic of violence and warfare.[4] Indigenous Northern Valley Yokuts people made the choice between resisting Spanish colonization in the hopes of remaining in their ancestral lands and relocation to the missions to build new lives.[5] Disease and epidemics took their toll on Indigenous peoples: villagers suffered frequent malaria outbreaks, while those who relocated to the mission experienced high rates of syphilis.[6] The increased militaristic engagement with Northern Valley Yokuts people took place at the same time as the Spanish colonial society grappled with a larger political transition into a Mexican nation.[7]

The 1810s and 1820s were also a time of increasing violence and warfare between Spanish colonizers and Indigenous peoples. During these decades warfare between Spanish and Mexican military expeditions and Indigenous horse raiders was commonplace throughout the greater San Francisco Bay Area. This violence and disruption connected to a larger pattern of increasing livestock raiding and military expeditions throughout the Southwest.[8] Fugitives from local missions worked together with unbaptized inland Yokuts individuals, families, and villages in raids and even outright warfare and rebellion against Spanish colonizers. Indigenous leaders such as Estanislao, Pomponio, and Yozcolo exemplified this in their resistance movements.[9] In many cases, such as with these three men, Indigenous leaders spent time at the missions and drew upon their knowledge and experiences with Spanish and Mexican society to inform their strategies against them. Their Indigenous armies brought together fugitives from the missions, including individuals from Mission Santa Cruz, and villagers who had thus far resisted relocation.

Indigenous community members used different strategies to survive and make the most out of their circumstances. For Yokuts individuals and families, such as Malimin, relocation to the missions involved complicated choices and compromises. Some chose to work closely in collaboration with the padres. The decision to work closely with the missionaries came with certain benefits and prestige within the mission hierarchy. Referred to by the Spanish and Mexican soldiers as Indian *auxiliaries* (assistants), these collaborating Indigenous people aligned with the Franciscans and Mexican military to help track down fugitives and defend the mission against hostile parties.[10] Malimin and his men drew on familiarity with their Yokuts homelands to help locate these escapees, visiting formerly neighboring villages to root out harbored fugitives. These auxiliaries offered their services to the padres in exchange for political and social prestige within the mission, exacerbating tensions in the mission community.

Chief Coleto Malimin and the Yokuts

Following Quintana's assassination in late 1812, the population surrounding Mission Santa Cruz grew, as the Villa de Branciforte slowly expanded while an increasing number of U.S. and European foreigners moved into the area and began to build their own settlements in the mountains. Some of the residents of the Villa de Branciforte were themselves Indigenous Californians, as seen with the family of Clementina Montero, daughter of the famous Mission San Gabriel rebellion leader, Toypurina.[11] Some of the foreign-born immigrants, such as Tennessee Native Joseph Ladd Majors and the Russian Creole Jose Bolcoff, naturalized as Mexican citizens and entered the local society by marrying local Spanish women.[12] Others maintained distance from the Mexican town and formed a community up in the mountain region known today as Zayante, the region named after the Sayanta people of the same area.[13] Tensions grew between the *pobladores* (colonists) of Branciforte and the growing foreign mountain settlement, which maintained its independence from local Spanish and Mexican authorities. It would not be until around 1834 that the local Indigenous population at Mission Santa Cruz ceased to be the majority in the region (see table 20).[14] But this simplistic demographic binary (Indian versus colonizer) overlooks the reality that Mission Santa Cruz was home to a complex diversity of peoples.

By the mid-1810s Yokuts outnumbered Ohlone people at Mission Santa Cruz. The Ohlone population consisted of local Awaswas and Mutsun speakers.[15] The Indigenous community at Mission Santa Cruz was in constant flux, as soldiers regularly captured new converts from Yokuts territories to fill the vacancies created by a combination of ongoing flights of fugitives and high mortality rates.

There is considerable debate about the methods and tactics used by soldiers and missionaries to bring Indigenous villagers into the missions.[16] In the early years of Spanish colonization, the majority of soldiers and missionaries, well aware of being vastly outnumbered by the large numbers of well-armed Indigenous villagers, actively sought to avoid forced relocation and confrontation. Instead, in those early years, "recruitment" consisted of a complicated mix of factors resulting in what anthropologist Milliken referred to as "a time of little choice" but to enter the missions.[17] This dynamic changed beginning in the 1810s, as increasingly aggressive militaristic forays into Yokuts territories attempted to retrieve fugitives and often involved the capture of unbaptized villagers.

Oral histories attest to tactics, including the kidnapping of women and children. Consider this story related by Maria Ascención Solórsano:

> I used to hear many stories of how they used to bring in the Tulareños to the Mission, after all the Indians that lived around here in the hills had already been captured, but there was only one woman who used to tell me what she herself had seen, for they captured her in the Tular and brought her to the Mission. I knew that old woman at Gilroy. She was named Maria Castro, she had been captured and the

Castros kept her. She always used to cry when she recalled what she had experienced.

When the soldiers from the Mission came over there in the Tular where she had been raised, there was a fight there at the sweathouse. This woman and her son eighteen years old, and her daughter, ran to the lake and put the babies, one belonging to the woman and the other to the daughter of the woman, in a big basket, and began to swim for the other side of the lake. The soldiers shot her son in the back of the head when he was swimming along in the water and right there he sank. Then Maria said to her daughter: "It is better that we give ourselves up, they have already killed your brother." And then Maria turned the basket upside down, and the breath of the little babies was bubbling in the water as they were drowning. And they kept on swimming ahead, and the soldiers went around to the other side of the lake on horseback, and the women hid themselves in the edge of the tules, but the soldiers hunted for them and found them. They did not have any clothes on. Some of the soldiers were tamed Indians and one of them gave his shirt to Maria and to the other woman they gave a handkerchief. Those Indians were very wild too, they wanted to kill the tame and civilized Indians. The interpreter had said: "It is better that you give yourselves up," but they were not willing to.

It was a very sad thing when they were capturing the Indians. They brought Maria and her daughter in along with other Indians. There were two or three babies in each saddle bag, the saddles used to have a bag at each side, and they made the mothers go along behind their babies, with their thumbs tied together, well tied together with hemp string that they sewed and made at the Mission. And they were tied at their arms and bodies with lariats and whenever a stop was made their babies were taken and given to their mothers so that would give them to suck. Some of the babies died in the saddlebag.[18]

Stories like this attest to the brutality of tactics remembered by mission survivors. While it is certainly possible that some Yokuts chose to relocate and receive baptism for a variety of reasons, many ended up at the missions through capture, kidnapping, and warfare. In total, from 1813 until the last year that the mission actively sought out new villagers for baptism, in 1834, 378 Indigenous people received baptism at Mission Santa Cruz. The overall Indigenous population at Mission Santa Cruz reached its peak in 1821 with 519 members, the only time in these years that the population reached more than 500.[19]

The appearance of relative demographic stability belied the high mortality rates and ongoing flights of fugitives (see table 21). For example, a letter in 1819 listed 104 fugitives, out of a total population of 381.[20] This meant that the actual Indigenous population in 1819 was 277, as over a quarter of the stated population remained fugitive, outside of the actual mission control. This issue of overreporting the mission population was similar to what Padre Fernández had done in 1798, suggesting that this was a pattern and that these reports frequently failed to report the actual population.[21]

The nearly four hundred tribal people who arrived at Mission Santa Cruz between 1813 and 1834 came from riparian lands one hundred miles eastward, from Yokuts village sites along the Chowchilla, Fresno, Mariposa, and San Joaquin Rivers. According to interviews conducted in the 1930s by ethnographer Frank F. Latta, the majority of Yokuts people taken to Mission Santa Cruz likely belonged to a couple of groups that lived on the western side of the San Joaquin River—the Honoumne, from the region around modern Gustine and just north of Los Banos; and the Kawachumne (People of the Grass Nut Place), whose lands encompassed Firebaugh and Mendota.[22] Referred to collectively as *tulareños*, or people of the tule, by the Spanish, a diversity of Northern Valley Yokuts tribal nations lived in this swampy riparian region, known today as the cities of Merced, Los Banos, Madera, Mendota, and Fresno.

Information regarding the names of villages and tribal groups of Yokuts from this region is sparse and difficult to ascertain. Much of what we know from baptismal registries and a few letters from Spanish expeditions in the region in the early 1800s appears to refer mostly to village names, while the tribal names mentioned earlier were provided to Latta much later. With regards to Yokuts who ended up at Mission Santa Cruz, there were two major waves between 1817 and 1821. The first included families and individuals from a variety of village sites in both Kawachumne and Honoumne territory. These included the sites of Nupchenches, Mallim,

Notualls, Luchamme, Osocalis, Cutucho, Copcha, Tape, Chanech, Sagim, Atsnil, and Tejey, among others.[23] The second wave of Yokuts people, those who arrived between 1820 and 1821, came predominantly from the Huocom and Hupnis tribes.[24] They also included sizable numbers of Quithrathre, Sipieyesi, and Hualquemne (see table 22).

The argument denying forced conversion stands in contrast with oral histories and remembrances from Indigenous families. For example, Amah Mutsun tribal chair Valentin Lopez, a descendant of Mission Santa Cruz families of Ohlone and Yokuts lineage, has frequently spoken about stories of violence and disruption passed down in his family:

> As a young boy, I listened to stories from my elders about the cruelty of the missions. There were tales of how native women were captured—with their thumbs tied together with leather straps to form human chains—and marched forcibly from their tribal lands to the missions. If the Indians did not cooperate, the soldiers, at times, killed them. In one incident, more than two hundred women and children of the Orestimba tribe (living near what is now the town of Newman) were being taken to Mission San Juan Bautista. When, after passing the summit at the Orestimba Narrows, these women refused to go any farther, the Spanish commander ordered the women and children killed with sabers and their remains scattered.[25]

Some historians and anthropologists question the veracity of oral histories like these, especially when they are not backed up by corroborating historical documents. Some have suggested that there is no evidence of tying women and children by their thumbs, proposing that perhaps this story could instead result from a misinterpretation of adobe handprints at the missions, where some thumbprints might not be visible.[26] Small details such as the tying of thumbs tend to be kept out of official accounts, making it difficult to prove. And yet, in this case, there are examples in the archives. One such example was offered in the story by Solórsano presented earlier in this chapter. A second example is found in another of her stories that she shared with John P. Harrington:

> The women were brought from the Tular tied together by their thumbs, one walking behind the other, or else by the side of the other. Just stand in front of somebody and tie your thumbs together and try to walk and you will see how it can be done.
>
> They did not bring them riding double behind them because they did not have enough horses.
>
> They were very bad to the women and it made no difference to them if the bushes slapped the women when they could not raise their hands up. They dragged them and pulled them around any old way.[27]

The vivid recollection of the impact of being tied in this manner and marched demonstrates the clarity of the memory and the trauma that induced it. In addition to the Indigenous oral histories, Spanish sources corroborate the tactic, as in the story told by soldier José María Amador, who described using a similar method of tying thumbs together when marching the Quintana assassination conspirators to the Presidio of San Francisco.[28] Furthermore, it is possible that this same thumb-tying practice was observed and incorporated by later immigrants, as one gruesome story from 1850 relates that the notoriously sadistic Andrew Kelsey and Charles Stone tortured enslaved Pomo workers by hanging them by their thumbs.[29]

With regards to Lopez's Orestimba story, confirmation is offered in stories told by the grandson of a Spanish soldier who claimed to have been involved in the massacre.[30] Latta recorded the story of José Antonio Águila, whose grandfather was a soldier in the early 1800s. This story took place at Orestimba (We Meet Here Again), a place, according to Latta's informants, that was named by Yokuts for the tragic encounter that took place there. The tragedy took place not far from the Orestimba Narrows that Lopez discussed. Note how the soldiers received instruction to remain silent about the massacre. It is not surprising that events such as these remain outside official documentation. Águila believed that these events to have taken place in 1809:

> My grandfather, Antonio Águila, was with the Spanish Cavalry when they made the agreement with the Indians to meet the next year and

he was with them when they came back. The Indians again refused to go to the mission. The Cavalry tried to take them and got into a hot fight and killed or ran away all the older people. They took the younger ones to Mission Santa Clara.

You know, the Spanish treated the Indians just like they did the wild horses—shot the old ones and broke the young ones.

That was the bloodiest battle the Spanish Cavalry ever had with the San Joaquin Indians [Yokuts]. They didn't intend to kill so many, but the Indians wouldn't quit, or run away and hide and so that was the way it turned out.

When the thing was over the priests swore all of the soldiers to secrecy. I heard my father tell about it once. We were working cattle with two Indians, vaqueros who had been captured as boys in that fight. I knew them for many years afterward and heard them tell about it several times.

One noon, when we were eating our lunch under an oak tree they told us that the fight had taken place near by, on the Orestimba Creek just about a mile above the upper end of the Narrows, and on the south side of the creek. They said that about two hundred Indians were killed or scattered.

As we rode away from our noon camp my father told me that the Indians had told the truth, that all of the soldiers had been sworn to secrecy about the fight, but his father was ashamed of his part in it and thought that I should know the truth about it.[31]

Latta found only one other reference to the massacre at Orestimba. This was in a letter by Padre José Viader in October 1810, as he led an expedition from Mission Santa Clara to the junction of the Merced and San Joaquin Rivers. Viader explained, "We reached the spot where we had the fight with some natives" but only found one person there at this later expedition. In the same letter Viader described passing "a dry creek named Ores timac [where] there is also tall pine and the soil the same as the spot described where we had the fight." He continued, describing an encounter nearby, "The Indians, fearing our object was to capture them and take them to the mission, so they would not come out."[32] It is hardly a wonder that a year after this massacre neighboring villagers would keep distance from the expedition party.

The Orestimba massacre story offers one example of an attempt at abduction or kidnapping, but it is far from the only one. In another story shared by Latta, an older Yokuts man recalled hearing about violent tactics used in the capture and kidnapping of people to the missions. The old man, named Pahmit, described a story passed to him by a man named Sopahno from the region: "One morning early they all 'sleep. They hear big noise, lots shoot, lots yell. Indian run 'way in tule. Spanish shoot, kill lots Indian men, women. They kill Sopahno['s] father. His mother run away in tule. Spanish take 'bout twenty-thirty Indian boy', girl. Sopahno stay at Mission San Juan 'bout twenty year. Then priest tell Indian, 'You all go away from Mission. You all go back your home.'"[33] The multitude of traumatic stories of capture and violence told by contemporary Indigenous families attest to the unreported tactics used by Mexican soldiers in these times.

Within Mission Santa Cruz the arrival of the incoming Yokuts families coincided with a political shift, mirroring the larger demographic influx of these diverse tribal nations (see map 3). This shift is reflected in the tribal affiliation of the alcaldes beginning in the 1820s (see table 23). Asisara claimed that the "padres nominated an alcalde and assistant for each of the different bands, of which there were about thirty."[34] While there were not thirty alcaldes, it does appear that the tribal affiliations of the alcaldes represented the shifting demographics in a broader sense. Yet the political climate at the mission was complicated by a combination of preexisting tensions between tribal nations and kinship networks and new conflicts or alliances formed through the violence of colonial disruption. The mission population continued to engage with the larger region through ongoing networks of trade and fugitive flights.[35]

Colonial contact with villages in the Honoumne region traced back as far as October 1806.[36] During an exploratory expedition, local Indigenous villagers invited Lieutenant Gabriel Moraga and his party to visit two distinct villages: Nupchenches and Cutucho, noting that Nupchenches had about 250 villagers, while Cutucho had around 400.[37] The expedition found these villages along the San Joaquin River from its big bend near Mendota to approximately the mouth of the Merced, between modern cities Newman and Mendota alongside the San Joaquin River. From the description in Padre Pedro Muñoz's diary from the Moraga expedition, the Nupchenche village was situated at or near the mouth of Santa Rita Slough. In November 1815 Sergeant José Dolores Pico, ostensibly chasing fugitive baptized Natives who had fled from various Bay Area missions, attacked the Chanech village site, which he described as being four leagues north of Nupchenches. Pico and his party captured sixty-six people but reported that the majority had escaped. Pico scouted Nupchenches but found that the villagers had decamped, possibly after hearing about the violence from fleeing Chanech villagers.

Pico's party moved on to raid the Copcha rancheria, eight leagues southeast of Nupchenches (just north of the modern city of Firebaugh). Copcha was likely in Kawachumne territory. Before continuing out of the area on his raiding expedition, Pico reported the name of another village site, Mallim, which he placed as near Chanech.[38] All in all, records identified six independent village sites. From north to south they were Chanech, Mallim, and Nupchenches, all in Honoumne territory, and Cutucho, Tape, and Copcha, in Kawachumne (see map 4). Estimates suggest that the six villages numbered no fewer than eighteen hundred people in 1816.[39]

The sequence of arrival of Yokuts from these regions was closely tied to expeditions into these territories. At Mission Santa Cruz the first Chanech to arrive was a young boy, Gilsic (Carlos), in July 1805.[40] Then, in April 1810, a group of 42 Chanech, listed as being from the Yeurata rancheria, received baptism at Mission Santa Cruz.[41] These Chanech were accompanied by a larger group of 73 Tejey. Between 1813 and 1834 a total of 378 incoming Indigenous people received baptism at Mission Santa Cruz from a diversity of Yokuts tribal nations (see table 22).[42] The influx of Yokuts also corresponded to the ongoing flights of fugitives from the missions returning to their homelands or refusing to return from their seasonal trips home. In turn, the recapture of these fugitives became a central objective of the military expeditions.

Some of the early Yokuts arrivals were able to negotiate political power. Chief Malimin, baptized and known by the Spaniards as Coleto, received baptism on May 24, 1810. He was the first in a group of seventy-five members of the Tejey rancheria.[43] Tejey territory was at the intersection of the Merced and San Joaquin Rivers. Ketchum observed that the Merced

River is the first significant tributary to the San Joaquin River after its turn northward, which would likely make the Tejey homeland a place of significant cultural value in the region.[44] Perhaps Malimin and his people were among the more powerful in that area, centrally located among the other Yokuts villages and trade routes. His baptism was immediately followed, in order, by one of his wives, Yguichegel (Coleta); his oldest son, Moctó (Agustin); Moctó's wife, Cachimtan; and Malimin's younger son, Guajsilii.[45] This family became key figures in the mission population; Malimin and Moctó quickly became the most visible Indian auxiliaries at Mission Santa Cruz. Malimin and his family would continue to dominate local Indigenous politics well into the latter part of the nineteenth century.

As was pointed out by Amah Mutsun tribal historian Ed Ketchum, Coleto's Indigenous name, Malimin, bears a striking resemblance to the Mutsun word for "coyote"—written as *mayan* or *mallin*.[46] Ketchum further speculated that perhaps Malimin was clever and so the Mutsun people gave him this name. That certainly makes sense. In fact, in his initial baptismal entry his Native name is spelled *Malin*, which is even closer to the phonetic spelling of *coyote* in Mutsun; it is only in later documents that it is written *Malimin*. As noted previously, a Tejey village was also listed as Mallim or Mallin. This similarity could either suggest that the village had some connection with Coyote, as we have seen with Mutsun villages discussed earlier, or that the Mexican community referred to the village by the name of its prominent chief. Considering Malimin's rise to power within the mission, it would not be surprising if Mutsun informants advised the missionaries to enter the name Malin, which would mean that Indigenous people helped shape the baptismal registries and documents into Indigenous archives in which some names held deeper layers of meaning.

While Malimin and his sons were able to find avenues to power and influence within the mission, it is interesting to consider the potential difficulties in translating power, at least spiritual power, for people coming from farther away. For many Indigenous peoples power came from familiarity with lands and environs.[47] Solórsano provided an interesting note to Harrington regarding the way power was constituted within the Mission San Juan Bautista community, as Harrington has an entry reading: "How the Medicine Men of the Coast Were More Powerful than Those of the Valley: The Indians of the [San Joaquin] Valley were very good medicine men but they could not bewitch the Indians of the coast. Their witchcraft did not avail over in this direction."[48] It is interesting to consider the ways in which relative foreigners would have struggled to maintain their powers after relocation. Perhaps Yokuts leaders replaced spiritual power and standing with social and political power.

In May 1816 tensions between the Chanech and Mallim villagers erupted, exacerbated by tensions between fugitives, auxiliaries, and villagers. The Mallim appear to have formed positive relations with the missionaries, as many members had already received baptism at Mission Santa Cruz. It is possible that this favorable relationship was connected specifically to Malimin, as the Mallim and Tejey villagers appear to have been closely tied through kinship. Sometime in May, Chanech villagers attacked and killed two baptized Mallim villagers who were fugitive from Mission Santa Cruz. Spanish sources reported that the Chanech had been telling the soldiers bad things about the Mallim villagers, possibly in an attempt to discredit Malimin and his family. The conflict suggests that tensions had long existed between the groups, which could trace back to before Spanish arrival. Alternatively, these tensions could have been exacerbated by the impact of violence and colonialism. In either case the Chanech allied with the villagers at the nearby rancherias of Luchamme and Notualls against the Mallim. The chief of the Notualls village, Cutsayo, was known for his antipathy toward the soldiers.[49]

While some Indigenous leaders, such as Malimin, chose to ally themselves with the Franciscans and thereby secured some political power, others aided the growing numbers of fugitives and livestock raiders. One particular conflict revolved around two main leaders whom the soldiers blamed for recent livestock raids: Ayaclo (Egidio) and El Chivero. Ayaclo was a Locobo man who had been baptized at Mission Santa Cruz as a child, in 1808.[50] In May 1816 Ayaclo had recently been captured and was being held at the presidio in San Francisco for the theft of a horse herd. Ayaclo confessed to working closely with his accomplice, El Chivero. El Chivero appears to have had a long, complicated history of interaction, both friendly and hostile, with soldiers. He went by various names, including his baptismal name, Francisco Xavier. El Chivero was valued not only for his knowledge of the physical landscape but also for his linguistic proficiency, as the padres frequently remarked upon his fluency in Spanish.[51]

Ultimately, Padre Marquínez requested that an expedition set out for the region and called for the wholesale capture of Mallim villagers, not just the fugitives. To justify this move, Marquínez argued that fugitives would continue to run to Mallim "as long as there's a single old woman remaining on their lands."[52]

By early June two of the three Indigenous auxiliaries returned after a trip to the Mallim rancheria. The padres had sent them in the hopes of persuading some of the fugitives to come back to Mission Santa Cruz. They had been sent with offers of pardons and promises for the fugitives, telling them that they would not be punished if they opted to return. The two auxiliaries who returned reported that the majority of fugitives from Mission Santa Cruz had rejected the pardons and chosen to stay at Mallim, that the fugitives were afraid to return to the mission and instead prepared for further flight. The third auxiliary, who did not return, was El Chivero, who had been apprehended by soldiers on the orders of Friar Marquínez for his involvement in the livestock raids with Ayaclo. After the return of the two auxiliaries, the padres and soldiers agreed that the time was right to lead an expedition to retrieve the fugitives. Lieutenant Luis Antonio Argüello requested that El Chivero serve as the guide, acknowledging that he knew the territory the best.[53] Padre Escude agreed, suggesting that El Chivero be given a pardon for his past crimes in exchange for his help.[54]

Ultimately, it was not the soldiers who recovered the fugitives but the Indian auxiliaries, specifically Chief Coleto Malimin. It took until December, but Malimin and his men cleared out the Mallim rancheria, killing four *gentiles* in the process. The padre exclaimed his delight at the return of forty-two fugitives.[55] At the Mallim rancheria they found a mix of Chanech, Luchamme, and Mallim fugitives. They left no one at the village, bringing everyone back to Mission Santa Cruz. They took with them the elderly, the crippled and blind, as well as their dogs. The only exceptions were three people apparently dying of disease, who were brought to the Chanech rancheria. Yet this capture of fugitives did not put an end to these flights, as a letter reports that while the Mallim rancheria had been emptied, other fugitives had taken refuge with their allies at the Notualls rancheria.[56]

Apparently, Ayaclo had escaped from the presidio and made his way to Mallim. Malimin claimed that Ayaclo had been at the Mallim village a few days before Malimin's arrival, planning more horse raids.⁵⁷ The letter did not elaborate on the extent of Ayaclo's raids, and they were never mentioned again. He must have returned to Mission Santa Cruz within a few years, as he married an Indigenous woman, Chiemiit (Egidia), there in early 1818.⁵⁸ The couple had a child, whom they named German, in May 1822, but German died within a few days. After Chiemiit's death, in 1829, Ayaclo remarried two more times: to Sayanit (Septima) in early 1830 and to Maria Concepcion in 1834. Ayaclo appears to have remained at the mission for many years, but he may have left the community in the early 1840s.⁵⁹

The dire situation facing inland Yokuts villages and villagers contributed to the difficult choices made by auxiliaries and fugitives alike. The loss of villagers through movement into the missions was further compounded by an epidemic of malaria that devastated remaining villagers throughout the San Joaquin Valley in 1833.⁶⁰ Malimin's homeland, populated by at least seven villages in the early part of the 1800s, was desolate with abandoned village sites, described by one traveler as "graveyards" in 1833.⁶¹ How could Malimin, Ayaclo, or others have interpreted this epidemic? At a time when many villagers were considering relocation—either to follow family and kin, enticed by offers of new political powers or social standing, or threatened by the military force of invading soldiers—the outbreak of new epidemics must have further undermined faith in traditional ways and lifestyles. Traditional medicines and prayers could not account and provide cures for these new diseases, which must have undermined faith in traditional spiritual and medicinal leaders.

Coleto Malimin was from the village of Tejey, and he is variously listed as being Tejey or Mallim.⁶² In all, Malimin had five sons enter Mission Santa Cruz, each of whom played a significant role, either as alcalde or as Indian auxiliary. Seven years after his arrival, Malimin brought back additional family members from the Mallim village. Perhaps he was emboldened by his success in navigating mission politics and knew that his family could also thrive. The 1817 Yokuts influx included three of Malimin's five sons (the other two had arrived with him in 1810), Malimin's second wife, and the wives of his three adult sons.⁶³ In February 1817, a few months after the arrival of this large group, the padres baptized thirty-four adults from a mix of families from the Achila, Atsnil, Chanech, Janalame, Mallim, and

Notualls villages.[64] Many of them were family members of Mallim or Tejey people who had arrived with Malimin's group back in 1810. Did Malimin's political ascent help convince them to enter the mission? Perhaps the fact that a majority of Mallim members had evacuated the village site finally convinced those who had held out over the previous six years that it was time to join their kin.

Within a short time Malimin and his people were working closely with the missionaries, acting as protectors of the mission in addition to capturing fugitives. In early May 1817 the arrival of unfamiliar ships in the Monterey Bay harbor prompted Padre Escude to arm Chief Coleto Malimin and twenty-five of his men in case the mission required protection.[65] The concern over foreign ships was linked to concerns about stability within the larger Spanish empire. Movements toward independence had been taking place in the Spanish Americas since the *grito de Dolores* (cry of Dolores) in Guanajuato, Mexico, in 1810.[66] Indeed, the sailor Bouchard, known to the Spanish as a pirate, had been attacking Spanish colonial settlements along the Pacific coast as far back as 1815.[67] In early October 1818 Bouchard and his people took over Monterey for six days, during which time they burned down the fort, the artillery quarters, and homes, including the governor's house. After ransacking Monterey and destroying the canons, Bouchard and his men repaired their ships and headed south. They burned a rancho just north of Santa Barbara and parts of Mission San Juan Capistrano. The Santa Cruz missionaries feared that Mission Santa Cruz might be the next target.

The threat of Bouchard's arrival led to the evacuation of all Indigenous people from Mission Santa Cruz, a flight from which many never returned. During the evacuation members of the neighboring Villa de Branciforte, whom Padre Ramon Olbés had ordered to protect the mission, instead looted, raided, and vandalized some of the iconography.[68] The scandal prompted an investigation and a steady tide of complaints from Padre Olbés.[69] While most accounts of the incident have focused on the tensions between the Villa de Branciforte residents and the missionaries, it does appear that Olbés suspected that some of the Natives sent back to check on the mission might have conspired with the Villa de Branciforte residents.[70] While the large group made their way to Mission Santa Clara, a group of five Indigenous men were sent back to the mission to check in on it, finding it vandalized.[71] Furthermore, many of the Indigenous people evacuated did not return to Mission Santa Cruz, instead likely returning to their homelands in Yokuts territories.[72] In the months that followed the incident, the missionaries complained about the slow return of many of these fugitives.[73] In 1819 Mission Santa Cruz padres listed 104 fugitives who had still not returned. Unsurprisingly, the majority of those listed were Chanech and Tejey, supporting the theory of a large-scale return to homelands.[74]

Women and Labor—Impositions of Patriarchy

Following Mexican independence, labor relations continued to reflect social inequalities similar to those found during the mission period. Social and labor hierarchies left Indigenous laborers in positions of servitude, even as Indigenous families expanded geographically from the immediacy of the mission. Yet the census documents finally acknowledged Indigenous laborers, listing their jobs for the first time in the 1820s. Unfortunately, these lists show that labor options for women diminished from the 1820s into the 1830s, or at least they reflect that census-taking officials failed to acknowledge women's labor except in special cases (see tables 24 and 25). In earlier chapters I have discussed the artisanal training received by some young members of the mission. Indigenous workers filled most labor roles to sustain life within Mexican society while continuing to perform some jobs more relevant to traditional practices. For example, both the 1825 letter and the 1834 census included a variety of highly skilled jobs such as masons, carpenters, bakers, smiths, shoemakers, and tanners (see table 25).[75]

The 1825 letter shows an interesting division of labor, as women appear to have worked alongside men in jobs like farming, gardening, general labor (almost certainly domestic labor), herding sheep, tending chickens, and even deer hunting (see table 24). There was even one woman who worked as a *vaquero* (cowboy).[76] Raising sheep and weaving became the main focus of production for Indigenous laborers, with large flocks of sheep held on mission-owned pasturelands stretching up San Gregorio, north of Año Nuevo.[77] Grinding corn was reserved for women only. Given the regional practice of acorn grinding, it is possible that this job entailed grinding a mix of different seeds and grasses, the tending of which had traditionally been in the realm of women's work. The job of weaver, which required working the loom to provide clothing, was divided almost evenly between men and women.[78]

The 1834 census offers a glimpse into Indigenous labor (see table 25).[79] The prevalence of skilled workers—shoemakers, hatmakers, and weavers—reveals that clothing was made by the Indigenous community.[80] Skilled Native artisans such as masons, smiths, and carpenters, many of whom had been trained around 1800, played a prominent role in many local construction projects. The corn doctor tended his crops, while many worked as day laborers, field hands, farmers, and gardeners. The horsebreaker, muleteer, and shepherd worked with the livestock. Eleven people are listed as overseers, a large number considering the relatively few workers in need of supervision. Of these all but two were Yokuts (see table 26). The overseer-worker ratio suggests that the role of the overseer went beyond work supervision and entered a realm of social and corporal control.

Some of the jobs listed in the 1834 census reveal interesting aspects of Indigenous life at the mission (see table 25). One Yokuts (Tejey) man named Atauque (Paterno) is listed as an arrow maker, which shows that the need to produce new arrowheads was substantial enough for him to be officially employed.[81] He was thirty-four years old upon arrival at the mission in 1810 with the large Tejey group led by Malimin. Did he make arrowheads before coming into the mission and continue to do so some twenty-five years later, or is this something he learned after arrival? Did he produce arrowheads for Malimin and the other Yokuts, or were these arrowheads used for hunting and available to everyone at the mission?

By the 1834 census the majority of these jobs were reserved for men (although there is a record of one female weaver, Yuñan, who had been married to Yachacxi and involved in the Quintana assassination). This change represented a shift in gendered labor divisions from the report in the mid-1820s or, more likely, the underreporting and invisibility of women laborers in the 1834 document. Most workers were listed as "day laborers," apparently doing assorted labor. Some of these jobs do appear to have signified status or special standing, including the overseers, who were most frequently Yokuts (see table 25).

The 1834 census is also the first to show surnames for many of the Indigenous population. Previous census rolls list Native people by one name.[82] Interestingly, these surnames include references to prominent Mexican officials, especially those who dealt with policies that had direct impact on Native people. These names included Echandía, Farias, and Gomes.[83] Other surnames include those of prominent Bay Area Californio community members such as Brabo, Fernandes, Gutierres, Higuera, Lopes, Olivares, and Ramires, among others. It is unclear whether these names were ascribed by the Mexican census takers or chosen.[84]

Along with the political and social powers negotiated by Malimin and the incoming Yokuts came additional responsibilities. These included military-style oversight of the mission population, which often involved violence and the corporal imposition of order on Indigenous bodies. The missionaries imposed hierarchies by designating social categories of power within the population. And while the missionaries helped to empower and impose this system, Indigenous politics played a part, as Malimin and his people negotiated most of these positions. Asisara gave an account of the social dynamics: "The Indians at the mission were very severely treated by the padres, often punished by fifty lashes on the bare back. They were governed somewhat in the military style, having sergeants, corporals, and overseers, who were Indians, and they reported to the padres any disobedience or infraction of the rules, and then came the lash without mercy, the women the same as the men. The lash was made of rawhide. I was never punished, except for a few slaps for forgetfulness. I was always busy in the padres' house, doing the work of a house servant."[85] The overseers at Mission Santa Cruz did include a mix of tribal and linguistic backgrounds, but beginning by the 1820s, the majority were Yokuts (see table 26). The description by Asisara suggests that along with this political and social prestige came the power over the physical well-being of others, reinforcing social isolation and distance between the Yokuts and the rest of the Native population.

By the mid-1820s Malimin's sons occupied many of these leadership positions. One of his sons, Punis, served as overseer, and Moctó worked as an alcalde (see tables 26 and 23).[86] Agustin Moctó, who was Malimin's oldest son, became a central figure in this social hierarchy, appearing throughout the mission records as informant and confidant. Moctó frequently helped the padres update their records on the fates of those living outside mission lands, appearing as informant in the burial records throughout the 1820s.[87] Around 1825 he also served as alcalde, fulfilling multiple leadership roles. He continued to make rounds outside the mission and report back on the deaths of missing individuals, frequently helped by a group of five other Yokuts.[88] Another of Malimin's sons, Guajsilii, would serve as one of the two elected regidores at Mission Santa Cruz in 1831.[89]

And yet, despite the political and social gains of Malimin and his sons, evidence suggests that there were severe limitations to their elevated status. The Franciscan missionaries continued to exercise control over all the baptized Indigenous people at the mission, even those they depended on for protection and reliable service. The ongoing flights of fugitives, which consistently included large numbers of Yokuts, suggest that despite attaining certain powers, many did not find life at Mission Santa Cruz to their liking. Even those individuals and families who worked closely with the missionaries were not immune to punishment and castigation at the hands of the padres.

While some Yokuts men were able to negotiate relative power within the mission, avenues to power were clearly not open to women. In fact, women often suffered, while their male counterparts experienced elevated status. This imbalance is extremely clear around issues of childbirth, fertility, and procreation. In many ways the missionaries treated Indigenous couples like livestock, in a way that mirrored animal husbandry practices. An account from Asisara shows how some padres at Mission Santa Cruz fixated on fertility and reproduction to the point of inflicting psychological torture on couples who were struggling with infertility. This story illustrates the types of physical, sexual, and psychological cruelty used by some padres, who utilized shame and public humiliation to exert control over the intimate lives of Indigenous people.

The story involves Padre Ramon Olbés, who worked at Mission Santa Cruz between 1818 and 1821. A Yokuts couple who had recently arrived at the mission were unable to bear children. After inquiring about why they were unable to give birth, Padre Olbés interrogated the couple about their sexual activities. Asisara related the incident:

> [Olbés] put them in a room in order to "level" them out, in other words, to have them perform coitus in his presence. The Indian

[male] refused but he was forced to show his member in order to make certain that it was functioning properly. Then, the padre took the woman and put her in a room; the husband was sent to the guards with a pair of shackles . . . she was asked again, why she did not give birth like other women. Padre Olbés asked her whether her husband slept with her and she answered yes. The Padre reiterated his question: "why can't you give birth?" "I do not know," answered the Indian woman. She was made to go to another room in order to check her private parts. She resisted and grabbed the Padre's cord. There was a vigorous, long struggle between the two, who were alone in the room. She tried to sink her teeth into his arm but only managed to bite his habit. Padre Olbés yelled out and the interpreter and the *alcalde* came to his aid. Then, Padre Olbés ordered that she be taken, by the arms, outside and that she be given fifty lashes. After being punished, he ordered that she be shackled and locked up in the nunnery. After this was done, Padre Olbés ordered that a wooden doll be made in the shape of a newly born baby, and took it to the flogged woman, and ordered her to take the doll as her child, and that she should carry it for nine days in the presence of the people. He forced her to present herself at the door of the Church with the doll as if it were her son until she completed the nine days.

As a result of these occurrences, the sterile women became highly alarmed.

The wicked Padre had cattle horns placed on the head of the woman's husband, and they were secured with a leather cord. At the same time, he had him shackled. In this condition, they would bring him daily to Mass from jail. The other Indians would mock him and bullfight him.[90]

This kind of psychological punishment or torment aimed at men and women unable to conceive children does not appear to be an isolated incident. Padres at Mission San Gabriel imposed a similar punishment of carrying wooden dolls for women suspected of infanticide.[91] In addition, Solórsano related this story to Harrington about a woman from Mission San Juan Bautista: "A woman who wanted to have children and never was able to was made by the Fathers to carry a calf across her shoulders. A number of men took her out through the door of the church and they carried her through the streets of the town, all shouting with one voice: 'This woman gave birth last night, she gave birth to a calf.' And the woman went along crying wherever they took her, begging God that she might give birth."[92]

Sometimes the Indigenous alcaldes refused to assist the padres in punishing others. In one of Lorenzo Asisara's stories he tells of the Cotoni man Samecxi (Dámaso), who returned late to his dormitory after having gone missing from his chores earlier in the day.[93] Padre Olbés confronted Samecxi upon his return, accusing him of gambling at the Villa de Branciforte. Olbés threatened, "I am now going to punish you, not on your ass but on your belly." Samecxi resisted. "No, Father, there is no reason for you to punish me in the belly. I went to find some wood for the people who take care of me; I have not committed any other offense."[94] Padre Olbés ordered the alcaldes to help grab and punish Samecxi, but they resisted, siding with Samecxi and "claiming he had done no wrong." Meanwhile, the others, locked in the dormitories, cheered Samecxi on. Some proceeded to pick up roof tiles and throw them at the padre, who took off running. It does appear that Olbés had his way; Samecxi eventually did receive punishment for some offense, as his burial record lists him as having died at the San Francisco Presidio.[95] As Asisara's story did not provide exact dates of the event, it is unclear how long Samecxi was at the presidio before his death. It is also curious that Asisara describes Samecxi's exploits in great detail but does not mention his fate in the presidio—Asisara was more interested in sharing stories of Samecxi's resistance than the punishment he received for it. Nevertheless, his fate reinforces our understanding of the harsh conditions and frequently fatal effects of corporal punishment administered at the presidios.

The clearest example of the limitations of the political powers gained by Malimin and the Yokuts is found in the story of Guajsilii, one of Malimin's sons. Guajsilii's story suggests that despite belonging to this prestigious family, his life was not free from abuse at the hands of the missionaries. Ultimately, the padres sought to maintain a level of control over the lives of even those who worked closely with them. Guajsilii and his wife, Segejate, resisted life at the mission as early as 1819, appearing on the list of fugitives.[96] While the reason for their flight is not explicitly expressed, later documents suggest that Segejate may have experienced sexual abuse at the hands of one of the padres or soldiers: her burial record lists her cause of death as syphilis.[97] The couple must have returned shortly after their flight, as between 1820 and 1831 there are records of Segejate's having given birth to eight children. Each of them died before the age of two.[98] Congenital syphilis frequently leads to difficulties in childbirth, birth defects, and high infant mortality rates. The couple appears in the 1834 *padrón*, or census, and again in 1836, but Guajsilii is absent from the official records after his wife's death in 1841.

The oral histories of Asisara claim that Padre Luis Gil y Taboada passed syphilis to Indigenous women of Mission Santa Cruz in his time at the mission. Spanish records also show that he was known for "being free and familiar in his relations" to Native people, "too much so in the case of the women."[99] Syphilis became endemic within the missions, with many believing that it had initially been introduced by Spanish soldiers.[100] Asisara recalled that Gil y Taboada "was very amorous. He hugged and kissed the Indian women, and he had contact with them until he had syphilis and skin eruptions broke out. Finding himself in this situation, he would celebrate mass sitting in his house. Many times he was unable to celebrate mass standing up because he was ulcerated."[101] Did Padre Gil y Taboada rape Segejate? It certainly seems possible.

Segejate's story, and the introduction of venereal disease, is far from an isolated incident. The potential sexual abuses of Padre Gil y Taboada illustrate the coloniality of sexual abuse, the exercise of power over Indigenous peoples that denied their basic human rights. Antonia, the daughter of a Chipuctac man named Seynte (Projecto), was likely the target of the padre's sexual predation. Seynte and his wife, Samórim, were important figures within the mission.[102] The couple had eight children together, but only two lived into adulthood.[103] Their daughter Antonia lived to about twenty-one years of age, but her death records suggest that she may have been targeted by the abusive padre. Her burial record includes a suspicious note by Padre Luis Gil y Taboada, suggesting that she was the object of particular importance for the padre. The burial record has a long entry praising her, including Gil y Taboada's observations that she was "exactly fulfilling the duties of a virgin and married woman: extremely modest, silent, and ready to perform the work to which she was destined."[104] While this note could appear to be righteous praise, it is more complicated when one considers the nefarious reputation of the padre. Consider a story related by Solórsano:

> I heard tell that they used to wall up people, they made a hole in the adobe wall only big enough to accommodate the body of the person and they put the person in there and left him there to die and dry up. This is what the priests did in Mexico and San Juan Mission, and especially to women. The priests always picked out a pretty girl, and if she did not let herself be used by the priests, they would wall her up, or else they would do away with her in some other way.[105]

As with the stories of violent coercion discussed earlier, some historians have questioned the veracity of stories like these, pointing out that if there were really bodies placed into the actual adobes at the missions, they would have been identified or otherwise become known. But the persistence of stories in the oral histories handed down by families, such as this one from Solórsano, points to the inherited trauma of sexual abuse at the hands of the missionaries. Whether this particular story was based on an actual account of a woman being abused in this manner or not, the horror, trauma, and fear conveyed in the story came from actual lived and witnessed abuses, and stories like these served to forewarn and alert children to the abusive tendencies of the missionaries.

New Kinship Connections and Prominent Women

The culturally and linguistically distinct Yokuts and the previously arrived Ohlone peoples eventually formed two separate communities within the mission, but a third group emerged out of the large numbers of marriages between Yokuts and Ohlone. This group was made up primarily of incoming Yokuts women and Ohlone men, both Mutsun and Awaswas speakers. In order to understand the marriage patterns and new kinship ties formed within these diversifying mission communities, it is important to see the gendered makeup of the shifting demographics.

The majority of incoming Yokuts were women. Of the 507 Yokuts to arrive between 1813 and 1834, 287 were women and 220 were men (chart 3). The large number of incoming women coincided with the condition of men outliving women at Mission Santa Cruz. Because few burial records include cause of death, it is impossible to say why women died in larger numbers. The passage of venereal disease and complications in childbirth certainly could have been factors. Furthermore, the ratio of burials of men to women mirrored almost exactly the ratio of incoming Yokuts men to women (chart 4). Was this pattern a matter of coincidence, or could it be that auxiliaries such as Agustin Moctó targeted women fugitives to bring wives back for the men? It is certainly possible, despite a lack of direct evidence. Unsurprisingly, marriage records reveal a pattern of incoming Yokuts women marrying Awaswas or Mutsun speakers in large numbers, although by far the majority of marriages between 1810 and 1834 were between Yokuts men and women (chart 5). The large number of marriages between Ohlone men, both Mutsun and Awaswas, and Yokuts women was more than just a by-product of demographic realities, as it reflected a pattern of marriage across tribal lines seen throughout Indigenous California.[106] While the imposition of Spanish and Franciscan patriarchal values meant that Indigenous men had access to relative power within the missions, as seen in the stories of Malimin and his sons, some women found avenues to express power and influence. Yaquenonsat, the driving force behind the Quintana assassination, continued to live at Mission Santa Cruz until her death at the end of 1831.[107] Though she does not appear in the archives after the assassination, it is worthwhile to wonder what influence she may have had outside the awareness of the missionaries. Similarly, Yuñan persevered within the mission community, last appearing in the records in the 1834 census.[108] Here the forty-five-year-old "Serafina Pinto" is listed along with her eight-year-old daughter, Rafaela Brabo, where she is noted as weaver—the only Indigenous woman listed with any occupation in this census. Yuñan does not have a burial record, so it is unclear if she left the area in the 1830s or if her death is simply unrecorded. Her daughter shows up in the 1845 census living with a Yokuts man, Jose Antonio, whom she would eventually marry, and with Hermenegildo, the godson of Yuñan.[109] Rafaela Maria and Jose Antonio had a son, the grandson of Yuñan, Jose Pedro, in 1848.[110] Jose Pedro and his family may have survived into the era

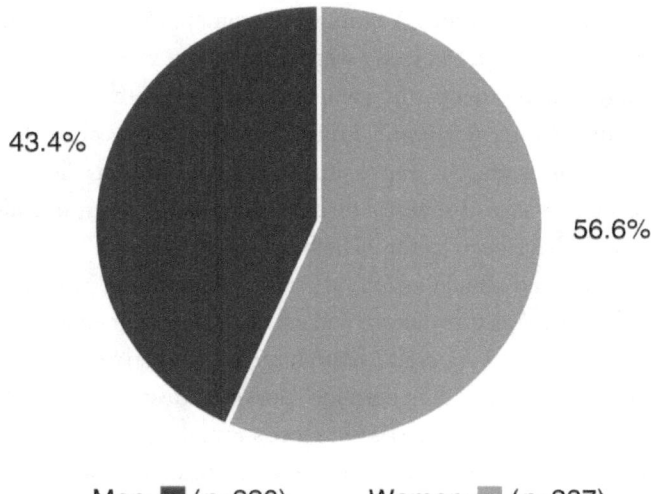

Men: ■ (*n*=220) Women: ■ (*n*=287)

Chart 3. Incoming Yokuts, by gender

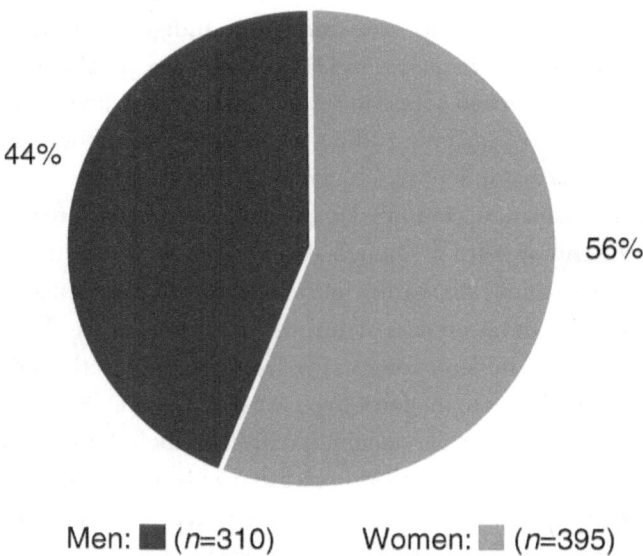

Men: ■ (*n*=310) Women: ■ (*n*=395)

Chart 4. Burials by gender at Mission Santa Cruz, 1813–34

		WOMEN			
		Awaswas	Mutsun	Yokuts	Totals
MEN	Awaswas	17	13	36	66
	Mutsun	3	25	39	67
	Yokuts	1	0	188	189
	Totals	21	38	263	322 Marriages

Chart 5. Marriage patterns between Awaswas, Mutsun, and Yokuts people at Mission Santa Cruz

of United States rule, and it is possible that their descendants are around today.[111]

Among the women for whom Yuñan served as *madrina*, one case stands out in its relation to the previously mentioned Padre Gil y Taboada, further shedding light on his abuses. Yuñan served as madrina for multiple children born to one particular couple, Taucha (Vicente Carlos) and Saeta (Vicenta), who had four children between 1821 and 1824.[112] None of the children survived longer than two months.[113] Saeta died in 1834, and her death record notes that she died of syphilis.[114] Padre Gil y Taboada served as the officiant for her baptism as well as for those of all four of her children.

The vast majority of cross-cultural marriages were between Yokuts women and Ohlone men. The single exception is significant in that it demonstrates the continued influence of the original Mission Santa Cruz families. The one marriage between an Awaswas-speaking Ohlone woman and a Yokuts man was that of the daughter of Lino and Humiliana, Petra Nicanor, and her husband, Chuyuco (Victoriano).[115] As a young man, the Tejey Chuyuco had arrived along with Malimin and his family back in 1810. Lino and Humiliana's daughter, Petra Nicanor, was born in early 1814, likely while Lino was imprisoned at the presidio in San Francisco for his involvement in the Quintana assassination. As the one exception to the larger pattern of intermarriage, it raises the question of why and how the couple married. Was this marriage a political one attempting to build kinship between the incoming Tejey community and the local leaders?

The Rise of the Yokuts

Patterns of intermarriage and kinship extension in other areas of California suggest that their marriage, along with other cross-tribal marriages, was indeed a strategy of alliance building and kinship.[116]

Independence amid Fugitivism, Violence, and Warfare

Following Mexican independence in 1821, the new liberal Mexican state enacted policies calling for a number of changes intended to broaden citizenship and alter colonial legacies relating to race and the power of the church.[117] This new government saw Spaniards as a security threat and set about dismantling certain colonial laws that had privileged them.[118] In an attempt to undermine the inequities produced by the racial system that privileged Spaniards, in 1821 the government officially abolished the colonial system of *castas*, and then in 1829 it abolished African slavery.[119] Despite these official policies, in Santa Cruz, as in other regions of Mexico, the social category of "Indian" continued to influence social hierarchies.[120] These concerns about Spaniards included the predominately Spanish-born Franciscan missionaries of Alta California, who held large tracts of land surrounding the missions. Secularization, the official transference of the missions from the clergy into governmental administration, became a focal point for Mexican officials.[121]

In 1821 missionaries ordered the building of new adobe homes in the plaza in front of Mission Santa Cruz.[122] It is likely that these homes were built as an enticement for families like that of Malimin and his sons, to help persuade them to stay at the mission.[123] Records show that members of the local Indigenous community began to demand liberation, so these new homes may well have been a concession to appease Indigenous demands and discontent.[124] These demands likely contributed to Padre Gil y Taboada's letter claiming he would be pleased if Mission Santa Cruz were closed altogether.[125] By 1824 Gil y Taboada reported that he had heard some of the baptized Natives "bemoaning the fact that they haven't been given their freedom."[126] The padre assumed that some of the colonists at the neighboring Villa de Branciforte must have "imbued the Indians with their liberal ideas." Gil y Taboada continued to report his opinion that "if they were free, the Province would be lost and even your wives and daughters would suffer for they would be treated abominably."[127] This is a telling revelation from the mind of the padre, considering his proclivity for Indigenous women. His report called out the sexual deviance of the Indigenous men of the mission, despite the reality that it was the padre himself who was victimizing Indigenous women. His fears about an emancipated Indigenous population more likely reflect sublimated guilt about his own sexual anxieties and improprieties.[128]

It is likely that the Indigenous people of Mission Santa Cruz had heard about the Chumash war for independence in 1824, which would only have reinforced their own desires for liberation, rather than being imbued with liberal ideas by the colonists at the Villa de Branciforte, as Gil y Taboada suggested.[129] A few months before the padre's letter, in Santa Barbara, Chumash leaders from Missions La Purisima, Santa Barbara, and Santa Inés organized a mass revolt. They organized two thousand Chumash and reached out to six Yokuts villages (two of which sent help). The Chumash war for independence was closely tied to Indigenous citizenship and the still unfulfilled promises of emancipation.[130] The war lasted four months, and more than one thousand Chumash went into exile in the inland territories of their Yokuts allies.[131] The Yokuts allies of the Chumash hailed from village sites farther south than the Yokuts at Mission Santa Cruz, but news of the well-organized rebellion would certainly have made its way to the local Indigenous community, as it clearly and understandably prompted considerable concern from the padres.

During this time of fugitive flights and escalating demands for liberation, Padre Gil y Taboada appears to have grown increasingly frustrated.[132] His anxieties about managing the mission appear to have overwhelmed him, as at one point he threatened to abandon Mission Santa Cruz and let the Indians flee if he did not receive more soldiers.[133] The padre's letters during the 1820s were more occupied with his ongoing health concerns (relating to outbreaks of syphilis), securing himself a return to Mexico City, and his involvement in illicit trade with Russian colonials than with setting up conditions for emancipation.[134] Likely a combination of frustrations left him, despite his instructions toward secularization, "fed up with dealing with the Indians."[135]

In 1826 Mexican governor of Alta California José María de Echeandía set forth steps toward provisional emancipation. Echeandía proposed that baptized Indians who had been Christians for at least fifteen years could apply to be disaffiliated from their mission.[136] He asked for missionaries to report on fugitives and to give qualifying fugitives a license to disaffiliate. He also gave instructions to find and force the return of those who did not fit the criteria.[137] Fugitives of Mission Santa Cruz, overwhelmingly Yokuts people who had entered the mission within the last decade, would not have qualified for disaffiliation. Instead, the instructions for provisional emancipation ended up helping justify and boost the frequency of militaristic fugitive incursions into Yokuts territories.

By the late 1820s Indigenous people affiliated with missions throughout California wrote or dictated petitions for release from their status of *neófia*, asking for liberation or demanding "what is owed."[138] They frequently justified their requests by testifying to their abilities as skilled laborers.[139] In Santa Cruz there are no records of any petitions for liberty, although the listing of occupations noted earlier suggests that there was a growing awareness of the importance of recognizing skilled labor. It is possible that some of these petitions are lost, but the total absence of written petitions suggests that either this practice was never conceived of as an option by the mission community or it was discouraged or otherwise prohibited by local missionaries.[140]

By the late 1820s the Bay Area was engaged in ongoing rebellions and anticolonial movements on a grand scale, as leaders such as Estanislao and Yozcolo mobilized thousands to fight the Mexican military. The absence of formal petitions for emancipation among the Santa Cruz Indigenous population did not mean that individuals and families were not concerned with their liberty and that they did not take matters into their own hands. The restrictions regarding fifteen years of Catholic immersion likely meant that Yokuts people throughout the greater Bay Area would have been denied the right to return to their homelands. Fugitives from Mission Santa Cruz joined with leaders such as Estanislao and Yozcolo, who themselves followed in the footsteps of the Miwok resistance leader Pomponio and others.[141]

Estanislao and Yozcolo drew upon their experiences within the missions while battling with Spanish or Mexican soldiers. Both men had served as alcaldes, Estanislao at Mission San José and Yozcolo at Mission Santa Clara. Estanislao was a Laquisamne Yokuts man whose Native name was Cucunuchi, baptized in 1821.[142] Estanislao left Mission San José and led a force of hundreds, including Miwok, Ohlone, and Yokuts, in defiance of the missionaries and Californio soldiers beginning around 1829, before his eventual death in 1838. Yozcolo similarly worked as an alcalde in Mission Santa Clara before becoming a rebel leader from 1829 until his death in 1839. Both resistance movements drew fugitives from missions throughout the Bay Area, including Mission Santa Cruz.[143] Meanwhile, Mexican soldiers took part in ongoing military expeditions into Yokuts territories.[144] Pan-tribal groups of Miwok, Ohlone, and Yokuts increasingly built coalitions of baptized Natives and villagers who resisted relocation to the missions, crossing tribal, linguistic, and ethnic boundaries to work together raiding livestock and fighting soldiers. If the padres did not grant them liberty from the mission, some took matters into their own hands. Perhaps Malimin's son, Estevan, was among these fugitive fighters.

Between 1813 and 1834 the introduction of large numbers of Yokuts shifted the politics within the Mission Santa Cruz Indigenous population. The most prominent of these new leaders were Chief Coleto Malimin and his sons, who became Indian auxiliaries (assistants). As such, they translated for missionaries and soldiers, supervised the mission population, took up arms to protect the mission from coastal threats, and tracked down fugitives. Malimin and his people navigated mission society by working closely with the padres and soldiers. By taking on these special roles, Malimin and his people were able to gain a small degree of political and social status, helping to facilitate their transitions from their homelands. But their relationship with the missionaries was complex. The Yokuts negotiated a limited degree of social and political power within a larger context of violent supervision by the padres, and at times new kinship bonds formed in marriages between Yokuts and Ohlone people worked to break down these hierarchies.

The eastern-lying Yokuts homelands during this period had become sites of regular military expeditions, resistance, warfare, and devastating epidemics of malaria, resulting in the abandonment of many village sites. And yet for many who fled the missions, these homelands continued to be a place where they could gather, organize, and actively resist forced relocation. This was a time when Indigenous leaders such as Estanislao, Pomponio, and Yozcolo organized movements to steal horses and cattle and battle the Spanish or Mexican soldiers. Fleeing from the missions offered a popular alternative to relocation. In some cases the line between auxiliary and fugitive became obscured, as some auxiliaries worked in collaboration with the fugitives they were sent to retrieve. Indeed, ongoing flights of fugitives and violent military encounters between Yokuts villagers, auxiliaries, and Mexican troops characterized this period in the Yokuts territories to the east.

Within Mission Santa Cruz linguistic and cultural divisions between the incoming Yokuts and the Awaswas- and Mutsun-speaking Ohlone already at the mission helped to shape these newly forming social and political hierarchies. Prominent women leaders such as Yuñan continued to exert influence despite their omission from the Franciscan-imposed alcalde system. Marriages and expanding kinship networks helped unite some Yokuts and Ohlone families. At times the divided communities within the mission were drawn together by their opposition to physical, sexual, and psychological abuse at the hands of a succession of padres. In the coming years policies of secularization and emancipation would eventually result in a limited degree of change and freedom. The choices made during these years would help to shape the politics, land base, and emancipation itself.

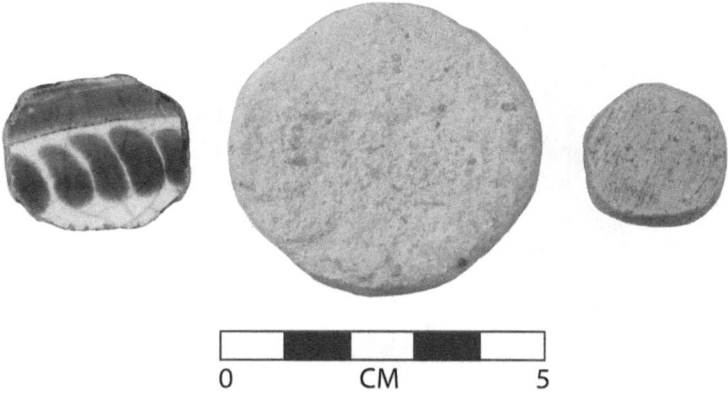

Fig. 1. Modified ceramic gaming pieces from Central California missions. *Left:* Majolica disk from Mission Soledad; photo disk courtesy of the Hearst Museum of Anthropology, University of California, Berkeley (1-84524). *Center*: Teja disk from Mission Santa Clara. *Right*: Teja disk from Mission San José. Center and left images by Lee Panich. Used with permission.

Fig. 2. Drawing of Indigenous people gaming at Mission Dolores (San Francisco), entitled *Jeu des habitants de Californie,* by Louis Choris, 1822. Original held at Library of Congress.

Fig. 3. The man sitting is believed to be Macedonio Lorenzana, while the man standing is his longtime neighbor and the husband of Pasquala Lorenzana, Jose Joaquin Juarez. n.d. Photo from Helen B. Collins collection, permission courtesy of James Zetterquist.

Fig. 4. Justiniano Roxas, who was most likely actually named Yrachis. A drawing of this image was used in *Harper's Weekly*, August 7, 1875. Photo taken by Edward Payson Butler 1873. Original held by Santa Cruz Museum of Art & History. Used with permission.

Fig. 5. Stereoscopic photograph of Justiniano Roxas. Photo taken by John Elijah Davis Baldwin in 1874. This photo is the basis for the illustration by Holtzman (fig. 6). Stereoscopic photos were a common source of entertainment in the late nineteenth century, as they were viewed through a stereoscope to create the illusion of three-dimensional depth. Original held by Santa Cruz Museum of Art & History. Used with permission.

Fig. 6. Illustration of Justiniano Roxas from Wallace W. Elliot's *Illustrations of Santa Cruz County* (1879). This image was painted by F. Holtzman. Original held by Santa Cruz Museum of Art & History. Used with permission.

Fig. 7. (*opposite top*) Jose "Cache" Lend. Original held by Santa Cruz Museum of Art & History. Used with permission.

Fig. 8. (*opposite bottom*) Rafael "Tahoe" Castro. Original held by Santa Cruz Museum of Art & History. Used with permission.

Fig. 9. (*above*) *Ruins of the Old Mission Church of Santa Cruz, in 1859* (photographic reproduction of painting most likely from 1878). University of California Berkeley, Bancroft Library, folder "Mission Era: California under Spain and Mexico and Reminiscences, ca. 1850–78," https://calisphere.org/item/ark:/13030/tf5m3nb4zp/.

Fig. 10. Possibly Maria Filomena, taken in the early 1900s. Courtesy of Casey Tefertiller.

Fig. 11. The Native American participants in the second annual Zayante Indian Conference in 1907. These nineteen men all came from places far from Santa Cruz. The photo is from Cornelia Taber, *California and Her Indian Children* (Northern California Indian Association, 1911), 28.

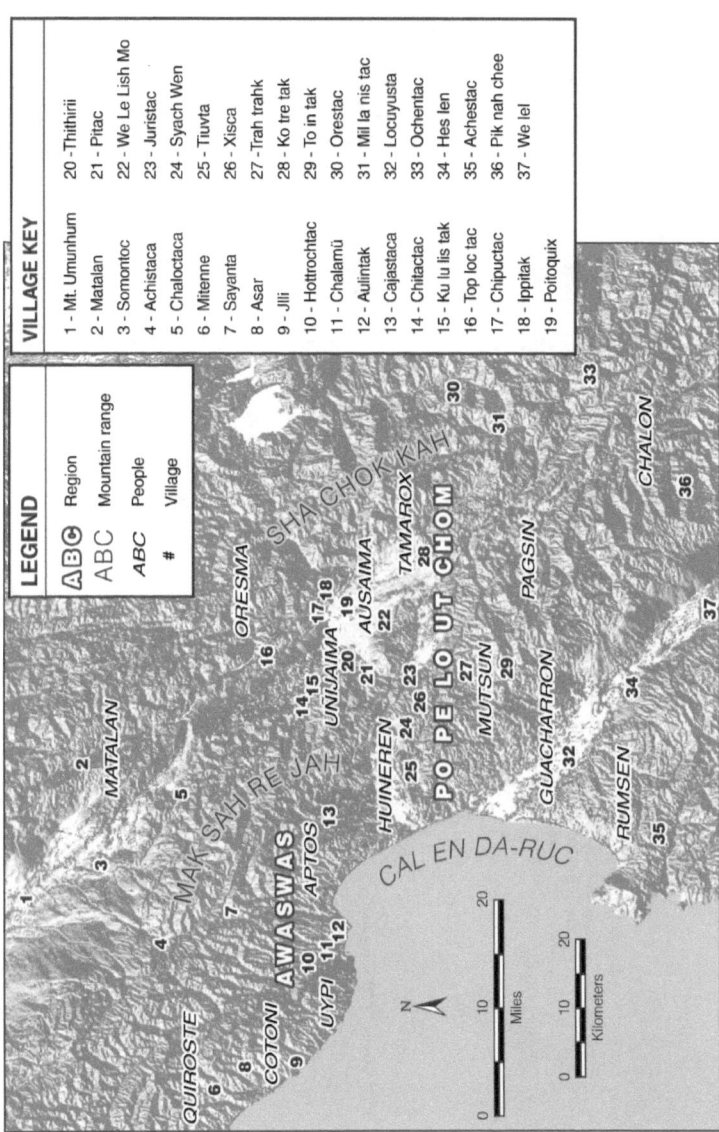

Map 1. Indigenous landscape of Po Pe Lo Ut Chom, with villages, people, and mountain ranges. Map created by Amah Mutsun tribal historian Ed Ketchum; this version made by Stella D'Oro.

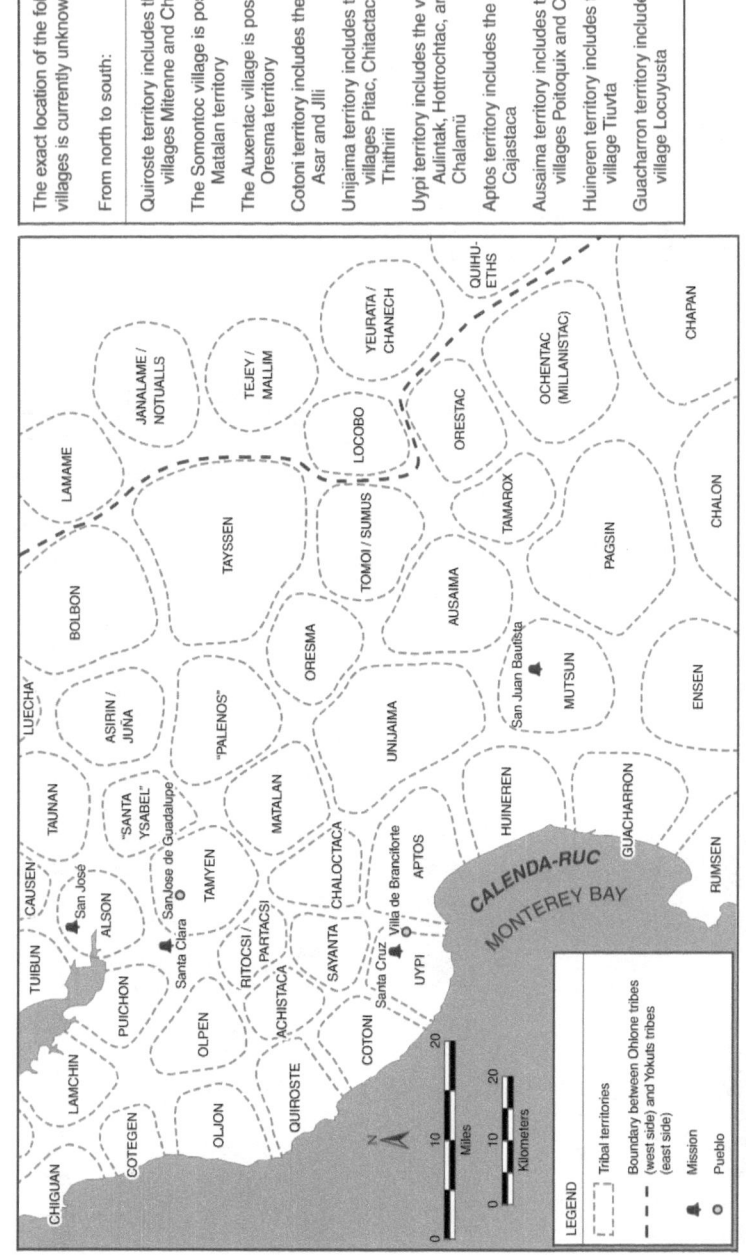

Map 2. Tribal territories, showing approximations of Indigenous territories prior to Spanish colonization and disruption. Villages are listed in connection with tribal affiliation. Created in consultation with Amah Mutsun tribal historian Ed Ketchum. Map by Stella D'Oro.

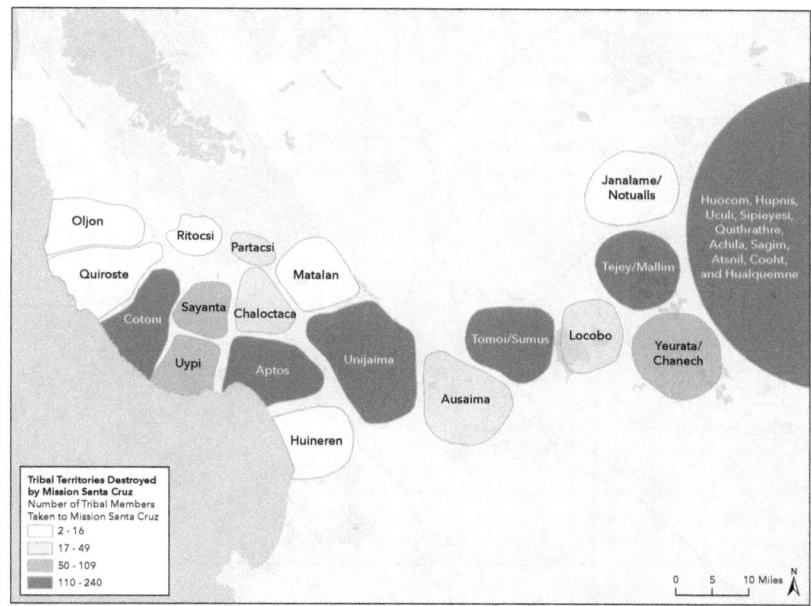

Map 3. Indigenous tribes impacted by Mission Santa Cruz, along with approximations of total tribal members relocated to Mission Santa Cruz. Map concept initiated by Amah Mutsun tribal chair Valentin Lopez; data and tribal territories provided by the author in consultation with Mark Hylkema. Map designed by Annie Taylor.

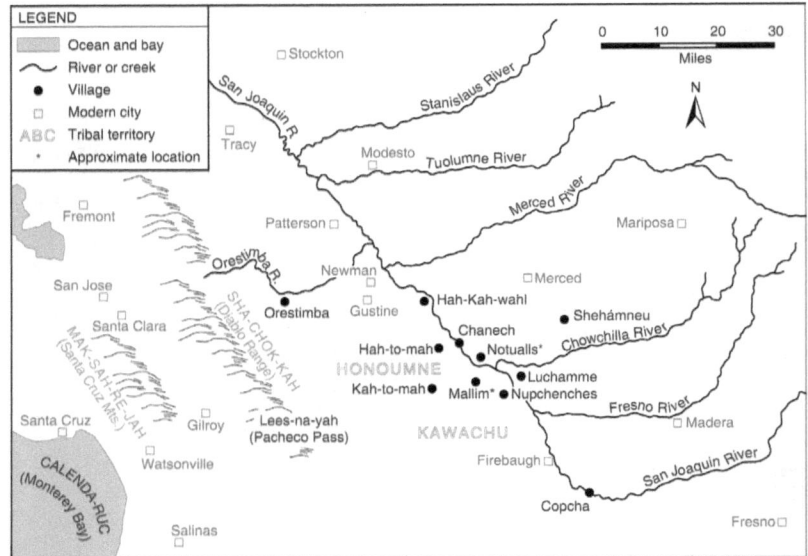

Map 4. Approximate locations of Yokuts villages. Map based on prototype originally made by Frank Latta that appeared in *Handbook of Yokuts Indians*, then augmented by author's research; this version updated by author and Stella D'Oro.

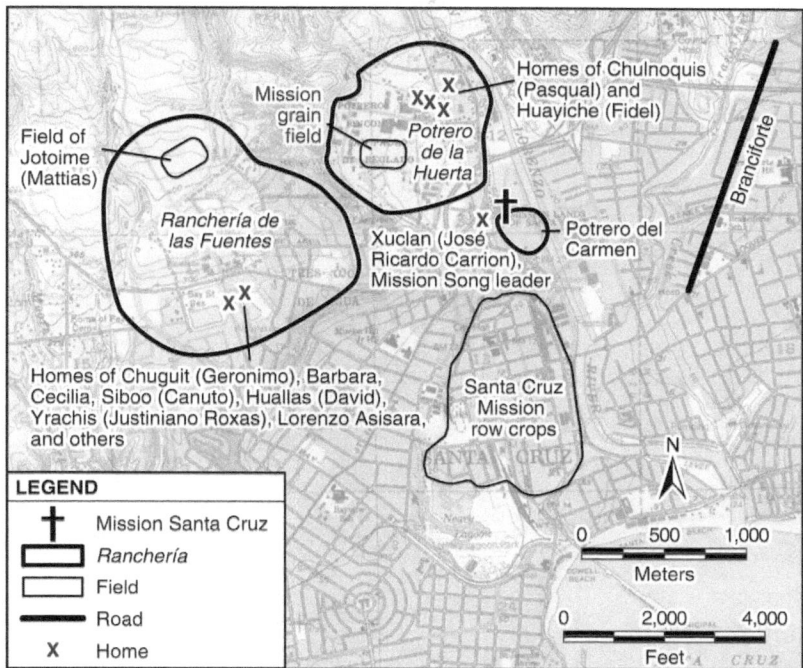

Map 5. Westside Santa Cruz, ca. 1840. Includes approximate locations of Indigenous homes surrounding Mission Santa Cruz after the closing of the mission around 1839, overlaid onto contemporary Santa Cruz city map. Map based on prototype originally made by Edna Kimbro; this version updated by author and Stella D'Oro.

Table 1. Number of baptisms, by tribe

Tribe or village	Baptisms at Mission Santa Cruz	Baptisms at other missions
Achistaca	85	0
Aptos	117	0
Cajastaca	67	0
Chaloctaca	40	9
Chipuctac	50	19
Chitactac	89	14
Cotoni	95	0
Partacsi	35	0
Pitac (Unijaima)	76	62
Quiroste	12	215
Ritocsi	8	0
Sayanta	69	5
Somontoc	8	20
Uypi	104	0
Subtotal	855	344
Total		1,199

Note: Amah Mutsun tribal historian Ed Ketchum sheds light about the Pitac: "I believe the Pitac are Unijaima people that lived in the hills southwest of Gilroy on Tick Creek. (Note that Pi means Tick in the Mutsun language.)"
Source: Figures compiled by author from a combination of the online Early California Population Project (www.huntington.org/information/ECPPmain.htm) and the Milliken database, generously donated.

Table 2. Livestock reported near Mission Santa Cruz, 1791–97

Year	Cattle	Sheep	Pigs	Mares and foals	Mules	Horses
1791	160	146	28	26	6	10
1792	180	170	0	36	7	15
1793	210	300	0	44	5	16
1794	350	400	0	60	5	19
1795	530	1,100	0	170	10	26
1796	650	1,140	0	360	48	9
1797	710	1,500	14	500	50	29

Source: Mission Santa Cruz annual reports, held at Santa Bárbara Mission Archive-Library (SBMAL).

Table 3. Agricultural yields at Mission Santa Cruz, 1791–97

Year	Wheat	Barley	Corn	Pinto beans	Chickpeas	Lentils	Peas	Beans
1791	12	—	—	—	—	—	—	6
1792	120	44	250	9	8	—	5	—
1793	100	20	180	24	—	—	5	—
1794	400	—	450	60	—	—	50	—
1795	1,100	—	600	60	—	—	26	—
1796	2,000	—	140	90	—	2	13	—
1797	1,400	—	200	5	—	3	—	—

Note: Amounts are in *fanegas*, or the amount of land required to plant a fanega of seed (1 *fanega* = 1.575 bushels).
Source: Mission Santa Cruz annual reports, held at SBMAL.

Table 4. 1796 Mission Santa Cruz baptisms, by month

Month	Baptisms	Percentage of total
January	112	15.2
February	227	30.9
March	121	16.5
April	18	2.5
May	50	6.8
June	15	2.0
July	13	1.8
August	5	0.7
September	8	1.1
October	41	5.6
November	89	12.1
December	35	4.8
Total	734	100

Source: Mission Santa Cruz annual reports, held at SBMAL.

Table 5. Baptisms, births, burials, and populations of Indigenous Christianized Indians

Year	Baptisms	Births	Burials	Population
1791	82	0	2	89
1792	74	1	5	158
1793	82	4	6	233
1794	130	11	27	332
1795	258	16	75	507
1796	111	14	91	523
1797	33	13	64	491

Source: Figures compiled by author from a combination of the online Early California Population Project (www.huntington.org/information/ECPPmain.htm) and the Milliken database, generously donated.

Table 6. Mission Santa Cruz baptisms before 1797, by tribe

Tribe	Date of first baptism	Number baptized	Percentage of total
Achistaca	October 9, 1791	84	11.4
Aptos	October 18, 1791	114	15.5
Cajastaca	February 7, 1795	15	2.0
Chaloctaca	January 28, 1792	40	5.4
Chipuctac	March 20, 1795	19	2.6
Chitactac	March 20, 1795	63	8.6
Cotoni	May 1, 1792	87	11.9
Partacsi	February 16, 1795	34	4.6
Pitac	January 12, 1796	26	3.5
Quiroste	February 17, 1793	12	1.6
Ritocsi	February 20, 1793	7	1.0
Sayanta	October 25, 1791	69	9.4
Somontoc	February 7, 1793	8	1.0
Tiuvta (Calendaruc)	February 3, 1795	3	0.5
Uypi	October 13, 1791	104	14.2
Mission-born	December 14, 1792	46	6.3
Unknown		3	0.5
Total		734	100

Note: "Unknown" are identified as two San Gregorio, likely from the north (Oljon or Cotegen?), and one Santa Agueda.
Source: Figures compiled by author from a combination of the online Early California Population Project (www.huntington.org/information/ECPPmain.htm) and the Milliken database, generously donated.

Table 7. Percentage of Awaswas speakers among overall Mission Santa Cruz population

Year	Total population	Awaswas speakers	Percentage of Awaswas speakers
1798	508	298	58.66
1810	507	116	22.88

Source: Overall population figures from Jackson, "Disease and Demographic Patterns," 33–57. Number of Awaswas speakers compiled by author.

Table 8. Agricultural crops planted at Mission Santa Cruz

Year	Wheat	Barley	Corn	Pinto beans	Chickpeas	Lentils	Peas	Beans
1791	12	—	—	—	—	—	—	6
1792	120	44	250	9	8	—	5	—
1793	100	20	180	24	—	—	5	—
1794	400	—	450	60	—	—	50	—
1795	1,100	—	600	60	—	—	26	—
1796	2,000	—	140	90	—	2	13	—
1797	1,400	—	200	5	—	3	—	—
1798	450	—	303	111	—	7	5	—
1799	333	—	103	8	—	34	46	—
1800	1,640	170	1,000	40	3	14	10	10
1801	1,097	200	700	23	17	10	—	70
1802	550	—	100	20	17	11	50	—
1806	2,074	414	680	40	—	—	—	—
1809	2,006	360	—	4	3	—	138	4
1810	1,178	400	80	68	5.5	—	17	136

Note: Amounts are in fanegas, which refer to the amount of land required to plant a fanega of seed (equivalent to 1.575 bushels).
Source: Mission Santa Cruz annual reports, held at SBMAL.

Table 9. Livestock count in Mission Santa Cruz pastures, 1791–1810

Year	Cattle	Sheep	Pigs	Horses: mares and foals	Mules
1791	130	146	28	36	6
1792	180	170	—	36	7
1793	260	300	—	44	5
1794	350	400	—	60	5
1795	530	1,100	—	183	10
1796	650	1,150	—	360	12
1797	750	1,500	14	500	47
1798	997	1,006	12	544	20
1799	1,015	1,457	34	775	34
1800	1,232	2,047	36	985	50
1801	1,300	2,203	52	1,013	53
1802	1,407	2,915	102	1,800	61
1806	2,400	5,400	120	3,200	20
1809	2,000	3,499	50	1,000	23
1810	800	4,944	33	800	19

Source: Mission Santa Cruz annual reports, held at SBMAL.

Table 12. Indigenous alcaldes, 1796–1811

Election year	Native name	Spanish name	Baptism year	Baptism number	Tribal or village affiliation	Age at election	Marriage witness prior?	Special title
1796	Geturux	Canuto	1795	389	Aptos	47	No	
1796	Lacah	Julian	1793	141	Chaloctaca	29	No	
1797	Guichiguis	Valerio	1793	179	Uypi	36	Yes	de hombre
1797	Lacah	Julian	1793	141	Chaloctaca	30	No	de mujere
1799	Cunumaspo	Erasmo	1797	754	Chitactac	38	Yes	
1799	Yucuquis	Antonio	1791	44	Uypi	40	No	
1809	Saguexi	Pedro Antonio	1793	220	Aptos	26	No	de mujere
1809	Tucumen	Rufino	1792	99	Uypi	43	Yes	de hombre
1810 and 1811	Yachacxi	Donato	1794	262	Cotoni (Achistaca)	19	Yes	de mujere
1811	Guallac	David Fluallas	1795	413	Sayanta	23	Yes	de hombr

Sources: 1796 election: AGN, Californias 17, vol. 65, exp. 8, March 30, 1796, 310-11; 1797 election: Fernández to Borica, December 13, 1797, SFAD, 120; 1799 election: Gonzalez and Carranza to Borica, January 15, 1799, SBMAL, CMD 421; 1809 election: margin notes, SCZM# 471, 472, and 274; 1810 election: padrino note on SCZB# 1440-43, 1445, and 1446, SCZM# 495 and 524-32; and 1811 election: notes on SCZM# 524-31.

Table 13. Indigenous regidores, 1797–99

Election year	Native name	Spanish name	Baptism year	Baptism number	Tribal affiliation	Age while serving
1797	Virguis	Pedro	1791	43	Uypi	36
1797	Orcheriu	Gaspar Pablo	1791	46	Cotagen or Oljon (San Gregorio)	32
1799	Luchuchu	Eufrasio	1795	550	Chitactac	38
1799	Virguis	Pedro	1791	43	Uypi	38

Sources: 1797: Friar Manuel Fernández to Governor Borica, December 13, 1797, SBMAL, CMD 346; and 1799: Gonzalez and Carranza to Borica, January 15, 1799, SBMAL, CMD 421.

Table 10. Missionaries assigned to Mission Santa Cruz

Padre name	Home region	Years in Americas	Years in California before Mission Santa Cruz	Age on arrival in Santa Cruz	First entry	Final entry	Baptisms performed
Baldomero Lopez	Valladolid, Spain	5	0	30	September 1791	June 7, 1796	384
Isidro Salazar	Cantabria, Spain	7	0	33	September 1791	March 29, 1795	168
Manuel Fernández	Galicia, Spain	2	1	28	February 25, 1795	October 15, 1798	229
Francisco Gonzalez	Spain (unknown)	unknown	0	23	June 24, 1797	August 17, 1805	287
Domingo Carranza	Calahorra, Spain	2	0	28	October 26, 1798	July 19, 1808	65
Andres Quintana	Calahorra, Spain	1	0	28	November 19, 1805	September 25, 1812	186

Source: Data on entries and baptisms taken from baptismal records via the Early California Population Project (ECPP) database hosted by the Huntington Library, www.huntington.org/ecpp. Biographical information taken from Geiger, *Franciscan Missionaries*.

Table 11. Fugitive deaths by 1810, by region

Deaths reported from afield	Tribes (or villages)	Language spoken (region)
20	Achistaca, Aptos, Cajastaca, Chaloctaca, Sayanta, Uypi	Awaswas
46	Auxentaca, Chipuctac, Chitactac, Orestac, Partocsi, Pitac, Somontoc, Sumus	Mutsun
4	Locobo	Yokuts

Source: Data compiled by author from ECPP records.

Table 14. Mission Santa Cruz population totals, 1791–1812

Year	Native baptisms	Natal baptisms	Burials	Reported population
1791	82	0	2	89
1792	73	1	5	158
1793	78	4	6	233
1794	119	11	27	332
1795	242	16	75	507
1796	97	14	91	523
1797	20	13	64	495
1798	72	16	45	504
1799	26	14	70	468
1800	41	11	51	472
1801	15	10	51	442
1802	42	14	61	437
1803	17	14	33	437
1804	63	12	49	461
1805	61	13	53	464
1806	90	15	105	466
1807	49	12	53	492
1808	31	15	49	485
1809	1	6	49	449
1810	120	11	61	507
1811	1	9	56	462
1812	0	9	30	437

Source: Santa Cruz Mission Libro de Padrones, Baptisms, and Burials, all at Monterey Diocese Chancery Archives, Monterey CA. These population numbers are from reports at the end of the year.

Table 15. Conspirators arrested in connection with assassination

Native name	Spanish name	Baptismal number	Tribal affiliation	Kinship connection
Unknown	Lino	226	Chaloctaca	Unknown
Lacah	Julian Apodeca	141	Chaloctaca	Unknown
Ules	Andrés Cañizares	97	Chaloctaca	Lino's father
Sirinte	Fulgencio Cañizares	111	Chaloctaca	Lino's uncle
Quihueimen	Quirico	65	Uypi	Unknown
Ètop	Antonio Alberto	755	Aptos	*Padrino* for Quihueimen's son Rustico (SCZB #1561), in 1811
Euxexi	Ambrosio	232	Somontoc	First wife was Ules's sister
Unknown	Leto Antonio	SCLB #1015	Mak-Sah-Re-Jah (San Carlos)	Parents baptized their sister at Mission Santa Clara (SCLB# 1902) along with Lino's older brother, Cucufate (SCLB# 1903)
Unknown	Secundino Antonio	SCLB #1016	Mak-Sah-Re-Jah (San Carlos)	Parents baptized their sister at Mission Santa Clara (SCLB# 1902) along with Lino's older brother, Cucufate (SCLB# 1903)

Source: Data compiled by author.

Table 16. Percentage of Awaswas tribal members still alive in 1812

Tribe	Total baptized	Deaths by end of 1798	Total still living in 1799	Deaths from 1799 to end of 1811	Total still living in 1812	Percentage of all baptized still living in 1812
Achistaca (Cotoni)	85	43	42	29	13	15.3
Aptos	116	38	78	53	25	21.6
Cajastaca (Aptos)	67	6	61	46	15	22.4
Chaloctaca	40	20	20	11	9	22.5
Cotoni	93	48	45	33	12	12.9
Sayanta	69	34	35	28	7	10.1
Somontoc	16	2	14	11	3	18.8
Uypi	104	47	57	40	17	16.3
Total			352		101	

Note: Spanish officials reported the sentences in 1816, after four of the conspirators had already died. While the burial records do not list details, it is likely that they died as a combination of the forced labor, excessive lashings, and poor conditions at the presidios. It is curious that the Spanish government still assigned sentences to these four dead men.
Source: Data compiled by author.

Table 17. Change in percentage of Awaswas-speaking tribes, 1799 vs. 1812

Year	Total population	Awaswas-speaking population	Awaswas-speaking percentage
1799	504	352	69.8
1812	462	101	21.9

Note: Awaswas speakers include Aptos/Cajastaca, Chaloctaca, Cotoni/Achistaca, Quiroste, Sayanta, Somontoc, and Uypi. The totals reflect the number of people at the beginning of the year. The aggregate population was officially recorded at the end of each year. For the purpose of these figures, it indicates the people who were still alive at the beginning of the year (i.e., the population totals from the previous year).
Source: Data compiled by author.

Table 18. Most frequent Indigenous padrinos at Mission Santa Cruz

Native name	Spanish name	Baptism number	Number of baptisms	Year of first baptism	Year of last baptism
Suména	Pedro Regalado	790	62	1810	1823
Gnibita	Santiago Menor	1213	61	1810	1810
Samórim	Fabiana Arraez	62	51	1812	1821
Unknown	Maria Rafaela	SD 1315	43	1794	1796
Moctó	Agustin	1480	40	1820	1821
Mullóc	Luciano	530	38	1817	1825
Yuñan	Serafina	381	37	1808	1830

Source: Data compiled by author.

Table 19. Conspirators arrested and sentenced, with burial dates and locations

Native name	Spanish name	Sentence	Death year	Location at death
Euxexi	Ambrosio	6 years, 200 lashes	1814	SF Presidio
Ules	Andrés Cañizares	2 years	1815	SF Presidio
Unknown	Leto Antonio	10 years, 200 lashes	1815	SF Presidio
Unknown	Secundino Antonio	10 years, 200 lashes	1815	SF Presidio
Unknown	Lino	10 years, 200 lashes	1817	SB Presidio
Sirinte	Fulgencio Cañizares	6 years hard labor	1819	SB Presidio
Lacah	Julian Apodeca	6 years, 200 lashes	1820	SB Presidio
Quihueimen	Quirico	6 years, 200 lashes	1838	Mission Santa Cruz
Ètop	Antonio Alberto	10 years, 200 lashes	1832	Mountains south of Mission San Carlos

Note: Spanish officials reported the sentences in 1816, after four of the conspirators had already died. While the burial records do not list details, it is likely that the men died from a combination of the forced labor, excessive lashings, and poor conditions at the presidios. It is curious that the Spanish government still assigned sentences to these four dead men.
Source: Data compiled by author.

Table 20. Population of Santa Cruz County, 1791–1860

Year	Villa de Branciforte	Native American	Foreigners	Santa Cruz region	Totals
1791	0	84	—	—	84
1795	0	507	—	—	507
1797	39	495	—	—	534
1800	66	492	—	—	558
1805	14	467	—	—	481
1810	40	507	—	—	547
1815	40	365	—	—	405
1820	83	461	—	—	544
1821	98	519	—	—	617
1825	140	496	—	—	636
1830	148	320	—	—	468
1834	201	238	—	—	439
1845	294	120	56	—	470
1852	—	110	—	1,109	1,219
1860	—	218	—	4,726	4,944

Note: The Federal Manuscript Census only recognized the region as Santa Cruz from 1850 onward. Official incorporation of the township occurred in 1866, at which time it was voted to keep the name Santa Cruz instead of Branciforte.

Sources: The 1791 to 1834 statistics are from Santa Cruz Mission Libro de Padrones, Monterey Diocese Chancery Archives, Monterey CA; the 1845 statistics are from Robert H. Jackson, "The Villa de Branciforte Census," *Antepasados* 4 (1980–81): 45–57; and the 1852 and 1860 statistics are from Federal Manuscript Census records.

Table 21. Mission Santa Cruz demographics, 1813–34

Year	Baptisms	Births	Burials	Population
1813	9	8	49	397
1814	16	6	26	388
1815	12	11	37	365
1816	27	12	34	358
1817	83	14	33	408
1818	50	21	31	410
1819	13	13	48	381
1820	113	19	33	461
1821	91	13	31	519
1822	20	20	39	499
1823	31	16	53	474
1824	29	16	48	461
1825	19	18	51	496
1826	31	12	32	484
1827	11	10	29	473
1828	16	10	61	434
1829	10	3	41	333
1830	16	13	29	320
1831	10	9	33	298
1832	7	7	35	284
1833	7	5	16	261
1834	27	14	15	238

Note: Baptisms are those of incoming children and adults as well as newborns born to couples already living there.
Source: Data compiled by author from baptismal and burial records.

Table 22. Identification of Yokuts baptisms, 1813–34

Tribe	Total baptized
Achila	16
Atsnil	12
Chaneche	32
Cooht	11
Huocom	83
Hupnis	35
Mallim	16
Notualls	11
Quithrathre	17
Sagim	13
Sipieyesi	20
Tejey	26
Various Yokuts	86
Mission-born	269
Total	647

Note: Those listed here as simply "Yokuts" come from forty-seven different Yokuts tribes. Included are tribal or village groups with at least ten members who received baptism at Mission Santa Cruz.
Source: Data compiled by author, from the Early California Population Project and the original baptismal documents held at the Monterey Archdiocese.

Table 23. Alcaldes elected, 1796-1831

Year of alcalde election	Native name	Spanish name	Baptism year	Baptismal number	Tribal affiliation	Age while serving	Special standing
1796	Geturux	Canuto	1795	389	Aptos	47	
1796, 1797	Lacah	Julian	1793	141	Chaloctaca	29	de mujeres
1797	Guchiguis	Valerio	1793	179	Uypi	36	de hombres
1799	Cunumaspo	Erasmo	1797	754	Chitactac	38	
1799	Yucuquis	Antonio	1791	44	Uypi	40	
1809	Saguexi	Pedro Antonio	1793	220	Aptos	26	de mujeres
1809	Tucumen	Rufino	1792	99	Uypi	43	de hombres
1810 and 1811	Yachacxi	Donato	1794	262	Achistaca	19	de mujeres
1811	Guallac	David	1795	413	Sayanta	23	de hombres
1813	Toquilme / Tuquinmen in burial	Mauricio	1800	941	Cajastaca	35	
1813, 1816, 1818	Chumanit	Dato	1796	676	Aptos	23, 26, and 28	
1823	Taucha	Vicente Carlos	1814	1594	Cooht	24	
1823	Autocrus	Juan Joseph	1808	1403	Locobo	23	
1825	Moctó	Agustin	1810	1480	Tejey	39	Coleto Malimin's son
1831	Chujes	Crisantos	1791	41	Uypi	35	

Sources: 1796: AGN, California (017), vol. 65, exp. 8, fojas 310-11; 1797: SBMAL, CMD346; 1799: SBMAL, CMD421; 1809: SCZM# 471, 472, 474; 1810: SCZB# 1440-43, 1445-46, SCZM# 495; 1811: SCZM# 524-32; 1813: SCZM# 541-42; 1814: SCZB# 1604; 1816: SCZB# 1641; 1818: SCZM# 599-600; 1823: SFD# 1444; 1825: SCZD# 1639-41; and 1831: SCZM# 780.

Table 24. Occupations of men and women in 1825

Job	Men	Women
Carpenter	7	—
Charcoal maker	3	—
Cook	1	—
Cornmeal grinder	—	18
Cowboy	16	1
Deer hunter	3	3
Drover	3	—
Farmer	14	7
Firewood gatherer	3	—
Gardener	2	2
Hay grower	30	—
Laborer	25	16
Mason	4	—
Pozole cook	2	—
Sacristan and *acólito*	2	—
Shepherd and chicken farmer	10	8
Sheriff or fiscal	5	—
Shoemaker	4	—
Smith	2	—
Weaver	40	46
Total	176	101

Source: Padre Luis Gil y Taboada, SBMAL, December 31, 1825, CMD 2840.

Table 25. Indigenous individuals' jobs, 1834 census

Occupation	Number performing job
Arrow maker	1
Baker	2
Carpenter	6
Charcoal maker	2
Corn doctor	1
Cowhand	1
Day laborer	26
Farmer	1
Field hand	3
Gardener	2
Hatmaker	1
Horse breaker	1
Mason	4
Muleteer	1
Laborer	1
Overseer	10
Sacristan	1
Seamstress	1
Shepherd	1
Shoemaker	4
Smith	3
Soap maker	2
Tanner	1

Source: Data compiled by author.

Table 26. Indigenous overseers, 1834 census

Overseer name on census	Native name	Age in 1834	Tribe	Baptismal number	Language
Oton Gimes	Tanite	35	Chipuctac	SJB 330	Mutsun
Jose Herrera	Palax	25	Sagim	1991	Yokuts
Hirineo del Campo	Yugunag	29	Locobo	1243	Yokuts
Agusto Machado	Nahuiyach	29	Huocom	1929	Yokuts
Ygnacio Hetes	Choropo	29	Cooht	1598	Yokuts
Apolinario (Aguilar)	Tsuyutiyúl or Teyoc	29	Huocom	1767	Yokuts
Bernardino Gomes Farias	Punis	30	Tejey	1648	Yokuts
Ysidro Echeandia	Sauset	29	Tejey	1627	Yokuts
Buenabentura Patron	None given	36	Hupnis	848	Yokuts
Javier de la Torre	Unknown	32	Churistac	?	Mutsun
Hasario Ydalgo	Characa	40	Yeurata	1067	Yokuts

Source: Taken from the 1834 Mission Santa Cruz Census, held in the *Libro de Padrónes*, Archives of the Monterey Archdiocese. Note the use of surnames of prominent Mexican officials involved in emancipation and secularization: Gomes Farias and Echeandía, most prominently.

Table 27. Distribution of Indigenous people

Year	Servants	Near mission	Total Indigenous population	Total population	Indigenous members of total population (%)
1834	0	238	238	439	54.2
1836	27	247	274	549	49.9
1839/40	36	121	157	342	45.9
1841	72	96	168	485	34.6
1843	90	25	115	455	25.3
1845	6	120	126	470	26.8

Source: Numbers are based on author's calculations from the various *padrones* contained in the *Libro de Padrónes*, Monterey Archdiocese, Monterey CA.

Table 28. 1841 Census of Indigenous communities

Location	Quantity	Households
Servants	72	18
Ranchería de los Fuentes	33	4
Potrero del Carmen	30	5
Potrero de la Huerta	33	4

Source: Data compiled by author.

Table 29. Overall populations, including "Indians"

Year	Vi la de Branciforte	Foreigners	Indians	Santa Cruz (County) totals
1845	294	56	120	—
1850	—	—	—	643
1852	—	—	110	1,219
1860	—	—	218	4,944
1880	—	—	131	12,802
1900	—	—	68	21,512
1910	—	—	15	26,140
1920	—	—	45	26,269

Source: Figures from U.S. census records. The 1890 census rolls were destroyed in a fire in 1921.

Table 30. Family of Meregildo and Maria Agueda

	Baptismal number	Baptism date	Burial number	Burial date	Age at death
Meregildo	2172	August 21, 1830	unknown	—	—
Maria Agueda	2194a	April 8, 1833	2707	May 31, 1875	42
Jose Miguel Antonio	2971	May 22, 1853	unknown	—	—
Maria Jesus	3033	December 27, 1854	unknown	—	—
Tomas Acantuviense	3251	February 5, 1860	2810	June 4, 1877	17
Ambrosiana	3341	February 16, 1862	2665	February 4, 1874	11
Maria Rosa	3442	January 17, 1864	unknown	—	—
Maria Delfina	3619	late 1866	2514	October 31, 1867	~1 year
Mariana	3815	December 24, 1868	2554	November 8, 1869	11 months
Maria Rafaela	3948	July 31, 1870	unknown	—	—
Jose Alfredo	4100	June 30, 1872	2647	July 15, 1873	1

Source: Data compiled by author.

5

Not Finding Anything Else to Appropriate

On a Sunday morning, September 28, 1839, a group of more than seventy members of the Indigenous community at Mission Santa Cruz lined up and met with a visitor, William Edward Petty Hartnell. Alta California governor Juan Bautista Alvarado had appointed the English-born turned Mexican citizen Hartnell as *visitador general de las misiones* (general inspector of the missions) and charged him with overseeing the process of closing down the missions (known as secularization).[1] When Hartnell spoke with the group, one man in particular, the Awaswas-speaking Ohlone man from the Sayanta village Chugiut (Geronimo), demanded his freedom. The sixty-year-old Chugiut had lived at the mission since his baptism in 1793. Chugiut told Hartnell that he was old and tired of waiting and that he wanted his lands and his freedom. As one of the elders of the local Indigenous community, he undoubtedly spoke for the rest of the Mission Santa Cruz survivors, who had heard rumors about freedom and the transfer of mission lands for years and yet had witnessed little change. During this meeting the survivors requested their freedom from Hartnell as well as the fulfillment of promises made by the new Mexican government that they would receive what was left of the mission cattle, horses, livestock, and lands—lands that they had tended over the years. Earlier in the decade local Californio administrators had granted much of these same lands to their own friends, so there was little left unclaimed by 1839. Freedom and rights had been a long time coming, and Chugiut and the others were tired of waiting.[2]

Chugiut and his wife, Barbara, would eventually receive lands. Before his death, around 1850, Chugiut became a well-respected and important member of the local community. Throughout the 1840s he and his extended kinship network lived on the resource-rich lands on what has become known as the Westside of Santa Cruz. He and his family kept multiple seasonal gardens, sold produce to members of the local Californio community, had access to the rich freshwater springs on his property, and participated in the economic and social worlds that developed after the closing of Mission Santa Cruz. A skilled mason himself, Chugiut sold access to the rock quarry on his lands to Californio builders. While he navigated the Californio community, Chugiut and his family continued to draw on traditional practices, moving homes seasonally, milling acorns and other traditional foods to supplement their agricultural yields, and speaking their languages.

Chugiut's move to the former mission lands took place following the eventual enactment of secularization and emancipation provisions. At that point the Indigenous residents of Mission Santa Cruz spread out into three distinct neighborhoods directly surrounding the mission. Yet while these neighborhoods formed and were identified on census documents, this reduction is itself an oversimplification of a much more complex social reality. Each of these rancherias were made up of a diversity of families and extended kinship networks.[3]

The elder Chugiut, a Sayanta man from local lands who had been living and working at Mission Santa Cruz from its earliest days, finally was able to expand into the lands that he had cultivated for many years. Chugiut's life during this era exemplified the promise of emancipation and Indigenous land ownership, when formerly mission-bound Indigenous families were emancipated from their conditions under *neófia*. And yet, despite the changing circumstances, this was not a time of unrestrained freedom, as new rules and restrictions governed Indigenous labor, mobility, land ownership, and citizenship.[4]

Not all received lands and accessed resources like Chugiut.[5] The overall Indigenous population in the area fell below two hundred following the smallpox epidemic that swept through in 1838 (see table 27). Distinct Indigenous communities expanded into the lands adjacent to the mission. A community of Yokuts, including the descendants of Malimin (Coleto), moved onto the Potrero—the low-lying pasture and orchards behind the mission. Others lived in mission adobes or small parcels of adjacent lands. Still other mission survivors found manual and domestic labor opportunities by working in the homes of wealthy Californio families throughout the larger region. Some, especially Yokuts families from the San Joaquin

Valley, returned to traditional homelands, sometimes joining with Indigenous horse thieves, who often returned to Santa Cruz to steal livestock. Emancipated from their subordinate neófia relationship with the mission, Indigenous survivors had witnessed most of their mission lands gifted in large land grants to Californio families before finally getting the opportunity to gain small portions for themselves.[6] This was a time of change with regards to questions of citizenship, land, and mobility.[7] For many the conditions limiting these rights overwhelmed the few gains, as subordinate relationships with local Californios persisted.[8]

Release of Mission Lands and Liberation

To understand the impact of secularization and emancipation, it is important to briefly examine the political changes that had been brought about by Mexican independence in 1821. The previous chapter introduced ideas regarding emancipation, showing how Natives at Mission Santa Cruz advocated for their liberation and rights. The new liberal Mexican government pushed to reform colonial policy, specifically challenging the racial *casta* system and the power of the church. One of the major subjects of reform concerned the large tracts of lands held by churches. The issue of secularization—the process of releasing lands controlled by the church—at this time was unique to California, as these issues had previously been dealt with throughout mainland Mexico.[9] In contrast with secularization, emancipation referred to the release from the conditions of neófia, the paternal relationship between Indigenous baptized peoples (*neofitos*) and the padres.[10] The combination of policies regarding secularization and emancipation raised new questions about citizenship, labor, and land.[11]

Debates about secularizing the missions had occupied governmental officials in mainland Mexico as early as 1813 and originally included plans for turning over mission lands to Natives with intentions to build Indian pueblos.[12] Governor Echeandía put forth a provincial plan for secularization in 1830, laying out specific rules for the missions to hand over lands and livestock to Indigenous converts, with the larger goal of releasing coveted mission lands to Mexican civilians.[13] His plans included using surplus goods to build schools and hospitals for former mission Indians. Because of Mexico's turbulent political climate, Echeandía was never able to put his plan into action. A new, conservative federal government replaced Echeandía with the brigadier general Manuel Victoria, an advocate for the mission system, in late 1830. Further unrest in Alta California led to the deposition of Victoria by Pío Pico and Echeandía in February 1832. In 1833 Brigadier General José Figueroa, a highly decorated veteran of Mexican independence, stepped into the role of governor.[14]

Figueroa was hesitant to enact Echeandía's secularization, worried that the removal of the missions as an economic force would badly damage the California economy. Figueroa echoed the patronizing concerns of the missionaries from the 1820s, who viewed baptized Native people as children incapable of functioning without ecclesiastic supervision, so he supported provisional emancipation, which included many restrictions.[15] But before Figueroa could implement his proposal, events in Mexico City once again altered the political order in Alta California.

President Antonio de Santa Anna chose Valentín Gómez Farías, a prominent and radical liberal, to be his vice president. The unstable Santa Anna handed over the presidency to Farías for the first time in 1833.[16] Farías was a fierce supporter of secularization and quickly moved to extend it into the frontier settlements of Alta California by announcing his own plans for secularization.[17] His plans, however, failed to address land redistribution to newly liberated Indigenous people.

Governor José Figueroa issued the Emancipation and Secularization Decree of 1834, which ended the conditions of neófia but brought with it new restrictions.[18] For one, emancipation did not grant Indians the rights of full citizens (*vecinos*), which often included rights to lands.[19] Figueroa's Reglamento Provisional para la secularización de la Misiones called for the secularization of ten missions and set forth plans for the rest.[20] The new law issued one hundred to four hundred *varas* (a *vara* equals 2.75 feet) of land as well as communal plots for emancipated Indigenous peoples. The pueblos were intended to hold their own jurisdiction and have their own government and elected officials.[21] While this order appeared to offer liberation for local Indigenous survivors, the actual implementation of these laws fell to a local *comisionado* (administrator). Santa Cruz had three such administrators.[22] Importantly, the decree stated that a non-Native administrator would be appointed to oversee this transition.[23] In each region Indigenous communities responded differently to emancipation and secularization.[24] In Santa Cruz official acceptance of secularization and emancipation was slow to come, and actual emancipation for the local Indigenous community was delayed until nearly 1840.[25]

Secularization at Mission Santa Cruz

Lorenzo Asisara, in an interview in 1877, offered specific details about secularization at Mission Santa Cruz. Asisara was born in 1820, and by the 1830s he was a young man who worked closely with the mission padres. In his own accounts he says that he was treated well, working in the homes alongside the padres.[26] Asisara recalled that in 1833, when Padre Antonio Suárez del Real was in charge, General Jose Figueroa came to Mission Santa Cruz on his way to his new post at the Presidio of Monterey, where he was received with great ceremony and fireworks.[27] This official visit lasted about ten days.[28] Conversations involving liberation and freedom from the missions expanded further as Indigenous individuals from neighboring missions made their way into the region.[29]

A succession of three administrators oversaw secularization at Mission Santa Cruz between the years 1834 and 1840. Juan Gonzales was the majordomo in August 1834, when secularization administrator Ignacio del Valle came to check on Mission Santa Cruz.[30] Asisara accused Gonzales of raiding mission storehouses for gold, silver, and supplies on the very night that del Valle arrived. Asisara recalled that he caught Gonzales, along with Padre Antonio Real, Gonzales's sister-in-law and mission housekeeper Maria de Alta Gracia Rodriguez, and two other Gonzales family members looting the supplies, after being alerted by del Valle about the possibility of such misappropriations. Asisara confessed that he was bribed to remain silent by Padre Real's gift of forty dollars in gold and a chest of beads for his father, Llencó.[31] For his time as mayordomo, Gonzales, who will be discussed shortly for his role in sending Indigenous orphans to local ranchos, received an adobe home in the mission plaza. Padre Real made three grants while Gonzales was mayordomo at the mission: one to Gonzales himself, one to his sister-in-law Maria de Alta Gracia Rodriguez, and one to the Indigenous mission song leader, Xuclan (José Ricardo).[32]

Asisara's retelling of secularization and emancipation suggests a high level of administrative incompetence or neglect.[33] In January 1839 Francisco Soto replaced Gonzales as mayordomo. Asisara recalls that Soto was a heavy drinker who physically abused his Indian charges.[34] This portrait of Soto is reinforced by the Hartnell report.[35]

During the 1830s Mexican authorities granted the vast majority of local lands to prominent members of the local Californio community, leaving very little land left to grant to the Indigenous residents.[36] Throughout the decade prominent Californio families received large rancho grants accounting for more than 160,000 acres. The Castro and Rodriguez families, the two most influential and land-rich families in the region, received the majority of these grants.[37] Land grants consisted of large-scale ranchos averaging more than seven thousand acres as well as smaller plots of land within the Villa de Branciforte given to local working-class Californios.[38] Reports of the time support this charge of nepotism in both land and livestock allotment; when French explorer Eugène Duflot de Mofras passed by Mission Santa Cruz in 1841, he reported that "the livestock [had been] divided among the governor's friends."[39]

Finally, in late 1839, likely as a result of the Hartnell report, it appears that some Indigenous people began to receive small plots of lands, although few received actual legally binding grants or paperwork supporting their land ownership. A new mayordomo, Don Jose Bolcoff, was appointed late in 1839.[40] Asisara reported that Bolcoff distributed the remaining animals among the few remaining Indians. Asisara also credits Bolcoff with bringing to light records regarding land concessions made by Figueroa to the Indians. Bolcoff was given instructions that while the "Indians may work freely in the fields of the establishment at whatever they wish," they remained subordinate to him and "subject to cooperate in whatever work is offered them in the interest of the establishment itself."[41] Thus, despite the apparent promises of secularization and emancipation from the mission, Indians remained second-class citizens.

Labor, Punishment, and Restrictions

The proliferation of large, Californio-owned and run rancho tracts within the area also resulted in the need for workers to attend to crops, livestock, and domestic requirements.[42] Californio rancho-owning families relied on Indigenous laborers, continuing the social and labor hierarchies that had formed in the colonial era. Rancho owners exercised a great deal of authority in inflicting physical punishment on Indigenous workers.[43] With the transition away from missionary oversight of the Indigenous community, the Californio administrators found themselves in a new position of managing the Indian population, whose members were still expected to provide labor to the community.[44] One way they did this was through the establishment of an office entitled "encargo de justicia," as happened in San Diego. This new official administered justice to baptized Native people who had committed petty crimes. These laws were extremely vague in defining these crimes, despite outlining punishments of imprisonment in chains and forced labor.[45] Crimes appear to have included drunkenness and "public scandal."[46] The creation of this administrative oversight further undermined the Indigenous alcalde's standing as an authority, and work conditions appear to have been difficult and oppressive, as witnessed by reports of Indigenous laborers fleeing from various ranchos.[47]

In the greater Santa Cruz region, laborers on local ranchos included a mix of incoming refugees from neighboring California mission communities and orphaned children of Mission Santa Cruz survivors.[48] The continuing high mortality rates often caused by epidemics and disease led to orphaned youth. Sometimes these children found homes with relatives or kin, but in many cases children ended up living with Californio families. In these cases census reports noted Indigenous children distinctly from the Californio families.[49] Though these orphans were not always listed as servants, as with most Native workers in Californio ranchos, they were frequently listed as *criados*. The term is connected with the Spanish word *criar*, "to raise or bring up," but the word was typically used for household servants.[50] Thus, the terms of their arrangement reinforced their second-class status and the paternal relationships tracing back to the colonial casta system.

At times the practice of exchanging Indigenous orphan servants had similarities to systems of slavery. Some Californio families appeared to use godparentage to establish control over orphaned children, allowing them to send these children to work on local ranchos. The situation with Gonzales and his wife, Maria Anna Rodriguez, is a particularly interesting one, as the couple appear to have lived close by the mission, while Gonzales served as its mayordomo from 1834 until 1839.[51] The couple served as *padrinos* for sixty-one baptisms, of which thirty-three were of Indigenous children.[52] The Gonzales family appear to have "adopted" some of these children into their own home, and others they might have loaned out or passed off to other Californio rancho families. For example, Maria Guadalupe, who arrived at the mission in 1834 as a ten-year-old Tejey orphan, appears in their household, listed as a criado, beginning with the 1836 census as "Maria Guadalupe del Tular" and continuing through at least the 1845 census.[53] In another case an eleven-year-old Yokuts girl, Maria Rosa, was baptized in 1839, with *madrina* Antonia Armas, with a note that reads: "Bought by Peres for 13 pesos from a Tular Chief (Capitan)." Maria Rosa appears in the household of Juan Peres and his wife, Antonia Armas, for at least five years.[54]

In contrast, some of these orphaned children ended up on neighboring ranchos, apparently sent by their padrinos to labor for other homes. For example, the children of the Sayanta man Huallas (David), lived in the household of Juan Gonzales, appear to have been sent elsewhere.[55] In the 1840 census one of Huallas's sons, Rogerio, appears in the home of Gonzales's neighbor and sister-in-law, Maria de Alta Gracia Rodriguez.[56] Another of his sons, Ybon, appears at Rancho San Andrés on the 1840s census and later.[57]

Separating Indigenous children and sending them to work at local ranchos appears to have been a pattern, often assisted by people like Gonzales and his family.[58] This pattern of godparentage by Californio families, which frequently led to the removal of Indigenous orphans from their kin and extended families and their placement as laborers, served as another way to separate Indigenous children from the teachings and culture of their ancestors. Growing up as servants, distanced from ceremony, language, and family practices, undoubtedly severed important ties and access to knowledge and practices. It is likely that some contemporary families descend from these orphaned children and have little knowledge of their lineage or heritage, unaware that their ancestors had survived the missions.

In some cases Indigenous families recently emancipated from neighboring missions, presumably after petitioning for their liberation, found work at these ranchos.[59] While authorities permitted laborers move to rancho sites, they required Indigenous people were required to use a system of passports and passes, not unlike the seasonal *paseos* used in the mission era. Mexican officials carefully monitored Indigenous people through this period, requiring passes and frequently complaining of unmonitored flights or movement or requesting workers be sent from one rancho to another.[60] Californio officials reported Indigenous workers who had left their rancho, stolen something, or were otherwise "fleeing from justice."[61] In this way Californio landholders retained a great deal of control over the movement and punishment of Indigenous workers.

Rancho San Andrés, for example, became home to nine people who worked as servants for the Castro family. These nine included two families and a few more individuals, all from neighboring mission communities like San Juan Bautista and Soledad. This included Carlos, Faustina, and their daughter, Ynocente, a family from Mission San Juan Bautista. A Pagsin (Mutsun-speaking Ohlone) man, Carlos was descended from some of the earliest Indigenous people at Mission San Juan Bautista, while his wife, Faustina, was from the Chapan or Chapant village (likely in Chalost territory), who had arrived at Mission Soledad as a one-year-old in 1805.[62] Their family appears to have moved between mission communities throughout the 1830s, settling at Rancho San Andrés by 1840. They are recorded as living and working at the rancho property in the censuses from 1840 until 1843, although they may have remained on the property in later years unreported in the official census.

Another Indigenous family to work at Rancho San Andrés was that of Guejais (Josefa Antonio) and Amonason (Jose Antonio, originally baptized as Beda) and their daughter, Crescencia. It appears that the family came from Mission San Luis Rey, where Guejais was born, while Amonason was likely from the Topome village.[63] The couple first appeared in the 1840 census and the 1843 census, which recorded them as living with Carlos, Faustina, and Ynocente. It is likely that the descendants of these families continued to live in the area, which would become known as Aptos, up through the 1860s. The presence of these Indigenous workers from neighboring communities points toward one labor possibility for recently emancipated Indigenous families during this time. Another option included returning to eastern homelands.

Disrupted Yokuts Homelands and Livestock Raiders
How the Indians Used to Go About Stealing

In those times the Indians used to go about much to see what they could steal. They kept stealing the horses from my father until he had only a few. The Tularenos used to come here from the Tular to steal but they were not the only ones that stole. The Indians from here used to go following them, and some horses would get separated from the rest when the Tularenos were carrying them away and used to come back one by one alone. The horses know their place and they come home.[64]

The violence and warfare that characterized tensions over liberty and freedom increased throughout the 1830s and 1840s.[65] As more and more Indigenous people left the Bay Area missions, the incidence of horse and cattle raids by Indigenous raiding parties increased.[66] Yokuts families returned to their ancestral homelands only to find the landscape transformed, many of their village sites destroyed or abandoned. With few left to manage the landscape and resources, they must have found it difficult if not impossible to return to traditional practices. Some turned to raiding Californio-owned ranchos and settlements, stealing livestock. These horse and cattle raiders became engaged in ongoing battles with the local Californios, who referred to them as "Tulareños." The colonists at the Villa de Branciforte and neighboring ranchos regularly complained about groups of horse-raiding Tulareños wreaking havoc. Furthermore, horses signified status within Mexican and Spanish culture, and the presence of skilled vaqueros among former mission-living Indigenous people reveals one way people used and developed skills taught in Spanish colonial culture for their own purposes.[67]

In 1838 a Branciforte resident's body was found hanging from a tree not far from Mission Santa Cruz, his body riddled with arrows, reportedly left dead by Indigenous horse raiders.[68] Cornelio Perez, another *poblador* from the pueblo, recalled raids by "Tulare Indians" in 1835 and 1838. Regarding the latter raids, Perez said: "In the year 1838, the Indians stole the horse of Don Carlos Castro of Soquel. As Juez de Campo [field judge], I gathered up the principal residents from Santa Cruz in order to go out in pursuit of the savages. We managed to catch up with them in the dangerous arroyo called the 'Lake of the Pot' . . . we defeated them, killing two Indians who were left there shot."[69] Californio military excursions in pursuit of horse thieves were commonplace.[70] Perez later recalled that "the Indians invaded Rancho Refugio to steal the horse herd of Juan Jose Feliz. Afterward, five men left in pursuit of the robbers . . . succeeding in catching them where the Sayanta Arroya ends up. The Indians threw a knife . . . they killed an individual named Antonio Amaya."[71] The interior of California formed a borderland of violent interaction between the Californios and Indigenous peoples.[72]

Not all local Indigenous people worked in solidarity with the raiders, as some aided the Californios in fighting against them. In 1843, for example, Jose Bolcoff enlisted a group including Chavan, Chulnoquis, Chuyuco, Cristobal, Guadalupe, and Yocoguehs to assist in defense. These were Yokuts men, including Chulnoquis, one of Malimin's sons; and Chuyuco, the Tejey husband of Lino's daughter, Petra Nicanor.[73] Only Chulnoquis and Cristobal had weapons of their own; presumably, the others were asked to fight barehanded.[74] Like the Indigenous *auxiliaries* and fugitive rebels in earlier years, Indigenous people navigated these times through a variety of alliances and rivalries, engaging in their own politics built around kinship ties and family connections.

Indigenous Rancherias

In the 1841 census three distinct Indigenous communities were noted for the first time.[75] Their appearance in the official record shows the expansion of Indigenous people into the lands surrounding Mission Santa Cruz (see table 28).[76] These three distinct rancherias existed as homes for local Indigenous people for only a short time, as only two remained as identifiable communities beyond the 1840s (see map 5). These three rancherias spread out adjacent to the mission. The first, called Rancheria de la Fuentes (Rancheria of the Fountains), formed on the former mission agricultural lands. Located in the area in front of Mission Santa Cruz, the second was called Potrero del Carmen and included a group of adobe homes that had been built in the 1820s.[77] The third, called Potrero de la

Huerta (Fields of the Orchards), appears to have been on orchard fields behind the mission.

The name Rancheria de la Fuentes was clearly a reference to the multiple springs on these lands, which formed a small portion of the larger coastal terrace of Santa Cruz's Westside. This land had been the agricultural fields tended by the Indigenous laborers of Mission Santa Cruz. The larger area included three freshwater springs, which had been the main water source for the mission.[78] The region, referenced as "de la Fuentes," became home to Chugiut and his family (see map 5). The 1841 census listed thirty-three members in four households made up primarily of Awaswas- and Mutsun-speaking Ohlone from local lands (see table 28). The story of Chugiut and his kinship network will be explored in depth shortly.

The second Indigenous neighborhood was the Potrero del Carmen, which by 1841 was home to thirty members in five households (see table 28). These lands appear to have been part of the larger pasturelands in front of Mission Santa Cruz. While the exact location of Potrero del Carmen cannot be mapped out with certainty, evidence found by tracing the movements of families listed as living there offers clues. For example, Petra Nicanor and her husband, the Tejey man Chuyuco (Victoriano), were listed as living in Potrero del Carmen immediately after secularization.[79] We know from archaeological evidence that by the 1840s their family lived in one of the adobe homes on the front side of the mission.[80] Petra Nicanor was the daughter of Quintana assassination conspirator Lino, and it seems likely that her status within the community allowed her access to the adobe home. The Potrero del Carmen families here were mostly Huocom but also included some Tomoi, a few Chaneche, Hupnis, Locobo, and Tejey—basically a mix of Yokuts along with a few Mutsun. It is worth remembering that the Tomoi lived on the edge of Mutsun and Yokuts territory, on the opposite side of Pacheco Pass from the Locobo (see map 2). The community included Chaujana (Simon), the chief of the Yokuts-speaking Hupnis tribe.[81] This area is only specifically mentioned in the 1841 census; it probably merged with the third neighborhood sometime in the 1840s, most likely as portions of both began to be settled and claimed by Californios.

The third neighborhood, Potrero de la Huerta, was home to the sons of Malimin and their kin (see map 5). By acquiring the lands around the orchard, where their homes had been built, this community was able to gain valuable resources. This is the area that became known more generally as the Potrero in later years, though it is likely that it had merged with Potrero del Carmen by then. One large household of mostly Tejey Yokuts lived communally alongside three other smaller mixed households of Mutsun Ohlone and Yokuts families, thirty-three people in four households altogether (see table 28). Malimin had died in 1822, and his oldest son, Agustin Moctó, died ten years later.[82] Malimin's son Guajsilii (Estevan) disappeared from the Mission Santa Cruz rolls in the early 1830s. Huich (Vicente Francisco) died a few months after the smallpox epidemic of 1838.[83] The two surviving sons, Chulnoquis (Pasqual) and Punis (Bernardino), became recipients of the Potrero lands behind the mission, along with the Quithrathre Yokuts man Huayiche (Fidel).[84] The prominence of the Malimin heirs in the Potrero suggests that they received these lands as a reward for the family's years of service to the mission, a notion that is supported by newspaper reports many years later.[85] The Potrero continued to serve as a home for the Yokuts community for decades.

At the same time that many found homes on nearby lands, a select few enjoyed new possibilities for social, economic, and geographic mobility that allowed them to travel and find opportunities throughout the greater Bay Area.[86] Some recently emancipated Indigenous families from neighboring missions such as San Juan Bautista, Santa Clara, Soledad, and even as far south as Santa Barbara moved into the area to find work on local ranchos, while others moved into the area through intermarriage with Californios or incoming foreigners.[87] Labor opportunities offered mobility for a select few, as these opportunities appear to have been tied to youth and service to the Mexican state.

Social, Racial, and Geographic Mobility

Lorenzo Asisara is the most well-known among surviving members of the Mission Santa Cruz Indigenous communities.[88] Born in 1820, Asisara came of age during the final years before the secularization of Mission Santa Cruz. Through his father, Llencó, Asisara held kinship connections with the early Mission Santa Cruz families, those involved with protecting the community from Padre Quintana. Like many of his generation born within the mission, Asisara came from a mixed Ohlone Yokuts lineage, as his father was a local Awaswas-speaking Cotoni, while his mother came from Yokuts territory.[89] Lorenzo and his father were key members of the local Indigenous community, as Llencó worked as the mission orchardist.[90] Asisara described his own changing roles within the mission as foreman, key keeper, sacristan, alcalde, and musician. He followed in the tradition of Lino and other mission-born children in holding stature and power within the mission community.[91]

Asisara's life was one of relative privilege within the mission community. He revealed that he avoided punishment at the hands of the padres by working closely with them. After describing the ways that the mayordomos administered punishments, Asisara reflected on how he was able to avoid punishment because of his status as a house servant.[92] He claimed that he had served as a sacristan in his youth, working closely with the padres in domestic as well as ecclesiastical servitude. His involvement with the choir points to the prominence of young Indigenous musicians.

Padre Antonio Real sent Asisara to Monterey for six months sometime around 1833 or 1834, shortly after Governor Figueroa's visit to Santa Cruz.[93] The trip is an example of the special status afforded musicians, as Asisara was sent southward along with four other unidentified young men. There he learned clarinet from Sergeant Rafael Estrada, adding to his previous skills with the flute.[94] It is likely that Asisara and the other musicians played string instruments like the violin as well. While there, Asisara was taught to read and write Spanish by Padre José María del Refugio Suárez del Real, the brother of Padre Antonio Real. Asisara's training in reading and writing demonstrates the special access offered to some musicians and is reflective of his high intelligence, as many contemporary Californio did not read and write.

Music was a central element of Indigenous participation in the social world of Santa Cruz, as it was throughout Indigenous California, and musicians formed an important class within mission communities.[95] Music and dance were not new to the Indigenous community, but the use of new Spanish instruments was. Where once they had used bird bone whistles, clapper sticks, turtle shell shakers, and other instruments made from local products, the choir was now introduced to horns, woodwinds, and other instruments common to Catholic practices. Mission musicians could receive special training or privileges, and they were frequently asked to perform for visitors, with one padre claiming, "Once a year at least each one of them was given a new suit, and other privileges were granted to them to encourage them to serve in the choir."[96] Of the local musicians one Mexican traveler said, "The orchestra was made up of a group of Indians who sang accompanied by violins, triangles, drum and bass drum, creating a din that almost equaled that of a small cannon they shot off outside from time to time."[97]

The elevated status of musicians is most visibly reflected in the distribution of lands following secularization. The lead song leader, Xuclan (José Ricardo Carrion), received a piece of land next to the mission.[98] Xuclan was a good friend of Asisara, and the two lived on his property at times into the 1860s. Xuclan would eventually become the last landholding Indian in Santa Cruz, giving up his parcel of mission lands following a court case in 1866.[99] And yet, despite Xuclan's lands, compensation for musicians was not always offered. Typically, musicians received little in the way of economic recompense for their work, especially during secularization, when Catholic administrators resisted paying their musicians in response to the statewide defunding of the church.[100]

Asisara represents a rare example of racial malleability, as he is identified in his marriage records as *razon* following his marriage in 1837 to Maria Tomasa Alvarado, a member of the Californio community of Mission San Gabriel. Perhaps it was during his time in Monterey that Asisara met his future wife. The Alvarado family had moved between Mission San Gabriel and the presidio at Santa Barbara in the early 1800s. Maria Tomasa's father, Juan Nepomuceno Dolores Alvarado, had been a soldier stationed at the Presidio of Santa Barbara.[101] Asisara's ability to transcend his racial and social status demonstrates the fluidity of these categories while illuminating marriage as a pathway to social mobility. For Asisara this social and racial transcendence proved to be transitory; following Maria Tomasa's death, sometime before 1845, Asisara returned to being classified as an "Indio."[102]

Smallpox Traumas and the Lost Generation

The Indigenous population in the Santa Cruz region changed from barely constituting the majority of the total population in 1834 to accounting for around a quarter of the total population by 1845 (see table 27). This downward trend was the result of a combination of factors, including the return of some Yokuts people to traditional homelands. The smallpox epidemic, known as the Miramontes epidemic, entered California through Fort Ross in 1837 and potentially killed hundreds of thousands of Native Californians.[103] It reached Santa Cruz in 1838 and took a great toll on the surviving community. The influx of Indigenous workers from neighboring missions to work on the new ranchos helped to augment the overall population of Indigenous people, from a demographic perspective, but the net result meant the local population with ties to Mission Santa Cruz experienced a substantial demographic collapse.

In June 1838 a smallpox epidemic began to sweep through the region. The burial records indicate that 38 Indigenous members of Mission Santa Cruz died that summer.[104] If the total population was somewhat less than the 274 listed in the 1836 census, this would have meant that somewhere around 14 percent of the Indigenous population died in the smallpox epidemic (see table 27). The last Indigenous person to die in this epidemic was Llencó, Asisara's father.[105] In later years Asisara recollected that "smallpox came through and killed off any of the survivors [of the mission]."[106] The losses were substantial but not total. Still, it was predominately members of the older generation who died during this period; tragically, they had made it through the rough years under mission control but did not survive long enough to see actual emancipation. It is easy to understand why Asisara felt that this disease had decimated his community, especially given the connection to the loss of his father.

The elders were hit the hardest during this epidemic, and the loss of these important figures must have been extremely difficult. One of the elders who died of smallpox was a survivor of the Quintana affair, Quihueimen. His life and that of his family shed light on psychological duress and transgenerational trauma.[107] While it is difficult to pinpoint historical psychological processes such as trauma, the records offer clues about it. The story of Quihueimen and his son Rustico suggests evidence of transgenerational trauma.

Quihueimen was the longest-living survivor among the Quintana assassination convicts; he survived his sentence and was the only one to return to Santa Cruz. Quihueimen must have returned to Mission Santa Cruz sometime in the 1820s. At that point he would have served somewhere between six and nine years of hard forced labor at the Santa Barbara Presidio.[108] Quihueimen had been sentenced to two hundred lashings, and it is likely he received even more physical abuse during his time in prison, considering the length of his sentence and the conditions of life at the presidios. In the process of his arrest itself, he was undoubtedly dragged along with the other convicts in front of his community, their thumbs fastened with twine, as they were marched up to San Francisco. It is hard to imagine the intensity of the psychological and corporal punishment that he experienced, but however he managed, Quihueimen was the only convict to survive his full sentence.[109]

Rustico was born in 1811 and would have been about three years old when soldiers marched his father to San Francisco. Young Rustico would have been raised by the Indigenous community, as his mother Chesente died in 1815.[110] Father and son would have reunited after their long separation sometime in the 1820s. In 1828 Quihueimen married Ulalixmi (Coleta), a Yokuts woman, and the couple had a child.[111] Quihueimen continued to serve as padrino in his later years, after his return to Mission Santa Cruz.[112] Among the people for whom he served in this godparent role was Catarina, the daughter of Xuclan, the mission song leader.[113] Xuclan was born shortly before the assassination, the son of a Sumus couple who entered the mission about eight months before Yaquenonsat.[114] The devastation of the smallpox epidemic meant the loss of the generation of heroes—including Quihueimen and Asisara's father—who had protected the mission.[115]

It is clear that Quihueimen was able to reintegrate into his community after serving his sentence at the presidio. His involvement in the padrino system, a system of kinship and honor, suggests that he was still well connected. The psychological impact of the years of imprisonment and physical labor is impossible to gauge, but it is likely that Quihueimen internalized his pain and anger in order to survive. How might this have impacted his son Rustico? Did he conflate his father's absence with his mother's death a few years later? By the time his father returned, Rustico must have been over ten years old. How did he respond to his father's return, and how did Quihueimen manage to return to fatherhood after his absence? Incidents in the 1840s suggest that Rustico dealt with trauma handed down from his father.

At some point in the 1840s, Rustico owned a home in the Potrero del Carmen area, close to the property of Lino's daughter, Petra Nicanor.[116] Rustico eventually married a Huocom Yokuts woman, Nonorochi (Maria Alvina), and the couple had four children.[117] In 1842 Rustico was arrested for pulling a knife on Nonorochi.[118] Rustico clearly had issues with anger and violence that he directed toward his family and loved ones. It is worthwhile to ponder the role played by Rustico's upbringing, his awareness of his father's punishments, and the influence that his father had upon his return. Quihueimen had managed to survive years of imprisonment and subjection to physical and psychological abuse. Clearly, some of this violence left its mark. Was Rustico modeling what he had learned from his father? Although it is impossible to identify psychological experiences and traumas in the historical records, these signs point to the inherited traumas and pains suffered by Rustico and undoubtedly by other mission survivors as well.

One of the most common ways for survivors of traumatic events to numb and self-medicate is through the abuse of alcohol. Records from these times that point toward alcohol usage among the Indigenous community highlight the frequency with which this community likely suffered from what we would now consider to be post-traumatic stress. The padres had long tried to control Indigenous access to alcohol, frequently attempting to prohibit baptized Native peoples from visiting Villa de Branciforte for fear they would drink and gamble. By the 1840s the growth of local distilleries coincided with ongoing complaints about Indians and drinking. Rustico was specifically mentioned, along with Lorenzo Asisara, in a story by a local padre. Padre Adam recalled Rustico, Lorenzo, and another unnamed musician drinking to excess and needing to be restrained to perform their musical duties.[119] Did Rustico drink to numb his own traumatic experiences, like so many others? How might others in the community have used alcohol or other vices to deal with colonial traumas and abuses?

A story from Maria Ascención Solórsano sheds light on the ubiquitous presence of alcohol in the missions. Note the reference to vineyards and stills within the mission culture, as the missionaries introduced alcohol and the means of producing wine and spirits:

The Drinking Horns

Many years ago they had drinking horns here. They were horns that were used for drinking liquor and or water, very well decorated, and they did not break when they fell on the floor. There was a machine at the Mission for making liquor. The kind that is called a still. As soon as they established the Mission they planted vineyards and began to make wine and brandy. The Indians were very heavy drinkers from the time that the mission was started and they drank it where ever they could get it. They drank much all the time and worse after the Americans arrived and there began to be much more whisky. There were many deaths and fights in the drinking bouts and they killed many people. The Indians of San Juan were bad enough but those of Carmel were worse and much more so when they got to drinking. We did not like to see the Carmel Indians come to San Juan fiestas, because they only came to get drunk at San Juan and to get into trouble with the Carmel and San Juan women.[120]

We are left only with occasional anecdotes about drunken Indians but should be asking how the survivors learned to cope with the traumas of colonial violence.[121] Evidence suggests that they did so through both ceremony and alcohol. Asisara's recollection of this time reveals his sense of loss: "The smallpox epidemic came and finished off the Indians. Not finding anything else to appropriate, Bolcoff took to his ranch the adobes, bricks, roof tile, timbers, and old beams also belonging to the mission. That is how the belongings to the mission came to vanish. The lands had been distributed to the Indians; those who survived sold their properties for liquor; those who died abandoned their lots and others took possession of them."[122]

Despite Asisara's portrait of staggering loss, it does not tell the whole story. Surviving Indigenous people looked to more than just alcohol for relief. The persistence of traditional song, dance, ceremonies such as the Kuksui, and the use of sweat lodges also attests to the various ways that people looked for comfort and healing. The continued use of Indigenous languages and stories handed down about histories and landscapes affirms the importance of community and the sharing of stories. Yes, these were clearly traumatic times of great loss, but survivors persevered and continued to build community the best that they could.

Asisara: Geographic Mobility

Returning to the story of Asisara, sometime in 1841, a few years after the burial of his father, Asisara and his wife, Maria Tomasa, moved up to San Francisco.[123] By 1845 Asisara was widowed.[124] In 1845 he served as part of the barefoot, unarmed Native American troops formed under the oversight of General Vallejo.[125] He later recalled witnessing U.S. soldiers arrive amid the tensions of the Bear Flag Revolt, which lasted from June to July 1846.[126] His participation with the army during these years helped build status within the Mexican community. In the 1870s American historian Hubert Bancroft sent his bilingual assistant, Thomas Savage, throughout California to interview Californios. During Savage's stop in Watsonville to visit the Californio soldier José María Amador, Amador invited his friend Asisara to share his stories. Asisara provided two interviews to Savage, relating stories about his father's involvement with the Quintana assassination, along with other stories of survival and struggle within Mission Santa Cruz. Asisara's involvement with the Mexican military played a large role in his relationship with the retired soldier Amador. Asisara eventually moved between Monterey, Santa Cruz, San José, and San Francisco, before returning to Santa Cruz by 1845.[127]

After his return to the area, Asisara lived on the Westside with Chugiut and his friend Xuclan but also continued to associate with the local Californios living across the river at the Villa de Branciforte. Local newspapers reported many years later that Asisara was involved in the story of the wife murderer Pedro Gomez in 1847. Gomez had killed his pregnant wife, Barbara, whom he suspected of having an affair. The heavily stylized article recalled that "Lorenzo, the Indian violinist, the choir master, the chanter of Latin hymns, the scholar, the teacher and the lover of little Barbara, shut his sinewy fingers into the strings of his violin and tore them asunder ever as the strings of his heart were torn."[128] Gomez was sentenced to die by firing squad, but Asisara killed him with a knife while he awaited his sentence.[129]

Asisara's complex life reveals much about the social and geographic mobility that some were able to achieve during the Mexican era. While his story is the most visible, largely because of the important and extremely rare interviews he gave later in his life, it is clear that some Indigenous youth explored the greater region in the hopes of finding new labor opportunities. At the same time, Asisara's close ties with numerous members of the Californio community suggest some degree of lessening of the social and racial hierarchies of the Hispanic colonial world. But what about families that stayed in the area following emancipation? The life of Chugiut, the most visible in the Westside community of the Rancheria de los Fuentes, demonstrates the possibilities of the time, as newly emancipated Indigenous people began to form an Indian pueblo, with multiple economic and social ties to the larger Californio society.

Chugiut, Barbara, and the Lands of the Springs

On a September morning in 1839, a group of seventy-one Indigenous people gathered to meet with William E. P. Hartnell, general inspector of the Alta California missions. According to the 1839 census, there were actually 121 Native people living near the mission, so Hartnell's group must only have met with representatives of the total community (see table 27). Hartnell reported:

> The Indians ask for their freedom and that the cattle, horses, etc. be apportioned to them. They do not like the Administrator; they are afraid of him. They do not want the orchard taken from them or their houses or the place del Refugio which it is said was given to Juan Jose Felis. There is a house roofed with the tile belonging to the Mission; they need the area from the Mission to the Arroyo del Matadero, adjacent to the Russian, for their plantings and livestock. Geronimo especially wants his freedom because of his old age. Jose Antonio Rodrigues is trying to administer the Mission and says that with the looms and orchard there is enough to maintain it. The Father also wants the orchard.[130]

The sixty-year-old Sayanta man known as Geronimo Miguel Pacheco Chugiut finally got his wish, although not all of the Indigenous community's demands were met.[131] The administrator Bolcoff and his family ended up with the Rancho Refugio (contemporary Wilder Ranch) and the Arroyo del Matadero. By November 1839 Chugiut received lands that he had previously tended, former Mission Santa Cruz grazing and agricultural lands on Santa Cruz's Westside.[132] He lived on these lands through most of the 1840s, becoming an integral part of the local economy, selling fruits and vegetables to local Californios. In choosing these rich lands of the Westside, Chugiut also gained control over the rock quarry and one of the local springs.[133] Chugiut and his family lived in a style that relied on Indigenous practices and incorporated elements of Spanish and Catholic customs.[134] They continued to speak a mix of Spanish and the Awaswas language, migrate seasonally, utilize traditional foods, practice their own dances, use their sweat lodges, and hold ceremonies.[135]

Chugiut lived on the Westside with his Cajastaca (Aptos) wife, Barbara, their immediate family, and extended kinship network.[136] Between 1819 and 1840 the couple had ten children.[137] Only three survived into adulthood: Cecilia, Acursio, and Luis de los Reyes. By the mid-1840s their two adult children, Cecilia and Acursio, and their families lived with Chugiut and Barbara.[138] Cecilia had married Gabriel, who was likely a Coast Miwok who had moved into the region sometime before 1840.[139] They all lived on the Westside, where they rotated seasonally between two homes. In the summer months they lived on the lower part of the bluff, where they planted their summer crops. In the winter they moved above the bluff by the small lake known these days as Westlake and planted their winter crops. Local Californio Roman Rodriguez testified: "When I first knew [Chugiut] he was one of the mission Indians living in the mission. After the secularization of the missions he then went to live near the corner of Majors Mill where there is a pear tree. Then he went to live above. When he sowed summer crops he lived at the place below but most of the time he was living above near the Laguna."[140]

Indigenous women during this period were not permitted even the limited rights that Native men enjoyed at this time. Mexican patriarchal practices, which Indigenous men and women had been exposed to since initial Spanish settlement, further cemented sexual hierarchies in these decades. Women were not permitted to vote or to petition for emancipation; instead, men had to petition on their behalf.[141] Few records remain to give a sense of the life of Barbara or their children, as all of the records, written or remembered by men, focus on Chugiut as head of the household.

The family raised and sold melons, onions, squash, tomatoes, potatoes, corn, mutton (sheep), eggs, and chicken.[142] When Chugiut did not have the produce that the Californios had come to buy, he, Barbara, or Cecilia would act as go-between and sell the produce of their Indigenous neighbors.[143] Chugiut had long worked these lands while living at the mission, and when finally emancipated, he continued to live on them.[144] His family's seasonal movement, which followed the crop cycle, echoed long-standing Indigenous practices, in which local tribal members followed resource availability. In addition to their crops, they continued to supplement their yields with traditional foods. Acorn grinding stones were later used to identify the old homestead, revealing the persistence of acorn grinding, so central to traditional practices.[145]

Chugiut was well respected by Californios and Indians alike. When asked in later years by U.S. court interviews if Chugiut had been a chief, Californio Roman Rodriguez responded: "He was an Indian like the rest of them—a mason by occupation and in the service of the mission. He was not a captain of the other Indians, or anything of that kind. He was esteemed by the other Indians and they worked for him for that reason." He was seen as a reliable businessman, someone to buy food from, and trustworthy.[146] Yet he lived and worked closely with his family, which included his Sayanta kin, Huallas (David), the Tomoi man Siboo (Canuto), Lorenzo Asisara, and in later years the Chipuctac man Yrachis (Justiniano Roxas).[147] Huallas served many functions within the mission's political structure for years, taking roles as early as 1811 and into the 1830s.[148] When Don Jose Bolcoff was asked, "Who was the head businessman and the most prominent one among the Indians?" he responded: "David [Huallas], Geronimo [Chugiut], and Lorenzo. . . . David was first and then Geronimo." Huallas died during the 1838 smallpox epidemic.[149]

The lands that Chugiut and his people lived on were rich in resources and included one of the three springs that flowed along the Westside as well as a rock quarry known then as the Calero.[150] Chugiut and his people came from local tribal nations, people who had intimate knowledge of these lands going back generations. His deep local knowledge may have informed his selection of these resource-rich lands. The Potrero lands of the Yokuts did have access to the mission orchards but did not include access to the rock quarry or springs. Members of the Californio community would purchase rock and lime from Chugiut's rock quarry on the upper bluff.[151] With his training in masonry, Chugiut would have been familiar with the rock quarry and known its potential use for building.[152] Picking these fertile lands, Chugiut also had access to the fresh water from the springs, as he frequently lived alongside the small lake made from one of the springs. In fact, he was known to have sold leeches from his pond to community members.[153]

While gaining control of important resources, Chugiut was also known for sharing and remembered for his generosity and kindness. French immigrant Joseph Frey arrived in Santa Cruz in 1847. He had worked as a blacksmith back home but sought a piece of land that he could cultivate. After his arrival, Frey farmed down on the Potrero with the permission of the Yokuts community. While working one day, Frey met Chugiut and shared with him that he would like to have another piece of land so he could plant a few potatoes. He later recalled that Chugiut offered him a piece of land up in his fields.[154] Frey reported that Chugiut told him: "Here is my land. You can have it just so long as you please and if you want to pay me something for the rent it is alright. And if you don't it is just the same."[155]

While Chugiut and his family expanded their landholdings and quickly integrated economically and socially with the Californio community, a closer examination of land transactions during the 1830s and 1840s reveals limitations on the extent of Indigenous landholding.[156] Records exist for the titles of a handful of Indigenous land recipients, including Xuclan, the song leader, and a Jotoime (Matias).[157] Records indicate that a "Geronimo Miguel Pacheco" (Chugiut) received title for his lands on November 27, 1839.[158] On the same day a similar title was given to the Tomoi man Siboo (Canuto)—the same man who had run away with Yaquenonsat in 1809 as a young boy—who was tied through kinship to Chugiut and his family.[159]

On the same page as these transfers is a record of a transfer of title from "Geronimo" to Joseph L. Majors dated April 4, 1843.[160] It appears that within a mere four years of receiving the lands, actual title was no longer held by Chugiut and his people. They continued to live on these lands regardless of title, and years later Majors claimed that he had bought up the titles to protect the Indians from being exploited by others. While it is tempting to dismiss Majors's comments for their paternal attitude, the records do show that Majors and his wife, Maria de los Angeles Castro, continued to provide homes for members of Chugiut's kin until the 1890s.[161]

Meanwhile, the Yokuts down at the Potrero held their lands collectively. These were lands that had been cultivated after the founding of Mission Santa Cruz, along the San Pedro Regalado River. Ownership of the Potrero lands is documented through their sale. The group of Yokuts men sold their lands to Thomas J. Farnham for two hundred dollars, a transaction that was overseen by Joseph L. Majors in 1847.[162] This document was signed by a group of Yokuts men, including Coleto Malimin's two surviving sons, Chulnoquis (Pasqual) and Punis (Bernardino), as well as Punis's stepson, Angel. The Potrero title is signed to a group that included "Bernardino Coleto, Pascual Coleto, Angel Coleto, Mariano Bassillo, Pedro Viejo, Fidel Viejo, Carlos Fidel, Andres Viejo, Alarahio Viejo—Indians of the Mission of Santa Cruz in Alta California, who according to law in such case made and provided are now the owners of the following described premises and free men and citizens by the law in such cases governing for and in consideration of the sum of two hundred dollars lawful money, the receipt whereof is hereby acknowledged. Do hereby sell and convey in full ownership the following described lands to whit The Potrero lying north of the church of the mission aforesaid."[163] Notice that Coleto Malimin's sons and grandson use their patriarch's Spanish name as their surname in this document, while others use the Spanish word *viejo* (old). Carlos similarly used his father's Spanish name, Fidel, as his surname. Despite the official sale, the Yokuts community continued to live on the Potrero lands, albeit a much smaller portion of them, well into the period of United States rule.

Despite the distinct kinship ties and ethnic differences that separated the communities that formed after the closing of the mission, at times members of these distinct communities found ways to support each other. Chugiut appears to have helped the Yokuts in fighting for their rights and lands. In 1844 the Californio Jose Arana petitioned for and received some of the Yokuts's Potrero lands without their permission.[164] In 1847 three Indigenous men petitioned the incoming United States officials to get their land back because their previous claims to Governor Micheltorena had been "put in the oven," presumably on the back burner.[165] The three men included Coleto Malimin's son Punis (Bernardino), Carlos Roun (likely the same "Carlos Fidel" from the previous title), and "Geronimo Real Pacheco."[166] By this time Chugiut and his kin were known to be living up on the Westside, not on the Potrero with Punis and Carlos. Did Chugiut attempt to use his clout and standing within the Californio community to help the Yokuts fight for their lands? In later interviews Arana defended Chugiut's character, saying that he was "honorable, not a common man, not a drunkard, a good man," someone whom Arana would trust with his children.[167] Did Chugiut join the complaint to lend his weight to their cause? The letter stated:

> We, Bernardeno Farias, Carlos Roun, Geronimo Pacheco Real, present ourselves before you as the principal authority of this jurisdiction of Santa Cruz of the Government of the United States. First, in the year 1834 the missions were secularized by the previous Mexican government and land was apportioned to us, a certain plot for cultivation to each person. In the year [18]44 Sr. Jose Arana took our land away from us without our knowing by whose order. We made some claims to the Mexican Government which was Sr. Micheltorena who put our petitions in the oven. We therefore beg you to bring this to the attention of the present Government of the United States so that Sr. Arana returns to us our lands which we need for our sustenance. Since our fathers worked for this land, the only gift left to us, we therefore humbly beg that you heed our petition and return to us the land that belongs to us, whereby we will receive mercy and grace.[168]

By the end of the 1840s, most of the landholding Indigenous people of the region had sold or lost their lands.[169] The exact conditions of these sales are not known, but the quick turnover shows how rapidly the promise of Indigenous land ownership passed. Xuclan retained title to his home, but it appears that everyone else had sold their lands or otherwise never received official title. Despite the legal dispossession, many surviving members of these Indigenous communities remained in the region, finding ways to live on former mission lands, often by working in the homes or fields of other colonists.

Chugiut is said to have died sometime around 1850, but there is no burial record for him at the mission. Instead, there is a note requesting reimbursement from the county "Indian fund, to J. L. Majors, for digging grave for Indian Geronimo (deceased) for $3; for making $6 (cut to $4), $7 paid, P. Tracy, clerk."[170] Did Chugiut make an intentional choice to be buried on his own lands, instead of within the mission cemetery? His wife, Barbara, also does not appear in the mission burial records, though other records show that she died a few years earlier than Chugiut.[171] Perhaps this is a statement of discontent by Chugiut and Barbara regarding the Catholicism offered at the mission, or it could reflect a desire to receive a traditional Indigenous burial. While many continued to receive a Catholic burial, recorded in church documents, the absence of notable community members Chugiut and Barbara strongly suggests that they chose to be buried outside of the church's oversight.

The 1830s and 1840s were yet another period of rapid change. After years of imposed ties to Mission Santa Cruz, Indigenous families finally experienced emancipation from the limits of their bondage to the mission. After its closing, three distinct Indigenous communities formed around the mission. Some left to work on Californio ranchos, while others moved into the area through marriage or for rancho work. Life for those on the rancho was carefully overseen by the Californios, and movement in general was subject to permissions and restriction by Californio officials. Some left the region to return to ancestral lands, though some among them came back to steal horses from local ranchos, likely drawing on regional familiarity and local ties formed during the mission days. A select few of the younger generation, such as Lorenzo Asisara, explored the greater region.

Chugiut's story best exemplifies the promise of social and economic integration with the Californio community. His success offers a glimpse of the possibilities during the Mexican national era. Yet despite his relative success, these gains were always held in check by remnants of the colonial racial and social laws that had established notions of second-class status.

During the 1840s large numbers of Europeans and U.S. immigrants began to distinguish themselves from the local Californio and Indigenous communities. The demographic shift of the 1840s, the first decade that the Native American population became a minority in the region, resulted in growing power and influence for the incoming immigrants. Locals such as Isaac Graham and his friends in Zayante became involved in California politics, helping to undermine Mexican authorities while building momentum for the eventual U.S. occupation.[172]

In 1848, after years of tensions between the incoming immigrants and Mexicans, the whole of the Southwest was turned over to the United States through the Treaty of Guadalupe Hidalgo. Despite the lack of a formal treaty or title to the large region that constitutes contemporary California, the Mexican government "gave" these lands to the United States. The consequences for local Indigenous families were immense, as new racial and political policies targeted Indians. The promises of the 1830s and 1840s quickly faded as new challenges and waves of violence arrived with the era of U.S. occupation.

6

Genocide and American Fantasies of Ancient Indians

In December 1873 a reporter from the *Santa Cruz Sentinel* came to visit and record the story of a man known in town as Justiniano Roxas. After surviving a fire that burned his small cabin and nearly suffocating from smoke inhalation, the elderly man had recently been placed in the county hospital on Mission Hill under the care of the local organization known as the Sisters of Charity, who managed the hospital.[1] The newspaper reporter wrote down the man's name and misidentified him as a similarly named man in the Mission Santa Cruz baptismal records, whose advanced age would have meant that this Roxas was 121 years of age. The reporter was apparently unaware that baptismal names were frequently reused and given to new generations in incoming Indigenous baptisms. In reality the man known as Roxas was named Yrachis and had been baptized at the mission in 1796 as an eight-year-old child from the Chipuctac village. The reporter failed to identify his Roxas and instead embellished his story with a fantasy about ancient Indians, romanticized notions of Roxas as the "last of his kind," setting in motion a series of events that posthumously gained Roxas international notice while evoking the ubiquitous extinction trope identified by historian Jean O'Brien.[2] And yet the true story of Yrachis is much more incredible than the fantasy of centenarian Indians that the journalist's imagination spawned.[3]

Before his death, in 1875, Yrachis had survived through an increasingly hostile time, well into the period of United States rule, when being Indigenous meant potentially being targeted by U.S. authorities for extermination.[4] Yrachis grew up at Mission Santa Cruz and witnessed the loss of family members, extended family and kin, and the vast majority of Indigenous people baptized at the mission. He survived the years following secularization, during the Mexican national period, when surviving community members were often compelled into labor at neighboring ranchos. Instead, Yrachis made a home on the Westside of town, on lands near Chuguit and his family. He survived into the period of U.S. rule, characterized by scalp bounties, frequent campaigns of military and militia raids into Indigenous villages, and the capture of Indigenous children for indenture into colonial households.[5] On top of all this, his actual story of struggle and perseverance was lost to the romanticized celebration of a mythical past.

Despite the short period of limited rights, mobility, and land ownership during the Mexican national years (approximately 1834–48), the surviving Native community found this brief window closing quickly as newly imposed racial, legal, and political structures pushed Indians to the margins of society. While the gold mines in the interior of California became the stage for genocidal military campaigns, militias, warfare, and the kidnapping of Indigenous children, Native families living within established Mexican settlements, speaking Spanish, and wearing Mexican-style clothes faced their own versions of this statewide campaign of anti-Indian violence.[6] Indigenous survivors in Santa Cruz developed strategies of racial passing, relocation, labor, and at times outright resistance, as seen in the fires of Tahoe and Cache.[7] At the same time, Californian newspapers celebrated stories embracing the vanishing remnants of the local Indigenous inhabitants, helping justify homesteading and land grabs.[8]

The surviving Indigenous community faced a dire situation in the years following American annexation and occupation in 1848. In these genocidal years Indigenous politics necessitated a politics of survival. Incoming European and United States immigrants targeted Mexicans and Indians alike through lynching, dispossession, and violent intimidation. Indigenous people survived state-sponsored violence and displacement by drawing on and seeking out connections and kinship ties with other Indigenous communities while relying on traditional practices to help facilitate their survival.

California Gold and Genocide

Santa Cruz became a site for relocating Indigenous Californians from throughout the state, who, upon arrival, formed new kinship ties with local survivors. Meanwhile, some members of the local Indigenous community sought larger groups of survivors in neighboring areas such as San Juan Bautista and Watsonville. Others found work on local ranches and in households, limited labor opportunities that frequently resulted in dividing families.[9] As historian Madley has explained there were many different types of servitude that impacted Native people during these years, including debt peonage, chattel slavery, and wage labor.[10] In spite of tremendous challenges as well as popular American narratives that celebrated the impending disappearance of the local Indigenous community, the survivors of the mission and their descendants continued to persevere.[11] Somewhere between one hundred and three hundred Native peoples lived in the area up through the 1880s. Immigration to California following the discovery of gold in the Sacramento region in 1848 resulted in a huge population boom. Existing Indigenous and Californio communities quickly became overwhelmed by incoming foreigners. While Indigenous people had become outnumbered in Santa Cruz for the first time in the 1840s, from the 1850s onward they formed only a small minority of the rapidly growing population (see table 29).

In many early census reports, Indigenous presence was severely undercounted. This was from a mix of misperceptions, ideas about citizenship, and poorly managed record taking. The accuracy of the 1850 census in California was so questionable that the state conducted its own census again in 1852. In Santa Cruz the 1850 census reported no people identified as Indians.[12] The 1852 census listed 110 Indians out of a total population of 1,219.[13] The 1860 census listed 218 Indians out of a total population of 4,944.[14] And then in 1870 the number of Indians fell to merely 2 out of total of 8,743 people in Santa Cruz County (see table 29).[15] These discrepancies and inconsistencies are more a reflection of the attitudes of the enumerators than Indigenous movement in and out of the region. For example, John J. Boyle of Watsonville, enumerator of the 1860 census, claimed in the *Santa Cruz Evening News* that "before I finished my count, I received instructions that Indians who are not taxed should not be enumerated. Consequently, there were a greater number of Indians I could not enumerate."[16] Despite the shortcomings of unreliable U.S. census numbers, census documents show that this community persevered through this period.

U.S. occupation of California resulted from the end of the U.S. Mexican War of 1848. The Treaty of Guadalupe Hidalgo ended the war, ceding the southwestern states while negotiating the preservation of rights and lands for those choosing to remain living on them. This meant that all Mexican citizens of California had legal and citizenship rights.[17] But questions remained regarding the limitations and qualifications of citizenship. U.S. politicians began to institute laws aimed to deal with the "Indian problem."[18] Newly arriving immigrants could see that Indigenous labor supported an economic system built on cattle, grains, and grapes, which was predominately unpaid labor.[19] U.S. officials sought to maintain systems of Indigenous servitude while avoiding language that embraced slavery, an issue that was gripping the nation at this time.

The political transition of California from a Mexican state to an American state meant changing status for Indigenous Californians. Along with the huge influx of foreigners following the discovery of gold, the switch to political and legal control by the United States resulted in new racial and identity conceptions and definitions. The Mexican national system, while officially outlawing the Spanish colonial *sistema de castas*, retained legacies of this complex and plural system of racial categorization. U.S. courts relied on a much less nuanced racial binary built around skin color, in which the ever-shifting category of whiteness stood in contrast with the "other"—predominantly Blackness or "Indianness."[20] The diversity within existing Mexican Californian communities meant that some Mexican citizens, specifically those considered to have one-half Indian blood or more, could be denied certain rights. The legal and racial category of Indian broadened in these years to exclude a larger number of people from rights of representation and citizenship.

From 1846 until eventual statehood in 1850, California was ruled by U.S. military leadership, an interim system of martial law. New decrees bound Indians to work, defining vagrancy laws that punished any Indian found "wandering" or "idle" by making him or her subject to arrest and punishment.[21] Additionally, U.S. army lieutenant Henry W. Halleck became the secretary of state under martial law, and he implemented a statewide Indian pass system, which criminalized all Indians not employed by non-Indians or even those employed who had left their employers without written permission.²² The transition to civilian control called for the formation of a state constitution.

By 1849 U.S. officials began putting together plans for the political transition of California into statehood. President Zachary Taylor sent his agent Thomas Butler King with instructions to apply for statehood as soon as possible. Officials made plans for a constitutional convention in Monterey to discuss things, including the rights of Indians. U.S. officials wanted to maintain compliance with the provisions of the Treaty of Guadalupe Hidalgo and feared that they risked statehood if they did not guarantee rights to the Californios. Two conventions eventually took place. The first one resulted in a very close vote on the rights of Indians. One vote prevented the recognition of full citizenship for Indians. A second debate was called a few months later to further discuss these issues.

A few Californio elites, along with a number of foreigners, took part in this second constitutional convention. Several participants had ties to Santa Cruz, including the Frenchman Pierre Sansevaine and Thomas Larkin.²³

Of the forty-eight delegates, eight were Californio, and another six included foreigners who had lived in California for ten years or more. Representatives from the United States included Larkin, Johann Sutter, John C. Frémont, and William Tecumseh Sherman. The Californio members included prominent figures such as Mariano Guadalupe Vallejo and Pablo de la Guerra y Noriega, eldest son of the legendary José de la Guerra y Noriega.²⁴ These two were the only Californio members who spoke some English and, unsurprisingly, were the two Californios who spoke up the most. Pablo de la Guerra served as representative of Santa Barbara, accepting an invitation from Manuel Jimeno of Monterey. The de la Guerra family had earlier resisted acknowledging the rule of the United States, but through their participation they hoped to preserve some of their own political powers.

At this second convention the delegates debated issues including slavery and citizenship. The question of voting rights and Indian enfranchisement was discussed in depth, an issue that threatened to derail the push for statehood. Members of the Californio community were asked to comment and answer questions regarding citizenship, status, and race. The Californio members of the meeting were called upon to speak for the state of "Indian affairs" at this point and drew on their experiences in colonial California, and members like de la Guerra fought hard to include a degree of Indian enfranchisement.[25]

De la Guerra spoke out on this issue, asking to clarify "whiteness." Here the colonial legacies of the more nuanced Spanish racial system came into conflict with U.S. racial binaries. U.S. legal systems rested on excluding Indians and Africans from citizenship. Meanwhile, following independence, the Mexican nation had abolished race-based exclusion in an effort to challenge Spanish colonial *casta* restrictions. De la Guerra responded to the question of whiteness by noting that "many citizens of California have received from nature a very dark skin; nevertheless, there are among them men who have heretofore been allowed to vote, and not only that, but to fill the highest public offices. It would be very unjust to deprive them of the privileges of citizens merely because nature had not made them white."[26] De la Guerra continued to push back, arguing that Indians had rights to vote under existing Mexican law and that the Treaty of Guadalupe Hidalgo guaranteed these rights to continue for all Mexicans, including Indians.

The conflict resulted from distinctions between Californio (Spanish/Mexican) and U.S. racial categories and histories. Mexican society had a much more complicated and nuanced understanding of race and heritage, in which Indigenous ancestry did not exclude one from citizenship or political power. For example, former Mexican governor of California Pío de Jesús Pico was himself of mixed Spanish, Indigenous, and African ancestry. The Californios understood Indigenous Californians as part of two groups—those who had been affiliated with the missions (and therefore Hispanicized through linguistic, cultural, and religious conversion) and those still living outside of colonial settlements.[27] These echoed the mission-era categories that classified them as either *neofitos* or *gentiles*.[28]

The U.S. did not define the racial and social category of Indian in the same way. They had their own preconceived notions formed through years of wars, treaties, and removal policies focused on Indigenous nations across the continent. A majority of the delegates recognized that they needed to guarantee rights for Mexican citizens but wanted to distinguish between former Mexican citizens, who would gain voting rights, and Indians, who would be disenfranchised.

Ultimately, the committee decided that the state constitution of 1848 would retain whiteness as a qualification for citizenship. They feared that incoming citizens would be outnumbered by the large majority of remaining Indigenous people throughout California. Following the decisions of the committee, new policies targeted tribal peoples for extermination. In 1851 and 1852 meetings between United States Indian agents and tribal representatives took place. At these meetings officials negotiated plans for eighteen treaties, but the U.S. senate refused to ratify them.[29] The treaties remained shelved for fifty years.[30] These unratified treaties were followed by policies that targeted Indian children for capture and forced indenture, vagrancy laws that targeted poor and unemployed Indians, scalp bounties, and funding to reimburse militias and military campaigns against Indigenous Californians.[31]

The society that emerged in the new state of California was one of outright genocide and terror for Indigenous Californians.[32] As reported by historian Benjamin Madley, California governors authorized at least twenty-four state militia expeditions between 1850 and 1861, killing 1,342 to 1,876 or more Indigenous Californians, while raising up to $1.5 million to fund these militia operations.[33] Between 1846 and 1873 a combination of "individuals, vigilantes, California state militiamen, and U.S. soldiers killed at least 9,492 to 16,094 California Indians, and probably many more," with the statewide Indigenous population dropping from an estimated 150,000 to around 30,000.[34]

For Indigenous survivors in Santa Cruz, experience with Spanish and Mexican language, clothing, and religious and cultural practices helped them hide within the Californio community or at least helped make the communities difficult for the typical Anglo immigrant to distinguish.

While the adobe structure of Mission Santa Cruz fell to an earthquake in 1857, remaining members of the mission community fought to protect their Potrero lands behind the mission from the hordes of incoming foreigners. Some families remained on these lands into the 1880s, while others moved to surrounding communities.

While Santa Cruz does not have any records or evidence of scalp bounties, local newspapers drew on the larger statewide environment and attitudes toward Indians as a source of satire.[35] In 1874 a notice ran in the *Santa Cruz Sentinel* that read "No More Bounty on Scalps: The Board of Supervisors having refused to levy any tax for scalps in this County, therefore no more bills will be audited or paid on this fund, and the Modocs can wear their long hair unmolested from henceforth and forever."³⁶ The notice referenced the Modoc War, which had ended in Northern California shortly before the publication of this notice.³⁷ The satirical attitude of the notice revealed the local Anglo-American perception that the so-called Indian problem found in Modoc territories farther north in California did not exist in Santa Cruz—as Santa Cruz did not have any "wild" long-haired Modocs. This perception helped to assuage potential feelings of guilt and to justify local land acquisitions.

A *Santa Cruz Sentinel* article from 1866, about seven years before the notice mentioning Modocs, suggested that some sympathy for the local Indigenous peoples did exist. The article began by discussing the arrest of two Indigenous men, Jose Maria and Alanjon, for assault and carrying concealed weapons. Note that the author addresses Indigenous use of alcohol as the focal point, without acknowledging the crucial context of multigenerational trauma and losses that this community dealt with. The article reveals some of the emphasis on extinction narratives and patronizing racial attitudes of the time but ultimately argues for the protection of the Potrero lands behind the mission:

> It may not be amiss, at this time, to allude at some little length to the history of these poor Indians, who have become almost extinct—owing to the vices that they contracted from their white neighbors, who have robbed them of their possessions. When the Santa Cruz Mission was established, the tribes of Indians at Aptos, Soquel and Santa Cruz numbered some three thousand. All are now scattered, or have passed away; their tribal character has become extinct—except about forty, who have their houses on the Potrero, within the limits of our Incorporation. These few keep up their tribal distinctions.
>
> Our Indians have not become extinct on account of losses in war, or pestilence, but the grasping avarice of the whites drove them from their lands and happy hunting grounds, and, disheartened, they roam unguided and without impulse through the land, and drop down and perish by the wayside, or become the victim of the white fiends who sell them the Indian's curse—whiskey. The firewater burns up their vitals as surely as the fire does the flax. Our few remaining Indians

live upon land granted by the Catholic clergyman to two Indian[s], for past service, and comprises a small tract on only twenty or thirty acres, one of whom still lives the other has passed to the "Indians hunting grounds." The two were kind-hearted, and their land was always the home of the whole tribe, and the few now on the Potrero, are there with their consent. But a few years ago a white man came here; he was a stranger, and envied the poor Indians their little home; came to them, said he was a stranger and poor, and wanted a little corner, whereupon to put a house. The Indians allowed him to put up a house, and let him use a garden-spot; he commenced encroaching upon his kind neighbors until he had surrounded quite a number of acres with a low and poor fence. After his death his representatives attempted to dispossess the Indians of nearly or quite all of the remainder, but through the humane exertions of some of our old citizens, they were prevented from executing their designs.

Would it not be well for the citizens of Santa Cruz to now determine that the Potrero, the land granted to two Indians, shall be forever set apart to those Indians and their children, and that no vandal shall ever despoil them of what the good priest gave them for services rendered? And would it not be well to take active measures to ascertain what white scoundrel sells or gives them strong drinks? Our laws are sufficient to punish the criminal.

The poor fellows are industrious, earn their own living, are a tax upon no person, and are quiet and inoffensive. Then, for humanity's sake, if not for the sake of law and justice, let us protect them in what is their right, and punish those who do them this great injury.[38]

The article attempts to offer historical context for the Indigenous community. It gestures toward a link between the persistence of historical trauma and susceptibility to alcoholism and fighting, though at the same time the patronizing language is overwhelming with stereotypes and racial tropes. The two men mentioned in the article as having received the Potrero were clearly the Yokuts men Huayiche (Fidel) and Chulnoquis (Pasqual).[39] It does appear that most of those who continued to live on the Potrero were Yokuts descendants, supporting the journalist's claims of keeping up tribal distinctions. But even this sympathetic call for protection of the

Potrero was ultimately part of an argument for more restrictive measures preventing Indians from access to liquor. Frequent court cases punished recently arrived immigrants for selling liquor to Indians.[40] Throughout these decades newspaper articles reported drunken Indians getting into trouble.[41] For the *Sentinel* editors the image of the hostile "savage Indian" became the image of the Modoc, while local Indigenous survivors fit a more patronizing pattern of the "poor, vanishing Indian," which allowed the settlers to see themselves as sympathetic and ease any potential guilt over ongoing land thefts.[42]

Other policies targeted Indian children for capture and servitude, under the guise of Indian indenture.[43] Indian indenture was eventually outlawed following the Civil War. In Santa Cruz, while no official documents record petitions for Indian indenture, the census shows that many families did indeed have Indigenous children as young as ten listed as servants.[44] When taking into account estimations that as many as one in every four households had Indian indentures along with the frequent omissions by census enumerators of indentures and wards from the census rolls, it is likely that many more households kept Indigenous servants than show up in the records.[45] This came at a time when other communities of color began to find work in white households, such as a small number of African Americans and the more numerous Chinese men. The Santa Cruz community in the era of United States rule was made up of a diversity of recently arrived immigrants, the majority composed of Germans, Italians, Portuguese (including fishing families from the Azores), and eastern-born U.S. citizens.

In this rapidly growing and diversifying community of settlers, Indigenous people were frequently left out of economic opportunities. In previous decades Indigenous horse and cattle thieves raided Mexican and Spanish livestock regularly. By the 1850s U.S. courts dealt with ongoing incidences of this kind of theft, which continued long-standing patterns of survival in the midst of shrinking opportunities. In 1866 an Indigenous man named Juan Antonio stole a horse and saddle from A. G. Wright, an immigrant from the East Coast. He rode the horse down to Watsonville and sold the horse for ten dollars and the saddle for five before his arrest.[46] He was sentenced to a year of hard labor in the San Quentin State Prison.[47] A year later two Indigenous men were arrested for stealing saddles, bridles, and lariats from a local stable.[48] Some locals found the pace of legal consequences unsatisfactory and resorted to taking the law into their own hands instead. Violence toward Indigenous people was ongoing. In 1877 a local Indigenous man, Carlos, was murdered at a saloon.[49]

Locally, a group of white vigilantes focused their anger on the local Californio community, including Mexican settlers and Indigenous people. Vigilante justice through lynching was common throughout the West, helping to foster an atmosphere of racial hostility aimed primarily at Latinos and Indigenous people. Watsonville resident Matt Tarpy and his group, the Pajaro Property Protective Society, played a central role in these vigilante movements.[50] The first documented lynching in Santa Cruz was in 1852. Sixteen more lynchings were documented in Santa Cruz County and neighboring townships between 1852 and 1877.[51] In addition to these extralegal vigilante killings, capital punishment was common. Newspaper articles often celebrated the hanging of Indians, as in the case of Jose Miguel of Mission Soledad.[52] Jose Miguel and another unnamed Indian had been arrested for the murder of Frank Williams, a Portuguese man living in Watsonville in December 1865.[53] Jose Miguel escaped from his cell while being held in San José, killing his jailor in the process.[54] The other unnamed Indian was hanged shortly after, while Jose Miguel evaded capture for a few months, before his apprehension in Los Angeles. His eventual hanging in Santa Cruz was a cause for local celebration.

The most infamous of these local public hangings is the lynching of Jose Chamales and Francisco Arias in 1877.[55] A photo of the two hanging on the downtown Water Street Bridge helped give visibility to this act.[56] The lynching of these two men has been much discussed, in large part because of this photograph, but this type of violence was common. In 1870 three Indigenous men, Valentine Varago and two brothers named Gremezes, were arrested for killing a man known as "Indian Bill" in Monterey County and put in jail in Watsonville. In the middle of the night the men were taken out of jail, gagged, and hanged from the bridge that ran over the Pajaro River.[57] It was a time of extreme violence, especially for darker-skinned community members. These hostilities extended to Californio civilians and important members of local society. The case of Macedonio and Romualda illustrates the effects of these shifting racial politics.

"Indian" as a Social Category of Exclusion

In 1851 a land trial in the new American courts highlighted the ways in which even members of the Californio community lost rights by falling into an increasingly restrictive racial category of Indian. This case involved a prominent family in the Villa de Branciforte community, early settlers of the region Macedonio Lorenzana and his wife, Maria Romualda (see figure 3). Young Lorenzana was ten years old in 1800, when he was one of the twenty orphans to make the voyage from Mexico City to Alta California.[58] Lorenzana, who had been identified as a mestizo on the ship rolls, was placed in the Pueblo of San José with Francisco Castro of the prominent Bay Area Castro family.[59] As an adult, he moved to the Villa de Branciforte. There he and his wife, herself the daughter of a Spanish soldier and a local Indigenous woman from Mission Santa Clara, raised their large family.[60] Lorenzana and his wife worked hard to provide for their large family yet due to their mixed-blood heritage, they were seen by newcomers as Indians—and thus could be excluded from certain rights.[61] Their story illustrates not only the downward trajectory of rights for those with Indigenous heritage in the new state but also a defiant stand taken by Lorenzana, as he defended his rights and, by implication, the rights of his wife and of others identified as Indian.

The Lorenzana family arrived at the Villa de Branciforte in the early years following Mexican independence. The court case in which Marciano was called upon to defend his role in drawing property lines involved issues of land ownership and grants from the Mexican era. Beginning in the 1830s, many local Californios petitioned for and received lands from the Mexican government. Politically prominent locals such as the Castro and the Rodriguez families received rancho plots of great acreage, whereas working-class members of the Villa de Branciforte, like Lorenzana, received smaller plots and shared communal pasturelands (*ejidos*) for their livestock. In Branciforte, Lorenzana worked as a manual laborer.[62] In the 1830s he began to fulfill roles of civil service for the growing Branciforte community, serving as regidor, or councilman, by 1838 and as second alcalde in 1841.[63] Lorenzana became known as a reputable and reliable member of the community.[64] After a fire consumed his home, he received a grant of land in the Villa de Branciforte in September 1841.[65] Eventually, his older children received lots, including his oldest son, Jose. Jose's home still stands as the lone adobe on old Villa de Branciforte lands and is known today as the Craig-Lorenzana Adobe.[66]

By the 1850s the influx of newly arrived immigrants looking for land targeted wealthy Californio families who held large ranchos.[67] They resorted to a variety of tactics, often in conjunction with new U.S. courts, to claim what they saw as unsettled lands, including squatting, homesteading laws, and legally mandated land cases. New legal regulations forced Californio landowners to defend their lands in U.S. courts.[68] These courts required translators, surveyors to confirm boundaries, and legal representatives, all of whom expected to be paid in land. The smaller landowners could not afford the legal costs to keep their lands, and newcomers claimed the common pasturelands.

The Mexican government taxed ranchers based on production, while the U.S. tax system was based on land, and with periods of floods and drought in the 1860s, this created huge problems for rancheros. After heavy flooding in 1861–62, California experienced one of its driest periods in recorded history in the drought of 1862–65. Unproductive ranchos were still required to pay taxes on their lands, which devastated a once thriving cattle industry, bankrupting many Californio ranchers.[69] Other rancho families lost lands to squatters, who used homesteading laws to occupy and claim portions of ranchos. In some cases families feuded over their lands, losing more lands in costly courtroom procedures.[70]

In the case of *Amesti v. Castro* (1874) two local Californio families fought over the boundary lines between their two ranchos. Macedonio Lorenzana played a role in this case—a role that would later affect his standing in the community. The dispute centered on the boundaries between two of the first rancho properties granted by Governor Luis Antonio Argüello following Mexican independence. Spanish-born Don José Amesti received Rancho Corralitos, while the locally born Jose Joaquin Castro received Rancho San Andrés. In the spring of 1846 Lorenzana, who was then serving as second alcalde, was called on to document the boundaries between the two ranchos. At the time, Jose Bolcoff, "El Ruso"—the Russian who had married into the Castro family—was serving as first alcalde.[71] Worried that this might be a conflict of interest, Bolcoff had instructed Lorenzana as second alcalde to oversee the mapping of the rancho lands. Amesti protested the boundary lines and was allowed to arbitrate before the alcalde of Monterey, Walter Colton. In May 1847 the Vermont-born former naval chaplain decided in favor of Amesti.[72]

After the death of Joaquin Castro, in 1850, his heirs sued Amesti. They claimed that the "extraordinary proceeding" of the arbitration hearing of 1847 had been fraudulent and fixed by Amesti's allies. Amesti lost the case and appealed the ruling, and the court proceedings lasted into the early 1870s. Ultimately, Amesti's wife, María Prudencia Vallejo de Amesti, won the court battle and was able to keep the lands.[73] The Castro heirs sold off much of the remaining Rancho San Andrés lands in 1873.[74]

During the hearing back in 1851, Lorenzana was called to testify, since he had signed and authorized the boundary lines in question. Under the new ironically named 1850 "Act for the Government and Protection of Indians," testimony given by anyone identified by the racial category Indian against a white defendant could be rejected by the judge and court.[75] Although Lorenzana had been classified as mestizo at his orphanage, the dark-skinned Lorenzana now identified himself as an Indian.[76] If Native Americans in Mexican and Spanish society were second-class citizens due to the legacies of the *casta* system, in U.S. society Indians had even less rights.[77] U.S. laws severely limited Native Americans from voting and representation in courts.[78] Lorenzana fell victim to these shifting racial politics.[79]

The judge inquired about Lorenzana's racial identity, and Peter Tracy, the county clerk, transcribed the court discussion:

> Macedonio Lorenzana being sworn duly says that he is of Indian descent, that he never knew his father and mother, that he has the right of holding property and voting in Mexico—was born in the City of Mexico. He cannot say how long he lived in Mexico. He came to this country when quite an infant. He came here by order of the government of Mexico—about six or seven years—to populate the land. He does not know the name of the person who brought him here. He came here one year before the year one—he lived in the Pueblo of San José about ten years working with Francisco Castro, deceased. Francisco Castro was uncle to the plaintiffs in this suit. He worked for Castro as a son. He belong[s] to the Kingdom of the Indians of Mexico and considers himself an Indian.

Cross examination:

Cannot tell about a subject so remote but believes he belongs to the tribe of the Monterunias [*sic*].[80] He knows his parents were Indians—he knows it because the Kingdom of Mexico is Indian—and by that he knows he is an Indian. Cannot give any other reason for believing that he is an Indian other than he came from an Indian Kingdom. He has held office under the Mexican Government nearly one year. He has but little recollection of the City of Mexico. . . .

The court decided the witness to be incompetent.[81]

U.S. justice was situated within assumptions about racial hierarchies and legal implications, and those belonging to the legal category of Indian did not possess the right to testify in court. U.S. law defined "Indian" as anyone with one-half Indian blood, meaning that Lorenzana's *mestizo* heritage would have left him clearly outside of the protections afforded to Mexican citizens like his Californio neighbors. Lorenzana argued that he had rights under Mexican law, the law that had ruled the land just a few years before this trial. When Lorenzana pointed out that he had full citizenship rights "in Mexico," he was not referring to the physical location of Mexico but instead to California, a part of Mexico only a few years earlier. He was asserting that he held full rights, including voting rights, in Mexican Santa Cruz in the years before U.S. statehood.

Lorenzana had been raised within Hispanic colonial society, in which racial identity signified status but did not necessarily exclude one from rights. This world encompassed both Indigenous communities and Spanish colonial towns. Branciforte was no exception, as the majority of people in the area before the 1850s had some degree of Native heritage. Lorenzana saw himself as a member of this diverse Indigenous society. Although he had long since left his childhood home in Mexico City, he proudly traced his heritage to the Aztecs of central Mexico.

Although it was not Lorenzana's own land and home at stake in this trial, his standing within the community was diminished. The orphan, citizen, family man, laborer, and former alcalde found himself excluded from the political process of the United States despite his years of hard work and community service. He found himself treated like an Indian despite his obvious connections to the Californio community. He never served in public office again. In February 1852 Lorenzana sold his lands to Peter Tracy, the same county clerk who had recorded his testimony.[82]

Macedonio Lorenzana died on January 29, 1863, a few months after a picture was taken of him alongside Jose Joaquin Juarez, his longtime neighbor and the husband of fellow orphan Pasquala Lorenzana (see figure 3).[83] Shortly after Macedonio's death, his son Faustino (known as "El Charole") began to have skirmishes with the law. Ironically, the younger generation of Californios, whose parents had been in frequent conflict with Native American horse and cattle raiders and bandits throughout the 1830s and 1840s, now found themselves resorting to similar tactics, after watching their parents lose their lands and rights.[84] This was especially true for dark-skinned Californios with clear Indigenous ancestry, like the Lorenzanas. Faustino ran alongside his cousin Tiburcio Vasquez and the local Robles and Rodriguez sons. As a response to these "bandits," vigilante mobs rounded up and harassed local Californio families.

In 1865 Ohio-born Santa Cruz resident Jack Sloan was shot and killed, the murder blamed on Macedonio's son Faustino. In response, a vigilante mob marched through town, arresting Macedonio's grandson Pedro, as well as Jose Rodriguez. Faustino escaped. The mob arrested other members of the local Californio community, including Faustino's brother, Mattias, and his wife, Concepción. It was this kind of indiscriminate rounding up some members of the Californio community that created an atmosphere of racially based violence.[85]

While the others were released after being held for nearly three months, Pedro was taken from jail by a mob and thrown into the bay with weights tied to his legs. In 1870 Faustino was eventually tracked down by a posse in Santa Barbara and shot more than a dozen times.[86] Macedonio's granddaughter, Josie, was arrested in connection with prostitution and involvement in running the local "house of ill fame" on Front Street in 1884.[87] Other members of the Lorenzana family similarly found themselves in trouble with the law throughout the latter decades of the nineteenth century.[88]

While Lorenzana did not survive to see his children's and grandchildren's struggles with the law, his wife, Maria Romualda, did. She lived until September 1884, though the Santa Cruz newspapers failed to recognize the rich history tying her to local Indigenous people.[89] At the time of her death, local papers clearly did not know her story; they referred to her only as Mrs. Lorenzana and mistakenly claimed that she was born in Santa Cruz and had lived to be 104 years old, the details of her life obscured in the romanticized *Santa Cruz Sentinel* account that fixated on imaginary centenarians.[90] Yet the article correctly linked her to her son Faustino, claiming that "one of her sons shot and killed 'Jack' Sloan at Arana Gulch about twenty years ago, and is well remembered by many."[91] The outlaw story, with its tales of the local bandidos, sold papers, while the struggles and perseverance of this hardworking family did not.[92]

In a brief period of time in a rapidly shifting cultural landscape, the Lorenzana family moved from a position of civic leadership to extreme marginalization. His Indigenous ancestry and that of his wife resulted in their family falling into the marginalized status of Indian. The U.S. courts nullified Lorenzana's right to testify, the family lost most of their lands, and his son and grandson had been brutally killed. Members of the local Californio community had once held great tracts of land and controlled local politics, but by the late nineteenth century they found themselves stripped of most of their land and power, now occupying the lower social rungs in a rapidly expanding state. Newly imposed racial categories had disenfranchised a complex society, no longer recognizing people's human or civil rights. The incoming society fractured the Californio community along racial lines, imposing restrictive categories of Indianness on dark-skinned Californios.

The Real Roxas: Yrachis's Story of Survival

The *Santa Cruz Sentinel* ran stories about "Old Times Roxas, the Oldest Inhabitant on the Earth."[93] Roxas received this attention in the local newspapers, helping promote a narrative of antiquity and disappearance. Father Adam had located the early entry in the Mission Santa Cruz baptismal book of a local Uypi man similarly baptized as "Justiniano Roxas."[94] Adam claimed that this was the same person, failing to discover the burial record of this early entry, and supported claims that Roxas was over 120 years old.[95] Father Adam commissioned local photographer Edward Payson Butler, proprietor of the Pioneer Gallery in downtown Santa Cruz, to take a photograph of Roxas, a copy of which was reportedly sent to the Vatican (see fig. 4).[96] Shortly thereafter, a second photograph was taken by John

Elijah Davis Baldwin, owner of the downtown Star Gallery (see figure 5). A portrait painted by a man named F. Holtzman from the Butler photo was eventually sent to the 1893 Chicago World's Fair (see figure 6).[97] This portrait now hangs in the Mission Santa Cruz chapel replica museum. The story of Yrachis's longevity, attributed to the California climate, spread farther after his death, on March 10, 1875, eventually reaching Australia. *Harper's Weekly* even ran a story on Roxas.[98] While journalists, priests, and other newcomers embraced the idea that Roxas represented the last of his race, the real story of Roxas is one of great loss.

The real Roxas was baptized at Mission Santa Cruz in January 1796 as an eight-year-old named Yrachis from the Chipuctac village site northeast of modern Gilroy.[99] He was one of thirty-three mostly infants and children from the Chipuctac villages baptized that day in a mass ceremony, including his five siblings and his parents, Tallup and Murejate.[100]

Although baptized into the community, Yrachis's family probably did not adapt easily to life at Mission Santa Cruz. Most of his family appears to have spent considerable time running away from the mission. Their burial records indicate that they died while far away from the mission.[101] Within a few years Yrachis's parents and all his siblings, except his brother Seynte, were dead. Did Yrachis and his brother choose to stay at the mission, or did they leave with their family, only to return after their other family members' deaths? Maybe they were captured and returned by Spanish soldiers. The details are unclear, but the temptation to stay with his family must have been strong. Perhaps Yrachis was emboldened to stay at the mission by the quick assimilation of Seynte, his older brother.

The story of Seynte reveals much about the experiences of that first generation of Indigenous children in the California missions. Four years older than Yrachis, he quickly became an integral figure within the mission community. By 1799 Seynte began serving as a frequent marriage witness.[102] The same year he married Samórim, a member of the local Achistaca tribe.[103] This marriage helped to build kinship with local members of the community and might have contributed to his quick integration into mission life. The couple had eight children together, but only two lived into adulthood.[104] Their daughter Antonia is mentioned in an earlier chapter; a suspicious note on her burial record from Padre Gil y Taboada suggests that she may have been a victim of sexual abuse at his hands.

Yrachis's life at the mission was marked by staggering loss. In 1804, at the age of sixteen, he married a young Tomoi woman named Quichuate, but she died just three years later, on April 1, 1807, without having any children.[105] Two years later Yrachis remarried, this time to a much older woman named Cosorom, probably from near his home village.[106] Nine months later almost to the day, the couple gave birth to a son, Benbenuto, but the boy did not live to see his second month, dying on September 20, 1810. Just ten weeks later, Cosorom also died.[107] Twice a widower, Yrachis married once again on July 21, 1811, this time to a recent convert from the Auxentaca village of Saipan, east of the Santa Cruz Mountains.[108] But five months later she died too.[109]

Yet despite the staggering losses that he experienced, Yrachis persevered by relying on and bonding with kinship relations. He lived on the Westside, not far from the family of Chugiut, with the family of the Achistaca Samectoi (Seferino Arce) and his wife, Gepeson (Maria de la Pieded Tapia), a fellow Ausaima member.[110] In the spring of 1837 Gepeson died of a respiratory illness. A few months later Samectoi died too, possibly of smallpox.[111] After their deaths, Yrachis appears to have moved in with another Ausaima family. By 1845 Yrachis was living with a fellow widower, the forty-year-old Huocom man Labarsec (Gabriel), and an Ausaima couple, the sixty-year-old Sipon (Alvino) and his twenty-six-year-old wife, Sergia.[112] In addition to the shared tribal connections between the Ausaima, Yrachis shared kinship directly with Sergia.[113] No burial records are to be found for Sipon and Sergia, but at some point in the mid-1850s it appears that Yrachis ended up living on his own on the Westside, the condition in which Father Adam and the local journalists found him in the early 1870s.[114]

Yrachis worked at a variety of occupations in these years. A *Santa Cruz Sentinel* article suggested that he had some connections with the New Almaden quicksilver mines.[115] Ohlone guides had first led Secundino Robles, a resident of the Villa de Branciforte, to the rich source of quicksilver and cinnabar in 1824.[116] It is possible that Yrachis was among those Indian guides. One oral history from the early twentieth century tells of his being compelled to work on the local ranchos: "He had been taken away from the Mission by Rodriguez to work for his board on his ranch where part of his duties were to raise Romey Rodriguez, but he always came home to the Mission and camped on Vista Point."[117] "Home" here meant on the lands of Chuguit, on the Westside near the mission.

Yrachis died on March 10, 1875, not long after gaining some recognition through the journalists and photographers, most likely from injuries suffered during his house fire.[118] At some point in the early twentieth century, Chester A. Wood and the Improved Order of Redmen, a nineteenth-century fraternal organization that embraced romanticized notions of Native Americans but only allowed white men to be members, placed a plaque marking Roxas's grave. Santa Cruz officials eventually named a street after him. In 1958 the Santa Cruz County Board of Supervisors—with the urging of local historian Margaret Koch but apparently without the support of local Indigenous communities—declared Roxas an honorary chief of the Costanoan tribe. And throughout the 1960s Italian American actor Malio Stagnaro performed the role of "Chief Roxas" in local plays and pageants in Santa Cruz.[119] His image and name became remembered in Santa Cruz, but the details of his life, his survival, and the many losses he experienced remained buried under the American fantasies of extinction. That Yrachis survived these trying times is a testament to his perseverance; how exactly he survived remains a mystery.

Genocide and U.S. Fantasies about Ancient Indians

How the Americans Waited until All Those Who Knew Anything Were Dead and Then Came All Eager to Make Records

It seems to me a very curious thing that if the scientists desired so much to know the San Juan language that they waited until all those that talked it best were dead and finished, and then came and just scribbled down a few words any old way.[120]

When first the Americans came to San Juan [Bautista] there were many Indians who had been born before the building of the mission. All the history of how they lived when they were still wild Gentiles could still have been obtained, and very easily, but they didn't do it.[121]

As local newswriters embellished the "vanishing Indian" narrative through the celebrations of "ancient" people like Yrachis, a handful of salvage ethnographers and interviewers were able to locate local Indigenous Ohlone and Yokuts survivors. In some ways both the ethnographers and the news writers bought into the same premise—that local Indians were few and dying out. They evoked what Madley has called the myth of inevitable extinction, a narrative that Californian journalists had begun employing in the 1840s.[122] This allowed them to lament a loss that they deemed inevitable while absolving them of any responsibility to step in and assist. While the ethnographers sought to preserve what they could, the news writers used the Native American story to justify land acquisition while lamenting the sad passing of a people. Neither worked to change the harsh conditions facing Native survivors. Ironically, while the ethnographers sought to preserve knowledge, language, and information regarding what they perceived as a vanishing people, the information they found confirms the persistence of Indigenous language and culture.

By the 1870s a number of ethnographers and linguists passed through the region, seeking out local Indians to consult. A couple of scholars, including John Wesley Powell, Alexander Taylor, and Henry Wetherbee Henshaw, sought out and collected information about California Indians. Powell led the charge as the director of the Bureau of Ethnology at the Smithsonian Institution. Taylor wrote a series of newspaper articles chronicling regional village site names and what information he could find, though it is not clear if he spent time locally. Henshaw did spend time in Santa Cruz collecting linguistic material from unnamed linguistic informants. He noted that two men, Lorenzo (almost certainly Asisara) from Santa Cruz and Felipe Gonzales of Watsonville, could speak the "Santa Cruz dialect," so it is likely that one of them was his informant.[123]

The other prominent ethnographer to pass through the area was the Frenchman Alphonse Pinart. Pinart traveled through California between June 24 and October 26, 1876. Along the way he sought out survivors of the missions, transcribing words and linguistic notes. He was in Santa Cruz between August 18 and 26. His notes include the most extensive list of Awaswas language that has been recorded as well as testimony to the continued use of the language. He stopped in Santa Cruz and interviewed local

Indians, including an interview with a woman, Eulogia, on August 23.[124] Later that day he appeared to review the words with Rustico from Aptos.[125]

Pinart recorded these notes during his travels to Santa Cruz:

> At about a quarter mile on the San Lorenzo road, is the "potrero": small piece of land where few Indians of Santa Cruz live. In groups of 6 to 7, they live in little wooden shacks, but I noticed that among them you can see cleanliness that is seldom found among the Indians as they are, for example, the old Eulogia, a woman of about 50 years old originally from Tulare. She has a flat face, a square nose, long nostrils and of yellowish brown skin, fairer than that of Indians of this part of the coast. The others: 3 bucks [*sic*] 2 women and a "criatura" present a mixed type. It's from the "Tulareño" that I get my vocabulary. I cannot know where she is from, however, she tells me that she speaks the language of the old Mariano, who died two years ago at the age of about 100 years old. According to the book of births of the mission, I can see that Mariano was from the Chaloctaca village, which to my understanding should be on the left bank of San Joaquin in the counties of Stanislaus or Merced. Eulogia told me that the language of Stanislaus is different from hers: she was born in Tulares, but was brought very young to the mission and does not remember her former years.

Pinart consulted the baptismal book to look up names in the case of Guimayach (Mariano), and just like the journalist, he found an earlier man with a similar name.[126] Pinart continued:

> 5 years ago, here died a man by the name of Justiniano Roxas, who was 123 years old. He was the last descendant of the tribe of the Branciforte or the Santa Cruz. Branciforte was the name of the pueblo established by the Spanish on the other side of the San Lorenzo. There is an Indian from Santa Clara called Santiago. He lives with his family on the other side of the San Lorenzo in a small shack and works at the tannery of San Lorenzo, but as soon as his work is done he is drunk and there is very little to obtain from him. I am told that he still speaks his dialect.
>
> Aptos on August 26—Left this morning from Santa Cruz—Soquel—the railroad follows the cliff on the mesa cañada of Aptos . . . Rustico,

Indian of Santa Cruz, small, robust, square shoulders, big head, all while in a shape of [illegible], short and pushed inward. His face flat, with very pronounced cheekbones and flat lips. Dark skin, like chocolate, he was once singer of the mission, and he remembers his language well. In the mission there are several Indians, but apart from Rustico, his child, from whom we cannot really get anything, there is also an Indian from San Luis Rey named Martin. Rustico claims that old Justiniano was native of Gilroy mission.[127]

Pinart's notes reflect and repeat some of the same mistakes made by ethnographers and journalists alike, by drawing on similar misperceptions about the local Indigenous population. He mirrors the mistake made by the reporter who spoke with Yrachis. Curiously, Pinart's account mentions another misconception—that "Justiniano was a native of the Gilroy mission." While there was no mission in Gilroy, the Chipuctac village was likely near Gilroy, so this note seems to help corroborate the identity of Roxas as Yrachis.

The salvage ethnographers looked for Indigenous survivors to provide information and vocabularies from local tribes while embracing narratives of their eminent disappearance. In contrast with those perspectives, one interviewer was able to record the thoughts of a local survivor. This being the interviews of Lorenzo Asisara conducted by Thomas Savage at the request of the historian Bancroft. Asisara's recollections emphasized both the traumas his community had endured and the ways in which they resisted and fought back, shedding light on a much more nuanced sense of history and Indigenous politics than that recorded by the salvage ethnographers.

In some cases, even while Anglo newspapers such as the *Santa Cruz Sentinel* reported the names of certain individual Indians, their larger stories and histories remained erased from official view. In September 1857, for example, the *Sentinel* reported a "Remarkable Case of Longevity": "An Indian by the name of Pedro died in this place on last Monday, who, it is supposed, had attained the remarkable age of one hundred and thirty years."[128] Despite the ongoing fascination with the ages of local Indians, this article obscures what was likely a much more fascinating story.

The simply named "Pedro the Indian" of this obituary was actually Suulu, the Indigenous chief of the Huocom. The Huocom were a San Joaquin Valley Yokuts tribe that had entered Mission Santa Cruz in large numbers around 1820.

Suulu and his wife, Atamay, arrived in November 1820, along with large numbers of their fellow Huocom.[129] Their two sons, Najaruy and Choótg, arrived with the first wave of Huocom some seven months before their parents.[130]

Like so many others in the mission world, Suulu saw many of his family members die before emancipation. His wife, Atamay, died a few years after their arrival, while his sons were both dead by 1832.[131] Unlike many of his contemporaries, Suulu does not appear to have remarried after his wife's death. The census records indicate that he continued to live among his fellow Huocom and Yokuts. By the time of his death, in 1857, the incoming settlers did not see him as the traditional chief that he was. The local newspapers did not always run obituaries for local Indians, so why was it that Suulu (or Pedro, as they called him) was one of the few to receive this, albeit limited, treatment? It is likely that his inclusion and recognition resulted from his continued prominence among the local Indigenous community. Yet Suulu was not alone; other members of his Huocom tribe lived among the survivors and no doubt were aware of his political and social standing within their community.

Incoming immigrants grappled with their conflicting and contradictory narratives about Native people. The government promoted narratives about savage Indians, whom they proposed to deal with through arming and funding militias and the theft of Indigenous children. At the same time, academics scoured the lands for signs of vanishing Indians whose stories and languages they could document. Little effort was made to understand the dire circumstances Indigenous survivors faced. Newspapers wrote about the drunken exploits of mission survivors but thought little about the traumas and injustices that drove them to seek comfort and solace.

And yet despite the genocidal policies of the early era of U.S. occupation, Indigenous people persisted in the Santa Cruz area.[132] Mission survivors banded together, when possible, to build community in neighborhoods throughout town. Some lived in ranchos or in nearby homes, working as servants or field hands. Orphaned children in particular often ended up as servants in homes throughout the area, part of a widespread pattern of Indigenous children ending up as servants in non-Indian homes.[133] The census reports show that the community persisted, with more than 200 reported in 1860 and 131 reported by 1880 (see table 29), despite underreporting by census enumerators. The largest group of local survivors held onto the last of the former mission lands owned by Indigenous people—the Potrero.

7

They Won't Try to Kill You If They Think You're Already Dead

On a cold December morning in 1884, two young Indigenous men known as Tahoe and Cache watched as a local barn burned, smoke rising up in the dawn sky. The fire was the latest in a series of arsons that had burned new barns and homes in the lands recently inhabited by the local Indigenous communities following the closing of Mission Santa Cruz.[1] The fires targeted homes of recently arrived Europeans and Anglo-Americans and barns built in the Potrero area behind the mission as well as in the former mission crop fields that had become the new downtown of the rapidly growing city (see map 5). In response to the latest fire, the local constable arrested two young men, Jose "Cache" Lend and Rafael "Tahoe" Castro (see figs. 7 and 8). Both men were from local Indigenous families that had survived difficult times at Mission Santa Cruz. Tahoe and Cache had done their best to adjust to the changing world, working a variety of jobs in town. They played catcher and shortstop, respectively, positions of advanced skill and athletic ability, for the local Santa Cruz Powder Works baseball team. The two young men were known throughout town for their knowledge of local plants and animals, for catching and selling local fish and game, as well as for being expert egg collectors who could find nests of even the rarest local birds.

The Santa Cruz County Superior Court sentenced the pair to six years in the State Prison after a brief hearing.[2] The *Santa Cruz Sentinel* reported that the "two 'dusky braves' were brought before Judge Logan to answer the charges of arson brought against them. They plead guilty and waived time for sentence."[3] In their initial interrogation regarding the fires, printed in the local paper, Cache testified that they had lit the fires "just for fun."[4] Cache confessed to the arsons, while Tahoe pleaded innocent, claiming that he had been home sleeping at the time.[5] The two young men declined legal representation, and the quick trial did not include a jury.[6] The responses given by Tahoe and Cache suggest that at least one other American man was involved, but nobody else was ever questioned about the fires.[7]

The judge sentenced the two men to six years at the newly built San Quentin facility and sent them away within a few weeks of their arrest.[8] These young men had been well liked before the incident. Cache's employer, Mrs. Fagen, attested to his character. She described Cache as "faithful and industrious . . . and [she] had invariably found him honest."[9] Yet despite their affability and relative success navigating their changing world, these two young men were under suspicion and quickly sentenced by an incoming U.S. justice system that criminalized those who fit the racial category of Indian.[10] The two young men died shortly after their sentencing. Jose Lend died on May 3, 1886, from tuberculosis of the lymph nodes, about sixteen months after being sent away. About a year after Lend's death, Rafael Castro was reported to have gone "insane" and in August 1887 was sent to the Stockton Insane Asylum, where he died.[11]

The motivations for the arsons will never be truly understood. There are many reasons that explain arson, pyromania being one of them. Perhaps the newspaper reporter had it right and they merely wished to see the firemen in action. An oral history shared nearly one hundred years after the events suggested that the young men had wanted to become firefighters but had been denied, prompting them to start setting fires.[12] If true, these young men wanted to take up what would have been one of the most dangerous and selfless of jobs at the time in order to help their community. Is it possible that the young men thought that by lighting these fires they might find a way to become firemen themselves? This speaks to the limitations of opportunities for young Native people during these times. Or is it possible that the arsons were committed as a reaction to the ongoing encroachment on what had been Indigenous lands? A reaction to the rapid encroachment experienced by the surviving Native community?

Whatever their motivations might have been, the two young men's involvement in the arsons has to be understood in the larger historical context of land loss and colonialism.[13] The arsons took place during a period of dangerous and grim circumstances facing Indigenous families after U.S. annexation of California in 1848. Local newspapers of the time embraced and reinforced long-standing stereotypes and racist tropes. One *Sentinel* article celebrated the arrest of these "two illiterate and drunken Indians.... those 'sons of the forest,' whose sole pleasure in life, aside from imbibing firewater, seemed to be an interest in the Fire Department."[14] The author observed that the young men did not own property, failing to take into account the dispossession of historical lands underway at this time.[15] The same article made a point to connect the arsons with the murder and robbery of a white community member from eight years earlier, in 1877, a crime that ended with the lynching of two Latino men, Francisco Arias and Jose Chamales.[16]

The *Santa Cruz Sentinel* report pointed out that the two "Indian firebugs" descended from "Maria" and her sister, two of the survivors of Mission Santa Cruz.[17] This was likely a reference to the mixed Mutsun Ohlone Ausaima and Yokuts Huocom Maria Filomena and her sister, Maria Guadalupe.[18] Maria Filomena, who survived locally into the twentieth century, was the stepdaughter of the Mutsun Ohlone Sumus man Xuclan (Ricardo), the former mission song leader who until 1866 had held the last parcel of mission lands granted to a local Indigenous person. Filomena and her son would have been well aware of Xuclan's dispossession, which likely shaped the sense of loss and injustice felt by his grandson, Tahoe.[19] Perhaps the lighting of these fires was intended as a challenge to the loss of their lands. Whether directly connected to the arsons or not, the ongoing encroachment on Indigenous lands and the larger violence and dispossession leveled at their community would have had an impact on the young men's lives.

The young men's involvement in the fires, despite these unanswered questions regarding their motivations, points to a long history of local Indigenous use of fires as tools for land management and at times for warfare.[20] The fire that led to the arrest of Tahoe and Cache came ninety-one years after the Quiroste-led attack of December 1793, when local Indigenous people attacked and used fire to burn down the first Mission Santa Cruz settlement. As mentioned in the first chapter, this Indigenous use of fire as a tool against colonial occupation was not exceptional, as it reflected a dynamic found throughout California. While the Quiroste-led attack fit a long-standing pattern of regional warfare, it also aimed to challenge initial Spanish occupation. The barn burnings of 1884 might very well have represented frustration over the increasing encroachment of incoming immigrants on lands that had been home to generations of local mission survivors.

In the course of the ninety years since the Quiroste-led attack, the demographics had changed dramatically. The surviving Indigenous community watched as large numbers of settlers moved onto these lands, a pattern that accelerated after the gold rush of 1848 (see table 29). Along with the new arrivals came new racial and social categories, which led to more violence directed at Indians and dark-skinned Californios. Much had changed over these ninety-one years, and these young men seem to have used an important traditional strategy—fire—as a tool of resistance in a time when their Indigenous community was frequently marginalized.

The story of Tahoe and Cache exemplifies the larger situation facing the surviving Indigenous community in the latter half of the nineteenth century, particularly the story of dispossession and removal. In these years Indigenous families persevered by relying on community, cultural practices, and knowledge—like sweat lodges, traditional songs and dances, and geographic familiarity built on ancestral knowledge.[21] As the American city of Santa Cruz grew exponentially in size, the surviving Indigenous families found themselves pushed to the margins of society. Incoming settlers continued to rapidly build homes, barns, and businesses on lands throughout the region, while Native families attempted to keep what little lands they had gained.

The majority of the surviving Indigenous community remained in homes in the Potrero—the orchards behind the former mission. The Potrero continued to serve as the local reservation up until the time of Tahoe and Cache. As incoming immigrants bought up property in the Potrero area, surviving families were forced to look elsewhere for homes. Families found refuge wherever they were able. Some remained on local lands up through the turn of the twentieth century, moving northward to Pescadero, while others moved southward, into towns like Aptos or Watsonville. Still others left the region entirely, moving inland to the San Joaquin Valley area, near traditional homelands of the Yokuts in cities like Firebaugh, Los Banos, and Madera. As discussed in the previous chapter, the incoming U.S. society treated Indigenous Californians with great hostility and instituted policies of genocide. The children and grandchildren of mission survivors, with their fluency in Spanish and familiarity with Californio families, often hid themselves and their Indigenous heritage within the growing Latino community to avoid being targeted by racially motivated hostility.

Indigenous Survival, Indigenous Lands: The Potrero

By the latter part of the nineteenth century, local Indigenous survivors found refuge in a variety of places throughout the county. One Indigenous man, Xuclan, the song leader, was able to hold onto his home next to the mission until 1866. A few individuals remained on lands on the Westside, which had been owned briefly by Chugiut and his kin. After losing their rights to these lands, those who remained were able to do so by working in households like that of Joseph Ladd Majors, his wife, Maria de los Angeles Castro, and their family. The Majors family consolidated much of the Indigenous-owned lands along the Westside and offered homes to Chugiut's kin.

The most prominent remaining Indigenous community, mostly descendants of the Yokuts, continued to live in the Potrero fields below the mission bluff. The Potrero area was the last of the former mission lands to be occupied by mission survivors, a remnant of the mission land-based communities that formed after secularization. This area became known throughout Santa Cruz as home to local Native people, as the local reservation.

The Potrero lands were of special significance to many Indigenous families, as they had been homelands for incoming families and individuals throughout the mission era. The lands had been formally granted to two Yokuts men, Huayiche (Fidel), from the Quitchas tribe, and the Tejey man Chulnoquis (Pasqual), and while the majority of these lands had been sold in 1847, the community continued to live there into the 1880s.[22] Among many others they were joined there by Huayiche's son, Carlos, his Yokuts wife, Rosa, and their four sons: Agustin, Juan Jose Rafael, Juan Bautista, and Jose Martial Carlos.[23] As late as 1866, newspaper reports argued for the protection of the Potrero as the last remnants of land for descendants of these two men.[24] When the linguist Alphonse Pinart traveled through the area in 1878, he visited the Potrero and described it as a "small piece of land where few Indians of Santa Cruz live. In groups of 6 to 7, they live in little wooden shacks."[25] These lands were used for more than just homes, as they were the site of important spiritual and cultural events as well.[26] One woman whose family had recently migrated into the area from West Virginia described the Potrero: "The Indian settlement was in the Potrero on the left side of the street by that name near Evergreen Cemetery, and was fenced in by a deep ditch so that their horses could not escape. Most of the [Indians'] houses were made of [wooden] slabs with shake roofs. They had a sweat house plastered with mud on the outside. A fire was built in the center with a small place for the smoke to escape. The Indians sat around the fire. When sufficiently sweated, they ran from the building and plunged into a hole of cold water in the creek. . . . They made their living by working for the white people. They were expert pickers of wild blackberries and got many where the golf links are now."[27] The Indigenous community at the Potrero must have regularly continued to use their sweat lodges for this young observer to casually remark about it.

The local Indigenous community did work as laborers in white households, but they also continued to find a variety of work. Some worked as gardeners, messengers, carriage drivers, drovers, delivery men, and field laborers, while others worked at local industrial sites like the tannery.[28] Labor options in the U.S. era diminished for members of the local Indigenous community, a result of the population boom that included the arrival of various other populations, such as large numbers of Chinese immigrants, who worked as domestic servants or for the railroads as well as running laundry services and vegetable gardens downtown.[29] For the first time local Indigenous survivors found themselves competing for jobs as domestic laborers or field workers.[30]

Some local community members continued to use Native laborers as domestic workers, such as Majors and his wife. For example, in 1851, the Majors family appears to have "adopted" two young Indigenous boys: twelve-year-old Juan de Dios and nine-year-old Tomas de Jesus.[31] The couple appear as the godparents for the two boys' baptisms, with their parents listed as deceased. Five years later the *Santa Cruz Sentinel* reported that Tomas, "who had been for some time in the employ of Joseph L. Majors . . . was found dead of unknown causes in a field on the west side."[32] While no official child indenture petition had been filed by Majors, godparentage facilitated the induction of orphaned Indigenous children into household labor bondage just as effectively as the child indenture laws of the time. The connection between the Majors family and the surviving Indigenous community appears to have lasted through the decades, as a sixty-five-year-old Lorenzo Asisara is listed as a laborer in the household of Robert H. and Mary C. Majors in Seaside (just south of Watsonville) in the 1880 census, and Maria Filomena appears as a servant for Maria de los Angeles in the 1900 census.[33]

Another example of older Indigenous survivors working in local households or businesses is seen with the story of the Huocom Yokuts man Guimayach (Mariano), who became known by the white community as Mariano Hablitas or "Cooper's Indian."[34] Guimayach married four times between 1821 and 1844.[35] He had one child, the boy Salvador, who died as an infant in early spring 1834.[36] In 1834 Guimayach worked in town as a day laborer.[37] By 1841 he lived in the Potrero area along with a large community of survivors of the mission era, before marrying his fourth wife, Andrea.[38] By 1860 Guimayach appears to have lived with Huocom kin and even to have helped them procure deeds to lands in the Potrero.[39] Yet despite the records indicating that he lived in the Potrero lands through these years, it appears that he spent the majority of his time working for two brothers who had moved into the area in 1849 from Pennsylvania, William and John Cooper.[40] Local legends claim that Guimayach accompanied the brothers on their trips to the gold mines, where he worked for them as an aide-de-camp.[41] In Guimayach's later years he continued to work for the Coopers in their general merchandise store on the corner of Front and Cooper Streets in downtown Santa Cruz, sometimes staying in the backroom. It is here that he became known as Cooper's Indian, at least by members of the white American settler community. Guimayach, who had become blind in his later years, died on December 28, 1876.[42]

The Potrero lands continued to serve as homelands for the Indigenous community long after the adobe structure of Mission Santa Cruz was gone. An earthquake in 1857 had left the old adobe mission in ruins, and the incoming community chose to leave it in disrepair (see fig. 9). The debris was eventually removed, but it was not until 1885 that the newly arrived Father McNamee began serious plans to build a new church where the adobe mission once stood.[43] After the fall of the original adobe mission, the lone adobe structure that remained standing from the mission era was one of the homes built for baptized Native families, which remains standing today, known as the School Street Adobe, part of Santa Cruz Mission State Historic Park. The rooms of this structure had continued to be used through the late 1840s by local Indigenous survivors such as the family of Maria Petra Nicanor, the daughter of Lino, a local hero of the Quintana assassination.[44]

Maria Petra Nicanor and her Tejey Yokuts husband, Chuyucu (Victoriano), lived in one of the rooms in this adobe until the 1840s.[45] Petra Nicanor eventually sold her lands to Joseph Majors in June 1848.[46] It is noteworthy that she sold the lands under her own name, not her husband's, which was unusual for the time and perhaps reflected the prominent standing of women within local Indigenous families, following long-standing patterns. Or perhaps her husband was in bad health at the time, as Chuyucu was buried near Mission Santa Clara a month after the sale.[47] The burial in Santa Clara suggests that he had spent time moving back and forth between the two communities, perhaps finding work there, or it could be that his family moved there for a time after they left the adobe. If they had moved, it looks as if the surviving family members found their way back, as Petra Nicanor died of cholera in January 1851 and was buried at Mission Santa Cruz. Her burial record indicates that she was the "daughter of the deceased Lino and Maria Vibiana [sic]."[48] Very few Indian burial records of this time included information about parents, suggesting that the padres were well aware of her father's legacy and involvement with Quintana's assassination.[49] By the end of the 1840s these adobe rooms had become homes for members of the Californio community.[50]

In the mid-1880s incoming immigrants made plans to replace the original adobe mission that had lain in ruins for decades with a new Victorian-style church. Before construction of the new church, they had to deal with the bodies of Native people that had been buried in the cemetery adjacent to the old mission. They removed the bodies, carried them in wagons, and reinterred them in a mass grave at the new Holy Cross Cemetery site across town.[51] The body of Padre Andres Quintana was reported to have been exhumed in October 1885, inspiring the *Sacramento Union*, the most prominent Californian newspaper of the time, to embrace romanticized stories about the "wild Indians" and their "acts of depredation."[52]

The removal of these bodies also led to interesting discoveries that suggest that local Indigenous peoples found ways to subvert Catholic burial and funereal practices in favor of more tradition-based practices. A local news item reported that "the bones of an Indian chief were unearthed; around the skull and pointing towards the mouth, were half a dozen pipes of rare make."[53] The inclusion of items like the pipes shows the continuity of traditional burial practices. Another article reported that "in one of the coffins dug up at the old Catholic cemetery Monday afternoon nothing was found but more silver ornaments, the bones having mysteriously disappeared."[54] It would seem that a body had been removed and replaced with an offering. Could this be evidence of an Indigenous body removed for burial or other funeral treatment? Perhaps the body was removed and buried in the mountains in a more traditional manner. The journalist's mention of the discovery of "more silver ornaments" suggests that this was not the first time the Americans had found missing bodies replaced by offerings or at least with other ornamentation. The evidence from both burials implies that there had been an ongoing subversion of traditional Catholic burial within the Indigenous community, outside the awareness of the mission friars.[55]

Trauma, Survival, and the Search for Healing

Members of the local Indigenous community continued to find their way into the local newspapers, oftentimes shedding light on the heartache and difficulties they faced, along with hints about ways they found to persevere and find strength through traditional practices and ceremonies. In April 1874 the renowned local gardener Meregildo was found with his throat cut in an attempted suicide.[56] After receiving stitches to repair his damaged windpipe, Meregildo initially claimed that he had been attacked by a masked man. Meregildo's friend Jose Santiago, an Indigenous man originally from Santa Clara who was working at Kron's Tannery at the time, was arrested and detained at the local jail in suspicion.[57] After blood was found in the local sweat lodge, Father Adam urged Meregildo to come clean about what had happened. Meregildo confessed to trying to take his own life "in a fit of despondency," and Santiago was subsequently released. (The same Santiago was the father of Jose "Cache" Lend, whose story will be examined in more depth shortly.) The article concluded that Meregildo was "out of danger" after receiving medical attention.[58]

Meregildo's depression and attempted suicide reflect the difficulties of his generation's struggles to survive and persevere while dealing with the impact of transgenerational trauma from his ancestors' time in the mission. His attempted suicide came about a year after another tragic event in which he was involved, along with his friend Jose Santiago, Cache's father. In March 1873 a night of drinking involving Meregildo, Jose Santiago, and their friend Jesus Maria ended with Jose Santiago fatally stabbing Jesus Maria. According to the testimony of Jose Santiago, Meregildo, Jose Santiago's wife, Isabella, and Jesus Maria's wife, Maria Petronilla, Jesus Maria was stabbed twice after getting into a drunken quarrel with his friend Jose Santiago.[59] The two men had started drinking early that night, after receiving two bottles of wine from their Californio friend and coworker Antonio, who had been given the wine by local U.S. immigrant Nelse Nelson. After nine o'clock that evening, the two men went to Nelson's house, asking for more wine. After being denied, they broke into the house and took over a gallon of wine from a barrel, along with a knife. They then went to the house of their friend Meregildo, where the three continued drinking.

The report of this tragedy claims that Jesus Maria was the larger of the two men and was also "noisy and quarrelsome." This is the same Jesus Maria who was the son of Rustico, who had been arrested for pulling a knife on his wife, and the grandson of Quihueimen, the conspirator arrested and imprisoned for the assassination of Padre Quintana. It is fair to once again question the role played by the traumas Quihueimen had experienced and the reverberations of this trauma within his family over generations. The same story attests that Jose Santiago "was always very quiet," and his employer of over seven years, Jacob Kron, testified to Jose Santiago's "good character." Jose Santiago pleaded "not guilty," and it was decided that "the deceased was the most quarrelsome, [and] the accused was discharged." One article reporting on the incident focused on advocating against the selling of liquor, pointing out that Jesus Maria left behind a wife and five children, while Jose Santiago himself was the main provider for his family, which included his wife and six children. The article pleaded against selling alcohol to the Native community, arguing that "when sober [they] are peaceable, quiet and industrious."[60] As Meregildo's attempted suicide took place just over a year after these events, it seems highly likely that the tragedy continued to weigh heavily on both Meregildo and Jose Santiago. Jose Santiago's central role in the death of Jesus Maria would explain why the police detained him after finding Meregildo in his wounded state.

Meregildo, born in 1830, was orphaned when his Huocom Yokuts parents died later in the decade.[61] After their deaths, he initially continued to live with Huocom kin.[62] By 1843 he was living in the household of Jose Bolcoff up the coast, along with the daughter of his baptismal *madrina*, Yuñan (Serafina).[63] The fifteen-year-old "Merigeldo" is listed in a household headed by Maria Juana Castro, as part of the three households that made up the Rancho de Refugio lands belonging to the three Castro sisters on the Westside of Santa Cruz.[64] This small household of five sat between the larger lands of Jose Bolcoff, married to Maria Candida Castro, and Joseph Majors, married to Maria de los Angeles Castro.

In 1852 Meregildo married Maria Agueda, the daughter of the Cajastaca man Jotoime (Mattias) and the Yokuts-speaking Chanech woman Nenoat (Maria Bibiana).[65] The couple had nine children altogether, but three had died by the end of 1873 (see table 30). A fourth child, eleven-year-old daughter Ana Ambrosiana, had died just two months before Meregildo's suicide attempt.[66] Although Meregildo and Maria Agueda still had five surviving children, the recent loss of Ana Ambrosiana certainly added to Meregildo's despondency. His wife, Maria Agueda, died about a year after Meregildo's suicidal incident.[67] While the burial records do not indicate the cause of death, it is possible that she was ill, adding to Meregildo's depression.

Despite these heavy losses, Meregildo persevered. He worked as a farm laborer, although it appears that he gained renown for his gardening. Known as "one of the best gardeners in town," he was hired by community members to tend their gardens.[68] Labor options at the time consisted of farm labor, domestic service, or working with cattle. Gardening provided one additional opportunity for some people like Meregildo. In a way this recalls the stories of Tahoe and Cache: Meregildo and other members of the local Indigenous community became known among the incoming community for their knowledge of local plants and the environment.

U.S. authorities called upon locals like Meregildo to locate freshwater sources and to work as gardeners or in the fields or lauded their skills finding local birds, eggs, or plants.[69] The incoming settlers' frequent association of the Indigenous community with the environment reflects both the importation of U.S. stereotypes about Native Americans and the reality of cultural and historical differences. Long-established U.S. stereotypes of the "noble savage" and the "ecological Indian" help explain why this was one of the few areas in which local newspapers reported Indigenous skill or aptitude.[70] Still, reading past these layers of projection, such reports reflect confirmation of the local community's generations of knowledge handed down about the local environment.

In 1866, Meregildo and his friend Jesus Maria, the man who would eventually die in the stabbing tragedy in 1873, unsuccessfully tried to claim lands on the Potrero.[71] The claims were denied, and instead Guimayach received rights to these lands, ostensibly for "all Indians."[72] This decision further supports the idea that Meregildo and others lived among kin with tribal connections, as Guimayach, an elder from the Huocom tribe, appears in the 1860 census as part of Meregildo's family.[73]

The *Santa Cruz Sentinel* reference to Meregildo's sweat lodge, which was situated in the Potrero lands behind the mission, demonstrates the continuation of traditional practices and rituals. Meregildo initially claimed that he had entered the sweat lodge to "call a sick man lying there to come to his assistance."[74] It is clear from his remarks that Meregildo and other members of the community used these lodges to help with illness, including depression, post-traumatic stress disorder (PTSD), and despondency resulting from the years of colonial trauma. These Potrero lands were more than just lands for homes; they included ceremonial lands set aside for places of health and healing like the lodges.

By 1880 Meregildo appears to have continued his work as a gardener in homes on the Westside, as he is listed as the forty-eight-year-old gardener for the household of Moses Meder.[75] Meregildo's twenty-eight-year-old son, Jose Miguel Antonio, and ten-year-old daughter, Maria Rafaela, also appear as servants in neighboring households.[76] While the census lists the family as having split up, living within neighboring households, it actually appears that the enumerators made a mistake and that the family continued to live together as laborers for the Majors family.[77] Their duplicate appearance in the census records suggests that the family lived with the Majors and worked among multiple neighboring households, and they were likely counted twice.

Meregildo's burial is not recorded in the Holy Cross records. It is unclear whether he moved from the area sometime near the end of the century or if he survived into the twentieth century. His family's ties to local families and farms suggest that they continued to pursue labor opportunities on local lands. Other families tried similarly to stay local, but ongoing exposure to disease sometimes decimated families, leaving survivors struggling to recover. The story of one of the young men involved in the 1884 arsons, Cache, illustrates these difficulties and sheds light on his responses to the authorities after his and Tahoe's arrest.

Cache and His Family

When asked why they had lit the fires after their arrest, Cache is reported to have testified that he "did not care what became of him, as he had nobody to care for him."[78] It is easy to read this as part of the larger story of great loss and dispossession facing all Indigenous survivors, but this statement comes into clearer focus upon examination of his family. He had certainly witnessed his father, Jose Santiago, being arrested at least twice in previous years, for the drunken stabbing of Jesus Maria as well as for the attempted suicide by Meregildo. The story of Cache's mother, Maria Ysabel, further reflects great loss and hardship. Her story shows how, despite survival into this era, Indigenous families were particularly vulnerable to disease and epidemics. Maria Ysabel was the daughter of a Tejey and Huocom Yokuts couple, both Yokuts: Sauset (Isidro) and Josotmin (Maria Buena).[79] Ysabel married Jose Santiago, who had been born at Mission Santa Clara.[80] Santiago's penchant for drinking caught the notice of the linguist Pinart, who wrote about it in his journals in 1878.[81] Santiago had kinship connections to Mission Santa Cruz, as his parents were a part of the Sumus tribe, which had been split between Missions Santa Clara and Santa Cruz.[82] Ysabel and Santiago had nine children between 1857 and 1877, yet only four of them survived past 1886.[83] One of their sons, born in 1862 and named Jose Primitivo in his baptism, was known in town as Jose "Cache" Lend, the catcher on the local baseball team and one of the two young men arrested for the burning of the barns near the Potrero.[84]

When he was about fourteen years old, Cache's family experienced terrible loss due to a diphtheria epidemic that hit the county for two years beginning in 1876.⁸⁵ The Native community had dealt with waves of deadly smallpox, syphilis, and malaria over the previous fifty-plus years, and they found themselves once again facing a dangerous epidemic. In the spring of 1878 Cache's nine-month-old sister, Augustina, died.⁸⁶ Nearly three weeks later, his five-year-old sister, Maria Vicenta, died as well, followed less than a month later by his mother, Maria Ysabel.⁸⁷ She was followed by her twenty-year-old daughter, Maria Guadalupe, one week later.⁸⁸ In less than two months four members of this family had died. The family hardships continued when, five years later, twelve-year-old Gregoria Elena died of unknown causes.⁸⁹ Her death came about a year and a half before the first of the barn burnings. It is not clear where his father was at the time, as few reports exist of Santiago past the end of the 1870s. It is possible that he had passed away as well or had fallen deeper into his drinking. The despondency Cache displayed during his interrogation could certainly have been a reaction to having lost most of his family over the previous five years.

The *Santa Cruz Sentinel* reported that Cache worked for the local doctor and his family, who lived on the Westside.⁹⁰ Dr. P. B. Fagen, his wife, Mary E., and their sons appear to have employed Cache as their gardener and carriage driver for over a year before the arsons. The wealthy Fagen family also employed two live-in servants, Katie Mitchell, a white seamstress, and Sam Lee, a Chinese domestic servant.⁹¹ Cache seems to have formed a close relationship with the family dog, a spaniel, who reportedly tracked Cache to the jailhouse, after which the dog "lies by the fence in front of the jail all day, and only returns to Dr. Fagen's residence at meal times, and returns to his post again as soon as he has been fed. No coaxing can get him away."⁹² In the *Santa Cruz Daily Sentinel* article about the arrests, Mrs. Fagen described Cache as "faithful and industrious . . . his simple tastes were like a child's. . . . [She] was very much surprised to hear that Cache was implicated and attributed his being led into it through strong drink. The lady trusted him with sums of money and had invariably found him honest, and, from his nature, concluded that he is unable to realize the enormity of the offense, or that he had committed any transgression at all."⁹³ The newly arrived family clearly valued Cache's work but were surprised by his involvement in the arsons.

New Kinship Ties through Godparentage

In the latter part of the nineteenth century, Indigenous families that had survived their time at neighboring missions moved into the area and intermingled with the local community. Many surviving families drew on networks and interconnections formed during the mission years in their search for new homes or to revisit familiar lands. These stories further illuminate the persistence of Indigenous communities that remained outside of the sphere of colonial influence.[94] Archaeological evidence demonstrates that small communities overlooking coastal areas rich in resources formed far outside the reach of the growing American cities in these years.[95] One report told about a group of fifty Yokuts from the Merced area who came to Monterey to collect mussels and abalones. The report claimed that the group arrived seated on horseback, armed with rifles, speaking a mix of Spanish and Indigenous Yokuts languages. It is likely that they were descendants of survivors from local missions who drew on their familiarity with these lands, given that the majority of Merced-area Yokuts people had been captured and transported to Missions Santa Cruz and San Juan Bautista during the mission era.[96]

Santa Cruz locals recalled annual trips by inland Native American families to resource-rich Año Nuevo, the territorial homelands of the once-powerful Quiroste. One local observed that "they'd trek here every summer along about the last of May. They would come from way over as far as Tulare, and Bakersfield and come with their travois. . . . They'd go from way over by Tulare and Bakersfield and that neck of the woods and come clear up by New Year's Island [Año Nuevo Point]. They lived there on the abalones and the mussels and clams. They'd stay there all summer, and then in the fall when the rains were starting to come, why they'd go trekking back."[97] Baptismal registries show that these newcomers to the area often connected with locals. Godparentage during the mission era was used to create new kinship ties, as discussed earlier. These patterns continued into the American era, as Indigenous godparentage continued to play a key role in extending kinship networks and building community by connecting incoming Indigenous families with local families.

An example of how kinship through godparentage connected incoming Indigenous families to those already in the area involves two people of special importance for the Santa Cruz Indigenous community—Lorenzo Asisara and Maria Filomena. Jose Roque and Maria Crescencia were a couple who moved into Santa Cruz as late as 1859, when they married there.[98] They had been emancipated from different missions, Jose Roque from Mission San Gabriel and Maria Crescencia from Mission San Luis Rey.[99] It is not clear if the couple moved to the area together or met there, but by the time of their marriage, they lived in Aptos.[100] The two witnesses for their marriage were Maria Filomena and her sister, Maria Guadalupe.[101] The couple's first daughter was born in 1860, and Lorenzo Asisara and Maria Filomena served as godparents.[102] The couple had seven children altogether, with Lorenzo Asisara serving as godparent for four of them, Maria Filomena for three.[103]

Did the couple form these new connections with Lorenzo and Filomena after moving into the area? It is impossible to know for sure, but another possibility exists. Asisara himself moved around the Bay Area, living for some time in San Francisco, San José, and Monterey. He spent some time in San Francisco in the 1840s, where he worked as a soldier under Vallejo.[104] It is possible that Asisara met Roque during his time in service or while moving around the region. In any case families such as that of Jose Roque and Maria Crescencia enjoyed a degree of mobility, moving throughout California and connecting and building ties between Indigenous families and communities. During this time of incredible struggle and displacement, Indigenous families would surely have looked for people to whom they could relate. Shared histories and disruption and loss as well as commonalities with cultural and spiritual practices would have helped build these new networks. Lorenzo Asisara and Maria Filomena helped facilitate the move into the region for this incoming family.

Displacement, Loss, and the Absence of Justice

The burning of the barns on the Westside reflects frustrations over the continued loss of lands that were historically significant to the local Indigenous community. Some resisted white encroachment on lands that had become Indigenous territories, including the Potrero behind the mission. Following emancipation in the 1830s, these lands had become homeland to a diversity of Indigenous survivors. For some of the younger generation of Indigenous residents, these lands represented the last remnants of community and land ownership. They would certainly have heard stories from their elders about the recent years when they had received lands of their own. For some of these youth, like Tahoe and Cache, steady American encroachment on the collective lands of the Potrero must have felt like the last of their lands was disappearing (see figs. 7 and 8).

The last local Native American to hold property granted from former mission lands was the Sumus man Xuclan, the former mission song leader. Xuclan was known in town by his baptized Spanish name, José Ricardo Carrion.[105] Xuclan was born in 1805 and baptized as a one-year-old shortly after his Sumus parents arrived at Mission Santa Cruz with their three children.[106] At least some members of his family appear to have preferred life on traditional lands, as both Xuclan's father and sister were reported dead while fugitive from the mission in 1810.[107] Xuclan grew up as an important member of the mission community, serving as *padrino*, marriage witness, page, and the lead singer of the choir.[108]

Shortly after his fellow mission choir member the Mutsun Ohlone Ausaima man Rafael de Jesus died, in January 1836, Xuclan married Rafael's widow, Chutupat.[109] The Yokuts-speaking Huocom woman Chutupat had two young daughters from her previous marriage, Maria Filomena and Maria de Jesus (later in life referred to as Maria Guadalupe).[110] Xuclan helped raise the two daughters, becoming their stepfather.[111] The family lived together in their home near the mission, although they may have spent some time in San José and in Pescadero, the ranching and fishing community just north of Santa Cruz.[112] In early 1851 Chutupat, Xuclan's wife, died.[113]

The older of the two daughters was Maria Filomena (see fig. 10). She was the mother of Rafael, known as "Tahoe," one of the young men arrested for arson. Maria Filomena lived into the twentieth century, and in her elder years she spoke about her memories to a young girl, Ruby Tefertiller, who would recall many years later: "Maria told stories of her two sons 'Ta-jo' and 'Ka-She.' They were in jail. They had wanted to become firemen, but somehow failed to make it. Other teams were accepted. The accepted applicants fooled the Indians by saying 'Our job was to put fires out. Yours is to set them.' Evidently, they did it on several occasions. Finally they set a fire to a lot near the Louden-Nelson

Community Center and accidently caught a barn on fire. The owner of the barn prosecuted the sons for the fire. Even though they told their story they were sent to jail."[114] Her story stands in contrast with the official narrative reported at the time. Her version suggests that the fires may have been in reaction to the limited opportunities for Indigenous youth. And yet the young men had close ties with Indigenous community members who had owned land, and it is likely that these stories of displacement played a role in the fires as well.

Maria Filomena would have been acutely aware of her stepfather Xuclan's struggle to retain his lands. She would have moved out of Xuclan's house long before his 1866 displacement, as she was living with her own family by the mid-1850s. Xuclan was able to hold onto his small plot of land until he was forced to defend his ownership and occupation of the lands in American courts in 1866.[115] Local business owner Henry Rice alleged that he had purchased Xuclan's lands back in 1834, the year of secularization. At the time of the trial, Xuclan (listed as Ricardo) was living with his good friend Lorenzo Asisara and another friend whose name is only given as José. All three men were listed as fellow defendants.

In his defense Xuclan used the language associated with homesteading by arguing that he had been in possession of said lands, including cultivating and enclosing them. The *Santa Cruz Sentinel* articles around the time focused on teaching American immigrants to occupy open lands for homesteading, characterizing existing rancho lands as "sparsely settled; and in many portions . . . an unbroken wilderness."[116] The Homestead Act of 1862 promised to "furnish a permanent home for bona fide settlers" and advised, "Within six months the homestead must be actually occupied or cultivated as the home of the claimant."[117] Land claims and homesteads emphasized the enclosure, improvement, and cultivation of lands while asserting the fallow nature of prior occupancy.

When Rice could not produce the deeds to prove his ownership, the court decided in favor of Xuclan. Yet the deeds records show that despite winning the legal right to keep his home, Xuclan ended up selling his lands to Rice for fifty dollars in the months following the trial.[118] He obviously wanted to keep them, considering the time he spent defending his rights, so it is unclear what motivated this sale. Perhaps the fifty dollars was incentive enough for him to sell? Whatever the circumstances, the sale meant the end of the last privately held property owned by a mission survivor, other than the Potrero.

Xuclan's stepdaughter, Maria Filomena, was an important member of the local Indigenous community, serving frequently as *madrina* for Indigenous baptisms alongside *padrino* Lorenzo Asisara. By the mid-1850s she had married an Indigenous man known as Andres Castro.[119] The couple had five children together between 1856 and 1873.[120] In 1863 they had their fourth child—Rafael, the boy who came to be known as Tahoe.[121] Tahoe was described as being "one of the very best shortstops in the city and [he] moved like lightning when running the bases." News reports incorrectly suggested that the boys were both sons of "Maria" and her sister, referring to Maria Filomena and her sister, Maria Guadalupe, who also appeared frequently as a godparent in Indigenous baptisms.[122] The two women were alternatively noted as living on Potrero Street or Evergreen, both in the Potrero lands. It was noted that they "always were seen together in their plain skirts and with black shawls over their heads and wrapped around their shoulders. They took in washing and had many customers."[123]

While Tahoe would have been too young to witness his grandfather's struggle to retain his lands, the story of Xuclan's displacement would have certainly been a familiar one. After the arrest of Tahoe and Cache, Tahoe continued to maintain his innocence, while Cache claimed that they had been involved in many of the frequent arsons.[124] Tahoe contended that he had been asleep at the time but had known about the fire.[125] A highly editorialized article focused on the two young men's apparent indifference, even claiming that "without compunction they can set buildings on fire. What do they care? They do not own property; they want some fun."[126] The writer emphasized the rights of the new landholding Americans yet conveniently ignored the historical displacement of the young men and their community.

It was Maria Filomena's recollections that suggest that the two young men had wanted to be firefighters but were prohibited because of their second-class status. It seems possible that the glass ceiling prohibiting Indigenous youth from having jobs such as firefighter combined with frustrations over the sense of loss and invisibility felt within their community contributed to the arsons. The Anglo journalists noted that "the two dusky 'braves'... received their sentences with a sardonic grin, and with as much nonchalance as if they were going to a place where they would be permitted to set fire to a barn before each meal. Cache and Tahoe calmly smoked cigarettes on the way to jail and seemed to be contented and happy."[127] The indifference that the journalists thought they saw on the men's faces was much more likely resignation or futility, the result of a short life of hardship and struggle, as each of the boys had witnessed overwhelming losses, including their community getting squeezed out of lands that held deep transgenerational meaning and connected them with their ancestors.

Survival—Hidden in Plain Sight

They won't try to kill you if they think you're already dead.[128]

Survival for the local Indigenous community in these years frequently meant being hidden from the eyes of the dominant American society. In 1891 the City of Santa Cruz planned and orchestrated a public celebration of the centennial of the founding of Mission Santa Cruz. City officials asked Lorenzo Asisara to attend, enabling the public to see one of the survivors of the mission. Asisara's participation was a quiet one, as he was not given the opportunity to speak to the crowds. Ironically, despite his silence in the official celebration, it is the precious words of Asisara, transcribed in the decades before the celebration, that provide one of the most nuanced reports of the life of Indigenous Californians. Asisara's participation in the centennial was his last recorded public appearance. To date, no burial records have been found for him, though it appears that he died sometime before 1902.[129] His absence in the church burial records seems to confirm reports that he, like many others, had not held onto his Catholic upbringing.[130] Lorenzo did what many of his community did—continued surviving despite disappearing from official view of American society.

Yet the disappearance from official American records is a superficial one. The real story is the perseverance of the Indigenous community. Indigenous people continued to be an active presence in the Santa Cruz community into the 1900s. The inclusion of Asisara as the only Native participant in the city's celebration seemed to suggest to the community that he was a lone survivor, all that remained of a once vibrant community. But this was clearly not the case. Some surviving children, especially those orphaned, ended up in American households.[131] While many members of this community had moved out of the immediate vicinity, others remained in town.

Surviving Indigenous families found ways to survive in the rapidly growing city. The 1900 census reported sixty-eight Indians living in twenty households throughout the greater county.[132] And these records only represent those who were outwardly identified as Indians, potentially missing any who passed as Mexican. Most of those who were enumerated worked on local farms; some worked as wood choppers, others as day laborers or servants in wealthier households. The youth attended local schools as Indigenous families persevered. In the early 1900s Santa Cruz expanded, industrialized, and became a prime Bay Area tourist destination known for its beaches and boardwalk entertainment. Simon Gonsaga, a thirty-year-old man of likely Chipuctac and Yokuts (Atsnil and Copcha) ancestry, owned a house in Soquel, not far from the San Andrés Castro Adobe that still remains today. There Simon lived with his mission-born parents, Teodora and Santos.[133] The region continued to be an Indigenous space, becoming home to descendants and more and more members of the Native American diaspora.

Maria Filomena, the Chipuctac Huocom woman known in the community as "Maria the Indian," continued to live on the Westside, near Chugiut's former rancheria. By 1900 the seventy-year-old Filomena worked as a servant for Maria de los Angeles Castro Majors.[134] Oral histories attest to her living into the early twentieth century, in an adobe by the Evergreen Cemetery, in the Potrero region. A *Santa Cruz Sentinel* article from 1902 claimed that "of all the Indians who once lived in Santa Cruz County, only two remain, and they are both [women]," likely a reference to Maria Filomena and her sister, Guadalupe.[135] Maria Filomena's young friend Tefertiller would many years later recall that the adobe was "probably about where the freeway cut through. I don't remember any windows and the inside of the house was a dark, smokey blue, no doubt from the fireplace where corn husks were always drying."[136] Filomena became blind in her later years but would take her daily walks around the site where Mission Santa Cruz had once stood, telling her stories to generations of newly arriving immigrant, pointing out the Indigenous history and connections to these lands (see fig. 10).[137] While Maria Filomena might have been the last Indigenous survivor of Mission Santa Cruz to remain on those grounds, some survivors had left the area to join others in places like Watsonville or found refuge in their own ways throughout the greater region.

After the Potrero

As members of the local Native community faced constant pressure to consolidate what little land they held, they looked for places to build community with other surviving Indigenous families. With the growing American population in Santa Cruz, some families looked southward to places like Aptos and Watsonville. These towns remained smaller in population, as the majority of incoming American settlers moved into the Santa Cruz and Soquel townships. Watsonville and, to a smaller extent, Aptos became places where local Californio and Indigenous families made homes and formed community, relative safe havens from the racially tinged violence of American dominant settlements like Santa Cruz. Some of these Indigenous families moved northward into small coastal towns like Pescadero. A select few found ways to remain on former Mission Santa Cruz lands, often working in households of local families.

Some of the Indigenous families living in Aptos descended from families that had moved into the region in the 1840s to pursue labor opportunities. Families, such as that of Amonason (Jose Antonio) and Guejais (Josefa Antonia), who worked at Rancho San Andrés in the 1840s, remained in the Aptos region well through the latter half of the nineteenth century.[138] It is possible that the Indigenous people living in Aptos in the twentieth century were related to these families. One oral history from the 1970s told of a man named Willy who had lived in the hills of Aptos. Willy and his family hunted clams along the coast and apparently had long ties to the area.[139] According to the same interview, "When they were putting in that golf course at Rio Del Mar, when they were grading it, the bulldozer dug out 125 mortars (rock bowls for crushing acorns); a fellow from Watsonville came over and packed them all up and took them to Watsonville."[140] This story attests to the persistence of an active Indigenous presence that was aware of local sacred and burial sites and took action to protect them.

Watsonville and the surrounding communities became places of refuge for Indigenous families throughout the greater area. Watsonville had also become home to many surviving Californio families that had long-standing ties with Indigenous survivors. Watsonville was close to Mission San Juan Bautista as well as Mission Santa Cruz, and it appears that survivors from both local missions found their way to Watsonville in these years. Maria Ascención Solórsano recalled economic ties between Mission San Juan Bautista survivors and the community at Watsonville, telling John Harrington that "the Indians made baskets and took them over to Watsonville to the store to sell them."[141] Solórsano also spoke about some Santa Cruz people living in surrounding areas like Gilroy, where she had met a woman named Rosa Arsola.[142] Solórsano was aware of surviving Santa Cruz Indigenous peoples, telling Harrington: "When I was young I used to hear mention [of] the name of Rustico. He was very old and surely he must have known much about the time of long ago."[143] The Watsonville chancery records reveal that quite a few Indigenous families lived in the area in the late nineteenth century. Chulnoquis (Pasqual), for example, the son of Malimin (Coleto), who lived for a long time in the Potrero, appears in the Watsonville burial records in 1887.[144]

Siboo (Canuto), the same Tomoi man who once fled Mission Santa Cruz with Yaquenonsat and later lived with Chugiut (Geronimo) on the Westside of Santa Cruz, eventually moved down to Watsonville.[145] Siboo was a Bear Doctor, along with another man named Lucas.[146] Solórsano met Siboo when she was still a child. She spoke about him (and Lucas) with Harrington:

> I knew an old Indian at San Juan who was called Canuto, he used to live at Watsonville on the Amestes Ranch [sic], he didn't wear any pants, only a gee-string and a blanket. He had been a bear formerly, but had done no harm to anybody. He had been one of the big captains, I think that he was a Santa Cruz Indian. . . . When I

knew him he was already very old, and had already confessed and had quit those practices already. He had confessed to Father Angel at Watsonville. He had all his blankets and belongings in a bundle, and when he died they burnt all those things, the earth resounded way down under the earth. I was seven years old when he died. He was very old when he died. I do not know where he was buried. . . . My mother and father were living at Las Aromas when he died. I got to see him at the Amestes Ranch. He had a shirt on and a blanket wrapped around his body and tied at the waist, of dark color, it is possible that it was one of those that they made on the looms of the missions. He was a large man, very old, about ready to die. He talked Indian, surely.[147]

At another point Solórsano described Siboo's use of Bear medicine. Siboo's story showed that he was able to harness his power to strike out against the colonizers.

Lucas and Canuto were two other Indians that used to turn into bears. . . . And Canuto, when the cowboys were going along with cattle, he would come out on them and go at the horses, and the cowboys would try to lasso him and could not do it. The bear would carry away their riatas and later they would go to Canuto's house to get them. When they would see him, at once those fellows knew that it was Canuto. He did this just to do injury to those men. Canuto used to do this at San Juan. That Indian used to live at San Juan and when he took a notion he would go over by Pacheco also to get the riatas away from the cowboys.[148]

As discussed in earlier chapters, cattle represented great disruption to Indigenous access to traditional lands and resources, with pasturelands quickly taking over areas that had been used for traditional plants, colonizing the environment in a parallel displacement to what Indigenous people experienced. Siboo's targeting of the cowboys and their cattle is a fascinating example of him using his power to attack a cardinal symbol of colonial destruction.

The relocations and movement to and from Watsonville demonstrate the ways in which Indigenous survivors in the latter part of the nineteenth century rebuilt a sense of community with survivors from neighboring missions. These re-formations would eventually contribute to the reconstitution of local tribes. Long-standing kinship and tribal ties between families throughout the area extended far beyond the scope of the mission institutions, so it is not surprising that families remained connected in this way. This bond was especially common among families surviving neighboring Missions San Juan Bautista and Santa Cruz. One family's story in particular exemplifies the ways in which survivors of these two missions built community: the story of Maria Josefa Velasquez, ancestor of contemporary Amah Mutsun families, including tribal chair Valentin Lopez.

There is contradictory evidence about whether Josefa was born at Mission Santa Cruz or San Juan Bautista, but nonetheless her story shows the interconnections and the perseverance of kinship ties between survivors of the two neighboring missions.[149] We do know that in the late 1840s she married a Native man from Mission San Buenaventura named Felix, who was likely Chumash. Josefa and Felix married at Mission San Juan Bautista but in the 1850s came to live in Santa Cruz, where Josefa gave birth to two children.[150] Josefa's second child had godparents from the local Indigenous community, the Huocon Yokuts man Meregildo and his wife, the Cajastaca (Aptos) Awaswas and Chanech Yokuts woman Maria Agueda. The connection between the family of Josefa and Felix and these godparents continued the trend of building kinship ties, connecting Josefa and Felix with the Indigenous community of Santa Cruz.[151] Felix died in 1856.[152] By the late 1850s Josefa moved down to Watsonville, where she married Antonio Velasquez.[153]

Josefa was an entrepreneur, as she ran a tamale factory and cantina in a place called Freedom, about seven miles north of Watsonville. According to Ketchum: "[Josefa] Velasquez and Ascención Solórsano's cousin Jose Magdelano Espinosa were partners in a Cantina near Watsonville. It was an important gathering place for the Californio and Indigenous peoples as well as Mexican immigrants in the late 19th century and into the 20th century."[154] By 1930 Josefa's son Ambrosio and his wife would have a tamale restaurant in Watsonville, following in her footsteps.[155] Solórsano recalled stories about her friend:

If They Think You're Already Dead   251

Doña Josefa had a saloon and dance hall right there where she lived, and the people used to be there drinking, dancing, and eating tomales [sic], and how many deaths used to be at those dances! They would kill somebody and they would not stop the dance, they kept right on dancing, they were already used to it. Doña Josefa was very nonchalant, she had no fear of anything. She had very nice clothes, that woman did. They played beautiful music there, and there one would see very constantly the native Californians. [Josefa's] sons were musicians too, Martin was musician as soon as he was grown up, and went about everywhere. Don Ambrosio [Josefa's son] plays the flute, guitar and accordion.

And that woman lasted! It seemed as if she was never going to change, all the time she was just the same, I remember that she looked the same for thirty years or more. They say that the Indians of long ago lasted long because they lived on pure and simple foods, but here in this case this woman lived like a rich woman, she ate of the best and drank of the best, and in spite of that she lasted long, surely she must have taken after her ancestors.[156]

Solórsano's recollections emphasizing the celebratory aspects of life remind us that despite the hardships and traumas experienced in this history, people found ways to build community, find time to celebrate, and persist. Her stories also show that survival continued to involve drawing on traditional practices like ceremonies with sacred songs and dances. Dances such as the Kuksui dance continued to be practiced by Indigenous families in the years after the closing of the missions. Velasquez recalled that she had witnessed a Kuksui spiritual ceremony in her youth, most likely at the location of Juristac.[157] The ceremony would have to have been in the 1840s or 1850s, given her age, potentially a few decades after the closing of the missions. The Kuksui dance is a sacred ceremony practiced between spiritual leaders from neighboring communities, helping to build and reinforce connections across tribal lines. The continuation of this meaningful ceremony in these later years is further evidence of its importance to the health of the community as well as a testament to the survival of Indigenous communities well beyond the mission institutions.

In the face of so much loss and devastation, ceremonies and communal gatherings would have been crucial to survival. The communities formed by the families of Solórsano, Velasquez, and others eventually would join together to become the San Juan Band of Indians and, more recently, the Amah Mutsun Tribal Band.

Indigenous survivors consistently built community and expanded kinship ties with other survivors by drawing on traditional cultural practices such as language, traditional ecological knowledge, sacred ceremonies, and sweat lodges. While forced into great changes by consecutive colonial regimes, Indigenous peoples engaged in their own politics to navigate these trying times, challenging oppression and fighting for survival all along the way. Generations of mission survivors drew on their strength, ingenuity, and hard work to persevere against the many obstacles they faced. At times they were forced to hide their identities from settling societies that sought either their complete subjugation or their annihilation. And yet despite erasure by the dominant settling society, these Indigenous histories of rebellion, persistence, and survival have remained present within contemporary communities through oral histories shared among family members. Today contemporary Indigenous communities are engaged in ongoing movements to recognize and sustain traditional ceremonies and practices, drawing on these histories of struggle and survival. The existence of contemporary Indigenous Californians is only possible because of the sacrifices, ingenuity, strength, and perseverance of Indigenous ancestors who found ways to survive tremendous challenges, through eras of colonization, subjugation, exploitation, and outright genocide.

Conclusion

Today there is a resurgence of activity and healing among the Amah Mutsun Tribal Band, the largest tribal organization of descendants of those who survived Missions San Juan Bautista and Santa Cruz. They are involved in diverse activities and programs designed to reconstitute cultural and historical knowledge and practices. They have developed a land trust to traditionally facilitate land stewardship, which has been their people's obligation for millennia.[1] They are relearning their Mutsun language, working toward conducting tribal business in Mutsun in the coming decades.[2] They work with ecologists at Native plant gardens focused on relearning traditional ecological knowledge, such as the Amah Mutsun Relearning Program (AMRP) at the UC Santa Cruz Arboretum & Botanic Garden, to learn about native plants.[3] They have stewardship programs in which Amah Mutsun youth work alongside archaeologists conducting research, learning historical ecological practices, and restoring traditional cultural knowledge. The Amah Mutsun have partnered with local California State Parks in stewarding lands such as Quiroste Valley.[4] They have worked with local land trusts in gaining access to sacred sites, such as Mount Umunhum.[5] They have taken active roles in working to remove historical markers that glorify trauma, such as the El Camino Real bells.[6] The histories of persistence discussed in this book did not end with the closing of the nineteenth century. Indigenous survivors in the area and throughout California found ways to persevere through the twentieth and into the twenty-first century, and it is these multigenerational struggles that have inspired and made possible recent revival movements.

In July 1906, three years after the much publicized visit to Santa Cruz by U.S. president Teddy Roosevelt, the Mount Hermon Christian Conference Center hosted the Zayante Indian Conference of Friends of the Indians. The interdenominational Mount Hermon Center, in the mountain town of Zayante, had been christened less than a week before the conference. The Zayante township had been named for the local Sayanta tribe, who lived along Zayante Creek.[7] In 1841 Rancho Zayante was granted to Tennessee-born Joseph Ladd Majors. After receiving a second land grant in Rancho San Agustin (modern Scott's Valley), Majors facilitated the sale of Rancho Zayante to Virginia-born American Isaac Graham. The Mount Hermon center was built not far from the site of Graham's old lumber mill and liquor distillery. The conference was the first of its kind for the Northern California Indian Association (NCIA).[8] The two-day meeting was the first of at least eleven annual gatherings.[9]

C. E. Kelsey, special agent for the Office of Indian Affairs and Indian rights reformer, had formed the San José chapter of the NCIA in 1894. The NCIA was a West Coast branch of the Philadelphia-based Women's National Indian Association, which was founded in 1879 by a group of educators and activists including Mary Bonney and Amelia Stone Quinton, in reaction to the opening of Oklahoma Indian Territory to white settlement.[10] These organizations were created to advocate for American Indian policy during what is known as the Assimilation era and especially reforms in education, Christianization, and sobriety.[11] Assimilation policies, including the federal boarding schools for Native Americans and the Dawes General Allotment Act, were the progressive U.S. alternatives to Indian removal and warfare.[12]

Two hundred people attended the 1906 NCIA conference, but very few of them were Indigenous Californians. Despite the meeting's Santa Cruz location, nobody from the local Native community attended. The Zayante Indian Conference official report articulated their understanding of local Indigenous history, proclaiming "when set free by the fall of the missions, these latter Indians, as a rule went home where they came from. Those of the Mission strip proper [the coastal zone from San Diego to Sonoma] proved unable to maintain for themselves; there was nothing for them to do, or very little, and they disappeared rapidly."[13] Articulating the myth of the vanishing California Indian, they did not expect to see Indians in towns, as they assumed that they had rejoined what was left of their tribes or simply "disappeared."[14]

The goals of the NCIA conference included bringing public awareness to the difficult conditions facing California Indians, along with a host of assimilation era policies and programs designed to "uplift" and "civilize" Indigenous Californians. These goals set the conference in contrast with the extermination policies in California that had been backed by U.S. military as well as state and federal governmental organizations since the beginning of U.S. rule in 1846.[15] A major part of the conference participants' goals included missionization. As the report declared: "Perhaps the most important thing needed is the *Christianizing of the Indians*. I think you will probably all agree with me that the Indian cannot attain his full stature as a man unless he is a Christian man."[16] Thus, the aims of even the most well-intentioned early twentieth century U.S. organizations were eerily reminiscent of those of the Franciscans from a century earlier.

A combination of day schools and off-reservation boarding schools for Indigenous children were key components of U.S. assimilation policy in the late nineteenth and early twentieth centuries. These institutions had much in common with the missions: they sometimes were run by religious organizations, their goals were to assimilate Indigenous children in order to replace their traditional culture and languages, and they taught children and young adults menial labor skills in order to prepare them for work on the bottom rung of society.[17] As early as 1871, day schools were established on reservations like Northern California's Hoopa Valley and Round Valley.[18] By the 1880s off-reservation boarding schools were established across the state in places like Tule River (1880), Round Valley (1881), Anaheim, Fort Yuma, and the Sherman Institute in Riverside, among others.[19] A Santa Cruz newspaper painted a rosy picture of these schools, stating that "the Indians are taking kindly to education. They have the evidence before them of its benefits, not only from their white surroundings, but in those of their schools and acquired proficiency in scholarship. The tribes also discover that their very existence depends upon adopting the arts of civilization, and yield, although in some instances it may be reluctantly, to the march of progress."[20] And yet students resisted and challenged their situations at these schools, with high incidences of arson and fugitivism, not unlike their ancestors' response to the missions.[21]

In this first annual Zayante Indian Conference meeting of 1906, one Indigenous man, Mr. William Ralganal Benson from Ukiah, addressed the NCIA members in attendance, asking for better educational advantages for Indian children (industrial training) and that liquor might be taken from them ("You brought it to us, and you ought to take it away!"). Benson was a Pomo activist, basket weaver, and scholar.[22] He spoke at length about the need for land for settled homes ("You have taken it from us, and you might give us a little bit!").[23] This initial conference recorded the presence of only this one Indigenous man. The NCIA must have realized the significance of the absence of American Indian faces and voices, as subsequent conferences included California Indians, mostly men, whom they were careful to photograph, images they displayed in their annual reports (see fig. 11).

At the second annual Zayante Indian Conference, twenty California Indian men attended. The minutes reported that these men had joined with some hesitation, claiming that one had said: "For forty years white men make promises, and no keep promises. Hope gone. Just come to hear."[24] The "Indian delegates" to the conference put together a list of five demands: land for homes, protection from liquor traffic, education, field physicians, and legal protection. The men are all listed as having come from their homelands in California regions to the north (Santa Rosa, Hopland, Fort Bragg, Guidiville, Potter Valley, Chico, Laytonville) or inland (Porterville, Visalia, Morongo), regions just outside the boundaries of Spanish colonial settlement.[25]

Yet even with the presence of twenty Native Californians, none of the participants included members of the Indigenous community living in the greater Santa Cruz region. It is unknown if the conference organizers even made attempts to contact local Indigenous people, but their absence supported the larger idea of Indian disappearance that the conference members held.[26]

Much like the centennial celebration of Mission Santa Cruz in 1891, local officials ignored the presence of an Indigenous minority in the region in favor of promoting the narrative of the vanishing California Indian. As discussed in this book and elsewhere, white Californians, even those who genuinely sought to protect and help Native Californians, had embraced ideas that California Indians were vanishing since the 1850s. They failed to recognize Indigenous people who spoke Spanish, worked in towns, owned houses, or otherwise did not conform to stereotypes and expectations of "Indian" behavior or practices. Thus, local Indigenous people managed to pass under the radar.

For members of the surviving local Indigenous community, this invisibility might have been a welcome relief from persecution and violence. Indigenous politics of the early twentieth century focused on survival, frequently through hiding "Indian" identities. Spanish, Mexican, and U.S. rule in California had made it clear that the racial category of Indian came with second-class-citizen status. Their absence from these conferences, "celebrations," and other public displays may have been a welcome respite. The threat of removal to places like Fort Tejon, in Southern California, loomed large.[27] When discussing how his ancestors kept their Indianness quiet because of fears of being removed to distant reservations, Ketchum explained in 2003:

> I heard people say it was because they were concerned about being taken to, as I remember it, Tehachapi [Fort Tejon]. That was somewhere down around Bakersfield that they were concerned about being taken to. You've got to remember that the Mutsun people were living in the San Juan Bautista area, and they were intermarrying with Tulare. There were intermarriages with people up at San Jose. There were intermarriages with people who were from the Carmel area, and with some people down in the south. So they knew what was happening to the Indian people all over the state, and they knew whenever there was a law passed that put some sort of restriction on Indians, and they took care to protect themselves because of what had happened earlier.[28]

As Ketchum's story demonstrates, fears of removal or extermination reverberated through Indigenous Californian families across generations.

I began this study looking at the fourteen hundred Indigenous people living in the seven independent polities in Santa Cruz during the 1770s: the Aptos, Uypi, Cotoni, Sayanta, Chaloctaca, and Quiroste. In the ensuing 130 years, the area became home to Indigenous people from over thirty-five tribes from throughout the larger San Francisco Bay Area and northern San Joaquin Valley as well as Indigenous individuals and families brought together through colonial displacement involving Great Britain, Mexico, Russia, Spain, and the United States. Throughout this time Indigenous people adapted and expressed themselves politically and culturally. Moreover, the nineteenth-century San Francisco Bay Area was a zone of incredible colonial violence and persecution for Indigenous people through encounters involving Mexico, Russia, Spain, and the United States.

The nineteenth century was a time of rapid change, violent disruption, and a struggle for survival. In the early 1800s the Indigenous population at Mission Santa Cruz and Mission San Juan Bautista continually expanded as a diversity of tribes entered the mission under conditions of increasing violence by first Spanish and then Mexican soldiers. Yet colonial subjugation was frequently challenged—in direct attacks, escapees, and most visibly in the assassination of the sadistic Padre Quintana in 1812. Indigenous politics between diverse tribes both within and outside of mission lands continually shaped intermarriages, alliances, and rivalries, as kinship networks expanded and shaped the social and political interactions between Indigenous individuals and families.

In the Mexican era (1821–46) many local Indigenous families received some limited rights, but they continued to hold tentative positions in the larger social world developing within the new Mexican state. Most lost their small plots of lands in just a few years, in an environment of violence, hostility, and second-class status. By the U.S. era (1846–present), when genocidal policies openly targeted California Indians, Indigenous politics became even more a struggle for survival than before. Native families used strategies to hide their identities, drawing on the use of the Spanish language, familiarity with Mexican culture, and newcomers' racial myopia to pass as Mexican, in order to survive and avoid institutional violence. Nevertheless, despite staggering losses, some Indigenous people in Santa Cruz persevered through the U.S. era of the second half of the nineteenth century.

By the turn of the twentieth century, surviving Indigenous families in the Santa Cruz region did their best to retain remnants of their traditional culture and history through the preservation of language and Indigenous cultural values and by seeking out community with other Indigenous families.[29] The survival of Indigenous families stands as a testament to the tenacity, strength, and perseverance of these survivors. Survival itself was an act of defiance. The dominant narratives of California history have overlooked or ignored the histories of Native Californians, while families have struggled to hold onto the stories of their elder generations. California education systems have practiced what one scholar refers to as "ritual avoidance" by whitewashing these histories and silencing Indigenous Californian history.[30] Yet the histories and stories of Indigenous survivors remain in the oral histories and in the written archives for those who can find and listen to these voices.

In the first four decades of the twentieth century, ethnographers and anthropologists sought out local Native families to interview. They sometimes met with surviving elders who still spoke Indigenous languages. These scholars searched for, located, and recognized prominent California Indian families interconnected throughout the region. These scholars included the ethnographer Jeremiah Curtin, the anthropologist Alfred Edward Kroeber, the anthropologist Edward W. Gifford, the anthropologist and linguist James Alden Mason, the ethnographer C. Hart Merriam, and the ethnologist and linguist John Peabody Harrington. These academics relentlessly sought signs of "traditional" practices and language. While many of these scholars considered their work as "salvage anthropology," or, the preservation of vanishing cultures and languages, in actuality their many interviews attested to the persistence of California Indian languages and cultural practices. Their recordings and interviews continue to help contemporary tribal members reconnect to ancestral lands, history, and language.

Around the greater San Francisco Bay Area, many Indigenous families relocated to ranchos or places where they could find other surviving communities of mixed Ohlone, Yokuts, and Miwok people. In the late twentieth century members of these communities and families organized themselves to form several reconstituted tribal nations. Of these at least four nations, each representing hundreds of members of Indigenous Bay Area peoples, have had active petitions for federal recognition: the Muwekma Ohlone Tribe of the San Francisco Bay Area, Ohlone Costanoan Esselen Nation (OCEN), the Costanoan-Rumsen Carmel Tribe (CRCT), and the Amah Mutsun Tribal Band. Each of these communities has filed multiple times for federal recognition.[31] Other mission descendant families have organized groups such as the Confederated Villages of Lisjan, the Confederation of Ohlone Peoples, the Chalon Indian Nation, and the Association of Ramaytush Ohlone (ARO).[32] None are currently federally recognized, a by-product of an inflexible recognition process that fails to take into account the specific colonial histories and historical processes that have shaped these groups.

The Muwekma Ohlone Tribe of the San Francisco Bay Area includes a combination of Ohlone and Miwok peoples from the East Bay and the Santa Clara region. The Muwekma formed out of at least six rancherias—one in San Leandro (1830s–60s), Alisal Rancheria near Pleasanton (1850s–1916), Sunol (1880s–1917), Del Mocho in Livermore (1830s–1940s), El Molino in Niles (1830s–1910), and a later settlement in Newark (ca. 1914–present day).[33] They brought together Chocheño- and Tamyen-speaking Ohlone, many who were also descended from Yokuts or Coast Miwok ancestors. During World War I, before all Native Americans officially received citizenship, at least six Muwekma members enlisted in the U.S. Army and fought in the war.[34] Between 1906 and 1928 the tribe had been federally recognized as the Verona Band of Indians of Alameda County.[35] Today, under the leadership of tribal chairwoman Charlene Njimeh, the Muwekma continue to fight to regain federal recognition and involve themselves in Indigenous issues throughout the Bay Area.[36] Muwekma tribal members are finding new ways to celebrate Ohlone culture, like Vincent Medina's Café Ohlone.[37]

The Ohlone Costanoan Esselen Nation was formed by survivors of the Monterey region.[38] It includes members of the two bordering Indigenous cultures of the Monterey area—Ohlone and Esselen—and descendants of speakers of Rumsen Ohlone and Esselen. Like the Muwekma and Amah Mutsun, many OCEN members have enlisted in the U.S. military. In the 1930s the Rumsen Ohlone elder Isabel Meadows worked as a frequent linguistic informant for John Peabody Harrington.[39] In 2021 the OCEN, under the leadership of tribal chairwoman Louise J. Miranda, represents more than six hundred enrolled members tracing back to at least nineteen distinct villages.[40]

A group of Rumsen Ohlone families who left the Monterey area in the nineteenth century, fleeing U.S.-era violence and persecution, formed the Costanoan Rumsen Carmel Tribe (CRCT). Many of these families relocated to Southern California, finding work on ranchos and remaining to the present day.[41] The CRCT continues to preserve and celebrate Ohlone culture through language classes, tule boat launches, traditional dances, and gatherings, including an annual Bear Ceremony and well-attended annual Big Time gathering held at the San Francisco Presidio. However, the CRCT's efforts to obtain land in the Monterey Bay area have so far proven unsuccessful.

The last of these four large groups is the one most directly connected to Mission Santa Cruz—the Amah Mutsun Tribal Band.[42] Members are descended from families with ties to both Mission Santa Cruz and Mission San Juan Bautista and speakers of both the Awaswas and the Mutsun Ohlone languages. In 1929 and 1930 tribal member Ascención Solórsano de Cervantes and her granddaughter Martha Herrera worked closely with J. P. Harrington, sharing linguistic and cultural knowledge.[43] They helped Harrington to record a substantial body of important linguistic and historical records including over sixty-seven thousand anthropological field notes, a small sampling of which is cited in the previous chapters. Like the three previously mentioned tribes, the Amah Mutsun survived by working in agricultural fields and served in the U.S. military.[44] Today, under the guidance of tribal chairman Valentin Lopez, the Amah Mutsun are involved in conservation and land trust programs to protect traditional tribal territories, native plant restoration and relearning programs, and a variety of other local movements. The land trust strategy points to innovative approaches to Indigenous land recovery that offer alternatives to traditional American Indian struggles for federal recognition.[45]

As this book has shown, Indigenous Californians deployed a variety of strategies to navigate the nineteenth century. In addition to the four larger reconstituted tribal nations, Indigenous Californian families found ways to persevere on their own or in smaller family groups. Some, like the Tachi-Yokut Tribe, returned to their homelands in the San Joaquin Valley and joined with others in reconstituting their own tribal entities.[46] Many have chosen to remain independent of these larger groups. Descendants of mission fugitives, including Ann Marie Sayers, found refuge in places such as Indian Canyon near Hollister, the only recognized and protected Native land base in the Bay Area.[47] Many, like Gregg Castro and his family, hid out of sight from the dominant society.[48] Some individuals, such as Rumsen Ohlone descendant Linda Yamane, have worked tirelessly to revitalize traditional Indigenous practices such as basketry and storytelling, despite not identifying with the larger organized California Indian nations.[49] Other Indigenous people from Mexico, other areas in California, and throughout North America moved into the traditional Ohlone homelands, forming communities with existing California Indian families.[50] To be clear, this is not intended as a definitive list by any means, as there are many descendants of mission-surviving families alive today, some affiliated with larger tribal nations and others choosing not to be. The intention here is to trace some of this history to make it clear that Indigenous families survived the missions and the genocidal U.S. policies and are very much alive and present today. The resurgence and reformation of many groups and families today is in part a result of many years of struggle for rights and recognition.

Since the 1970s the struggles to protect burials and sacred sites have frequently brought increasing activism and organization among Indigenous families and individuals. In 1975 there was nearly a violent showdown over construction at the stie of multiple Indigenous burials on Lee Road, near Watsonville.[51] This site dated back to around 500 BCE.[52] Patrick Orozco, a Watsonville-based member of the Rios family mentioned briefly in the previous chapter, a family of Chumash and other California Indian ancestry, had watched over this graveyard. Orozco's grandmother had told him about how his grandfather would pray at the cemetery and tell his family: "Your people are there. Respect them and protect them."[53] In spring of 1975 developers began to bulldoze the cemetery to build a warehouse. When construction began, Orozco reached out to the local Indigenous community in the hopes of protecting the sacred burial site.[54]

After reports of looters opening one of the graves on March 13, the local Indigenous community responded by posting armed guards on site.[55] Armed with rifles, bows, and arrows, Orozco and others from the local Indigenous community entered the graveyard one night and occupied the site.[56] More local Native Americans joined within a few weeks, including members of the San José chapter of the American Indian Movement (AIM), members of the Northwest Indian Cemetery Protective Association, along with Cherokee, Lakota, Cheyenne, Yaqui, and even a group of Hopi elders, who performed a ceremony at the occupation site.[57] Other allies also rallied to support the occupation and protect the burial ground. Members of the Santa Cruz chapter of Vietnam Veterans Against the War / Winter Soldier Organization (VVAW/WSO) arrived and brought food for the occupiers.[58]

Rob Edwards, Cabrillo College professor of archaeology, also intervened on behalf of Orozco, supporting the Natives' claims.[59]

The developers agreed to halt construction until the bodies were reburied, avoiding violent conflict.[60] On March 23 a settlement was reached, allowing the developers to build the warehouse on the already bulldozed half of the graveyard in agreement for selling the other half of the cemetery to the Pajaro chapter of the Northwest Indian Cemetery Protective Association for $17,500.[61] The action invigorated and inspired the local Indigenous community. Families that had hidden their Indigenous roots from public view now found that they could choose to gather publicly. In response, to advocate for future site protections, Orozco and others involved helped form a local branch of the Northwest Indian Cemetery Protective Association, which eventually evolved into the Pajaro Valley Ohlone Indian Council.[62]

Thirty-five years later, in 2011, a similar situation occurred when developers KB Home encountered the remains of a child buried near a six thousand-year-old village site near the San Lorenzo River.[63] KB Home was founded in 1956 and grew to become a nationwide corporation, the first home building company to be traded on the New York Stock Exchange, and a company that frequently appeared on the Fortune 500. The most likely descendant, Anne Marie Sayers (Mutsun Ohlone), was notified. Local Indigenous leaders and non-Indigenous allies formed the Save the Knoll Coalition, raising public awareness through marches and threats of occupation. After a series of protests and meetings, the Santa Cruz City Council halted construction while they met with representatives from the developers and the Ohlone. Sayers helped to organize a council of local Ohlone elders, who met with the city council and representatives from KB Home.[64] This council was composed of a diverse group of Ohlone people from throughout the greater region.[65] Ultimately, after ongoing meetings, marches, and organizing, on September 19 KB Home elected to cancel building plans on the portion of the site containing known human burials, agreeing to establish an easement protecting the burial area in perpetuity, with provisions to allow Ohlone tribal members to access the grounds for ceremony.[66] Considering the size and corporate standing of KB Home, this victory was an impressive one and a testament to the potential of coordinated resistance and coalition building. Successful organizing around the protection of the knoll and negotiations with a major corporation inspired further collaborative movements to protect other sites throughout the region, such as the fight to protect the Ulistac village site in Santa Clara in 2013. As Ketchum explained: "Ulistac I believe is the equivalent place as Juristac in the Monterey Bay Ohlone world. It means Big Head Place. Big Head is a term used for the dancers in the various ceremonies of the 'Ohlone.' Their head dresses certainly made the heads big. The Spanish/Mexican seem to use 'L' and 'R' interchangeably for example 'Charon' and 'Chalon.'"[67] The fight to protect these sacred sites continues.

As I have argued throughout the book, the Indigenous landscape of the Santa Cruz region is a complex one of difference and diversity. Indigenous leaders had different goals and used different tactics for navigating these trying times of this colonial history. Some California Indians worked closely with missionaries and soldiers to chase down escapees, while others worked in direct opposition to the colonizers. In the late 1800s local leaders such as Lorenzo Asisara and Maria Filomena built new kinship connections through godparentage with Indigenous newcomers. California Indian survival in the Santa Cruz region has always involved the creation of new alliances and connections, a constant reorganizing of social and political relations before and after 1769. This pattern continues today, as more and more descendants use a variety of strategies and approaches to persevere and protect their families, culture, and lands.

Contemporary San Francisco Bay Area Indigenous people continue to contend with a development-centered regulatory environment that affords few formal protections for Native burial sites and sacred places. The Amah Mutsun have organized to protect their sacred lands of Juristac from development plans to turn it into a gravel pit.[68] The federal government's denial of access to Indian Health Services, designed for all non–federally recognized tribes such as those in the Santa Cruz region, results in a federal government failure to address the needs of generations of California Indian families impacted by more than two centuries of psychological and physical violence. Meanwhile, without adequate land bases, many have moved far from their traditional homelands in search of affordable living. Many California Indian groups continue to fight for federal recognition. Ironically, contemporary struggles continue to seek many of the same rights that those twenty Indigenous men at the second annual Zayante Indian

Conference asked for more than one hundred years ago. The legacies and consequences of the failed attempts to address issues of land and health concerns in the nineteenth and twentieth centuries continue to impact generations of Indigenous Californians today.

The twenty-first century has the potential to be one of revitalized Native American presence in Santa Cruz, the greater San Francisco Bay Area, throughout California, and beyond. The canonization of Junípero Serra in 2015, while celebrating the California mission era, also invigorated an already growing sense of Indigenous Californian pride and identity. In the fall of that year, the San Fernando–based Tataviam woman Caroline Ward and her son, Kagen Holland, embarked on a "780-mile pilgrimage to each of the twenty-one California Missions, to honor the Indigenous ancestors who suffered and perished in the Mission system and assert California Indian rejection of sainthood for Junipero Serra."[69] Along the way they met with Indigenous Californian leaders, elders, and community members, the vast majority of whom enthusiastically supported the group's message. At each mission they held ceremonies and shared stories of the ancestors, fostered by the offerings of diverse members of regional Indigenous communities who joined the walkers. The gatherings testified to the fact that Native Californians endured, persevered, and remain. The pilgrimage has inspired ongoing conversations and communications across the state between the diverse contemporary Indigenous Californian communities that share a common history of survival and trauma from the last 250-plus years. Today we are fortunate to have more and more Indigenous academics and new approaches to the archives that embrace Indigenous epistemologies, categories, and methodologies as well as methods drawn from a variety of fields ranging from anthropology to genocide studies to medical history. These new studies have the potential to help bring this history to light and, most importantly, support the efforts of contemporary Indigenous Californian communities.[70] It is my hope that by illuminating these important histories and recognizing the strength and tenacity of the Indigenous families that fought against great odds in times of tremendous loss and upheaval, we can all learn to better understand the history of these lands and peoples, learn to listen to and honor the descendants of these families, and ultimately to recognize that the incredible work being done today by contemporary Indigenous Californian communities is a testament to the strength and ingenuity of their ancestors.

Notes

Foreword

1. Elias Castillo, *Cross of Thorns*, 154.

2. It is widely accepted that the California Indian population at first contact was somewhere around 310,000, see Cook, *Population of the California Indians*, 43. The California Native American Heritage Commission website, also drawing on Cook's work, notes that the California Indian population in 1900 was 16,000.

Introduction

1. Solórsano to Harrington, "San Juan Report," 1930, JPH, microfilm, reel 59, p. 28. This story has been reprinted from this original interview, most notably by Yamane, *Snake That Lived in the Santa Cruz Mountains*.

2. Email to author, September 26, 2016.

3. Other studies that examine this perseverance include, among others, Chavez, "Indigenous Artists, Ingenuity, and Resistance," Panich, *Narratives of Persistence*, Deborah A. Miranda, *Bad Indians*, Phillips, *Chiefs and Challengers*.

4. Other historical studies that privilege Indigenous voices include historian Denetdale, *Reclaiming Diné History*; anthropologist Cruikshank, *Social Life of Stories*; historians Miller, *Coacoochee's Bones*; Sleeper-Smith, *Rethinking the Fur Trade*; and Cavender Wilson, *Remember This*. This approach is also discussed by Pleasant, Wigginton, and Wisecup, "Materials and Methods in Native American and Indigenous Studies." My work is far from the only work centering Native Californian perspectives, and is written in hopes of being in dialogue with many who are already doing this. For example, William J. Bauer has written books specifically about centering Native Californian perspectives; see *California through Native Eyes*. Deborah A. Miranda (Rumsen Ohlone / Esselen) has written numerous articles and a book, *Bad Indians*, offering critical Indigenous perspectives and readings of the archival sources. Additionally, Risling Baldy, *We Are Dancing for You*, helps reveal how Native feminisms have always existed in Indigenous oral histories.

5. My interest in the larger themes of colonialism and Indigeneity spring from learning about my own family history. My paternal grandfather was born in Gal-

lup, New Mexico, and moved to California in the 1920s. Our family stories trace back to early colonial settlement in Santa Fe. I grew up hearing stories about colonialism in New Mexico, about our family's involvement in Indian wars, and about my grandfather's mixed-blood (New) Mexican and Indigenous heritage. These stories planted seeds and raised questions in my young mind about the relationship between place, identity, and colonialism. Upon moving to Santa Cruz, the same questions led me to wonder about local Indigenous history and compelled me to pursue these questions academically, despite my being a first-generation college student.

6. The Amah Mutsun continue to fight to protect sacred sites such as Juristac; see Amah Mutsun Tribal Band, "Protect Juristac," protectjuristac.org. For more on historical resistance informing contemporary struggles, see Alfred and Corntassel, "Being Indigenous"; Estes, *Our History Is the Future*; and Kauanui and Warrior, *Speaking of Indigenous Politics*.

7. Amador, "Memorias sobre la historia de California," Bancroft Library (BL), BANC MSS C-D 28, 58–77. This is the interview of Santa Cruz Mission–born Lorenzo Asisara contained in the notes of Bancroft's field historian, Thomas Savage, who conducted two interviews with Asisara in 1877. Asisara continued in his second interview with stories of life within the mission (90–113). A third interview in 1890, by Santa Cruz historian E. L. Williams, "Narrative of a Mission Indian, etc.," was published in Harrison's *History of Santa Cruz County*, 45–48. Asisara's interviews by Savage have been published in translation twice, the first time in a series of two articles by historian Castillo, "The Assassination of Padre Andrés Quintana by the Indians of Mission Santa Cruz in 1812" and "An Indian Account of the Decline and Collapse of Mexico's Hegemony over the Missionized Indians of California," 391–408. The account was later provided in Spanish and translated into English by Mora-Torres, *Californio Voices*.

8. Dunn, *Santa Cruz Is in the Heart*, 2:1–13. Dunn provides an excellent introduction to Asisara and overview of local Indigenous history. For other accounts of life within the missions, see Haas, *Pablo Tac*. Tac and Asisara are the only two mission survivors whose stories are publicly available. More accounts exist from later generations, including that of the Chumash man Fernando Librado Kitsepawit, born at Mission San Buenaventura, who was interviewed extensively by ethnographer Harrington in the early 1900s. See Librado, *Breath of the Sun*. Librado was born in 1839, around the time of secularization, when the missions closed. Johnson, "Trail to Fernando," 132–38.

9. Solórsano to Harrington, "San Juan Report," JPH, microfilm, reels 58 and 59.

10. The original books with these are held in various archives, while copies are to be found in the Santa Barbara Mission Archive Library (hereafter SBMAL). The books pertaining to Mission Santa Cruz, San Juan Bautista, and San Carlos

are all at the Monterey Archdiocese archives in Monterey. The information in these books can also be found online, with the Early California Population Project (ECPP): http://www.huntington.org/ecpp. In 1998, under the guidance of historian Steven Hackel, members of the Huntington Library began work on the ECPP. This incredibly important project digitized these records until 1850 and made them available to the public online in the early 2000s. Hackel, "Early California Population Project Report," 73–76. The construction of this database builds on the work of anthropologists Randall Milliken and John R. Johnson. Beginning in the 1970s, Milliken and Johnson gathered these records pertaining to each mission and meticulously copied, transcribed, and compiled tens of thousands of individual sacramental registry entries documenting each baptism, marriage, and burial record. Milliken compiled the records for the northern missions, Johnson for the southern. With this data the two scholars have been able to illuminate a greater understanding of individuals, families, and tribes across the missions. The late Milliken's database is currently located at the Bancroft Library in Berkeley: Randall Milliken Papers, BANC MSS 2013/157, University of California (UC), Berkeley. I was fortunate to know Milliken and was able to work with his database and materials before he submitted them to the Bancroft. The anthropologists' many works include Milliken, *Time of Little Choice* and *Native Americans at Mission San Jose*; Johnson, "Chumash Social Organization" and *Chumash Indians after Secularization*; and Smith and Johnson, "Lengua de los Llanos," 299–313.

11. I have built my own database from a combination of the records from the ECPP, the original missionary books, and the Milliken database. My approach extends the reach of these archives, as I have worked closely with additional data from the chancery records, including a close look at the godparentage and confirmation records. While the ECPP contains much information, there are a few limitations to the database. First, the records only extend until 1850, while my book covers a longer period. Second, there are the occasional minor errors or misreadings of smeared, smudged, or otherwise tough-to-read records, often necessitating a rereading of the originals. Third, the ECPP does not include confirmation records, which I have used in my research. Fourth, the ECPP and original records have little geographic information about tribal positioning. Milliken, who frequently worked in the field, added his own insights into the tribal geographic landscape in notes that are contained in his own database. About halfway through the writing of my dissertation I had the fortune to meet and work with Milliken, after which he shared a copy of his database. Additional studies that center on ideas of kinship include historian Brooks, *Our Beloved Kin*.

12. By focusing on the stories of individuals and families, I follow in the steps of historian De Danaan, *Katie Gale*. While my methodology and scope are different,

De Danaan's book provides an excellent framework for examining an Indigenous individual in the nineteenth century to reveal dynamics relevant to a larger scale.

13. For more on settler colonialism, see historian Ostler, "Locating Settler Colonialism."

14. For example, I have been in dialogue with historian Robert Michael Morrissey, who has used a methodology called "social network analysis" to examine interconnections in godparentage data in Native communities in Illinois. Morrissey, "Kaskaskia Social Network," 103–46. I hope to apply a similar method in future work to tease out further interconnections and patterns in the California records. This type of nuanced reading of documents to locate hidden stories is in line with other works, such as Scott, *Domination and the Arts of Resistance*.

15. For examples of works proposing the centering of Indigenous perspectives in retelling California history, see historian Bauer, *California through Native Eyes*; and Sarris, *Keeping Slug Woman Alive*.

16. Most scholars who emphasize decolonization suggest that colonial relations and legacies continue to impact everyone, not just Indigenous peoples, as colonialism has shaped epistemological categories such as gender, individualism, time, space, authenticity, and race, to name but some. Miller and Riding In, *Native Historians Write Back*; Tuhiwai Smith, *Decolonizing Methodologies*; Champagne, "Centering Indigenous Nations"; and Mihesuah and Cavender, *Indigenizing the Academy*. Similar works address Latin American histories; see Hill Boone and Mignolo, *Writing without Words*; Quijano, "Coloniality of Power," 533–80; Lugones, "Heterosexism and the Colonial/Modern Gender System," 186–209; and Mallon, *Decolonizing Native Histories*.

17. These epistemological categories include cultural differences in concepts such as individualism, family, space, time, authenticity, race, and gender. See Tuhiwai Smith, *Decolonizing Methodologies*.

18. Deloria, *World We Used to Live In*; and Praet, "Shamanism and Ritual in South America."

19. Along the lines of Silverman, *This Land Is Their Land*. For more on the myth of the missions, see Lorimer, *Resurrecting the Past*. For more on "ritual avoidance" in the treatment of missions in California classrooms, see Keenan, "Mission Project." Other important works are engaging with landscapes and public spaces around the missions; see Kryder-Reid, *California Mission Landscapes*; and Helmbrecht, "Revisiting Missions."

20. One of the most important of the works that highlight TEK and Indigenous Californian knowledge is Anderson, *Tending the Wild*. Some historians have looked at ecological reorganization in Spanish colonization; see the essays by Hackel, "Land, Labor, and Production"; and Anderson, Barbour, and Whitworth, "World in Balance and Plenty." See also Kimmerer, *Braiding Sweetgrass*.

21. Brave Heart, "American Indian Holocaust," 60–82; Duran and Duran, *Native American Postcolonial Psychology*; and Gone, "Community-Based Treatment," 751–62.

22. Van der Kolk, *Body Keeps the Score*; and Wolynn, *It Didn't Start with You*.

23. A great example is found by anthropologists such as Basso, *Wisdom Sits in Places*. Basso illustrates how Indigenous categories of history, language, and knowledge are inescapably intertwined with local geographies. See also Cruikshank, *Do Glaciers Listen*, and important new research by Indigenous anthropologists like that of Carolyn Smith, "Weaving *pikyav* (to-fix-it)."

24. Historian Newell, *Constructing Lives at Mission San Francisco*; archaeologist Silliman, *Lost Laborers in Colonial California*; historians Teixeira, *Costanoan/Ohlone Indians*; and Bean Lowell, *Ohlone Past and Present*.

25. Archaeologists Panich, "Archaeologies of Persistence," 105–22; Tsim D. Schneider, "Heritage In-Between," 51–63; Panich and Tsim Schneider, *Indigenous Landscapes and Spanish Missions*; and Panich, *Narratives of Persistence*. The theme of persistence has also recently been explored by sociologist Cordero, "Native Persistence." Furthermore, some new scholarship is challenging the concept of persistence, instead preferring a model of survivance, which emphasizes the actual survival of Native people, and is built on the work of Vizenor, *Survivance*. Acebo and Martinez, "Towards an Analytic of Survivance."

26. Anthropologist Lightfoot, *Indians, Missionaries, and Merchants*, 239. Many of the aforementioned archaeologists build on the pioneering work of Lightfoot.

27. Physiologist turned historian Cook, *Conflict between the California Indian*; Cook, *Population of the California Indians*; and historian Heizer, *Destruction of California Indians*.

28. Engelhardt, *Missions and Missionaries of California*; Guest, *Examination of the Thesis of S. F. Cook*; Bancroft, *California Pastoral*. One recent study shows how Indigenous people in California responded to epidemics in creative ways, emphasizing survival; see anthropologist Hull, *Pestilence and Persistence*. My work is more similar to Hull's.

29. The topic of the "vanishing Indian" and other harmful narratives have been explored in depth in historians Deloria, *Indians in Unexpected Places*; O'Brien, *Firsting and Lasting*; and Dunbar-Ortiz and Gilio-Whitaker, *"All the Real Indians Died Off."*

30. Costo and Henry Costo, *Missions of California*. This compilation was put together as a response to the movement to canonize Junípero Serra in the 1980s. While it similarly embraces arguments of genocide and extermination at points, it is notable for its inclusion of a diversity of Indigenous Californian perspectives. See also Secrest, *When the Great Spirit Died*; and Heizer, *Destruction of California Indians*.

31. Anthropologists Bean and Blackburn, *Native Californians*. The Chicano studies movement is the best example of this shift toward cultural and social history. For a small sampling of these early works, see Acuña, *Occupied America*; Prago, *Strangers in Their Own Land*; and Camarillo, *Chicanos in a Changing Society*.

32. Historians Hurtado, *Indian Survival*; and Phillips, *Indians and Intruders*. On gender, see Hurtado, *Intimate Frontiers*; and Chávez-García, *Negotiating Conquest*. More recently, Bouvier argues that "gender ideology was one of the ingredients in the glue that held together the conquest project . . . [and] also shaped indigenous behavior toward the Spanish conquerors" (*Women and the Conquest of California*, xv), while Miranda and Risling Baldy have pushed this analysis into exciting new directions. See Deborah A. Miranda, "Extermination of the *Joyas*" and "'They Were Tough, Those Old Women before Us'"; and Risling Baldy, *We Are Dancing for You*.

33. Historians Jackson, *Indian Population Decline* and *Race, Caste, and Status*; and Jackson and Castillo, *Indians, Franciscans, and Spanish Colonization*.

34. Jackson, "Disease and Demographic Patterns," 33–57.

35. This new historiographic shift has recently been explored by Zappia in "California Indian Historiography," 28–34.

36. Historian Sandos, *Converting California*; and Sandos and Sandos, "Early California Reconsidered," 592–625. The latter article, in particular, stands out for its engagement with the baptismal registries in a similar way as this book. The issue of conversion and baptism is further explored by Cordero, "California Indians."

37. Hackel, *Children of Coyote*; "Staff of Leadership," 347–76; and "Sources of Rebellion," 643–69.

38. Hackel, *Children of Coyote*, 11.

39. Other studies that similarly relied upon these binaries are found with Hurtado, *Indian Survival*; Jackson and Castillo, *Indians, Franciscans, and Spanish Colonization*; Hackel, *Children of Coyote*; and Castillo, *Cross of Thorns*. These studies have contributed much to our understanding of Indigenous history but did not move beyond this dichotomy. Hackel identified tribal difference but did not examine these differences in his analysis of Indigenous politics. Castillo's study, important for its contribution to our understanding of Spanish cruelty, does not examine Indigenous difference and diversity. An excellent study that shows the limitations of these binaries is Raibmon, *Authentic Indians*. Furthermore, this binary erases difference among the Spanish settling community, many of whom traced back to mestizo or even Indigenous heritage from Guanajuato, Guadalajara, or Mexico City. Langer traces the historical context of Italian Franciscan missionaries in Bolivia in *Expecting Pears from an Elm Tree*. Beebe and

Senkewicz similarly explore the histories of the Franciscan missionaries in California in "What They Brought," 17–46, as does Rex Galindo, *To Sin No More*. Others have explored identity formation and Spanish colonialism; see Radding Murrieta, *Wandering Peoples*, and Voss, *Archaeology of Ethnogenesis*.

40. Cutcha Risling-Baldy, "In Which I Finally Explain My One Star Rating of Steven Hackel's Children of Coyote Book or Why I Will Probably Never Be Hired in a History Department or I Often Write LOL in the Margins of My Books—It's True (Now with Picture Evidence!)," *Sometimes Writer-Blogger Cutcha Risling-Baldy*, May 21, 2013, https://www.cutcharislingbaldy.com/blog/in-which-i-finally-explain-my-one-star-rating-of-steven-hackels-children-of-coyote-book-or-why-i-will-probably-never-be-hired-in-a-history-department-or-i-often-write-lol-in-the-margins-of-my-books-its-true-now-with-picture-evidence. From Risling-Baldy's excellent and in-depth blog post critiquing Hackel's work.

41. Haas offers a more nuanced approach to Indigenous California, emphasizing questions of Indigenous identity construction while demonstrating how cultural continuities allowed for the formation of "quiet opposition to Catholicism and Spanish culture" (*Conquests and Historical Identities*, 27).

42. Haas, *Saints and Citizens*; and Chavez, "Indigenous Artists, Ingenuity, and Resistance."

43. Haas, *Saints and Citizens*, 7.

44. Gutiérrez and Orsi, *Contested Eden*; and Hackel, *Alta California*. Hackel's book is a compilation that brings together some of the more cutting-edge historical works on Indigenous California, including essays by Haas and Sandos.

45. Some recent articles have effectively used these records in innovative ways as well. Some examples include Sandos and Sandos, "Early California Reconsidered," 592–625; Newell, *Constructing Lives*; Stoll, Douglass, and Ciolek-Torrello, "Searching for Guaspet," 1–9; and Fischer, *Cattle Colonialism*. Still, none of these engages deeply with the godparentage data, which is crucial to understanding kinship ties through the mission era and beyond. This book is also in dialogue with archaeologists such as the previously mentioned Newell, Panich, Tsim Schneider, and Silliman.

46. Lightfoot, *Indians, Missionaries, and Merchants* (Spanish and Russian); and Madley, *American Genocide* (which traces how the U.S. Indian policy grew out of Spanish and Mexican policies).

47. Trafzer and Hyer, *Exterminate Them*; and Phillips, *Indians and Indian Agents*.

48. Lindsay, *Murder State*; and Madley, *American Genocide*.

49. Bauer, *We Were All Like Migrant Workers*; and Phillips, *Vineyards & Vaqueros*.

50. Cothran, *Remembering the Modoc War*.

51. Some examples include Shackley et al., *Early Ethnography of the Kumeyaay*; Haas, *Pablo Tac*; Hull and Douglass, *Forging Communities*; Dartt-Newton and Erlandson, "Little Choice for the Chumash"; Gamble, "Subsistence Practices and Feasting Rites"; Gamble, *Chumash World at European Contact*; Roy, "Tongva People"; John, "Toypurina"; O'Neil, *Acjachemen (Juaneño) Indians*; and Sepulveda, "Our Sacred Waters."

52. Arkush, "Native Responses to European Intrusion," 62–90; Tsim D. Schneider and Panich, "Landscapes of Refuge and Resiliency"; Allen, *Native Americans at Mission Santa Cruz*; and Skowronek, "Sifting the Evidence," 675–708.

53. Khal Schneider et al., "More than Missions."

54. Kimbro, Ryan, and Jackson, *Como La Sombra*. The late Kimbro, a local architectural historian, provides an excellent architectural history of Mission Santa Cruz. This report contains much of her findings and served as an outstanding resource for my research. Her notes are stored in the Edna Kimbro Archives, cared for by archivist Charlene Duvall. Allen, *Native Americans at Mission Santa Cruz*. Allen provides the most complete archaeological study of the sole standing adobe structure, which was home to Indigenous community members. Her study reveals the persistence of traditional practices.

55. Tsim D. Schneider, "Placing Refuge," 695–713. Schneider describes "hinterlands" as "landscapes that, in time, provided contexts for continuity and adjustment among Indian communities making social, material, and economic choices in the wake of missionization." Panich and Schneider similarly discuss a "landscape" approach, which seeks to "expand mission archaeology by illuminating the opportunities for indigenous autonomy in social, political, and economic relationships that intersected colonial modes in various ways across time and space" ("Expanding Mission Archaeology," 48–58). Another exciting project is helping to locate examples of macropolitical forms of autonomy and prosperity in the colonial hinterlands: Acebo, "Re-Assembling Radical Indigenous Autonomy."

56. This book is in dialogue with studies that examine Indigenous peoples outside the realm of European encounters, notably Blackhawk, *Violence over the Land*; James Brooks, *Captives and Cousins*; and Hämäläinen, *Comanche Empire*.

57. For example, Spanish records refer to the Aleutian seal hunters whom Russians brought southward in the early 1800s as "Russian Indians" and the Nuu-chah-nulth people of Vancouver Island, a number of whom English and Spanish colonizers brought to the San Francisco area in the 1790s, as "Indians."

58. For a look at the racial system of the Spanish (*sistema de castas*), see Martínez, *Genealogical Fictions*. On colonial relations on the Spanish frontiers,

see Radding Murrieta, *Wandering Peoples*. For an overview of the changing categories extending into the Mexican years, see Gloria Miranda, "Racial and Cultural Dimensions," 265–78. With regards to Alta California, see Johnson and Lorenz, "Genetics and the *Castas*."

59. American and Latin American scholars alike have explored methodological problems in Indigenous encounters. For key examples that influence my research, see Burns, *Into the Archive*; and Van Young, "Cuautla Lazarus," 3–26. Burns turns a critical eye to the notaries and record keepers themselves, while Van Young explores the difficulties in discerning "truth-value" in contested encounters.

60. I avoid these terms throughout the book, as they evoke a condescending interpretation of Indigenous people. For example, all baptized Native people are seen as neophytes—spiritual novices. This term was used on children and adults alike, on newborns and incoming spiritual leaders, failing to recognize or acknowledge existing spiritual expertise or knowledge. The term highlights the paternalistic approach of Spanish colonial settlers, who failed to recognize Indigenous ingenuity or knowledge. Throughout the book I instead choose to refer to people as baptized or unbaptized, as that corresponds to the underlying distinction between the categories of *neofito* and *gentile*. Of *neófia* Haas says, "A condition of unfreedom, it involved being renamed and the new name inscribed on the baptismal and census roles; unable to leave the mission without permission; required to work and live under mission regulations; and subject to the severe discipline of the missionary and guards" (*Saints and Citizens*, 5).

61. Voss, *Archaeology of Ethnogenesis*. Voss has explored the forging of new racial identities on this northern outpost of Spanish colonial society, which led to the creation of a new Californio culture.

62. Other works that examine Indigenous racial construction in American society, albeit in later periods, include Lowery, *Lumbee Indians in the Jim Crow South*.

63. Throughout the book I choose to prioritize the Indigenous names of people whenever possible. Missionaries imposed Spanish names at the time of baptism, and most Spanish, Mexican, and American records reflect these colonial names, with the lone exception of the baptismal registries, which often recorded Indigenous names. In this book I make the deliberate choice to use the Indigenous name and to provide the Spanish name in parentheses at first mention. This was a complicated decision, and I consulted contemporary tribal members in making it. It is important to recognize that, historically, Bay Area Indigenous peoples had a prohibition about speaking the names of the deceased in the years following their passing. I discussed whether to include Indigenous names or only Spanish with multiple Bay Area Indigenous community members, and

while a few expressed concerns about these historical prohibitions, the majority of people I spoke with, including Amah Mutsun tribal chair Valentin Lopez, felt that it was more important to illuminate and restore knowledge of these historical names, which are otherwise difficult to trace.

64. Milliken, *Time of Little Choice*. Milliken's book is the most thorough study of San Francisco Bay Area Indigenous history and serves as a starting point for my study. Milliken correctly characterized the Spanish colonial occupation of the region as "a time of little choice" for local Indigenous families.

65. Awaswas and Mutsun describe two distinct linguistic groups within the fifty-plus tribes identified today under the broad category of Ohlone. Like Ohlone, *Yokuts* refers to numerous linguistically and culturally distinct people, these of the inland San Joaquin Valley.

66. These numbers are based on my calculations built from the chancery records. I calculated these numbers by looking at all the baptisms, subtracting non-Native baptisms, taking into account those who moved from one mission to another, and other adjustments. This 90 percent loss is among the higher death rates but not an isolated situation. Missions San Carlos, La Purisima, and San Buenaventura all also had over 90 percent burial rates. Overall, not counting the two missions whose burial books have been lost (San Luis Rey and Soledad), for the other nineteen missions, I calculate 88,616 baptisms and 65,960 burials—a death rate of 80.9 percent.

67. These numbers are based on my calculations. I chose to end the range at 1831 because the burial and baptismal records become less complete in the 1830s, as the mission lost funding during secularization and eventually, by the late 1830s, emancipation freed Native people from their bondage to the mission, making the tracing of individual records more difficult. Mission Santa Cruz lists 476 Indigenous children as being born at the mission. But of these, I removed five children, as they were born over six months before arriving at the mission, leaving 471. This includes three children listed as having been born three months or less before baptism, which I included in my calculations. Of the 471 mission-born children, 239 died before reaching their first birthday (50.7%), 120 died between the age of one and five (25.5%), sixteen died between age five and ten (3.4%), and three died between ten and fifteen (0.6%). Ninety-six reached at least fifteen years or had insufficient records to know with certainty. Of those without sufficient data, seven were listed as fugitives. I counted them as potentially reaching adulthood due to an abundance of caution, and, frankly, unwarranted optimism, out of hope that they may have lived out their lives somewhere in their homelands. Another forty-eight that I counted as potentially reaching adulthood (over fifteen) did not have any burial records, meaning that they may have died at any point and somehow not been in the vicinity of the mission or

otherwise avoided recordation by the church. It is likely, though not certain, that this is because they moved away from the mission at some later point in their lives (possibly after secularization). This strong possibility justified counting them among those having reached adulthood.

68. I am drawing from multiple studies of precontact cemeteries in the San Francisco Bay Area. At the CA-SCL-732 Kaphan Umux (Three Wolves) site in southern San Jose, one study showed that of the 102 bodies, 22 were under the age of seventeen (21.6%). Cambra, "Archaeological Investigations," 4.5. A study at the CA-SCL-38 Yukisma site in Milpitas found 38 out of 244 individuals under the age of sixteen (16%). Bellifemine, "Mortuary Variability in Prehistoric Central California," 91. In slight contrast, the Sií Túupentak CA-ALA-565/H site just north of Fremont, California, found 30 out of 76 to be under the age of seventeen (39.5%). However, Byrd and his team compared these rates with fifteen neighboring precontact Indigenous cemeteries and found all but one to have much lower percentages of child burials (with regards to the varying age definitions used to define "child" in these studies, Byrd et al. note that "there are discrepancies in the way that adolescents are defined between projects, but generally the upper age limit is about 16 years old"). Though the total numbers of burials for each of the sixteen sites was not provided in the report, the average percentage of child burials among these sites, including the relatively high count at Sií Túupentak, was 24 percent. Byrd et al., *Protohistoric Village Organization and Territorial Maintenance*, 256–58. Hylkema's report on the Tamien Station CA-SCL-690 site in San Jose found 23 under the age of sixteen out of a total of 142 burials (16.2%). This study also compared neighboring precontact cemeteries (including many also listed in the Byrd report) and included the actual number of burials. For the eight sites compared, Hylkema found 271 subadults (under sixteen years) out of a total of 1,036 burials (26.2%). Hylkema, *Santa Clara Valley Prehistory*.

69. Scholars have typically used the word *recruitment* to describe relocation of Indigenous people into the California missions. The word clearly understates and erases what was always disruptive and at times a violent process of forceful coercion by suggesting an incentive driven enticement into the missions. I put the word within quotation marks at times within this book to signify this erasure and draw attention to the debate around this topic. But for the most part, in this book I use words that more directly describe the circumstances of relocation and intake in the given example.

70. Lindsay, *Murder State*; and Madley, *American Genocide*.

71. Peelo, "Baptism among the Salinan Neophytes." Peelo argues "that the reasons Native Californians chose baptism are geographically, temporally, and culturally contingent."

72. Friar Estévan Tapis to José de la Guerra, April 29, 1818, SBMAL, DLG 955, letter 2. Tapis refers to the "Misión de Mata Frayles" (mission of friar killers). Tapis is not alone in characterizing the mission this way, as Friar Marcelino Marquinez also refers to "la misión de los patricides de P Quintana" (the mission of padre killers of Padre Quintana). Marquinez to Governor Solá, August 25, 1819, SBMAL, CMD 1145.

73. The Kumeyaay of San Diego had killed Father Luís Jayme in 1774, but Mission Santa Cruz was the only site in the Bay Area with a successful assassination. The killing of Father Jayme is discussed by Bokovoy (*San Diego World's Fairs*, 1–2) and Saunt (*West of the Revolution*, 61–65). Mission Santa Cruz was a site of particular rebellion in the context of northern missions in the early Spanish colonial era. Southern California missions were also places of rebellion in those years, such as Mission San Gabriel with Toypurina's rebellion, see Hackel, "Sources of Rebellion." In later years, during the Mexican era and onward, these rebellions increased dramatically, as with the rebellions of Estanislao, Yozcolo, and Pomponio in the northern missions and the Chumash uprising, among others. See Sandos, "Levantamiento! The 1824 Chumash Uprising" and "Levantamiento! The 1824 Chumash Uprising Reconsidered"; and Flores, "Native American Response and Resistance."

74. Engelhardt, *Missions and Missionaries*; and Geiger, *Franciscan Missionaries in Hispanic California*. One exception is found in the work of Hackel, who focused on Mission San Carlos (*Children of Coyote*).

75. As such, this chapter is in dialogue with works that examine national identity formation in the Spanish Americas, including Reséndez, *Changing National Identities*; Joseph and Nugent, *Everyday Forms of State Formation*; and O'Hara, *Flock Divided*. O'Hara argues that despite official overtures toward abolishing racial categories, "the colonial category of Indian continued to shape religious practice and community litigation in many Mexican parishes" (237). It is also in dialogue with González, *This Small City*. González argues that Mexicans in Los Angeles defined themselves through warfare with their Indian neighbors, whom they saw as inferior. The Mexican villagers in the Santa Cruz region did not follow this pattern, due in part to their more complex mixed-blood heritage.

76. Earle, *Return of the Native*. Earle explores the ways that "Indians" and colonial ideas about them have been used in national memories and narratives, despite liberal policies to abolish the racial and social category.

77. Amador, "Memorias sobre la historia de California," BL, BANC MSS C-D 28, 60 (emphasis mine).

78. Madley, "California's First Mass Incarceration System."

79. By centering on Indigenous power, this book is in dialogue with other similar studies such as the works of historians Blackhawk, *Violence over the Land*; and Hämäläinen, *Comanche Empire*.

80. Schneider, Schneider, and Panich, "Scaling Invisible Walls," 3–4.

81. Mora-Torres, *Californio Voices*, 80–81. It is clear that Mora-Torres comes to the same conclusion about the relationship between Spaniards—in this case Padre Quintana—and the Indigenous community, but I prefer a more literal translation here. I believe this literal take maintains the direct challenge in Lino's statement.

82. Solórsano to Harrington, "San Juan Report," JPH, microfilm, reel 58, p. 45.

83. This quotation is used by Milliken, *Time of Little Choice*, 35 (original is in Tibesar, *Writings of Junípero Serra*, 2:87).

84. Solórsano to Harrington, "San Juan Report," JPH, microfilm, reel 58, pp. 79, 42.

1. *First Were Taken the Children*

1. Santa Clara baptism (SCLB) number 2718. I am choosing to prioritize Indigenous names, when available. Henceforth, when giving names, I will give Indigenous names first and add Spanish baptismal names in parentheses at the first mention of the person. Thereafter I will use the Native name. In the case in which no Native name is recorded, I will use the Spanish name alone. This attack and the conditions leading to it will be examined in detail later in this chapter.

2. These attacks and the red tile roofing response are explored by Madley, *American Genocide*, 34–35. Ipai and/or Tipai attackers used flaming arrows to attack Mission San Diego in 1775, while others used them on Mission San Luis Obispo in 1776 and over the next few years, resulting in the change to red tiles. The Chumash burned down buildings in a multi-mission war for independence in 1824.

3. Lightfoot and Parrish, *California Indians and Their Environment*, 14–36.

4. Keeley, "Native American Impacts," 316.

5. Governor José Joaquín de Arrillaga to Father Fermin de Lasuén, May 31, 1793, SBMAL, CMD 168 and 169. By 1793 Governor Arrillaga had formalized fire restrictions, ordering soldiers to prevent Indian fires in the open country around Santa Barbara.

6. Milliken, *Time of Little Choice*.

7. Sandos, *Converting California*. Sandos correctly observes that "accepting the ritual of Baptism after eight to thirty days of rote recitation of Christian prayers did not mean Indians expelled other beliefs from their hearts and heads" (xv). Sandos argued that conflating baptism with conversion justified, in their minds, the missionaries' interpretation of behavior that violated Catholic doctrine as sinful. For more on conversion, see Rex Galindo, *To Sin No More*, 169–227; and Kugel, "Religion Mixed with Politics." Kugel examines conversion

among the Ojibwa, concluding that it related more closely to ongoing political concerns than to Christianity.

8. Mutsun elder Barbara Solórsano told this story to anthropologist C. Hart Merriam in the early 1900s. This version comes from Hylkema, "Mount Umunhum Environmental Restoration ASR," 26.

9. Merriam to Harrington, December 26, 1929, JPH, microfilm, reel 59, p. 55. It is likely that this is a Mutsun word for these mountains, as Merriam notes in parentheses that this "may be in another language." Merriam received his information from Mutsun-speaking Barbara Sierra de Solórsano, mother of Ascención. We do not know if others, including the Awaswas speakers in the Santa Cruz area, knew it by a different name. In this book I choose to refer to the mountain range by the name Mak-Sah-Re-Jah, as it is the only Indigenous name we have for this region.

10. Local stories credit Hummingbird with bringing fire, stealing it from Badger, and turning his throat vermillion red in the process. Yamane, *When the World Ended*. Hylkema speculates that the presence of reddish cinnabar deposits on Mount Umunhum might correlate to the red throat of Hummingbird in "Mount Umunhum Environmental Restoration ASR" (16). Mount Umunhum was the site of the Almaden Air Force Station from 1958 to 1980. In 2017 the Midpeninsula Regional Open Space District Board of Directors voted to grant permanent property rights of Mount Umunhum to the Amah Mutsun Tribal Band. On September 14, 2017, the Amah Mutsun held a ceremony on the summit celebrating this as well as the opening of the area for public visitation.

11. The name Aulintak comes from two sources. The first mention appears in an 1890 interview with Mission Santa Cruz–born Lorenzo Asisara conducted by E. L. Williams, in Harrison, *History of Santa Cruz County*, 45–48. Asisara mentions "Aulinta" as the name for Santa Cruz given by the Uypi. "Aulintac, the rancheria proper to the Mission" is recorded by ethnographer Alexander S. Taylor in his article on the Awaswas Ohlone language. See Taylor, *Indianology*, 6. Taylor credits this name (along with others) to a currently missing letter from Friar Ramon Olbes to Governor Sola, dated November 1819, "in reply to a circular from him, as to the Native names, etc., of the Indians of Santa Cruz, and their rancherias." It is also repeated as "Aulin-tak" by Alfred L. Kroeber, presumably taken from the Taylor records, in "Handbook of the Indians of California," 465. As pointed out to me by Dean Silvers, in the Rumsen Ohlone language the word *Aulun* translates to "red abalone." While it is not confirmed that the translation is the same in the Awaswas Ohlone language (more about these different languages soon), the dearth of Awaswas word lists leaves open the possibility that *Aulun* was a word used by both Rumsen and Awaswas speakers. Awaswas words for abalone include *xasan, achkis,* and *tuppenish,* but it is possible that these refer

to other species, such as black abalone. These translations are found in Pinart, *California Indian Linguistic Records*, 23. In addition to Aulintak, ethnographer C. Hart Merriam notes that the "Santa Cruz tribe (Hor-de-on) lived in a field called Indian Potrero, near where the powder mill at Santa Cruz now stands" ("Ethnographic Notes," 372). The name appears a few times in the notes of Merriam as well as in an interview by John P. Harrington in which one woman is noted as being a "member of the Hordeon tribe." Solórsano to Merriam, November 11, 1930, "San Juan Report," JPH, microfilm, reel 59, p. 33. It is possible that the people of the Aulintak village identified as Hordeon. Alternatively, ethnographer Henry W. Henshaw notes that his Awaswas-speaking informant identified a tribal name, which he guessed to be referring to the people of Santa Cruz, as "he-mĕt-ra-kat." Henshaw, California Indian Linguistic Records, 186. As for the location of Aulintak, it seems most likely that the village site was on what is now called Mission Hill, which sits by the mouth of the San Lorenzo River.

12. "Spanish" colonizers were not homogeneous themselves, comprised of a mix of Franciscan friars (typically born in Spain and trained at the College of San Fernando in Mexico City), soldiers, servants, and guides—typically previously baptized Indigenous peoples from the Baja California missions. For more on the history of the Spanish Franciscan friars, including their relocation from Spain, recruitment, and training, see Rex Galindo, *To Sin No More*, 71–168.

13. The history of this naming has been explored in depth by Milliken, Shoup, and Ortiz, *Ohlone/Costanoan Indians*, 42–43. In sum, the name Ohlone has two possible sources. One possibility is that the name is taken from the coastal tribe living just north of the Quiroste, between modern San Francisco and Half Moon Bay, whose name was written by the Spanish as *Oljon*. The other possibility is that the name is a variant of the Sierra Miwok word indicating the direction west—*O'lo'no wit*. The shared linguistic roots of Ohlone and Miwok suggest that the tribal name for the Oljon, who lived on the westerly edge of the bay, may arise from the same root. The name Ohlone has come to be used by many contemporary Indigenous communities, including the Amah Mutsun Tribal Band of Ohlone Indians, the Muwekma Ohlone, and the Costanoan Rumsen Ohlone Tribe. Malcolm Margolin's classic overview of Ohlone culture, *Ohlone Way*, has helped to popularize the Ohlone name.

14. The Amah Mutsun Tribal Band are descended from Indigenous survivors affiliated with Missions San Juan Bautista and Santa Cruz. While they are the largest contemporary group of survivors of these missions, they are not the only families to have survived, as some families descended from these missions chose to remain unaffiliated with the Amah Mutsun or other San Francisco Bay Area tribes. To pick one example, the Sayers family are Mutsun and trace back to Mission San Juan Bautista but are not affiliated with the Amah Mutsun.

15. These names describe larger political units, recorded by Franciscan padres in the baptismal, confirmation, marriage, and death records at the various regional missions and as such are phonetic Spanish-language reconstructions of self-identified tribal names. The names of some villages are much harder to confirm, as the records rarely distinguish specific village affiliations. The suffix *-tac*, *-taka*, or *-ta* means "home" or "house" and therefore typically indicates a name of a village. You can see this in those listed here (and rewritten by me) as *Sayan-ta*, *Chaloc-taka*, and *Achis-taka*. The other names likely refer to the region and or the name for the people of those regions.

16. The word *Awaswas* first appears through Solórsano, who related the term *A-kwas-was* to Merriam as the name of the "Tribe from Santa Cruz" in a list of San Francisco Bay Area tribal and place names. JPH, microfilm, reel 59, p. 67. Amah Mutsun tribal historian and great grandson of Maria Ascención Solórsano, Ed Ketchum, in an email to the author September 26, 2016, suggests that many of the names we have for Bay Area places come from Mutsun words, which is corroborated by Merriam's list of Barbara's words. Additional Ohlonean dialects include the Ramaytush of the San Francisco Peninsula, Karkin of the North Bay, Chocheño of the East Bay, Tamyen of the Santa Clara Valley, Mutsun of San Juan Bautista, Rumsen of Monterey, and Chalon of Salinas. Ketchum also suggests that the words *Awaswas* and *Ramaytush* may refer to directions in the Mutsun language. According to the Mutsun dictionary, the word *awas* translates to "north," and *rammay* translates to "west." Warner, Butler, and Geary, *Mutsun-English, English-Mutsun Dictionary*, 9. Blevins and Golla make the further distinction that since the linguistic information comes from mission or post-mission times, these dialect labels (Chocheño and Awaswas, for example) should be understood as "referring to a mix of regional varieties brought together at specific missions rather than the aboriginal dialect pattern." "New Mission Indian Manuscript," 36. Furthermore, Association of Ramaytush Ohlone (ARO) chairman and scholar Dr. Jonathan Cordero theorizes that the Tamyen language is really misidentified as Chocheño. His theory is based on the extreme similarity between the two in the few sources that contain proposed "Tamyen" words. Conversation with the author, September 23, 2020. Historically, the linguistic family has been known as Costanoan languages, a term used by Kroeber. The use of *Ohlonean* traces back to Forbes, who adjusted the term *Olhonean* used by ethnographer Merriam. See Forbes, *Native Americans of California and Nevada*, 184.

17. Levy, "Costanoan." Levy argues that speakers utilized linguistic differences to mark sociocultural borders, but his conclusions have been effectively challenged by Field and Leventhal ("'What Must It Have Been Like!'" 103).

18. Much of this work has been done by archaeologist Mark Hylkema; see "Tidal Marsh," 250. While a few studies along the coast occurred earlier, begin-

ning with digs at SMA-22 in 1915 by researchers at the University of California, Berkeley, the vast majority of this work began in the 1970s. Furthermore, it was not until 1991 that the first study recognized cultural patterns distinguishing the southern coastal region from other larger Ohlone sites.

19. Panich, "Archaeologies of Persistence," 105–22.

20. *California Archaeology* 5, no. 2 (2013). The best example is the collaboration between Amah Mutsun tribal members, an archaeological team headed by UC Berkeley professor Kent G. Lightfoot, and Mark G. Hylkema and his staff at California State Parks, resulting in an exploration of traditional land management practices of the Quiroste tribe. The archaeological team included some tribal members, as collaborator and archaeologist Chuck Striplen was a member of the Amah Mutsun, and archaeologist Tsim D. Schneider is a member of the Federated Indians of Graton Rancheria, the contemporary name for the Coast Miwok, whose homeland is just north of San Francisco.

21. Jones and Klar, *California Prehistory*, 125. Archaeological excavations from the Scotts Valley site SCR-177 suggest these early dates. It is possible that human habitation goes back further, as it is generally believed that sites of earlier habitation have been washed away by stream action or submerged on the continental shelf. See Rosenthal and Meyer, *Landscape Evolution and the Archaeological Record*, 1.

22. Hylkema, "Tidal Marsh," 235, 390–91. Many of the coastal archaeological sites served as collection sites and important sites of gathering that turned into shell mounds, which archaeologists call "middens," after generations of repeated use. For more on the importance of these mounds, see Schneider, "Placing Refuge," 695–713.

23. Milliken, Shoup, and Ortiz, "Ohlone/Costanoan Indians," 73. The "banjo" ornaments and the Kuksui society will be talked about later in this chapter. For information regarding the recovery of the ornaments, see Breschini and Haversat, "Archaeological Data Recovery."

24. Peninsula tribes such as the Yelamu used tule reed boats, though none were observed along this coast.

25. Hornbeck, Fuller, and Kane, *California Patterns*, 36–37.

26. Hylkema, "Prehistoric Native American Adaptations," 25.

27. Anderson, *Tending the Wild*.

28. Lightfoot, Cuthrell, Striplen, and Hylkema, "Rethinking the Study of Landscape Management Practices," 290. The complexity of these practices is explored in detail in this article, which effectively disproves the misconception of Indigenous Californians as passive foragers.

29. Keeley, "Native American Impacts," 303–20.

30. Lightfoot and Parrish, *California Indians and Their Environment*, 124–30.

31. Fine, Misiewicz, Chavez, and Cuthrell, "California Hazelnut," 353–70. Though the California hazelnut (*Corylus cornuta* var. *californica*) is currently absent from the Quiroste Valley, it was historically present.

32. Jones and Hildebrandt, *Archaeological Test Excavation*.

33. Gifford-Gonzalez and Marshall, "Archaeological Assemblage," 16.

34. Keeley, "Native American Impacts," 311.

35. Keeley, "Native American Impacts," 311.

36. Harrington, *Culture Element Distributions*, 15. This report compiles data from Harrington's interviews with numerous Ohlone informants in the 1930s.

37. Shanks, *Indian Baskets*, 34–35.

38. Harrington, *Culture Element Distributions*, 7. His notes indicate that only Southern Ohlone ate raccoon. For more on dogs in Indigenous California, see Ensminger, *Dogs in California Aboriginal Cultures*.

39. Jones and Hildebrandt, *Archaeological Test Excavation*.

40. Bocek, "Ethnobotany of Costanoan Indians," 240–55. Ketchum informed me about the use of doveweed. Email to author, September 26, 2016.

41. Long discussed by Native scholars, kinship has been the subject of some recent studies across Native North America. See "Kinship with the World" in Deloria, *Spirit & Reason*; Lisa Tanya Brooks, *Our Beloved Kin*; and James Brooks, *Captives & Cousins*.

42. "Wife stealing" was commonly reported by the Spanish. To what extent this is a Spanish interpretation of polygamy, more complicated exogamic marriage patterns, or other practices outside the understanding of Spanish Catholics is hard to say for certain, though numerous reports suggest that intertribal warfare was fought over these incidences. For example, Governor Pedro Fages gave instructions on how to deal with issues of stolen women among newly baptized and pagan Indians. Fages to Castro, January 2, 1790, BL, C-A 44, 27–29.

43. According to Mark Hylkema, an archaeologist involved with the site CA-SCL-476 project along the Guadalupe River in San Jose, which dates back to circa 2000 BCE, multiple skeletons were found with parry fractures, defensive wounds to the forearms received when individuals shield themselves from blows to the face or head. They also found "animal effigy burials as well as dismembered people, several exhibiting large dart points embedded in the bodies. Others were left where they lay. It's a very unusually preserved site that I suspect was silted over by the adjacent Guadalupe River shortly after the event. I had long proposed that the river was a no-trespass zone between the Meganos intrusion and the pre-existing bay area people. The Meganos was a cultural group that expanded into the south bay from the interior central valley, and are characterized by extended burials rather than flexed. . . . The Meganos tradition ended by around AD 900, and some think that they are the ancestral Yokuts." Email to

author, July 21, 2020. The dig in question is recorded by Wiberg, "Archaeological Investigations." The broader theme is explored by Allen and Jones, *Violence and Warfare*.

44. Taylor, *Indianology*, 6. In his 1850s newspaper reports, Taylor suggested that "Santa Clara Indians" had protected these resources and traded cinnabar with Yokuts people from the interior San Joaquin Valley and possibly even with Miwok to the north. Taylor related: "The Indians of Santa Cruz and Santa Clara seem to have always been in fights about the possession of the Cinnabar mine, now the immensely rich New Almaden. The Indians, away from the Tules and Sacramento, were also accustomed to come often to get their share of the 'red paint,' and great battles were always fought in these 'vermillion expeditions.' One of them occurred even as late as 1841 or 1842, when several of the intruders were killed by the Santa Clara Indians." It seems likely that the "Santa Clara Indians" refer to the Somontoc, who will be discussed later in this chapter. With regards to trade with northern Miwok, Hylkema cites another story from Taylor, saying that "the tribe that had possession of the mines was wealthy as it monopolized the trade in vermillion, a paint that was ever in demand. . . . These Indians did a considerable commerce with their neighbors to the north, who visited them in canoes." Hylkema, "Mount Umunhum Environmental Restoration ASR," 28.

45. Skowronek, "Sifting the Evidence," 680.

46. Milliken, *Time of Little Choice*, 22.

47. Geiger and Meighan, *As the Padres Saw Them*, 68. This book contains the responses to a questionnaire given to California missionaries between 1813 and 1815, commonly known as *Preguntas y Respuestas*. In response to question 14, about marriages, the San Juan Bautista padres note, "They looked more to the procreation of children than to the stability of the marriage bond."

48. Typically, scholars have recognized male chiefs as holding multiple wives, including examples of sororal polygyny, in which a chief marries multiple sisters, as discussed by Newell (*Constructing Lives*, 86). At Mission Santa Cruz there are examples of women who had children from multiple male partners. For example, Paxit (a Cotoni woman baptized as Maria Severa), Santa Cruz baptismal number (SCZB) 290, had five children with three different men from different local tribes or villages—SCZB 461 (Sayanta), SCZB 311 (Cotoni), and SCZB 299 (Achistaca). In Paxit's case this is not a case of serial monogamy, as she had multiple children with one partner (Sipi, SCZB 461) before and after having a child with another (Anastasio, SCZB 311). This pattern of polygamy—the practice of multiple spouses for men and women, as opposed to polygyny (multiple wives for men)—within Santa Cruz mountain tribes, including a detailed analysis of the families cited here as well as comments on the pattern of wife stealing, has been explored in depth by King ("Central Ohlone Ethnohistory," 221–26). Addi-

tionally, Ketchum related a story: "I am aware of people today who have similar cases that do not involve wife stealing but rather gambling. A man lost his wife in the 'Stick Game.' He won her back several years later. She had children with both men. It was not that the woman was won. It was that the one man had the power at the time as revealed by winning the game." Email to author, September 26, 2016.

49. The existence of these third-gender peoples in Native California is examined in an excellent article by Deborah A. Miranda (Ohlone Costanoan Esselen Nation, Chumash), "Extermination of the *Joyas*," 253–84. For example, Miranda discusses one individual at Mission Santa Clara. Spanish authorities became confused when encountering a biological male in women's clothing. After an unsuccessful attempt by Spanish officials to force the individual to identify as male, this person returned to village life rather than face life in the mission re-gendered. Sandos remarks about similar encounters in Chumash territory (*Converting California*, 23–26), as does Newell (*Constructing Lives*, 116–17). The larger theme is also discussed by Morgensen (*Spaces between Us*).

50. Harrington, *Central California Coast*, 33–34.

51. Basso, *Wisdom Sits in Places*. This connection between land and identity is found throughout Indigenous societies.

52. Barbara Lee Jones, "Mythic Implications," 27. Padres reported that "spirits of places and objects could cause sickness or environmental problems if they were not honored by correct ritual means" (Geiger and Meighan, *As the Padres Saw Them*, 50–51).

53. Milliken, *Time of Little Choice*, 58–59. Milliken reports on a number of these shrines as well as the common Spanish response of burning them. This stood in contrast with the Native response to Spanish religious items. For example, when Pedro Font encountered cross poles left by Father Palóu from the previous year at Llagas Creek in the Santa Clara Valley, local Natives had already decorated the Spanish Catholic poles with feathers and offerings and left them protected.

54. Applegate, *Atishwin*. Applegate synthesized information from Yokuts, Chumash, and Salinan sources. Given the similarities and overlap of many spiritual practices among Indigenous Californians, it is likely that the Ohlone had similar conceptions of dream helpers. One padre once remarked, without irony, "Their principal superstition is their extremely obstinate belief in everything they dream about to such an extent that it is impossible to convince them of the unreality of their dream content." Geiger and Meighan, *As the Padres Saw Them*, 51.

55. Ketchum related that his "grandmother's grandmother told Harrington that her healing methods sometimes came in dreams." Email to author, September 26, 2016.

56. I use the term *narrative*, rather than *myth* or *folklore*, following Ortiz, who points out that the latter are generally associated with quaint, unbelievable stories. Instead, I recognize these as "sacred narratives," serving social purpose in communicating life lessons. See her excellent analysis of these differences in Ortiz, "Chocheño and Rumsen Narratives," 100.

57. The surviving narratives have been collected from the various salvage ethnographic interviews of the 1920s and 1930s by Linda Yamane (Rumsen). See Yamane, *When the World Ended*. However, as many of these narratives, dances, songs, and ceremonies tended to be private, they were rarely performed in public or shared with academics and, as such, remain outside of the public archive. This knowledge remains within the oral histories of descendants.

58. Most of these are the stories shared by Solórsano with Harrington, at least the ones recorded by academics. Contemporary families may have their own stories that they preserved and kept for themselves.

59. Lightfoot and Simmons, "Culture Contact," 149. The word *Kuksui* means "Big Head," in reference to the large headpiece that characterized the Kuksui regalia.

60. Solórsano to Harrington, "San Juan Report," JPH, microfilm, reel 58, p. 73.

61. The word *shaman* is an English translation of the Tungus word *šamán*, originating from Siberia, therefore I avoid using it here. Instead, I use the terms *sorcerer*, *medicine person*, or *doctor*, though these terms do not encompass the totality of the roles these people played within their communities.

62. Barbara Lee Jones, "Mythic Implications," 36.

63. Harrington, *Central California Coast*, 39–40.

64. These lodges were called *tupentak* by Chocheño speakers, though they were commonly referred to by the Spanish as *temazcals*, the Nahuatl word for "house of heat." From the Mission San Carlos response to question 15, relating to traditional medicine: "The men have the daily custom of entering an underground oven known as the temescal. A fire is built within and when the oven has become sufficiently heated the men enter undressed. They perspire so freely that upon coming out they give the appearance of having bathed. It is our experience that this is very beneficial for them. For a time the attempt was made to stop this practice but as a result skin diseases, boils, and other ailments appeared among the men. When they betook themselves of the temescal again scarcely a man was found afflicted with the itch, a disease common to the women and children who do not make use of such baths." The padres at Santa Cruz similarly responded: "What is quite common use among them is the sweat house which is built in the earth. A great fire is built therein and they sweat extremely much." Geiger and Meighan, *As the Padres Saw Them*, 77–78.

65. Barbara Lee Jones, "Mythic Implications," 34.

66. Harrington, "San Juan Report," JPH, microfilm, reel 58, pp. 34, 64.

67. Harrington, *Central California Coast*, 32.

68. Barbara Lee Jones, "Mythic Implications," 53.

69. Tuyshtak is called Mount Diablo today. The name Tuyshtak was in common use by East Bay Chocheño speakers. Mount Umunhum was discussed earlier. Ortiz, "Mount Diablo as Myth and Reality."

70. Barbara Lee Jones, "Mythic Implications," 54–55.

71. Yamane, *Snake*.

72. Harrison, *History of Santa Cruz County*, 47. Lorenzo Asisara spoke of how tribal names reflected regional names. Missionary baptismal registries report an often confusing mix of village or tribal names, which ethnographers, historians, and anthropologists continue to sift through to reconstruct regional names. See also Escobar, Field, and Leventhal, "Understanding the Composition."

73. It is possible that some names recorded reflect clan affiliation or other animal-related identity. For example, one man whose Native name is listed as Conejo (Telesforo Fidalgo), SCZB 102, had six children from two different mothers, SCZB 26–29, 35, and 39. The Spanish word *conejo* translates to "rabbit." This could be a coincidence, or, given his numerous children, it could be a playful name given by the padres reflecting the fertility of rabbits, or the name reflected an affinity with the animal, either through clan or spirit animal.

74. Field and Leventhal, "'What Must It Have Been Like,'" 114.

75. Barbara Lee Jones, "Mythic Implications," 51. Perhaps the term for the affiliations described here should be something other than *moiety*, as Newell points out the word comes from the French word *moitié*, meaning "half," and is applied by anthropologists to societies that divide into two groups, *Constructing Lives*, 87. While these affiliations do follow a similar pattern of conferring rights and obligations from one group to another, they appear to include more than just the two groups, Deer and Bear, as described by others.

76. Barbara Lee Jones, "Mythic Implications," 50–53. Many academic studies based on the work of Harrington and Kroeber, such as this one, claim that moieties were affiliated with one of two animals, Bear or Deer. Ketchum argued against this, claiming that there existed many different affiliations aligned with different villages and peoples. Here I'm going against academic convention and following the suggestions of Ketchum. Email to author, September 11, 2019.

77. Ketchum, email to author, September 11, 2019. Ketchum's theory is a solid one, and I suspect that Tamarox may indeed have some connection to Hawk. The villages that he is describing are in Mutsun territory. Unfortunately, translations for villages in Awaswas territory are more difficult to piece together, as very little of the Awaswas language is still in circulation or on record; otherwise, we might see similar patterns in the Santa Cruz mountain territories.

78. Harrington, "San Juan Report," JPH, microfilm, reel 58, p. 76. Solórsano notes that this was called "gome" at Mission San Juan Bautista.

79. Harrington, *Central California Coast*, 25–27.

80. Blackhawk, *Violence over the Land*.

81. Erlandson and Bartoy, "Protohistoric California," 304–9; and Preston, "Serpent in Eden," 3–37. Also see Jones and Klar, *California Prehistory*, 144–45.

82. It is difficult to estimate exactly how many there were, but given that approximately 1,199 were baptized among the various missions and the fact that quite a few chose not to receive baptism, it is likely that population numbers may have been as high as 1,400. This is my estimation. Milliken estimates that Santa Cruz mountain people numbered around 700, but it appears that the discrepancy is because he and I are considering different tribes as being from the Santa Cruz mountain range. Milliken was likely including some of the eastern slope mountain people as Santa Clara Valley people, whereas I am including them in these numbers. Overall, the average village population throughout the coastal side of Mak-Sah-Re-Jah was considerably smaller than those of villages in the valleys. For example, Milliken, Shoup, and Ortiz estimate Santa Clara Valley tribes had a population density of 6.28 people per square mile, compared to only 1.82 people per square mile in the mountains. Milliken, Shoup, and Ortiz, "Ohlone/Costanoan Indians," 64.

83. Sir Frances Drake's encounter with northern Coast Miwok during the time of their Kuksui ceremony is analyzed in detail in Lightfoot and Simmons, "Culture Contact in Protohistoric California" (148–51).

84. Wagner, "Spanish Voyages," 50. Juan Rodriguez Cabrillo, who passed along the coast without encounter in November 1542, recorded the first account of passage. Around fifty years later Sebastian Rodriguez Cermeño passed in a small boat "within musket-shot" of the shore. See Cermeño and Wagner, "Voyage to California," 15. Sebastián Vizcaíno followed in 1602. See Ascension and Wagner, "Spanish Voyages," 295–394. The exploration of the Monterey coast is examined in depth from the Spanish perspective in Hackel, *Children of Coyote* (27–37).

85. Cabrillo, for example, was told about foreigners on eight separate occasions on his travels. The prevalence of these reports is explored by Lightfoot and Simmons ("Culture Contact," 138–70).

86. Milliken estimated boundaries based on marriage patterns. The theory is that by tracing the pattern of tribal baptism, we can estimate proximity, since tribes that lived closest to the mission site tended to receive baptism earliest and in greatest numbers. By corroborating these records with letters recounting Spanish encounters, we get a sense of where each tribe was located. Meanwhile, archaeologist Mark Hylkema has been involved in archaeological research in

these mountains for nearly four decades. While I draw on the work of Milliken and also examine these patterns, I have had an ongoing dialogue with Hylkema about the tribal geography, as he and I have tried to combine his insights into the archaeological records with my familiarity with the Mission Santa Cruz records. Much of the considerations in this section on Indigenous landscapes and geography have been shaped and informed from these conversations with Hylkema. I will cite specific comments and feedback, but even when not noted directly, the influence is there, as Hylkema's insights and sense of this Indigenous geographic and political landscape is unparalleled.

87. The Franciscans renamed local tribes after saints. Used in the reports of the missionaries, the imposed titles varied by mission. Individuals continued to identify by tribal affiliation, which was reflected in the persistence of tribal names in census records up through the 1830s. The Franciscans labeled the Aptos as San Lucas.

88. Molegnis, SCZB 42, was renamed by the Spanish as Baltasar Dieguez at the time of his baptism, as was customary. The inclusion of a surname was primarily reserved for captains or other prominent figures. He is listed as fifty years old at his baptism on November 27, 1791.

89. Milliken, "Spanish Contact," 31. My estimates of geographic location of these local tribes here rely on those of Milliken, unless otherwise stated. Milliken worked extensively with these records and did the most to establish geographic relations between tribes.

90. The Calenda-ruc, which this study will not focus on but only briefly examine, refers to the region divided among two neighboring groups—the Guacharron and the Huineren. Village sites in this area included Locuyusta to the south and Tiuvta to the north. The name Tiuvta means "place of the elk," and, interestingly, the Portolá expedition of 1769 observed a herd of twenty-two tule elk in the region when they passed southward in November that year. The name Locuyusta appears to mean "Place of the Liar" (translations from Ketchum). Regarding this translation, Ketchum relates: Locuyusta was "only used when taken to Mission San Carlos. When taken to Mission San Juan Bautista, often called Guacharron de la Playa. This I believe means Condor/Eagle People. There are Guacharron de la Sierra in the hills." Email to author, August 30, 2019. Analysis of the names of villages and people of the larger region has been complied by King, "Appendix I: Documentation of Tribelet Boundaries, Locations and Sizes."

91. The Cajastaca were identified by the Spanish as a separate group, but based on the large number of people who identified as Cajastaca and Aptos on mixed baptismal, death, marriage, and census records, it is safe to say the Cajastaca were a subgroup of the larger Aptos, living to the south. The Spanish

renamed the Cajastaca as San Antonio. Of the last thirty-eight baptisms of Aptos members, eleven were identified as Cajastaca in later death records or census lists—SCZB 676, 682, 687, 689, 691, 692, 695, 696, 702, 718, and 719.

92. Harrison, *History of Santa Cruz County*, 46.

93. Harrison, *History of Santa Cruz County*, 46. Asisara mentions a "Captain Balthazar" and followed this by saying "these different tribes fought with bows and arrows." Though it is not entirely clear, it seems likely that he is implying that it was Molegnis (Baltasar) and his people who fought with the others.

94. The Spanish renamed the Uypi as San Daniel.

95. SCZB 2 and 3, respectively.

96. Olbes to Sola, November 1819, recorded in Taylor, *Indianology*, 6.

97. Patterns of intermarriage are established through tracing tribal identities of parents listed in baptismal records.

98. This theory comes from conversations between me and archaeologist Hylkema. In discussing the Achicstaca village (considering that the suffix *-taca* implies that the name refers to a village site rather than the name of a people), Hylkema was able to propose—based on geography, archaeological sites, and available resources—a likelihood of overlap between the coastal Cotoni and the upland Achistaca villagers. I was able to find corroborating evidence in the archives to show strong interconnection between the two groups. Two people baptized as Achistaca have burial records that list them as Cotoni (SCZB 303 and 335; and SCZD 236 and 598, respectively). Another child, Tehanu (Bernardina Olibares, SCZB 123), is listed as Achistaca with a Cotoni father, Guesguel (Theodomiro, SCZB 388), and a Cotoni mother, Echiem (Theodomira, SCZB 393). This interconnection is further corroborated in reverse. A four-year-old child, Pellécs (Santés, SCZB 472), is listed as Achistaca with Cotoni parents: father Atuis (Fronton, SCZB 493) and mother Ucsán (Frontona, SCZB 506).

99. Hylkema wrote: "Lots of bedrock mortars towards Buzzard's Roost on Empire Grade directly above Little Basin. Could be another village from Bonny Doon but all likely to be Cotoni. And Achistaca may refer to all the upland sites in a plural sense. Coastal edge villages will be by drainages and that is where many middens also occur. Uplands and lowland seasonal cycles. And villages/houses need to move around for hygiene." Email to author, June 8, 2021. With regards to hygiene, Hylkema is observing the need to vary village sites to rotate bathrooms and trash as well as the need to rotate to find firewood sources and other resources.

100. The Spanish renamed the Achistaca as San Dionisio. Achistaca was likely the name of a village but was used to designate this group of people, whose lands are not specifically identified. According to Ketchum, the word *Achistaca* translates in Mutsun to "place of the enemy or competitor." This sug-

gests that the village might be a name first suggested by another, hostile group. Email to author, September 18, 2019.

101. Upejen (Serafina Josefa), SCZB 90, was the first adult Achistaca to be baptized at Mission Santa Cruz. Roiesic (Pascual Antonio Arenaza), SCZB 137, was baptized along with Tuicam (Margarita de Cortona), SCZB 136, and Chitemis (Rafaela Gazetas), SCZB 135. He had children with both women.

102. The diplomatic visits to Mission Santa Clara are discussed in more detail later in this chapter.

103. Email to author, June 7, 2021.

104. The Spanish renamed the Chaloctaca as Jesus. Gelelis (Gabriel Cañizares), SCZB 113, seventy years old at his baptism in 1792, and his wife, Ypasin (Juana Eudovigis Pinedo), SCZB 153, sixty years old at her baptism at the same time. These ages were estimates made by the Franciscan missionaries and could be wrong. It is likely that Ypasin was younger, given that the youngest of the couple's six children were three, five, nine, and fourteen. This family was baptized with the surname of Cañizares.

105. Gelelis's elder son, Cholmos (Acisclo), SCZB 443, had three children with a Sayanta woman, Ullegen (Aciscla), SCZB 449, and two with a Cholactaca woman, Nisipen (Maria Guadalupe Cruz), SCZB 154.

106. Ules (Andres Cañizares), SCZB 97, was the first of the Chaloctaca to be baptized, followed by Lluillen (Maria de la Purificacion de Landa), SCZB 107. Ules will be discussed in more depth in following chapters. He was eventually convicted, along with his son and brother, in the retaliatory killing of the abusive Padre Quintana in 1812. Complaints of an "incorrigible" Andres appear in an undated letter to Governor Diego de Borica from Friars Francisco Gonzalez and Domingo Carranza, at the San Francisco Archdiocese (hereafter SFAD), document 126. Judging by the padres involved, this letter must have been written sometime after May 1798.

107. Most of these are identified in the Mission Santa Clara records under the broad name of San Carlos. The priests at that mission divided the surrounding valleys into districts, each with multiple villages. For example, they called those villages situated within one hundred yards of the first mission church by the name Our Mother Santa Clara; villages along the lower Guadalupe River were called Our Patron San Francisco. Others were named San Juan Bautista or San Joseph Cupertino. The end result makes it much harder to trace tribal identities among Mission Santa Clara recruits. The peoples of Mak-Sah-Re-Jah were often referred to in Santa Clara baptisms as being within the district of "San Carlos de la Sierra." The district designations at Mission Santa Clara are explained and accounted for by Hylkema ("Archaeological Investigations," 36–41; a map of the various districts in relation to the mission church is on p. 39).

108. Lorenzo Asisara, SCZB 1832, was born in 1820 and gave three interviews in the late nineteenth century. He recounted stories related by his father, Llencó (Venancio), SCZB 215. Note that one Cotoni child mentioned in a previous note, Tehanu, was given the surname Olibares, along with two of her siblings, Nugait (Simon Olibares, SCZB 159) and Sasuest (Theresa Olibares, SCZB 131), which suggests that this family might have included the tribal leader. Though there is no clear connection between this family and that of Lorenzo Asisara, other than his father also being Cotoni, Asisara and his father appear in the 1836 *padrón* both with the surnames Olibares. It would seem that either there was a familial or kinship tie between the two families or that the Olibares surname was one that different Cotoni members used.

109. Harrison, *History of Santa Cruz County*, 47. Asisara here is referring to the numerous shell mounds that are indeed still in existence throughout the Bonny Doon area.

110. Amador, "Memorias," BL, MSS C-D 28, 58. It is not clear what to make of this discrepancy, other to note that identity was clearly very plural and Indigenous people understood themselves in multiple ways—in relation to their lands, village sites, kinship networks, extended families, moiety or animal clan affiliations, and more.

111. The Spanish labeled them as San Juan Capistrano.

112. The elusive nature of their geographic origins explains why they do not appear on most maps.

113. These estimates come from Hylkema. Los Capitancillos Creek is part of Rancho Cañada de los Capitancillos, or "the Valley of the Little Captains." According to Hylkema, the valley received its name because the Spanish recognized that the tribes living in the region, presumably the Matalan people living in the Somontoc village area, had many different leaders or chiefs, the "little captains."

114. At Mission Santa Cruz the Somontoc were renamed as Santa Clara, possibly a reference to many of them already having been baptized at that mission.

115. This account was reported by settler William Trevethan, reprinted in the *Santa Cruz Sentinel*, July 2, 1870, 1. A similar version of the story was also recorded by journalist Taylor (*Indianology*, 6). Cinnabar was an important red clay used in ornamentation on baskets and bodies as a red paint. Stories such as previously cited account by Taylor spoke about battles between the "Santa Clara" and "Santa Cruz" Indians over this important resource. The Somontoc, identified in the Santa Cruz Mission baptismal book as the "Santa Clara Indians," lived in territories near the source of cinnabar, suggesting that they were indeed the ones in control of this resource, perhaps even into the 1840s.

116. Euxexi (Ambrosio), SCZB 232, had a child with a Chaloctaca woman, Ocot (Nicolasa), SCZB 253, and married a Sayanta woman, Florentina (Native name not given), SCZB 205, after his own baptism.

117. At Mission Santa Cruz the Spanish renamed the Quiroste as San Rafael. Only a handful of Quiroste were baptized at Mission Santa Cruz, as they were split between Missions Dolores (San Francisco), Santa Clara, and Santa Cruz.

118. Mission San Francisco baptismal number (SFB) 679, October 27, 1787. The Oljon tribe lived along the coast, just north of the Quiroste (see map 3).

119. SFB 711, October 19, 1788. *Quirogtes* is a variation on the phonetic Spanish interpretation of *Quiroste*. The Cotegen lived farther north up the San Francisco Peninsula from the Oljon.

120. Stranger and Brown, *Who Discovered the Golden Gate*, 73.

121. Crespí and Brown, *Description of Distant Roads*. The original diary entries are found in Costansó, Carpio, and Teggart, *Portola Expedition*, 85–87.

122. Crespí, Brower, and Bolton, *Fray Juan Crespi*, 240. In his November 26 entry Crespí noted: "On the road we found a new village of heathen who were building a town, making their spherical-shaped houses of poles and tule. According to what the explorers said these were the same ones whom they had seen in the village of El Pájaro."

123. Crespí and Brown, *Description of Distant Roads*; and Ketchum, email to author, August 31, 2019. Ketchum further elaborated on this: "A little more information on how I came to my conclusion. Many years ago, I read about the encounter between Portola's scouting party and the Guacharron. . . . I asked Mr. Lalo Franco, he was the Director of the Cultural Department for the Santa Rosa Rancheria Tachi-Yokuts, if he knew about the encounter. As I recall, he replied, 'Don't you know this was a Condor ceremony where messages were taken to and from the land of the dead.' He said that it probably occurred about every 11 to 13 years and was associated with the Pleiades. I could not find a relationship between the Pleiades and the time of the encounter. I had read in several places that the Condor was associated with the planet Mars. . . . I went to the UC Davis Astronomy Department to see if they could help me find a relationship. I was told that there were several online places where I could see the skies at any time. . . . Here I found that Mars and the Sun intersected at the time of the encounter. In addition, I suggest you also read *Wings of Spirit: California Condor* by John W. Foster and the Gashowu Yokuts story Coyote, the Hawk and the Condor for more background. . . . The Gashowu Yokuts story I believe was a bit incorrect as the Condors don't normally fly in a straight line but weave across the sky. While the planet Mars flies straight across the sky each night. So I believe the magic arrows that his brothers the dogs shot him with made him fly straight for eternity. Lalo Franco may be correct, as the fall is when the winds blow to the west in the Monterey Bay area. So maybe the conjunction may have to occur after the autumnal equinox and before the winter solstice as well." Ketchum is referring to the Gashowu Yokuts story found in Kroeber, "Indian Myths," 205–9; and Foster, "Wings of the Spirit."

124. Stranger and Brown, *Who Discovered the Golden Gate*, 79. Accounts of recently burned grasslands and evidence of Indigenous land management practices are described here.

125. Stranger and Brown, *Who Discovered the Golden Gate*, 83.

126. Panich, "Native American Consumption," 730–48. Spanish encounters with Indigenous peoples had been informed by two hundred years of experience, and explorers regularly carried goods to trade and offer as gifts. Archaeologists have pointed out that these glass beads were subsequently incorporated into existing Indigenous monetary systems. The central role of cloth in trade is explored in detail by Lacson, "Making Friends and Converts."

127. Stranger and Brown, *Who Discovered the Golden Gate*, 87.

128. The overland expedition was shadowed by two Spanish ships, which traced the coast. The expedition was hoping to find these ships in order to receive provisions.

129. It is probable that the Quiroste had left their village to gather acorns and hunt in the redwoods by this time.

130. Hackel, *Children of Coyote*, 50–61. Hackel explores the context of Spanish colonization in the history of Mission San Carlos (Monterey).

131. After the 1774 expedition led by military captain Fernando Rivera y Moncada, which encountered great difficulties crossing the numerous wetlands along the coast, Spanish authorities decided to use the inland valley passage as the thoroughfare between Monterey and the San Francisco Peninsula.

132. The Esselen are a group of tribes, culturally and linguistically distinct from the Ohlone. The modern Ohlone Costanoan Esselen Nation descend from Mission San Carlos survivors.

133. Hackel, *Children of Coyote*, 74–77. Hackel breaks down the four waves of entry into Mission San Carlos, noting that each wave came from farther from the mission and correlated with expansion of Spanish livestock and agricultural production (typically by Indigenous laborers).

134. Mission Dolores, on the San Francisco Peninsula, was founded June 29, 1776, a year before Santa Clara.

135. Milliken, *Time of Little Choice*, 51–55. The establishment of Spanish order through small episodes of violence is explored by Milliken. It is probable that word of Spanish retaliation and military prowess would have traveled.

136. The theory about children as spies is that of Ketchum, who also pointed out that it was often children without parents who first arrived at the missions. Email to author, September 26, 2016. This theory helps explain why so many parents brought their children to the missions in the early days, while waiting sometimes years before receiving baptism themselves. Hackel, *Children of Coyote*, 67. Hackel suggests that disease might explain why the majority of early baptisms were

performed on children, pointing out that the children and the elderly were most susceptible to illness. I do agree that disease may have played a role (see notes 138, 140), in addition to a combination of missionary and Indigenous strategy.

137. The one exception was named Manuel. At seventy he was baptized on his deathbed, SCLB 55, reinforcing Hackel's theory of disease as a factor (see note 137).

138. Milliken, *Time of Little Choice*, 221. Milliken suggests that two contextual factors contributed to these early baptisms. First, the stunning technology and complex social order of the Spanish challenged traditional criteria for economic and social success, and second, Spanish soldiers proved to be the most dangerous fighting men in the region when they killed any opponents during the first few weeks of settlement. See also Lacson, "Making Friends and Converts."

139. For more exceptions of adults receiving baptism, see the cases of seventy-year-olds receiving baptism on their deathbeds in 1777–78, SFB 54, SFB 57, and SCLB 55.

140. Confirmation books at each mission attest to the ongoing teachings. Copies of these books are held at the SBMAL.

141. This distinction as *neofito* (neophyte) or *gentil* (gentile) is ubiquitous in the archives. I avoid using this distinction, recognizing the inherent diminutive implication of the term, which relegated even advanced spiritual leaders to the status of a novitiate or beginner. Instead, I will refer to them as baptized Natives or baptized people in order to distinguish them from those who had not received baptism.

142. SCLB 80, baptized on March 29, 1778.

143. Pablo's older brother, Francisco Maria (Native name not given), SCLB 69, was baptized three months before Pablo, on December 28, 1777, among the first group of teenagers. Their father had been baptized a few months later, on February 28, 1778 (SCLB 76), while their mother was baptized on November 25, 1778 (SCLB 122).

144. Pablo first served as *padrino* (godparent) in SCLB 909 (July 26, 1786), and then appears to have continued to serve as *padrino* frequently from the 1790s until 1811 and assisted with baptisms until shortly before his death in 1818. He assisted in three baptisms in 1817: SCLB 6527, 6552, and 6557. His death is recorded in Mission Santa Clara death registry number (SCLD) 5076, on November 27, 1818. He assisted in baptisms at Mission San Juan Bautista for four Calenda-ruc children on November 29, 1801 (SJB 761–64).

145. Pablo accompanied Spanish soldiers in the fields assisting with three baptisms (SCLB 1362, 1608, and 1786) that took place away from the missions.

146. Pablo is listed as *padrino* for the majority of male confirmations, beginning with Mission Santa Cruz confirmation registry number (SCZC) 178 on May 9, 1793, and continuing through 1794.

147. This is recorded in SCZB 622, which lists the *padrino* as Pablo, translator from Mission Santa Clara.

148. As mentioned before, Mission Santa Clara records are particularly negligent in listing tribal origins. Large groups of "San Carlos" people started arriving as early as 1779 (SCLB 149). By 1787 large numbers began arriving (SCLB 1011–25, 1376–1404, as examples).

149. Lasuén, Memorandum regarding Confirmations, May 4, 1790, BL, CC-24, 66–67.

150. Romeu to Lasuén, July 11, 1791, SBMAL, California Mission Documents (hereafter CMD), 129. Lasuén described a visit to the site, reporting that he encountered many peaceful Indians.

151. Soquel's name is recorded in a variety of spellings: *Suquel*, *Sugert*, *Suquer*, and *Suquex*. By 1810 Spanish accounts began to call the Uypi tribe the Soquel or Zoquel tribe. The name remains, given to the Rancho property and later the township of Soquel, as well as the modern street that connects the cities of Santa Cruz, Soquel, and Aptos (another tribal name). As pointed out to me by Dean Silvers, the word *Soquel* may have linguistic connections in addition to those with the Uypi chief. Awaswas-speaking informants told linguist Pinart that the word for the laurel tree, found commonly in the region, is šokkoče or šokoči (Pinart, *California Indian Linguistic Records*, 17). The Mutsun language has a similar translation, with the word for laurel given as *sokkoci* or *sokco* (Warner, Butler, and Geary, *Mutsun-English, English-Mutsun Dictionary*, 350). There is some speculation in the public about the name Soquel coming from a village site in the area called Osocalis (there is even a distillery by this name in the area which is named for this possible village site). In my research I have not come across Osocalis in reference to this area but do find mention of an Osocalis village in Yokuts territory (see chapter 4). In any case, it is possible that a village named Osocalis and the Uypi chief both might share linguistic connections with the laurel tree.

152. The two daughters were baptized as Maria Lorenza, SCLB 1897, nine years old, and Clara de la Cruz, SCLB 1904, one year old, on May 29 and May 21, 1791, respectively. In Clara de la Cruz's baptismal records, her parents are listed with a note that identifies them as "Uypi in the place called Santa Cruz, the rancheria intended for the foundation of the mission by this name." The padres were clearly aware of Soquel's and Rosuem's status as well as plans to build on their territories. The chief received gifts of cattle and birds from Spanish officials following the foundation, possibly the result of discussions at Mission Santa Clara.

153. Ten children of Mak-Sah-Re-Jah parents were baptized in May 1791 (SCLB 1896–1905). The parents included not only Soquel and Rosuem, but also Achistaca elder Ules and his wife Llulle, as well as Quesues (SCLB 3115) and Usiam, a tribally unidentified couple closely connected to Mak-Sah-Re-Jah families.

154. These seven (SCLB 1965–71) had Sayanta, Chaloctaca, and Somontoc parents, the majority of which were eventually baptized later at Mission Santa Cruz.

155. Sal, Alférez Habilitado y Comandante del Presidio, Diario del reconocimiento de la Mision de Santa Cruz, September 25, 1791, BL, C-A 54, 270. Orders to found Mission Santa Cruz (along with Mission Soledad) had begun in late 1789; see Noriega to Lasuén, October 31, 1789, SBMAL, CMD 99. Sal was involved in the Rivera y Moncada expedition of 1774 and knew the area.

156. Sal, Alférez Habilitado y Comandante del Presidio, Diario del reconocimiento de la Mision de Santa Cruz, September 25, 1791, BL, C-A 54, 270–73. Sal commented in his report that no other mission from San Diego to San Francisco could boast access to as much wood as Santa Cruz.

157. Though never identified in the documents, it is clear that these six were not among the seven who had been baptized two weeks prior, since those had been infants.

158. Sal, Alférez Habilitado y Comandante del Presidio, Diario del reconocimiento de la Mision de Santa Cruz, September 25, 1791, BL, C-A 54, 270. Sal reported that Soquel "bore malice, *for the Indian was serious, reserved and of a melancholy disposition.* So much that the missionaries and guard were careful to watch the conduct of Suquel" (emphasis mine).

159. Geiger and Meighan, *As the Padres Saw Them*, 26.

160. Direct environmental reorganization had occurred at other missions, but this was the first instance of it in the Santa Cruz area.

161. The initial site of Mission Santa Cruz was destroyed due to flooding during the first winter after settlement, and it appears that the weather was particularly harsh in the winters of the early 1790s.

162. Sal also imparted his name to the chief, as the padres christened Soquel as "Hermenegildo." Despite Sal's promise to baptize Soquel first, Soquel was the second baptized at the new mission. A few days before Soquel received his baptism, a young girl, Micaela (Native name not given), daughter of an Achistaca couple tied through kinship with Soquel, received the first baptism. The reason for this is unclear. Perhaps it reflects intent by the Spanish to subvert Soquel's authority, or perhaps Soquel allowed his kin to receive the first baptism. Micaela's mother, Florentina (Native name not given), SCZB 205, married the Somontoc Euxexi, whose child had been baptized at Mission Santa Clara two weeks before the founding of Mission Santa Cruz. It is possible that the baptism of Micaela was tied to some arrangement made during that visit.

163. Sal, Instrucción al cabo de la escolta de Santa Cruz, September 21, 1791, BL MSS, C-A 54, 274–81.

164. Serra to Antonio María de Bucareli y Ursua, April 22, 1773, Tibesar, *Writings of Junípero Serra*, 1:341. Serra wrote that "there is not a single mission

where all the gentiles have not been scandalized, and even on the road, so I have been told . . . a plague of immorality had broken out." This theme is explored in depth in Hurtado, *Intimate Frontiers*.

165. It is important to consider these intermarriages within a complicated larger colonial context. In *Women and the Conquest of California* Bouvier argues that the "inscription of idyllic gender relations between the conquerors and the Indians may have sanitized a more violent frontier reality," xvi. Alternatively, in *Peace Came in the Form of a Woman* Barr suggests that intermarriage acted as a "political ritual," arguing that "those moments when women acted as mediators of peace did not simply signal cross-cultural rapport, but rather the predominance of native codes of peace and war" (2). Ultimately, Barr argues that Indigenous conceptions of kinship shaped Spanish-Indian politics in Texas. In Santa Cruz kinship was frequently reflected in godparentage relationships, but also may have influenced patterns of intermarriage between Spanish and Indigenous people as well as between diverse Indigenous groups, continuing and extending previous intertribal relations.

166. Beginning in 1790, twenty-four Nuu-chah-nulth people of the Mowachaht village received baptism at Mission San Carlos. These were brought by ships engaged in the Nootka Crisis conflict between England and Spain, which took place in the territory of the Mowachaht village on the west coast of Vancouver Island in 1789. Maria Jesus, "India de Nutka," as she was referred to by the Spanish padres, San Carlos baptism number (SCAB) 2088, married Jose Francisco de Tapia, San Carlos marriage number (SCAM) 529, on May 3, 1796. Their marriage was authorized after discussion, with a report by Sergeant Macario Castro (BL MSS, C-A 55, 84–91).

167. Lasuén to Arrillaga, July 8, 1785, SFAD, document 28. Father Lasuén requested permission from Governor Arrillaga for the marriage of the soldier Marcos Villela and twelve-year-old María Bibiana (baptized at birth as Viridiana Maria, SCAB 173). María Bibiana's parents were Rumsen, from the village of Achasta near the site of Mission San Carlos (Monterey).

168. Ojoc (Feliciana Ormachea), baptized on May 27, 1792, at age twelve, nearly two years before the marriage takes place. Azebes served as Ojoc's father's *padrino*, SCZB 106, while Ojoc received Azebes's mother's name at baptism. (His mother, Maria Feliciana, resident of San Carlos, is listed in the Santa Cruz marriage record [SCZM 61].) One wonders if Azebes did not have his eye on the young girl earlier or if her parents had somehow arranged the marriage. Ketchum suggests that this may have involved a "bride price" or other negotiation with the parents. Email to author, September 26, 2016.

169. Harrison, *History of Santa Cruz County*, 47; Asisara, in 1890 interview with E. L. Williams.

170. Of these eighty-nine, eighty-six had been baptized at Mission Santa Cruz. Three had been baptized at Mission Santa Clara but followed their parents to Santa Cruz. See annual report for 1791, at SBMAL.

171. For example, the Achistaca/Sayanta couple whose daughter Micaela received the first baptism at Mission Santa Cruz—Ynoc (Pancracio), Achistaca, SCZB 492, and Florentina, Sayanta, SCZB 205—did not receive baptism until 1795 and 1793, respectively. Florentina also had a fifteen-year-old son with Ynoc, Llumetu (Jose Maria), SCZB 330.

172. The friars gave passes to baptized youth to visit and aid the missionaries in recruiting their families.

173. Father Joaquin Adam, MS, n.d., California History Room, California State Library, box 1306, folder 21, 30. Many years after the fact, Adam recalled that tribal and familial separation and reorganization characterized the Mission Santa Cruz community in labor and in living. Adam was in charge of Mission Santa Cruz from 1868 to 1883. The endurance of these kinship networks is reflected in the 1813–15 reports, as the Mission Santa Cruz missionaries replied to question 9 about generosity: "They are charitable and compassionate but only to those who are relatives." In the Santa Cruz response to question 25 about charity: "They show charity towards none except their relatives . . . [they] will leave anyone else to die of hunger if he does not happen to be a blood relative." Geiger and Meighan, *As the Padres Saw Them*, 108.

174. These are recorded in the Mission Santa Clara Confirmation book, entries 1522–26, dated February 18, 1792. In all, nine received confirmation there (SCZB 66, 73, 74, 83, 111, 112, 152, Soquel, and Soquel's elder daughter, Maria Lorenza). Seven of them were between seven and ten years old, along with one fourteen-year-old, and Soquel. They were five Uypi (counting Soquel and his daughter), one Aptos, and three Chaloctaca siblings—all children of Gelelis and Ypasin.

175. Pablo shows up first in SCZC 184, dated May 9, 1793.

176. Catholic confirmation traditionally involves the formal teaching of Catholic doctrine, while baptism is the process of initiation via exposure to water, via sprinkling or pouring of water blessed by the priests onto the head.

177. Molegnis (Baltasar Dieguez), SCZB 42, was baptized on November 27, 1791, the first adult to receive baptism following the Uypi leaders.

178. Molegnis is recorded as SCZC 1; his wife, Solue (Ana de la Relde, SCB 47), was the first woman to receive confirmation, SCZC 93. They both received confirmation on November 27, 1791. The confirmation records first list men (*adultos*), followed by boys (*parvulos*), before then listing women (*adultas*) and subsequently girls (*parvulas*). This accounts for the distance between the two records, even though they are both listed first among their respective genders.

179. Geiger and Meighan, *As the Padres Saw Them*, 106. In their accounts the padres frequently complained about Indigenous sexuality. On the 1813–15 questionnaire, in response to question 24 regarding vice, the Santa Cruz padres responded, "Unchastity is the vice most common among them," while the Santa Clara padres replied, "The most dominant among these Indians are first, fornication; second, stealing; games [gambling], dances, and among women, abortion."

180. Bancroft, *California Pastoral*, 227–28. This related to those who were already coupled prior to baptism. Another account is in the 1813–15 questionnaire; the Mission Santa Cruz missionaries' answer to question 14 about marriage suggests that young men replaced traditional gifts of beads and shells to the intended girls' parents with prayer and petition to the reverend fathers. Geiger and Meighan, *As the Padres Saw Them*, 68. Ed Ketchum points out: "This would appear to some as though the groom is buying his wife, 'bride price.' Anthropologist Jack Goody contends that in societies in which women provide most of the labor for food there is a 'bride price,' while in societies where the men farmed 'plough agriculture' the women bring dowry to the marriage. 'Plough agriculture' is associated with private property and monogamous marriages. It appears this was another way in which the Catholics where imposing their will on the Native societies. It also demonstrates the de-masculation of the males in this new society." Email to author, September 26, 2016.

181. Ten-year-old Luis (Native name not given), SCZB 4, and seven-year-old Tumuzc (Policarpo Dieguez, SCZB 96). Luis's mother was a Uypi woman named Caujan (Rufina Peña, SCZB 101), while Tumuzc's mother was unlisted. If his mother was Caujan, it would have been stated as such, given that Caujan was baptized at the same time as Tumuzc. Evidence that Tumuzc's mother was another Uypi woman is suggested by Tumuzc's death record (SCZD 22), which lists him as Uypi, not Aptos like his father. Meanwhile, Caujan had a total of five children by five different men.

182. Recorded in SCZM 5.

183. Cholmos (Acisclo), SCZB 443, Nisipen (Maria Guadalupe Cruz), SCZB 154, and Ullegen (Aciscla), SCZB 449.

184. Panuncio (Native name not given), SCLB 1969, on September 10, 1791.

185. Ypasin's and Cholmos's children were baptized at this time—Tipan (Maria del Carmen Hablitas), SCZB 147, and Lassac (Onesimo Saturnino Hablitas), SCZB 151. The third, sixteen-year-old Tejos (Mariano Hablitas), SCZB 115, had received baptism three months earlier.

186. Nisipen died October 31, 1794, SCZD 35, her daughter on March 7, 1793, SCZD 8, and Gelelis on November 22, 1793, SCZD 10.

187. Tanca (Pantaleon) was baptized on February 16, 1795, SCZB 420, his parents eight days later, on February 24, 1795.

188. Cholmos and Ullegen received Catholic marriage after baptism, on February 24, 1795, SCZM 92.

189. SCZB 141. His baptism record does not state his tribal affiliation, but his confirmation record does, SCZC 23. Milliken, in his database, identified Lacah as Unijaima, which leads Ketchum to suggest that this might demonstrate a tie between the Chaloctaca and Unijaima. Email to author, September 26, 2016.

190. Village named in his baptism record. There are no other records of the same name.

191. Record at the Archivo General de la Nación (hereafter AGN), March 30, 1796, Californias (017), vol. 65, exp. 8, fjs. 310-11. The first election at Mission Santa Cruz took place in January 1797. These elections and the role of alcalde will be discussed at more length in following chapters.

192. AGN, Californias (017), vol. 65, exp. 8, fjs. 303-29.

193. These alcaldes did not always conform to Spanish control, as we will see in later chapters, as Lacah eventually played a key role in the murder of Padre Quintana in 1812.

194. Jackson, "Disease and Demographic Patterns," 33-57. The incidence of dysentery, respiratory disease, pneumonia, and tuberculosis appears to have ravaged Mission Santa Cruz in the early years, while outbreaks of measles (1804) and smallpox (1830) came later. Meanwhile Friar Lasuén reported a plague ravaging a village within a dozen leagues of Mission San Carlos in a letter to Governor Borica, June 15, 1795, AGN, Provincias Internas, 8:153-54. I do agree with Hackel, who argued that the spread of disease hastened relocation into the missions (*Children of Coyote*, 65-66).

195. Jackson, "Disease and Demographic Patterns," 38. Jackson explores the incidence of disease and pathogens, including those from wool, at Mission Santa Cruz.

196. Llaggen (Angela), SCZB 87, SCZD 2. She is listed as coming from the "San Gregorio" tribe, of which there were only two at Mission Santa Cruz, the other being her husband, Orcheriu (Gaspar Pablo), SCZB 46, who received baptism a month before Llaggen. Orcheriu appears to have moved later to Santa Clara, perhaps to be closer to kin, as he dies there in 1830, SCLD 1632. I believe that this indicated that Llaggen was from north of the Quiroste, in modern San Gregorio, along the coast, which would make sense with her husband later moving to Santa Clara.

197. Lasuén observed this in a memorandum to Governor Fages (July 8, 1789, SBMAL, CMD 95), stating "as death approaches, a deeper and better attachment to the true religion." A critical look at the conflation of Native baptisms with conversion to Catholicism is examined by Cordero, "California Indians."

198. Six of these records are incomplete, as they do not have burial records, which likely means that at some point they ran away (possibly taken by their parents) from the mission.

199. Lino, SCZB 226, only has a Spanish name recorded, as was typical with mission-born children.

200. Lino is listed as "Paje de Padre Quintana" in SCZB 1563, dated October 11, 1811. He served as marriage witness in SCZM 388-407, 444-47, 533-34, 538-40, and 548-51; and as godfather in SCZB 1563.

201. Twelve of these young infants, like Lino, appear in the confirmation book. They were all under three years at the time of "confirmation," which did not reflect typical Catholic teachings but, rather, a different kind of indoctrination. Monroy recognized a similar complication involving confirmation, due to the lack of Spanish understanding for many new converts. He noted the fact that "the Indians did not learn the language of their acculturators suggests that they probably did not comprehend much of the religion either." Monroy, *Thrown among Strangers*, 47-48.

202. SBMAL, Annual Report for 1793.

203. Harrison, *History of Santa Cruz County*, 46. Years later Asisara recalled being a "key-keeper." By 1797 new roles of political leadership within the mission had formed, including the alcalde, which will be explored in later chapters. The alcalde role, unique to Mission Santa Cruz, was divided along gender lines—with men (always) being either the *alcalde de mujeres* or *alcalde de hombres* (the mayor of women or of men, respectively). I understand this to mean that the elected official was in charge of locking up the women or men. The *monjeríos* and *jayuntes* are discussed in Jackson and Castillo, *Indians, Franciscans, and Spanish Colonization*, 144. For more on the *monjeríos*, see Deborah A. Miranda, "Extermination of the Joyas."

204. Bouvier, *Women and the Conquest of California*, 82. The separation of young women from older married women is explored in Newell, *Constructing Lives* (99-100).

205. Voss, "Domesticating Imperialism," 196.

206. Deborah A. Miranda, *Bad Indians*, 23-24. This story was related by the Chumash man Fernando Librado Kitsepawit to Harrington and described in detail by Miranda. It is worth noting that Kitsepawit was born in 1839, about the time of secularization, when the missions closed, so he did not himself live in the mission. Therefore, his story is secondhand, likely shared by his family and others who did survive them. Johnson, "Trail to Fernando," 132-38.

207. Sepulveda, "Our Sacred Waters," 40-58.

208. Hurtado, *Intimate Frontiers*, 12.

209. Vancouver, *Voyage of Discovery*, 2:13. This quotation comes from English captain George Vancouver, who visited Mission Dolores and Mission Santa Clara in 1792.

210. Kotzebue, *New Voyage Round the World*, 36. This quotation also appears in Jackson and Castillo, *Indians, Franciscans, and Spanish Colonization*, 81.

211. Street, *Beasts of the Field*, 42.

212. Geiger and Meighan, *As the Padres Saw Them*, 105, question 24.

213. Amador, "Memorias," 90. This quotation also appears in Jackson and Castillo, *Indians, Franciscans, and Spanish Colonization*, 81.

214. The Mission Santa Cruz Book of Confirmations shows that the first group confirmations took place in May 1793, a year and a half after founding (SBMAL).

215. Borica to Marcelino Cipres, Monterey, September 29, 1796, in SBMAL, CMD 279. In Monterey, by the mid-1790s, reports show that a number of baptized people fled the mission eastward into the tule-filled swamps, which the Spanish hesitated to cross.

216. Hackel, *Children of Coyote*, 65–74. Hackel similarly examines the impact of Spanish livestock and agriculture on Indigenous grasses and resources.

217. Informe al Commandante General, Monterey, August 24, 1796, BL, BSS, Provincial State Records, C-A 50, 206–8. Governor Borica recognized that Indigenous theft of cattle around Mission Santa Clara in 1796 was a response to food shortages due to three years of drought.

218. Soler to Governor Fages, April 10, 1787, BL, BSS, Provincial State Records, C-A 4, 139. An incident occurred at Mission San Carlos (Monterey) in April 1787, in which a number of cattle were attacked by a mixed group of unbaptized Calenda-ruc people and recently baptized runaways. This incident resulted in Spanish soldiers giving chase. Eventually, they negotiated with the Calenda-ruc chief for the arrest of the runaways.

219. Allen, *Native Americans*, 95. Allen noted the persistence of shellfish and traditional foods. This pattern has been studied throughout the greater San Francisco Bay Area. See Silliman, *Lost Laborers*.

220. This account was written a few years after the event and was reported by Governor Fages to Viceroy Miguel de la Grua Talamanca y Branciforte, August 12, 1793, BL, C-A 7, 405–13.

221. Monroy, *Thrown among Strangers*, 54–56. Monroy similarly recognized these complexities, noting that "for Indians to use an ox-driven wooden plow required a tremendous transformation of their orientation toward the cosmos. The ox and the tree lost the old spirits that had animated them and formed part of their essence."

222. Haas, *Saints and Citizens*, 113–14. Haas explores the centrality of the horse to Indigenous artwork in the California missions. Lacson also explores the centrality of horses to Spanish colonization in "Born of Horses."

223. Governor Fages to Lasuén, Monterey, August 20, 1787, SBMAL, CMD 64. Fears around Indigenous use of horses and firearms is explored in detail by Hackel (*Children of Coyote*, 338–39). Spanish officials feared that skilled horse riding Indians would become a military threat, but due to the necessity of horses to livestock management it was not practical to prohibit Indigenous use of horses.

224. Tibesar, *Writings of Junípero Serra*, 2:87.

225. Sullivan and McLeod, *Travels of Jedediah Smith*, 76–77.

226. Kugel, "Of Missionaries and Their Cattle." Kugel examines Ojibwa perceptions of missionaries and their cattle, and how they saw the two intertwined through spiritual power.

227. Harrison, *History of Santa Cruz County*, 58. Asisara recalls the prevalence of bear drawn to the cow pastures.

228. Bancroft, *History of California*, 1:495. The account of soldiers using bears for target practice at Mission Santa Cruz is given here.

229. Ketchum, email to author, September 26, 2016. Ketchum further noted, "I have read that the bears were usually not healthy." This is certainly likely, as capturing and holding a full-strength adult grizzly bear before the fight would have been, if not logistically impossible, extremely challenging.

230. Fages and Priestly, "Historical, Political, and Natural Description of California," 58.

231. SFB 1002, on November 18, 1791. Milliken identifies Charquin as the chief based on his appearing first among a mixed group of Quiroste and Olpen. The second in line that day was Lachi (Pacifico), SFB 1003, chief of the Olpen. The ordering of baptisms often reflected political hierarchies.

232. Starting in 1786, the missionaries at Mission Dolores opened the San Pedro outstation twelve miles down the coast, which helped ease conditions of overcrowding, provided additional food resources, and increased outreach down the coast into the Santa Cruz mountain region. This began the recruitment of coastal people such as the Quiroste.

233. Cuc chítí (Ninfa), SFB 991, Puchute (Marina), SFB 993, both on November 11, 1791. Yaccham (Emerenciana), SFB 1011.

234. San Francisco (Dolores) marriage registry number (SFM) 242, on November 19, 1791.

235. Sal to Arrillaga, February 27, 1793, BL MSS, C-A 55, 160–64. One eighty-year-old Quiroste elder, Lonsom, did receive baptism at Mission San Francisco (SFB 200) back in 1780 and lived in the community until his death two years later. The majority of the twenty-plus referred to were baptized at the San Pedro outstation. They are SFB 676–80, 711, 725, 871, 930, 976, 977, 981–83, and 985–93. The exceptions are 871 and 930, who were baptized at Mission San Fran-

cisco. Another fifteen Quiroste children were baptized at Mission Santa Clara during the spring of 1790 under the alias San Bernardino: SCLB 1581, 1684, 1688-89, 1691, 1699, 1707-10, 1720-21, 1723-24, and 1736.

236. San Francisco (Dolores) death registry number (SFD) 480, burial date November 17, 1792.

237. Evidence of Obera's trip is found in a note on the baptism of a Quiroste woman, Momioste, whom Olbera baptized in her sickness (SFB 1165), on January 3, 1793. She survived for almost another year (SFD 593).

238. Sal to Arrillaga, February 27, 1793, BL MSS, C-A 55, 160–64.

239. Uetex (Secundino Maldanado, SCZB 186) and Tuiguimemis (Manuela Yrien, SCZB 189), Uayas (Bartolome Lopez, SCZB 187) and Miscamis (Bonifacia Ubartondo, SCZB 190), all baptized on February 17, 1793. Their weddings were the same day, SCZM 33 and 34.

240. Sal to Arrillaga, February 27, 1793, BL MSS, C-A 55, 160–64.

241. Arrillaga, March 26, 1793, BL MSS, C-A 22, 359. This record in the provincial documents suggests a report on March 26, 1793, about Charquin—either that he had been captured or that attempts were being made to capture him. Unfortunately, the original was lost in the San Francisco fire of 1906.

242. SFD 541 and 542.

243. SFB 1290–1306 received baptism on May 2, 1793. SFB 1307–29 received baptism on May 6, 1793.

244. BL MSS, C-A 22, 361–62.

245. SFD 590. The other six included the previously mentioned Momioste, whom Olbera had baptized in his search for Charquin earlier in the year, SFD 593. The others are SFD 588–89, 591–92, and 594.

246. Chuchigite, listed as six or seven years old, SCZB 230.

247. Kenneally, *Writings of Fermín Francisco de Lasuén*, 1:299–300. Here the Spanish appear to be, somewhat unknowingly, operating within Indigenous protocols by stealing the women away via baptism and relocation. Lasuén served as president of the Franciscan missions of Alta California following the death of Friar Junípero Serra in 1784 until his own death in 1803. Lasuén, stationed in neighboring Monterey, personally visited Mission Santa Cruz on a number of occasions, including in May 1793, when he served as *padrino* for SCZB 214. James A. Sandos explores the life and policies of Lasuén in *Converting California* (83–98). Sandos argued that Lasuén employed a more cautious approach, in contrast with his predecessor Serra, for example, by favoring the education and training of baptized Natives (95–96).

248. SCZB 234, SCZD 13. It is possible that Juanchita's father was a Sayanta, as her father, whose name is listed as Cholos (and who does not appear to have been baptized himself), has the same name as the father of a Cotoni boy bap-

tized four days after her death (December 29, 1793). The boy's name was Susiur (Vicente Reyes), SCZB 239. Juanchita's mother is listed as the Quiroste woman Sanite (Fortunata), SCZB 254, from the Mitenne village. Sanite was baptized about a month after her daughter, on January 8, 1794.

249. BL MSS, Provincial State Papers, C-A 14, 176.

250. Second Lieutenant José Perez-Fernández to Arrillaga, February 1, 1794, BL MSS, Provincial State Papers, C-A 7, 55–56. Perez-Fernández was commander of the San Francisco Presidio.

251. Perez-Fernández to Arrillaga, February 1, 1794, BL MSS, Provincial State Papers, C-A 6, 336–67. This is the only mention of Pella. He was never listed under baptismal records.

252. Perez-Fernández to Arrillaga, February 1, 1794, BL MSS, Provincial State Papers, C-A 6, 336–67.

253. Perez-Fernández to Arrillaga, March 15, 1794, BL MSS, Provincial State Papers, C-A 7, 50–54.

254. SCZB 315 and 316.

255. The reason for their move is not noted, but the first of the two women, Quisuam, had an infant son, Cucufate, SCLB 2301, who had been previously baptized at Mission Santa Clara, on May 4, 1793,. The father, Aniceto, SCLB 2463, April 16, 1794, was baptized at Mission Santa Clara a few months after the Santa Cruz baptisms, so it is possible that they were relocated around then. The couple were joined by their thirteen-year-old daughter, Cipres (Prima), SCLB 2540, on September 20, 1794. The second Quiroste woman, Mañem, had a daughter, Gregoria, SCLB 2457, who received baptism at Mission Santa Clara merely a month later, on March 25, 1794.

256. BL MSS, Provincial State Papers, C-A 22, 367.

257. BL MSS, Provincial State Papers, C-A 22, 367.

258. BL MSS, Provincial State Papers, C-A 7, 188–200.

259. Milliken, *Time of Little Choice*, 123. Milliken makes the same argument.

260. A total of sixty-two Quiroste receive baptism in groups at Mission Santa Clara between September and December 1794. It is possible that some of them were not Quiroste, as they may have been allied neighbors. They were all recorded as "San Bernardino," which indicated from the western direction of the village of Mitenne. These baptisms are SCLB 2517, 2526, 2530, 2532–35, 2539–40, 2620, 2622–25, 2627, 2629–30, 2632–38, 2640–45, 2647–53, 2661, 2704–5, 2709–13, 2717–23, 2727–28, 2732–36, 2761, 2763, and 2768.

261. Overall, the majority lived at Mission Santa Clara, as 119 received baptism there, along with the 2 from Santa Cruz who moved there. Only 12 received baptism at Mission Santa Cruz, while 95 received baptism at Mission Dolores, the last receiving baptism on May 19, 1793 (SFB 1334).

262. Perez-Fernández to Borica, BL MSS, Provincial State Papers, C-A 15, 49. Reports indicated that unbaptized rebels were assisted by baptized Natives living at the mission. These collaborations persisted, as supported by evidence of Indigenous trade networks throughout the early 1800s.

263. BL MSS, Provincial State Papers, C-A 24, 53.

264. BL MSS, Provincial State Papers, C-A 8, 176–78.

265. BL MSS, Provincial State Papers, C-A 24, 82–84.

266. SFD 1189 and SCLD 2032.

267. Lasuén to Salazar and Lopez, August 22, 1793, in Kenneally, *Writings of Fermín Francisco de Lasuén*, 1:286–87. Lasuén is responding to numerous complaints from the two friars. He points out that the workload responsibilities (temporal affairs) would be similar at any mission. On the lack of harmony between the two friars, see Geiger, *Franciscan Missionaries*, 143 and 214.

268. Fages to Viceroy Miguel de la Grua Talamanca y Branciforte, August 12, 1793, BL MSS, State Provincial Records, C-A 7, 405–13. Spanish laws prohibited bows and arrows around Spanish settlements. Unbaptized workers were quickly disarmed, as seen in the previously discussed employment of Indigenous laborers in Monterey.

269. Lasuén to Fray Tomas Pangua, August 19, 1794, in Kenneally, *Writings of Fermín Francisco de Lasuén*, 1:317. In the course of assigning him to the region, Lasuén reported that "I am told that nothing suits him; and I notice that none of the missionaries who have known him like him." Like the majority of padres assigned to Alta California, Fernández was born in Spain (Villar) and trained at the College of San Fernando in Mexico City before being assigned and sent northward.

270. Commissioner Gabriel Moraga to Lieutenant Jose Arguello, October 30, 1794, BL, C-A 7, 125–33.

271. The second pueblo, El Pueblo de Nuestra Señora la Reina de los Ángeles del Río de Porciúncula, was founded in 1781.

272. Fernández's last baptism at Mission Santa Clara took place on November 27, 1794 (SCLB 2679). He first appears in the Mission Santa Cruz baptismal record on February 25, 1795 (SCZB 457). He performed sixty-five baptisms over the next month.

273. Lasuén to Fray Antonio Nogueyra, July 21, 1796, in Kenneally, *Writings of Fermín Francisco de Lasuén*, 1:387. Fray Salazar left Santa Cruz in July 1795, while Fray Lopez left in July 1796. Fray José de la Cruz Espi complained immediately after his assignment. Lasuén observed that "he adapts himself poorly in any mission . . . he has no taste for the work for which missionaries should come here. He gives signs of wishing to leave."

274. Jose Antonio Sanchez to Borica, March 7, 1796, in BL, C-A 55, 230.

275. Lasuén to Fernández, May 23, 1796, in Kenneally, *Writings of Fermín Francisco de Lasuén*, 1:380.

276. Fernández to Borica, SFAD, document 134, April 29, 1798. For example, Ynoc, SCZB 492, the father of Micaela, the young girl who received the first baptism at Mission Santa Cruz, received baptism at the hands of Fernández in 1795. Fernández later noted that "some Gentiles from the far side of the Pajaro [River], relatives of the earliest Christians of this Mission, have been subdued, by which we will give much glory to God and benefits to the Mission."

277. After 1796 it was only small groups of local peoples, most of them elders, that continued to enter the mission.

278. Geiger and Meighan, *As the Padres Saw Them*, 50. To a question about Indigenous superstitions, Mission Santa Cruz padres responded: "They hold at times secret, nocturnal dances always avoiding detection by the fathers. We are informed that at night, only the men gather together in the field or the forest. In their midst they raise a long stick crowned by a bundle of tobacco leaves or branches of trees or some other plant. At the base of this they place their food and even their colored beads."

279. Allen, *Native Americans*, 96–97.

280. The persistence of knowledge of traditional land management practices is explored in Anderson, *Tending the Wild*. As for the perseverance of herbal usage, quite a few Californios claimed to have learned California herbology from Native peoples, including the famous Juana Briones of San Francisco, who was raised across the San Lorenzo from Mission Santa Cruz, at the Villa de Branciforte. Another example is Catholic mystic and friar Magin Catalá, who was stationed at Mission Santa Clara for thirty-six years. Dona Pilar Larios, from neighboring San Juan Bautista, is another famous example from the Californio community, along with the Santa Cruz–based Maria de los Angeles Majors, known locally as a healer, who spoke of her childhood connections with Indians at Mission Santa Cruz in an interview with Belle Dormer (*San Francisco Chronicle*, August 16, 1896, 16:3).

281. The theme of psychological disruption is one explored in depth by Milliken. Documents repeatedly report evidence of malaise, depression, and confusion in the face of rapid social, ecological, and political transformation, in which traditional knowledge was unable to provide answers to new problems. Milliken, *Time of Little Choice*.

282. This quotation was used effectively by Milliken (*Time of Little Choice*, 223). It is found in Palóu, *Life and Apostolic Labors*, 211. Though not discussed in depth in this study, the missionaries created rules around the distribution of clothing for baptized Indigenous people at the missions. The specific allotments and rules around clothing is discussed in response to question 7 in a letter written

in 1800 (Friars Juan Cortés and Estévan Tapis to Friar Lasuén, October 30, 1800, SBMAL, CMD 497). Asisara recalled, about one missionary from the 1820s, that "he dressed the Indians well, each according to his class" (Castillo, "Indian Account of the Decline," 400). Note how clothing was used to impose hierarchy and define class distinctions, much as the presence of clothing helped padres to distinguish Indigenous people who had received baptism from those who had not.

283. The debate between voluntary and coerced conversion is explored by Madley ("California's First Mass Incarceration System," 16–17). Sandos claimed that there was "no forced recruitment of gentiles for missionization," while Milliken argued that Native people "were not marched to baptismal font by soldiers with guns and lances" (*Converting California*, 103; and *Time of Little Choice*, 1, respectively). Madley argued that the "Franciscans and their military allies established the system between 1769 and 1790, before deploying more overtly carceral practices between 1790 and 1836" ("California's First Mass Incarceration System," 16–17). In Santa Cruz and the greater San Francisco Bay Area, this shift happened in the early 1800s, as this book will argue.

284. Preparation for systems of punishment and control was an integral part of Spanish expansion. For example, Sal ordered that shackles and restraints be available shortly after the founding of Mission Santa Cruz. See Provincial State Papers, BL MSS C-A 55, July 31, 1792, San Francisco, 69.

285. These deaths are recorded as Soquel (SCZD 162, on June 16, 1796), Rosuem (SCZD 9, on March 11, 1793), and Gelelis (SCZD 10, on November 22, 1793).

2. Diverse Nations within the Mission

1. The use of games is ubiquitous across the Indigenous Americas. Voorhies, *Prehistoric Games*.

2. Harrington, "San Juan Report," JPH, microfilm, reel 58, p. 76.

3. Mexico, December 31, 1801, AGN, Californias 49. Raymundo Carrillo complains that their vices and bad conduct were a corrupting influence.

4. Allen, *Native Americans*, 84. Evidence of bone, shell, beads, and even roof tile fragments fashioned into gaming pieces have been observed in Native housing at Mission Santa Cruz.

5. *Refutation of Charges*, Lasuén to Lull, June 19, 1801, SBMAL, CMD 510. This important document is one of the most in-depth descriptions by missionaries of Indigenous Californians and their treatment, through Lasuén's response to an extensive questionnaire from Father Guardian at the College of San Fernando, Martin Lull. The questionnaire was ultimately a response to the charges made in 1797 by Fray Antonio de la Concepción Horra of cruelty by California missionaries against Indians. Horra's charges prompted concern by Spain's new Viceroy, Miguel José de Azanza Alegría. Viceroy Azanza in turn required

California Governor Diego de Borica to follow up on these charges by sending a questionnaire to the Presidio commanders. The charges by Horra and responses are discussed in Sandos, *Converting California*, 272; Beebe and Senkewicz, "Uncertainty on the Mission Frontier"; and in great depth by Sladeck, "Padres Descontentos," 193–250. In response to question 44, regarding games, Lasuén wrote that "all the games which the Natives of either sex knew in their pagan state are permitted them, with the exception of those which are in conflict with Christianity. Card playing is one of the things they have picked up from the white people, and to this they have become inordinately addicted . . . some of our neophytes, and even some pagans, have become so adept at cards that they win from their teachers. There is an Indian at this Mission of San Carlos, and at a single sitting he won more than thirty pesos from two of the gente de razon." While Lasuén believed that they became "addicted" to playing, perhaps they found some familiarity or relief through gaming, which was hard to find in an otherwise stressful situation. The presence of both baptized and unbaptized people playing these games is an important point, as it reveals the social ties that persisted outside of the dichotomies imposed by the Franciscans, between Native people at the mission and those living outside its boundaries.

6. Monroy, *Thrown among Strangers*, 35–39. Monroy argued that military pursuits of and the retrieval of fugitives along with unbaptized Indigenous people helped to fuel the expansion of the spiritual conquest. A similar pattern is found in Santa Cruz.

7. Hackel, *Children of Coyote*. Hackel's work, which explores the history of Indigenous peoples of Monterey from a perspective of forced assimilation, includes an example of this narrative. While the book does a fine job of exploring the intricacies of Spanish conquest, little attention is given to the perseverance of tribal or preexisting influences or connections.

8. Panich, "Archaeologies of Persistence," 105–22.

9. The best examples of these are found in Newell, *Constructing Lives*; and Sandos, "Early California Reconsidered," 592–625.

10. Lieutenant Perez-Fernández to Governor Diego de Borica, January 1, 1794, BL, C-A 7, 78. Fears of Indigenous confrontation echoed between Santa Cruz and San Francisco. In January 1794, at the height of the Quiroste rebellion, three additional guards were sent from San Francisco to Santa Cruz to reinforce Spanish military presence. This was met with anxiety in San Francisco, as reflected in a letter from Perez-Fernández to the governor, who noted that they were concerned about the reduced battalion "because at any moment the Indians could have bad thoughts."

11. Milliken, *Time of Little Choice*, 136–46. The initial flight, skirmish, and aftermath are discussed here at length.

12. Milliken, *Time of Little Choice*, 144. The outbreak was likely typhus and was limited to Mission Dolores, unlike later outbreaks that passed from one mission community to another. The reasons for this event are given in a number of recorded testimonies, kept at AGN.

13. Report by Commander Jose Arguello, April 29, 1796, BL, C-A 8, 3, and Commander Hermenegildo Sal to Governor Borica, January 31, 1796, BL, C-A 8, 4. Arguello released from San Francisco Presidio a group of six prisoners who had served time for killing and eating some mares and cattle belonging to settlers at the pueblo of San José. Curiously, one is named Ambrosio, who could be one of two people—Yamnisi (SCLB 2198, baptized as Ambrosio), who lived at Mission Santa Clara until he was killed by a bear in 1800, or Euxexi (SCZB 232, also baptized as Ambrosio), a Somontoc who lived at Mission Santa Cruz but baptized his daughter at Mission Santa Clara two weeks before the founding of Mission Santa Cruz.

14. Guest, "Establishment of the Villa de Branciforte," 29–50. These ambitions were intertwined, as Spanish expansion required a larger military presence. The recent Nootka confrontation and concerns that the English sought to disrupt the Spanish monopoly on trade in the Pacific had led to the 1793 attempt to settle on Bodega Bay. As Viceroy Marques de Branciforte made plans to expand civilian settlement of the region, letters from engineer Miguel Costansó advocated for military support for the expansion.

15. Weber, *Spanish Frontier*. The Spanish colonial frontier consisted of three types of settlements: missions, pueblos, and presidios. The missions served as sites of relocation of Indigenous peoples for Catholic instruction, Spanish acculturation, and the production of goods for the other settlements. Pueblos were to be homes for settling Spanish citizens, while the presidios housed and equipped Spanish soldiers.

16. While the division between Awaswas-speaking and Mutsun-speaking peoples is not known with certainty, I use the best guess given our current information and refer to the Santa Cruz Mountain tribes discussed at length in the first chapter as "Awaswas-speaking peoples."

17. Renya K. Ramirez, *Native Hubs*. The idea of "Native hubs" suggested by Ramirez suggests, like the hub of a wheel, a center of Native community in which individuals continue to have connections to homelands and other communities. While her study examines nearby Silicon Valley in the twentieth century and the circumstances and individuals differ, a similar framework helps to understand the persistence of Indigenous networks and the creation of connections that took place within the new setting of the mission in the nineteenth century.

18. Jackson, "Disease and Demographic Patterns," 38.

19. McNeill, *Plagues and Peoples*. The transmission and impact of smallpox and other diseases outside the realm of European settlement and official documentation is explored effectively in Fenn, *Pox Americana*.

20. Discussed in three separate letters, all found in BL, C-A 11, Monterey, January 30, February 27, and February 28, 1802, 186–88, 193, and 197, respectively.

21. Conclusive evidence of this outbreak was first discussed in depth by Jackson ("Disease and Demographic Patterns," 40).

22. As with most of the statistical work in this book, these numbers are based on my own computation of baptismal records. I have built my own databases, heavily aided by both the online baptismal records of Stephen Hackel and Huntington Library's Early California Population Project as well as Randall Milliken, who generously shared his personal database, which contains forty years of notes and research. I have added my own findings in order to trace tribal identities, helping to locate patterns along tribal and kinship lines, which were often omitted by the Franciscan missionaries, especially in the case of children born within the mission.

23. Commander Jose Arguello to Governor Arrillaga, San Francisco, December 31, 1805, BL, C-A 16, 281. "In the missions of this jurisdiction exist various diseases including syphilis, tuberculosis, dysentery of the blood, and other unknown maladies, and the neophytes are frequently dying from them."

24. Cinnabar clay, which leaves a red coloring, was used traditionally in ceremony and for paint and decoration. Cinnabar ore has been used to produce mercury, which led to the development of the New Almaden mines during the gold rush. Cinnabar is also found in the New Idria Mercury Mine, east of Pinnacles National Park. Ketchum informed me about tar resources located nearby the Pitac village.

25. Information regarding the Orestac and their quarry came from Ketchum. Email to author, September 26, 2016.

26. Allen, *Native Americans*, 95.

27. Allen, *Native Americans*, 61.

28. *Refutation of Charges*, Lasuén to Lull, June 19, 1801, SBMAL, CMD 510. In response to charge 53, Friar Lasuén observed that the gathering of goods in the forest "is something the pagans can enjoy because they have greater freedom, and because they have the assurance that the neophytes, because of the orders they have received [will not appear]." This quotation refers to unbaptized Indigenous peoples as *gentiles* (pagans), as was customary for the missionaries, as opposed to the baptized *neofitos* (neophytes). The terms reflect colonially imposed categories of identity and did not reflect the much more complex and nuanced tribal or kinship terms of identity used by Indigenous people.

29. While the Spanish eventually referred to the Yokuts as Tulareños, due to the swampy San Joaquin Valley, in these early days it appears that they confused

the boundaries and included eastern Mutsun territories within their understanding of Tulareños.

30. Governor Borica to Friar Marcelino Ciprés, Monterey, September 29, 1796, SBMAL, CMD 279. Borica responded to Padre Ciprés's worries about having to deal with runaways in the *tulares*, noting that the Tulareños "tried to run over and kill the missionaries the year before." Borica later noted, "Our system of conquest is peaceful . . . which will be impossible or more difficult if we try to engage with the Tulare Indians."

31. Blackhawk, *Violence over the Land*. To truly understand colonial and Indigenous encounters, it is important to recognize how colonialism impacted people across distances. Blackhawk uses violence as a lens to understand colonial encounters, pointing out the impact of years of warfare and occupation on tribes beyond of the realm of immediate encounter with Europeans.

32. Vallejo to Borica, December 14, 1797, BL, C-A 8, 359.

33. Allen, *Native Americans*, 49. The governor of Monterey informed Russian explorer Georg von Langsdorff of this in 1806. The slaughter was ostensibly to prevent overpopulation, but it is likely that Spanish fears of mounted Indigenous resistance played a role. Local settlers would have been aware of the transformation and mobility that horses brought to the Comanche (to name one example). For a look at this dynamic, see Hämäläinen, *Comanche Empire*.

34. Rick Flores, conversation with author, March 31, 2015. Flores is the curator of the California Native Plant Collection and associate of the Amah Mutsun Land Trust. Flores works closely with the Amah Mutsun tribe in the Amah Mutsun Relearning Program, which is a collaborative effort between the tribe and the UCSC Arboretum & Botanic Garden to assist tribal members in efforts of cultural revitalization, recuperation, and relearning of dormant cultural knowledge. The impact of swine on the ecology is also examined in Crosby, *Ecological Imperialism*.

35. Gonzalez and Carranza to Governor Borica, January 14, 1799, SBMAL, CMD 420. In 1799 Friars Gonzalez and Carranza reported that the henhouse (*gallinero*), which engineer extraordinaire Alberto Cordoba had spent considerable time building, had fallen in the rains, burying some hens beneath the ruins.

36. Borica, Monterey, June 7, 1799, BL, C-A 10, 327–30. In an email to author, September 26, 2016, Ketchum says that the name Ausaima most likely translates into "Salt People," as the word *awse* means "salt" in Mutsun. This name likely corresponds to both the resource and moiety affiliation. From now on I will present translations of village or tribal names in parentheses like this, and all come from Ketchum unless stated otherwise.

37. This theory is supported by the incident discussed in the first chapter, when tribal villagers from the Santa Clara area labored near Monterey in exchange for access to abalone and seashells.

38. Grossinger, *South Santa Clara Valley Historical Ecology Study*. Ketchum says that Unijaima translates into "Fish People," likely corresponding to moiety affiliation of the Unijaima people. Email to author, September 26, 2016.

39. Sal to Arrillaga, September 30, 1792, BL, C-A 55, 70–71. While delivering goods from Mission Santa Cruz, a Spanish soldier accompanied by two baptized men from said mission was robbed by a group of unbaptized villagers.

40. The villagers most likely attacked the cattle, which have similarities with local deer and elk, in an attempt to stave off hunger, but they may well have seen it as an exchange of cattle and livestock for the grasslands and resources that the cattle destroyed.

41. Father Lasuén to Fray Manuel Fernández, May 23, 1796, in Kenneally, *Writings of Fermín Francisco de Lasuén*, 1:380. The majority of the Guacharron relocated to Mission San Carlos (Monterey), with a smaller number at Mission San Juan Bautista. Mission Soledad had many people from a tribe called Chalon. Ketchum theorizes that they were also Guacharron.

42. Ketchum believes Chipuctac village was on the north shore of present-day San Felipe Lake, while Poitoquix was on the southeast shore. Poitoquix is the Mutsun name for both the village and the lake.

43. Geiger, *Franciscan Missionaries*.

44. The missionaries at Mission Santa Clara tended to use designations for directional homelands. People arriving from the south received the designation "San Carlos" (in the direction of Mission San Carlos), those from the west received "San Bernadino," and so on.

45. Salazar left in July 1795, while Lopez left a year later, in July 1796. Friar José de la Cruz Espi served the interim alongside Fernández, from the end of 1795 until the arrival of Gonzalez in May 1797.

46. Friar Manuel Fernández finally received permission to depart, as Governor Borica reported that he had permission "considering his indifference (disdain) and violence that was due" BL MSS C-A 10, December 12, 1798, 187 (translation mine). Apparently, as he was leaving, he took two barrels of mescal from the mission, more than his fair share. Commander Jose Arguello to Borica, December 11, 1798, BL MSS, C-A 10, 63.

47. The first to be marked as "San Juan" are found in entries by Baldomero Lopez, made about a month after the arrival of Fernández, in SCZB 529, March 12, 1795. This group included members of the Chitactac (Unijaima) and Chipuctac (Ausaima) peoples.

48. The geographical designation of these tribes comes from a combination of the theories by Randall Milliken, the insights of Ed Ketchum, and most crucially, the insights of archaeologist Mark Hylkema, who has conducted archaeological work for over forty years throughout the Santa Cruz Mountains and greater area.

49. As previously mentioned, Mission Santa Clara missionaries used a system of directional districts in recording village and tribal identities. The Ritocsi site was one of the villages in the San Josef de Cupertino district, although some appear to have been aggregated into the San Juan Bautista district. Archaeologist Mark Hylkema gave an example: "The SCL missionaries referred to everything north of Sunnyvale all the way to the coast as 'San Bernardino district.' Today's Bernardo Ave. in Sunnyvale still marks that boundary, along with Pastoria (the pastures), and El Camino Real." Email to author, June 7, 2021. The grouping together of multiple village sites under one district makes it extremely difficult, if not impossible, to determine the specific tribal identity of many of those who arrived in large groups. The closest approximation for translating the designations at Mission Santa Clara is found by Hylkema, who aggregated the work of Milliken and Chester King, along with his own insights ("Archaeological Investigations," 38). My approximations of the geographies of the Ritocsi and Partocsi village sites heavily rely on Hylkema's work and shared insights.

50. SCZB 197, 481, 485, 517, 522, 526, 527, 589–94, and 957.

51. Hylkema provides tantalizing evidence that archaeological site SCL-951 along upper Stevens Creek revealed a complicated mix of precontact and postcontact data. Analysis of a mussel shell found in Feature 2 at this site "produced a calibrated date with a 95% probablility that the shell specimen's age ranged between AD 1700 and AD 1950; with a 68% probability that the date ranged from AD 1810 to AD 1950. In other words, Feature 2 was used sometime during the Historic [post contact] period, and was not a prehistoric period cultural deposit." See "Historic Properties Survey Report," 17.

52. SCZB 411, 412, 415–17, 421, 426, 427, 446–48, 454–56, 460, 466, 500, 512, 585–88, 595–600, 614, and 1151.

53. Gillette, "Rock Art," 117–29. Also see Mark and Newman, "Cup-and-Ring Petroglyphs," 13–21.

54. Ketchum believes that multiple Juristac, or "Big Head Place," sites were found throughout the greater region, theorizing that they were spaced about twenty miles apart, allowing for various tribes to have space to practice the important Kuksui ceremony. Email to author, September 26, 2016.

55. Complicating this geography is the fact that some Chitactac members identify in later census documents as Chiputac. An example of this is Yrachis (Ostiano, SCZB 629). Yrachis shows up in the 1834 Padron as "Chiputac [*sic*]," despite being listed as Chitactac in his baptismal record.

56. Carchas (Doroteo, SCLB 3699), a nine-year-old boy, was baptized on December 8, 1798. His father, Elelis (Tomas, SCZB 1143), was baptized at Mission Santa Cruz on January 16, 1805. The boy was later relocated to Mission Santa Cruz, as noted on his burial record, SCLD 3245.

57. SCZB 912, 915, 980, 1040, 1058, 1059, and 1201. Juristac is the site of the important Kuksui (Big Head) ceremony, which brought together spiritual leaders from local lands. Juristac, one of the last undeveloped Kuksui sites in the region today, is currently under threat of development into a gravel pit, the proposed Sargent Quarry. The Amah Mutsun Tribal Band have been organizing to protect this site in recent years; see Campaign to Protect Juristac, protectjuristac.org.

58. The theory of Xisca or Risca village being short for Juristac comes from Ketchum.

59. Milliken, Shoup, and Ortiz, "Ohlone/Costanoan Indians," 144. Ketchum states: "The Tomoi controlled Pacheco Pass, the traditional trade route between the Central Valley and the coast. There were several other passes, but Tomoi was the most important. It is also [one of] California's 'Trail of Tears' as thousands of Yokuts were brought to the missions through this pathway." Email to author, September 26, 2016.

60. For example, two of the seven Sitectac were later identified as Tomoi in burial and census records, SCZB 1080 and 1087 in SCZD 903 and 1561, respectively.

61. The reference to the hills of the Sumus (*de la sierra de Sumus*) suggests that these may have been a subgroup of Tomoi, whose homeland included the eastern hills. This notation is found in the notes on SCZB 1292, Chaparis (Bruno), who was one of the first Sumus to arrive.

62. For example, Coayat (Justa), SCZB 1287, was baptized at Mission Santa Cruz, which notes that her father, Jesecori, SCLB 5236, was baptized as Tayssen at Mission Santa Clara, while her mother, Najasa (Odorica), SCZB 1109, was baptized at Mission Santa Cruz.

63. Friar Mariano Payeras to Borica, August 2, 1798, SFAD, document 148. The Ausaima were certainly not the only people who challenged Spanish colonization. The coastal Guacharron, who lived along the Calenda-ruc and the inland Mutsun, also received specific condemnation for their resistance, as seen in this letter complaining that tribal members were not conforming to Catholic practices. These two peoples, the majority of whom received baptisms at Missions San Carlos and San Juan Bautista, respectively, fall outside the parameters of this study. Ketchum believes that part of the reason that these tribes resisted Spanish colonization so passionately "is because these two areas were central to the precontact tribal religion." I think that in addition, as time passed, neighboring Indigenous communities learned more about the consequences of relocation to the missions, saw what became of other tribes, learned from fugitives, and developed stronger tactics to resist and challenge the colonizers.

64. This is in addition to the twenty at Mission San Carlos who had received baptism in years before the establishment of Mission San Juan Bautista.

65. The Ausaima were not alone, as many tribes formed complicated relationships with Spanish colonizers. The Ausaima case, being more visible, serves as an example of this complexity.

66. Governor Borica to Virrey, November 27, 1798, BL C-A 24, 430–31.

67. BL, C-A 10, 327–30.

68. Raymundo Carrillo to Arrillaga, February 1, 1802, BL, C-A 11, 192.

69. A large group of ninety-seven Ausaima entered Mission San Juan Bautista during 1800, a few years after the baptism of Ausaima chief Tetimure (Bernabe), San Juan Bautista baptism (hereafter SJBB) 212, and his family in August 1798. A second Ausaima chief, Llomoi (Jose Maria Estudillo), SJBB 1215, entered in October 1803. It is likely that Tetimure was chief of the Chipuctac village, as his nephew, Uthaña (Jose Domingo), SJBB 610, who married and relocated to Mission Santa Cruz, was listed as Chipuctac in the 1834 Santa Cruz census.

70. Von Kotzebue, *Visit of the "Rurik,"* 62. The first part of this passage is quoted in Milliken, *Time of Little Choice*, 219.

71. Harrington, "San Juan Report," JPH, microfilm, reel 59, p. 4. The Chauchilas were a Yokuts tribe living at Mission San Juan Bautista.

72. Historian Phillips noted that "fleeing from the missions became a collective expression of rebellion," *Indians and Intruders*, 82. Madley discusses patterns of escapees and fugitives at length; see "California's First Mass Incarceration System," 26–27.

73. Soler to Fages, April 10, 1787, BL, C-A 4, 139. Reports of runaways existed along with the first missions. Mission San Carlos reported groups returning to homelands as early as 1787, as seen in this report about a Calenda-ruc group returning to their village. The phenomenon of fugitivism in California, and specifically in Monterey, has been explored by Hackel (*Children of Coyote*, 90–95). Hackel argues that "because most mission-born Indians did not live to adulthood, and life outside required skills that many mission-born Indians did not have, fugitives were far more likely to have been baptized as adults" (95). Many fugitives from Mission Santa Cruz were indeed adults, but many of them are listed along with their children. I believe that Hackel overestimates the amount of cultural knowledge lost for this first mission-born generation. Later chapters will show evidence of cultural retention in post-mission eras.

74. Hopper mortars are shallow mortars intended to be used with baskets with open bottoms that are then affixed, often with asphaltum or pine sap, to the shallow pecked mortar depression. They contrast with sedentary deeper bedrock mortars. Hopper mortars are suggestive of mission-era adaptations by fugitive groups who needed to pack up and move to avoid capture. They are discussed by Hylkema ("Discovery," 15–16). They also further support Schneider's discussion of refuge sites outside of the mission walls ("Placing Refuge," 699–702).

75. The most in-depth analysis of the paseos is found in Newell, *Constructing Lives*. Newell argues that paseos were used for food gathering (57–58) and as opportunities to return to homeland to give birth or die (151–52). See also Arkush, "Native Responses to European Intrusion," 62–90. Arkush argues that these paseos played a key role in facilitating the retention of Indigenous worldviews and semitraditional cultural practices.

76. *Refutation of Charges*, Lasuén to Lull, June 19, 1801, SBMAL, CMD 510. This quotation is in response to questions 56 and 57, regarding *paseos*. The padres discussed the *paseos* in response to the fourth question from a letter written in 1800. Friars Juan Cortés and Estévan Tapis to Friar Lasuén, October 30, 1800, SBMAL, CMD 497. This questionnaire was written in response to allegations about the mistreatment of Indians made by Santa Barbara Presidio commander Felipe de Goycoechea.

77. Milliken, *Time of Little Choice*, 137–46. Milliken explores this large flight in detail.

78. Borica to Friar Marcelino Cipres, September 28, 1796, SBMAL, CMD 279.

79. Lasuén to Fages, August 18, 1788, SBMAL, CMD 84.

80. The Spanish referred to the Indigenous scouts and assistants, typically baptized, as auxiliaries.

81. Borica to Mission San Juan Bautista, July 22, 1799, "Recovery of Runaway Indians," BL, C-A 24, 565.

82. Of course, they were not the first to flee from Mission Santa Cruz. Small groups of runaways were involved with the Charquin-led Quiroste movement that began in 1793.

83. The first records to list people who had died "in their rancheria" appear in the burial records of a group of three males, SCZD 206–8. All three came from the eastern side of the mountains, away from the mission. One was an eleven-year-old Chipuctac boy, SCZB 367, and the other two were a sixty-year-old Chitactac and twenty-five-year-old Pitac who had arrived together, SCZB 623 and 624.

84. August 3, 1798, BL, C-A 24, 542.

85. Fernández to Borica, January 27, 1798, SFAD, Alexander Taylor Collection, 128.

86. Fernández to Borica, April 29, 1798, SFAD, Alexander Taylor Collection, 134.

87. SCZD 337–51. This document suggests that Mesa reported, "I think they have died, as Joaquin found out," while also noting that Mesa helped to locate missing relatives of some of the earliest baptized at Mission Santa Cruz.

88. Madley, "California's First Mass Incarceration System," 38.

89. Borica, February 6, 1798, BL, C-A 24, 393. Borica argued that the mission's small, overreported population could survive the influx of additional settlers.

90. Parenthetical added by Harrington. "San Juan Report," JPH, microfilm, reel 59, p. 14.

91. Friars Juan Cortés and Estévan Tapis to Friar Lasuén, October 30, 1800, SBMAL, CMD 497. Regarding food (question 6), Santa Barbara Presidio commander Goycoechea complained that the food was insufficient for Indians to maintain themselves from fatigue. He claimed that Indians were given pozole and atole and meat was given only a few days a week. He suggested that hunger led Indians to search for traditional foods and to escape from the mission. The friars refuted this, interestingly pointing out, in defense, that some Indians had taken to raising chicken. They argued that they must have excess food to share with the chickens, though they do not consider the possibility that the Indians were raising chickens to address their hunger in the first place.

92. These include two Uypi, SCZB 44 and 91; two Aptos, SCZB 162 and 696; three from Achistaca, SCZB 59, 120, and 475; one from Sayanta, SCZB 306, and one from Cajastaca, SCZB 441. As previously noted (see table 11), ten others were confirmed as having died while fugitive from the mission. The Franciscans' obsession with accounting and documentation supports the theory that Native people frequently fled and lived out their lives outside of the sphere of the mission.

93. May 15, 1799, BL, C-A 24, 563.

94. March 4, 1798, BL, C-A 24, 430–31.

95. Friar Marte to Borica, May 9, 1799, SFAD, no. 193.

96. BL, C-A 10, June 7, 1799, 327–30.

97. Haas, *Saints and Citizens*, 39. For more on horse riding and care, see Zappia, "Indigenous Borderlands."

98. Undated correspondence from Friar Gonzalez and Friar Carranza to Governor Borica, SFAD, no. 126.

99. Carranza worked at Mission Santa Cruz between October 1798 and August 1808, while Gonzalez was assigned there from May 1797 to June 1805. The letter mentions that they were unfamiliar with Ules, except through his reputation, and that the previous padres were unsuccessful in containing him, suggesting that this letter was written shortly after they arrived.

100. Missionaries frequently commented on the Natives' fluid partnerships in the 1814 questionnaire. For example, in the Mission San Juan Bautista response to question 14 regarding matrimony, the priests recorded that "they were readily satisfied, even in the case of adultery of one of the parties or both, to come together again even if the man had two or three wives if it was feasible to keep them all, for they looked more to the procreation of children than to the stability of the marriage bond."

101. The missionaries' use of a "child-focused strategy" of conversion is discussed in Newell, *Constructing Lives*, 93; and Bouvier, *Women and the Conquest of California*, 90–92.

102. Webb, *Indian Life*, 35.

103. Lasuén to Fages, July 9, 1789, SBMAL, CMD 95.

104. Friar Fernández to Borica, January 27, 1798, SBMAL, CMD 355.

105. A similar example of an Indigenous man finding ways to work around Catholic monogamy is found at Mission Dolores (San Francisco); see Newell, *Constructing Lives*, 100–103.

106. Toyup (also spelled *Toyop*, *Toiop*, *Collop*, and *Taupo*), SCZB 660. His children included (ages in 1796): twelve-year-old Seynte (Projecto), SCZB 626; one-year-old Tallap (Prisco), SCZB 627; eight-year-old Yrachis (mentioned earlier); six-year-old Apuch (Hipacio), SCZB 634; five-year-old Sichirimas (Novato), SCZB 640; three-year-old Megeroa (Vicencia), SCZB 643; one-year-old Satguit (Zanitas), SCZB 653; four-year-old Ceyuén (Rita), SCZB 655; five-year-old Guazon (Lucia), SCZB 776; and newborn Yanasta (Pacifica), SCZB 866 (Yanasta was likely born in 1796 but received baptism with her mother in 1799). Toyup had two other children: the mission-born Tiburcio, SCZB 901, born in 1800, and another child born in 1800 but baptized in 1804, Unsueta (Maria Dolores), SCZB 1133. Toyup was from the Pitac village. Yanasta was baptized in 1799, as a three-year-old, and entered with his mother, Niceya (Petrona), SCZB 865, a Somontoc woman. The mother of Seynte, Yrachis, Sichirimas, Megeroa, and possibly Ceyuén is listed as Murejate (also spelled *Morejaste* or *Mugerate*) and does not appear to have been baptized. (Ceyuén's mother is listed as Yumuraste, which could be an alternate spelling of *Murejate* or a fifth woman.) The mother of Tallap, Guazon, and the mission-born Tiburcio was Aschi (Nicefora), SCZB 667, whom Toyup married after entering the mission, SCZM 155. The mother of Apuch and Satguit was Comoguen, who also did not receive baptism. It is possible that some of the children fled with the father to be with their mother. The baptismal records of the children note that they came from the villages of Chitactac and Pitac, while later census records of Yrachis claims he was from Chipuctac.

107. A second wife, Niceya (Petrona), did enter the mission in 1799 and subsequently married (SCZM 255) Topoc (Desiderio), SCZB 560, a man with similar ties to the villages of Chitactac and Chipuctac. Topoc is listed as from Chitactac in his baptism but from Chipuctac in his burial record, SCZD 488, in 1801.

108. See SCZD 467, 468 (Toyup), 472, 701, 704, 708, 713, and 719. Toyup and two of his children were reported dead at the end of 1800, and his five other children were reported dead at the end of 1805.

109. Of Toyup's other children, one died in 1800, SCZD 455; one died in 1810, SCZD 992; one in 1820, SCZD 1427; one in 1825, SCZD 1613; and the fifth, Yrachis, died in 1875, SCZD 2699. Yrachis was famously known as Justiniano Roxas, whose story is discussed at length in an article cowritten by me and Cothran, "Many Lives of Justiniano Roxas," 168–204.

110. Tapis and Quintana to governor, May 22, 1809, SBMAL, CMD 801b.

111. Yaquenonsat (Fausta), SCZB 1318, will be discussed in detail in this chapter and the next.

112. Madley, "California's First Mass Incarceration System," 40.

113. Harrington, "San Juan Report," JPH, microfilm, reel 59, p. 8.

114. Monterey, September 26, 1796, BL, C-A 24, 496–97.

115. Friar Tapis and Friar Quintana, May 22, 1809, SBMAL, CMD 801a. The padres wrote of having told the 1809 runaways "that they could be pardoned, those that voluntarily returned to the mission within fifteen days; but only two of the plains people returned with those sent to deliver the notice."

116. This social stratification will be looked at more closely in the chapter 4.

117. Amador, "Memorias," BL, C-D 28, 77.

118. The imposition of systems of crime and punishment within the California missions is explored in depth by Elias Castillo, *Cross of Thorns*.

119. Borica to Comandande de Escolta de San Francisco, October 23, 1796, BL, C-A 24, 94–95. An example of the public display took place in 1796, when Borica ordered that one baptized Native be put in chains and administered whippings as punishment.

120. Monterey was the home of the closest presidio to Mission San Juan Bautista, so it is here that people were sent to be punished for their crimes. Harrington, "San Juan Report," JPH, microfilm, reel 59, p. 56.

121. July 31, 1791, San Francisco, BL, C-A 55, 69.

122. Borica to Friar Fernández, Monterey, September 15, 1796, SBMAL, CMD 276.

123. Borica, March 12, 1799, BL, C-A 24, 557.

124. Harrington, "San Juan Report," JPH, reel 59, p. 74.

125. BL, C-A 11, February 1, 1802, 198.

126. Carrillo to Arrillaga, May 1, 1802, BL, C-A 11, 201. This must be Gonzalo Jose, SCAB 521, baptized as an infant in 1778.

127. Gonzalo connected with his friend Pomponio after his escape. Pomponio, SFB 2546, is the outlaw who vexed Spanish authorities through the early 1820s, eventually dying at soldiers' hands in 1824. The cause of Gonzalo's death is not listed, but it is likely that it was also at the hands of soldiers. Information on his death and connection to Pomponio is found in the notes of his death record, SCAD 2472.

128. Five Cajastaca received baptism on December 3, 1802 (SCZB 1023, 1025–27, and 1029). The youngest of these was thirty-four-year-old Ojeti (Justina, SCZB 1029); the others ranged from forty-five to seventy years old, fitting the pattern of elders resisting baptism longer than the targeted youth.

129. Governor of Baja California Felipe Antonio de Goycoechea report, December 20, 1805, BL, C-A 12, 15. In this report Goycoechea unsuccessfully

advocated the closing of Mission Santa Cruz and dividing of the baptized Natives between Missions Santa Clara and San Juan Bautista.

130. Haas examines the introduction of Indigenous people into Spanish identity politics as a process of "becoming Indian." This is the focus of her second chapter in *Saints and Citizens*, 50–82.

131. Jackson, *Race, Caste, and Status*. Jackson explores ways in which the *de razon* and *sin razon* designations, as well as the *sistema de castas* and Spanish classifications of race, have worked in California. These themes continue to be explored in Latin American historiography. See Martínez, *Genealogical Fictions*; and Fisher and O'Hara, *Imperial Subjects*.

132. Branciforte to Borica of California, November 28, 1797, BL, C-A 8, 464. Regarding goods and people arriving in Monterey, "the 17 Indians [were] transported in the ship *Concepcion*." For a discussion on how Spanish racial categories changed and adapted in the San Francisco Bay Area, see Voss, *Archaeology of Ethnogenesis*.

133. Commander Jose Arguello to Arrillaga, September 19, 1810, BL, C-A 12, 275–79.

134. The only observation of the usage of tule boats along the Pacific in this region comes from Fray Palou during the Rivera Moncada expedition in 1774. Cuthrell, "Eco-Archaeological Study," 80.

135. Arguello to Arrillaga, March 30, 1811, BL, C-A 12, 306–9.

136. José Maria Estudillo, April 9, 1811, California Pre-Statehood Documents (hereafter CPSD), MS 105, Special Collections and Archives, University Library, UCSC, box 1:5, 44. This letter reports that a group of Russian Indians woke up to find their *cayuco* (seal-skin boat) stolen. Local officials suggested that an inquiry be made with "Zoquel," from the late Uypi chief Soquel, which started to be used to refer to the Uypi around this time.

137. For an in-depth look at the racial system of the Spanish, see Martínez, *Genealogical Fictions*.

138. On colonial relations on the Spanish frontiers and the development of social status, see Radding Murrieta, *Wandering Peoples*.

139. Authorities stationed in Mexico City spoke frequently of anxiety about English challenges to Pacific control, yet their local counterparts continually emphasized their fears about growing discontent and challenges by Indigenous peoples.

140. Florian Guest, "Establishment of the Villa de Branciforte," 32.

141. Florian Guest, "Establishment of the Villa de Branciforte," 33.

142. December 27, 1796, BL, C-A 55, 308–9. Instructions to provide two warships and weapons in preparation for the construction of the villa.

143. Garr, "Villa de Branciforte," 98–100. This is examined in depth by Garr, who contextualizes this order as following the 1780 plan by Teodoro de Croix

to establish this type of multifunctional town along the Colorado-Gila frontier. His suggestions were met with ridicule by missionaries such as Friar Francisco Palou, who wanted to keep the rowdy, typically mestizo frontier settlers away from the Catholic teachings of the missions.

144. The intention of these liberal governmental members was not necessarily altruistic, as they shaped policy more in the interest of expanding the tax base and diminishing the power—and subsequently the land base—of the church.

145. Governor Borica to missionaries of Mission Santa Cruz, May 2, 1797, SBMAL, CMD 322.

146. Lasuén to Fray Pedro Callejas, San Carlos, May 1, 1797, in Kenneally, *Writings of Fermín Francisco de Lasuén*, 1:26.

147. San Fernando College, headquarters of the Franciscan order in Mexico City, Friar Pedro Callejas, SBMAL, October 23, 1797, CMD 337.

148. The details of these debates are covered in depth in Garr "Villa de Branciforte"; and Guest, "Establishment of the Villa de Branciforte."

149. Governor Borica, February 6, 1798, BL, C-A 24, 393.

150. Friar Andrés Quintana and Friar Domingo Carranza to Governor Arrillaga, Santa Cruz, June 28, 1807, SBMAL, CMD 745.

151. AGN, Californias (17), vol. 49, fjs. 172. This document includes a list of these men, their crimes, their sentences, marital status, job qualifications, and their *casta* (racial) status.

152. The area of Guadalajara was homeland to the Caxcán, Tecuexes, Chichimeca, and Cocas, until Spanish occupation in the 1530s, culminating in the Mixtón Rebellion (1540–42). Actual Indigenous identity of the three settlers is not recorded, and while it is possible that they trace their lineage to local Indigenous peoples, Spanish colonialism involved a process of reorganization that left large numbers of Huichol or Nahua speakers, forming the majority of Indigenous residents in these locations today.

153. Mexico, December 31, 1801, AGN, Californias (017).

154. AGN, Californias (017), vol. 49.

155. This quotation comes from Solórsano and refers to a group of children brought from Mission San Miguel, probably in the 1830s or 1840s. Harrington, "San Juan Report," JPH, microfilm, reel 59, p. 11.

156. Jose Antonio Hernandez shows up as the third witness in SCZM 574–85, for a group of recently arrived Tejey (Yokuts tribe), including the chief, Malin (Coleto), SCZB 1478, and his son Moctó (Agustin), SCZB 1480. The other two marriage witnesses are the mission interpreters, Chachoix (Silvestre), SCZB 304, and Chogiore (Macario), SCZB 1320.

157. María Bibiana, SCAB 173 (her baptismal name is recorded as Virdiana Maria, which changed in later records). They lived in the area as early as June

1800, when María Bibiana gave birth to her daughter Gertrudis Jesus Villela, Villa de Branciforte baptismal number (VBB) 5.

158. Maria was one of the Nuu-chah-nulth people of the Mowachaht village baptized in Monterey in 1790, SCAB 2088. She was subsequently married to Tapia, SCAM 529. The couple first appears in local records in the Villa de Branciforte baptisms book on September 22, 1800, with the birth of their daughter, Maria Mauricia Tapia, VBB 7. Ketchum mentions that "some claim her father was Maquina de Nootka, Chief of the Nootka." This is certainly a possibility, as it is suspected that he was the chief during the Nootka Crisis of 1789, which precipitated Maria's arrival.

159. Toypurina's children are Cesario Antonio (San Luis Obispo baptismal number [hereafter referred to as SLOB] 906), Juana de Dios (SLOB 1095), and Maria Clementina (SCAB 1988).

160. The story of Toypurina has been explored in depth by scholars, including Hackel ("Sources of Rebellion," 643–69). The first documentation of the family's presence in the area appears in the Villa de Branciforte baptisms book, with the birth of Juana de Dios's daughter, Maria Policarpa Bonavides, VBB 48, January 27, 1809. Johnson and Williams, "Toypurina's Descendants," 31–55.

161. *Refutation of Charges*, Lasuén to Lull, June 19, 1801, SBMAL, CMD 510. In response to question 53, Lasuén wrote that Baja missions did not encounter "the same incidence of card-playing or drunk Indians."

162. Harrington, "San Juan Report," JPH, microfilm, reel 58, p. 51.

163. Bouvier, *Women and the Conquest of California*, 83–89. Bouvier examined the changing gender roles in relation to labor and age within the missions.

164. Deborah A. Miranda, "Extermination of the *Joyas*." Miranda (Ohlone Costanoan Esselen Nation, Chumash) explores the existence of queer or non-heteronormative identities in local Indigenous history.

165. See Lacson, "Making Friends and Converts."

166. Retired Governor Pedro Fages to Viceroy Miguel de la Grua Talamanca y Branciforte, August 12, 1793, BL, C-A 7, 405–13. An example of this is given in chapter 1 in which villagers from Santa Clara were hired in San Carlos (Monterey) and allowed to gather abalone in exchange for their labor.

167. Milliken, *Time of Little Choice*, 76–77. Friars Naboa and Peña complained about those who did business with the pueblo of San José without joining the mission, that their "conversion is being hampered by their frequent stays at said pueblo, in which many of both sexes have taken up nearly full-time residence, employed as servants and laborers by the citizens ... through their work they receive their food, they refuse to take up the yoke of evangelism and the laws of Christianity."

168. Alejo Miranda to Commander Jose Arguello, San José, July 3, 1797, BL, C-A 9, 91.

169. Schuetz-Miller, *Building and Builders*, 28.

170. January 22, 1799, BL, C-A 53, 553.

171. Milliken, *Time of Little Choice*, 89. These authorities at times included Indigenous overseers.

172. Arguello to Borica, September 30, 1797, BL, C-A 9, 31. The letter reports that one man who had been sentenced to two months of work at the presidio fled for his homelands while still in shackles.

173. Sandos, *Converting California*, 9–10. Sandos argues that the padres organized the mission community in hierarchies replicating Spanish society, with skilled artisans at the top of the order. In Santa Cruz it does appear that members of the community learned different skills, but the hierarchies are not as clearly defined. Additionally, some Indigenous individuals appear to have changed jobs over time.

174. Schuetz-Miller, *Building and Builders*, 16; and Hackel, *Children of Coyote*, 277. Hackel has pointed out that learning these skills helped some Indigenous people to "mix with and assimilate into the soldier-settler society of California." I agree that these skills helped some to navigate the Mexican era, but I disagree about the extent of integration with the Californios, as I will discuss at length in chapter 5.

175. Lasuén to Borica, July 23, 1796, AGN, Californias 49, 265–67.

176. Census of 1834, *Santa Cruz Mission Libro de Padrónes*, Monterey Diocese Chancery Archives, Monterey CA.

177. Chugiut, SCZB 184, was known by many names, including Geronimo Miguel Pacheco Leal. Like many others at Mission Santa Cruz, he continued to incorporate his Native name in the baptism records of his children. Chugiut, as well as the continuance of Native names, will be discussed in detail in chapter 5.

178. Chalelis (Roque Guerrero), SCZB 68, was baptized on November 29, 1791.

179. Chomor (Daniel), SCZB 345, was baptized in 1795, while Gemos (Sebastian Aparicio), SCZB 456, arrived from the eastern side of Mak-Sah-Re-Jah in 1796.

180. Annual report for 1795, original at SBMAL.

181. Allen, *Native Americans*, 10.

182. Schuetz-Miller, *Building and Builders*, 26.

183. Allen, *Native Americans*, 96–97.

184. *Refutation of Charges*, Lasuén to Lull, SBMAL, CMD 510. This is contained in the long response by Lasuén to charges of abuse and mistreatment: "Our neophytes sell one measure of wheat, or corn, etc. (it is true; they sell them, and they even keep them in order to sell them) for four strings of beads. They can buy a like quantity of forest seeds for just two. The Indians themselves have established this rate of exchange."

185. Geiger and Meighan, *As the Padres Saw Them*, 87–88. Ketchum noted: "I remember well my father telling me that the time to plant corn was when the new leaves on the oak trees reached the size of squirrel ears." Email to author, September 26, 2016.

186. John P. Harrington, "San Juan Report," JPH, microfilm, reel 59, p. 72.

187. Hackel, "Staff of Leadership." Hackel examines the powers and limitations of the alcalde system, along with patterns found within the alcaldes at Mission San Carlos. Newell did a similar study at Mission Dolores (San Francisco), in *Constructing Lives* (69–70). They both found that alcaldes tended to have been born outside the mission, to have accepted baptism earlier than their tribal counterparts, to have been previously married or widowed, and usually to have served as marriage witness as an important counterpart. Some patterns are similar here: alcaldes tended to have been born outside the mission and previously married or widowed. They did not always receive baptism before others of their tribe, and only some of them served as marriage witness before becoming alcalde (see table 12).

188. Connell, *After Moctezuma*.

189. Borica, September 22, 1796, Circular sobre eleccion de Alcaldes, BL, C-A 24, 496.

190. Fages, 1787, BL, C-A 52, 144.

191. Hackel, "Sources of Rebellion." Hackel discusses an example of both with Nicolás José, former leader and one of the principal organizers of the rebellion at Mission San Gabriel in 1785.

192. Hackel, *Children of Coyote*, 235–58; and Sandos, "Between Crucifix and Land," 210–11.

193. For the flogging of and right to flog Indian officials, see Tibesar, *Writings of Serra*, 3:407–17 and 4:3–11. For restrictions on charges against the padres, see general report by Governor Pedro Fages, 1787, para. 33, BL, C-A 52, 144.

194. Cutter, *Legal Culture of Northern New Spain*. Unlike Alta California, New Mexico offered legal options, as the *protector de Indios* played a key role in assisting Indians with judicial matters.

195. Haas, *Pablo Tac*. Pablo Tac, a Luiseño who wrote about his experiences and life within the missions, spoke of the *alcaldes* gathering with the missionaries in order to relate and translate their instruction.

196. AGN, Californias (017), March 30, 1796, vol. 65, exp. 8, 310–11. Geturux (Canuto), SCZB 389; and Lacah (Julian), SCZB 141. Ketchum points out: "Canuto was not christened until February 1795 at 46 years and elected in 1796 even though his children were at the mission in 1793 and 1802. He must have lived with the Neophytes for years before becoming a Christian. He was from Aptos as was Balthazar, maybe they were related?" I find no record indicating a rela-

tion between them, but that does not mean there are not strong kinship ties beyond the scope of the archives. It is true that Geturux's daughter Cunete (Barbara Borboa), SCZB 170, arrived much earlier, so it is likely that Geturux had been at the mission before his baptism. Ketchum also noted: "Julian on the other hand is the first Unijaima christened at Mission Santa Cruz in 1792 at the age of 26. Julian sure had trouble with wives dying. Perhaps he was chosen because he was an Indian Auxiliary?" My notes have him as Chaloctaca, not Unijaima, as his confirmation record lists him as such (his baptismal record lists him from the village Sucheseu, the only such notation in all the records). Lacah will be discussed at length in the next chapter.

197. Geiger and Meighan, *As the Padres Saw Them*, 127.

198. *Refutation of Charges*, Lasuén to Lull, June 19, 1801, SBMAL, CMD, 510. Father Lasuén claimed that "only in very few of the missions unmarried men are kept under lock at night." Mission Santa Cruz was one of them. Ketchum points out that Mission San Juan Bautista also had a similar separation.

199. Years later Lorenzo Asisara recalls special roles within the mission of "key-keeper." In his recollections of the Padre Quintana assassination, discussed in detail in chapter 3, Asisara mentions the unlocking of the dormitories.

200. Regarding superstitions, the padres reported that Native people at Mission Santa Cruz held "secret, nocturnal dances always avoiding detection by the fathers. We are informed that at night, only the men gather together in the field or the forest. In their midst they raise a long stick crowned by a bundle of tobacco leaves or branches of trees or some other plant. At the base of this they place their food and even their colored beads. Then they prepare for the dance bedaubing their bodies and faces. When all the men are together the old man whom they respect as their teacher or soothsayer goes forth to listen to and to receive the orders from the devil. The old man returns after a short interval to make known to the miserable and innocent listeners not what he heard from the father of lies but what his own perversity and malice dictated. After this they proceed with the dance and continue with it till daybreak. In order to dissuade them from such harmful deception there is no better remedy than preaching and punishment. This is what we missionaries do and with good results." Geiger and Meighan, *As the Padres Saw Them*, 50. The accuracy of the padres' report is highly questionable, sensationalized in its fixation on Catholic notions of the devil, and revealing in its admission to frequent castigation. From numerous reports by foreign travelers of dances and songs performed publicly within mission spaces, we know that song and dance continued; see, for example, von Langsdorff, *Voyages and Travels*, 192. Still, it is easy to believe that Indigenous spiritual leaders performed sacred songs and dances out of view of the padres.

201. Geiger and Meighan, *As the Padres Saw Them*, 127.

202. Examples of this will be discussed at length in chapter 3.

203. The most extensive study of Indigenous godparentage within the California missions is found in the fifth chapter of Newell, *Constructing Lives* (125–50). Newell effectively argues that Indigenous people utilized godparentage to create new bonds and extend kinship networks, as I similarly found at Mission Santa Cruz.

204. The role of *padrino* was sometimes symbolic, as in cases in which visiting dignitaries performed this role for adults. Examples of this include Bernardo Jauregui (*padrino* for SCZB 149), who served as master carpenter on the frequently used ship *Concepcion*, and Commander Hermenegildo Sal (*padrino* for SCZB 88, 89, 90, 119, and 120).

205. Haas, *Conquests and Historical Identities*, 21. Haas found a similar pattern at Mission San Juan Capistrano.

206. Maria Rafaela, San Diego baptismal number (SDB) 1315, was from the village of Matamó and baptized at Mission San Diego in 1788. On May 7, 1792, she married Antonio Domingo Enrríquez, a master weaver from the state of Querétaro, north of Mexico City. The baptism record of their second child, SCAB 2033, lists the family as living in San Carlos. It is likely that they spent considerable time at Mission Santa Cruz, working and possibly instructing baptized people. Both Maria Rafaela (forty-three times) and her husband (twenty times) were listed on numerous baptisms as *padrinos*. Enrríquez is credited with instructing baptized Natives in weaving earlier at Mission Santa Bárbara; see Schuetz-Miller, *Building and Builders*, 187.

207. Ojoc (Feliciana Savedra), SCZB 140, and Uychilli (Columba), SCZB 73. Their marriage records are SCZM 61 and 62, both dated March 3, 1794. Ojoc served as *madrina* sixteen times, Uychilli twice. It is possible that, while infrequent, these intermarriages between Indigenous women and Spanish men were part of a strategy to build kinship ties between local tribes and colonizers. This theory is first suggested in Newell, *Constructing Lives* (116).

208. Chaitin (Agueda), SCZB 77, served as *padrino* for Joaquin, SCZB 726, on November 22, 1796.

209. Their father was Maguen, SCZB 203, and Joaquin's Aptos mother was Oregit (Marcelina), SCZB 302. Maguen's first wife, Vuiles (Thomasa), SCZB 204, had died in late 1795, SCZD 93.

210. Carlos's baptism is listed as SCZB 738. His father, Sucul (Marcelo), SCZB 310, was the son of deceased Tugilua (also recorded as Tujilo, baptized as Jose Antonio), SCZB 217, an elder Cotoni. Tugilua's wife, Masilon (Maria Trinidad), SCZB 218, was young (twenty-two at her baptism in 1793, compared to the sixty-year-old Tugilua).

211. In 1795 there were also thirty-six Indigenous *padrinos*, but forty-three baptisms between 1794 and 1796 were all performed by Maria Rafaela, the Indig-

enous woman from the San Diego region (village of Matamó) who had married and moved north with the Spanish master weaver Antonio Domingo Enrríquez.

212. Indigenous women held influence within the community, despite being excluded from the imposed Franciscan political order. This will be explored in depth in the next chapter. Other studies have examined the role of godparentage in kinship relations; see Morrissey, "Kaskaskia Social Network."

213. Yuñan (Serafina), SCZB 381 and Samórim (Fabiana Arraez), SCZB 62. Women served as *madrina* 53 times out of the total 333 times that local Indigenous people served as godparent. I start with 1797, as in previous years, nonlocal Indigenous women such as Maria Rafaela frequently performed the role. This dynamic shifted in later years. All in all, between 1791 and 1831 women served as *madrinas* in 35.6 percent of local Indigenous godparent situations.

214. The terms *paje* and *acólito* are used interchangeably, see SCZM 742–45.

215. The note is made in SCZB 1563. The relationship between the two is suspect, not only for the antipathy between the friars and Lino's father but also for the central role that Lino would later play in the assassination of said Padre Quintana, to be discussed at length in chapter 3.

216. The first record that listed an identified *sacristan* is SCZM 562, February 26, 1816.

217. Acogüen (Urbano), SCZB 67, arrived November 29, 1791.

218. Serafin, SCZB 1573, had been named after his *madrina*, the aforementioned Yuñan (Serafina). Serafin, who had previously been noted as page, is first mentioned as *sacristan* in SCZM 709, on October 21, 1824. Acogüen may have been sick, as he died six months later, on April 15, 1825, SCZD 1602.

219. Hackel, *Children of Coyote*, 135–43. Hackel examines the need and development of interpreters in religious instruction as well as the difficulties of the missionaries in learning local Ohlone languages.

220. Harrington, "Culture Element Distributions," 33.

221. I say *worlds* plural. Despite the obvious overlap between Spanish and Franciscan cultural values, increasing disconnects between ecclesiastical and civilian life existed throughout the Spanish Americas. Growing discontent between government and church officials characterized the shifting culture before the independence wars against Spain, 1810–21. This is reflected in official complaints and tensions between the two local communities.

222. Borica to Virrey, Monterey, November 27, 1798, BL, C-A 24, 431. Governor Borica used two men captured in a confrontation near Mission San Juan Bautista, singling out the captives to "guide the two Indians to the mission to teach them Spanish and to employ them as guides and interpreters. There are a thousand jobs for those who do this thing [interpret] that happens between the gentiles because of the variety of languages, within a distance of 12 leagues there

are three or four distinct [languages or dialects]—they don't understand some rancherias more than others."

223. June 7, 1899, BL, C-A 10, 330. The letter delineating Spanish rules of engagement with the Ausaima mentions "sending free from Santa Cruz the Indian who is going to serve as guide and interpreter for the Padre Ministers, and who will inform them so that the [runaways, and/or enemies] are made to behave."

224. Borica to the padre of Mission Santa Cruz, Monterey, March 4, 1798, BL, C-A 24, 530–31. The letter relates that one unidentified man offered to assist in the recapturing of *huidos* (escapees) who had returned to their homelands near Mission San Juan Bautista. The governor, in supporting the use of this man's skills and knowledge, pointed out that he was enemies with some of them and that he himself was from nearby lands.

225. SCZB 29.

226. Aror appears as *padrino* first in SCZB 1361a, 1362a, 1363a, and 1364a, in June 1807. He served in this role seven times, the last one SCZB 1575, on September 8, 1812, before his death on November 6, 1814 (SCZD 1196). He appears as a witness to marriages along with a note of having served as "Interprete" on records beginning in 1809 (SCZM 461, 462, 551–53). Altogether he served as marriage witness twenty-three times.

227. SCZB 304, baptized February 16, 1794.

228. SCZB 945, August 17, 1800.

229. SCZB 1320. As previously mentioned, the Tomoi lands lay in Pacheco Pass, which connected the Yokuts to Mutsun-speaking territories, which makes it likely that Tomoi people would need translators.

230. Hackel, "Staff of Leadership," 356. Years later the staff used at Mission Santa Cruz appeared in an exhibit at the State Fair held in Sacramento in 1892. The staff was used in the "Santa Cruz" section. The article read: "An Alcalde's cane, formerly called the 'staff of justice,' because it was used by him as a warrant of arrest, is a relic of the Alcalde's office in Santa Cruz. It was in th emission in 1783 and used in an official manner until the office of Alcalde was abolished in 1850." "Visitors Pleased with What They Have Seen at the State Fair: The Pavilion Exhibit," *Sacramento Record-Union*, September 13, 1892, 5:1.

231. Smith and Johnson, "Lengua de los Llanos," 299–313. The article argues that Putiltec worked with Friar Andrés Quintana in translating this prayer from similar catechisms written in his Native Ohlone dialect, based on the particular phrasing used. It further concludes that the Yokuts dialect used was that of the Locobo tribe, who were the first of the Yokuts speakers to arrive at Mission Santa Cruz between 1806 and 1807.

232. Putiltec worked as translator and interpreter prior to his role as *padrino*, given his involvement with the catechism (see previous note). His work as

padrino began with a group of Achila, Sagim, Copcha, and Notuall Yokuts in SCZB 1683–93. The first of these baptisms was Cholé (Leon), chief of the Sagim village.

233. Putiltec appears as interpreter in Mission San Francisco Solano in modern Sonoma, San Francisco Solano baptismal number (SFSB) 1031, January 19, 1834.

234. Huilgen (Juan Bautista), SCAB 2920, was baptized on September 11, 1814, as a military group led by General Vallejo encountered the injured eleven-year-old in the field. He recovered and was brought back to the coastal mission. His specific tribal affiliation is unknown, as his baptismal record notes "Tulares."

3. Mission of Padre Killers

1. The most famous example of targeting of a padre for assassination was the 1775 Kumeyaay revolt against Padre Luís Jayme at Mission San Diego. See Carrico, "Sociopolitical Aspects of the 1775 Revolt at Mission San Diego de Alcala." In 1781 the Kw'tsa'n (Quechan) targeted and killed four padres in the Yuma Revolt. See Santiago, *Massacre at the Yuma Crossing*.

2. Edward D. Castillo, "Assassination of Padre Andrés Quintana."

3. The reported population over this seventeen-year span averaged 474.76, while there were an average of 59.76 burials per year over the same period. I start with 1795 because this is the first year the population reached 500.

4. The continuation of traditional mourning rituals within mission communities as a means of social cohesion is explored in depth in Dietler, Gibson, and Vargas, "'A Mourning Dirge Was Sung.'" See also Hull, Douglass, and York, "Recognizing Ritual Action and Intent."

5. Skowronek, "Sifting the Evidence," 685.

6. Edward D. Castillo, "Assassination of Padre Andrés Quintana," 123. His note 44 makes a similar point about the use of wailing to protect the living.

7. The difficulties endured by Indigenous women would have shared characteristics with the horrendous losses facing African women in slavery, and more work needs to be done to find similarities between these communities. Turner, "Nameless and the Forgotten."

8. This is based on my own research and calculations. Details of these figures are given in notes 67 and 68 in the introduction. Of the 471 Indigenous children born at the mission between founding in 1791 and 1831, 239 died before reaching their first birthday (50.7%), and another 120 died before reaching their fifth birthday (25.5%). And, as explained in the previous note, these numbers are conservative estimates, as I have counted all individuals with uncertainty or missing data as surviving into adulthood.

9. The theory of infanticide or abortion as practices of protest was first suggested academically by Heizer, in "Impact of Colonization." Castañeda relates

that the padres at Mission San Gabriel attributed all miscarriages to infanticide and punished Gabrielino women for their suspected crimes; see "Engendering the History of Alta California," 234.

10. Throughout colonial California, Spanish authorities requested that missionaries respond to a questionnaire of thirty-six questions relating to social, political, tribal, and family life of local Indians. Padres Marcelino Maquinez and Jayme Escudé wrote the responses for Mission Santa Cruz on April 30, 1814, a year and a half after the assassination. As they were newly appointed and had very little experience with the Indigenous people living at Mission Santa Cruz, there is reason to doubt the accuracy of these friars' words and insights. For an example of the cultural bias clouding their vision, in response to question 20 the Santa Cruz friars claim with a degree of certainty that the local Indians are "descendants of the ten tribes of Israel." Most of the original responses are held at SBMAL, though the Santa Cruz books are at the archives of the Monterey Archdiocese. Father Maynard Geiger collected and published the responses for all the missions in 1976; Geiger and Meighan, *As the Padres Saw Them*, 106.

11. SCZB 1431–33, 1553–66, and 1568–70.

12. SCZB 1432, 1554, and 1561.

13. Four of the conspirators served as *padrinos* in SCZB 1554, 1561, 1562, and 1563. Two of these children died within months after their births. The two who served as their *padrinos* were the two principal conspirators, Lino (for SCZB 1563) and Yaquenonsat (for SCZB 1562).

14. Territories of the many Yokuts tribes span throughout a large region of contemporary central California. These independent tribes and villages of Yokuts language speaking people are frequently divided into three regional groups: the Northern Valley Yokuts, Southern Valley Yokuts, and Foothills Yokuts. Each of these designations included numerous independent tribes and villages, similar to the larger linguistic Ohlone groupings (Mutsun, Awaswas, etc). All of the Yokuts tribal members and familes discussed in this book are from the Northern Valley Yokuts tribes. Northern Valley Yokuts territories traced northwards a little more than one hundred miles through the San Joaquin Valley, from the modern city of Mendota to Stockton. To simplify, I will primarily refer to them as Yokuts rather than Northern Valley Yokuts, or by their specific tribal name whenever possible. Wallace, "Northern Valley Yokuts."

15. By the beginning of 1812, there were 101 Awaswas-speaking people out of a total population of 462 (21 percent).

16. Robert H. Jackson argues that population stability at Mission Santa Cruz related to increased "recruitment," as the number of children in relation to the total population remained small. In addition to high infant and child mortality rates, the mission suffered heavy mortality rates for women and girls. By 1812,

children under ten represented merely 6 percent of the total population, according to Jackson, "Disease and Demographic Patterns," 42.

17. Jackson, "Disease and Demographic Patterns," 40. See also Hurtado, *Indian Survival on the California Frontier.*

18. SCZB 1434–1552, which included families identified as being Yeurata and Tejey. The Chaneche, based in modern Los Banos, went by various names. They were known at Mission Santa Cruz as Yeurata or Yeunata, at Mission San Juan Bautista and Mission Soledad as Tchanécha, Tsanechán, or Chanechan (SJBB 2109 and 2115, Soledad baptismal number [hereafter referred to as SOLB] 1695).

19. The first Locobo was Uc Ahigi (Santiago Maior), SCZB 1212, followed shortly by around thirty others, SCZB 1212–39, all baptized on February 2, 1806. SCZB 1240–43 were Locobo children, baptized on February 7, 1806.

20. Malimin (Coleto) was the first Tejey baptized (SCZB 1478). His Native name is confusingly listed on his baptismal record as "Col[e]ta ò Malin," but in both his own and his wife's burial records, he is listed as Coleto Malimin (SCZD 1465 and 1493). The lives of Malimin and his sons, many of whom became political leaders within the mission, will be explored in depth in chapter 4.

21. The Tomoi homelands were on Pacheco Pass, an important region connecting Mutsun and Yokuts lands. Given their geography, these tribes likely had many bilingual members. An example of Tomoi involvement in Yokuts baptisms is found with Chogiore (Macario, SCZB 1320), who is listed as interpreter in many of the incoming Yokuts baptisms. The Native name listed on Chogiore's baptismal record is Putiltec. As later accounts consistently list him as "Macario Chogiore," this is either a mistake or an example of someone who changed his name at some point. Norval S. H. Smith and Johnson have determined that it was this same Chogiore who wrote a Catechism in the Yokuts language sometime before 1810. See Smith and Johnson, "Lengua de los Llanos," 299–313.

22. Hackel, "The Staff of Leadership," 348. Hackel argues that Indian alcaldes and leaders "protected the interests of the Indian community and, in some cases, ultimately rebelled against the Spanish order." This was one of those cases.

23. José María Amador, "Memorias sobre la historia de California," BL, C-D 28, 58–77.

24. Haas, *Pablo Tac, Indigenous Scholar*. There are very few firsthand accounts by Indigenous people who lived in the California missions. Asisara and his contemporary, Pablo Tac, represent two of the most vivid accounts that remain. Another important account is that of the Chumash man Fernando Librado Kitsepawit, although he was born around 1839, after the close of the missions, found in Johnson, "Trail to Fernando," 132–38; and Librado, *Breath of the Sun.*

25. Asisara's interview came at the request of Californio retired soldier José María Amador. In 1877 Thomas Savage, as part of Bancroft's oral history project, interviewed Amador, who called upon his friend Asisara to share his stories. The two almost certainly knew each other from their shared military experience. Asisara's life has only been studied on a cursory level. I plan to focus on the complicated story of Asisara in a future book-length project.

26. The validity of some details of the Asisara account was debated following its initial publication by Edward D. Castillo. See Nunis and Castillo, "California Mission Indians." Nunis argues that many details do not stand up, including the use of silver coins and the lack of correspondence of dates cited. He further charges that Castillo "simply doesn't take the [Spanish reports] at face value" (211). Castillo effectively rebuts Nunis's dismissal of the Asisara account by arguing that Asisara's testimony lies within the realm of oral tradition, as "non-literate peoples treat the spoken word more carefully than do those from literate cultures," and that one "can hardly expect Native documents to conform explicitly with documents authored by colonial authorities. To do so would assume that only one truth and one reality existed, that of the colonist" (212–13).

27. Governor Pablo Vicente de Solá, February 5, 1816, AGN, Californias (017), exp. 15, foja 501. Solá similarly relates his account of the conspirators' testimonies given in a manifesto dated June 2, 1816, SBMAL, CMD 1145.

28. Solá, February 5, 1816, AGN, Californias (017), exp. 15, foja 501. Solá reports that Indian motivation included that Quintana had "made a whip of iron for lashings." Asisara's account described it as "a new horsewhip, made with wire straws," which was to be unveiled the next day. See Amador, "Memorias sobre la historia de California," 61. At the time of this attack, ironworker and blacksmith José María Larios lived in Las Aromas, which is halfway between Santa Cruz and San Juan Bautista, in present-day Aromas, supporting the availability of local skilled labor able to make this weapon. See Schuetz-Miller, *Building and Builders*, 76–77.

29. Solá, AGN, Californias (017), exp. 15, fojas 500–505. The recent beatings are mentioned in numerous documents, including the defense of Quintana by Governor Solá, who reports that "the two punished with the said whip were both dying." Solá, April 5, 1816, BL, Provincial Records, 9:139.

30. McCormack, "Conjugal Violence"; and Elias Castillo, *Cross of Thorns*. Ketchum notes: "My interpretation was the public humiliation was worse than the physical." With regards to the practice of torture in *Alta* California, see Saunt, "My Medicine is Punishment." Indeed, psychological assault was a key and lasting part of the traumatic mission experience. Aspects of this psychological torture will be explored in depth in later chapters.

31. Harrington, "San Juan Report," microfilm, reel 59, p. 8.

32. Lacah (Julián), SCZB 141, and Yaqunonsat (Fausta), SCZB 1318.

33. Yachacxi (Donato) was baptized on January 12, 1794, at the age of five, SCZB 262. The story is related in Amador, "Memorias sobre la historia de California," BL, C-D 28, 58–77. Here I am using the translation by Mora-Torres (*Californio Voices*, 81).

34. Ules (Andrés), SCZB 97, and Lino, SCZB 226.

35. Lino's statement about taking Quintana before a judge raises some interesting questions. To what extent was Lino aware of legal rights in colonial Spain? His assertion suggests an awareness of potential means for appealing to higher legal or perhaps spiritual judgement, despite being on the peripheries of the Spanish colonial empire. For more on Indian justice, see Owensby, *Empire of Law and Indian Justice in Colonial Mexico*.

36. Mora-Torres, *Californio Voices*, 81.

37. Amador, "Memorias sobre la historia de California," BL, C-D 28, 63.

38. Amador, "Memorias sobre la historia de California," BL, C-D 28, 64–65.

39. While Asisara does not provide explicit details, it is clear that this is a rejection of Spanish sexual impositions, which frequently discussed the forced separation of the sexes. Bouvier, *Women and the Conquest of California*, 135. I agree with Bouvier, who examined Asisara's account to conclude, "The seeds of rebellion were nourished by Franciscan efforts to control indigenous sexuality." It is difficult to imagine the entire community keeping quiet about Quintana's murder. It is possible that the celebration and opening of the dormitories is an imagined fantasy added to the story by Asisara or others. Nonetheless, the significance of this act of rebellion and release from the dormitories reflects frustration with these restrictions, regardless of whether this happened or was imagined.

40. Certainly suspicions existed, as seen in the call for autopsy and in later letters. Padre Luís Jayme to José de la Guerra, September 3, 1814, SBMAL, De La Gierra Collection (hereafter referred to as DLG) 537, letter 1. Here Jayme asserts, possibly around the time that the conspirators were caught, that he never believed that Quintana had died of natural causes. While the exact date of the soldiers learning about the assassination and subsequent arrest is not known with certainty, multiple oral histories suggest it was close to two years, meaning that the arrests would have been made in late 1814. With the letter dated September 1814, perhaps Padre Jayme's statement was made after learning of the arrest, suggesting that the arrest could have happened in late August or early September 1814. Bancroft, *History of California*, 12:388.

41. Commandante Luis Antonio Argüello to Governor José Joaquín de Arrillaga, October 13, 1812, BL, Provincial State Papers, C-A 12, 1805–15, 323.

42. Padre Marcelino Marquínez to José Maria Estudillo, October 15, 1812, in 1797–1850, Santa Cruz Pre-Statehood Documents (hereafter referred to as

SCPSD), MS8, B3:16, Special Collections and Archives, University Library, UCSC. The autopsy is considered to be the first conducted in California and has been written about as such. See Moes, "Manuel Quijano and Waning Spanish California," 78–93. It appears that the coroner was looking primarily for the presence of poisoning, given attempts at poisonings farther south.

43. José Eusebio Galindo, "Apuntes para la historia de California," Santa Clara, 1877, BL, C-D 87, 64. This story is told in two separate accounts, one by former soldier Galindo and the other by Asisara. Asisara gives more detail. See Amador, "Memorias sobre la historia de California," BL, C-D 28, 60. Amador claims that he was among the soldiers who marched the sixteen prisoners with their thumbs tied together. This harsh tactic of thumb tying is discussed in more depth in chapter 4.

44. Haas, *Pablo Tac*. An excellent example of this social translator and communicator is seen in the life of Pablo Tac.

45. Of the 133 children born at the mission by 1807, Lino was the oldest of the 27 who were still alive.

46. Lino is listed as "Paje de Padre Quintana" in SCZB 1563, dated October 11, 1811.

47. SCZM 388–407, 444–47, 533–34, 538–40, and 548–51 and SCZB 1365 and 1563.

48. SCZB 1365, on May 23, 1807, was administered to the child (Christina) of the Sumus chief and his wife, Chitecsme and Yachename (Mateo and Matea, SCZB 1314 and 1315), respectively. As will be discussed later in this chapter, Yaquenonsat's marriage to Lacah five months after the baptism, on October 18, 1807, helped reinforce the ties between the Sumus and the Awaswas-speaking leaders.

49. Quihueimen (Quirico) is recorded as SCZB 65, one of the earliest baptisms on record. His original baptismal record lists his Native name as Ququen, but it is listed as Quihueimen in SCZB 2194, his daughter's baptismal record. I follow the later record, as it was taken in 1833, despite not appearing in earlier records, though the inconsistency could either be due to error or a name change. Chesente (Maria Concepcion) is listed in SCLB 3705. Their marriage is recorded in SCZM 447.

50. Yuñan (Serafina) is listed as SCZB 381. Their marriage is recorded in SCZM 535. Although Yachacxi was not convicted of the assassination, he is credited in the oral histories as being the one who was nearly beaten to death and called the meeting with the conspirators.

51. Amador, "Memorias sobre la historia de California," BL, C-D 28, 60.

52. Lino's death in the Presidio of Santa Barbara is recorded in April 1817, SCZD 1288, whereas Asisara was born in August 1820, SCZB 1832.

53. Lluillin (Maria de la Purificacion de Landa, SCZB 107) was baptized just over one month after her husband, Ules.

54. Cucufate, SCLB 1903. In this baptismal record Lluillin's Native name is written as "Maltam Llules." I use Lluillin, as this is the name repeated in the Santa Cruz baptismal books. The stories of Soquel's family, the two daughters baptized at Mission Santa Clara, and the exchange regarding the founding of Mission Santa Cruz are told in the first chapter.

55. SCZD 1, recorded in November 1791, about five months after his baptism.

56. There do seem to be some connections between the Chaloctaca and the Somontoc, as will be discussed later.

57. Ules's father, Gelelis, and his wife, Ypasin, were both baptized in August 1792, seven months after their son, Ules.

58. There were sixty-nine Sayanta and forty Chaloctaca baptized, and only sixteen remained living in 1812.

59. Friars Francisco Gonzalez and Domingo Carranza to Governor Diego de Borica, undated, SBMAL, CMD 474a. While the letter is undated, judging by the padres involved, this letter must have been written sometime after May 1798 and before 1805.

60. Sirinte (Fulgencio), SCZB111.

61. Whether these statements are from Lino himself or have been modified by Asisara, the point is still the same: The Indigenous community remembered the assassination of Quintana as a consequence of failure to fulfill his spiritual obligations to the community.

62. Amador, "Memorias sobre la historia de California," BL, C-D 28, 60.

63. The more plural relationship to spiritual systems by Indigenous Californians stands in contrast with Catholic teachings, which saw alternative systems as teachings of the devil, or heretic.

64. Geiger and Meighan, *As the Padres Saw Them,* 50, 77–78. The persistence of sweat lodges and gathering to practice ceremony in the forests was previously noted in chapter 1, notes 60 and 263. The use of these lodges continued far beyond the closing of the mission, as later chapters will attest.

65. Harrington, *Central California Coast,* 32. This information is reported in Harrington's Culture Element Distribution (CED) interviews of northern and southern Ohlone in the 1930s.

66. Governor Pablo Vicente de Solá, AGN, Californias (017), exp. 15, foja 501. His defense of Quintana is found at BL, the Provincial Records, vol. 9, 138–39. The transcripts of the conspirators' testimonies are not found in the archives, only the statements by Solá, which offer summaries.

67. Sexual abuse by Franciscan missionaries in the Spanish colonies is explored in depth by Chuchiak, "Sins of the Fathers." Chuchiak argues that, in addition to frequent sexual abuses by the missionaries, in some cases Indigenous Maya used accusations of abuse and rape as a strategy to limit the authority

of Spanish friars. This situation is clearly different, as no formal accusations are on record.

68. Amador, "Memorias sobre la historia de California," BL, C-D 28, 65. Franciscan historian Maynard J. Geiger discusses Quintana's torture "in pudendis" (in the privates). See Geiger and Ritchie, *Franciscan Missionaries*, 206. For an excellent examination of abuses, sexual and otherwise, as well as the impact of trauma across generations, see Deborah A. Miranda, *Bad Indians*. Other works that examine sexual abuse in colonial California and beyond include Hurtado, *Intimate Frontiers*; and Bouvier, *Women and the Conquest of California*.

69. "Quintana, then a priest of Santa Cruz, forgot one of his vows in the society of a certain squaw, who, through penitence, or indignation, or vanity, or some other motive, let her husband into the secret of her conquest. After watching his opportunity, the man at length succeeded in mutilating the lover in the most brutal manner, leaving him insensible, but was himself dragged to the *calabozo* [prison], whence, according to common rumor, he was soon afterwards carried off by the Devil for his impiety." Simpson reported these rumors in his *Narrative of a Voyage*, 105–6. This account is also skeptically addressed by Geiger and Ritchie, *Franciscan Missionaries in Hispanic California*, 205–6.

70. Humiliana, SCZB 235. No Native name was listed for her, as was always the case for children born at the mission. In future endnotes, children born at the mission will only have Spanish names, unless a Native name is provided elsewhere in the archival documents.

71. SCZM 535.

72. SCZM 543.

73. Humiliana served as *madrina* for SCZB 1585, 1602, 1610, 1623, 1624, and 1784. Petra Nicanor's baptism was SCZB 1589.

74. Chuyucu (Victoriano), SCZB 1515, was Tejey (Yokuts) and arrived at Mission Santa Cruz as a six-year-old in the large wave of Yokuts who arrived in 1810. His Native name is alternatively given as Yuelile or Chuiucuu. Humiliana's death, in January 1851, is recorded in SCZD 2179. For archaeological evidence of her and her husband's cohabitation in the adobe that still stands on School Street, see Allen, *Native Americans at Mission Santa Cruz*, 29. Nicanor (under her own name, not her husband's) eventually sold her lands to Joseph Majors for fifty dollars on June 7, 1848. See Santa Cruz County Office of the Recorder (SCCR), Deeds 1:100.

75. It is very rare for burial records to list parents of adults, so the mention of Lino in this record stands out as unique in the Mission Santa Cruz burial records.

76. Notes in Asisara's account identify the women. See Amador, "Memorias sobre la historia de California," BL, C-D 28, 73. Shomam (Maria Tata), SCZB 689,

was an Aptos woman like Humiliana. Her name (Maria Tata) is given in the Asisara account, in which she is misidentified as the wife of the cook (Ètop or Antonio Alberto). Shomam married the young Uypi man Justiniano (SCZB 605) on the same day that Lino and Humiliana married (two of a group of five weddings that day), SCZM 545.

77. Galindo, "Apuntes para la historia de California," Santa Clara, 1877, BL, C-D 87, 64.

78. Bancroft, *History of California*, 12:388.

79. The accounts suggest that women's "gossip" was at fault. Deborah A. Miranda offers a critique of the dismissal of "gossip" as a colonial interpretation, and instead suggests that gossip can create "a narrative containing both Indigenous historical testimony *and* an autonomous self-empowerment,'" "'They Were Tough,'" 377. While it is not certain that this analysis is applicable to this situation, it is important to approach the archival accounts with skepticism. In this case, the distinctly male archive writers, seem to place blame squarely on the women and their private and largely unknown conversation.

80. Ules death is recorded on March 20, 1815, in SCZD 1219. The other three who died in San Francisco included Euxexi (Ambrosio), SCZD 1201, along with two brothers named Leto Antonio and Secundino, both of whom will be discussed at length later in the chapter.

81. All of the sentences are recorded in AGN, Californias (017), exp. 15, foja 501.

82. Lino's death is recorded in SCZD 1288, Sirinte's in SCZD 1368. Curiously, a note about the death of Lino appears in a book. Franciscan friar and former Los Angeles jail chaplain Joseph A. Thompson, descendant of José de la Guerra, captain of the Presidio of Santa Barbara at the time of Lino's death, wrote: "Then there was the case of Lino, a neophyte prisoner from Santa Inés [*sic*], held at Santa Barbara presidio on account of his crimes. De la Guerra informed the governor that this Indian died at the Mission Santa Barbara 'because seeing that he was seriously ill, I sent him to the mission hospital where a lady out of charity applies medication, and since this is the only temporal consolation that a poor person can receive, it did not seem right to deprive him of this aid, during the unfortunate situation in which he found himself'" (*El Gran Capitán*, 168). Thompson wrote this book as a hagiography, celebrating the story of his ancestor, and this passage is intended to exemplify the good character of de la Guerra.

83. Marichimas (Wenceslao) is listed as SCZB 1075. The Tomoi were closely related to the Sumus, like Yaquenonsat. Both came from the second wave of Ohlone baptisms, from farther inland around modern Henry W. Coe State Park. Marichimas died in November 1828, SCZD 1752.

84. Humiliana's death is recorded in SCZD 1801. The children of Humiliana and Marichimas include Ysabel, SCZB 1770, born in 1818 and died in 1819 (SCZD

1376); Tecla, SCZB 1836, born in 1820 and died in 1840 (SCZD 2061); Aquiléo, SCZB 2039, born in 1823 and died in infancy (SCZD 1536); Victoriana, SCZB 2055, born in 1824 and died in infancy (SCZD 1583); and Judas Tadeo, SCZB 2087, born in 1825. Only Judas Tadeo survived into later years, but his burial is not recorded.

85. Vicente, SCZB 951, and Miguel Antonio, SCZB 1016.

86. Zuem (Agapito de Albiz), SCZB 83.

87. Miguel Antonio married a Tomoi woman, Ysanti (Constantina), SCZB 1322, in February 1821, SCZM 654. Nicanor is listed as SCZB 2073. The baptisms that he served as witness for are listed as SCZB 2187 and 2226.

88. Miguel Antonio's burial is recorded in SCZD 2014, in July 1838. Vicente's burial is recorded in SCZD 1864, in December 1831.

89. The Mission Santa Cruz Biannual Reports for 1791 and 1792 list three people originally baptized at Mission Santa Clara, while reports beginning in 1824 list individuals baptized at San Francisco, Santa Clara, and San Juan Bautista, along with a few individuals who moved from Mission Santa Cruz to neighboring missions. The original Biannual Reports are held at SBMAL.

90. Allen, *Native Americans at Mission Santa Cruz*, 95; Peelo, "Creating Community in Spanish California," 108–9; and Schneider and Panich, "Landscapes of Refuge and Resiliency," 21–47.

91. Milliken, Shoup, and Ortiz, "Ohlone/Costanoan Indians," 144.

92. A survey of Santa Cruz marriage records shows more than thirty marriages of Native peoples of Santa Cruz to those of other missions. For example, Oton Tanite (SJBB 330) married five times: three times in Santa Cruz and twice in San Juan Bautista. He is alternately listed as Ausaima or Chipuctac. Oton shows up in the census taken in Santa Cruz for the majority of the 1820s and 1830s.

93. Leto Antonio, SCLB 1015, and Secundino Antonio, SCLB1016, were both baptized on April 14, 1787. Their death records (SCLD 4746 and 4747) state that they both died as prisoners in San Francisco. They had another brother, Llelleg (Fulgencio), SCLB 1566, who does not have a death date on record, suggesting that he lived outside the bounds of the mission. It is possible that he was the third participant hailing from Santa Clara and that he evaded capture.

94. Chacualis (Toquato), SCLB 1896, and Clara de la Cruz (no Native name recorded), SCLB 1897. The Uypi were alternately called the "Soquel" or "Zoquel" Indians by Mission Santa Cruz padres as early as 1811 (José María Estudillo to Comisionado de Branciforte, April 9, 1811, SCPSD, letter 44, b1:5).

95. Soquel and Rosuem's other daughter, Maria Lorenza, SCLB 1904, was baptized along with Cucufate, SCLB 1903, the child of Chaloctaca leader Ules.

96. Leto Antonio and Secundino Antonio's baptismal registries, as well as that of their families, list them as originating from "San Carlos," which stands as

a directional reference pointing southwest toward Mission San Carlos (Monterey) from Mission Santa Clara, where they had been baptized. The directional basically means that they were from villages in the Mak-Se-Re-Jah region and could have belonged to any of the local mountain tribes, which were closely tied with the Uypi.

97. Leto Antonio served as *padrino* in eleven baptisms (SCLB 3894, 4090, 4127, 4128, 4361, 5103, 5105, 5106, and 5109–11) and witness in twenty-nine marriages (SCLM 770, 771, 796–99, 833, 873–83, 992–99, 1079, 1163, and 1278). He is listed as "*paje*" in the notes on SCLB 3894, 4090, 4127, and 4128.

98. Vaughn, "Locating Absence," 141–74. The absence of marginalized women in the archives is explored in depth by Trouillot, *Silencing the Past*.

99. The most famous example is that of Tongva leader Toypurina, who led a rebellion at Mission San Gabriel in 1785. Hackel, "Sources of Rebellion." Less famous is the case of Bárbara Gandiaga, the Indigenous woman at Mission Santo Tomás in Baja California, who was accused of orchestrating the murder of two missionaries. Her story is examined by Reyes, *Private Women, Public Lives*. Additionally, within Coast Miwok society existed the *maien*, a women's secret society that held more power than the men, see Truesdell Kelly et al., *Interviews with Tom Smith and Maria Copa*, xvii and 479–81.

100. Examples today include (but are not limited to) Chairwoman Louise J. Miranda of the Ohlone–Costanoan Esselen Nation, Chairwoman Rosemary Cambra of the Muwekma Ohlone Tribe, Corrina Gould (Chocheño and Karkin Ohlone), and Ann Marie Sayers and her daughter Kanyon (Mutsun). The late Maria Ascención Solórsano of the Amah Mutsun Tribal Band also exemplified this common pattern of female leadership.

101. Asisara similarly fails to identify the names of the two women who alerted the Spanish soldier about the assassination—Humiliana and Maria Tata. In the original transcription, they are identified as "muger de Lino" and "muger del cosinero," with the names "Emiliana" and "Maria Tata" written above. This appears to be an afterthought, as if the interviewer, Thomas Savage, asked Asisara for their names later. Amador, "Memorias sobre la historia de California," BL, C-D 28, 73. In later stories, Asisara appears to overlook women's concerns with regards to sexual abuses by Padre Gil y Taboada, which will be discussed in chapter 4.

102. Yaquenonsat and Yuñan and the ways in which Indigenous women preserved power within the missions are examined in my article "'If They Do Not Fulfill.'"

103. These two notations (*monja*) appear in the records SCZB 1562 and SCZB 1567, indicating Yaquenonsat and Yuñan, respectively. On SCZB 1562, the *madrina* record lists a "Fatita" whose occupation is listed as *monja*. As there

is no Fatita listed in any California baptism records, no other similar sounding names, and only one "Fausta" at Mission Santa Cruz, I am confident that this record is a reference to Yaquenonsat.

104. While there are no other *madrinas* listed as being *monjas* in baptismal records at any of the California missions, Newell identified examples of women at Mission Dolores identified as *monjas* in burial records, *Constructing Lives*, 155–60.

105. For example, see Hackel, "Staff of Leadership."

106. SCZM 443, on October 18, 1807.

107. Ketchum, "Maria Ascención Solórsano." Ketchum quotes historian Ralph Milliken's 1930s interviews with the Mutsun woman María Antonia Sánchez, stating that the marriage of Solórsano's grandparents "joined the Mutsun speaking people and Yokuts people into one tribe." Perhaps Yaquenonsat and Lacah's marriage had similar political implications.

108. Friar Estévan Tapis and Quintana to Arrillaga, May 22, 1809, SBMAL, CMD 801b. Yaquenonsat appears at the top of a list of women fugitives.

109. SCZB 1262. Siboo (Canuto) received baptism on March 15, 1806, as a five-year-old boy from the Tomoi Rancheria.

110. She referred to him as Canuto from Mission Santa Cruz while corroborating data including his family members show that it is indeed the same person. Harrington, "San Juan Report," microfilm, reel 59, p. 34.

111. Harrington, "San Juan Report," reel 59, p. 64.

112. Tapis and Quintana to Arrillaga, May 22, 1809, SBMAL, CMD 801b. There is no direct evidence explaining why Yaquenonsat and the other forty-seven Sumus/Tomoi entered the mission together. I suggest Spanish soldiers brought them in. The tribal members arrived at a time (1807) of increased military exploration into the eastern lands, and it was atypical for large groups to abandon traditional homelands without provocation. This is further supported by the subsequent flight of forty fugitives in 1809, of which twenty-eight were Tomoi and Sumus.

113. Milliken, *Time of Little Choice*, 185–91. The accounts of this are found in a series of seven letters, in BL, C-A 12, 29–43.

114. Argüello to Arrillaga, February 28, 1805, BL, Provincial State Papers, Bancroft MSS C-A 12, 39–40. Eighteen Spanish soldiers and fifteen townspeople, under the direction of Sergeant Luís Peralta, retaliated and attacked the Luecha village, killing eleven, and captured four men and twenty-five women and children. This was followed by another expedition the following month, capturing two more in connection with the initial attack, thus bringing the majority of Luechas into the mission.

115. Geiger and Ritchie, *Franciscan Missionaries in Hispanic California*, 58–59.

116. Von Langsdorff, *Voyages and Travels*, 192. The dance was presumably in honor of the assistance that Langsdorff and his Russian counterparts provided to help the mission population recover from a recent measles epidemic that had killed 16 percent of the 852 Indians living at the mission.

117. Von Langsdorff, *Voyages and Travels*, 192.

118. Milliken addresses this incident and suggests that by the description of the ceremonies performed, the people of Mission San José were more likely to have been celebrating their survival of the recent measles epidemic than performing for the Russian visitors, *Time of Little Choice*, 199. Sandos challenges this, suggesting a closer look reveals that their behavior and dress reveals more about their internal dynamics, reflecting distinctions between coastal Ohlone and inland Yokuts, as well as an interesting example of imitation of Spanish military attire, which, as Sandos points out, could have served both as an acknowledgement of military conquest and a mockery of it. This is noted by Sandos in the cover-art note opening the 2015 Santa Barbara Mission Archive Library—produced "Keepsake" publication of his article "Early California Reconsidered." Sandos's interpretation is corroborated in von Langsdorff's account, *Voyages and Travels*, 195.

119. Geiger and Ritchie, *Franciscan Missionaries*, 59.

120. Geiger and Ritchie, *Franciscan Missionaries*, 58. Geiger claimed that de la Cueva was lured to the village, suggesting that the claim of a dying baptized Native needing last rites was a ruse by one of the Indigenous guides.

121. Barbara Lee Jones, "Mythic Implications," 50–53.

122. Email to author, September 26, 2016. Ketchum credits Lao Franco of the Tachi Yokuts for teaching him about the Eagle and Condor people's responsibilities to care for the dead.

123. This theme is explored in depth in Dietler, Gibson, and Vargas, "'A Mourning Dirge Was Sung'"; and in Hull, Douglass, and York, "Recognizing Ritual Action and Intent," 24–47.

124. Lacah is one of two gardeners identified specifically by Asisara, as he also mentions that Lacah's father, Llencó, worked as mission gardener.

125. Comandante Hermenegildo Sal to Governor Borica, March 30, 1796, AGN, Californias (017), vol. 65, exp. 8, fojas 303–29.

126. The most notable examples are in the stories of *alcaldes* Nicolás José at Mission San Gabriel in the Toypurina uprising and Andrés at Mission Santa Barbara in the 1824 Chumash uprising. See Hackel, "Sources of Rebellion," 653' and Sandos, "Levantamiento! The 1824 Chumash Uprising," 8–20.

127. His confirmation record (SCZC 23) lists him as being from the Jesus tribe—the padre-imposed name for the Chaloctaca. It is likely that the Sucheseu rancheria indicates a village separate from that of Ules and his family (given the

surname Cañizares), as none of their records include the Sucheseu label. As Ketchum pointed out, Milliken listed Lacah as being from the Unijaima tribe; email to author, September 26, 2016. On this I disagree with Milliken, and I believe he formed his hypothesis without seeing the notation from the confirmation records.

128. His marriages are recorded as SCZM 27, 81, 185, 314, and 443. Yaquenonsat arrived at Mission Santa Cruz about eight months before marrying Lacah. His first daughter, Maria, SCZB 334, was stillborn, while his second child, Jose de la Cruz, SCZB 724, survived only three and a half months.

129. Governor Solá to José de la Guerra, November 16, 1820, SBMAL, DLG 924, letter 9.

130. SCZD 1423.

131. Euxexi (Ambrosio) is listed as SCZB 232. His death is recorded in SCZD 1201, on October 10, 1814, before sentences were administered in 1816. The men were imprisoned in the San Francisco Presidio while awaiting sentencing.

132. SCLB 1384, 1387, 1418, 1791, and 1891.

133. SCLB 1971. The baptism was performed by Friar Baldomero Lopez, one of the two founding fathers of Mission Santa Cruz.

134. Ocot (Nicolasa) SCZB 253. Ocot had a daughter, Micaela, the first baptism performed at Mission Santa Cruz, SCZB 1. Micaela's father was Yñoc (Pancracio), SCZB 492. Euxexi married a Sayanta woman, Florentina, SCZB 205, shortly after entering the mission community, in SCZM 41. These partnerships reflect a more complex pattern of intermarriage and kinship over which the Spanish sought to impose Catholic notions of monogamy.

135. His marriages are recorded as SCZM 41, 80, 234, 364, and 539.

136. Sajuero (Nila), SCZB 666, in August 1812 (SCZM 539).

137. Llencó (Venancio), SCZB 215.

138. Tuquion (Maria Rafaela), SCZB 336. Their marriage was in December 1794, SCZM 76.

139. It is unclear if Jlli and Asar are two different names of the same village or if they were closely related. Asisara says that his father came from the "rancheria of Asar" in one interview and from "Jlli rancheria" in another. He calls his father Venancio Asar (using his baptized name), suggesting that Llencó took on his village name as his surname. Asisara himself went by various names, including Olivares and Asisara. Note that the surname "Asisara" could be an alteration of "Asar," taken from his father's village.

140. Asisara mentions that his father was the mission gardener but gives no further details. Amador, "Memorias sobre la historia de California," 59. As mentioned earlier, Asisara also describes Lacah as the mission gardener at the time of the assassination. Since Lacah was arrested and removed from Mission

Santa Cruz shortly after the assassination, Llencó replaced Lacah at some point thereafter.

141. Tuquion (Maria Rafaela), SCZB 336, SCZM 76, SCZD 431.

142. Luasatme or Lihutsatme (Manuela) is recorded in SCZB 1803. She is listed as being from the Chalahua rancheria, the only one with that title. She is baptized along with a group of Yokuts from the Huocom, Apil, and Tejey rancherias, so it is likely that she is from the same region.

143. SCZM 596–98.

144. SCZD 2039.

145. SCZM 535. The marriage took place on July 25, 1812.

146. Yachacxi or Yachasi, Spanish name assigned as Donato, is listed as SCZB 262.

147. Listed as "*Alcalde de Mugeres*" [*sic*] in the *padrino* notes in SCZB 1440–43 and 1445–46 and in witness notes for SCZM 495. He also appears as "*Alcalde actual de mujeres*" on witness notes for SCZM 524–32.

148. Yachacxi served as *padrino* in SCZB 2024, the birth of the son of the serving *alcalde*, Juan Joseph Autocrais, in 1823. His death is recorded in SCZD 1911.

149. Lleguix (Angel) is listed as SCZB 273, and Sauten (Antonia Ynés) as SCZB 287, on January 21, 1794. Yachacxi and Sauten married in June 1799 (SCZM 244).

150. Their children were the aforementioned *paje* Miguel Antonio; Cecilia, SCZB 1412; and Señorina, SCZB 1431. Cecilia died just two weeks after her birth, in July 1808, SCZD 906. Sauten died in December 1811, SCZD 1093. Señorina survived just over two years, dying in March 1812, SCZD 1105.

151. The five children with Yachacxi: Ysabel Josefa Joaquina Francisca, SCZB 1581; Maria Quiteria, SCZB 1641; Juana, SCZB 1784; Joseph Prudencio, SCZB 1997; and Rafaela Maria Engracia, SCZB 2141. With a previous husband, she had had another son in 1809, Pedro Celestino, SCZB 1427.

152. There is an unnumbered page at the end of the Book of Confirmations (SCZC) with additional, undated confirmations listed. Yuñan appears, alongside her baptismal number, 381, at the top of a short list of eleven girls (*parvulas*).

153. Yuñan serves as *madrina* in the following baptisms: SCZB 1414, 1567, 1569, 1573, 1609, 1836, 1921, 2002, 2032–36, 2041, 2055, 2071, 2083–84, 2100, 2103–19, and 2172 (the last taking place in April 1830).

154. SCZB 1414, 1567, 1569, 1573, 1609, 1836, 1921, 2002, 2032–36, 2041, 2055, 2071, 2083, 2084, 2100, 2103–19, and 2172.

155. SCZB 1414, 1569, 1609, 1836, 1921, 2002, 2041, 2055, 2071, 2083, 2084, 2100, and 2172.

156. SCZB 2103–19.

157. Manocchio, "Tending Communities," 75–81.

158. This is an area in need of more study with regards to Indigenous women. See Chowning, *Rebellious Nuns*; Díaz, *Indigenous Writings from the Convent*;

and Díaz, "Native American Women and Religion in the American Colonies," 205–31.

159. Ètop (Antonio Alberto), listed as SCZB 755. He also shows up in the Spanish records as "Antonio" or "Antonino."

160. See *padrino* notes for SCZB 755.

161. Provincial State Papers: Benicia, Military, 1767–1845, BL, C-A 17, 49:59–61. Ètop's is the only surviving testimony from the Quintana investigation and was given four years after the original testimonies and trials (the originals were taken in 1816, Ètop's in 1820). In Asisara's account he is referred to only as Antonio the cook, yet after his sentence he reappears in the records at Mission San Carlos. He is listed in both his burial and marriage records as Antonio Alberto (see SCAD 2803 and SCAM 921), and in his daughter's baptism record it is noted that he also goes by Antonio (see SCAB 3460).

162. Marriages are found at SCZM 277 and 279. Rustico's baptism is listed in SCZB 1561.

163. Asisara claims that Shomam (Maria Tata), the wife of the cook, was the one soldiers overheard talking with Humiliana. At the time of the assassination, Ètop was married to Najam (Victoriana), a Chipuctac listed as SCZB 808. Najam died about six months after the assassination (SCZD 1411), about a month after Shomam married Justiniano, so it is possible that Asisara confused the names and relationships. Another possibility, considering that the mission had multiple cooks, is that Justiniano was another cook involved but heretofore unidentified.

164. Sostenes is listed at SCZB 894, and Fidel is SCZB 1052.

165. Friar Narcisco Duran to Friar Vincente Francisco Sarría, December 28, 1817, SFAD, document 721. In Friar Duran's letter he explains that two baptized Native people poisoned a third. Duran laments that his task in keeping the baptized Indigenous people content and avoiding large-scale flights of fugitives is made more difficult by the resulting imprisonment of a spiritual leader, "for the principal prisoner is the capitan of a large rancheria, and is well respected and venerated as an oracle." The fear of poisonings and Indigenous access to and knowledge of local poisonous plants was frequently a subject of concern for the padres.

166. Friar Estévan Tapis to José de la Guerra, April 29, 1818, SBMAL, DLG 955, letter 2. Only Ètop, of all the convicts, is mentioned specifically as a cook. It is possible that others, such as Euxexi or Quihueimen, worked as cooks as well.

167. Street, *Beasts of the Field*, 62–63. Rumors of poisonings were common, and a few cases of successful poisonings are recorded, such as the poisoning of three padres at Mission San Miguel in 1801 and the killing of Padre José Pedro Panto by his cook, Nazario, at Mission San Diego in November 1811. This story has been explored in depth by McCormack, "Conjugal Violence," and Nunis, "The 1811 San Diego Trial of the Mission Indian Nazario."

168. Sentences were given in 1816 and did not appear to take into account the time the conspirators were held in San Francisco awaiting verdict. His sentence called for six years *in addition* to time in custody in the Presidio of San Francisco.

169. Provincial State Papers: Benicia, Military, 1767–1845, BL, C-A 17, 49:59–61. Nothing in the testimony explains why he was allowed to testify for his innocence, while none of the others were given the opportunity.

170. Provincial State Papers: Benicia, Military, 1767–1845, BL, C-A 17, 49:59.

171. Provincial State Papers: Benicia, Military, 1767–1845, BL, C-A 17, 49:60.

172. Ètop said that he came down to Año Nuevo, Quiroste territory, which, by this time, had become the local outpost where they kept the sheep. By the time of Ètop's release in 1820, his son had died, apparently from an accident related to falling off a horse. Sostenes' death is recorded in SCZD 1342. Spanish law typically prohibited Indians from riding horses, unless given special permission. Sostenes' death in this manner may suggest special standing, a pattern not unlike that found in other descendants of the conspirators, who often held land or other special status. Provincial State Papers: Benicia, Military, 1767–1845, BL, C-A 17, 49:60.

173. Provincial State Papers: Benicia, Military, 1767–1845, BL, C-A 17, 49: 59.

174. Provincial State Papers: Benicia, Military, 1767–1845, BL, C-A 17, 49: 60.

175. Unijunis (Catarina, SCAB 2675). Her Native name is listed in her marriage record (SCM 921) despite being born in the mission—an anomaly, as most mission-born children are not listed with Native names. Names like these that appear only in records well after the baptism serve as evidence that Indigenous parents continued to surreptitiously give Native names to their children, while not sharing these names with the Spanish Catholic officials.

176. SCAB 3460.

177. Baptismal notes read "in the mountain, where her parents ordinarily spend their time."

178. Breschini and Haversat, "Post-Contact Esselen Occupation."

179. SCD 2803. The exact date is unknown, due to his living away from the mission.

180. Monguis (Liberata) is recorded as SCZD 417. Their marriage is recorded in SCZM 230.

181. Rustico, SCZB 1561,

182. Tuliám (Prudencio) was SCZB 823. Their marriage is recorded as SCZM 262. Tuliám died in 1802, SCZD 543.

183. SCZM 232, 238, 262, 299, 348, 356, 447, and 467a. This is a little misleading, however, as quite a few of these marriages are remarriages. Overall there were four women from Santa Clara who married men at Santa Cruz. The

women include Satus (Gila), SCLB 3704, who married three different times, each after her previous husband's death. Satus was probably connected to Chesente through kinship, as the two women were baptized at the same time, with both listed as being from the "San Carlos" tribe (which meant from the local mountains).

184. Thirty-six marriages occur at Mission Santa Cruz between people baptized there and partners from either Mission San Carlos, Santa Clara, Dolores (San Francisco), or San Juan Bautista. Twenty-eight Indigenous people baptized at Mission Santa Cruz married partners at other missions: four at Mission San Carlos, fourteen at Mission Santa Clara, two at Mission Dolores (San Francisco), and eight at Mission San Juan Bautista.

185. These patterns are explored in Peelo, Panich, Spellman, Ellison, and D'Oro, "Marriage and Death in the Neophyte Village."

186. He served as *padrino* in baptisms SCZB 1406–11, 1432, and 1554 and witness for marriages SCZM 479 and 519–21.

187. Padre Olbés to Solá, June 23, 1819, SCPSD, box 4, letter 975. We know that he was in Santa Barbara from the letter by Padre Olbés of Santa Cruz, who writes to Solá to inquire about the status of Quihueimen and Lacah.

188. Quihueimen is incorrectly named by Galindo as being released due to his innocence. Galindo's account suggests that he is talking about Ètop, given Ètop's testimony and subsequent release. See Galindo, "Apuntes para la historia de California," 64.

189. SCZD 1240.

190. Ulalixmi (Coleta) is from a rancheria called Piluri. She arrived at Mission Santa Cruz in October 1826, SCZB 2112. Their child, Rosa Maria, is recorded in SCZB 2194.

191. Quihueimen's burial is recorded in SCZD 2034. Interestingly, two other people died of smallpox the same day as Quihueimen. One of them is Chalognis (Vicencio Salvador), another Uypi, like Quihueimen, who was baptized as a two-year-old two days before the seven-year-old Quihueimen, listed as SCZB 64.

192. He served as *padrino* in SCZB 2157, 2184, and 2280, the last taking place in 1837.

193. Xuclan (José Ricardo), SCZB 1377, will be discussed in later chapters. His daughter, Catarina, SCZB 2280. Catarina's mother is Tupat (Maria Margarita), a Yokuts from the Huocom rancheria, SCZB 1745. In almost all records he is listed as Ricardo, José Ricardo, or Ricardo Carrion (on 1834 census); it is only in his marriage record that his Native name is given (SCZM 706). His father, Chaparis (Bruno), is recorded in SCZB 1292, while his mother, Legem (Bruna), is recorded in SCZB 1295. I mention Yaquenonsat here, as another Sumus. Xuclan would eventually become the last landholding Indigenous survivor of Mission Santa

Cruz, giving up his parcel of the mission lands following a court case in 1866. Santa Cruz County Clerk's Office, Rice v. Ricardo, case 577, M.R.3.11. This story will be explored in depth in later chapters.

194. Friar Estévan Tapis to José de la Guerra, April 29, 1818, SBMAL, DLG 955, letter 2. Tapis refers to the "Misión de Mata Frayles" (mission of friar killers). Tapis is not alone in characterizing the mission thusly, as Friar Marcelino Marquínez also refers to "la misión de los patricides de P Quintana" (the mission of padre killers of Padre Quintana). Marquínez to Governor Solá, August 25, 1819, SBMAL, CMD 1763.

195. Friar Estévan Tapis to José de la Guerra, April 29, 1818, SBMAL, DLG 955, letter 2.

196. County deeds records indicate that around twenty-five former Mission Santa Cruz Indians held real property interest between 1834 and 1866. Most had relinquished claims by 1850, with Ricardo holding out until 1866. Indigenous landholding will be explored in depth in later chapters.

4. The Rise of the Yokuts

1. Padre Jayme Escude to Governor Solá, May 10, 1817, SFAD document 766.

2. Arkush, "Yokuts Trade Networks," 619–40. Arkush argues that the Yokuts were major facilitators of cultural exchange, introducing elements of Spanish and Mexican material culture to other interior tribes while maintaining a large degree of relative independence. This chapter looks at a group of Yokuts who served in similar roles but did so from their new home in Mission Santa Cruz. One study that focuses on the story of the Yokuts people is Phillips, *Indians of the Tulares*. As mentioned in the previous chapter, all Yokuts tribes and villages in this book are in the Northern Valley Yokuts region. Wallace, "Northern Valley Yokuts."

3. I refer here to the soldiers as being Spanish or Mexican, because of the complexities of identity formation in the years surrounding Mexican independence. At other times in this and later chapters I will also refer to this community as "Californio." In "Becoming Californio" Publos argues that the Californio identity emerged out of debates over the meaning of the terms *Spanish, Mexican,* and *Californio*. For convenience I use the terms *Californio, Mexican, and Spanish* to refer to these citizens, who came from a diversity of ethnic and regional backgrounds.

4. Caplan, "Indigenous Citizenship," 225–47. Caplan examines the move toward Indigenous citizenship in multiple regions following Mexican independence. This chapter will look briefly at the move toward liberation, while the next chapter will examine the issue of citizenship and rights more directly as it intersects with secularization and emancipation. This theme is explored regarding Indigenous Californians in Haas, *Saints and Citizens*, 117.

5. Haas, *Saints and Citizens*, 141–46. Haas discusses Indigenous petitions for liberty from southern missions following the 1826 provisional emancipation. There are no surviving petitions from people at Mission Santa Cruz, meaning either that nobody petitioned for their liberty or that those documents have been lost. As this chapter will show, local Indigenous people talked about emancipation and liberty, but fugitivism became the more common route.

6. Cook, *Epidemic of 1830–1833*; and Ahrens, "John Work."

7. Michael J. González, *This Small City*; Haas, *Conquests and Historical Identities*; Monroy, *Thrown among Strangers*; Sánchez, *Telling Identities*; and Voss, *Archaeology of Ethnogenesis*. These works examine this period of transition in Alta California, characterized by increasing violence and warfare similar to what González described in Southern California. The next chapter, which examines the period following official Mexican independence, will look closely at the impact of this political change on Indigenous rights.

8. Zappia examines warfare, trading, and raiding that linked the Yokuts of California to the larger Southwestern Indigenous world, *Traders and Raiders*. DeLay analyzes the roots of frontier warfare between Indigenous nations of the Southwest, *War of a Thousand Deserts*. See also Blackhawk, *Violence over the Land*; James Brooks, *Captives and Cousins*; Barr, *Peace Came in the Form of a Woman*; and Hämäläinen, *Comanche Empire*.

9. Here I am referring to the situation throughout California. In the Bay Area a diversity of Ohlone, Miwok, and Yokuts gathered under these leaders. To the south, Chumash and Yokuts collaborated during the Chumash war for independence in 1824. For more on Pomponio, Estanislao, and Yozcolo, see Flores, "Native American Response and Resistance"; James D. Adams, *Estanislao*; Holterman, "Revolt of Yozcolo"; and Gray, *Stanislaus Indian Wars*.

10. Sandos, *Converting California*, 102–5. Sandos explores the role of these Indian auxiliaries, finding similar patterns of elevated status and assistance to missionaries and soldiers. The term *Indian auxiliaries* came from early Spanish conquest in the Americas and referred to Indigenous peoples who allied themselves with Spanish conquerors. See Matthew and Oudijk, *Indian Conquistadors*.

11. Toypurina was, of course, infamous among Spanish missionaries. She was exiled to Monterey in the late 1790s, where she married Spanish soldier Manuel Montero. She died in 1799, and her widow and three children had relocated to the Villa de Branciforte by 1808, as discussed by Johnson and Williams, "Toypurina's Descendants," 31–55. Almost certainly as a result of her heritage, Montero herself became the target of Mission Santa Cruz padre Olbés, who tried to remove her children from her care, accusing her of having "mother's milk of venom."

12. Majors and Bolcoff married two sisters of the prominent Castro family. Both men will be discussed in the next chapter. This pattern of foreign men marrying prominent Californio women has been explored in depth by Casas, *Married to a Daughter*. Casas successfully argues that Californio women actively negotiated their rights in these marriages. For more on Bolcoff's mixed-blood (Creole) heritage, see Farris, *Far from Home*, 126–28.

13. Haas, *Saints and Citizens*, 149. Haas discusses the erasure of Native spaces and the rare use of Native names in rancho property titles. In Santa Cruz, three rancho properties were given names reflecting Indigenous tribes: Zayante, Soquel, and Aptos. The Zayante grant (and contemporary township) were named for the Sayanta tribe.

14. This chapter focuses primarily on the decades of the 1810s and 1820s. However, Mission Santa Cruz continued to baptize incoming Yokuts people until 1834, when the Alta California missions were officially secularized. Therefore, this section on demographics extends into the early 1830s to trace patterns of migration and baptism.

15. E. L. Williams, "Narrative of a Mission Indian," 47. Lorenzo Asisara, in his 1890 interview, spoke about the mission community as being divided along linguistic lines: "The padres nominated an alcalde and assistant for each of the different bands, of which there were about thirty. Those tribes nearest to the mission, such as up the coast a way, and as far south as Aptos, could understand each other, but those from a few miles farther off did not. Those of Gilroy were in their own language called Pasen [Pagsim]; San Juan, Uiuhi; Pajaro [south], Nootsum [Mutsun]; Aptos, Aptos; Soquel, Soquel; up the coast Tili and Ulsicsi; at Red Bank Dairy, up the coast, Posorou; on the San Vicente Creek, Sorsecsi; near the old limekilns of Williams' Landing, Coyulicsi." Asisara's understanding of Indigenous linguistic and territorial politics is much more complicated than the Awaswas Mutsun binary. I choose to simplify into the two broad categories to show the larger patterns while also arguing that some of these complex identity politics collapsed into broader alliances and kinship networks in the larger context of demographic collapse.

16. Sandos, for example, argues that "charges of 'forced conversion' of Indians made against the Franciscans in California episodically from the 1820s onward are nonsensical within the framework of Franciscan theology; they are also without historical proof and should be dismissed as yet another mission myth" (*Converting California*, 103). While Sandos was talking about the internal spiritual conversion to Catholicism as opposed to a superficial conversion, his comments here suggest a repudiation of the question of force and certainly contribute to the arguments against forceful "recruitment."

17. Milliken, *Time of Little Choice*.

18. JPH, microfilm, reel 58, p. 51.

19. Jackson, "Disease and Demographic Patterns," 37.

20. SBMAL, November 20, 1819, CMD 1822a. These were likely fugitives dating back to earlier in the year. In February 1819, Padre Gil y Taboada reported that the entire Mission Santa Cruz population fled after hearing from *pobladores* at the Villa de Branciforte that soldiers were threatening to take them prisoner. Gil y Taboada to Governor Arguello, February 24, 1819, Santa Cruz, SFAD document 922 and 922-2.

21. This was discussed in chapter 2. It is possible that these reports overrepresented the actual mission population numbers in order to justify requests for supplies.

22. Latta, *Handbook of Yokuts Indians*, 141–54. The most complete study of the Yokuts to date was written by Latta, born about thirty miles north of Los Banos, near Orestimba Creek in Stanislaus County. Both creek and county are named for Indigenous tribes (Orestimba) and individuals (Estanislao, who will be discussed briefly in this chapter). He spent much of his life interviewing, researching, and getting to know the local Yokuts people. Coincidently, Latta moved to Santa Cruz in 1956, living there until his death in 1983.

23. The names of these villages have been written using various spellings; for example, the Mallim, Notualls, and Copcha have been written as *Malim*, *Notoalls*, and *Copicha* by Cook, *Aboriginal Population*, 52. Here I have adopted the most frequent spellings in the Santa Cruz baptismal registry.

24. The exact location of these tribes is uncertain. Neither received mention in the military or ecclesiastical documents. Based on the timeline of their baptisms, it seems that the Huocom and Hupnis tribes were from slightly farther east than the earlier wave of Yokuts villagers.

25. Elias Castillo, *Cross of Thorns*, ix.

26. Conversations with author. Several prominent historians and anthropologists have brought up these points in conversation to suggest that there is a lack of evidence to support the claims made in these oral history accounts.

27. JPH, microfilm, reel 59, p. 4.

28. Amador, "Memorias sobre la historia de California," 78.

29. Historian Benjamin Madley brought this detail to my attention. The Pomo killed Stone and Kelsey for their abusive behavior in 1850, prompting the U.S. military to respond by massacring at least sixty of the local Pomo in what is now known as the Bloody Island Massacre. *American Genocide*, 110.

30. This massacre has been discussed previously by Madley, "California's First Mass Incarceration System," 30–31.

31. Latta, *Handbook of Yokuts Indians*, 151.

32. This is all cited by Latta, *Handbook of Yokuts Indians*, 152–53.

33. Latta, *Handbook of Yokuts Indians*, 145. Sopahno was likely referring to secularization in the 1830s, when he was told to leave the mission. That would place his initial story of capture in the 1810s, if he was there for twenty years.

34. E. L. Williams, "Narrative of a Mission Indian," 47; Hackel, "Staff of Leadership," 347–76. Hackel argues that in the early years at Mission San Carlos, Indigenous *alcaldes* were predominately traditional leaders, while in the later years they were elected from outside Indigenous political leadership. At Mission Santa Cruz there was not such a clear-cut pattern. In fact, the arrival of Yokuts resulted in Yokuts leaders and their families serving as *alcaldes*, along with Ohlone *alcaldes*.

35. Recent studies demonstrate the continuation of trade networks at Mission Santa Clara. Panich, "Native American Consumption," 730–48, and "Beyond the Colonial Curtain," 521–30. At Mission Santa Cruz the perseverance of underground trade between missions is evidenced by caches of beads found by archaeologists in the lost-adobe research. Tsim Schneider, conversation with the author, January 9, 2020.

36. While Nupchenches appears to be the name of a village site, Sherburne F. Cook has referred to the group of villages alongside the San Joaquin River collectively as Nupchenches. I am following his lead on this while acknowledging that there is a lack of clarity regarding the village and tribal names of the Yokuts from this region. Furthermore, these lands bordered the territories of Ohlone (to the east), Miwok (to the north), and Yokuts (to the south). While they have generally all been considered Yokuts, there is some uncertainty about whether they were Yokuts or Miwok.

37. Muñoz, "Gabriel Moraga Expedition of 1806," 245.

38. Cook, *Aboriginal Population*, 48–54. Cook chronicled the military expeditions into the region in depth and translated and transcribed the diaries of Father Pedro Muñoz, who recorded the Moraga expedition. Muñoz described one village encounter thusly, "It is called Nupchenche and has around 230 people under a chief named Choley. They gave us a welcome as follows: a very old woman came forward to shower us with grain, followed by their camptains who led us to the place prepared for the reception. Here they had spread some soft rush mats and deer hides upon which they served an abundance of dishes and two loaves of very white bread made with a grain resembling our rice," "Gabriel Moraga Expedition of 1806," 227. Milliken noted in his baptismal record database that eleven years later, a then 45-year-old man listed as Cholé was taken to Mission Santa Cruz (Leon, SCZB 1683). This Cholé was the first of around thirteen people identified as "Sagim" Yokuts to arrive at Mission Santa Cruz between 1817 and 1824. Milliken notes that Cholé is identified as a chief, likely making him the same one mentioned by Muñoz. The difficulty in tracing Yokuts

village and tribal identities is demonstrated by the small group of Sagim, who appear to be the Nupchenche. One woman, Yojoilit (Maria Teresa, SCZB 1699) is listed as being "Nopchinche" while her mother Tumna (Cucufata, SCZB 1711) is listed as being Sagim and father, Chachagua (Cucufato, SCZB 1438) as from the Yeurata Rancheria (Chanech).

39. Cook, *Aboriginal Population*, 52. Mallim is likely the village name of the Tejey people. Many of these villages coincide with contemporary cities: Chanech with Los Banos, Nupchenches with the Santa Rita Slough, Copcha with Firebaugh, and Cutucho and Tape with Mendota.

40. SCZB 1311. Gilsic (Carlos) is listed as being from the Chieuta rancheria, but his parents' names and information show that his father, Socoües (Patricio), from the Luchamme village, was baptized at Mission Santa Cruz in 1817 (SCZB 1689), while his mother, Oyocat, from Chanech rancheria, was baptized at Mission San Juan Bautista in early 1822 (SJBB 3005). It is unclear how twelve-year-old Gilsic arrived in 1805, a few months before the Moraga expedition. It seems likely that his arrival was connected in some way, perhaps prompting the expedition, or that he was brought back by scouts in anticipation.

41. SCZB 1434–50, 1452–72, 1474–77. Muñoz described the "Yunate" village site as having around 250 villagers. This is surely the same as the Yeurata village of the Chaneche. "Gabriel Moraga Expedition of 1806," 245.

42. This total is compiled from the mission baptismal records. Santa Cruz missionaries performed 654 baptisms between 1813 and 1834, the final year of mission operation, which was also the last year Yokuts arrived. Of those 654, many were newborns (269) and a few others were baptisms of Californio villagers (7).

43. It is likely that the Tejey and Mallim were closely connected. Coleto's Native name, Malimin, may also be connected with the village name Mallim, given the similarities and his acknowledged leadership of the group.

44. Email to author, September 26, 2016. Ketchum elaborated: "This location is where the Merced River and San Joaquin Rivers [*sic*] meet. Probably an important cultural place because the Merced River is the first significant tributary to the San Joaquin River after it turns to the north. I don't know if the other tributaries flowed all year into the San Joaquin south of this point. I believe they die in the sandy soils of the valley."

45. Malimin (Coleto), SCZB 1478, was listed as being fifty-eight years old. His family included his wife, forty-year-old Yguichegel (Coleta, SCZB 1479); twenty-four-year-old Moctó (Agustin, SCZB 1480); twenty-three-year-old Cachimtan (Agustina, SCZB 1481); and twelve-year-old Guajsilii (Estevan, SCZB 1482). He also had three sons who arrived later, the three-or four-year-old Huich (Vicente Francisco, SCZB 1639 in 1816), twenty-eight-year-old Chulnoquis (Pasqual, SCZB 1647

in 1817), and thirteen-year-old Punis (Bernardino, sczb 1648). Yguichegel is listed as the mother of Guajsilii, but Moctó's mother, Huasiuta, entered Mission Santa Cruz seven years later, receiving baptism on February 22, 1817 (sczb 1667), after the death of Yguichegel, who died five months after her baptism, in late 1810 (sczd 1006). Huasiuta, who was also the mother of the two later-arriving sons, was also christened with the name Coleta and married Malimin shortly after arrival (sczm 574, March 3, 1817). This suggests that Malimin had at least two wives before entry, with Huasiuta remaining outside the mission, presumably with her other sons, and likely receiving visits from Malimin during his seasonal passes.

46. Email to author, September 26, 2016; Warner, Butler, and Geary, *Mutsun-English, English-Mutsun Dictionary*, 92.

47. Basso, *Wisdom Sits in Places*.

48. jph, microfilm, reel 59, p. 63.

49. Padre Marcelino Marquínez to Governor Solá, May 25, 1816, sfad document 488.

50. Ayaclo (Egidio, sczb 1410), listed as being from the Locobo rancheria, was baptized on June 5, 1808, as a twelve-year-old. The *padrino* for his baptism was Quihueimen, the conspirator involved in the Quintana assassination.

51. Padre Marcelino Marquínez to Governor Solá, May 25, 1816, sfad document 488. The actual identity of El Chivero is not certain, although it is likely that he was from Mission Santa Cruz. Father Jayme Escude to Governor Solá, June 10, 1816, sfad document 401. Escude claims that El Chivero was baptized at Mission Santa Cruz, in which case he would be Sagián (Francisco Xavier, sczb 980) from the "San Juan" rancheria, most likely the Auxentaca village, according to Randall Milliken's database. Lieutenant Argüello to Governor Solá, June 10, 1816, sfad document 392. In this letter El Chivero is cited as being affiliated with Mission Santa Clara, but there is no corresponding "Francisco Xavier" baptized at that mission who would have been alive at that time. Ignacio Peralta to Governor Solá, May 25, 1816, sfad document 387. El Chivero was the subject in this report, mentioning that he was last known headed for the Mallim rancheria to summon the Christian fugitives staying there, suggesting that El Chivero both robbed livestock and aided the missionaries in tracking down fugitives.

52. Padre Marcelino Marquínez to Governor Solá, May 25, 1816, sfad document 488. While some historians have argued that there were not enough soldiers to actually remove entire villages, letters like these and the aforementioned oral histories attest to the military might exercised to intimidate villagers into wholesale removal and relocation.

53. The story of their report is told in two documents: Lieutenant Argüello to Governor Solá, June 10, 1816, sfad document 392, and the letter in the following footnote.

54. Padre Escude gives his account of the report from the two men and said it was "a good time to fall upon them before they move for they are so rebellious they sent to tell us they will not come back because they are afraid," Friar Jayme Escude to Governor Solá, June 10, 1816, SFAD document 401.

55. Padre Marquínez to Governor Solá, December 13, 1816, SFAD document 578. "My heart can scarcely be contained within my breast for the great abundance of joy. . . . Would not your heart be flooded with joy and satisfaction if, after you had lost forty-two children and had over a period of many years taken the most vigorous measures to recover them, all in vain, someone came to tell you, 'Señor, here come your forty-two children?'" This was the response to the recovery of people who clearly did not want to be at Mission Santa Cruz, mostly adults.

56. Padre Marquínez to Governor Solá, December 13, 1816, SFAD document 578.

57. Padre Marquínez to Governor Solá, December 13, 1816, SFAD document 578.

58. Chiemiit (Egidia, SCZB 1734), a twenty-year-old Chanech woman, received baptism on February 7, 1818. She arrived in a group of eighteen Chanech, Osocalis, Quithrathre, and Achila people. Ayaclo and Chiemiit married on March 5, 1818, shortly after her baptism. It is likely that the two met while in eastern lands, and it is also possible that Ayaclo convinced her to return to the mission with him, given that he likely returned around the same time.

59. I believe that he left, as he last appears in the 1841 padron in the "Potrero de la Guerta" as Egidio Caballero. His listed surname suggests that he was skilled with horses, which would certainly make sense considering his horse-thieving ways. The significance of his placement in this padron, which reflected the three different Indigenous communities that formed around former mission lands, will be made clear later in this chapter. His marriages: SCZM 769, January 25, 1830, to Sayanit (Septima, SCZB 1665), and SCZM 808, January 1, 1835, to Maria Concepcion. The latter appears to have been a widow from San Juan Bautista; their marriage document listed Ayaclo as Egidio "Cabayero."

60. Cook, *Epidemic of 1830–1833*, 308–22; Ahrens, "John Work, J. J. Warner," 1–32. Ahrens argues that it was indeed malaria, brought by Work and the Hudson Bay Company, that devastated Native populations in the San Joaquin and Sacramento Valleys.

61. Cook, *Aboriginal Population*, 54. The American J. J. Warner described the region in 1833: "We did not see more than six or eight Indians; while large numbers of their skulls and dead bodies were to be seen under almost every shade-tree near water, where the uninhabited and deserted villages had been converted into graveyards; and on the San Joaquin River, in the immediate neighborhood of the larger class of villages, which, in the preceding year, were the abodes of a large number of those Indians, we found not only graves, but the vestiges of

a funeral pyre. At the mouth of King's River we encountered the first and only village of the stricken race that we had seen after entering the great valley."

62. Tejey and Mallim could be two different village sites, closely bound through kinship ties. Ketchum suggests that Tejey could be the village name and Mallim the name for the people; email to author, September 26, 2016. The Spanish referred to some villages by the names of prominent chiefs or leaders, and Mallim is the home village of Coleto Malimin. As mentioned earlier, it is possible that this name is a reference to him. Whatever the case, the two names seem interchangeable. Malimin's youngest son, Huich, is identified as Tejey, while Malimin's other son, Chulnoquis, is listed as Mallim.

63. On December 14, 1816, the day after the group's arrival, Huich, the three or four-year-old son of Malimin, received baptism. His other two sons who arrived then, Chulnoquis and Punis, ages twenty-eight and thirteen, respectively, would eventually gain title to the Potrero lands following secularization, as will be discussed in the next chapter. The group of women who received baptism that day included Malimin's second wife, Huasiuta (Coleta, SCZB 1667), Moctó's wife Yenulate (Agustina, SCZB 1668), Chulnoquis's wife, Hueiete (Pasquala, SCZB 1669), and Guajsilii's wife, Segejate (Gervasia, SCZB 1672).

64. SCZB 1647–80.

65. Padre Jayme Escude to Governor Solá, May 10, 1817, SFAD document 766. The arming of Indian auxiliaries in response to Bouchard was not isolated to Malimin and his men at Mission Santa Cruz. Sandos observed a similar move in Santa Barbara, where auxiliaries received some instruction in European military methods in preparation for a potential attack by Bouchard, *Converting California*, 103–4.

66. Padre Mariano Payeras to Padre Baldomero López, July 4, 1819, Soledad, SBMAL, CMD 1754. Locally, the impact of these independence movements was financial. Missionaries complained about the lack of funds available because of the insurgents. For example, Payeras complained to López about the condition of the missions because of this. You may remember López as one of the founders of Mission Santa Cruz, who by this time had become the head of the local Franciscan order.

67. Bouchard's exploits are recalled in the memoirs of Antonio María Osio, *History of Alta California*, 44–54.

68. Padre Ramón Olbés, October 26, 1818, SBMAL, CMD 1588. Olbés reported the misdeeds after receiving word at Mission Santa Clara from his mayordomo and Silvestre Chachoix (SCZB 304), the interpreter and informant sent back to check on the mission. Silvestre Chachoix's Native name appears spelled in multiple ways, including *Chachoix* in his baptismal record, *Chachanis, Chacharis,* and *Chachara*. As one of the principal translators at the mission, he served

as *padrino* many times and in those records is frequently recorded as Silvestre Chachanis (or some variation).

69. Fray Maríano Payeras to Fray Baldomero Lopez, SBMAL, February 9, 1819, San Miguel, CMD 1668. Payeras reported the damage done to Mission Santa Cruz to López, the founder of Mission Santa Cruz, who had received a promotion to Guardian of the Colegio de San Fernando in Mexico City a few months earlier. In the letter Payeras acknowledges López's connection with Mission Santa Cruz, referring to it as his "favorite daughter" (*su hija predilecta*).

70. Olbés to Solá, SBMAL, December 1, 1818, CMD 1607. The padres frequently complained about relations between Indians at the mission and Branciforte villagers, citing Indians gambling and drinking with the settlers. It is certainly possible that they found more in common with the mestizo and predominately mixed-blood villagers than the padres. Michael J. González argues that debates about the capabilities of Indians were at the center of conflict between missionaries and civilians, in "Child of the Wilderness Weeps." Local conflicts follow this same pattern but also stem from initial settlement of the villa on lands the padres considered far too close to Mission Santa Cruz.

71. California Archives, December 8, 1818, Provincial State Papers, BL, Benicia Military, 1:275. The five men appear to have been from local tribes, suggesting that the padres continued to acknowledge the importance of this older community. The group included the Cotoni translator Silvestre Chachoix, the Chipuctac man Causúte (Gregorio, SCZB 797), the Sayanta man Chugiut (Geronimo Miguel Pacheco, SCZB 184), the Auxentaca man Picothe (Victorino, SCZB 1059), and the Chipuctac man Checello (Hilario, SCZB 860).

72. Padre Mariano Payeras to López, July 4, 1819, Soledad, SBMAL, CMD 1754. Payeras, after visiting Mission Santa Cruz, reported that of the fugitives, "there are still many in the mountains, and in the great valley of the Tular."

73. Padre Marcelino Marquínez to Governor Solá, August 25, 1819, SBMAL, CMD 1763.

74. November 20, 1819, SBMAL, CMD 1822a. Santa Cruz was not the only mission with large numbers of fugitives reported at this same time. For example, Mission Soledad reported forty-seven fugitives, Padre Jayme Escude to Solá, November 30, 1819, SBMAL, CMD 1826.

75. Padre Luis Gil y Taboada, December 31, 1825, SBMAL, CMD 2840; and census of 1834, *Santa Cruz Mission Libro de Padrónes*. "They worked as basket weavers, blanket weavers, carpenters, blacksmiths and tanners, besides tending the fields and the herds. The cultivated fields were fenced with posts driven in the ground and tied with hazel bark or withes. Ditches were run along the outside. In plowing time from 100 to 130 oxen were used. . . . Surplus crops were sold by the priests. Spanish vessels took beans, corn, dried peas and horse

beans. English vessels took hides and tallow. Russian ships took wheat and barley." From UCSC, McHenry Library, Pre-Statehood Documents, Rowland Files, B-2, 366.04, Indians.

76. Padre Luis Gil y Taboada, December 31, 1825, SBMAL, CMD 2840.

77. As will be discussed in chapter 5, the Hartnell report notes that there were 1,026 sheep, 127 horses, 10 oxen, and 16 cows in 1839. "Diary and Blotters of the Two Inspections Made by W. E. P. Hartnell, General Inspector of Missions in Alta California, 1839–1840," September 28, 1839, Starr P. Gurcke Papers, MS 8, box 3:12, Special Collections and Archives, University Library, UCSC. The sheep pastures of San Gregorio Valley are discussed in Brown, "Indians of San Mateo County," 21: "The missioanires complained about the problems of distance from Santa Cruz: the [Indigenous] ranch hands were always falling sick 'in those frigid mountains' and could not come to church even when healthy. The headquarters of the sheep ranch seem to have been at the head of the valley, just west of La Honda, and in the 1830's they passed into the ownership of Antonio Buelna."

78. Padre Gil y Taboada to Padre Mariano Payeras, November 24, 1821. Gil y Taboada reported that "the Indians are destitute and disgusted and do nothing without a flogging which causes me great anguish." He was referring to their reluctance to labor and provide resources, including saddles and clothing for soldiers and settlers. Confessions of anguish aside, the letter also states that wool was scarce due to bad weather and the prevalence of wolves and bears eating the younger animals up at the Año Nuevo outstation, where many of the cattle were kept by this point. Baptized Indigenous people from Mission Santa Cruz managed pasture lands for livestock up the coast. In addition to the cattle at Año Nuevo, they managed thousands of sheep about 25 miles north of Año Nuevo, in what is today known as San Gregorio.

79. Census of 1834, *Santa Cruz Mission Libro de Padrones, Baptisms, and Burials*, all at Monterey Diocese Chancery Archives, Monterey CA. In contrast, Haas found that for Southern Californian Indians, the 1836 and 1844 censuses did not list occupations other than "servants" (*Conquests and Historical Identities*, 43).

80. Haas, *Conquests and Historical Identities*. Haas found that many Indigenous people "pointed to the skills they had learned at the mission in an effort to obtain their freedom," 40. The 1834 padron offered the first official recognition of the many skilled-labor roles performed by local Natives, despite the many years of practice that most of these skilled laborers had. The early learning of artisan skills is discussed in depth in chapter 2. The implementation of secularization and emancipation policies will be explored in chapter 5.

81. The man listed as a *flechero* is Atauque (Paterno, SCZB 1492).

82. There are a few early exceptions, where some prominent Native people had surnames. This was discussed in chapter 2.

83. The Mexican officials from whom these names come will be discussed in chapter 5, which will look more closely at the policies of emancipation and secularization.

84. Haas, *Saints and Citizens*, 159. Haas suggests that the last names were given by administrator Ignacio de Valle. The long history of imposing names supports her claim, but I am less certain in this case, because the evidence suggests that tribal identities listed on the document were not taken from baptismal records. The large number of discrepancies between tribal affiliations on baptismal records and the 1834 padron (Pitac versus "Chiputac," Sipieyesi versus Janil, or Auxentaca versus "Hanjentasa," to cite a few examples) suggests to me that there was a degree of self-identification involved. It is possible that the same was true for names, and that people chose their own surnames.

85. E. L. Williams, "Narrative of a Mission Indian," 46–47.

86. Moctó is listed as *alcalde* in SCZD 1639–41 and 1753–56.

87. He appears in the following burial records: SCZD 1466–69, 1639–41, and 1753–56, a total of eleven times between 1822 and 1828. Each time he is mentioned by his full name, Agustin Moctó, which is a hybrid of his Spanish and Indigenous names. As there was already an Agustin (Sachat, SCZB 57, a Sayanta man), it is possible that his Indigenous name was used to make this distinction. But this particular pattern of name usage, with the first and last being Spanish and Native, respectively, throughout the 1820s and the census of 1834 suggests that it was a common practice. I deviate from previous chapters at this point by referring to Agustin Moctó and others, including his father, by their hybrid names, as I believe they would have used both at the time.

88. In SCZD 1639–41 the padres identified "The Alcalde Agustin, and five other tulareños" as the informants reporting the three dead individuals.

89. Thomas Savage, Records in the Parish (ex Mission) Church of Santa Cruz, CA: Copies & Extracts by Thomas Savage for Bancroft Library 1877, box 3:16, BL, University of California, Berkeley. The annual reports of the Mission Santa Cruz elections are incomplete, so while this is the only recorded year that Guajsilii served as regidor, he may have served other years.

90. Mora-Torres, *Californio Voices*, 123–25. This story is also related in Castañeda, "Engendering the History of Alta California," 235.

91. Castañeda, "Engendering the History of Alta California," 234.

92. JPH, microfilm, reel 58, p. 46.

93. Samecxi (Dámaso, SCZB 233).

94. The story is told in Amador, "Memorias sobre la historia de California," 91–94.

95. Samecxi's death is recorded at Mission Dolores, where he is listed as having died while held in the presidio, SFD 4574, on February 23, 1818. His story is told years later by Asisara, who was born in 1820. The persistence of Samecxi's story of rebellion points to the types of memories that were handed down by members of the community. These stories highlight both abuse and resistance and remember those who sacrificed their lives to stand up for Indigenous people.

96. November 20, 1819, SBMAL, CMD 1822a.

97. SCZD 2069. Written in Spanish as *gálico*. Gálico was a reference to what the Spanish referred to as the "French disease," referencing Gaul, the historical name for France.

98. Guajsilii and Segejate married in 1817 (SCZM 588) and had their first child in 1820. Their children: SCZB 1790, 1923, 2003, 2052, 2090, 2127, 2159, and 2185. Burial records, respectively, SCZD 1415, 1447, 1529, 1566, 1631, 1769, 1824, and 1862. Their names were, respectively, Estevan, Benvenuta, Ramona, Erasma, Lucia, Francisco Fabriano, Mercurio, and Maria de los Angeles.

99. Bancroft related in a footnote about Padre Gil y Taboada, that "to his neophytes he was indulgent and was well liked by them, being free and familiar in his relations with them—somewhat too much so in the case of the women it is said, and it is charged that his infirmities of body were aggravated by syphilitic complications. In 1821 he was accused of improper intimacy with a married woman who often visited his room and was found in his bed by the husband under circumstances hardly explained by the padre's plea of services as amateur physician; but his superiors were inclined to regard him as innocent, though imprudent." Bancroft, "The Works of Hubert Howe Bancroft," 681. Additionally, a letter from 1824 reported about a local scandal where an unidentified missionary in Santa Cruz having sex with baptized Indigenous women, Gervasio Soto, June 8, 1824, BL MSS, C-A 18, 179–83. Gil y Taboada wrote a defense against allegations against him, but the original has so-far proven unreadable to this author, Padre Luís Gil y Taboada to Herrera, April 6, 1826, SBMAL, CMD 2872.

100. Sandos, *Converting California*, 111–27. Sandos looks closely at the prevalence of syphilis, gonorrhea, and other venereal disease and concludes that syphilis was "one of the previously underappreciated factors contributing to the process of precipitous native population decline." The spread of the venereal disease was exacerbated by the crowded living conditions of the missions, as discussed by Monroy, *Thrown among Strangers*, 83–86.

101. Amador, "Memorias sobre la historia de California," 99. While Asisara recalls Gil y Taboada's violations, he also claims that the same priest "came to be greatly loved by all the Indians, especially by the Tulareños, whose language he understood to some extent." As Bouvier has pointed out, "His comments

rendered virtually invisible the separate female experience of sexual vulnerability," in *Women and the Conquest of California*, 135. Newell suggests that Asisara's claim that the padre passed syphilis to the women was in error, since the men loved Gil y Taboada, *Constructing Lives*, 91–92. I strongly disagree with Newell's interpretation and instead attribute the inconsistency to Asisara's internalized patriarchal leanings.

    102. Seynte (Projecto, SCZB 626). Seynte was the older brother of Yrachis (SCZB 629), better known as Justiniano Roxas, whose life is examined in Rizzo and Cothran, "Many Lives of Justiniano Roxas," 168–204. As early as 1799, Seynte had begun serving as marriage witness, the same year that he himself married Samórim (SCZB 62), a member of the local Achistaca tribe, SCZM 256. Samórim (alternatively written as Sambray and baptized as Fabiana Arraez) was herself an important member of the spiritual community, serving as *madrina* in thirty-five baptisms between 1815 (SCZB 1607) and 1821 (SCZB 1911). She died in January 1823 (SCZD 1499).

    103. Their children: Lazaro Domingo (SCZB 1014), Francisco Solano (SCZB 1129), Francisco (SCZB 1165), Antonia (SCZB 1364), Tomas (SCZB 1429), Hana Maria de la Espectation (SCZB 1578), Vicenta Rafaela (SCZB 1612), and Alvaro (SCZB 1758).

    104. SCZD 1721, on April 26, 1828.

    105. JPH, microfilm, p. 73, reel 59.

    106. Chase-Dunn and Mann, *Wintu and Their Neighbors*. This pattern is explored in relation to the Northern California Wintu, but the pattern of intermarriages between neighbors is seen with many Indigenous Californian tribes.

    107. SCZD 1867, on December 22, 1831.

    108. Taucha (Vicente Carlos, SCZB 1594) was a Yokuts man from the Cooht village, while Saeta (Vicenta, SCZB 1710) was from the neighboring Sagim village. They had four children: Pasquala (SCZB 1921), baptized on May 18, 1821; Silveria (SCZB 2015), baptized on June 20, 1822; Bibiana (SCZB 2054), baptized on November 3, 1823; and Octaviana (SCZB 2084), baptized on November 1, 1824.

    109. Pasquala (SCZD 1446) died on May 24, 1821; Silveria (SCZD 1486) died on August 21, 1822; Bibiana (SCZD 1543) died on December 13, 1823; and Octaviana (SCZD 1584) died on November 15, 1824.

    110. SCZD 1710.

    111. Census of 1834, *Libro de Padrónes*, Monterey Archdiocese.

    112. Jackson, "Villa de Branciforte Census." Rafaela Maria married Jose Antonio on April 28, 1846 (SCZM 870).

    113. Jose Pedro was baptized on May 15, 1848 (SCZB 2794).

    114. U.S. Census takers did not do a good job documenting Indigenous families in the latter half of the nineteenth century.

115. Victoriano Chuyucu (his Native name alternatively spelled *Chuiucuu* or *Chugucu* and his alias given as Yeulile, SCZB 1515) and Petra Maria Nicanor (SCZB 1589) married on February 17, 1829 (SCZM 755).

116. Chase-Dunn and Mann, *Wintu and Their Neighbors*; and Peelo, "Creation of a Carmeleño Identity." Peelo argues that multiple new identities were formed by intermarriages between tribal members who would have been outside of the traditional intermarriage regions. At Mission Santa Cruz, I argue here, a similar process took place between Yokuts women and Ohlone men. As the one exception to this pattern, the marriage of Petra Nicanor suggests that she held special status, almost certainly due to her heritage and Lino's significance to the local community.

117. The negotiation of rights, voting, and citizenship for those identified within the social and political category of "Indian" living in the "borderlands" of New Mexico and Arizona during the political transitions between Spanish colonial, Mexican national, and U.S. statehood is the subject of study in Crandall, *These People Have Always Been a Republic*. Crandall's fascinating and wide-ranging study, which curiously omits California, despite the parallel racial and colonial landscape, focuses on voting rights while arguing that different Indigenous communities found a variety of strategies to use their shifting rights in the struggle for sovereignty against colonial powers. This examination of Indigenous rights and citizenship constitutes a case study in Californian counterparts, adding to the examples in Crandall's important study.

118. These major legislative policies include "Decreto del Congreso Mejicano secularizando las Misiones, 17 de Agosto de 1833," in Lozano and Dublán, *Legislación Mexicana*.

119. Haas, *Saints and Citizens*, 117. The Plan de Iguala put forth the "three guarantees," which included universal citizenship for all, regardless of racial or casta designation.

120. O'Hara, *Flock Divided*. O'Hara argues that despite official overtures toward abolishing racial categories, "the colonial category of Indian continued to shape religious practice and community litigation in many Mexican parishes" (237).

121. Missionaries had officially had civil and political control over mission lands and baptized Natives. Secularization placed this power in the hands of the government. The most exhaustive study to date on secularization in California is found in Salomon, "Secularization in California," 349–71. Salomon's case study has many parallels with the situation at Mission Santa Cruz. In both cases the ambitious secularization policies dictating the return of lands and goods to Native workers were thwarted by corrupt officials and land grabs by local elites. Haas has argued that as emancipation and secularization were enacted, conversations about Indigenous citizenship ceased. Haas, *Saints and Citizens*, 157–63.

122. Padre Ramon Olbés to Governor Solá, July 22, 1821, SBMAL, CMD 2194. Allen, *Native Americans at Mission Santa Cruz*. The lone remaining adobe building stands today on School Street and is part of Mission Santa Cruz State Park. The Mission Santa Cruz annual reports for 1822 and 1824, originals at SBMAL, give updates on the construction of homes "where the new citizens are living," a nod to the transition toward Indigenous citizenship. Ketchum adds: "Adobe homes were constructed at San Juan Bautista at the same time. The first report was made in 1815" (email to author, September 26, 2016). See also Glenn J. Farris, senior state archaeologist, "Indian Family Housing at Mission San Juan Bautista," California State Parks, www.parks.ca.gov/?page_id=22731, accessed January 10, 2020.

123. Newell, *Constructing Lives*, 61. Newell cites archaeologist Allen and points out that the internal arrangement of adobe homes at Mission Santa Cruz reflected traditional usage, with fire pits positioned in the middle of the adobe. Padre Ramon Olbés to Governor Solá, July 22, 1821, SBMAL, CMD 2194. The letter was written in thanks to the governor for building these new homes for the mission Indians. The motivation I cite for construction was suggested by Edna Kimbro in a speech given at Mission Santa Cruz shortly before her death in 2003 (uncataloged video). I agree with her assessment, as the previously cited annual report of 1822 and its use of the language of citizenship support this idea.

124. Padre Gil y Taboada to Governor Luís Argüello, May 6, 1823, SFAD document 1525. Gil y Taboada reported that the "Indians have been wanting to leave the mission, in order to return to their lands that God had given them [ancestral lands], where they have worked and lived."

125. Padre Gil y Taboada to Governor Luís Argüello, Santa Cruz, April 5, 1823. There was a discussion about closing Mission Santa Cruz (*suppression*) and sending all Indians to Mission San Juan Bautista, although this did not happen. Padre Vicente Sarría to Padre José Francisco de Paula Señan, San Carlos, April 23, 1823, SBMAL, CMD 2418. Gil y Taboada apparently reversed his thinking, as by June 1823 he no longer advocated the closing of Mission Santa Cruz. Padre Gil y Taboada to Governor Luís Argüello, Santa Cruz, June 8, 1823, SBMAL, CMD 2441.

126. Padre Gil y Taboada to Governor Luís Argüello, Santa Cruz, April 5, 1824, SFAD 1650. Later in the letter Gil y Taboada expresses concern about the Chumash uprising, pointing out "that mission will soon be left with the Epitaph, *Here existed the Mission of Santa Ines.*" The Chumash uprising took place in February 1824, two months before this letter was written.

127. Padre Gil y Taboada to Governor Luís Argüello, Santa Cruz, April 5, 1824, SFAD document 1650.

128. Bouvier, *Women and the Conquest of California*; Hurtado, *Intimate Frontiers*; and Deborah A. Miranda, *Bad Indians*. Sexual violence against

Indigenous women has been explored in depth by these scholars, among others. Miranda is particularly relevant, as she unearthed the Solórsano story about Vicenta Guttierez, Indigenous woman at Mission San Carlos, who identified Padre Antonio Real as her rapist, before his assignment at Mission Santa Cruz between 1833 and 1844. *Bad Indians*, 22-24.

129. An account of this is provided by Rafael González, "1824: The Chumash Revolt," 323-28. While it is frequently referred to as the Chumash Revolt or uprising, I am choosing here to consider it larger than a revolt and instead choosing to refer to it as the Chumash war for independence.

130. Haas, *Saints and Citizens*, 117. These promises came with the provisional constitution (Cortes of Cádiz) of 1812. This will be discussed in more depth in chapter 5.

131. Sandos, "Levantamiento! The 1824 Chumash Uprising," 8-20; "Levantamiento! The 1824 Chumash Uprising Reconsidered," 109-33, and Beebe and Senkewicz, "End of the Chumash Revolt." More recently, Haas has explored the Chumash war from the perspective of the Chumash and their Yokuts allies, *Saints and Citizens*, 116-39. Her account details the alliances between Chumash and Yokuts. Along with issues of citizenship, emancipation, and rights, the Chumash rebellion also involved a rejection of Catholic sexual politics, Monroy, *Thrown among Strangers*, 94-95. Monroy points out that the Chumash war involved a degree of "rebellion against the sexual discipline the missions had instituted," as participants reported a reorganizing of marriage partners according to pre-Catholic arrangement. Monroy also correctly connects this particular dynamic to the assassination of Quintana, which involved the unlocking of the dormitories when the "young people of both sexes gathered and had their fun" (93). I would add that the challenging of imposed Catholic marital practices also mirrors issues surrounding the Quiroste-led attack, discussed in chapter 1. Given the length and breadth of the ongoing fight, I am choosing to refer to it as the Chumash war, rather than the more commonly accepted Chumash uprising.

132. As an example of the ongoing stresses with fugitives, recall the previously cited wholesale evacuation of the mission in February 1819, after a few Indians were told by civilians at the Villa de Branciforte that angry soldiers were headed to arrest them all. Padre Gil y Taboada to Governor Argüello, February 24, 1819, Santa Cruz, SFAD documents 922 and 922-2.

133. Padre Gil y Taboada to Governor Luís Argüello, Santa Cruz, 1824, SBMAL, CMD 2549.

134. For more on his involvement with illicit trade, likely aided by the local Russian Creole Bolcoff, see Farris, *So Far from Home*, 90-96. Geiger also mentions allegations of gambling, smuggling, and "occasional immorality" made against Gil y Taboada (*Franciscan Missionaries in Hispanic California*, 105).

135. Padre Gil y Taboada to Padre Herrera, Santa Cruz, February 8, 1826, SBMAL, CMD 2858. Although Gil y Taboada clearly did not support emancipation, other padres had reason to support some degree of emancipation. With ongoing flights of fugitives and the threat of losing more to disaffiliation, much of the missionaries' concerns related to retention. For example, Padre José Joaquin Jimeno wrote in October 1831 that he believed that the Indians were the rightful owners of the mission goods, and that freedom would further obligate them to continue working the mission lands and not prompt them to leave. Padre José Joaquin Jimeno to Fray Narciso Durán, October 2, 1831, SBMAL, CMAD 3342. Jimeno was a relatively recent arrival at Mission Santa Cruz, performing his first baptism there on December 29, 1830 (SCZB 2175). Haas, *Saints and Citizens*, 119. Gil y Taboada was not alone, as Haas points out that many of the padres of Alta California advocated leaving the state following Mexican independence.

136. Hackel, *Children of Coyote*, 376–77. Hackel, among others, notes that the same decree set forth restrictions on corporal punishment, limiting it to no more than fifteen lashings a week for children. Hackel argues that once Indians learned that they had options and of the missionaries' restrictions, they assumed more power over the padres, citing evidence of work stoppages at Mission San Carlos. At Mission Santa Cruz the evidence suggests that Indigenous residents challenged authority throughout the mission years, not necessarily in response to any imposed restrictions, though it is possible that unreported work stoppages took place.

137. Haas, *Saints and Citizens*, 141. Haas explores the steps toward emancipation in her work, noting that these early movements focused on release from the conditions of *neófia*, the official status of baptized Indigenous "neophytes," and disaffiliation from the missions. They did not include wording about freedom, although many petitions evoked terms like *liberty*.

138. Haas, *Saints and Citizens*, 141–46.

139. Haas, *Saints and Citizens*, 142; Hackel, *Children of Coyote*, 378–79. Haas and Hackel discuss how Indigenous petitioners listed their skilled labor occupations in many of these petitions. Hackel argues that select skilled workers "found opportunities amidst the upheavals of the 1820s and 30s." In Santa Cruz this does not appear to be the case.

140. A Mission Santa Cruz *alcalde* book from that period is missing. Details are discussed in the following chapter, as the missing book appears to have contained records of lands given to emancipated Natives. It is possible that this book also contained records of petitions for emancipation, although the absence of any mention of emancipation or petitions in any other correspondence of the time suggests that petitioning was not practiced at Mission Santa Cruz.

141. Miwok man Lupugeyun or Supegeyun (baptized in 1803 as Pomponio, SFB 2546) served as *alcalde* at Mission Dolores before leading raiding parties in 1818. Fugitive members of Mission Santa Cruz also worked with Pomponio, who took refuge in the mountains of Mak-Sah-Re-Jah north of the mission, near present-day Pomponio Beach and Pomponio Creek. The life of Pomponio is discussed by Goerke, *Chief Marin*, 110–19; and Flores, "Native American Response and Resistance." Ygnacio Martínez to Governor Echeandía, San José, May 21, 1827, SBMAL, CMD 3047. This document mentions that fugitive members of Missions Santa Cruz, San Juan Bautista, and Santa Clara joined a large group of fugitives from Mission San José. This was yet another large group of fugitives who resisted the missions, this one led by a man named Narciso.

142. Cucunuchi (Estanislao, SJB 4471).

143. Estanislao and Yozcolo are discussed in detail by Flores, "Native American Response and Resistance." Earlier studies have explored these individuals and their movements; see Holterman, "Revolt of Yozcolo," 19–23, and "Revolt of Estanislao," 43–44; Gray, *Stanislaus Indian Wars*; and Hurtado, *Indian Survival*, 43–44. Gray's study focuses on the history of Estanislao's people, the Laquisamne, but he also discusses Yozcolo and another revolutionary Yokuts leader, José Jesús, who witnessed the public execution of Yozcolo and followed in the steps of these two leaders.

144. Cook, *Expeditions*, 184–86. Cook transcribes and translates the diaries of Sebastian Rodriguez from the spring of 1828. Rodriguez's accounts include multiple mentions of aid by Indian auxiliaries.

5. Not Finding Anything Else

1. Hartnell, Diary and Copybook. The London-born Hartnell became a naturalized Mexican citizen in 1830, while marrying Maria Teresa de la Guerra, daughter of the one of the wealthiest and most powerful men of Alta California, Don José de la Guerra y Noriega of Santa Barbara. Hartnell visited each mission during the fall of 1839 on the orders of the Governor. He was charged with inspecting the conditions at each mission, and in particular he was checking to see if the Indians were receiving the lands, animals, and equipment promised to them in the secularization laws. His story and role as *Visitador General* are discussed by Pubols, *The Father of All*, 216.

2. Hartnell, "Diary and Blotters." Chugiut's outspoken demands are reminiscent of those of Mission San Carlos Indigenous man Manuel Ventura. Ventura's petition for emancipation included reference to "with profound respect to what is owed"; cited in Haas, *Saints and Citizens*, 143. In this chapter I will often refer to the colonists as Mexicans or Californios, interchangeably. It was in this period that many began to refer to themselves in regional terms more than in Mexican national terms.

3. In this chapter I frequently refer to three distinct Indigenous groups by linguistic and cultural markers: Awaswas Ohlone, Mutsun Ohlone, and Yokuts. Each of the three groups refers to multiple distinct tribal nations. These categories are used here to help trace larger patterns.

4. Haas, *Saints and Citizens*, 9. Haas elaborates: "Emancipation from the condition of *neófia* constituted the first step toward citizenship for Indigenous people in the California missions. . . . The government used the term *emancipation* in its official decrees, but the nature of unfreedom under neófia, and the smaller scale of emancipation, distinguishes this emancipation from emancipation from slavery. The important point is, however, that the process in California involved the problems raised in post-emancipation societies elsewhere and produced similar political resolutions to questions concerning the organization of labor, land, and citizenship." This chapter explores this process for the Indigenous people living in the Santa Cruz region in the 1830s and 1840s.

5. Hackel, *Children of Coyote*, 370. Hackel argues: "After secularization, no matter what their circumstances, Indians had more freedom than in the preceding decades. Perhaps to a greater degree than they had ever known." I strongly disagree with his suggestion that this period offered greater freedoms than before the period of Spanish colonization. For some, like Chugiut and his family, this was probably the case, but for many others it was a time of violence and limited rights.

6. Hackel commented that "the privatization of land holdings in California occurred at a dizzying pace" ("Land, Labor, and Production," 132). In Santa Cruz the Mexican government granted more than 160,000 acres in twenty-one land grants between 1833 and 1844. Over half (56 percent) of these were given to members of the two local elite families: the Castros and Rodriguezes. Rizzo, "Americanos Came like Hungry Wolves," 4.

7. Haas, *Conquests and Historical Identities*, 12. Haas argues that national identities "were forged . . . through the struggles between contending social groups over who had access to the land and to the rights of citizenship." Conflicts about access to land and rights of citizenship similarly characterized the formation of identity in Santa Cruz. This chapter will examine these dynamics, while highlighting examples of fluid identity politics. See also Crandall, *These People Have Always Been a Republic*.

8. Geiger, *Fray Antonio Ripoll's Description*, 11. The failure of the promises of the liberal Mexican era are summed up by Fray Ripoll's report on the testimony of three Chumash men, Andrés, Jayme, and Cristóval. These three men, who had worked closely with the padres, testified about the reasons for the Chumash war (which was discussed briefly in chapter 4). The men reported that conditions had gotten worse in the Mexican era, and one of the men reportedly said,

"Now that they should treat us with even greater kindness, they act in a worse manner."

9. Haas, *Saints and Citizens*, 140.

10. Haas, *Conquests and Historical Identities*, 42. Haas identified the common conflation of the two policies, emancipation and secularization. Secularization, the redistribution of church lands and goods, has usually been the center of analysis, while emancipation, which focused on individual and collective freedoms, has been historically understudied. Meanwhile, Sandos clarified that for Spanish and Mexican officials, emancipation meant "termination of parental control over someone" (*Converting California*, 106). Haas later argued that despite these distinctions, conversations around emancipation similarly dealt with "questions concerning the organization of labor, land, and citizenship" (*Saints and Citizens*, 9).

11. Caplan, *Indigenous Citizens* and "Indigenous Citizenship," 225–47. Caplan argues that Indigenous identities persisted in distinct ways according to regional dynamics, while tracing conversations about Indigenous citizenship and rights to the provisional constitution of 1812 (Cortes of Cádiz). In Santa Cruz, the question of Indigenous citizenship developed slowly and never abolished the subordinate social status, in ways that are similar to other regions of Alta California.

12. Geary, *Secularization of the California Missions*; Hutchinson, "Mexican Government and the Mission Indians," 335–62; Jackson, *From Savages to Subjects*; Jackson and Castillo, *Indians, Franciscans, and Spanish Colonization*, 88–89; Haas, *Saints and Citizens*, 143; Hackel, *Children of Coyote*, 376. Geary offers a comprehensive recounting of the process of secularization, tracing back to early debates around 1813. Hutchinson examines the larger Mexican context alongside regional Californio interests. Jackson examines the larger history of secularization throughout the borderlands, while Jackson and Castillo explore the history of these debates. Haas points out that while the aforementioned Cortes of Cádiz of 1812 included "forming Indian pueblos from mission land and redistributing mission goods among their populations, Echeandía's emancipation plan did not include those rights."

13. Echeandía, Plan para convertir en pueblos las misiones de la alta California, Julio y Agosto de 1830, Huntington Library, Guerra Family Collection, box 6, folder 256. Monroy traces the steps of the liberal Mexican nation toward secularization and the release of mission lands to help stimulate migration to the peripheries, such as in Alta California, *Thrown among Strangers*, 117–25.

14. Hutchinson, "Mexican Government and the Mission Indians"; Hackel, *Children of Coyote*, 384–88; and Salomon, "Secularization in California," 352–53. All three carefully trace these political changes.

15. José Figueroa, Provenciones provisionales para la emancipación de Indios reducidos, 15 de Julio, 1833, in Bancroft, *History of California*, 3:328–29; and Informe en que se opone al proyecto de secularización, October 5, 1833, Bancroft Library, Archives of California, State Papers, Missions and Colonization, book 2, C-A 53, 72. Figueroa argued that "neofitos" were "only recently domesticated" and that they must be "led by the hand towards civilization."

16. Farías would eventually serve as president for Santa Anna on five separate occasions in the 1830s and 1840s.

17. English translation of this plan is found in Decreto del Congreso Mejicano secularizando las Misiones, August 17, 1833, in Bancroft, *History of California*, 3:336.

18. This is discussed by many, but Haas has carefully analyzed the differing steps of emancipation and secularization, arguing that they granted emancipation but also restricted access to land and mandated continued labor in support of "public good" (*Saints and Citizens*, 158). In Santa Cruz much of the mission lands ended up in the hands of the administrators or their Californio allies, and the Indigenous population would not receive any until after 1839.

19. Haas, *Saints and Citizens*, 145. Haas points out that emancipation stood in contrast to the rights of *vecinos* and *pobladores* (working-class citizenry), especially in relation to land rights. In Santa Cruz, the working-class citizenry at the Villa de Branciforte did receive small lots of land.

20. José Figueroa, Reglamento provisional para la secularización de las Misiones de la Alta California, 9 de Agosto 1834, Bancroft Library, Archives of the Californias, Missions and Colonization, C-A 53, Tomo 2: 166–74.

21. A step-by-step rundown of secularization in California is explained in Salomon, "Secularization in California," 355. The formation of "Mexican pueblos" is explored by Michael J. González, *This Small City*. González analyzes the formation of a Mexican pueblo in Los Angeles, pointing out that the Mexican colonists defined themselves in contrast to the local Indians. In Santa Cruz, unlike in Los Angeles, the Mexican populace did fight with Indigenous horse-raiding parties but did not seek to exterminate local Indians. Instead, they integrated them into the lower rungs of their social order. Local Indians were viewed as workers and laborers. Indigenous families who remained independent of the Californio households formed distinct rancherias.

22. The details of the secularization of Mission Santa Cruz were explored in depth by the late Edna Kimbro. Kimbro put together her research on this important area in notes, apparently in the hope of publishing an article to be titled "The Aftermath of Secularization at Santa Cruz Mission, Alta California." My work here draws heavily on her notes and research. See notes in the folder titled Secularization at SCM, Kimbro Archives. Kimbro relied on both Mexican

documents and the account provided by Lorenzo Asisara, found in Amador, "Memorias sobre la historia de California," 102–13. In these accounts Asisara offers insights into the character of the three administrators.

23. Haas, *Saints and Citizens*, 158. Haas points out that this changed from earlier plans, which would have allowed Indigenous *alcaldes* to supervise secularization. According to Lorenzo Asisara's account, he was the *alcalde* at this time, which suggests that he would have overseen the transition. In Santa Cruz, Asisara recalled these administrators for their mismanagement and unwillingness to look out for the interests of the Indigenous community. The consequences of this alteration were significant. It is tempting to consider how Asisara might have handled it. Amador, "Memorias sobre la historia de California," BL, BANC MSS C-D 28, 113.

24. Haas explores the varied Indigenous responses to emancipation at Missions San Juan Capistrano and San Luis Rey, including refusals to work, open revolt, and demands for mission lands or village sites, *Conquests and Historical Identities*, 38–44. Despite these demands, Haas contends, few received legal title to lands they occupied. There was a similar dynamic in Santa Cruz, where land demands resulted in small gains, with even fewer receiving official legal title.

25. The corruption and slow movement toward emancipation at Mission Santa Cruz is similar to other communities in Alta California, as shown by Salomon at Mission San Luis Rey. José María de Echeandía, Decreto de emancipación á favor de neófitos, July 25, 1826, Bancroft, *History of California*, 20:103.

26. E. L. Williams, "Narrative of a Mission Indian, etc.," 47.

27. Padre Antonio Suárez del Real was the brother of Padre José María del Refugio Suárez del Real, who was remembered by Isabel Meadows in her interviews with Harrington for raping a young Indigenous woman, Vicenta Gutierrez, at Mission San Carlos. Meadows's story is explored in detail by Deborah A. Miranda ("Saying the Padre Had Grabbed Her," 93–112). Padre José María Real's story is explored in depth, though without mention of the sexual assault story, by Bacich ("Surviving Secularization," 41–57). Asisara knew both brothers, as Padre José María taught Asisara to read and write in Monterey. Asisara stated, "Like his brother, José María was inclined to vices, especially women" (Mora-Torres, *Californio Voices*, 131).

28. Amador, "Memorias sobre la historia de California," 105. Asisara reported this.

29. Friar Antonio Real to Figueroa, July 14, 1934, SFAD document 2117. Padre Real complained about the potential that the Natives would be troublemakers if freed. In this letter, he mentioned freed Indians from other missions loitering in the area, as well as Clareños (Indigenous people affiliated with Mission Santa Clara) loitering in San José. This suggests that some Indigenous people from

neighboring missions experienced an increase in mobility, revealing uneven practices around liberation between the mission padres.

30. Kimbro notes that Gonzales (VBB 38) was officially appointed *mayordomo* of Mission Santa Cruz on October 31, 1834, and paid forty dollars per annum. She cites "records in Parish Church." Handwritten notes in folder titled Secularization Notes, Kimbro Archives. While I have not encountered this document, the timeline matches up with Asisara's account. Kimbro also claimed that Gonzales served as mayordomo until 1839, when Francisco Soto took over; Kimbro, Ryan, and Jackson, *Como la Sombra Huye la Hora*, 66.

31. Amador, "Memorias sobre la historia de California," 103–10.

32. These are recorded in the Santa Cruz County Deeds (SCCD) book. Gonzales received an adobe house on the west side of the mission plaza, January 1, 1834, SCCD 4:739; Gracia Rodriguez received a home next to Gonzales, SCCD 1:118, 119; and Xuclan (José Ricardo, SCZB 1377) received an adobe house north of Gonzales's adobe on July 11, 1835, SCCD 1:96. Perhaps Xuclan received this home as a reward for concealing the theft that Asisara described. Asisara and Xuclan were longtime friends, and Asisara lived in the home with him by the 1860s.

33. Phillips, *Chiefs and Challengers*, 5–13. Phillips argues that the unwillingness of a group of Southern Californian Indians to work for an administrator after emancipation led to the decline of the mission.

34. Amador, "Memorias sobre la historia de California," 110–12.

35. The Hartnell report on the state of the California missions in 1839 was referenced at the beginning of this chapter. Later in this chapter I will present transcripts of the relevant parts of this report.

36. Haas, *Conquests and Historical Identities*, 45. Haas describes similar patterns in Southern California.

37. A detailed exploration of the distribution of large rancho lands and smaller plots within the Villa de Branciforte, as well as the ensuing loss of lands in the era of United States rule, is found in my master's thesis, "Americanos Came like Hungry Wolves." Indigenous families observed large tracts of lands granted to others before finally receiving some lands for themselves. In *Negotiating Conquest* Chávez-Garcia argues that *Californianas* (Californio women) who held rancho properties were better able to hold power than Native people in the era of U.S. rule. In Santa Cruz three Castro sisters received 36 percent of the total rancho land grants. The largest of these was Martina Castro's Soquel Rancho, which totaled 34,370.4 acres. Martina Castro had lost much of her land by the mid-1850s, as women's land claims fell into "a more subordinate position under the U.S. system" (Montoya, *Translating Property*, 16). For a full examination of Castro's legal battles, including transcripts of the court proceedings, see Powell, "Castros of Soquel," McHenry Library, UCSC, 1994.

38. Michael J. González, "Child of the Wilderness." González argues that debates about the capabilities of the Indians were at the center of disputes between the missionaries and civilians. This pattern does characterize tensions in Santa Cruz. Monroy points out that in Southern California the padres "saw secularization as a nefarious plot the lazy *gente de razón* perpetrated so that they could reap the material harvest of the padres' spiritual sowing. Everyone agreed that the Indians, sixty-two years after the founding of the first mission, remained unready for independence from the priests; but to give the mission lands over to the rancheros, whose minds and bodies lay as fallow as much of the mission lands, would be a scandal." Aside from the correction that "everyone" here did not include the Native peoples, the attitudes of padres like Gil y Taboada in Santa Cruz were similar to those reported by Monroy (*Thrown among Strangers*, 125).

39. Mofras, *Exploration du territoire de l'Orégon*, 216.

40. Pokriots, "Don Jose Antonio Bolcoff," 97–107. Bolcoff was a Russian Creole resident of the local Californio community. He had arrived in the area originally as a translator for the Aleutian seal hunters brought down by Russian colonists. Bolcoff was stationed in Monterey, where he came to work for the Mexican governor before settling into the Villa de Branciforte and marrying one of the prominent Castro sisters. Pokriots points out that Bolcoff's mother, Ana Macoris, was of Itelmen or Kamchadal ethnicity, indigenous to the Kamchatka Peninsula. His mixed heritage is likely how he was conscripted to translate. Bolcoff's story and mixed-blood heritage is also examined by Farris (*So Far from Home*, 126–28).

41. Manuel Jimeno, October 16, 1839, from Kimbro, "Biographical data concerning Lorenzo Olivara."

42. Hackel, "Land, Labor, and Production," 134–35; and Monroy, *Thrown among Strangers*, 100–102. Monroy characterizes this system as a form of peonage, while Hackel synthesizes several views to conclude that it was a system "based upon an exploitation and degradation of Indian labor," 144n. The rancho labor in the Santa Cruz region appear to follow a similar pattern, suggested by the absence of records indicating any type of payment for service. Here I add to their findings by tracing patterns of movement, suggesting that rancho workers more frequently came from mission communities a distance away, not from the mission in closest proximity.

43. "Private letter from Jesus Rodriguez to Rafael Castro asking Indian labor for his wheat," n.d., CPSD, MS 105, Special Collections and Archives, University Library, UCSC, box 2:1, document 148. Castro was notorious for the harsh treatment of his Indian workers. The request from his nephew mentioned the poor work of the Indigenous laborer named Faustino but pleaded, "Don't punish him for this."

44. Monroy, *Thrown among Strangers*, 186. Monroy claims that the rancho labor system "was easier for the Indians than what had come before in the missions and came later on the Anglo ranches," suggesting that the absence of guards supported their satisfaction. In contrast, Haas cites compelled conditions of labor for public works and the lack of respect for Indigenous land rights as reasons why labor relations in this period "continued to bind the former neophytes to many of the same conditions of coercive labor that had characterized their previous state." Haas, *Conquests and Historical Identities*, 40.

45. José María de Echeandía, Reglamento para los encargados de justicía y de la policia de las misiónes del Departamento de San Diego, January 29, 1833, Archives of California, State Papers, Missions and Colonization, Tomo 2:112–15. This law was enacted along with Echeandía's secularization plans. Article 8 states that crimes committed near the missions could be punished by imprisonment in chains for between sixty hours and eight days, with the possibility of an eight-day period of forced labor.

46. Salomon, "Secularization in California," 357–58. Salomon notes that these laws were vague enough to allow for punishment for failure to work for the administrator.

47. In Santa Cruz the situation more closely resembled that described by Haas in *Conquests and Historical Identities*, as rancho owners retained substantial power over Indian laborers. Rafael Castro, owner of the Aptos Rancho, requested that the Indian Petron of San Juan Bautista not only be sent to work for him, but also reimburse Castro "ten pesos and two trips which it cost me to make search for him." "Rafael Castro to William Thompson asking him as *Juez* (Justice) to order Vicente Alviso to send the Indian Petron back to him," March 13, 1847, CPSD, MS 105, Special Collections and Archives, University Library, UCSC, box 3:10, document 337.

48. The common usage of Indigenous people as domestic and field laborers in Mexican and, eventually, U.S. households is examined in depth by Hurtado, "Hardly a Farm House."

49. In the 1840 census, for example, nine-year-old "Juliana, Yndia" is listed under the Mexican couple Guillermo Marce, thirty, and Maria Estefania Robles. This is clearly the recently orphaned Juliana (SCZB 2177), born in January 1831, daughter of Criños (alternatively spelled as *Ynox* at the time of his baptism, Spanish name given as Eleutherio, SCZB 319) and *Mororoli* (alternatively spelled as *Mororoti* at the time of her baptism, Spanish name given as Pantaleona, SCZB 1811). Criños died in 1838 (SCZD 2032), and Mororoli died in 1839 (SCZD 2052).

50. Zappia addresses this term and its linguistic connection to *creer* (to raise): "Spaniards employed this gentler euphemism to justify coercive forms of bondage in towns and missions across New Spain" (*Traders and Raiders*, 2).

51. Like many others, Maria Anna Rodriguez went by various names, as she is also listed as Maria Antonia de Gracia Rodriguez. Juan Gonzales. Kimbro suggests that Gonzales may have been replaced as mayordomo in 1839 after having been caught stealing from the mission during Hartnell's visit, as recounted by Asisara. See Kimbro, Ryan, and Jackson, *Como La Sombra Huye La Hora*, 66.

52. Juan Gonzales served as *padrino* in SCZBS 1928, 1929, 1930, 1931, 1932, 2095, 2239, 2240, 2241, 2243, 2246, 2252, 2254, 2257, 2291, 2292, 2308, 2311, 2312, 2327, 2333, 2334, 2647, 2672, 2674, 2715, 2735, 2748, 2759, 2760, 2771, 2791, and 2860. Of those 1928, 1929, 1930, 1931, 1932, 2095, 2241, 2257, 2312, 2333, 2334, and 2647 were all Indigenous children; the rest were Californio children. Maria Anna Rodriguez served as *madrina* in all but 1928, 1930, 1929, 1931, 1932, 2095, 2333, 2748, 2715, and 2860. Rodriguez also served as *madrina* (and sole godparent) on SCZB 2058, 2059, 2060, 2061, 2062, 2063, 2064, 2065, 2066, 2067, 2068, 2139, 2142, 2169, 2170, 2208, 2216, 2217, 2231, 2238, 2242, 2255, 2272, 2296, 2633, 2660, 2691, and 2710. Of these, twenty-one were Indigenous children: SCZB 2058, 2059, 2060, 2061, 2062, 2063, 2064, 2065, 2066, 2067, 2068, 2139, 2142, 2169, 2170, 2208, 2216, 2217, 2238, 2296, and 2255. They were often godparents for multiple children in the same family. For example, they both served as godparents for the children of Xuclan (José Ricardo, SCZB 1377) and Tupat (Maria Margarita, SCZB 1745), Juan Jose (SCZB 2334) and Maria Guadalupe (SCZB 2647); and also for the children of Chaplica (Agaton, SCZB 1432) and Turiralt (Agustina, SCZB 1808), Maria Prudencia de Jesus (SCZB 2208), Maria Josefa (SCZB 2257), and Pedro Pablo (SCZB 2312). The last family is notable, as Maria Josefa is most likely the same woman who survived into the early 1900s and the ancestor of Amah Mutsun Tribal Band's Lopez family. Josefa Velasquez would tell ethnographer John Aldon Mason in 1916 that she was born at Mission Santa Cruz but "reared in the ranchos around Watsonville." J. A. Mason, October 1916, to San Juan Bautista and Watsonville to see Costanoan informants, reel 23, Ethnological Documents of the Department and Museum of Anthropology, University of California, Berkeley, Banc Film 2216, Bancroft Library.

53. Maria Guadalupe (SCZB 2231) in 1836, 1839, 1840, 1841, 1843, and 1845 censuses, all in *Santa Cruz Mission Libro de Padrónes*.

54. Maria Rosa (SCZB 2314) appears in their household in the 1839, 1840, and 1843 censuses. She then married Carlos (SCZB 2007) in May 1845 (SCZM 857), and from the 1845 census until possibly the 1860 census she appears with her husband and family. In the 1860 U.S. Census a family appears on p. 602, visit 934, with forty-five-year-old Juan Carmel (likely Juan Carlos), thirty-year-old Rosa Carmel, and their ten-year-old son, Jose S. (likely José de los Santos, SCZB 2840, born in April 1850).

55. Testimony of Manuel Rodriguez, 472, Land Case 285 SD, Rancho Tres Ojos de Agua, Documents Pertaining to the Adjudication of Private Land

Claims in California, ca. 1852–92, BANC MSS Land Case Files 1852–92; BANC MSS C-A 300 FILM, Bancroft Library, University of California, Berkeley. David Huallas (SCZB 413), as he was known by the 1840s, was originally named Guallac and baptized as David in 1795, when he arrived at Mission Santa Cruz as a nine-year-old. A Sayanta, Huallas was Chugiut's cousin.

56. Rogerio (SCZB 2076). The 1840 census actually lists this entry as "Rodrigo, Yndio," but he was the same age as Rogerio, and there was no "Rodrigo" in the area at this point. Maria de Alta Gracia Rodriguez had served as housekeeper for Padre Antonio Real and had received an adobe residence on the west side of the mission plaza, next to Gonzales. SCCD 1:118 and 1:119; also discussed in Kimbro, Ryan, and Jackson, *Como la Sombra Huye la Hora*, 178.

57. Census of 1841, *Santa Cruz Mission Libro de Padrónes*.

58. They also appear to have taken in Pedro Pablo (SCZB 2312), the brother of Amah Mutsun Tribal Band ancestor Josefa Velasquez, in the 1843 census, while his siblings appear as *criados* in other households. A young woman, most likely Josefa Velasquez, appears in the household of Juan Jose Castro at the San Andreas rancho in the 1840 census.

59. Haas, *Saints and Citizens*, 140–46. Haas presents multiple petitions stating that "we solicit our freedom." I have found a few similar petitions, although none of them by members of Mission Santa Cruz. For example, Nasario of Mission San Fernando Rey petitioned for liberty for himself and his family in a letter to Don José Castro, prefect of Alta California, August 5, 1839, Monterey Historical Society, Robert B. Johnston Archival Vault, book 9, 495.

60. "Pass from San Jose for two Indians," March 30, 1843, CPSD, MS 105, Special Collections and Archives, University Library, UCSC, box 3:7, document 308; "Pass signed by Ricardo Juan for the Indian Cibero to go to San Andres to work for Juan Jose Castro apparently in 1846," March 28, 1846, CPSD, MS 105, Special Collections and Archives, University Library, UCSC, box 1:14, document 33.

61. "San Jose Juez writes Bolcoff to return two Indians who have run away," November 30, 1841, CPSD, MS 105, Special Collections and Archives, University Library, UCSC, box 4:3, document 386. Villa de Branciforte *alcalde* Joaquin Buelna sent word to Santa Cruz that "natives Jose Artes and Sinforoso are leaving for your jurisdiction, fleeing from justice and taking their wives with them. I hope you will be kind enough to order their apprehension and deliver them to Citizen Jose Maria Flores who is commissioned for the purpose of conducting them to court."

62. Carlos (SJBB 673) and Faustina (Native name unknown, SOLB 1158). The couple married at Mission Santa Cruz (SCZM 840, March 2, 1840). Ynocente (SJBB 3784) was Faustina's daughter from a previous marriage.

63. Amonason (listed as Jose Antonio while living at Rancho San Andrés but baptized as Beda, San Luis Rey baptismal record number [hereafter referred

to as SLRB] 2289) and Guejais (Josefa Antonia, SLRB 1045). A marriage in Santa Cruz in 1859 (SCZM 972) includes the following regarding the bride: "Maria Crecencia, born in San Luis Rey, daughter of Jose Antonio Verona and of Josefa Antonia, both Indigenous and living in Aptos." Crescencia would appear to be SLRB 5129, born in 1830. Rancho San Andrés was in the town that would become Aptos, which suggests that the family continued living in the area into at least the late 1850s.

64. Harrington, "San Juan Report," JPH, microfilm, reel 59, p. 8.

65. Cook, *Expeditions*; and Zappia, *Traders and Raiders*. Cook documents military expeditions into Yokuts territories, while Zappia examines the larger web of trading, raiding, and warfare that connected the Indigenous Southwest, including California.

66. Broadbent, "Conflict at Monterey," 86–101; Phillips, *Indians and Intruders in Central California*. Both authors explore the increase in Indigenous raiding during this period. Broadbent ultimately argues that the horse raiders must been nonmissionized Indians, a mix of Yokuts, Miwok, and Ohlone. I agree that the proliferation of horses helped the Indigenous raiders, but, as Phillips also points out, those involved included many former mission-based people. In fact, familiarity with the local terrain, as well as with the local Indigenous and Californio population, might have been what brought these raiders into the region. For example, late in her life, Californio rancho owner Maria de los Angeles Castro Majors related a story of being spared by a group of these raiders who had chased her on horseback. The attackers relented after one member of the group recognized her from his childhood, when she had helped to heal his wounds. "Once Heiress to a Vast Californian Domain Who is Now Supported by Charity: Maria de los Angeles Castro Majors, the Oldest Survivor of the Castros," Interview by Belle Dormer, *San Francisco Chronicle*, August 16, 1896.

67. Panich, "Indigenous Vaqueros in Colonial California," 187–203. Panich offers an in-depth analysis of the use of horses by mission-based Indigenous people.

68. Reader, "History of the Villa de Branciforte," 16. Reader identifies the body as that of Eugenio Soto, but the murdered man could not be this person, as Soto continued to live in the area at least into the 1850s. In fact, in 1839 Soto married Leandra Ventura Ramos, SCZM 835. His wife, Ramos, SFDB 4179, was an Indigenous woman with parents who were Coast Miwok from the Saclan village and Ramaytush from the San Francisco Peninsula. The couple are ancestors of the Association of Ramaytush Ohlone Chair Jonathan Cordero.

69. Perez, "Reminiscences of Cornelio Perez," 121. The story of a local man, Jose Antonio Amaya, who was killed by arrows during an expedition to recover stolen horses is related in Cook, *Expeditions*, 203. His burial is recorded in SCZD 2104, on October 2, 1844.

70. "Serrano to Santa Cruz 2nd Alcalde relative to a hunt for Indian horse thieves," July 8, 1844, CPSD, MS 105, Special Collections and Archives, University Library, UCSC, box 3:7, document 301.

71. Perez, "Reminiscences of Cornelio Perez," 121.

72. Haas, *Saints and Citizens*, 177–79. Haas points out that the Yokuts formed a similar boundary comparable to the *apacheria* or *comancheria* described in New Mexico territories. See also Hämäläinen, *Comanche Empire*.

73. In addition to these two, the group includes the Huocom man Yocoguehs (Domingo, SCZB 1828) and the Hupnis man Chavan (Buenaventura, SCZB 2182). The exact identities of Cristobal and Guadalupe are less certain, though it is likely that they are also Yokuts. Censuses of 1834 and 1839, *Santa Cruz Mission Libro de Padrónes*. The 1834 census lists a twenty-year-old Tejey man, Cristobal Sandobal, and the 1839 census lists twenty-year-old Cristobal Santual. Although I have yet to corroborate his baptismal entry, this is almost certainly the Cristobal mentioned here, who also shows up living among the other Yokuts in later census lists. I believe that the identical age noted on both records (twenty years) is likely just a mistake made by the enumerator. These include the 1836 census, which lists a Cristobal, Bentura (short for Buenaventura), and Guadalupe in order, and the 1841 census, which lists Cristobal and Guadalupe together in the same Potrero de la Guerta, along with Chulnoquis.

74. "Indians Named to Hunt Down Horse Stealing Indians," June 4, 1843, CPSD, MS 105, Special Collections and Archives, University Library, UCSC, box 4:2, document 377-C.

75. The 1841 census refers to these three areas as "rancherias." *Rancheria* had multiple meanings tracing back to Spanish colonial times. It often referred to Indigenous villages, and during the Mexican years it was used for lands Indians lived on. Lacking the land base and the legal protections of the rancho entities, they were clearly not ranchos like the large land grants handed out to wealthy Californio families. In the case of Santa Cruz, the rancheria designation was simply a diminutive reference to a neighborhood or community. As will show throughout this chapter, there were few legal and civic protections for the rancherias, and local Californios quickly took possession of most of these lands.

76. Hackel, *Children of Coyote*, 393. Hackel shows that in Monterey, Indigenous people gained small tracts spread throughout the greater region. Options appear to have existed in all directions, in small Native pockets. In contrast, Indigenous lands spread out in the direct vicinity of Mission Santa Cruz. The only options for Santa Cruz Indigenous society lay in local lands, movement out of the region, or work on the Californio ranchos.

77. The meaning of "Potrero del Carmen" is not quite clear. The Virgin of Carmel, or *Nuestra Señora de* Monte Carmelo, is a Catholic version of the Virgin

Mary celebrated in coastal towns and often adopted by sailors and fishermen as a patron saint, which could make sense considering the coastal nature of Santa Cruz. Alternatively, in Granada, Spain, a Carmen is a traditional house that includes an annexed enclosed green space, garden or orchard, typically as an extension of the house. There does not appear to be any local connections to Granada, so this seems less likely.

78. The *zanja*, or aqueduct, built to bring spring water to the mission, is currently the site of High Street, which traces a straight line from the entrance of UCSC to the site of Mission Santa Cruz. Much of Santa Cruz Westside became the property of Joseph Ladd Majors, who was granted Rancho Tres Ojos de Agua (Three Eyes of Water), also named for the springs.

79. Their placement is shown on the 1841 census, Libro de Padrones, Monterey Archdiocese.

80. Allen, *Native Americans at Mission Santa Cruz*, 29. Chuyuco is listed in the 1845 census as the shoemaker, the only one in the community. Allen found evidence of shoe leather and materials in one of the adobe rooms, suggesting that Chuyuco and his family had lived there and worked in their home.

81. Chaujana (Simon, SCZB 1866). His status as chief is noted in the baptismal record of his wife, Yujuhilil (Simona, SCZB 1881).

82. Coleto Malimin (SCZD 1493, December 18, 1822), and Agustin Moctó (SCZD 1880, July 2, 1832).

83. SCZD 2043, on December 26, 1838. The records indicate that Huich died of throat issues, the first to appear in the burial records following the smallpox victims.

84. The Quithrathre man Huayiche arrived at the mission four years after Pasqual and Bernardino, in 1821, in a wave of Yokuts. Though it is not clear if he was directly related to them, their proximity in the baptismal rolls and continued collaboration suggest that they were connected through kinship.

85. An 1866 article advocated the protection of the potrero lands, asking, "Would it not be well for the citizens of Santa Cruz to now determine that the Potrero, the land granted to two Indians, shall be forever set apart to those Indians and their children, and that no vandal shall ever despoil them of what the good priest gave them for services rendered?" "Lo! The Poor Indian." *Santa Cruz Weekly Sentinel*, June 23, 1866, 2:6.

86. Movement between mission communities and even between villages and missions had continued since the earliest days of Spanish colonization, as witnessed by the ongoing flights of fugitives and seasonal passes. By the 1820s larger numbers of families began to officially move between missions. For example, the 1822 *Mission Santa Cruz Bi-Annual Report*, original held at the SBMAL, reports that "in these two years four Indians from Mission San Juan Bautista

have settled at this Mission and from here seven have moved there, one has moved to Mission San Carlos and one to Mission Soledad."

87. One example of intermarriage is the union of the New England–born Paul Sweet and the Chumash woman Margarita. The couple, who lived off modern Paul Sweet Road, had children and grandchildren that lived in the area well into the twentieth century.

88. SCLB 1832. Asisara's name is written out in a variety of ways—Asisara, Olivares, and Olivaras. Asisara was born and baptized on August 10, 1820.

89. There is some uncertainty about the origins of Asisara's mother, Luasatme (baptized as Manuela, SCZB 1803). Her baptismal record indicates that she was from the Chalahua village. Edward Castillo believed that she was from the Salinan village, Chalome, near the confluence of Estrella Creek and the Salinas River, "Indian Account of the Decline," 394. Milliken disagrees, and believes that she was from a Yokuts village inland (conversation with the author, December 16, 2013). I agree with Milliken's assessment, considering that she was baptized along with a group of seven others, all from Yokuts nations: Huocom, Tejey, and Apil. Two of the other youth included the children of Huocom chief Suulu (discussed in more depth in the next chapter).

90. Harrison, *History of Santa Cruz County*, 46. Luasatme died in 1833 (SCZD 1908). Asisara described his father as the mission orchardist. This is confirmed by the 1834 census, which lists the sixty-one-year-old Cotoni gardener as "Benancio Olivares" along with his fourteen-year-old son, "Lorenso Olivares." Between them a name is crossed out, that of Llencó's fourth wife, a fifteen-year-old woman from the Yokuts-speaking Hualquelmne people, Maria Blandina (SJBB 3739). She died in late 1836 (SCZD 1973), so it seems that her name was crossed out sometime after her passing. Llencó may have begun taking care of the mission orchard following the arrest of his friend Lacah (Julían Apodeca).

91. Asisara's story is a complex one, worthy of its own study. I have plans to examine his life and accounts in greater detail in a future manuscript. For just a small example of this complexity, the way that Asisara and his father form their names appears to suggest connections to Indigenous linguistic practices. In the 1877 interview with Savage, Lorenzo stated that his father was from the "Asar Rancheria on the Jarro Coast." El Jarro was the name of a mission rancho near modern Davenport, on traditional Cotoni lands. Did the surname 'Asisara' derive from their village, Asar? Furthermore, given the similarity between the names Llencó and Lorenzo, could this be another example of crossover between Indigenous and Spanish names?

92. Harrison, *History of Santa Cruz County*, 46–47.

93. Mora-Torres, *Californio Voices*, 131.

94. Amador, "Memorias sobre la historia de California," 103.

95. Mann, *Power of Song*; Sandos, *Converting California* and "Identity Through Music." Sandos argues that "Spanish occupation offered upward social mobility to Indians who could replicate European sound in European song," 112. One study focuses on the archaeoacoustics of Yokuts rock art, examining links between Indigenous Californian rock art, acoustic settings, and sonic landscapes and spiritual ceremony. The study suggests that artists selected specific acoustic environments for their artwork, arguing that they viewed "songs as essential carriers of knowledge, that sounds assisted the entrance to the underworld or allowed communication with the ancestors" (translation mine), Alarcón and Díaz-Andreu, "Paralelos Etnográficos Sobre Chamanismo y Acústica," 241.

96. Adam, "Rare Old Books," 154. Father Adam related the quotation about giving mission musicians new suits. Eliza Farnham described her experience with the Mission Santa Cruz choir, which she witnessed before a bear-and-bull fight, by noting: "What particularly amused Charlie and myself in the festivities of this day, was the sight of the church choir turned out, after the rites were over, into a street band. Their instruments consisted of a bass and kettle drum, two violins, a triangle and a banjo. The performers, all Indians, appeared to have suffered in some recent encounter; for every head was more or less damaged, the eyes, foreheads, noses, and cheeks, being badly battered, and patched; doubtless a reverent, but certainly not a very reverend choir!" Farnham, *California, In-Doors and Out*, 134.

97. Veytia, *Viaje a La Alta California*, 58.

98. Xuclan (José Ricardo Carrion, SCZB 1377).

99. Xuclan's story will be discussed in more detail in the next chapter. For the trial over his land, see Santa Cruz County Clerk's Office, Rice v. Ricardo, Case 577, M.R. 3.11. Ricardo, with Lorenzo Asisara listed as fellow defendant, successfully defended his title to the lands but then sold his lands to Rice for fifty dollars in the months following the trial. Little has been written about landholding Indians during the Mexican and U.S. eras. For one such study exploring land held in nearby San José, see Shoup and Milliken, *Inigo of Rancho Posolmi*.

100. "Nicolas Gutierres to Administrator of Santa Cruz," March 2, 1836, CPSD, MS 105, Special Collections and Archives, University Library, UCSC, box 1:5, document 43. "Orders that 'the communal funds of the ex-Mission not be burdened' with salaries and gratifications for musicians and singers. He should advise them to assist as they did formerly in the communal functions of the Church without remuneration—for private functions they should be fairly paid by the Father Minister."

101. Maria Tomasa's baptism is found in Mission San Gabriel baptismal record number (SGB) 5472. Her father is found in Mission Santa Barbara baptis-

mal record number (SBB) 93. Asisara and Maria Tomasa's marriage is found in SCZM 823, on February 7, 1807.

102. His return to *Indio* status is reflected in the census of 1845, available in the Libro de Padrones, archive of the Monterey Diocese.

103. Historian Benjamin Madley kindly pointed out the larger impact of the *viruelas Miramontes*, as it was known. Madley brought these sources to my attention. Former Governor Juan B. Alvarado estimated that between 200,000 and 300,000 California Indians died from this epidemic, "Historia de California," 1876, BL, BANC MSS C-D 4:165–66. Henry Cerruti described the spread of the epidemic from Fort Ross through Northern California, "Establecimientos Rusos de California," 1875, BL, BANC MSS, 8. Cook was much more conservative in his estimation, believing it to have killed around 10,000, "Smallpox in Spanish and Mexican California," 183–87.

104. SCZD 2003–40. All but one of these burials were of Indigenous people. The final entry with the words *virulas* written on it (2040) belonged to Jose Joaquin Castro, the owner of the San Andrés Adobe.

105. SCZD 2039, on September 1, 1839.

106. Amador, "Memorias sobre la historia de California," 112.

107. Brave Heart, "American Indian Holocaust," 60–82; Duran, *Native American Postcolonial Psychology*; and Gone, "Community-Based Treatment," 751–62. Within the field of psychology, recent studies, including these by Indigenous scholars, have developed theories and language around the idea of transgenerational trauma. These studies can be applied to historical situations to help understand dynamics of abuse, violence, trauma, and survival.

108. Padre Olbés to Solá, June 23, 1819, SCPSD, box 4, letter 975. We know from Olbés's letter that Quihueimen was in Santa Barbara, as Olbés inquires about the status of Quihueimen and Lacah.

109. As discussed at length in chapter 3, Ètop reduced his sentence and survived. He died before Quihueimen while living in the forests on the periphery of Mission San Carlos.

110. Chesente's burial, SCZD 1240. Rustico's baptism is listed in SCZB 1561, January 7, 1811.

111. Ulalixmi (Coleta) was from a village called Piluri. She arrived at Mission Santa Cruz in October 1826, in SCZB 2112. They married on June 1, 1828 (SCZM 748). Their child, Rosa Maria, is recorded in SCZB 2194.

112. He served as *padrino* in SCZB 2157, 2184, and 2280, the last taking place in 1837.

113. Xuclan was previously mentioned in relation to Asisara. His daughter, Catarina, is recorded in SCZB 2280. Her mother is Tupat (Maria Margarita), a Yokuts from the Huocom village, recorded in SCZB 1745. In almost all records

Xuclan is listed as Ricardo, José Ricardo, or Ricardo Carrion (on the 1834 census); only in his marriage record is his Native name given as Xuclan (sczm 706).

114. His father, Chaparis (Bruno), is recorded in sczb 1292, while his mother, Legem (Bruna), is recorded in sczb 1295. I mention Yaquenonsat here as another Sumus.

115. Quihueimen's burial is recorded in sczd 2034. Two other people died of smallpox the same day. Coincidently, one of them is Chalognis (Vicencio Salvador), another Uypi, like Quihueimen, who was baptized as a two-year-old two days before the seven-year-old Quihueimen, listed as sczb 64.

116. For details on property owned by Rustico, see Allen, *Native Americans*, 29. Rustico, who survived into the late 1870s, would later serve as linguistic informant for Pinart, *Mission Indian Vocabularies*. He will be discussed further in the next chapter.

117. Nonorochi (Maria Alvina), sczb 1900. Their children are Maria Faviana Sebastiana (sczb 2249), Vicente de los Reyes (sczb 2298), Jesus Maria Guadalupe (sczb 2693), and Maria Apolonia (sczb 2745).

118. "Bolcoff sentences Indian Rustico to labor for having menaced his wife with a knife," October 30, 1842, cpsd, ms 105, Special Collections and Archives, University Library, ucsc, box 4:4, document 393. This letter claimed that "the Indian Rustico has threatened his wife with a short dagger" and requested that Rustico be sentenced to labor on public works.

119. Adam, "Rare Old Books," 154–56. Father Joaquin Adam recalled the following story in 1898: "Some years ago while pastor of Santa Cruz I had the pleasure of hearing three survivors of the old mission musicians—Lorenzo, Rustico, and another whose name I cannot recollect. They sang for me on Holy Thursday, Good Friday, and Holy Saturday, and it was a treat to hear them. They sang and played their violins. After service Saturday morning one of them came to my house to know if their services would be needed for Easter Sunday. I told him no; he asked the same question three or four times. I could not see then what his object was in asking so often. I paid them and soon after one of the altar boys ran to me saying, 'Father one of the Indian singers is lying down drunk outside the church door.' As soon as they found out they were free they indulged in their old habit. Another priest told me that when he wanted to secure the Indian musicians for the choir he had to lock them up in a room a day or two before in order to be sure of their services. And the amusing part of it was that, knowing their weak points, they would present themselves and say: 'Father, here we are, lock us up if you wish to have us sing on such a day.'" Despite Adam's misguided suggestion that the relatively recently introduced liquor was an "old habit," this story suggests that liquor became a common means of coping with incredible loss, generations of physical and psychological abuse, and displacement. While

alcohol abuse was commonly reported regarding the former mission Indians, it is worth wondering what role these traumas played in connection with the use of alcohol.

120. Harrington, "San Juan Report," JPH, microfilm, reel 59, p. 22.

121. Testimony of Jose Arana, 93, Land Case 285 SD, Rancho Tres Ojos de Agua. Stories of the "drunken Indian" continued through the ensuing years, which will be explored in the next chapter. It is worth noting that some Californios classified Indians by whether they were drunks or not, as seen with Jose Arana, when he described Chugiut as being "honorable, not a common man, not a drunkard, a good man."

122. Amador, "Memorias sobre la historia de California," 113.

123. The couple appear in the Santa Cruz censuses of 1839, 1840, and 1841. They next appear in the 1842 San Francisco census. In this document Asisara was listed as age twenty-six, employed in the household of Jesus Noe along with two other Indigenous people from Mission Santa Cruz: Francisco and Concepcion.

124. There is no burial record for Maria Tomasa, and she does not appear in any census after 1842. In the 1845 Santa Cruz census, Asisara is listed as a widow. There is a chance that SCAD 3311 of an unidentified Maria Tomasa, buried in 1845, is Asisara's wife, but it seems unlikely, despite the appropriate time frame. The burial note says that Maria Tomasa was an Indian woman from Mission San Carlos.

125. Little study has been devoted to the Indigenous forces under Vallejo. It is unclear whether they were compelled into service or whether this was a voluntary strategy to earn status.

126. Harrison, *History of Santa Cruz County*, 46. Asisara claims he was at the San Francisco Presidio when Fremont arrived. The participation of Native people in the Californian theater of the Mexican-American War has been severely understudied. Passing mention is given by Phillips, *Chiefs and Challengers*, 61; and Rawls, *Indians of California*, 82–105. This absence is best addressed by Haas, "War in California, 1846–1848." DeLay explores the central role played by Indigenous southwestern nations in this war in *War of a Thousand Deserts*.

127. In the 1845 Santa Cruz census, twenty-six-year-old widow "Lorenso Olivara" is the first listed for the Native American portion. He is listed as the head of Chugiut's household, which I will consider shortly.

128. "When P. Gomez, Slayer, Defied *Alcalde* Blackburn after Killing Gomez' Wife, Belle Dormer," *Santa Cruz Sentinel*, October 8, 1932, 7:1. Dormer claimed that she heard this from E. L. Williams, the man who interviewed Asisara in 1877. Asisara was not the only local Indigenous man to have an affair with a Californiana. A few years before the Gomez affair, the Partacsi Cajastaca youth

Jubenal de la Cruz (SCZB 1998) was involved in a scandal with Lucia Bolcoff, the daughter of the Russian Jose Bolcoff. Jubenal and Lucia ran away together, infuriating her father and starting a scandal that resulted in numerous testimonies regarding the couple's activities north of town. The complex story testified to a high degree of social mixing between local Indigenous people and the Californios and included mention of Lucia staying at the home of Xuclan and his Huocom wife, Tupat (Margarita, SCZB 1745). Another person mentioned in this account is Cecilia (SCZB 1951), the daughter of Chugiut. Lucia Bolcoff, uncataloged Mexican Archives of Monterey County, March 8, 1842, Starr Gurke translations, UCSC, McHenry Library.

129. "When P. Gomez, Slayer, Defied *Alcalde* Blackburn After Killing Gomez' Wife," Belle Dormer, *Santa Cruz Sentinel,* October 8, 1932, 7:1.

130. Hartnell, "Diary and Blotters." As seen with the Potrero de la Huerta (orchard), the padre did not appear to get his wish to keep the orchard.

131. In the mission documents he appears repeatedly as Geronimo Miguel Chigiut, Chaguit, Chugiat, Chugiut, or some other variation of his Native name. In the 1834 census the fifty-one-year-old Sayanta mason appeared as "Geronimo Pacheco Leal." His baptismal *padrino* was a Spanish soldier named Miguel Pacheco, which was likely the source of his surname. Like many at Mission Santa Cruz, he appeared to have kept his Native name (Chugiut) as his surname into the 1840s.

132. SCCD 1:47, November 27, 1839. See also Hackel, *Children of Coyote*, 369–70. Hackel points out that "select Indians—namely craftsmen, former mission officials, survivors with political and economic ties to the Franciscans or influential californios, and those with large and extended family networks—found opportunities in the midst of the upheavals." Chugiut was both a skilled craftsman (mason) and had an extended kinship network, and his acquisition of these resource-rich lands fits the pattern identified by Hackel.

133. Haas, *Saints and Citizens*, 100–101. Haas argues that rocks played a significant role in Indigenous spiritual life, as their "cracks, crevices, and holes served as portals to the supernatural." Furthermore, Haas points out that shaman often gained control of special rock sites. Chugiut's control over the rock quarry may have held meaning beyond the control of a significant resource. Also see Rivera Andía, *Non-Humans in Amerindian South America*; Kimmerer, *Braiding Sweetgrass*; and Cruikshank, *Do Glaciers Listen*.

134. Testimony of claimant Nicolas Dodero, 591, land case 285 SD, Rancho Tres Ojos de Agua. Details regarding Chugiut, his family, and his engagement with the Californio community were revealed in a series of interviews concerning the land grant known as Tres Ojos de Agua (Three Eyes of Water), referring to the three freshwater springs in the region. The more than six hundred pages

of interviews concerning the boundaries of this land grant focus repeatedly on the exact location of Chugiut's lands, as they marked one of the boundary lines. The interviews, recorded in 1862, provide many details regarding the lives, work, and social standing of Chugiut, his family, and his extended kin network. Not surprisingly, while many of the European and U.S. newcomers interviewed knew little about Chugiut, members of the Californio community provide great detail.

135. Joseph Frey responded that Chugiut spoke "Spanish and Indian" (Testimony of Frey, 300, Land Case 285 SD, Rancho Tres Ojos de Agua). Chapter 6 will examine examples of the continued use of sweat lodges. In 1916 Maria Josefa Velasquez related to ethnographer John Aldon Mason stories of witnessing Kuksui dances in her youth, in the 1840s. This too will be discussed in more detail in the next chapter. Both practices continued into the era of United States occupation.

136. Barbara (SCZB 976) was born at Mission Santa Cruz on January 8, 1802, to two parents from the Cajastaca village. Barbara and Chugiut married on July 29, 1817 (SCZM 593).

137. SCZB 1783 (Barvara), 1829 (Norverta), 1951 (Cecilia), 2045 (Rudesindo), 2094 (Acursio), 2136 (Dolores), 2162 (Fortunato), 2186 (Maria Candelaria), 2205 (Maria del Carmen), and 2238 (Luis de los Reyes).

138. Acursio married a woman named Carmen (most likely the mission-born Taratac-, Chitactac-, and Cajastaca-descended woman baptized as Maria del Carmen, SCZB 2189) on November 12, 1844 (SCZM 856).

139. Gabriel is listed on the 1845 census as being from Bodega, a reference to Bodega Bay, Coast Miwok territory just north of San Francisco. The couple married on March 2, 1840 (SCZM 838).

140. Testimony of Roman Rodriguez, 172, Land Case 285 SD, Rancho Tres Ojos de Agua. Their seasonal movement was noted in the interview with Rodriguez, who lived in the mission plaza. Later in the interview, when asked about Chugiut's home, Rodriguez answered, "I saw the house for the first time forty years ago—the house was only there for the Indian to take care of his crop but not for the Indian to live in for the Indian was living in the mission" (198). Juan Jose Castro recalled that Chugiut "had two sowing places. In the upper one he sowed wheat and in the lower one summer crops" (230).

141. Haas, *Saints and Citizens*, 141.

142. Testimony of Arana, 93, Land Case 285 SD, Rancho Tres Ojos de Agua.

143. Testimony of Arana, 93, Land Case 285 SD, Rancho Tres Ojos de Agua. Arana, when asked whom he bought from when Chugiut was not around, replied, "Of his daughter [Cecilia] or his wife [Barbara]." When asked how he knew it was Chugiut's produce, Arana replied: "I did not know. Geronimo

would go and cut what I wanted. At times I considered that what I purchased was raised there, Geronimo was the head of the other Indians and when he had not what I wanted he would take from the other Indians and pay them for it."

144. Testimony of Roman Rodriguez, 195, Land Case 285 SD, Rancho Tres Ojos de Agua. Rodriguez: "Before he had his liberty from the Priests he used to go out there to cultivate these same lands, and after he had his liberty from the Priests he went there to live."

145. Testimony of Roman Rodriguez, 195, Land Case 285 SD, Rancho Tres Ojos de Agua, 273. Bautista Dabadio, a fifty-five-year-old carpenter who had arrived in the area in 1843, when asked how to locate where exactly Chugiut's home had stood, testified that he had found "pieces of large stones that had had holes in the centre with which the Indians used to ground the acorns."

146. Testimony of Roman Rodriguez, 195, Land Case 285 SD, Rancho Tres Ojos de Agua.

147. Testimony of Roman Rodriguez, 195, Land Case 285 SD, Rancho Tres Ojos de Agua, 93.

148. This is the aforementioned Huallas (Davis), whose orphaned children worked on the rancho of Juan Gonzales. Siboo (Canuto) was a Tomoi man who arrived at Mission Santa Cruz in early 1806 (his name sometimes appearing as Sieboo or Siboó). In the land case documents, multiple interviewees referred to Siboo as a relative or cousin of Chugiut. In response to a question regarding Chugiut's second house, Rafael Castro said that "there lived there also a man named Canuto, living there together in a body or as one family. Canuto had land sowed there and living together like wolves." Testimony of Castro, 214, Land Case 285 SD, Rancho Tres Ojos de Agua. The last comment is seemingly a critique of the more expansive Indigenous kinship conception of family and communal living. The presence of Yrachis was also noted by Castro. Testimony of Castro, Land Case 285 SD, Rancho Tres Ojos de Agua, 284–85.

149. January 16, 1823, SFD 1424. David served as *alcalde de hombres* (mayor of the men), SCZM 524–31 (1811) and 556a–59 (1815), SCZB 1568. He also served as *procurador* (deputy).

150. SCZD 2017, July 28, 1838.

151. Testimony of Elihu Anthony, 138, Land Case 285 SD, Rancho Tres Ojos de Agua. Anthony, an American entrepreneur who moved here from New York, like many of his countrymen, could not identify Chugiut or any other Indian specifically (this theme will be explored in depth in chapter 6). Yet he offered his description of these lands: "There was near the Laguna or springs that makes the stream that passes Majors house this mill, to the south and west side of the spring to the best of my recollections. There was a kind of Indian village, part of them on one side and part of them on the other. I will not be certain, they were

there circling about the spring." It is possible that he was observing the distinct Potrero and Westside lands, although he may have just noted the distribution of houses among Chugiut's kin. Regardless, his observations about the centrality of the spring testify to its importance.

152. Testimony of Paul Sweet, 118, Land Case 285 SD, Rancho Tres Ojos de Agua. Sweet reported that he would buy rock from Chugiut. Rafael Castro testified that he had "taken lime out from there [the rock quarry] by the permission of Geronimo" (222).

153. Chugiut was listed as a mason in both the 1836 and 1845 census. He would have learned it early on and was surely one of the young men trained in the early 1800s, as discussed in chapter 2.

154. Dabadio testified in response to a question about how long Chugiut had lived near the laguna: "All the time that I knew him I have known him to live in that house. The house was well known, being covered with tile. He was living there when I came to Santa Cruz in 1843. I then went there to buy leeches from him that were found in the laguna" (273).

155. Testimony of Frey, 301, Land Case 285 SD, Rancho Tres Ojos de Agua.

156. Testimony of Frey, 302, Land Case 285 SD, Rancho Tres Ojos de Agua.

157. Unfortunately, the majority of Indian land grants and documents are lost. As the late Edna Kimbro explains: "Early Santa Cruz land ownership is nearly impossible to research successfully because the official land records previous to 1847, including those of the mission and the Villa de Branciforte are missing and have been well over 100 years. Such records are known to have existed up until 1841 when Bolcoff mentions having recorded a grant 'in the respective book in my charge.' They seem to have gone astray sometime between then and 1847 when William Blackburn began 'Alcalde Book A' August 1, 1847, in which to record his indiscriminate grants of Mission lands to all comers. In 1862 when the validity of some of Blackburn's grants to San Franciscans was challenged in court, the Supreme Court of California heard testimony from Emmanuel Rodriguez, former *alcalde* of Santa Cruz. Rodriguez said of the land records, 'They were destroyed at the time Fremont came here; I mean by their being destroyed, the house [courthouse] was locked up and they thrown away.'" See folder titled Secularization at SCM, Kimbro Archives.

158. The surviving records are found in the SCCD. For Xuclan (José Ricardo Carrion), see SCCD 1:96. Jotoime (Matias, SCZB 934), SCCD 1:29. A 1986 study by archaeologist Rob Edwards and Edna Kimbro examined a 1931 aerial photo that revealed lines of cultivated fields on the Great Meadow area of the UCSC campus. They concluded that the fields most likely belonged to Jotoime, "Mission Fields in the Great Meadow, University of California, Santa Cruz," November 1986, copy on file in the Edna Kimbro Archives. This conclusion and a brief sketch of

Jotoime are also printed by Edwards, Cabrillo College Archaeological Program, Annual Report 1986-87. Jotoime also died during the smallpox epidemic of 1838 (SCZD 2019). His brother Aspan (Pacifico, SCZB 937), appears to have died of a fever a few months before smallpox hit the area (SCZD 1996). Their father, Rojuisi (Juan Antonio, SCZB 991), may have been a Cajastaca chief, as he had multiple wives and at least six children. Could his standing have influenced Jotoime's land title? Jotoime's daughter, Maria Agueda (SCZB 2194a), will be discussed in chapter 6.

159. This record is rewritten into the SCCD, as the originals were likely lost with the *alcalde's* book. SCCD 1:47. The record was written by Jose Bolcoff and states that "Miguel Geronimo Pacheco has petitioned for his benefit and that of his family a 100 vara lot for tilling."

160. SCCD 1:47. This title was given to an "Indian Correcto Fondador," which most likely is a reference to "Canuto," Siboo's baptized Spanish name.

161. SCCD 1:47.

162. SCCD 1:47. The connection between the Majors family and local Indigenous families will be discussed in chapter 6. The transfer to Majors claimed that "On [April 4, 1843] there appeared the Indian Miguel Geronimo in my office to have transferred his rights to the tilling land and the house lot as expressed in the title, to Don Jose Majors, to which there appeared as witness Don Rafael Castro."

163. SCCD 1:590-1. Farnham died shortly after the exchange, but his wife, the famous feminist Eliza Farnham, came to Santa Cruz and lived on these lands for many years. Her memoirs and recollections of Santa Cruz are discussed by Jo Ann Levy, *Unsettling the West*. Throughout her account there are numerous mentions of unnamed Indians who tended lands around her, presumably Yokuts individuals (59). The title included the names of Punis (Bernardino), Chulnoquis (Pasqual), Punis's stepson Angel (SCZB 2296), the Huocom man Guimayach (Mariano, SCZB 1799), Huocom chief Suulu (Pedro, SCZB 1862), the Quitchas Yokuts man Huayiche (Fidel, SCZB 1976), his son Carlos (SCZB 2007), the Chipuctac Mutsun man Chacello (Hilario, SCZB 860), and the Huocom man Cuyoju (Andres, SCZB 1864).

164. Records of Jose Arana's petition to Mexican authorities is copied into the Santa Cruz deeds book. Original land petitions from the Mexican era (1821-48) are mostly lost in the aforementioned missing *alcalde's* book. Arana's petition claimed that "having negotiated to make a garden of fruit trees I petition to be granted me a piece of land situated on the bank of the river and also at the edge of the Camino Real which leads to the pueblo, below or adjoining the land of the Indians Pascual and Fidel, the dimensions of which are 500 varas north and south and 150 from east and west, that said land may be used for the work

of agriculture and, to the best advantage provide for the maintenance of my increasingly numerous family. . . . Santa Cruz, March 10, 1844." SCCD 1:11.

165. University of California, Santa Cruz, McHenry Library, Pre-Statehood Documents, Uncatalogued Starr Gurke Translations, February 12, 1847, reel 13, p. 1013.

166. Carlos (SCZB 2007) and Punis appear on the previously cited sale of some of these lands.

167. This quotation by Arana was previously cited, 93, Land Case 285 SD, Rancho Tres Ojos de Agua.

168. UCSC, McHenry Library, Pre-Statehood Documents, Uncatalogued Starr Gurke Translations, February 12, 1847, reel 13, 1013. There is no record for the outcome to the petition request.

169. Hackel, *Children of Coyote*, 404. Hackel finds the same pattern in Monterey.

170. Rowland Files, Pre-Statehood Documents, McHenry Special Collections, Rowland Files, B-1, 1062.01, County Government, UCSC. The county clerk, Peter Tracy, will reappear briefly in chapter 6, benefitting by gaining lands at a time when Indians were forbidden from holding them. It appears that Tracy learned how to navigate U.S. legal policies regarding Indians.

171. Barbara last appears in the census of 1841. The 1845 census lists Chugiut as a widower.

172. By the 1840s Graham and his followers began to actively challenge Mexican authorities, leading to numerous skirmishes and even the arrest and temporary deportation of Graham. See Nunis, *Trials of Isaac Graham*. This book does not examine the Mexican-American War in depth, as I focus on the perspective of Indigenous people. For the most complete study of the war, see Harlow, *California Conquered*.

6. Fantasies of Ancient Indians

1. Story of the fire was reported in a short newspaper blurb as follows: "The oldest resident of Santa Cruz, Justiniano Roxas, came near ending his earthly career this week. He sloops in his little cabin, and is cared for by another Indian living near. During the night the cabin took fire, and he was nearly suffocated by the smoke, before his guardian rescued him." "Local," *Santa Cruz Enterprise*, March 5, 1875, 3:1. He must have gone in and out of the Sisters of Charity's care, as an article from the fall before this fire mentioned that Roxas was "still alive and enjoying the hospitalities of the Sisters' Hospital in Santa Cruz," "The Oldest Living Inhabitant of California Photographed—A Cabinet Picture for the Vatican," *Santa Cruz Weekly Sentinel*, September 5, 1874, 3:3.

2. O'Brien, *Firsting and Lasting*, 116–18. O'Brien examines narratives that celebrate the supposed extinction of Indigenous peoples by recognizing someone as the

"last" member of their community. She points out that these narratives celebrated Indigenous extinction as a necessary step in the maturation of U.S. modernity.

3. "Old Times Roxas," *Santa Cruz Sentinel*, December 27, 1873, 3:2. The story of Roxas has been explored in depth by Rizzo and Cothran, "Many Lives of Justiniano Roxas."

4. SCZD 2699 on March 12, 1875, just over a year after the *Sentinel* article.

5. Madley, "Unholy Traffic in Human Blood and Souls."

6. A recent study has shown that during the gold rush, tribal communities in Central California "actively resisted, negotiated, adapted and endured in the face of colonial violence." This study also reveals the rich and complicated history of Indigenous migration and diaspora in those years, as a diversity of tribal peoples relocated to California during that time. See Shaler, "Mariposa and the Invasion of Ahwahnee," ix.

7. The genocidal policies of early U.S. occupation are explored in depth by Lindsay, *Murder State*; Madley, *American Genocide*; and Trafzer and Hyer, *Exterminate Them*.

8. Cothran, *Remembering the Modoc War*. Cothran focuses on the ways that narratives about the Modoc War worked to justify land grabs and genocide while absolving guilt.

9. Much of the labor opportunities for Native Americans in California and Mexico could be considered debt peonage; see Reséndez, "North American Peonage."

10. Madley, "Unholy Traffic in Human Blood and Souls."

11. Many historians have repeated these misconceptions about extinction, referring to the "demise of the Indians" who "stood at the brink of doom" in the era of United States occupation; see Monroy, *Thrown among Strangers*, xvii and 189, respectively. See also Secrest, *When the Great Spirit Died*; and Heizer, *Destruction of California Indians*.

12. 1850 U.S. Federal Manuscript Census.

13. 1852 California Manuscript Census.

14. 1860 U.S. Federal Manuscript Census.

15. 1870 U.S. Federal Manuscript Census.

16. "First Federal Census Gave Us Six Hundred," *Santa Cruz Evening News*, March 25, 1930, 12:1. Copy of article found in Edna Kimbro Archives, folder on "Indians and Census." While Boyle was referencing the 1860 census, which did report more than two hundred Indians, it is likely that the 1850 and 1870 census enumerators were similarly instructed.

17. Griswold del Castillo, *The Treaty of Guadalupe Hidalgo*, 72–86.

18. Here I provide an overview of the development of legal implications for Indians and the California Conventions. A detailed account of this is provided by Madley, *American Genocide*, 145–56.

19. Almaguer, *Racial Fault Lines*.

20. See Jacobson, *Whiteness of a Different Color*, and Roediger, *Wages of Whiteness*.

21. Sandos, "Between Crucifix and Land."

22. Madley, *American Genocide*, 146–49.

23. Fourcrier, "Sailors, Carpenters, Vineyardists." Sansevaine, the nephew of Californio Jean-Louis Vignes, one of the original viticulturists in the state, had lived at the Villa de Branciforte since the early 1840s. Larkin was closely tied with the local Californio community and is the namesake of Larkin Valley Road, which runs between Aptos and Corralitos.

24. Pubols, *Father of All*, 284–87. José de la Guerra would have been nearly seventy at the time of these meetings. By this time, his sons were in control of his estate and political responsibilities. Pubols explores the de la Guerra family's perspectives on these meetings in depth.

25. The details of these debates is covered by Madley, *American Genocide*, 152–56.

26. Ross Browne, Debates in the Constitutional Convention of California. These debates have been examined in other works, most prominently in Heizer and Almquist, *Other Californians*, and Montes, "See How I am Received." For more on one of the principal opponents to Indian enfranchisement, California senator William Gwin, see St. John, "Unpredictable America of William Gwin."

27. These distinctions are explored in more depth in earlier chapters. Of course, colonial contact changed Spanish and Indigenous people alike; the idea that those outside of the missions lived in an uninterrupted continuum of tradition is flawed.

28. This distinction is also similar to the *casta* designations *de razon* (with reason) and *sin razon* (without reason), which were used to distinguish between those living in accordance with Spanish values and those not.

29. The treaties were negotiated as an exchange for the gold mining, as examined by Phillips, *Indians and Indian Agents*.

30. Larisa K. Miller, "Secret Treaties with California's Indians."

31. Johnston-Dodds, *Early California Laws and Policies*. Indian indenture in relation to Rancho Guajome in San Diego County is specifically examined by Magliari, "Free Soil, Unfree Labor," 349–89. A more recent study focuses on Sacramento; Magliari, "Free State Slavery," 155–92.

32. For the most comprehensive study of California genocide, see Madley, *American Genocide*. Following publication of Madley's book in 2016, California governor Jerry Brown publicly acknowledged this history of genocide. In June 2019 Governor Gavin Newsom issued an apology. McNally, "Dark History Hits Home."

33. McNally, "Dark History Hits Home," 354.

34. McNally, "Dark History Hits Home," 351. The devastating effects of these policies of outright extermination have been explored by a few scholars beginning with Heizer, *Destruction of California Indians*; and Secrest, *When the Great Spirit Died*. Survival in the face of these campaigns is emphasized by Hurtado, *Indian Survival*. Also see Lindsay, *Murder State*.

35. To date, I have been unable to locate any records of actual payments for Indian scalps in Santa Cruz County. This is substantiated by the work of Madley, who also found no local ties to scalp bounties.

36. "No More Bounty on Scalps," *Santa Cruz Weekly Sentinel*, November 8, 1873, 3:1. Ten years earlier the same paper had run an ad informing that "the territorial Legislature of Arizona has passed a law giving a bounty of $100 for each scalp of an Apache Indian. Here is a chance for enterprising hunters to make a fortune." "Scalp Bounties," *Santa Cruz Weekly Sentinel*, November 26, 1864, 3.

37. Madley, "California and Oregon's Modoc Indians." The Modoc War, which was really the war waged against the Modoc people who attempted to retain access to their homelands, has been analyzed by Madley. The ways in which narratives about the Modoc war were used to justify settler colonialism have been examined by Cothran, *Remembering the Modoc War*. See also McNally, *Modoc War*.

38. "Lo! The Poor Indian," 2:6. Later the same year an article appeared about the sale of lands to a Mr. Phillips. The land in question was referred to as "the tract of land known as the King Estate, situated on the Potrero, and occupied in part by Indians." "Improvements," *Santa Cruz Weekly Sentinel*, November 3, 1866, 3:1.

39. Huayiche (Fidel, SCZB 1989) and Chulnoquis (Pasqual, SCZB 1647), discussed in chapter 5. Chulnoquis was one of Coleto's sons. He eventually died in Watsonville (Watsonville burial record 197, on July 10, 1887), while Huayiche's burial is unrecorded. The article suggests that one of them had recently died, which must mean that Huayiche died in the 1860s.

40. The newly established U.S. courts in Santa Cruz had prosecuted incoming immigrants for selling liquor to Indians as early as 1848; see Rowland Card Files, SCPSD, box B-1, card 289.01–.05, June 16, 1848, and box C, cards 150–52: Court of Sessions, December 1–February 4, 1851. The Alcalde Records, Santa Cruz Pre-Statehood Documents, box B-1, card 361.02, 1850, report that "any person who shall be convicted of selling or giving any intoxicating liquors to any Indian shall for each offense be fined in a sum of not less than $50 nor more than $200 at the descrssion [*sic*] the court." Still, it is clear that alcohol was a problem for the local Indigenous community, although, as I elaborated in chapter 5, alcohol abuse was likely closely tied to transgenerational trauma.

41. Some examples of the more intense incidents will be discussed in depth in the next chapter. Some newspaper reports reported single incidents like this: "Manual Schicano, a poor deluded Indian, who had got too much of the pale face's tangle-foot, so that he was unable to navigate, was taken in by the local police. Judge Curtis looked Manual in the eye; fined him ten dollars for his frolic, to go henceforth and sin no more. Paid eight dollars, laid one day in jail, and was allowed to hunt up the other dollar among his friends" ("Police Jottings," *Santa Cruz Weekly Sentinel*, September 28, 1878, 3:5).

42. Ironically, the same year this article was written, 1866, the last landholding Mission Santa Cruz survivor, Xuclan (José Ricardo), would lose his lands. His story will be discussed later this chapter.

43. Stacey L. Smith, *Freedom's Frontier*. Smith's study examines the contradictions of slavery and freedom in early U.S. California. Other studies that have looked at this include Sandos, "Between Crucifix and Land"; and more in depth, Madley, "Unholy Traffic in Human Blood and Souls."

44. Official requests for Indian children as indentured servants can be found in the Center for Sacramento History, Indian Indentures: 1861 and 1862, filed March 4, 1861, and January 28, 1862. None of these examples is from Santa Cruz, yet the practice existed before official legislation. In the 1860 census, for example, the following youth were listed as Indian servants in white households: ten-year-old Samuel Offen, p. 634, visit 1101; sixteen-year-old Louis Cannarth, p. 625, visit 1009; sixteen-year-old Francisca (no last name), p. 577, visit 491; and fifteen-year-old Refugio (no last name), p. 584, visit 554.

45. For the one in four household estimation, see Madley, "Unholy Traffic in Human Blood and Souls," 656–57. For the omission of indentures and wards, see Magliari, "Masters, Apprentices, and Kidnappers."

46. "In Jail," *Santa Cruz Weekly Sentinel*, July 16, 1864, 2:2.

47. "Lo! The Poor Indian," 2:1.

48. "Thieves About," news of the crime, *Santa Cruz Weekly Sentinel*, March 3, 1866, 3:1. "Convicted," news of the trial of "Ramon Queunto, the Indian," *Santa Cruz Weekly Sentinel*, March 10, 1866, 3:1. The last article mentions that in addition to his theft from Theodore Winterhalder, Ramon was also tried for stealing a bridle from Mr. Imus. Curiously, both Imus and Winterhalder would be among the settlers to have their properties targeted for arson in the story discussed in the next chapter.

49. Carlos (SCZB 2007). Carlos was killed by John Cantwell at the local Bausch Brewery on February 28, 1877. Cantwell was tried and sentenced to fifteen years for the murder, see Pre-Statehood Documents, UCSC, Rowland Collection, A-2, card 53.

50. Reader, *Brief History of the Pajaro Property Protective Society*. Reader covers the history of local vigilantism and Matt Tarpy, who himself was lynched in March 1873.

51. Gonzales-Day, *Lynching the West*. Nine lynchings are documented within Santa Cruz County; seven more in the township of Pajaro, which is situated on the Monterey County side of the boundary between Santa Cruz and Monterey Counties; and one more documented in San Juan Bautista, in San Benito County. Of the seventeen men lynched, all were noted as being Mexican, Californio, Mestizo, or Indian, except for the aforementioned Tarpy and a Scottish man named John Clare.

52. "Execution," *Santa Cruz Weekly Sentinel*, September 22, 1866, 2:2.

53. *Santa Cruz Weekly Sentinel*, December 23, 1865, 3:1.

54. "Terrible," *Santa Cruz Weekly Sentinel*, February 17, 1866, 2:1.

55. Geoffrey Dunn, "Santa Cruz's Most Notorious Lynching," *Good Times Santa Cruz*, November 12, 2013.

56. Gonzales-Day, *Lynching in the West*. The photo of Arias and Chamales is the focus of Gonzales-Day's third chapter. He argues that these photos, which were often used as postcards and western memorabilia, were intended to strike fear in Mexicans and Indigenous peoples.

57. "Murder and Lynching," *Santa Cruz Weekly Sentinel*, May 21, 1870, 2:3.

58. The details of the voyage are found in the testimonies of Apolinaria Lorenzana. See Beebe and Senkewicz, *Testimonios*, 165–92.

59. The report of the specific assignments of each of the orphans is found in AGN, Californias, vol. 41, expediente 1 BIS, 209. Jackson, *Race, Caste, and Status*. In the Spanish colonial world, an elaborate hierarchical caste system (*sistema de castas*) was used to explain race and heritage—built around many variations of Native American, African, and Spanish ancestry. *Mestizo* was one of these categories and designated a person with Native American and Spanish parents. The *sistema de castas* was used to justify racial hierarchies, as Spanish-born people (*peninsulares*) held higher positions than American-born Spaniards (*criollos*). In California, for example, the Spanish prohibited local Native people (*Indios*) from using firearms, lighting fires, or riding horses. These ideas were spread through *casta* paintings from Spain, which taught stereotypes of superiority and inferiority; see Carrera, *Imagining Identity in New Spain*.

60. Maria Romualda Petronila Vasquez's baptism is recorded at Santa Barbara Presidio baptismal number 187. Her mother was Maria Leocadia (SCLB 338, born March 3, 1782), an Indigenous woman born at Mission Santa Clara to her father Huajolis or Gusilis and mother Yunen or Ylinen. Huajolis (Pablo, SCLB 738) and Yunen (Pelagia Maria, SCLB 714) were among the earliest Native Ameri-

can families to relocate to Mission Santa Clara, from a Tamyen Ohlone-speaking tribe south of the mission, listed as "Rancheria de San Juan Bautista."

61. Details about the life of Maria Romualda and the migration of young Macedonio, along with the group of children from the Lorenzana orphanage, are examined in my article for the *Santa Cruz Museum of Art & History Journal*, "He Came from an Indian Kingdom."

62. Lorenzana is listed as a "laborer" in the censuses of 1839 and 1845. For these, see *Santa Cruz Mission Libro de Padrónes*; and Jackson, "Villa de Branciforte Census."

63. Lorenzana was cited as regidor in the notes in "Proceedings of the trial of Francisco Pinto for not having done right by Margarita Castro," May 14, 1838, CPSD, MS 105, Special Collections and Archives, University Library, UCSC, box 2:3, 170. He is also noted as "secretario" in 1834, in Rowland Collection, C-878, 396, and as second alcalde in 1841 by Cornelio Perez in testimony about the land grant of Tres Ojos de Agua (modern Westside Santa Cruz). See BL, Documents Pertaining to the Adjudication of Private Land Claims in California, circa 1852-92, BANC MSS Land Case Files 1852-92, BANC MSS C-A 300 FILM, Land Case 285 SD, Tres Ojos de Agua, transcript 591: "Tres Ojos de Agua" Nicolas Dodero, Claimant, 150. The late local historian Leon Rowland noted that Lorenzana "served as second *alcalde* under Buelna and Bolcoff in 1845 and the first half of 1846, and at various times in the preceding two decades was regidor or sindico [*sic*]"; see Pre-Statehood Documents, UCSC, Rowland Collection, C-636.

64. "Book of Trials and Municipal Affairs of Branciforte Alcalde for 1833 and 1834," January 29, 1834, CPSD, MS 105, Special Collections and Archives, University Library, UCSC, box 2:3, 169. In the book of Settlement of Disputes, 1833-34, reliable members of the local Californio community called upon "good men" (*hombres buenos*) to testify. Lorenzana was called upon in this manner.

65. His petition for a new piece of land adjoining the San Lorenzo River and approval by Jose Bolcoff are found in Santa Cruz County Book of Deeds, 1:11-12, September 18, 1841.

66. The Craig-Lorenzana, or Branciforte, Adobe is today a private residence on the corner of Branciforte and Goss Avenues.

67. Details of this dispossession are examined in my master's thesis; see Rizzo, "Americanos Came like Hungry Wolves."

68. Many of the settlers did not know that the 1848 Treaty of Guadalupe Hidalgo obligated the United States to honor Mexican land claims. U.S. Congress enacted the California Land Act of 1851, formally titled "An Act to Ascertain and Settle the Private Land Claims in the State of California." This act set up the Board of Land Commissioners, which established strict guidelines for proving land ownership.

69. Igler, *Industrial Cowboys*, 56. Many historians credit this drought for breakdown of the cattle industry. Meanwhile, some industrious immigrants profited from the subsequent sales of rancho lands. A broader study that looks at cattle, environment, and colonialism in California and Hawai'i can be found in Fischer, *Cattle Colonialism*.

70. Pitt, *Decline of the Californios*. Pitt was the first to explore the particularly rapid change in Northern California following the gold rush.

71. Pokriots, "Don Jose Antonio Bolcoff," 97–107.

72. Goode, "American Conquest of Alta California," 4–23. Goode relates the story of the former naval chaplain appointed as the Monterey *alcalde* by Commodore Robert F. Stockton following the United States' seizure of Monterey in July 1846.

73. María Prudencia was a member of the Bay Area Vallejo family. Don Amesti died in 1855. While she won this case, she was forced to sell much of her lands to cover court costs in dealing with squatters who moved onto her lands in the 1860s. Records of her land sales are found in SCCD, 36:158, 35:113, 34:486, and 34:491. She sold the majority of her lands to the family's San Francisco—based attorney William Patterson, SCCD, 2:87–91.

74. Kimbro, et al, *Historic Structure Report*, 22–29. Ironically, they also sold the majority of the lands to Amesti attorney Patterson, for two thousand dollars, to recover court costs and damages from the trial. Kimbro pieced together records to find that Guadalupe Castro had actually "sold more of the rancho than finally existed making it necessary that the lawsuit against Amesti be won. Losing the lawsuit ensured the ruin of all," 29.

75. California, *Statues of California*, 409. The shifting legal rights for California Indians in the early years of U.S. statehood is examined in detail by Madley, *American Genocide*, 157–63. Article II, Section 1 of the California State Constitution of 1849 outlined voting rights for "every white male citizen of the United States, and every white male citizen of Mexico." It allowed the legislature to, by two-thirds vote, admit "Indians or the descendants of Indians, in such special cases."

76. Martínez, *Genealogical Fictions*. These racial categories (*sistema de castas*) were somewhat fluid, as people shifted in classification over time. Martínez examines the origins of this system, its connection to Spanish concepts of *limpieza de sangre* (purity of blood), and the limitations of these categories.

77. Johnston-Dodds, *Early California Laws and Policies*. Along with California statehood came laws targeting Indigenous Californians.

78. Madley, *American Genocide*, 158–9.

79. Lorenzana was not the only person to find himself on trial over his racial identity and Indigenous heritage. In 1858, during the land case regarding the

Rancho el Pescadero in modern Pebble Beach (Monterey County), claimant Jose Armenta was similarly questioned about his Indian heritage. See Documents Pertaining to the Adjudication of Private Land Claims in California, Land Case 157 SD, circa 1852–92, BANC MSS Land Case Files 1852–92; BANC MSS C-A 300 FILM, BL, University of California, Berkeley.

80. There is no tribe named "Monterunias." Lorenzana was likely referencing Moctezuma or Montezuma, the legendary emperor of the Aztecs. Alternatively, Monterunias is similar to the two Spanish words *monte* and *ruinas*, which translate to mountain ruins. In either case, certainly Lorenzana's sense of identity is informed by stories and legends that likely circulated in California regarding the Aztecs. Earle, *Return of the Native*. Earle describes the dynamics of myth-making, Indigenous histories, and national memory. Similarly, Haas discusses "visions of Aztlan" and the making of California as a Native story, *Saints and Citizens*, 151.

81. Museum of Art & History, Santa Cruz County Records, Superior Court Material, File 10, *Amesti v. Castro* (1874), Evidence in Case, 2.

82. Records of the sale of Macedonio Lorenzana's lands are found in SCCR, Deeds, 1:275.

83. Lorenzana's death is recorded in SCZD 2415.

84. Stories of these Yokuts raiders and horse thieves and their local connections are discussed in chapter 4.

85. Reader, "*Charole*," Kimbro, *Historic Structure Report*, 36–41. In this climate of violence from the 1850s through 1870s, local vigilantes indiscriminately rounded up Californios: widows, elderly couples—anyone.

86. Reader, "*Charole*." The story of the burning of the jail by suspected arsonists, though never confirmed, is found in "Fire," *Santa Cruz Sentinel*, June 17, 1865, 3:1. Pedro was the only inmate at the time of the fire.

87. Reader, *Harlots and Whorehouses*. Reader tells the story of Josie Lorenzana and the brothel at Number 10 Front Street. For the article on the arrest of Josie Lorenzana, see "Sentinel Jottings," *Santa Cruz Sentinel*, August 7, 1884, 3:1. Public support for the closing of the Number 10 Front Street brothel is found in "Sentinel Jottings," *Santa Cruz Sentinel*, August 9, 1884, 3:1.

88. Jesus Lorenzana was arrested for stabbing Alex Bernard; see "Stabbing Affray," *Santa Cruz Sentinel*, June 14, 1884, 2:2. Jesus Lorenzana and Jose Jesus Juarez were arrested for fighting and disturbing the peace (*Santa Cruz Daily Surf*, October 19, 1885); James Lorenzana was arrested for the shooting of Joe Rodriguez (*Santa Cruz Daily Surf*, July 5, 1893); and Julia Lorenzana was arrested for assault with a knife (*Santa Cruz Daily Surf*, September 2, 1895).

89. Maria Romualda's death is recorded in SCZD 3055, September 26, 1884.

90. Maria Romualda would have been eighty-five at the time of her death. The early American fixation on centenarians in California is discussed by Boyd and Rizzo, "Many Lives of Justiniano Roxas."

91. "Sentinel Jottings," *Santa Cruz Sentinel*, September 27, 1884, 3:2.

92. Boessenecker, *Bandido*. Boessenecker examines the story of local bandido Vasquez and his local connections in detail.

93. "Old Time Roxas," 3:2.

94. Father Joaquin Adam arrived in Santa Cruz in 1868 and stayed until he was relieved by Father Hugh McNamee in 1884. Adam first appears as administrator of baptism on December 24, 1868 (SCZB 3815). In a 1916 account reported by Frances R. Smith, Adam described the Santa Cruz Indigenous community as follows: "The Indians at the mission were not all of the same tribe, but perfect harmony prevailed, and when the season of work was over, many paid visits to their countrymen and seldom returned alone, for the good friars had the art of making labor attractive. As it was the custom of the Indians to live in bands, or groups, and various groups used different languages, it was quite a matter of necessity that the success of the Indians or the friars depended upon the organization of these men. The groups were divided with respect to the various languages, and according to Father Adam they did their labor in 'respective bands,' avoiding conflicting tribal relations." See California History Room, California State Library, Sacramento, Owen C. Coy Collection, 1860–1940, box 1306, Mission Santa Cruz, folder 21 Manuscripts—"Mision de Exaltacion de la Santa Cruz," by Frances R. Smith, written in Palo Alto, March 4, 1916, by Frances R. Smith, under the guidance of Father Adam, 30. While Adam appears to have romanticized the labor opportunities, his account does speak to the ongoing tribal, linguistic, and kinship lines within this diverse community.

95. SCZB 109, and SCZD 885 in April 1808.

96. "The Oldest Living Inhabitant of California Photographed—A Cabinet Picture for the Vatican," *Santa Cruz Weekly Sentinel*, September 5, 1874, 3:3.

97. The portrait is mentioned in an article in 1875, which also notes that Roxas "would like to go to the Centennial Exposition, but has not the cash, so he must needs stay at home until next Centennial Anniversary in Philadelphia." "Splendid Portrait," *Santa Cruz Weekly Sentinel*, February 20, 1875, 3:1. One newspaper blurb sold copies of the painting, stating: "We have had the pleasure of seeing a very fine painting of the celebrated Indian, Justiniano Roxas, by Holzman. This artist intends to have the painting lithographed, and will sell copies at a very reasonable price. Every one should secure a copy of this celebrity of Santa Cruz. Orders may now be left at the Enterprise office. The likeness is perfect," "Local," *Santa Cruz Enterprise*, February 12, 1875, 3:1.

98. Justiniano Roxas has been the subject of multiple articles and studies. The first was by Jackson, "Justiniano Roxas Hoax," 44–54. Jackson proves that the man Adam had identified was not the surviving Roxas. Dunn further analyzes the story, retracing the photographs and development of the myth around Roxas, as Roxas became a public figure in Santa Cruz well into the twentieth century. Dunn, "Deconstructing Roxas." Roxas's death was reported in the "Roxas Is No More," *Santa Cruz Weekly Sentinel*, March 13, 1875, 2:5.

99. I believe that the real Roxas was Yrachis, baptized as Ostiano (SCZB 629, on January 15, 1796). I reached this conclusion for several reasons. Ostiano's aunt, Masihúmu (Sabina, SCZB 1425), lists her nephew as Justiniano in her baptism record on March 15, 1809. It is not uncommon for names to change over time within the mission community, and his aunt's record shows that Ostiano also went by the name Justiniano. Furthermore, the 1834–35 census lists "Hostiano Tapia," a forty-six-year-old Chipuctac man. The 1845 census lists an "Ustiano" living on the Westside, which fits with the reports contained in the land case regarding these lands. See Documents Pertaining to the Adjudication of Private Land Claims in California, Land Case 285 SD, 660 pp., transcript 591: "Tres Ojos de Agua," Nicholas Dodero, Claimant, ca. 1852–92, BANC MSS Land Case Files 1852–92; BANC MSS C-A 300 FILM, BL, University of California, Berkeley. These records indicate that Justiniano moved onto the west side sometime in the late 1830s. This "Ustiano" is listed as being a sixty-year-old from the Tulares (Yokuts), but I believe that the "Tulares" identification is a mistake made by the enumerator. The other possible identity for Roxas would be the Tomoi man baptized as Justo (SCZB 1279a, March 17, 1806, eight years old at baptism). But I believe this is the man known as Justo Gonsales (1834 census) and Jose de Justo (1845 census). This man died at age seventy (SCZD 2447a) and was buried on June 20, 1864.

100. Yrachis's family arrived with a group the padres identified as being from the "San Juan" tribe. Missionaries frequently renamed tribes according to Catholic saints, and at Mission Santa Cruz the "San Juan" people typically referred to any of the various tribes living on the eastern side of the local mountain range. Yrachis's siblings include Seynte (Projecto), SCZB 626; Tallap (Prisco), SCZB 627; Sichirimas (Novato), SCZB 640; Megeroa (Vicencia), SCZB 643; and Ceyuén (Rita), SCZB 655. His parents were Tallap (SCZB 660, his name also spelled *Taupo*, *Toyop*, or *Toiop* in his children's records) and Murejate (alternatively spelled *Morejaste* or *Mugerate*), who appears to have never received baptism, indicating that either she was dead before her family came to Mission Santa Cruz or that she avoided baptism and relocation altogether. Tallap entered with his second wife, Aschi (Nicefora, SCZB 667).

101. Their deaths are recorded in SCZD 468, 701, 708, and 713. Family members who died at Mission Santa Cruz, so appear not to have run away, include his stepmother, Aschi, who died on May 22, 1804 (SCZD 637), and younger brother Tallap (Prisco), who was buried at the mission on May 27, 1810 (SCZD 992).

102. Seynte appears as witness for forty-one marriage ceremonies, between 1799 (SCZM 239) and 1805 (SCZM 363). Seynte eventually served as witness for the marriage of his brother, Yrachis, SCZM 342.

103. SCZM 256. Samórim (alternatively written as Sambray, and baptized as Fabiana Arraez, SCZB 62) was herself an important member of the spiritual community, serving as *madrina* in thirty-five baptisms between 1815 (SCZB 1607) and 1821 (SCZB 1911). She died in January 1823 (SCZD 1499).

104. Their children include Lazaro Domingo (SCZB 1014), Francisco Solano (SCZB 1129), Francisco (SCZB 1165), Antonia (SCZB 1364), Tomas (SCZB 1429), Hana Maria de la Espectation (SCZB 1578), Vicenta Rafaela (SCZB 1612), and Alvaro (SCZB 1758).

105. Quichuate (Pacifica, SCZB 1124) and Yrachis married on November 23, 1804, SCZM 342, and her death is recorded in SCZD 848.

106. Cosorom was baptized on March 2, 1802, at the age of twenty-seven and given the name Genoveva, SCZB 1005. When she married Yrachis on October 23, 1809, she was thirty-four and he was twenty-one, SCZM 475. Her tribal and village information is uncertain, as she was baptized in 1802 at the age of twenty-seven, in a large group identified as being from "San Juan." This is likely in reference to Mission San Juan Bautista, suggesting that her home village was in Mutsun territory, near to Yrachi's.

107. Cosorom's death was recorded in SCZD 1019 on December 1, 1810. Cosorom had a son from a previous marriage, Chalema (Raymundo, SCLB 3803), who was baptized at Mission Santa Clara and moved to Santa Cruz with his parents. Cosorom and her family fit a larger pattern of parents who visited the missions, allowing their children to receive baptism, possibly in exchange for goods like cloth and beads. Some of these parents chose to receive baptism as well, while others remained outside of the mission system. Some joined other mission communities, ostensibly caught in the splitting of tribal members between missions, as seen with the Ausaima/Chipuctac.

108. The Auxentac village site was situated along Coyote Creek, in the vicinity of modern Gilroy Hot Springs and Henry W. Coe State Park, just east of Morgan Hill. Saipan (baptized as Alexandra, SCZB 1204). Their marriage, SCZM 531, on July 21, 1811. She died five months later, SCZD 1097, on December 16, 1811.

109. SCZD 1097, on December 16, 1811.

110. His connections to Gepeson (Maria de la Piedad, SCZB 902) seem to be familial as well, given that they both appear with the surname "Tapia" in the

1834–35 census. The Native name of the Achistaca Samectoi (Seferino Arce, SCZB 320) is alternatively spelled *Samecloi* or *Samedoi* in his children's baptismal records. The repetition and alteration of his Native name in documents through the 1830s is further evidence of the retention of Indigenous names throughout the postmission years, despite the recording of only Spanish names in official documents like the census. Chugiut and his family's connection with the west side rancheria is explored in chapter 5.

111. Gepeson was buried on May 24, 1837, SCZD 1986. Samectoi was buried the following year, on August 8, 1838, SCZD 2029.

112. Labarsec (Gavriel or Gabriel, SCZB 1874). Sipon (Alvino, SCZB 538) and his wife, Sergia (SCZB 2069). Sergia's father was Utana (Eutropia, SJBB 610), an Ausaima baptized at Mission San Juan Bautista. Utana moved to the Santa Cruz region and married Sergia's mother, Benvenuta (SCZB 868), daughter of two local Uypi parents baptized in the earliest days at Mission Santa Cruz—Yucuquis (Antonio Pantoja, SCZB 44) and Sipan (Andrea Pico, SCZB 49).

113. Sergia's baptismal *madrina* was the Ausaima (Chipuctac) Constantina (SCZB 787), who was married to Chalema (Raymundo, SCLB 3803), son of Yrachis's second wife, Cosorom. Chalema was born at Mission Santa Clara in 1799 to parents who lived at Mission Santa Cruz, another example of families dividing and moving along kinship lines between mission communities.

114. The presence of Yrachis living on the Westside was noted by Castro in his interview over land boundaries in the U.S. Courts. Castro estimated that "Justiano" moved onto these lands around 1856. Curiously, the interview included a question about Yrachis: "Is this the same Indian there now watching gophers? Castro: I saw him there the other day, I don't know what he is doing." Testimony of Castro, Land Case 285 SD, Rancho Tres Ojos de Agua, 284–85.

115. "Old Times Roxas," 3:2.

116. Secundino was the son of Don José Antonio Robles and Gertrudis Merlopes, one of the founding families of the Villa de Branciforte. Secundino was born at the Villa de Branciforte in June 1811 and baptized in July, VBB 61. The Villa de Branciforte baptismal registry is not included in the ECPP, as the original was recently unearthed and now sits in the archives of the Monterey Archdiocese. Snell, "New Almaden."

117. This story is from an interview in 1981 with Ruby Tefertiller. Her family has lived on lands adjacent to Mission Santa Cruz since the early American era and had known Maria Filomena, a local Indigenous woman who will be discussed in the next chapter, as a young girl and told of her stories. See Tefertiller, "Oral History from Ruby Tefertiller."

118. SCZD 2699, burial on March 12, 1875. The fire was reported in "Local," *Santa Cruz Enterprise*, March 5, 1875, 3:1.

119. Margaret Koch, "The SC Mission Indian Whose Life Spanned Three Eras," *Santa Cruz Sentinel*, February 8, 1966; "Chief Roxas Appears Again," *Santa Cruz Sentinel*, April 12, 1963; Marian Goodman, "Last of His Race," *Santa Cruz Mobile Keno*, April 14, 1972; "Clippings Relating to Justiniano Roxas," all in clipping box "Biography—R," Santa Cruz Public Library, Santa Cruz, CA. "Roxas, Our Oldest Inhabitant," *Santa Cruz Sentinel*, 1919, in "Roxas Notes," cabinet E, drawer 4, folder 18, Kimbro Archives.

120. Harrington, "San Juan Report," JPH, microfilm, reel 59, p. 14.

121. Harrington, "San Juan Report," JPH, microfilm, reel 59, p. 7.

122. Madley, *American Genocide*, 185–86.

123. Henshaw, *California Indian Linguistic Records*, 89.

124. Pinart, *California Indian Linguistic Records*. Eulogia is really Paylat (SCZB 1680), the woman from the Jasnil rancheria, in Atsnil (Yokuts) territory. As such, it casts some doubt on the veracity of Pinart's vocabulary list. Confusion on the ethnographer's side about geography and tribal and linguistic heritage likely led to mixing of the various linguistic informants.

125. This is the same Rustico (SCZB 1561) discussed in chapter 5. Rustico was the son of the Uypi man Quihueimen (baptized as Quirico, SCZB 65). Quihueimen was one of the two surviving convicts of the Quintana assassination. Rustico survived until September 1879 (SCZD 2895).

126. Guimayach (Mariano, SCZB 1799) is actually from the Huocom Yokuts people, which makes more sense, as, according to Paylat, they are closely related to her Atsnil people. Pinart looked up a different Mariano—the Chaloctaca man Tejos (Mariano Hablitas, SCZB 115), baptized in 1792 as a sixteen-year-old, who died in 1796 (SCZD 203).

127. Alphonse Louis Pinart Papers, BL, BANC MSS Z-Z, 9:17. The original is in French; the translation was generously provided to me by Anastasiia Cherygova and Erica Jomphe. The comments by Pinart regarding Roxas's age and identity reflect the misunderstandings discussed at the beginning of the chapter. Santiago from Santa Clara will be discussed in the next chapter.

128. The obituary ran September 12, 1857, 2:1. The burial is recorded in SCZD 2248, on September 7. The burial record notes his age as "a widow of 100 years or more."

129. The Huocom entered along with large numbers of Hupnis, Tejey, and Sipieyesi—all Yokuts-speaking tribes. Suulu and Atamay received baptism on November 15, 1820, the first man and woman listed among a group of thirty from the abovementioned tribes. A note on Suulu's baptism identifies him as the "capitan de la Ranchera de Huocom." The baptisms appear to have been followed by marriage ceremonies, as fifteen marriages are recorded on

the same day, all involving the thirty new arrivals. On Suulu and Atamay's marriage record, sczm 628, the names are alternatively listed as "Suuler" and "Alamay."

130. Najaruy (Miguel), sczb 1796, and Choótg (Anastasio), sczb 1800, both received baptism on April 2, 1820, along with six other adolescents from the Tejey, Huocom, and Apil Yokuts tribes.

131. His sons' burials are recorded in sczd 1690 and 1873, in 1827 and 1832, respectively. Atamay's burial is recorded in sczd 1588.

132. The genocidal policies inflicted across the state did not take place in Santa Cruz, as the massive toll of deaths, disease, and trauma had already taken place within the mission. In nearly 200 pages of appendices, Madley did not document any massacre in Santa Cruz, *American Genocide*, 361–554.

133. Magliari, "Masters, Apprentices, and Kidnappers."

7. If They Think You're Already Dead

1. Previous fires include the fire at the Imus property, noted in "Here, There, Everywhere," *Santa Cruz Weekly Sentinel*, September 1, 1883, 3:2; and the home of S. W. Field, "Sentinel Jottings," *Santa Cruz Sentinel*, April 22, 1884, 3:1.

2. Copies of the court proceedings, including transcripts of their testimonies, are on microfilm at the Superior Court of California, County of Santa Cruz Civil Division. *People of the State of California v. Raphael Castro*, CA Superior Court Case 829 (1884), microfilm roll 4.17, 922 and *People of the State of California v. Joe Lend*, CA Superior Court Case 830 (1884), microfilm roll 4.17, 967.

3. "Bad Injuns: Their Childish Innocence in Having a 'Little Fun' at the Expense of Property Owners—the Community Can Now Sleep in Peace," *Santa Cruz Daily Sentinel*, December 10, 1884, 3:3. Deputy Sheriff Alzina and officer majors arrested the two young men on Friday, December 5; they appeared before a judge on Monday, December 9, and were sent to San Quentin two weeks later, on December 24. Details about their appearance with Judge Logan are in "New To-Day," *Santa Cruz Daily Sentinel*, December 24, 1884, 3:3. In addition to his work as attorney and judge, James Harvey Logan was an amateur botanist credited with the 1881 creation of the loganberry, a cross between raspberry and blackberry. He also built the Brookdale Lodge, which still stands today.

4. "The Barn Burners: Two Indian Boys Arrested for Arson—One Confesses, the Other Denies," *Santa Cruz Sentinel*, December 9, 1884, 3:2. Santa Cruz officials brought the two men before Justice Spalsbury, and the interrogation was conducted by the district attorney.

5. "Barn Burners," 3:2.

6. "Barn Burners," 3:2. This article states that the two young men "did not want an attorney."

7. "True's Tesimony: Council Takes It While He Is on His Death Bed," *Daily Alta California*, April 13, 1884, 1:1. The article mentions Henry Martin True as a person of interest. Tahoe and Cache testified that True had given them liquor in exchange for burning the barn of True's son-in-law a few months earlier. True was also involved, possibly as an extortionist, in the infamous Senator Sharon scandal in San Francisco, a connection pointed out to me by Santa Cruz local historian Geoffrey Dunn. True had died suspiciously in the midst of the Sharon investigation earlier in 1884, testifying for the Sharon case on his deathbed. Since True had "gone to a higher tribunal, over which the Justice Court of Santa Cruz Township has no control," American authorities focused only on the two young men. "Their Childish Innocence in Having a 'Little Fun' at the Expense of Property Owners—the Community Can Now Sleep in Peace," *Santa Cruz Daily Sentinel*, December 10, 1884.

8. "New To-Day," 3:3.

9. "Bad Injuns," 3:3.

10. Dunn, "Conquest and Destiny," 19–26. Dunn tracked down records of their deaths and made similar arguments about the circumstances of the boys' arrests. This book expands Dunn's argument by examining, in depth, the family histories of these two men and their community, while providing a larger context of Indigenous Santa Cruz in the American era.

11. Dunn, "Conquest and Destiny," 19–26. Research on their fates was conducted and reported by Dunn.

12. Tefertiller, "Oral History from Ruby Tefertiller." This oral history will be discussed in more depth later in this chapter.

13. See Tefertiller, "Oral History from Ruby Tefertiller."

14. "Bad Injuns," 3:3.

15. "Bad Injuns," 3:3. It is probable that Duncan McPherson wrote the article. McPherson was the owner of the *Santa Cruz Daily Sentinel* and a leader of the local anti-Chinese movement.

16. "Bad Injuns," 3:3. American officials arrested Jose Chamales and Francisco Arias for the murder and accused them of having used the stolen money to attend a local circus. This event resulted in the lynching of the two men on the Water Street Bridge and is the focus of the third chapter in Gonzales-Day, *Lynching in the West*, 93–100; and Dunn, "Santa Cruz's Most Notorious Lynching," *Good Times*, November 12, 2013. The *Sentinel* article drew connections between Tahoe and Cache, claiming that "two Indians, in their childish innocence may kill a man for the fun of seeing him kick, and then rob him of money

with which to purchase tickets for a circus, and spend the balance, if any is left, in buying peanuts for their copper-colored squaws. Without any compunction they can set buildings on fire." There are no actual connections between the two events, or the people involved, other than race and class. Dunn's article points out that they were considered "half-breeds" and "Indians," the thirty-five-year-old Arias was said to be from up the coast a bit in neighboring Pescadero, and twenty-one-year-old Chamales from Branciforte.

17. *Santa Cruz Sentinel*, December 24, 1884. The reference to the "Indian firebugs" came from a short article about the sentencing of the two young men, stating that "the Indian firebugs were taken to their future home in San Quentin." The reference to "Maria" came from undated articles by local historian Ernest Otto, who penned a column on local history in the 1940s and 1950s. For more on Otto, see Dunn, "Historian for All Time."

18. SCZB 2191; and Maria Guadalupe, SCZB 2647.

19. Rafael "Tahoe" Castro, SCZB 3428. Maria Filomena "Castor" [sic] appears in the 1900 U.S. census as a seventy-five-year-old servant to Maria de los Angeles Majors, who herself was listed as eighty-three years. As will be discussed in more detail later in this chapter, the Majors family provided a home for a number of local Indians, including Filomena's stepfather, Xuclan (Ricardo), as noted in the previous chapter.

20. See Anderson, Lewis, and Stewart, *Forgotten Fires*.

21. Throughout this chapter will be examples of stories, many related by white settlers, of local Indigenous people and their familiarity with natural resources like water and springs, knowledge of local plants and animals, and other stories connecting Indigenous survivors with these types of skills. To some extent this speaks to romanticized notions of the noble savage, with white settlers seeing Indigenous people in animalistic terms, not unlike the approach of the missionaries. On the other hand, this awareness of the local environment does speak to the deep ancestral knowledge and intimacy with the local ecosystem.

22. Chulnoquis (Pasqual, SCZB 1647) was the son of the Tejey chief Coleto Malimin. The Quitchas Yokuts man Huayiche (Fidel, SCZB 1976) was the other recipient of the lands. The sale of these lands to Thomas Farnham, SCCR Deeds Book 1, 590–91. The lawyer Farnham, who received these lands after his help in freeing the notorious Isaac Graham in what is known as the Graham affair, never lived on these lands, as he died in 1848. His wife, the famous abolitionist Eliza, did live on these lands and wrote about it. See Jo Ann Levy, *Unsettling the West*, 59.

23. Carlos (SCZB 2007), Rosa (SCZB 2314), and their four sons: Agustin (SCZB 3001), Juan Jose Rafael (SCZB 3102), Juan Bautista (SCZB 3234), and Jose Martial Carlos (SCZB 3476). This is the Carlos mentioned in chapter 5 who was killed by

John Cantwell at the local Bausch Brewery on February 28, 1877. Pre-Statehood Documents, UCSC, Rowland Collection, A-2, card 53.

24. This article was quoted at length in the previous chapter. "Lo! The Poor Indian," 2:6.

25. Pinart Papers, vol. 9, BL, BANC MSS Z-Z 17, trans. Anastasiia Cherygova and Erica Jomphe.

26. In the 1980s Edna E. Kimbro attempted to protect these lands, recognizing their historic importance. Kimbro, who compiled much information about the local Indigenous community before her passing in 2005, filed an Environmental Impact Report to recognize the "post mission period dwellings of Fidel and Pasqual, located immediately north and south of Pogonip Creek in the precise area where the Salz pond is today." She noted that "Pasqual and Fidel were among those granted the Potrero area as a rancheria upon secularization of Mission Santa Cruz. This site is potentially one of the most significant remaining in the City of Santa Cruz and must be assessed prior to approval of any project." See Kimbro Archives, File on Indians and Census, document dated October 23, 1986, Re: 1111 River Street, PD-SUP-DP-85-292.

27. Gourley, "My Early Childhood Memories," 72–74. The golf links refers to modern Pogonip Park, near the Potrero lands. Pogonip was home to the local golf course. Gourley's account described two young Indian boys, "Lahugh" and "Kajesus" (Jose or Tomas de Jesus?), who she believed had developed crushes on her and her friend. Gourley recalled that the two boys frequently brought the girls berries. She further tells a story in which her friend's brothers attempted to humiliate one of the Indian boys, suggesting that he ask her father for her hand. The father, Gourley relates, "told him it would be a terrible thing to do for a white girl to marry an Indian. So that was the end to the Indian beaus when we were young girls."

28. Gourley, "My Early Childhood Memories," 78. Gourley also mentions that Indians worked delivering groceries, stating that "the Cooper Brothers had a grocery and dry goods store on Front St. The only means of delivery they had was a clothes-basket filled with goods carried on the shoulders of an Indian." The various census reports identify these other listed jobs as being performed by Indians, while newspaper reports on Tahoe and Cache mention Cache's work as a buggy driver. Examples of Indigenous workers at the tanneries will be discussed shortly.

29. Lydon, *Chinese Gold*. The arrival of Chinese immigrants in the Monterey Bay has been explored in depth by Lydon. He points out that in Santa Cruz the majority of the incoming Chinese community found domestic labor in the households of white settlers.

30. Bauer, *We Were All Like Migrant Workers Here*. Bauer explores how Indigenous people from the Round Valley confederated tribes used work and labor opportunities to survive and persist. Another study that examines Indigenous labor during this period but in Los Angeles is found in Phillips, *Vineyards & Vaqueros*. Both works recognize Indigenous Californians as laborers rather than as passive victims.

31. On August 4, 1851, the two received baptism: Juan de Dios (SCZB 2898) and Tomas de Jesus (SCZB 2899).

32. "Dead Indian," *Santa Cruz Weekly Sentinel*, December 13, 1856, 2:1. Tomas de Jesus's burial is recorded in SCZD 2233, on December 7, 1856.

33. Asisara appears in the 1880 U.S. Federal Census, p. 49, visit 8, in Seaside, alongside the Majors couple and their three children. Maria Filomena, who will be discussed at length later this chapter, appears in 1900 U.S. Federal Census, p. 9, visit 158. A seventy-five-year-old Filomena is listed as Maria Filomena "Castor" [*sic*], servant to the eighty-three-year-old Maria de los Angeles, on Mill Street.

34. Guimayach or Quimayach (Mariano, SCZB 1799), was baptized on April 2, 1820, as a seventeen-year-old Huocom man, along with a group of eight Tejey, Huocom, and Apil teenage men and women. This group included two sons (Najaruy and Choótg, SCZB 1796 and 1800, respectively) of the Huocom chief, Suulu, discussed in the previous chapter, as well as the future mother of Lorenzo Asisara, Luasatme (Manuela, SCZB 1803), who was listed as being from a village site called Chalahua, most likely a village in the Yokuts territories near Huocom and Tejey territories. This is the same Mariano mentioned by Pinart as having passed away a few years before his arrival in town. Louis Pinart Papers, vol. 9, BL, BANC MSS Z-Z, 17. His obituary noted that he was "known as 'Cooper's Indian, he having been provided for for the last twenty-five years by W. Cooper," "Brevities," *Santa Cruz Weekly Sentinel*, January 6, 1877, 3:2. A newspaper blurb incorrectly identified Guimayach, noting: "On the 25th of April 1792, was baptized a boy of 16 years, called Telos, son of Chalmos and Nisipen Gentiles. In baptism he was given the name of Mariano Hablitas," "Local," *Santa Cruz Enterprise*, March 5, 1875, 3:1. The real Tejos (SCZB 115) died in 1796 (SCZD 203). It is notable that the unidentified author of this blurb referenced the Mission Santa Cruz Baptismal Book to try and find information on Guimayach and published Indigenous names, a rarity, even while mistaken. Tejos parents were both from the Chaloctaca village, Cholmos (Acisclo, SCZB 443) and Nisipen (Maria Guadalupe Cruz, SCZB 154). Hablitas was a family name given at baptism to Tejos and his sister (Tipan, Maria del Carmen Hablitas, SCZB 147) and brother (Lassac, Onesimo Saturnino Hablitas, SCZB 151). It is not clear why Guimayach, baptized as "Mariano," eventually became known as Mariano Hablitas, but it

is possible that the local Indigenous community had associated the two names from this previous Mariano Hablitas.

35. He first married the Huocom woman Huslalsme (Bernardina, SCZB 1853) on June 24, 1821 (SCZM 660). Huslalsme died on January 3, 1822 (SCZD 1460). He then married a mission-born Tejey woman, Luisa Daniela (SCZB 1587), on January 12, 1827 (SCZM 736). Luisa Daniela died on July 28, 1832 (SCZD 1882). His third marriage was to a mission-born Notuall (Yokuts) woman, Felipa de Jesus (SCZB 1752), on June 26, 1833 (SCZM 793). Felipa de Jesus died December 24, 1840 (SCZD 2064). His final marriage was to a mission-born Hupnis woman, Andrea (SCZB 1894), on February 4, 1844 (SCZM 853). Andrea died shortly after, in July 1845 (SCZD 2110).

36. Salvador (SCZB 2206), born March 28, 1834, died May 5, 1834 (SCZD 1922).

37. 1834–35 census, on file at the Monterey Archdiocese.

38. SCZM 853 in February 1844.

39. Guimayach, whose age is unlisted, appears as "Mariano" in the 1860 U.S. census, Santa Cruz County, p. 623, visit 992. He is listed as living with the family of the Huocom Meregildo and Maria Agueda, who will be discussed later in this chapter. A "Mariana Narcissa" appears to have received a partial grant to some Potrero lands along River Street in 1866, at the same time that one was denied to a "Merehelda" [Meregildo] and Jesus Maria. The record indicates that the two young men were unsuccessful claimants, while "Mariana" received the property, "probably for joint use of remaining redmen in this city." See Rowland Card Files, Santa Cruz Pre-Statehood Documents, McHenry Library, UCSC, box C, card 305, Property Distribution 1866.

40. These brothers are relatives of the famous James Fenimore Cooper, a key figure responsible for popularizing the romanticized notion of Indigenous people as "noble savages" as well as for writing fictional stories that romanticized the trope of the "vanishing Indian" (for example, *The Last of the Mohicans*). Information regarding his connection to the Cooper brothers is related in Reader, "'Missing' Pioneers," 14. Reader repeated the misidentification from the previously cited *Santa Cruz Enterprise* blurb, calling Guimayach Tejos.

41. Guimayach's involvement in the gold rush is related by the late Phil Reader, "'Missing' Pioneers," 14. Reader was a Santa Cruz historian who conducted extensive research, but often failed to properly cite his sources. The source for this story is unknown, though Guimayach's connection with the Cooper brothers is documented. His 1877 obituary claimed that the Coopers had taken care of Guimayach for the final twenty-five years of his life, "Brevities," *Santa Cruz Weekly Sentinel*, January 6, 1877, 3:2. Apparently, the Cooper brothers regularly helped out elderlymen, as the obituary of New York City–born George H. Plum mentioned that Plum's "friends, the Messrs. Coopers, have kindly and charitably provided for his

every want through the weary years of his affliction, and for the last twenty months, have daily visited his bed side and rendered his dying hours as bearable as possible." "An Old Citizen Gone," *Santa Cruz Enterprise*, August 14, 1874, 2:1.

42. "Brevities," *Santa Cruz Weekly Sentinel*, January 6, 1877, 3:2. His burial is recorded in SCZD 2740, two months after the report of his death. It is not clear why he was buried two months later.

43. Friar McNamee took over for Father Adam in 1883. These plans are discussed in a bulletin requesting that "those having friends or relatives buried in the lot adjoining the old adobe to have them removed within two weeks. From this it is evident that preparations for laying the foundation for the new church building will soon commence." "Sentinel Jottings," *Santa Cruz Sentinel*, July 14, 1885, 3:1. Eight days later it was reported that "the old cemetery will be leveled to the grade of the rest of the ground and those who desire will remove the remains of friends buried there. Others will remain under the new church, which however, will cover only a portion of the ground devoted to the cemetery." "Santa Cruz Minus the Mission," *Santa Cruz Daily Surf*, July 23, 1885, 2:2.

44. Allen, *Native Americans at Mission Santa Cruz*, 29.

45. Petra Nicanor's Tejey (Yokuts) husband, Chuyucu, alternatively spelled *Chuyuso, Chugucu, Chuiucuu*, oeven once as *Yeulile* (Victoriano, SCZB 1515).

46. See SCCD, 1:100, June 7, 1848.

47. SCLD 8267.

48. SCZD 2179.

49. Her mother's name is incorrectly given. It is possibly a reference to the Chaneche Yokuts woman Viviana Maria (SCZB 1725), wife of Jotoime (Matias, SCZB 934) and mother of Maria Agueda, although the two would have been about the same age. Maria Bibiana died nearly a decade earlier, in March 1839 (SCZD 2049). Maria Agueda is discussed later in this chapter.

50. Kimbro et al., *Como La Sombra Huye La Hora*. Kimbro's report provides much detailed information regarding the local Indigenous population and their relation to the mission lands, including some family trees. Details about the Potrero, as well as the deeds of those who sold their rooms in the adobe, are on p. 68.

51. The mass grave used to bury these bodies remained unmarked until June 2017. The Holy Cross Cemetery worked together with the Amah Mutsun Tribal Band to build a plaque with the Spanish names of 2,583 people believed to be buried there. The Amah Mutsun held a ceremony on the summer solstice for the buried. "Solstice Ceremony at Santa Cruz Mass Grave Lays Ancestors Finally to Rest," *Santa Cruz Sentinel*, June 21, 2017.

52. "The Dead at Santa Cruz: Excavations at the Cemetery—Traditions and Superstitions," *Sacramento Union*, October 1, 1885, 2:4. This was not an isolated report, as a poem honoring the late Quintana appeared a year earlier,

in the same edition that reported about Tahoe and Cache; see "Santa Cruz," by Amelia Woodward Truesdell, *Santa Cruz Sentinel*, December 10, 1884, 1:5. The long poem includes these lines: "Neophytes' rebellion and the press of / Mejico's [*sic*] hard strife / Lacked it not the martyr record—here by / Indian hate was slain, Fray Quintana when the midnight hid; the brow with brand of Cain."

53. "More Bones Unearthed," *Santa Cruz Sentinel*, September 29, 1885, 5:3.

54. "Sentinel Jottings," *Santa Cruz Sentinel*, September 29, 1885, 5:1.

55. Skowronek, "Sifting the Evidence," 687. Skowronek discusses archaeological evidence of syncretic burials at the missions, with the inclusion of shell beads and pendants as a form of passive resistance.

56. Meregildo, SCZB 2172.

57. This is the Tayssen (Ohlone) man Jose Santiago (SCLB 8415). The Taysen or Taysenn tribe may be either neighbors of or from the same group as the Sumus. Milliken suggests that Taysen is the tribal name recorded by the priests at Mission Santa Clara for the same group known at Mission Santa Cruz as the Sumus. In either case they appear to have kinship ties with the Sumus, which may explain Santiago's movement to the area. This is the same Jose Santiago who was the father of Jose "Cache" Lend, one of the two men arrested for arson. The same Santiago from Santa Clara was mentioned by Pinart in the previous chapter.

58. "Cutting His Own Throat: A Monday Morning Sensation—An Indian Attempts to Commit Suicide and Then Tells an Improbably Story," *Santa Cruz Sentinel*, April 18, 1874, 3:5. The article details the events leading up to Meregildo's confession.

59. Jesus Maria, baptized as Jesus Maria Guadalupe (SCZB 2693), is the son of the Uypi man Rustico and his Huocom Yokuts wife, Maria Alvina. Jesus Maria's wife, Maria Petronilla, baptized as Maria Petronila de la Concepcion (SCLB 10042), is the daughter of an Indigenous couple from the Ululatos village in Patwin territory, near modern Vacaville. Her parents, Mouloia (Simon, SFB 6414) and Chouylquel (Eustaquia, SFB 6421), were baptized at Mission Dolores, married at Mission Santa Cruz (SCZM 816) in 1836, then gave birth to Maria Petronilla in Santa Clara in 1840.

60. There are two reports on this incident, on two different pages of the same edition of the same newspaper. "Indian Homicide" and "Selling Liquor to Indians," both in *Santa Cruz Weekly Sentinel*, March 29, 1873, 2:2 and 3:2, respectively.

61. Meregildo was born in 1830 to Huocom Yokuts parents. His mother, Silsueail (Clementina, SCZB 1981), who died in 1833, and his father, Carachúl (Roque, SCZB 1980), both arrived with a large group of Yokuts-speaking Huocom in 1821.

62. In the 1839 census, a nine-year-old Meregildo is listed as living with the Huocom Yocoguehs (Domingo, SCZB 1828) and his wife, Maria Manuela (SCZB 1822). This is the same Yocoguehs who had been enlisted by Bolcoff to help defend the mission in 1843. In the 1841 census Meregildo is listed in a large household headed by the same Yocoguehs and Maria Manuela but including many other Huocom, Tejey, Chanech, and Hupnis people in the Potrero del Carmen.

63. Yuñan has been discussed at length in previous chapters. A thirteen-year-old Meregildo is listed in the 1843 census as being in the Bolcoff household as a *criado*, or servant, alongside Rafaela (SCZB 2141). The two are again listed in the Villa de Branciforte community in the 1845 census as household 41, alongside another servant José Antonio (SCZB 2210), whom Rafaela would eventually marry.

64. These lands sat near those of Chugiut and others who held Westside lands near the old mission site, discussed at length in chapter 5.

65. Maria Agueda, SCZB 2194a. Her Cajastaca father, Jotoime (Matias, SCZB 934), died in 1838 (SCZD 2019), while her Chaneche Yokuts mother, Nenoat (Maria Bibiana, SCZB 1725), died in 1839 (SCZD 2049). Jotoime was mentioned in chapter 5 as the recipient of a parcel of land on what is currently the lower campus of the UCSC. Meregildo and Maria Agueda married in July 1852 (SCZM 920).

66. Ana Ambrosia (Ambrosiana, SCZB 3341), died on February 4, 1874 (SCZD 2665).

67. SCZD 2707, on May 31, 1875.

68. In the 1860 U.S. census Meregildo appears listed as a farm laborer. "Cutting His Own Throat," 3:5. The article remarked that he was "one of the best gardeners in town and was recently employed by W. Brown."

69. Two unidentified Indigenous men were called upon to help locate water wells on an Eastside development; see "Enterprising East Santa Cruz: Improvements That Indicate a Substantial and Healthy Growth," *Santa Cruz Daily Surf*, February 14, 1889, 3:3. Similarly, the stories of Tahoe and Cache remark about the two men's knowledge of local plants and animals, along with their egg-finding skills. The perception of local Indians' knowledge of local berries is related in the previously cited recollections in Gourley, "My Early Childhood Memories."

70. For more on the myth of the noble savage, see Berkhofer, *White Man's Indian*; Philip Joseph Deloria, *Playing Indian*; Porter, *Native American Environmentalism*; Harkin and Lewis, *Native Americans and the Environment*; and LaDuke, *All Our Relations*.

71. This is almost certainly Jesus Maria Guadalupe (SCZB 2693). He also was arrested in 1866 for assault and carrying a concealed weapon. "Lo! The Poor

Indian," 2:6. This appears to be the same person who died in March 1873 (SCZD 2635).

72. UCSC, Pre-Statehood Collections, Rowland Files, box C, card 305, Property Distribution in 1866.

73. U.S. census 1860, p. 623, visit 992. Curiously, in addition to Guimayach, Meregildo's 1860 household included two-year-old Domingo (Jose Domingo Ismael, SCZB 3166), the son of Maria Agueda and the Atsnil Yokuts man Higinio, not Meregildo. *Padrinos* are Joseph Majors and Maria de los Angeles Castro. Higinio, variously spelled *Yginio* or *Egidio* in his baptism (SCZB 2173), is the son of an Atsnil Yokuts couple from Santa Clara, Sacats (Teodomiro, SCLB 7792) and Cutinalme (Teodomira, SCLB 7793), who moved into the area by the 1830s. This couple shifted their Spanish names by the time they appeared in Santa Cruz; they are listed in the records consistently as Turmino and Turmina. Higinio was married at the time to Maria Rosa (SCZB 2194), the daughter of Quihueimen. They were married two months prior to the marriage of Meregildo and Maria Agueda (SCZM 918), in May 1852. Higinio and Maria Rosa served as *padrinos* for the son of Meregildo and Maria Agueda, Tomas Acantuviense (SCZB 3251), born in December 1859. The ties between the two couples suggest that they held a more fluid relationship to monogamy, possibly revealing cultural values regarding relationships that were closer to those reported within precontact local Indigenous communities.

74. "Cutting His Own Throat" 3:5.

75. 1880 U.S. census, p. 3, visit 20. He is listed here as "Meryildo Rayuna." In the 1834 census the first local census to contain surnames for Native people, Meregildo's father is listed as "Roque Rayon," suggesting that Meregildo continued to use his father's surname. Meder is the person who tricked Jose Bolcoff and his family into signing away their Rancho Refugio by the mid-1850s. Museum of Art and History, Santa Cruz County Records, Superior Court Material, file 163. Meder was known in Santa Cruz for being the first banker of the American era. The Rancho Refugio lands are now Wilder Ranch State Park, home to the Bolcoff Adobe and Meder House.

76. Jose Miguel Antonio (SCZB 2971) and Maria Rafaela Vasquez (SCZB 3948) are listed in the 1880 census, p. 3, visit 21, of M. V. Bennett, and visit 23, of D. D. Dodge, respectively. They are listed as "Miguel Rayund" and "Rafaela Rayuna."

77. 1880 U.S. census, p. 39, visit 364, lists them as fifty-year-old "Rayone Hildo," ten-year-old "Emma," and twenty-eight-year-old "Mike," all listed as laborers for the head of house, Mary A. Majors.

78. "Barn Burners," 3:2.

79. Sauset (baptized as Isidro, sometimes noted as Jose Ysidro, SCZB 1627, on April 13, 1816). He became known as Isidro Sauset, with his Indigenous name

retained as his last name, a practice common within the surviving Indigenous community in Santa Cruz. The Tejey are a large Yokuts group from the San Joaquin Valley, discussed in more detail in chapter 4. Of the nine Tejey and Chaneche people baptized the same day as Sauset, four of them died while fugitives (SCZB 1625, 1629, 1631, and 1633), and another remains unaccounted for (SCZB 1626)—likely a fugitive whose fate the missionaries never learned. Overall, about one hundred Tejey were baptized at Mission Santa Cruz, the majority of them in 1810 (see chaps. 3 and 4). Sauset and his small group were among the second wave of Tejey to arrive. The twelve-year-old Huocom girl Jorsotsmin (alternatively Josotmin or Jocsotsinin, Maria Buena, SCZB 1941), on September 27, 1821. She was listed as the daughter of the unbaptized couple Tatijim and Liliguinati. Following secularization, the family lived in the Potrero del Carmen Rancheria, in the adobe homes in front of the mission.

80. SCLB 8415. Santiago is referred to as being from Mission Santa Clara in their marriage record, SCZM 949, on July 21, 1856. He is also referenced as "Jose Santiago from Santa Clara" by the French linguist Alphonse Pinart, mentioned in the previous chapter.

81. Pinart Papers, vol. 9, BL, BANC MSS Z-Z 17.

82. Santiago's parents, Uresses (Santiago, SCLB 6001, on May 12, 1812) and Pascasia (SCLB 6208). His mother, Pascasia, was the daughter of two Sumus, Aluns (Neofito, SCLB 4760) and Hichuela (Policarpa, SCLB 5487). Santiago's father and maternal grandparents are all listed as being from the Taysenn tribe along the Orestimba River. This was the name given to the Sumus at Mission Santa Clara.

83. Maria Guadalupe (SCZB 2353, on February 1, 1856), Benito (SCZB 3270, on June 10, 1860), Jose Primitivo (SCZB 3359, on July 6, 1862), Luciana (SCZB 3513, on March 26, 1865), Maria (SCZB 3668, on May 30, 1867), Gregoria Elena (baptism record not found, but burial record of a twelve-year-old Gregoria Elena, daughter of Santiago and Isabela Elena, is SCZD 3011, on April 23, 1883), Juan Francisco (SCZB 4085, on April 14, 1872), Maria Vicenta (SCZB 4247, on June 21, 1874), and Augustina (SCZB 4483, July 29, 1877).

84. I believe Jose Primitivo (SCZB 3359, on July 6, 1862) to be the young man known as Cache, or Jose Lend. Dunn believed that Cache was really Jose Fernandez (SCZB 3529) because of the latter's birthday on June 18, 1965. While this would make sense given the stated age of Cache, this Jose Fernandez has a burial record, SCZD 2537, which claims he died on May 25, 1869, as a four-year-old. The only two Joses who are close enough in age and still alive at the time are the aforementioned Jose Primitivo and Jose Gregorio Calles (SCZB 3518, born on April 16, 1865). While it is possible that either of the two could be Cache, the convicted Jose Lend testified that he "had nobody to care for him," see "Barn

Burnerss," 3:2. Jose Gregorio was the son of Santos and Teodora, who survived into old age past 1900; see U.S. Federal Census 1900, Soquel Township, p. 34, visit 527. The differing family stories and circumstances of the two Joses lead me to think that Jose Primitivo is the real Cache.

85. Over two years beginning in 1876, at least 175 people died in the community, many of them children. Reader, "Voices of the Heart."

86. SCZD 2856 on April 6, 1878.

87. Maria Vicenta, SCZD 2857 on April 26, 1878. Maria Ysabel, SCZD 2859 on May 21, 1878.

88. SCZD 2861 on May 28, 1878.

89. SCZD 3011 on April 23, 1883.

90. "The Barn Burners: Two Indian Boys Arrested for Arson—One Confesses, the Other Denies," *Santa Cruz Sentinel*, December 9, 1884, 3:2.

91. 1880 Federal U.S. Census, p. 32, visit 287. Chinese servants, launderers, fishermen, and agricultural workers had begun to move into the Monterey Bay area in the early 1850s. In Santa Cruz many members of the Chinese community worked in households, although a number of Chinese Laundromats, garden markets, and businesses existed throughout the second half of the nineteenth century. See Lydon, *Chinese Gold*.

92. The story of the dog's affection for Cache is included as a note under the principal report in the "Barn Burners," 3:2. Representations of city-dwelling Indigenous Californians by American newspapers focus condescendingly on their assumed childishness or romanticize their connections to local lands and animals. See previous notes in this chapter about the stories regarding Native American knowledge of local waterways, wildlife, plants, or eggs. As previously noted, the ease in connecting local Indians with animals was partly a result of preexisting American stereotypes that saw "Indians" as less than human, but it is possible that Cache formed a strong bond with the dog. The history of local Indigenous spiritual connections with canines is seen in the inclusion of canine bones in burial sites such as CA-SCL-732, in Coyote Creek, Santa Clara County, CA. See also Field and Leventhal, "What Must It Have Been Like," which explores the significance and implications of this site.

93. "Bad Injuns," 3:3.

94. Schneider, "Placing Refuge."

95. A recent finding of village sites up along the ridge of the local mountain range with usage that implies the postmission period suggests that some survivors put down roots in the mountain range north of Santa Cruz and returned to ancestral lifeways. See Hylkema, "Discovery of Two Previously Un-Recorded Ancestral Native American Archaeological Sites."

96. Reports by Alexander Taylor of visits by Yokuts to the Monterey area were explored by Pilling, "Archeological Implications of an Annual Coastal Visit," 438–40. Here Pilling notes this report by Taylor in May 1859.

97. Spedding Calciano, "Frank L. Blaisdell," 123. This is reported in an oral history transcript made in 1967.

98. SCZM 972, on June 4, 1859. The marriage record notes that Jose Roque was a widow, having been married before to an Indigenous woman named Joaquina. It also says that Roque was born in San Gabriel, the son of Indigenous parents, Roca and Nicolrata. Based on this it appears that Jose Miguel Roque is SGB 7355, baptized as Miguel. This entry lists father Guaspet (Roque, SGB 2369) and mother Atumibam (Nicostrata, SGB 5556), both from the Cochovipabet village.

99. The marriage record notes that Maria Crescencia, from San Luis Rey, was the daughter of Jose Antonio Veronea and Josefa Antonia. It is likely that Maria Crescencia is SLRB 5129, born in 1830. Her mother is listed as Guejais (Josefa Antonia, SLRB 1045) and father as Amonason or Hasutamamason from the Topome village (SLRB 2289). Alternatively, there are two couples at San Luis Rey, both named Jose Antonio and Josefa Antonia, who have children. Neither couple has a daughter named Crescencia, but that could be because of a name change at some point. These couples are: Tamanacuix (Jose Antonio, SLRB 4190) and Aulenguagix (Josefa Antonia, SLRB 4208), both from the Cupa village, or Tobac (Jose Antonio, SLRB 4617) from the Topome village and Ommoix (Josefa Antonia, SLRB 4636) from the Cuqui village.

100. Also noted in their marriage record. Missions San Gabriel and San Luis Rey are two of the least recorded missions. The original baptismal registries for both missions are lost, leaving a lack of clarity on the exact identities of the couple.

101. Maria Guadalupe (named Maria de Jesus at baptism, SCZB 2232).

102. SCZB 3266, on April 13, 1860.

103. Lorenzo served as *padrino* in SCZB 3266, 3375, 3568, and 3692, while Maria Filomena was *madrina* for SCZB 3266, 3375, and 3568.

104. Asisara's experience as a soldier at the San Francisco Presidio is mentioned in an interview he gave in 1890. See E. L. Williams, "Narrative of a Mission Indian," 46.

105. SCZB 1377, on March 11, 1808.

106. Xuclan's parents, Chaparis (Bruno, SCZB 1292) and Legem (Bruna, SCZB 1295), received baptism at Mission Santa Cruz on June 12, 1806, as part of a large group of Sumus. This was the same group that included the Quintana assassination conspirator and key player Yaquenonsat (Fausta). Curiously, Xuclan's baptism took place when he was one year old, in March 1808. Xuclan's mother, Legem, remarried in September 1808 (SCZM 449). Chaparis was reported dead at the end of 1810 (see note below), so Legem's remarriage suggests that Chaparis

had left the mission sometime in 1808. Why was the infant Xuclan baptized almost two years after his parents? His baptismal record noted that he had been born at the mission. Perhaps his parents resisted having him baptized? Was he taken from the mission when his family fled? Or does this suggest the limitation of missionary control over the growing Indigenous population? Five young children received baptism the same day as Xuclan (SCZB 1375–79), suggesting that this was a group of overlooked or missing youth.

107. His father was reported dead at the end of 1809, SCZD 974, and his sister Ulgem (Eulalia, SCZB 1303) was reported dead at the end of 1810, SCZD 1030. At the end of most years the padres entered records of fugitives found to be dead outside of the mission bounds, typically with notes about the reporting of this data from Indian auxiliaries, such as Agustin Moctó or others.

108. Xuclan is noted as *"paje"* in his entry as marriage witness in SCZM 665–77, on November 27, 1821; a month later, on December 21 (SCZM 689); and again on December 26, 1821 (SCZM 690). He served as *padrino* in SCZB 1991, 2110, 2028–31, and 2875.

109. The mission-born Rafael de Jesus (SCZB 1413), whose father was Pitac and mother Ausaima (Chipuctac), died on January 5, 1836 (SCZD 1954). His burial record explains that he "died of sores after having them all his life," suggesting that he might have suffered from syphilis. His burial record listed him as Rafael Cantor—"Rafael the singer." Xuclan and the Yokuts-speaking Huocom woman Chutupat (Margarita, SCZB 1745) married on May 12, 1836 (SCZM 815), four months after Rafael's death.

110. The older daughter, Filomena, SCZB 2191, was born on July 5, 1832, and Maria de Jesus, SCZB 2232, was born on December 24, 1834.

111. The family is listed in the census of 1839, in Mission Santa Cruz Libro de Padrones, on file at the Monterey Archdiocese. The family is listed as including twenty-five-year-old Ricardo "Carion," his twenty-year-old wife, Margarita (her 1818 baptismal record lists her as a four year old, suggesting that she was closer to twenty-five at the time of her marriage), her two daughters—nine-year-old Maria Filomena and seven-year-old Maria Jesus—as well as two-year-old Maria Catarina (SCZB 2280), daughter of the couple. Quihueimen, the surviving convict of the Quintana assassination, served as the *padrino* to Maria Catarina, who died of a fever in December 1842 (SCZD 2079).

112. Xuclan's connection to Pescadero is related in the chapter 5 story of Luisa Bolcoff. His connections to San José come from a record in 1834, which noted that Xuclan (as Jose Ricardo) and Chuyucu (as Jose Victoriano), husband of Lino's daughter, Maria Petra Nicanor, were called to appear before the justice of the peace in San José to answer charges brought against them. Kimbro, *Como La Sombra Huye La Hora*, 138. Document in San José Pre-Statehood Documents, Alcalde of San José, June 28, 1834.

113. SCZD 2183, on February 22, 1851.

114. Tefertiller, "Oral History from Ruby Tefertiller." Tefertiller had met Maria Filomena as a young girl and discussed her and her stories when interviewed shortly before her passing in the 1980s.

115. Transcription of court records found in the collections of Santa Cruz Museum of Art and History, Santa Cruz County Clerk's Office, Rice v. Ricardo, Case 577, M.R. 3.11. The court proceedings took place on July 23, 1866. Little has been written about landholding Indians during the Mexican and American eras. One such study explores land held in nearby San José; see Shoup and Milliken, *Inigo of Rancho Posolmi*.

116. "Unsurveyed Public Lands—Santa Cruz County," *Santa Cruz Weekly Sentinel*, February 9, 1867, 2:1.

117. "Homestead Law," *Santa Cruz Weekly Sentinel*, August 4, 1866, 4:1.

118. The sale of these lands to Rice is recorded in the transcripts of the case, see Santa Cruz Museum of Art and History, Santa Cruz County Clerk's Office, Rice v. Ricardo, case 577, M.R. 3.11

119. It is not clear who Andres is or where he is from, as no records give much information. He goes by Andres or Jose Andres Castro at times, though it is clear on multiple records that he is Indigenous. To date, I have not found a marriage record between a Filomena and an Andres in the area, but I estimate that they were married between 1854 and 1856, based on the baptismal records of her children. Maria Filomena has a child out of wedlock in 1854 (Hipolita Carrana, SCZB 3104), and then the couple have their first child in in 1856 (Jose de Jesus Reynaldo, SCZB 3118). Her first child died as an infant (SCZD 2200). One clue potentially about Andres's identity is that he eventually went by the name Andres Castro, suggesting that he might have had some connection with the local Castro family. In the 1843 census there is a servant named Andres listed in the household of Joaquin Castro and Maria Eusabia Balencia, living on or near the Castro Adobe. No more information exists about this Andres, and he does not appear in that household in later censuses.

120. Their children included the aforementioned Jose de Jesus Reynaldo, Teresa de Jesus (SCZB 3219), Rafael (SCZB 3428), Margarita (named after Filomena's mother, SCZB 3602), and Francisco Xavier (SCZB 4157).

121. Rafael (SCZB 3428), born on November 13, 1863.

122. Maria Guadalupe (SCZB 2647), daughter of Xuclan and Chutupat, Filomena's mother. Alternatively, the sister could be Maria de Jesus (SCZB 2232), born on December 24, 1834. She married an Indigenous man named Manuel (baptism currently unknown, although he is recorded as an "Indio" in their child's baptismal record). They had a child, Clodomiro (SCZB 3764), in June 1868.

123. The various notes in this paragraph about Tahoe and Cache, his mother, and aunt were reported by local historian and newspaper journalist Ernest Otto, who was alive at the time of the arsons. These notes were recorded in numerous undated historical columns in the 1940s and 1950s and collected and reprinted in Dunn, *Santa Cruz Is in the Heart*, vol. 2.

124. His testimony is transcribed in "Barn Burners," 3:2. The conditions of his confession are unclear, as the article notes that they refused legal representation. It is not entirely clear if they refused or were not allowed any.

125. Given the prevalence of violence and discrimination against local Californios and Indians at the time, it is entirely possible that Tahoe was not involved in this arson. However, as I argue here, it is not difficult to understand that the continual encroachment of American families could have motivated both him and Cache.

126. "Bad Injuns," 3:3.

127. "New To-Day," 3:3. It is interesting that the journalist mentioned their smoking. Many Indigenous Californians, including the Yokuts, smoked local tobacco for ceremonial and other purposes.

128. This quotation came from informal discussion following a talk given by Castro at Cabrillo College on October 1, 2015. Castro spoke to Stan Rushworth's English class that evening, telling stories of local history and about Indigenous survival and perseverance. Here Castro was explaining why his family had hidden their Indian heritage. See also Castro, "Mission Accomplice (but NOT Accomplished)."

129. "The Spectator's Comments," *Santa Cruz Sentinel*, May 9, 1902, 1:4. This article includes some of E. L. Williams's interview with Asisara, provided by Williams, and mentions that the "Indian Lorenzo has since died at the County Hospital of this place," suggesting that Asisara had died in Santa Cruz before the article's printing.

130. His leaving the church is recorded in two reports. The first is that cited above, which notes that "Lorenzo dropped out of the ways of the new religion. He again followed that of his forefathers, the ways of the Great Redman's Spirit and the happy hunting grounds. Lorenzo died in the first part of the 60's and was interred in the Evergreen Cemetery," in "Old Coins Unearthed in Evergreen Cemetery," *Santa Cruz Weekly Sentinel*, February 2, 1908, 9:3. This is noted by Santa Cruz historians Randall Brown and Traci Bliss, in *Evergreen Cemetery of Santa Cruz*, 65. Another article, similarly cited by Bliss and in an early chapter here, tells of Asisara's involvement in the revenge killing of the wife-slaying Pedro Gomez. The article goes on to say that "Lorenzo went back to his people and forgot in five years all that he had learned in 25. He refused to have anything to do with the Spaniards, their church or their religion. He died

with the name of the woman he loved best on his lips." "When P. Gomez, Slayer, Defied Alcalde Blackburn after Killing Gomez' Wife," by Belle Dormer, *Santa Cruz Sentinel*, October 8, 1932, 7:1. Despite the extravagant rhetoric and other errors (for example, the former article erroneously claimed that Asisara died in the 1860s) these two reports corroborate and explain his burial in the Evergreen cemetery, as opposed to the Catholic cemetery at Holy Cross, confirming Asisara's separation from the church.

131. A brief newspaper blurb noted that "two little Indian girls in need of a home secured one temporarily Monday, but we hope it will be permanent." "Sentinel Jottings," *Santa Cruz Sentinel*, April 26, 1892, 3:1.

132. This includes the 1900 U.S. Federal Manuscript Census for the following townships: Soquel, Santa Cruz, and Branciforte. In this census most of the Indians are listed separately on the Indian Census. Unfortunately, the enumerators did not list addresses for Indians on this supplemental page, preventing us from knowing exactly where they lived.

133. The family is listed in the 1900 U.S. Federal Manuscript Census, Soquel Township, p. 34, household 527. Unfortunately, the address is not reported, as it is in the Indian Census supplemental form. However, the family has ties to the contemporary local family of Patrick Orozco (discussed in the conclusion). The Gonzaga family lived next door to the Rios family, Patrick's grandmother, Rose Rios, and her parents (household 528 in census listing cited here). The families lived on Trabling Road, a few blocks away from the Castro Adobe on Rancho San Andreas. Teodora is buried alongside their neighbors, Daniella Lugo Rios and Jesus Lugo. Santos is most likely one of two people. The first possibility is that he is the grandson of the aforementioned Sayanta man Geronimo Chugiut, nee Jose Chrisantos Francisco (SCZB 2679). The other possibility is that he is Guadalupe del Espiritu Santo (SCZB 2661), the son of the Chipuctac father Hilario (SCZB 860) and Atsnil (Yokuts) mother Eulogia (SCZB 1680). Teodora's identity is less certain, but she is most likely from Mission San Juan Bautista, SJBB 3800, the daughter of a Copcha (Yokuts) couple from the Firebaugh region: Consic (Columbo, SJBB 2537) and Chahualat (Columba, SJBB 2538). Her mother, Chahualat, died at Mission San Juan Bautista in October 1838 (SJBD 3306). Santo and Teodora appear to have married in November 1849 at Mission San Juan Bautista (SJBM 1205).

134. Maria Filomena is one of the few Indians whose place of residence was known, because she was listed as a servant within a non-Indian household (p. 9, household 155, visit 158). Filomena is listed as Maria Filomena "Castor."

135. *Santa Cruz Sentinel*, May 6, 1902. The story calls the two women "squaws," a common derogatory term for Indigenous women. It very possibly comes from the Algonquian or Iroquois languages and could be a reference to

women's genitalia. While commonly used in American society, the word is generally considered demeaning and insulting.

136. See Tefertiller, "Oral History from Ruby Tefertiller," 15.

137. See Tefertiller, "Oral History from Ruby Tefertiller," 7, 9, and 17.

138. Their story is mentioned in chapter 5. As noted in that chapter, the couple appears in the marriage record of their daughter (SCZM 972), noting that they live in Aptos.

139. Johnston, "Paul D. Johnston," 77–78. Johnston and interviewer Spedding Caliciano had the following exchange: "Calciano: Were there any Indians around in 1900? Johnston: Well, there was a lot of half-breeds around, you know. They're practically all gone now. The last one was one that lived up at Valencia [Aptos] for years. We called him Willy. I don't know what his name was. That's all I ever heard. He was harmless, but he was a wild-looking bird I'll tell you. (Laughter) Kids were all afraid of him. Never forget; the game warden arrested him down here for getting clams out of season one time, you know. But the Indians had a privilege; they could hunt or fish anytime they wanted. The game warden took him in and the judge turned him loose. (Laughter) But he was a real old original Indian. I don't know where he came from. He lived in Valencia for years. Calciano: When did he die? Johnston: Oh, he died ten, fifteen years ago."

140. Johnston, "Paul D. Johnston," 78.

141. Solórsano to Harrington, "San Juan Report," JPH, microfilm, reel 59, p. 9.

142. Solórsano to Merriam, November 11, 1930, "San Juan Report," JPH, microfilm, reel 59, p. 33. Solórsano explained: "At Gilroy many years ago I talked with a very bright old woman named Rosa Arsola, who said she came from Santa Cruz and was a member of the Hordeon tribe. She said she had forgotten her language." It is possible that this woman was the same Tular-born Rosa (SCZB 2314) adopted by the Majors family and widower of Carlos, or Rosa Maria (SCZB 2194), daughter of Quihueimen, who later married Euginio.

143. Solórsano to Harrington, "San Juan Report," JPH, microfilm, reel 59, p. 45. Rustico was buried in Santa Cruz in September 1879 (SCZD 2895).

144. Immaculate Heart of the Blessed Virgin Mother at Watsonville burial number (WID) 197, dated July 10, 1887.

145. SCZB 1262. Ascención mentions Siboo's mother, Tapuiube or Tapuyube (Vicenta, SCZB 1268), and someone who is thought to be his sister, Sacet (Brigida, SCZB 1276), confirming his identity. Ascención spoke about all three of them using their Spanish names. Given the ages at baptism, it does not seem possible that Sacet was the biological sister of Canuto, as this "Brigida" would have been older than Tapuiube. Perhaps the term *sister* is used to connote kinship ties. It is possible that this is actually a Canuto from Mission San Carlos (SCAB 3825), who has a sister named Maria Brigida (SCAB 4346) and mother

named Vicenta (SCAB 2626). However, this Canuto would have been born in 1833, which would have meant he was in his thirties when Solórsano met him in the 1860s.

146. Ketchum suggests that Lucas is SJBB 1791, a man from Millanistecos, "which is closely associated with Orestacos, Bear Place." Email to author, February 20, 2020. Ketchum also points out that Siboo is Tomoi, whose lands are closely aligned with Orestacos as well. The two men's connections with Orestacos may explain why these men were bear doctors.

147. Solórsano to Harrington, "San Juan Report," JPH, microfilm, reel 59, p. 34. Siboo's death is either recorded at St. Patrick's Church in Watsonville 182 on June 8, 1876, or in Santa Cruz. St. Patrick's Church was established in 1869, the second church in Watsonville. Immaculate Heart of the Blessed Virgin Mother was the name of the first Watsonville Catholic church, established in 1855. In 1930 the name of this church was changed to Our Lady Help of Christians Church, commonly called "Valley Church." For the purposes of notation here, I will refer to the Immaculate Heart of the Blessed Virgin Mother as Watsonville 1 (abbreviated W1) and St. Patrick's Church as Watsonville 2 (abbreviated W2), so that this Canuto's burial will be noted as W2D 182. There is also an eighty-year-old Canuto who was buried on September 29, 1864, in Santa Cruz, SCZD 2394. The date for the 1864 burial lines up more closely with the story from Ascención. It seems likely that he was buried in Santa Cruz, which might explain why Ascención did not recall where he was buried, as she was living in Watsonville at the time. Perhaps one of them is the Canuto from San Carlos mentioned in the previous note.

148. Solórsano to Harrington, "San Juan Report," JPH, microfilm, reel 59, p. 64.

149. There is uncertainty about the exact identity of Josefa Velasquez. In Josefa's conversation with Aldon Mason in 1916, Mason wrote down that Josefa had been born in Santa Cruz, raised in the ranchos of Watsonville, and that her mother had died when she was young. Velasquez to J. A. Mason, October 1916, reel 23, Ethnological Documents of the Department and Museum of Anthropology, University of California, BL, Banc Film 2216. If Josefa was born at Mission Santa Cruz, then she is most likely SCZB 2257, born June 8, 1836, to Achistaca/Chipuctac father, Chaplica (Agaton, SCZB 1432), and Huocom mother, Turiralt (Agustina, SCZB 1808). Chaplica's father was the Achisataca man Tomisiqua (Miguel, SCZB 10), while his mother, Gepeson (Maria de la Piedad, SCZB 902), came from the Chipuctac village, in Unijaima territory. Mason worked under Alfred Kroeber and received his doctorate from UC Berkeley in 1911. His dissertation was an ethnographic study of the Salinan group, who lived just south of Ohlone territory. But there is strong evidence to suggest that Josefa was not born at Mission Santa Cruz. In 1930, after Josefa's death, Ascención Solórsano told

Harrington that Josefa was "pure Juañeno" while also telling him that she spoke Mutsun, Awaswas, and likely the language spoken at Mission Soledad (either a Yokuts dialect or maybe Chalon). Solórsano to Harrington, "San Juan Report," JPH, microfilm, reel 59, p. 49. Some descendants of Velasquez have identified a marriage record between Josefa Maria and Antonio Velasquez in 1858 (WIM 17), which notes that Josefa Maria's parents were named Josef and Martina; see email from Quirina L. to Randy M. regarding Josefa Velasquez, "Santa Cruz—SJB—Velasquez / Luna," carton 4, folder 113, Randall Milliken Papers, BANC MSS 2013/157, BL. This record suggests that Josefa Velasquez is really SJBB 4042, although that entry lists the baptismal name as Perpetua, not Josefa. But names did frequently change during these years, so it is certainly possible. Perpetua, or Josefa, was the daughter of the Ausaima man Xanttaroa (Bernardo Jose, SJBB 1293) and his wife, the Pagsin woman Martina (SJBB 305). Note that her parents' names closely match the Josef and Martina from the 1858 marriage record. Solórsano also mentioned that Josefa had a first husband named Feliz and that the couple had multiple children who had died a long time ago. Solórsano to Harrington, "San Juan Report," JPH, microfilm, reel 59, p. 49. There is a marriage record between unenumerated Josefa and "Felix" dated 1849, SJBM 1207. This record states that the groom is from San Buenaventura and the bride is from "this mission" (meaning San Juan Bautista). This same Feliz and Josefa appear to have moved to Santa Cruz, where they had two children (see next note). Feliz's burial record (SCZD 2231) from 1856 says, "Feliz, Yndio, born in San Buenaventura, married to Maria Josefa." The question of her heritage highlights the difficulties in dealing with records from this era, in which Indigenous identities were often overlooked. Taken as a whole, the evidence does suggest that most likely Josefa was born at Mission San Juan Bautista and moved to Santa Cruz after her marriage to Feliz. The one record that does not reconcile with this interpretation is the only one that is provided directly from Josefa (the Mason notes), whichstates that she was born in Santa Cruz. However, it could be that she she was simply telling Mason that she had lived in Santa Cruz (in the 1850s with Feliz), and that Mason misinterpreted this to mean that she had been born at Mission Santa Cruz.

150. Francisco in 1852 (SCZB 2954) and Maria Dubisa de Alta Gracia in 1859 (SCZB 3233). The date of Feliz's death in 1856 brings into question the identity of Josefa's second child's father, especially considering she would have married Antonio before the birth of this second child.

151. SCZD 2231.

152. This would appear to be WIM 17.

153. The note about Meregildo and Maria Agueda as *padrinos* is in SCZB 3233.

154. Email to author, September 26, 2016. The 1900 census shows Jose M. Espinoza, listed as "partner," living with Josefa and her son, Ambrosia. U.S. Federal Census 1900, Pajaro Township, p. 9, visit 135.

155. U.S. Federal Census 1930, Watsonville Township, sheet 2B, visit 44. This lists a sixty-eight-year-old Ambrosio Velasquez and his wife, Maria. Maria is noted as running a tamale restaurant, following in the footsteps of Josefa.

156. Solórsano to Harrington, "San Juan Report," JPH, microfilm, reel 59, p. 48.

157. Notes about the Kuksui dance as remembered by Velasquez are found in the reports cited above. Juristac is near modern Gilroy. The Amah Mutsun Tribal Band have been working to protect this sacred place, as there is a threat to turn it into a gravel pit. See protectjuristac.org.

Conclusion

1. "Santa Cruz County Land Trust Restores Native American Stewardship," *Santa Cruz Sentinel*, September 11, 2018.

2. For more on language reclamation and its potential for decolonizing, see Leonard, "Producing Language Reclamation"; McCarty, "Hear Our Languages"; and Leonard, "Reflections on (De)colonialism in Language Documentation."

3. "UC Santa Cruz Arboretum's Relearning Garden Reawakens Traditional Amah Mutsun Plant Knowledge," *Santa Cruz Sentinel*, November 20, 2011.

4. "Amah Mutsun Tribe Lands First Land Preservation Agreement," *Santa Cruz Sentinel*, August 22, 2013.

5. "Agency Grants Mount Umunhum Property Rights to Tribe," *Santa Cruz Sentinel*, December 14, 2017.

6. "Call for Historic Bell Removal Begins at UC Santa Cruz," *Mercury News*, June 23, 2019. See also Ramirez and Lopez, "Valentin Lopez, Healing, and Decolonization." Similar Indigenous-led discussions are occurring regarding statues as well. Sepulveda, "Discussion of San Francisco's 'Early Days' Statue."

7. It is likely that some Sayanta descendants still lived in the region. In addition to Santos, mentioned earlier, who may have been a grandson of Sayanta Geronimo Pacheco Chugiut, three other grandchildren still may have been alive: SCZB 2344, 2740, and 2773, Maria de la Resurreccion [*sic*], Maria Ynocencia, and Maria Luisa, respectively. In addition, the whereabouts of Geronimo's nephews—SCZB 2076, 2096, 2128, 2134, 2192, and 2227—are unknown. The Rodriguez family apparently trace their heritage to Chugiut.

8. The Mount Hermon center was dedicated on July 24, 1906, and the first of the annual conferences took place a week later, on July 30 and 31. The story of the Mount Hermon retreat center is related by Ross Eric Gibson, *San Jose*

Mercury News, October 4, 1994, 1B. The notes from the first meeting are found in "Northern California Indian Association Assembled in the Zayante Indian Conference," July 17-20, 1907, Mount Hermon CA, prospectus (1907), Stanford University Library. More information on these are found at the Northern California Indian Association Newsletters and Bulletins, Early 20th Century, Autry National Center, Los Angeles, MS 1311, folder 1.

9. For more on the early days of the NCIA, see Castaneda, *Marie Mason Potts*.

10. C. E. Kelsey was an officer of the Northern California Indian Association and a special agent for the Office of Indian Affairs, advocating for California Indians in the early 1900s. Miller, "Primary Sources on C. E. Kelsey."

11. Mathes, *Women's National Indian Association*.

12. Cahill, *Federal Mothers and Fathers*.

13. Taber, "Northern California Indian Association," 3.

14. For more on this myth, see Madley, *American Genocide*, 185-86.

15. Madley, *American Genocide*.

16. Taber, "Northern California Indian Association," 13.

17. For more on the Indian boarding schools, see Adams, *Education for Extinction*; Child, *Boarding School Seasons*; and Trafzer, Keller, and Sisquoc, *Boarding School Blues*.

18. Madley, "California Indians," 8.

19. Madley, "California Indians," 9.

20. *Santa Cruz Weekly Sentinel*, January 26, 1884, 3:4.

21. For example, Madley discussed stories of students setting these schools on fire in Round Valley in 1883, Tule River in 1890, and Pechanga in 1895 ("California Indians," 9). See also Whalen, *Native Students at Work*; and Samantha Williams, *Assimilation, Resilience, and Survival*.

22. Benson's biography is related along with his firsthand report of the Clear Lake Massacre, see Radin and Benson, "Stone and Kelsey 'Massacre.'" His story is also discussed by Madley, *American Genocide*, 103-8.

23. "Northern California Indian Association," 15.

24. "Northern California Indian Association." The second annual conference is discussed in *Santa Cruz Weekly Sentinel*, April 13, 1907, 9:5.

25. "Northern California Indian Association Assembled in the Zayante Indian Conference," July 17-20, 1907, Mount Hermon CA, prospectus (1907), Stanford University Library, 8.

26. The photo for the fourth annual conference, in 1909, includes a woman who looks similar to Maria Ascención Solórsano. The fuzzy image does not list names of participants, but it is possible that some locals, like Solórsano, attended some of these meetings. The image in question is found in Taber, *California and Her Indian Children*, 28. This image, and the larger role of Taber

and Christian-run "Indian charity" organizations, has been analyzed by Cahill, "Reassessing the Role of the 'Native Helper.'"

27. Frank and Goldberg, *Defying the Odds*, 35–41; and Phillips, "Bringing Them under Subjection."

28. From interview of Ed Ketchum by Beverly R. Ortiz in 2003, published in Milliken, Shoup, and Ortiz, *Ohlone/Costanoan Indians*, 212.

29. Ramirez, *Native Hubs*; and Rosenthal, *Reimagining Indian Country* and "Rewriting the Narrative." Ramirez's and Rosenthal's important studies illuminate how Indigenous communities formed and navigated the urban landscapes of twentieth-century San Jose and Los Angeles, respectively.

30. Keenan, "Mission Project."

31. For an overview of the complications surrounding federal recognition for Bay Area tribal nations, see Field, "Complicities and Collaborations," 193–210. An overview of all Ohlone groups to petition for federal recognition is provided in Milliken, Shoup, and Ortiz, *Ohlone/Costanoan Indians*, 305–7. For a look at Federal Recognition for the San Luis Rey Band of Mission Indians, see Chilcote, "Time out of Mind."

32. For more on the Confederation Villages of Lisjan, see https://villagesoflisjan.org/tribal-history. For more on the Chalon Indian Nation, see https://chalontribe.com. For more on the ARO, see https://www.ramaytush.org. The ARO founder and chair, Jonathan Cordero (Ramaytush), is assistant professor of sociology at Cal Lutheran University. He has published multiple important articles exploring Ramaytush and Bay Area Indigenous history and cultural persistence, while also supporting outreach and awareness of this history in the community through the ARO. See Cordero, "California Indians, Franciscans, and the Myth of Evangelical Success" and "Native Persistence."

33. In the early 1900s special Indian agent Charles E. Kelsey identified this group as the Verona Band of Alameda County residing near Pleasanton, Sunol, and Niles. As a result of Kelsey and through the Appropriation Acts of Congress of 1906, the Verona Band was federally recognized between 1906 and 1927. This ended in 1927 when Sacramento superintendent Colonel Lafayette A. Dorrington, who had a notorious drinking habit and frequently fabricated reports, was asked to provide a list of California tribes who had yet to receive lands. Dorrington responded by dismissing the needs of approximately 135 tribal bands, effectively terminating their status. These 135 tribal bands included the Muwekma, the OCEN, and the Amah Mutsun. All three lost their status at this time. Field, "Unacknowledged Tribes."

34. More served in World War II and later wars. Details about Muwekma Ohlone veterans can be found on their website: www.muwekma.org/thepeople/veterans.html.

35. Ortiz, *Ohlone/Costanoan Indians*, 199 and 207.

36. For a more complete overview of the Muwekma and their efforts to gain federal recognition, including the work of former Chairwoman Rosemary Cambra, see Field et al., "Contemporary Ohlone Tribal Revitalization," 412–31.

37. Zappia, "Original 'Farm-to-Table.'"

38. In the early 1900s special Indian agent Charles E. Kelsey and Reno superintendent James Jenkins identified the tribe that would later become known as OCEN as the Monterey Band of Monterey County. Previously, in 1883, special Indian agent Helen Hunt Jackson identified the tribe as the "San Carlos Indians, living near the old San Carlos Mission at Monterey." Further details about their history can be found on the nation's website, www.ohlonecostanoanesselennation.org. Jackson's story is a fascinating one, as she was a poet and author before becoming an Indian agent in 1882. For more on her, see Mathes, "Helen Hunt Jackson."

39. Yamane, "Profile: Isabel Meadows," 14.

40. Tribal enrollment numbers are cited at the OCEN website: www.ohlonecostanoanesselennation.org/index.html.

41. "Costanoan Rumsen Tribal History," Costanoan Rumsen Carmel Tribe website, www.costanoanrumsen.org/history.html.

42. Amah Mutsun website, http://amahmutsun.org. In the early 1900s Kelsey recognized the Amah Mutsun as the "San Juan Band."

43. In 2003 the Gilroy Unified School District named a newly built middle school in the Gilroy Unified School District was named Ascención Solórsano Middle School in her honor.

44. Ortiz, *Ohlone/Costanoan Indians*, 201–2.

45. For example, see information regarding the Amah Mutsun Land Trust, http://amahmutsun.org/land-trust. Another example of land trust is being developed by Corrina Gould (Chochenyo and Karkin Ohlone): the Sogorea Te' Land Trust. http://sogoreate-landtrust.com/.

46. Tachi-Yokut Tribe website, https://www.tachi-yokut-nsn.gov.

47. Imrie, "Costanoan-Ohlone Indian Canyon Resource," 208–9. Sayers has made her Indian Canyon lands into a center for Native peoples. Many events and gatherings have taken place on these lands.

48. Castro, "T'epot'aha'l, the Salinan Nation: Always, Now, Forever," 218–20.

49. Linda Yamane (Rumsen Ohlone) has been instrumental in reviving traditional Ohlone basketry. See Yamane and Aguilar, *Weaving a California Tradition*. She has also worked to preserve and publish stories recorded by ethnographers like Harrington: Yamane, *When the World Ended*; Yamane, *Snake That Lived in the Santa Cruz Mountains*; and Ramirez and Yamane, *Tjatjakiymatchan (Coyote)*.

50. Robin and Orozco, "Pajaro Valley Ohlone Indian Council," 216–17.

51. For more on the formation of the Red Power Movement, see Smith and Warrior, *Like a Hurricane*; and Blansett, *Journey to Freedom*. In the San Francisco Bay Area the nineteen-month occupation of Alcatraz Island, which began in late 1969, helped inspire the large local Indigenous population. This population had grown following the Indian Relocation Act of 1956, which relocated Native American families from reservations to urban centers including San Francisco and Oakland. Fixico, *Termination and Relocation*.

52. "Indian Remains Date Set Back," *Santa Cruz Sentinel*, March 7, 1975, 16:1.

53. Orozco and Robin, "I'm an Indian, but Who Am I," 18–27.

54. "Indians Ask Halt to Digging at Their Site," *Register-Pajaronian*, Monday, March 17, 1975.

55. "Opening Indian Graves Suspected," *Santa Cruz Sentinel*, March 14, 1975, 30:1.

56. "Indians Digging In as Talks Break Down," by Marj Von B, *Register-Pajaronian*, Thursday, March 20, 1975, 1:1.

57. "Vandalism Found at Burial Site," by Mark Lawshe, *Santa Cruz Sentinel*, Sunday, March 16, 1975, 1:3. The Hopi elders were discussed in this article and in an separate one, "Bird Watching, Flowers Watching," *Santa Cruz Sentinel*, March 16, 1975, 2:1.

58. "Ohlone Burial Ground: Armed Indians Appear," by Tom Honig, *Santa Cruz Sentinel*, Thursday, March 20, 1975, 1:1.

59. Orozco and Robin, "I'm an Indian, but Who Am I," 26.

60. "Settlement on Burial Ground," by Tom Honig, *Santa Cruz Sentinel*, March 21, 1975, 1:1.

61. "Building Resumes at Burial Site," by Bill Akers, *Register-Pajaronian*, Monday, March 24, 1975, 1:6.

62. Orozco and Robin, "I'm an Indian, but Who Am I," 19.

63. "Native American Remains Unearthed at Santa Cruz Housing Development Site; Protesters Rally for Halt to Construction," *Santa Cruz Sentinel*, August 14, 2011.

64. "A Victory for the Ancestors—KB Home Agrees to Not Build on Burial Ground," *Save the Knoll* (blog), September 20, 2011, https://web.archive.org/web/20111126164645/http://savetheknoll.org.

65. This group included elders from established groups like the Amah Mutsun as well Ohlone individuals involved in protecting Indigenous San Francisco Bay Area sacred sites, such as Corrina Gould (Chocheño and Karkin Ohlone) and Charlene Sul (Rumsen Ohlone). Gould is involved with the Indian People Organizing for Change, which has been leading the Shellmound Peace Walks in the East Bay since 2005, http://ipocshellmoundwalk.homestead.com/about.html. Sul is the chair of the Advisory Council for the Confederation of Ohlone Peoples, http://www.ohlonenation.org.

66. "Housing Builder Agrees to Preserve Knoll: KB Home Reaches Agreement with City, Native American Elders over Burial Ground," *Santa Cruz Sentinel*, September 20, 2011.

67. "Ohlone Indians Join Rally to Save Santa Clara Nature Preserve," *Mercury News*, October 21, 2013. Ketchum quotation from email to author, September 26, 2016.

68. Protect Juristac website, protectjuristac.org.

69. *Walk for the Ancestors* (blog), walkfortheancestors.org. Yet even with Serra's legacy, not all Bay Area Ohlone are in agreement with the walkers' mission. While many united in opposition to Serra's canonization, others did not. The diversity of Ohlone experiences and histories have shaped and continue to shape differing perspectives. For example, Chocheño Ohlone cousins Andrew Galvan and Vincent Medina have debated the Serra legacy: Julia Prodis Sulek, "Cult of Serra: A Nun and a Pair of Mission Indian Cousins Come to Terms with Junipero Serra's Sainthood," *Mercury News*, February 7, 2015.

70. Panich argues that "archaeologists and other scholars of colonial California can support the efforts of Native Californians by providing intimate details about how indigenous people negotiated the challenges of missionary colonialism." Panich, "After Saint Serra," 244.

Bibliography

Acebo, Nathan Patrick. "Re-Assembling Radical Indigenous Autonomy in the Alta California Hinterlands: Survivance at Puhú." PhD diss., Stanford University, 2020.

Acebo, Nathan, and Desireé Reneé Martinez. "Towards an Analytic of Survivance in California Archaeology." *Proceedings of the Society for California Archaeology* 32 (2018): 144–52.

Acuña, Rudolfo. *Occupied America: The Chicano's Struggle toward Liberation.* San Francisco: Canfield, 1972.

Adam, Joachim. "Rare Old Books in the Bishop's Library." *Annual Publication of the Historical Society of Southern California and Pioneer Register, Los Angeles* 4, no. 2 (1898): 154–56.

Adams, David Wallace. *Education for Extinction: American Indians and the Boarding School Experience, 1875-1928.* Lawrence: University Press of Kansas, 1995.

Adams, James D. *Estanislao: Warrior, Man of God.* La Crescenta CA: Abedus, 2006.

Ahrens, Peter. "John Work, J. J. Warner, and the Native American Catastrophe of 1833." *Southern California Quarterly* 93, no. 1 (Spring 2011): 1–32. https://doi.org/10.2307/41172554.

Alarcón, Ana María, and Margarita Díaz-Andreu. "Los paralelos etnográficos sobre chamanismo y acústica entre los yokuts: una reflexión histórica sobre la (ausencia de) interacción entre la antropología y el estudio del arte rupestre." In *Sociedades prehistóricas y manifestaciones artísticas. Imágenes, nuevas propuestas e interpretaciones*, edited by G. García Atiénzar and V. Barciela González, 231–46. Colección Petracos 2. Alicante, Instituto Universitario de Investigación en Arqueología y Patrimonio Histórico (INAPH) de la Universidad de Alicante, 2019.

Alfred, Taiaiake, and Jeff Corntassel. "Being Indigenous: Resurgences against Contemporary Colonialism." *Government and Opposition* 40, no. 4 (2005): 597–614. https://doi.org/10.1111/j.1477-7053.2005.001166.x.

Allen, Mark W., and Terry L. Jones. *Violence and Warfare among Hunter-Gatherers*. London: Routledge, 2016.

Allen, Rebecca. *Native Americans at Mission Santa Cruz, 1791–1834: Interpreting the Archaeological Record*. Los Angeles: Institute of Archaeology, University of California, Los Angeles, 1998.

Almaguer, Tomás. *Racial Fault Lines: The Historical Origins of White Supremacy in California*.
Berkeley, Calif.; London: University of California Press, 2009.

Amador, José María. *Memorias sobre la historia de California*. Bancroft Library (BL). Provincial State Records. University of California, Berkeley, C-D 28.

Anderson, M. Kat. *Tending the Wild: Native American Knowledge and the Management of California's Natural Resources*. Berkeley: University of California Press, 2005.

Anderson, M. Kat, Michael G. Barbour, and Valerie Whitworth. "A World in Balance and Plenty." In *Contested Eden: California before the Gold Rush*, edited by Ramón A. Gutiérrez and Richard J. Orsi, 12–47. Berkeley: University of California Press, in Association with the California Historical Society, 1998.

Applegate, Richard B. *Atishwin: The Dream Helper in South-Central California*. Socorro NM: Ballena, 1978.

Archivo General de la Nación (AGN). Mexico City, Mexico.

Arkush, Brooke S. "Native Responses to European Intrusion: Cultural Persistence and Agency among Mission Neophytes in Spanish Colonial Northern California." *Historical Archaeology* 45, no. 4 (2011): 62–90. https://doi.org/10.1007/BF03377306.

——. "Yokuts Trade Networks and Native Culture Change in Central and Eastern California." *Ethnohistory* 40, no. 4 (1993): 619–40. https://doi.org/10.2307/482590.

Ascension, Antonio de la, and Henry R. Wagner. "Spanish Voyages to the Northwest Coast in the Sixteenth Century. Chap. 11: Father Antonio de la Ascension's Account of the Voyage of Sebastian Vizcaino." *California History* 7, no. 4 (December 1928): 295–394.

Bacich, Damian. "Surviving Secularization: A Mexican Franciscan in a Changing California, 1833–1851." *California History* 94, no. 2 (May 1, 2017): 41–57. https://doi.org/10.1525/ch.2017.94.2.41.

Bancroft, Hubert H. *California Pastoral*. San Francisco: A. L. Bancroft, 1888.

——. *History of California*. 5 vols. San Francisco: A. L. Bancroft, 1884.

——. *The Works of Hubert Howe Bancroft*. Vol. 20 of *History of California*, vol. 3: *1825–1840*. BC Historical Books. San Francisco: History Company. 1886. http://dx.doi.org/10.14288/1.0376061.

Barr, Juliana. *Peace Came in the Form of a Woman: Indians and Spaniards in the Texas Borderlands*. Chapel Hill: University of North Carolina Press, 2009.

Basso, Keith H. *Wisdom Sits in Places: Landscape and Language among the Western Apache*. Albuquerque: University of New Mexico Press, 1996.

Bauer, William J., Jr. *California through Native Eyes: Reclaiming History*. Seattle: University of Washington Press, 2016.

———. *We Were All like Migrant Workers Here: Work, Community, and Memory on California's Round Valley Reservation, 1850–1941*. Chapel Hill: University of North Carolina Press, 2009.

Bean Lowell, John, ed. *The Ohlone Past and Present: Native Americans of the San Francisco Bay Region*. Menlo Park CA: Ballena, 1994.

Bean Lowell, John, and Thomas C. Blackburn, eds. *Native Californians: A Theoretical Retrospective*. Menlo Park CA: Ballena, 1976.

Beebe, Rose Marie, and Robert M. Senkewicz, eds. *Testimonios: Early California through the Eyes of Women, 1815–1848*. Norman: University of Oklahoma Press, 2015.

———. "The End of the 1824 Chumash Revolt in Alta California: Father Vicente Sarría's Account." *Americas* 53, no. 2 (October 1996): 273–83. https://doi.org/10.2307/1007619.

———. "Uncertainty on the Mission Frontier: Missionary Recruitment and Institutional Stability in Alta California in the 1790s." In *Francis in America: Essays on the Franciscan Family in North and South America*, edited by John Frederick Schwaller, 295–322. Washington DC: Academy of American Franciscan History, 2008.

———. "What They Brought: The Alta California Franciscans before 1769." In *Alta California: Peoples in Motion, Identities in Formation, 1769–1850*, edited by S. W. Hackel, 17–46. Berkeley: University of California Press, 2010.

Bellifemine, Viviana. "Mortuary Variability in Prehistoric Central California: A Statistical Study of the Yukisma Site, CA-SCL-38." Master's thesis, San Jose State University, 1997. https://doi.org/10.31979/etd.66wn-2z5b.

Berkhofer, Robert F. *The White Man's Indian: Images of the American Indian, from Columbus to the Present*. New York: Vintage, 1979.

Blackhawk, Ned. *Violence over the Land: Indians and Empires in the Early American West*. Cambridge: Harvard University Press, 2006.

Blansett, Kent. *A Journey to Freedom: Richard Oakes, Alcatraz, and the Red Power Movement*. New Haven CT: Yale University Press, 2018.

Blevins, Juliette, and Victor Golla. "A New Mission Indian Manuscript from the San Francisco Bay Area." *Boletín: The Journal of the California Mission Studies Association* 22 (2005): 33–61.

Bliss, Traci, with Randall Brown. *Evergreen Cemetery of Santa Cruz*. Charleston SC: History Press, 2020.

Bocek, Barbara R. "Ethnobotany of Costanoan Indians, California, Based on Collections by John P. Harrington." *Economic Botany* 38, no. 2 (April–June 1984): 240–55. https://doi.org/10.1007/BF02858839.

Boessenecker, John. *Bandido: The Life and Times of Tiburcio Vasquez*. Norman: University of Oklahoma Press, 2012.

Bokovoy, Matthew F. *The San Diego World's Fairs and Southwestern Memory, 1880–1940*. Albuquerque: University of New Mexico Press, 2005.

Bouvier, Virginia M. *Women and the Conquest of California, 1542–1840: Codes of Silence*. Tucson: University of Arizona Press, 2004.

Brave Heart, Maria Yellow Horse, and Lemyra M. DeBruyn. "The American Indian Holocaust: Healing Historical Unresolved Grief." *American Indian and Alaska Native Mental Health Research* 8, no. 2 (1998): 60–82. https://doi.org/10.5820/aian.0802.1998.60.

Breschini, Gary S., and Trudy Haversat. *Archaeological Data Recovery at Ca-Scr-44, at the Site of the Lakeview Middle School, Watsonville, Santa Cruz County, California*. Archives of California Prehistory. Salinas CA: Coyote, 2000.

———. "Post-Contact Esselen Occupation of the Santa Lucia Mountains." Paper presented at the Annual Meeting of the Society for California Archaeology, Riverside CA, April 2000.

Broadbent, Sylvia M. "Conflict at Monterey: Indian Horse Raiding, 1820–1850." *Journal of California Anthropology* 1, no. 1 (1974): 86–101. https://doi.org/10.2307/25748316.

Brooks, James. *Captives and Cousins: Slavery, Kinship, and Community in the Southwest Borderlands*. Chapel Hill: University of North Carolina Press and the Omohundro Institute of Early American History and Culture, 2002.

Brooks, Lisa Tanya. *Our Beloved Kin: A New History of King Philip's War*. Henry Roe Cloud Series on American Indians and Modernity. New Haven CT: Yale University Press, 2018.

Brown, Alan K. "Indians of San Mateo County." *La Peninsula* (San Mateo County Historical Association) 17, no. 4 (Winter 1973–74): n.p.

Burns, Kathryn. *Into the Archive: Writing and Power in Colonial Peru*. Durham NC: Duke University Press, 2010.

Byrd, Brian, Laurel Engbring, Michael Darcangelo, and Allika Ruby. *Protohistoric Village Organization and Territorial Maintenance: The Archaeology of Síi Túupentak (ca-ala-565/h) in the San Francisco Bay Area*. CARD Publication 20. Davis: University of California, Center for Archaeological Research at Davis, 2020.

Cahill, Cathleen D. *Federal Fathers and Mothers: A Social History of the United States Indian Service, 1869–1933*. Chapel Hill: University of North Carolina Press, 2013.

———. "Reassessing the Role of the 'Native Helper': Christian Indians and the Women's National Indian Association." Paper presented at the Women and American Religion: Reimagining the Past Conference, Martin Marty Center, University of Chicago, October 2003.

California State Government. *The Statues of California, Passed at the First Session of the Legislature. Begun the 15th Day of Dec. 1849, and Ended the 22nd Day of April, 1850, at the City of Pueblo de San José*. San Jose: J. Winchester, 1850.

Camarillo, Albert. *Chicanos in a Changing Society: From Mexican Pueblos to American Barrios in Santa Barbara and Southern California, 1848–1930*. Cambridge: Harvard University Press, 1979.

Cambra, Rosemary, Alan Leventhal, Laura Jones, Julia Hammett, Les Field, Norma Sanchez, and R. Jurmain. "Archaeological Investigations at *Kaphan Umux* (Three Wolves) Site, CA-SCL-732: A Middle Period Cemetery on Coyote Creek in Southern San Jose, Santa Clara County, California." Manuscript on file, California Department of Transportation, District 4, Oakland, 1996.

Caplan, Karen D. *Indigenous Citizens: Local Liberalism in Early National Oaxaca and Yucatán*. Stanford CA: Stanford University Press, 2009.

———. "Indigenous Citizenship: Liberalism, Political Participation, and Ethnic Identity in Post-Independence Oaxaca and Yucatán." In *Imperial Subjects: Race and Identity in Colonial Latin America*, edited by Andrew B. Fisher and Matthew D. O'Hara, 225–47. Durham NC: Duke University Press, 2009.

Carrico, Richard L. "Sociopolitical Aspects of the 1775 Revolt at Mission San Diego de Alcala: An Ethnohistorical Approach." *Journal of San Diego History* 43, no. 3 (1997): 143–57.

Carrera, Magali M. *Imagining Identity in New Spain: Race, Lineage, and the Colonial Body in Portraiture and Casta Paintings*. Austin: University of Texas Press, 2003.

Casas, María Raquél. *Married to a Daughter of the Land: Spanish-Mexican Women and Interethnic Marriage in California, 1820–1880*. Reno: University of Nevada Press, 2007.

Castañeda, Antonia I. "Engendering the History of Alta California, 1769–1848: Gender, Sexuality, and the Family." *California History* 76, nos. 2–3 (1997): 230–59. https://doi.org/10.2307/25161668.

Castaneda, Terri A. *Marie Mason Potts: The Lettered Life of a California Indian Activist*. Norman: University of Oklahoma Press, 2020.

Castillo, Edward D. "The Assassination of Padre Andrés Quintana by the Indians of Mission Santa Cruz in 1812: The Narrative of Lorenzo Asisara." *California History* 68, no. 3 (Fall 1989): 116–25. https://doi.org/10.2307/25462397.

———. "An Indian Account of the Decline and Collapse of Mexico's Hegemony over the Missionized Indians of California." *American Indian Quarterly* (Fall 1989): 391–408. https://doi.org/10.2307/1184523.

Castillo, Elias. *A Cross of Thorns: The Enslavement of California's Indians by the Spanish Missions*. Fresno CA: Craven Street, 2015.

Castro, Gregg. "Mission Accomplice (But NOT Accomplished)." *News from Native California* 28, no. 2 (2014–15): 59–62.

———. "T'epot'aha'l, the Salinan Nation: Always, Now, Forever." In *A Gathering of Voices: The Native Peoples of the Central California Coast*, edited by Linda Yamane, 218–20. Santa Cruz CA: Museum of Art & History, 2002.

Cavender Wilson, Angela, and Eli Taylor. *Remember This! Dakota Decolonization and the Eli Taylor Narratives*. Lincoln: University of Nebraska Press, 2005.

Cermeño, Sebastian Rodriguez, and Henry R. Wagner. "The Voyage to California of Sebastian Rodriguez Cermeño in 1595." *California Historical Society Quarterly* 3, no. 1 (1924): 3–24.

Champagne, Duane. "Centering Indigenous Nations within Indigenous Methodologies." *Wicazo Sa Review* 30, no. 1 (2015): 57–81. https://doi.org/10.5749/wicazosareview.30.1.0057.

Chase-Dunn, Christopher K., and Kelly Marie Mann. *The Wintu and Their Neighbors: A Very Small World-System in Northern California*. Tucson: University of Arizona Press, 1998.

Chavez, Yve B. "Indigenous Artists, Ingenuity, and Resistance at the California Missions after 1769." PhD diss., University of California, Los Angeles, 2017.

Chávez-García, Miroslava. *Negotiating Conquest: Gender and Power in California, 1770s to 1880s*. Tucson: University of Arizona Press, 2004.

Chilcote, Olivia. "'Time Out of Mind.'" *California History* 96, no. 4 (November 1, 2019): 38–53. https://doi.org/10.1525/ch.2019.96.4.38.

Child, Brenda J. *Boarding School Seasons: American Indian Families, 1900–1940*. Lincoln: University of Nebraska Press, 2000.

Chowning, Margaret. *Rebellious Nuns: The Troubled History of a Mexican Convent, 1752–1863*. New York: Oxford University Press, 2009.

Chuchiak, John F. "The Sins of the Fathers: Franciscan Friars, Parish Priests, and the Sexual Conquest of the Yucatec Maya, 1545–1808." *Ethnohistory* 54, no. 1 (January 1, 2007): 69–127. https://doi.org/10.1215/00141801-2006-040.

Connell, William F. *After Moctezuma: Indigenous Politics and Self-Government in Mexico City, 1524–1730*. Norman: University of Oklahoma Press, 2011.

Cook, Sherburne F. *The Aboriginal Population of the San Joaquin Valley, California*. Berkeley: University of California Press, 1955.

———. *The Conflict between the California Indian and White Civilization*. Vol. 17. Berkeley: University of California Press, 1943.

———. *The Epidemic of 1830–1833 in California and Oregon*. Berkeley: University of California Press, 1955.
———. *Expeditions to the Interior of California, Central Valley, 1820–1840*. Berkeley: University of California Press, 1962.
———. *The Population of the California Indians, 1769–1970*. Berkeley: University of California Press, 1976.
———. "Smallpox in Spanish and Mexican California, 1770–1845." *Bulletin of the History of Medicine* 7, no. 2 (1939): 153–91. http://www.jstor.org/stable/44440416.
Cordero, Jonathan F. "California Indians, Franciscans, and the Myth of Evangelical Success." *Boletín: The Journal of the California Mission Studies Association* 33, no. 1 (2017): 62–79.
———. "Native Persistence: Marriage, Social Structure, Political Leadership, and Intertribal Relations at Mission Dolores, 1777–1800." *Journal of California and Great Basin Anthropology* 35, no. 1 (2015): 133–49.
Costansó, Miguel. *The Portola Expedition of 1769–1770, Diary of Miguel Costanso*. Edited by Frederick John Teggart. Translated by Manuel Carpio. Berkeley: University of California Press, 1911.
Costo, Rupert, and Jeannette Henry Costo, eds. *The Missions of California: A Legacy of Genocide*. San Francisco: Indian Historian Press, 1987.
Cothran, Boyd. *Remembering the Modoc War: Redemptive Violence and the Making of American Innocence*. Chapel Hill: University of North Carolina Press, 2014.
Crandall, Maurice. *These People Have Always Been a Republic: Indigenous Electorate in the U.S.–Mexico Borderlands, 1598–1912*. David J. Weber Series in the New Borderlands History. Chapel Hill: University of North Carolina Press, 2019.
Crespí, Juan, and Alan K. Brown. *A Description of Distant Roads: Original Journals of the First Expedition into California, 1769–1770*. San Diego CA: San Diego State University Press, 2001.
Crespí, Juan, Robert Weldon Brower, and Herbert Eugene Bolton. *Fray Juan Crespi: Missionary Explorer on the Pacific Coast, 1769–1774*. Berkeley: University of California Press, 1927.
Crosby, Alfred W. *Ecological Imperialism: The Biological Expansion of Europe, 900–1900*. New York: Cambridge University Press, 1986.
Cruikshank, Julie. *Do Glaciers Listen? Local Knowledge, Colonial Encounters, and Social Imagination*. Vancouver: University of British Columbia Press, 2007.
———. *The Social Life of Stories: Narrative and Knowledge in the Yukon Territory*. Lincoln: University of Nebraska Press, 2000.

Cuthrell, Robby Quinn. "An Eco-Archaeological Study of Late Holocene Indigenous Foodways and Landscape Management Practices at Quiroste Valley Cultural Preserve, San Mateo County, California." PhD diss., University of California, Berkeley, 2013.

Cutter, Charles R. *The Legal Culture of Northern New Spain, 1700–1810*. Albuquerque: University of New Mexico Press, 1995.

Dartt-Newton, Deana, and Jon Erlandson. "Little Choice for the Chumash: Colonialism, Cattle, and Coercion in Mission Period California." *American Indian Quarterly* 30, no. 3 (2006): 416–30. https://doi.org/10.1353/aiq.2006.0020.

De Danaan, Llyn. *Katie Gale: A Coast Salish Woman's Life on Oyster Bay*. Lincoln: University of Nebraska Press, 2013.

DeLay, Brian. *War of a Thousand Deserts: Indian Raids and the U.S.-Mexican War*. New Haven CT: Yale University Press, 2008.

Deloria, Philip Joseph. *Indians in Unexpected Places*. Lawrence: University Press of Kansas, 2004.

———. *Playing Indian: Otherness and Authenticity in the Assumption of American Indian Identity*. New Haven CT: Yale University Press, 1998.

Deloria, Vine. *Spirit and Reason: The Vine Deloria, Jr., Reader*. Golden CO: Fulcrum, 1999.

———. *The World We Used to Live In: Remembering the Powers of the Medicine Men*. Golden CO: Fulcrum, 2006.

Denetdale, Jennifer. *Reclaiming Diné History: The Legacies of Navajo Chief Manuelito and Juanita*. Tucson: University of Arizona Press, 2007.

Díaz, Mónica. *Indigenous Writings from the Convent: Negotiating Ethnic Autonomy in Colonial Mexico*. Tucson: University of Arizona Press, 2010.

———. "Native American Women and Religion in the American Colonies: Textual and Visual Traces of an Imagined Community." *Legacy* 28, no. 2 (2011): 205–31.

Dietler, John, Heather Gibson, and Benjamin Vargas. "'A Mourning Dirge Was Sung': Community and Remembrance at Mission San Gabriel." In *Forging Communities in Colonial Alta California: The Archaeology of Indigenous-Colonial Interactions in the Americas*, edited by Kathleen L. Hull and John G. Douglass, 62–87. Tucson: University of Arizona Press, 2018.

Dunbar-Ortiz, Roxanne, and Dina Gilio-Whitaker. *"All the Real Indians Died Off": And 20 Other Myths about Native Americans*. Boston: Beacon Press, 2016.

Dunn, Geoffrey. *Santa Cruz Is in the Heart: Selected Writings on Local History, Culture, Politics and Ghosts*. Capitola CA: Capitola, 1989.

———. *Santa Cruz Is in the Heart*. Vol. 2. Capitola CA: Capitola, 2013.

Duran, Eduardo, and Bonnie Duran. *Native American Postcolonial Psychology*. Albany: State University of New York Press, 1995.

Earle, Rebecca. *The Return of the Native: Indians and Myth-Making in Spanish America, 1810–1930*. Durham NC: Duke University Press, 2007.

Early California Population Project (ECPP). *A Database Compiled and Developed at the Huntington Library*. General editor, Steven W. Hackel; lead compiler, Anne M. Reid. Henry E. Huntington Library, San Marino CA, 2006.

Engelhardt, Zephyrin. *The Missions and Missionaries of California*. Vol. 1. San Francisco: James H. Barry, 1908.

Ensminger, John J. "Dogs in California Aboriginal Cultures." *California Cultures: A Monograph Series* 5 (August 2017). https://rectangle-sparrow.squarespace.com/monographs/ccms-05-pdf.

Erlandson, Jon M., and Kevin Bartoy. "Protohistoric California: Paradise or Pandemic?" *Proceedings of the Society for California Archaeology* 9 (1995): 304–9.

Escobar, Lorraine, Les Field, and Alan Leventhal. "Understanding the Composition of Costanoan/Ohlone People." Paper presented at the California Indian Conference, San Francisco State University, February 27–28, 1998.

Estes, Nick. *Our History Is the Future: Standing Rock versus the Dakota Access Pipeline, and the Long Tradition of Indigenous Resistance*. New York: Verso, 2020.

Fages, Don Pedro, and Herbert I. Priestley. "An Historical, Political, and Natural Description of California." *Catholic Historical Review* 5, no. 1 (1919): 71–90.

Farnham, Eliza Woodson Burhans. *California, In-Doors and Out; or, How We Farm, Mine, and Live Generally in the Golden State*. New York: Dix, Edwards, 1856.

Farris, Glenn J., ed. *So Far from Home: Russians in Early California*. Berkeley CA: Heyday and Santa Clara University Press, 2012.

Fenn, Elizabeth A. *Pox Americana: The Great Smallpox Epidemic of 1775–82*. New York: Hill and Wang, 2001.

Field, Les W. "Complicities and Collaborations: Anthropologists and the 'Unacknowledged Tribes' of California [and Comments]." California Forum on Anthropology in Public. *Current Anthropology* 40, no. 2 (April 1999): 193–210. https://doi.org/10.1086/200004.

———. "Unacknowledged Tribes, Dangerous Knowledge: The Muwekma Ohlone and How Indian Identities Are 'Known.'" *Wicazo Sa Review* 18, no. 2 (2003): 79–94. https://doi.org/10.1353/wic.2003.0012.

Field, Les W., and Alan Leventhal. "'What Must It Have Been Like!': Critical Considerations of Precontact Ohlone Cosmology as Interpreted through Central California Ethnohistory." *Wicazo Sa Review* 18, no. 2 (2003): 95–126.

Field, Les W., Alan Leventhal, Dolores Sanchez, and Rosemary Cambra. "A Contemporary Ohlone Tribal Revitalization Movement: A Perspective from the Muwekma Costanoan/Ohlone Indians of the San Francisco Bay Area." *California History* 71, no. 3 (1992): 412–31. https://doi.org/10.2307/25158653.

Fine, Paul V. A., Tracy Misiewicz, Andreas S. Chavez, and Rob Q. Cuthrell. "Population Genetic Structure of California Hazelnut, an Important Food Source for People in Quiroste Valley in the Late Holocene." *California Archaeology* 5 (2013): 353–70. https://doi.org/10.1179/1947461X13Z.00000000019.

Fischer, John Ryan. *Cattle Colonialism: An Environmental History of the Conquest of California and Hawai'i.* Chapel Hill: University of North Carolina Press, 2015.

Fisher, Andrew B., and Matthew D. O'Hara. *Imperial Subjects: Race and Identity in Colonial Latin America.* Durham NC: Duke University Press, 2009.

Fixico, Donald Lee. *Termination and Relocation: Federal Indian Policy, 1945–1960.* Albuquerque: University of New Mexico Press, 1992.

Flores, Gustavo Adolfo. "Native American Response and Resistance to Spanish Conquest in the San Francisco Bay Area, 1769–1846." Master's thesis, San Jose State University, 2014.

Forbes, Jack. *Native Americans of California and Nevada.* Healdsburg CA: Naturegraph, 1969.

Foster, John W. "Wings of the Spirit: The Place of the California Condor among Native People of the Californias." California Department of Parks and Recreation. Last modified 2009. https://www.parks.ca.gov/?page_id=23527.

Fourcrier, Annick. "Sailors, Carpenters, Vineyardists." *Santa Cruz County History Journal* 3 (1999): 135–44.

Fryberg, Stephanie A., Arianne E. Eason, Laura M. Brady, Nadia Jessop, and Julisa J. Lopez. "Unpacking the Mascot Debate: Native American Identification Predicts Opposition to Native Mascots." *Social Psychological and Personality Science* 12, no. 1 (January 2021): 3–13. https://doi.org/10.1177/1948550619898556.

Gamble, Lynn H. *The Chumash World at European Contact: Power, Trade, and Feasting among Complex Hunter-Gatherers.* Berkeley: University of California Press, 2011.

———. "Subsistence Practices and Feasting Rites: Chumash Identity after European Colonization." *Historical Archaeology* 49, no. 2 (June 2015): 115–35. https://doi.org/10.1007/BF03377142.

Garr, Daniel. "Villa de Branciforte: Innovation and Adaptation on the Frontier." *Americas* 35, no. 1 (July 1978): 95–109. https://doi.org/10.2307/980927.

Geary, Gerald J. *The Secularization of the California Missions (1810–1846)*. Washington DC: Catholic University of America, 1934.

Geiger, Maynard. *Franciscan Missionaries in Hispanic California, 1769–1848: A Biographical Dictionary*. San Marino CA: Huntington Library, 1969.

———. *Fray Antonio Ripoll's Description of the Chumash Revolt at Santa Barbara in 1824*. Santa Barbara CA: Mission Santa Barbara Archive Library, 1980.

Geiger, Maynard, and Clement W. Meighan. *As the Padres Saw Them: California Indian Life and Customs as Reported by the Franciscan Missionaries, 1813–1815*. Santa Barbara CA: Santa Barbara Mission Archive Library, 1976.

Gelya, Frank, and Carole E. Goldberg. *Defying the Odds: The Tule River Tribe's Struggle for Sovereignty in Three Centuries*. New Haven CT: Yale University Press, 2010.

Gifford-Gonzalez, Diane, and Francine Marshall. "Analysis of the Archaeological Assemblage from CA-SCR-35, Santa Cruz County, California." Archives of California Prehistory. Salinas CA: Coyote, 1984.

Gillette, Donna L. "The Rock Art of Chitactac-Adams Heritage Park and Environs." In *A Gathering of Voices: The Native Peoples of the Central California Coast*, edited by Linda Yamane, 117–29. Santa Cruz CA: Museum of Art & History, 2002.

Goerke, Betty. *Chief Marin: Leader, Rebel, and Legend*. Berkeley CA: Heyday, 2007.

Gone, Joseph P. "A Community-Based Treatment for Native American Historical Trauma: Prospects for Evidence-Based Practice." *Journal of Consulting and Clinical Psychology* 77 (2009): 751–62. https://doi.org/10.1037/a0015390.

González, Michael J. "The Child of the Wilderness Weeps for the Father of Our Country." In *Contested Eden: California before the Gold Rush*, edited by Ramón A. Gutiérrez and Richard J. Orsi, 147–72. Berkeley: University of California Press, 1998.

———. *This Small City Will Be a Mexican Paradise: Exploring the Origins of Mexican Culture in Los Angeles, 1821–1846*. Albuquerque: University of New Mexico Press, 2005.

González, Rafael. "1824: The Chumash Revolt." In *Lands of Promise and Despair: Chronicles of Early California, 1535–1846*, edited by Rose Marie Beebe and Robert M. Senkewicz, 323–28. Norman: University of Oklahoma Press, 2001.

Gonzales-Day, Ken. *Lynching in the West, 1850–1935*. Durham NC: Duke University Press, 2006.

Goode, Barry. "The American Conquest of Alta California and the Instinct for Justice: The 'First' Jury Trial in California." *California History* 90, no. 2 (2013): 4–70. https://doi.org/10.2307/41936498.

Gourley, Sarah Elizabeth. "My Early Childhood Memories." *Santa Cruz County History Journal* 2 (1995): 65–80.

Gray, Thorne B. *The Stanislaus Indian Wars: The Last of the California Northern Yokuts*. Modesto CA: McHenry Museum, 1993.

Griswold del Castillo, Richard. *The Treaty of Guadalupe Hidalgo: A Legacy of Conflict*. Norman: University of Oklahoma Press, 1990.

Grossinger, Robin. *South Santa Clara Valley Historical Ecology Study, Including Soap Lake, the Upper Pajaro River, and Llagas, Uvas-Carnadero, and Pacheco Creeks*. Oakland CA: San Francisco Estuary Institute, 2008.

Guest, Francis F. "The Establishment of the Villa de Branciforte." *California Historical Society Quarterly* 41, no. 1 (March 1962): 29–50. https://doi.org/10.2307/25155449.

———. "An Examination of the Thesis of S. F. Cook on the Forced Conversion of Indians in the California Missions." *Southern California Quarterly* 61, no. 1 (1979): 1–77. https://doi.org/10.2307/41170811.

Gurcke, Starr P. Papers. Special Collections and Archives. University Library, University of California, Santa Cruz.

Gutiérrez, Ramón A., and Richard J. Orsi, eds. *Contested Eden: California before the Gold Rush*. Berkeley: University of California Press, 1998.

Haas, Lisbeth. *Conquests and Historical Identities in California, 1769–1936*. Berkeley: University of California Press, 1995.

———. *Pablo Tac, Indigenous Scholar: Writing on Luiseño Language and Colonial History, c. 1840*. Berkeley: University of California Press, 2011.

———. *Saints and Citizens: Indigenous Histories of Colonial Missions and Mexican California*. Berkeley: University of California Press, 2014.

———. "War in California, 1846–1848." In *Contested Eden: California before the Gold Rush*, edited by Ramón A. Gutiérrez and Richard J. Orsi, 331–56. Berkeley: University of California Press, 1998.

Hackel, Steven W. *Children of Coyote, Missionaries of Saint Francis: Indian-Spanish Relations in Colonial California, 1769–1850*. Chapel Hill: University of North Carolina Press, 2005.

———. "Early California Population Project Report." *Journal of California and Great Basin Anthropology* 26, no. 1 (2006): 73–76. https://doi.org/10.2307/27825823.

———. "Land, Labor, and Production: The Colonial Economy of Spanish and Mexican California." In *Contested Eden: California before the Gold Rush*. edited by Ramón A. Gutiérrez and Richard J. Orsi, 111–46. Berkeley: University of California Press, 1998.

———. "Native Insurgent Literacy in Colonial California." *California History* 96, no. 4 (November 1, 2019): 2–10. https://doi.org/10.1525/ch.2019.96.4.2.

———. "Sources of Rebellion: Indian Testimony and the Mission San Gabriel Uprising of 1785." *Ethnohistory* 50, no. 4 (2003): 643–69.

———. "The Staff of Leadership: Indian Authority in the Missions of Alta California." *William and Mary Quarterly* 54, no. 2 (1997): 347–76. https://doi.org/10.2307/2953277.

Hämäläinen, Pekka. *The Comanche Empire*. New Haven CT: Yale University Press, 2008.

Harkin, Michael Eugene, and David Rich Lewis, eds. *Native Americans and the Environment: Perspectives on the Ecological Indian*. Lincoln: University of Nebraska Press, 2007.

Harlow, Neal. *California Conquered: The Annexation of a Mexican Province, 1846–1850*. Berkeley: University of California Press, 1989.

Harrington, John P. "Culture Element Distributions: XIX Central California Coast." *University of California Anthropological Records* 7, no. 1 (1942): 1–46.

———. Papers (JPH). "San Juan Report." Northern and Central California: Costanoan. National Anthropological Archives, Smithsonian Institution, Suitland MD.

Hartnell, William E. P. *The Diary and Copybook of William E. P. Hartnell*. Edited by Glenn J. Farris. Translated by Starr Pait Gurcke. Santa Clara CA: Arthur H. Clark, 2004.

Heizer, Robert F. *The Destruction of California Indians: A Collection of Documents from the Period 1847 to 1865 in Which Are Described Some of the Things That Happened to Some of the Indians of California*. Lincoln: University of Nebraska Press, 1993.

———. "Impact of Colonization on the Native California Societies." *Journal of San Diego History* 24 (Winter 1978): 121–39.

Heizer, Robert F., and Alan J. Almquist. *The Other Californians: Prejudice and Discrimination under Spain, Mexico, and the United States to 1920*. Berkeley: University of California Press, 2000.

Helmbrecht, Brenda. "Revisiting Missions: Decolonizing Public Memories in California." *Rhetoric Society Quarterly* 49, no. 5 (2019): 470–94. https://doi.org/10.1080/02773945.2019.1668048.

Henshaw, H. W. *California Indian Linguistic Records: The Mission Indian Vocabularies of H. W. Henshaw*. Edited by Robert F. Heizer. Berkeley: University of California Press, 1955.

Hill Boone, Elizabeth, and Walter Mignolo, eds. *Writing without Words: Alternative Literacies in Mesoamerica and the Andes*. Durham NC: Duke University Press, 1994.

Holterman, Jack. "The Revolt of Estanislao." *Indian Historian* 3 (Winter 1970): 43–54.

---. "The Revolt of Yozcolo: Indian Warrior in the Fight for Freedom." *Indian Historian* 3 (Spring 1970): 19–23.

Hornbeck, David, David L. Fuller, and Phillip S. Kane. *California Patterns: A Geographical and Historical Atlas*. Palo Alto CA: Mayfield, 1983.

Hull, Kathleen L. *Pestilence and Persistence: Yosemite Indian Demography and Culture in Colonial California*. Berkeley: University of California Press, 2009.

Hull, Kathleen L., and John G. Douglass, eds. *Forging Communities in Colonial Alta California: The Archaeology of Indigenous-Colonial Interactions in the Americas*. Tucson: University of Arizona Press, 2018.

Hull, Kathleen L., John G. Douglass, and Andrew L. York. "Recognizing Ritual Action and Intent in Communal Mourning Features on the Southern California Coast." *American Antiquity* 78, no. 1 (2013): 24–47. https://doi.org/10.7183/0002-7316.78.1.24.

Hurtado, Albert L. "'Hardly a Farm House—A Kitchen without Them': Indian and White Households on the California Borderland Frontier in 1860." *Western Historical Quarterly* 13, no. 3 (July 1982): 245–70. https://doi.org/10.2307/969413.

---. *Indian Survival on the California Frontier*. New Haven CT: Yale University Press, 1988.

---. *Intimate Frontiers: Sex, Gender, and Culture in Old California*. Albuquerque: University of New Mexico Press, 1999.

Hutchinson, C. Alan. "The Mexican Government and the Mission Indians of Upper California, 1821–1835." *Americas* 21, no. 4 (1965): 335–62. https://doi.org/10.1017/S0003161500012967.

Hylkema, Mark G. *Discovery of Two Previously Un-Recorded Ancestral Native American Archaeological Sites: ca-scl-951 and ca-scl-952*. Past Lifeways Archaeological Studies. Report prepared for the Midpeninsula Regional Open Space District, January 2017. Manuscript on file, Northwest Information Center, California Historic Resources Information Center, Rohnert Park CA.

---. *Historic Properties Survey Report (HPSR) and a Finding of No Effect to Cultural Resources, Stevens Creek Steelhead Passage Improvement Project, Santa Clara County, California*. Report prepared for Friends of Stevens Creek Trail, April 2021. Manuscript on file, Northwest Information Center, California Historic Resources Information Center, Rohnert Park CA.

---. "Mount Umunhum Environmental Restoration ASR: Negative Archaeological Survey Report (NASR): A Finding of No Effect to Archaeological Resources, Mount Umunhum Restoration and Public Access Project, Santa Clara County, California." Report prepared for the Midpeninsula Regional Open Space District, January 2011. Manuscript on file, Northwest Information Center, California Historic Resources Information Center, Rohnert Park CA.

———. "Prehistoric Native American Adaptations along the Central California Coast of San Mateo and Santa Cruz Counties." Master's thesis, San Jose State University, 1991.

———. "Tidal Marsh, Oak Woodlands, and Cultural Florescence in the Southern San Francisco Bay Region." In *Catalysts to Complexity: Late Holocene Societies of the California Coast*, edited by Jon Erlandson, Terry L. Jones, and Jeanne E. Arnold, 233–62. Los Angeles: Cotsen Institute of Archaeology at UCLA, 2002.

Hylkema, Mark G., and Kenneth R. Bethard. 2007. *Santa Clara Valley Prehistory: Archaeological Investigations at ca-scl-690, the Tamien Station Site, San Jose, California*. Davis: Center for Archaeological Research at David, Department of Anthropology, University of California.

Hylkema, Mark G., with contribution by Thad M. Van Buren. *Archaeological Investigations at the Third Location of Mission Santa Clara de Asis: The Murguia Mission, 1781–1818 (ca-scl-30/h)*. Report prepared for the California Department of Transportation, District 4, Oakland, 1995. Reprinted through Coyote Press, Salinas CA.

Igler, David. *Industrial Cowboys: Miller & Lux and the Transformation of the Far West, 1850–1920*. Berkeley: University of California Press, 2001.

Imrie, Russell, for Anne Marie Sayers. "Costanoan-Ohlone Indian Canyon Resource." In *A Gathering of Voices: The Native Peoples of the Central California Coast*, edited by Linda Yamane, 208–9. Santa Cruz CA: Museum of Art & History, 2002.

Jackson, Robert H. "Disease and Demographic Patterns at Santa Cruz Mission, Alta California." *Journal of California and Great Basin Anthropology* 5, no. 2 (1983): 33–57.

———. *From Savages to Subjects: Missions in the History of the American Southwest*. Latin American Realities. Armonk NY: M. E. Sharpe, 2000.

———. *Indian Population Decline: The Missions of Northwestern New Spain, 1687–1840*. Albuquerque: University of New Mexico Press, 1995.

———. "The Justiniano Roxas Hoax: The Story of the Oldest Man on Earth." *Californians* 4, no. 6 (1986): 44–54.

———. *Race, Caste, and Status: Indians in Colonial Spanish America*. Albuquerque: University of New Mexico Press, 1999.

———. "The Villa de Branciforte Census." *Antepasados* 4 (1980–81): 45–57.

Jackson, Robert H., and Edward D. Castillo. *Indians, Franciscans, and Spanish Colonization: The Impact of the Mission System on California Indians*. Albuquerque: University of New Mexico Press, 1996.

Jacobson, Matthew Frye. *Whiteness of a Different Color: European Immigrants and the Alchemy of Race*. Cambridge: Harvard University Press, 2002.

John, Maria. "Toypurina: A Legend Etched in the Landscape." In *East of East: The Making of Greater El Monte*, edited by Romeo Guzmán, Caribbean Fragoza, Alex Sayf Cummings, and Ryan Reft, 25–36. New Brunswick NJ: Rutgers University Press, 2020.

Johnson, John R. *The Chumash Indians after Secularization*. San Diego: California Mission Studies Association, 1995.

———. "Chumash Social Organization: An Ethnohistoric Perspective." PhD diss., University of California, Santa Barbara, 1988.

———. "The Trail to Fernando." *Journal of California and Great Basin Anthropology* 4, no. 1 (1982): 132–38.

Johnson, John R., and Joseph G. Lorenz. "Genetics and the *Castas* of Colonial California." In *Alta California: Peoples in Motion, Identities in Formation, 1769–1850*, edited by S. W. Hackel, 157–96. Berkeley: University of California Press, 2010.

Johnson, John R., and William M. Williams. "Toypurina's Descendants: Three Generations of an Alta California Family." *Boletín: The Journal of the California Mission Studies Association* 24, no. 2 (2007): 31–55.

Johnston-Dodds, Kimberly. *Early California Laws and Policies Related to California Indians*. Sacramento: California State Library, California Research Bureau, 2002.

Johnston, Paul D. "Paul D. Johnston: Aptos and the Mid–Santa Cruz County Area from the 1890s through World War II." Interviewed and edited by Elizabeth Spedding Calciano. Santa Cruz: Regional History Project, University Library, University of California, Santa Cruz, 1973.

Jones, Barbara Lee. "Mythic Implications of Faunal Assemblages from Three Ohlone Sites." Master's thesis, San Francisco State University, 2010.

Jones, Deborah A., and William R. Hildebrandt. *Archaeological Test Excavation at Sand Hill Bluff: Portions of Pre-Historic Site ca-scr-7, Santa Cruz County, California*. Report on file, Northwest Information Center, California Archaeological Site Inventory, Department of Anthropology, Sonoma State University, Rohnert Park CA, 1990.

Jones, Terry L., and K. A. Klar. *California Prehistory: Colonization, Culture, and Complexity*. New York: Altamira, 2007.

Joseph, Gilbert Michael, and Daniel Nugent. *Everyday Forms of State Formation: Revolution and the Negotiation of Rule in Modern Mexico*. Durham NC: Duke University Press, 1994.

Kauanui, J. Kēhaulani, and Robert Allen Warrior. *Speaking of Indigenous Politics: Conversations with Activists, Scholars, and Tribal Leaders*. Minneapolis: University of Minnesota Press, 2018.

Keeley, Jon E. "Native American Impacts on Fire Regimes of the California Coastal Ranges." *Journal of Biogeography* 29, no. 3 (March 2002): 303–20. https://doi.org/10.1046/j.1365-2699.2002.00676.x.

Keenan, Harper Benjamin. "The Mission Project: Teaching History and Avoiding the Past in California Elementary Schools." *Harvard Educational Review* 91, no. 1 (March 1, 2021): 109–32. https://doi.org/10.17763/1943-5045-91.1.109.

Kenneally, Finbar, ed. *Writings of Fermín Francisco de Lasuén*. 2 vols. Washington DC: Academy of American Franciscan History, 1964.

Ketchum, Ed. "Maria Ascención Solórsano (de Garcia y de Cervantes)." *Amah Mutsun Land Trust Newsletter* 1, no. 2 (July 2016). http://amahmutsun.org/land-trust-newsevents/maria-ascencion-solorsano-de-garcia-y-de-cervantes.

Kimbro, Edna E. "Biographical Data Concerning Lorenzo Olivara, Santa Cruz Mission Indian." Kimbro: Sec. at SCM [Secularization at Santa Cruz Mission]. Unpublished notes.

Kimbro, Edna E., A. Crosby, E. L. Tolles, E. Moore, and K. Hildebrand. California Department of Parks and Recreation, Monterey District. *Historic Structure Report for Rancho San Andres Castro Adobe: State Park*. Davenport CA: Historical Investigations, 2003.

Kimbro, Edna E., MaryEllen Ryan, and Robert H. Jackson. *Como la Sombra Huye la Hora: Restoration Research: Santa Cruz Mission Adobe: Santa Cruz Mission State Historical Park*. Davenport CA: Historical Investigations, 1985.

Kimmerer, Robin Wall. *Braiding Sweetgrass: Indigenous Wisdom, Scientific Knowledge, and the Teachings of Plants*. Minneapolis: Milkweed Editions, 2013.

King, Chester. "Central Ohlone Ethnohistory." In *The Ohlone Past and Present: Native Americans of the San Francisco Bay Region*, edited by John Bean Lowell, 203–47. Menlo Park CA: Ballena, 1994.

Kotzebue, Otto von. *A New Voyage Round the World*. Vol. 2. N.p.: Outlook Verlag, 2020.

———. *The Visit of the "Rurik" to San Francisco in 1816*. Edited by August C. Mahr. Stanford CA: Stanford University Press, 1932.

Kroeber, Alfred L. "Handbook of the Indians of California." *Bureau of Ethnology Bulletin* 78 (1925).

———. "Indian Myths of South Central California." *American Archaeology and Ethnology* 4, no. 4 (May 1907): 169–244.

Kryder-Reid, Elizabeth. *California Mission Landscapes: Race, Memory, and the Politics of Heritage*. Minneapolis: University of Minnesota Press, 2016.

Kugel, Rebecca. "Of Missionaries and Their Cattle: Ojibwa Perceptions of a Missionary as Evil Shaman." *Ethnohistory* 41, no. 2 (1994): 227–44. https://doi.org/10.2307/482833.

——. "Religion Mixed with Politics: The 1836 Conversion of Mang'osid of Fond Du Lac." *Ethnohistory* 37, no. 2 (1990): 126–57. https://doi.org/10.2307/482539.

Lacson, Paul Albert. "'Born of Horses': Missionaries, Indigenous Vaqueros, and Ecological Expansion during the Spanish Colonization of California." *Journal of San Diego History* 60, no. 3 (2015): 207–29.

——. "Making Friends and Converts." *California History* 92, no. 1 (May 1, 2015): 6–26. https://doi.org/10.1525/ch.2015.92.1.6.

LaDuke, Winona. *All Our Relations: Native Struggles for Land and Life*. Chicago: Haymarket, 2015.

Langer, Erick D. *Expecting Pears from an Elm Tree: Franciscan Missions on the Chiriguano Frontier in the Heart of South America, 1830–1949*. Durham NC: Duke University Press, 2009.

Langsdorff, Georg H. von. *Voyages and Travels in Various Parts of the World during the Years 1803, 1804, 1805, 1806 and 1807*. N.p.: printed by George Phillips, 1817.

Latta, Frank F. *Handbook of Yokuts Indians*. Exeter CA: Bear State, 1977.

Leonard, Wesley Y. "Producing Language Reclamation by Decolonizing 'Language.'" In *Language Documentation and Description*, edited by Wesley Y. Leonard and Haley De Korne, 14:15–36. London: EL, 2017.

——. "Reflections on (De)colonialism in Language Documentation." In *Reflections on Language Documentation 20 Years after Himmelmann 1998*, edited by Bradley McDonnell, Andrea L. Berez-Kroeker, and Gary Holton, 55–65. Honolulu: University of Hawai'i Press, 2018.

Levy, Jo Ann. *Unsettling the West: Eliza Farnham and Georgiana Bruce Kirby in Frontier California*. Berkeley CA: Heyday, 2004.

Levy, Richard. "Costanoan." In *California*, edited by Robert F. Heizer, vol. 8 of *Handbook of North American Indians*, 485–95. Washington DC: Smithsonian Institution, 1978.

Librado, Fernando. *Breath of the Sun: Life in Early California*. Edited by Travis Hudson. Banning CA: Malki Museum, 1979–80.

Lightfoot, Kent G. *Indians, Missionaries, and Merchants: The Legacy of Colonial Encounters on the California Frontiers*. Berkeley: University of California Press, 2005.

——. "The Study of Indigenous Management Practices in California: An Introduction." *California Archaeology* 5, no. 2 (2013): 209–19. https://doi.org/10.1179/1947461X13Z.00000000011.

Lightfoot, Kent G., and Otis Parrish. *California Indians and Their Environment: An Introduction*. California Natural History Guides. Berkeley: University of California Press, 2009.

Lightfoot, Kent G., Rob Q. Cuthrell, Chuck J. Striplen, and Mark G. Hylkema. "Rethinking the Study of Landscape Management Practices among Hunter-Gatherers in North America." *American Antiquity* 78, no. 2 (April 2013). https://doi.org/10.7183/0002-7316.78.2.285.

Lightfoot, Kent G., and William S. Simmons. "Culture Contact in Protohistoric California: Social Contexts of Native and European Encounters." *Journal of California and Great Basin Anthropology* 20 (1998): 138–70.

Lindsay, Brendan C. *Murder State: California's Native American Genocide, 1846–1873.* Lincoln: University of Nebraska Press, 2012.

Lorimer, Michelle Marie. *Resurrecting the Past: The California Mission Myth.* Temecula CA: Great Oak, 2016.

Lowery, Malinda Maynor. *Lumbee Indians in the Jim Crow South: Race, Identity, and the Making of a Nation.* Chapel Hill: University of North Carolina Press, 2010.

Lozano, José María, and Manuel Dublán. *Legislación Mexicana: Ó, Colección Completa De Las Disposiciones Legislativas Expedidas Desde La Independencia De La República.* Official edition. Mexico: Dublán y Lozano, 1876.

Lugones, Maria. "Heterosexualism and the Colonial/Modern Gender System." *Hypatia* 22, no. 1 (2007): 186–209.

Lydon, Sandy. *Chinese Gold: The Chinese in the Monterey Bay Region.* Capitola CA: Capitola, 1985.

Madley, Benjamin. *An American Genocide: The United States and the California Indian Catastrophe, 1846–1873.* New Haven CT: Yale University Press, 2016.

———. "California and Oregon's Modoc Indians: How Indigenous Resistance Camouflages Genocide in Colonial Histories." In *Colonial Genocide in Indigenous North America*, edited by Andrew Woolford, Jeff Benvenuto, and Alexander Laban Hinton, 95–130. Durham NC: Duke University Press, 2014.

———. "California Indians." *Oxford Research Encyclopedia of American History*, edited by Jon Butler. New York: Oxford University Press, 2021. https://doi.org/10.1093/acrefore/9780199329175.013.117.

———. "California's First Mass Incarceration System: Franciscan Missions, California Indians, and Penal Servitude, 1769–1836." *Pacific Historical Review* 88, no. 1 (February 2019): 14–47. https://doi.org/10.1525/phr.2019.88.1.14.

———. "Unholy Traffic in Human Blood and Souls." *Pacific Historical Review* 83, no. 4 (2014): 626–67. https://doi.org/10.1525/phr.2014.83.4.626.

Magliari, Michael. "Free Soil, Unfree Labor." *Pacific Historical Review* 73, no. 3 (2004): 349–90. https://doi.org/10.1525/phr.2004.73.3.349.

———. "Free State Slavery: Bound Indian Labor and Slave Trafficking in California's Sacramento Valley, 1850–1864." *Pacific Historical Review* 81, no. 2 (2012): 155–92. https://doi.org/phr.2012.81.2.155.

———. "Masters, Apprentices, and Kidnappers: Indian Servitude and Slave Trafficking in Humboldt County, California, 1860–1863." *California History* 97, no. 2 (May 1, 2020): 2–26. https://doi.org/10.1525/ch.2020.97.2.2.

Mallon, Florencia E. *Decolonizing Native Histories: Collaboration, Knowledge, and Language in the Americas*. Durham NC: Duke University Press, 2011.

Mann, Kristin Dutcher. *The Power of Song: Music and Dance in the Mission Communities of Northern New Spain, 1590–1810*. Stanford CA: Stanford University Press, 2010.

Manocchio, Regina Teresa. "Tending Communities, Crossing Cultures: Midwives in 19th-Century California." *Journal of Midwifery & Women's Health* 53, no. 1 (January 2008): 75–81. https://doi.org/10.1016/j.jmwh.2007.03.006.

Margolin, Malcolm. *The Ohlone Way: Indian Life in the San Francisco–Monterey Bay Area*. Berkeley CA: Heyday, 1978.

Mark, Robert, and Evelyn Newman. "Cup-and-Ring Petroglyphs in Northern California and Beyond." In *Rock Art Studies in the Americas: Papers from the Darwin Rock Art Congress*, edited by Jack Steinbring, 13–21. Oxford, England: Oxbow, 1995.

Martínez, María Elena. *Genealogical Fictions: Limpieza de Sangre, Religion, and Gender in Colonial Mexico*. Stanford CA: Stanford University Press, 2008.

Mathes, Valery Sherer. "Helen Hunt Jackson: Official Agent to the California Mission Indians." *Southern California Quarterly* 63, no. 1 (April 1981): 63–82. https://doi.org/10.2307/41170915.

Mathes, Valerie Sherer, ed. *The Women's National Indian Association: A History*. 1st ed. Albuquerque: University of New Mexico Press, 2015.

Matthew, Laura E., and Michel R. Oudijk, eds. *Indian Conquistadors: Indigenous Allies in the Conquest of Mesoamerica*. Norman: University of Oklahoma Press, 2007.

McCarty, Teresa L., Sheilah E. Nicholas, Kari A. B. Chew, Natalie G. Diaz, Wesley Y. Leonard, and Louellyn White. "Hear Our Languages, Hear Our Voices: Storywork as Theory and Praxis in Indigenous-Language Reclamation." *Daedalus* 147, no. 2 (March 2018): 160–72. https://doi.org/10.1162/daed_a_00499.

McCormack, Brian T. "Conjugal Violence, Sex, Sin, and Murder in the Mission Communities of Alta California." *Journal of the History of Sexuality* 16, no. 3 (2007): 391–415. jstor.org/stable/30114190.

McNally, Robert Aquinas. "A Dark History Hits Home." *California History* 96, no. 4 (November 1, 2019): 78–87. https://doi.org/10.1525/ch.2019.96.4.78.

———. *The Modoc War: A Story of Genocide at the Dawn of America's Gilded Age*. Lincoln; London: University of Nebraska Press, 2017.

McNeill, William Hardy. *Plagues and Peoples*. Garden City NY: Anchor, 1976.

Mihesuah, Devon Abbott, and Angela Cavender Wilson, eds. *Indigenizing the Academy: Transforming Scholarship and Empowering Communities.* Lincoln: University of Nebraska Press, 2004.

Miller, Larisa K. "Primary Sources on C. E. Kelsey and the Northern California Indian Association." *Journal of Western Archives* 4, no. 1 (2013). https://digitalcommons.usu.edu/westernarchives/vol4/iss1/8.

———. "Secret Treaties with California's Indians." *Prologue* 45 (Fall–Winter 2013): 38–45. https://www.archives.gov/files/publications/prologue/2013/fall-winter/treaties.pdf.

Miller, Susan A. *Coacoochee's Bones: A Seminole Saga.* Lawrence: University Press of Kansas, 2003.

Miller Susan A., and James Riding In, eds. *Native Historians Write Back: Decolonizing American Indian History.* Lubbock: Texas Tech University Press, 2011.

Milliken, Randall. *Native Americans at Mission San Jose.* Banning CA: Malki-Ballena, Malki Museum, 2008.

———. "The Spanish Contact and Mission Period Indians of the Santa Cruz–Monterey Bay Region." In *A Gathering of Voices: The Native Peoples of the Central California Coast*, edited by Linda Yamane, 25–36. Santa Cruz CA: Museum of Art & History, 2002.

———. *A Time of Little Choice: The Disintegration of Tribal Culture in the San Francisco Bay Area, 1769–1810.* Menlo Park CA: Ballena, 1995.

Milliken, Randall, Laurence H. Shoup, and Beverly R. Ortiz. *Ohlone/Costanoan Indians of the San Francisco Peninsula and Their Neighbors, Yesterday and Today.* San Francisco: National Park Service, Golden Gate National Recreation Area, 2009.

Miranda, Deborah A. *Bad Indians: A Tribal Memoir.* Berkeley CA: Heyday, 2013.

———. "Extermination of the *Joyas*: Gendercide in Spanish California." *GLQ: A Journal of Lesbian and Gay Studies* 16, nos. 1–2 (2010): 253–84. https://doi.org/10.1215/10642684-2009-022.

———. "'Saying the Padre Had Grabbed Her': Rape Is the Weapon, Story Is the Cure." *Intertexts* 14, no. 2 (2011): 93–112. https://doi.org/10.1353/itx.2011.0005.

———. "'They Were Tough, Those Old Women before Us': The Power of Gossip in Isabel Meadows's Narratives." *Biography* 39, no. 3 (2016): 373–401. https://doi.org/10.1353/bio.2016.0047.

Miranda, Gloria E. "Racial and Cultural Dimensions of 'Gente de Razón' Status in Spanish and Mexican California." *Southern California Quarterly* 70, no. 3 (1988): 265–78. https://doi.org/10.2307/41171310.

Moes, Robert J. "Manuel Quijano and Waning Spanish California." *California History* 67, no. 2 (June 1988): 78–93. https://doi.org/10.2307/25177243.

Mofras, Eugène Duflot de. *Exploration du territoire de l'Orégon, des Californies et de la mer Vermeille, exécutée pendant les années 1840, 1841 et 1842: ouvrage publié par ordre du roi, sous les auspices de M. le maréchal Soult, duc de Dalmatie ... et de M. le Ministre des affaires étrangères.* Paris: Arthus Bertrand, 1844.

Monroy, Douglas. *Thrown among Strangers: The Making of Mexican Culture in Frontier California.* Berkeley: University of California Press, 1995.

Montes, Amelia María de la Luz. "See How I Am Received: Nationalism, Race, and Gender in *Who Would Have Thought It?*" In *Decolonial Voices: Chicana and Chicano Cultural Studies in the 21st Century*, edited by Arturo J. Aldama and Naomi Helena Quiñonez, 177–94. Bloomington: Indiana University Press, 2002.

Monterey Diocese Chancery Archives, Monterey CA.

Montoya, María E. *Translating Property: The Maxwell Land Grant and the Conflict over Land in the American West, 1840–1900.* Berkeley: University of California Press, 2002.

Mora-Torres, Gregorio, ed. and trans. *Californio Voices: The Oral Memoirs of José María Amador and Lorenzo Asisara.* Denton: University of North Texas Press, 2005.

Morgensen, Scott Lauria. *Spaces between Us: Queer Settler Colonialism and Indigenous Decolonization.* First Peoples: New Directions in Indigenous Studies. Minneapolis: University of Minnesota Press, 2011.

Morrissey, Robert Michael. "Kaskaskia Social Network: Kinship and Assimilation in the French-Illinois Borderlands, 1695–1735." *William and Mary Quarterly* 70, no. 1 (2013): 103–46. https://doi.org/10.5309/willmaryquar.70.1.0103.

Mt. Pleasant, Alyssa, Caroline Wigginton, and Kelly Wisecup. "Materials and Methods in Native American and Indigenous Studies: Completing the Turn." *William and Mary Quarterly* 75, no. 2 (2018): 207. https://doi.org/10.5309/willmaryquar.75.2.0207.

Muñoz, Fray Pedro, Robert Glass Cleland, and Haydée Noya. "The Gabriel Moraga Expedition of 1806: The Diary of Fray Pedro Muñoz." *Huntington Library Quarterly* 9, no. 3 (1946): 223–48. https://doi.org/10.2307/3816007.

Newell, Quincy D. *Constructing Lives at Mission San Francisco: The Making of Mexican Culture in Frontier California.* Albuquerque: University of New Mexico Press, 2009.

Nunis, Doyce B., Jr. "The 1811 San Diego Trial of the Mission Indian Nazario." *W. Legal History* 4 (1991): 47–58.

———. *The Trials of Isaac Graham.* Vol. 7: *Famous California Trials.* Los Angeles: Dawson's, 1967.

Nunis, Doyce B., Jr., and Edward D. Castillo. "California Mission Indians: Two Perspectives." *California History* 70, no. 2 (Summer 1991): 206–15. https://doi.org/10.2307/25177268.

O'Brien, Jean M. *Firsting and Lasting: Writing Indians Out of Existence in New England*. Minneapolis: University of Minnesota Press, 2010.

O'Hara, Matthew D. *A Flock Divided: Race, Religion, and Politics in Mexico, 1749–1857*. Durham NC: Duke University Press, 2010.

O'Neil, Stephen. *The Acjachemen (Juaneño) Indians of Coastal Southern California*. Malki Museum Brochure, no. 5. Banning CA: Malki-Ballena, 2014.

Orozco, Patrick, and Lois Robin. "I'm an Indian, but Who Am I?." *Journal of California and Great Basin Anthropology* 17, no. 1 (1995): 18–27.

Ortiz, Beverly R. "Chocheño and Rumsen Narratives: A Comparison." In *The Ohlone Past and Present: Native Americans of the San Francisco Bay Region*, edited by Lowell John Bean, 99–163. Menlo Park CA: Ballena, 1994.

Osio, Antonio María. *The History of Alta California: A Memoir of Mexican California*. Edited and translated by Rose Marie Beebe and Robert M. Senkewicz. Madison: University of Wisconsin Press, 1996.

Ostler, Jeffrey. "Locating Settler Colonialism in Early American History." *William and Mary Quarterly* 76, no. 3 (July 2019): 443–50. https://doi.org/10.5309/willmaryquar.76.3.0443.

Owensby, Brian Philip. *Empire of Law and Indian Justice in Colonial Mexico*. Stanford CA: Stanford University Press, 2008.

Palóu, Francisco. *The Life and Apostolic Labors of the Venerable Father Junípero Serra*. Edited and translated by George Wharton James. Pasadena CA: Private Press of George Wharton James, 1913.

Panich, Lee M. "After Saint Serra: Unearthing Indigenous Histories at the California Missions." *Journal of Social Archaeology* 16, no. 2 (2016): 238–58. https://doi.org/10.1177/1469605316639799.

———. "Archaeologies of Persistence: Reconsidering the Legacies of Colonialism in Native North America." *American Antiquity* 78 (2013): 105–22. https://doi.org/10.7183/0002-7316.78.1.105.

———. "Beyond the Colonial Curtain: Investigating Indigenous Use of Obsidian in Spanish California through the pXRF Analysis of Artifacts from Mission Santa Clara." *Journal of Archaeological Science: Reports* 5 (2016): 521–30. https://doi.org/10.1016/j.jasrep.2016.01.008.

———. "Indigenous Vaqueros in Colonial California: Labor, Identity, and Autonomy." In *Foreign Objects: Rethinking Indigenous Consumption in American Archaeology*, edited by Craig N. Cipolla, 187–203. Tucson: University of Arizona Press, 2017.

———. *Narratives of Persistence: Indigenous Negotiations of Colonialism in Alta and Baja California*. Tucson: University of Arizona Press, 2020.

———. "Native American Consumption of Shell and Glass Beads at Mission Santa Clara de Asís." *American Antiquity* 74, no. 4 (2014): 730–48. https://doi.org/10.7183/0002-7316.79.4.730.

Panich, Lee M., and Tsim D. Schneider. "Expanding Mission Archaeology: A Landscape Approach to Indigenous Autonomy in Colonial California." *Journal of Anthropological Archaeology* 40 (2015): 48–58. https://doi.org/10.1016/j.jaa.2015.05.006.

Panich, Lee M., and Tsim Schneider, eds. *Indigenous Landscapes and Spanish Missions: New Perspectives from Archaeology and Ethnohistory*. Tucson: University of Arizona Press, 2014.

Peelo, Sarah M. Ginn. "Baptism among the Salinan Neophytes of Mission San Antonio de Padua: Investigating the Ecological Hypothesis." *Ethnohistory* 56, no. 4 (2009): 589–624. https://doi.org/10.1215/00141801-2009-023.

———. "Creating Community in Spanish California: An Investigation of California Plainwares." PhD diss., University of California, Santa Cruz, 2009.

———. "The Creation of a Carmeleño Identity: Marriage Practices in the Indian Village at Mission San Carlos Borromeo Del Río Carmel." *Journal of California and Great Basin Anthropology* 30, no. 2 (2010): 117–39.

Peelo, Sarah, Lee M. Panich, Christina Spellman, John Ellison, and Stella D'Oro. "Marriage and Death in the Neophyte Village at Mission Santa Clara: Preservation of Ancestral and Elite Communities." In *Forging Communities in Colonial Alta California: The Archaeology of Indigenous-Colonial Interactions in the Americas*, edited by Kathleen L. Hull and John G. Douglass, 162–90. Tucson: University of Arizona Press, 2018.

Perez, Cornelio. "Reminiscences of Cornelio Perez." Translated by Phil Reader. *Santa Cruz History Journal* 3 (1997): 122–23.

Phillips, George Harwood. *Bringing Them under Subjection: California's Tejón Indian Reservation and Beyond, 1852–1864*. Lincoln: University of Nebraska Press, 2004.

———. *Chiefs and Challengers: Indian Resistance and Cooperation in Southern California, 1769–1906*. Norman: University of Oklahoma Press, 1975.

———. *Indians and Indian Agents: The Origins of the Reservation System in California, 1849–1852*. Norman: University of Oklahoma Press, 1997.

———. *Indians and Intruders in Central California, 1769–1849*. Norman: University of Oklahoma Press, 1993.

———. *Indians of the Tulares: Adaptation, Relocation, and Subjugation in Central California, 1771–1917*. Temecula CA: Great Oak, 2016.

——— . *Vineyards and Vaqueros: Indian Labor and the Economic Expansion of Los Angeles, 1771–1877*. Vol. 1 of *Before Gold: California under Spain and Mexico*. Norman OK: Arthur H. Clark, 2010.

Pilling, Arnold R. "The Archeological Implications of an Annual Coastal Visit for Certain Yokuts Groups." *American Anthropologist* 52, no. 3 (July–September 1950): 438–40. https://doi.org/10.1525/aa.1950.52.3.02a00350.

Pinart, Alphonse. *California Indian Linguistic Records: The Mission Indian Vocabularies of Alphonse Pinart*. Edited by Robert F. Heizer. Berkeley: University of California Press, 1952.

Pitt, Leonard. *The Decline of the Californios: A Social History of the Spanish-Speaking Californians, 1846–1890*. Berkeley: University of California Press, 1966.

Pokriots, Marion D. "Don Jose Antonio Bolcoff: Branciforte's Russian Alcalde." *Santa Cruz History Journal* 3 (1997): 97–107. Special Branciforte edition. Santa Cruz County Historical Trust.

Porter, Joy. *Native American Environmentalism: Land, Spirit, and the Idea of Wilderness*. Lincoln: University of Nebraska Press, 2014.

Powell, Ronald G. "The Castros of Soquel." 11 vols. Unpublished manuscript, on file at McHenry Library, University of California, Santa Cruz, 1994.

Praet, Istvan. "Shamanism and Ritual in South America: An Inquiry into Amerindian Shape-Shifting." *Journal of the Royal Anthropological Institute* 15, no. 4 (December 2009): 737–54. https://doi.org/10.1111/j.1467-9655.2009.01582.x.

Prago, Albert. *Strangers in Their Own Land: A History of Mexican-Americans*. New York: Four Winds Press, 1973.

Preston, William. "Serpent in Eden: Dispersal of Foreign Diseases into Pre-Mission California." *Journal of California and Great Basin Anthropology* 18 (1996): 2–37.

Pubols, Louise. "Becoming Californio: Jokes, Broadsides, and a Slap in the Face." In *Alta California: Peoples in Motion, Identities in Formation, 1769–1850*, edited by S. W. Hackel, 131–56. Berkeley: University of California Press, 2010.

——— . *The Father of All: The de La Guerra Family, Power, and Patriarchy in Mexican California*. Berkeley: University of California Press, 2009.

Quijano, Anibal. "Coloniality of Power, Eurocentrism, and Latin America." *Nepantla: Views from the South* 1 (2000): 533–80. https://doi.org/10.1177/0268580900015002005.

Radding Murrieta, Cynthia. *Wandering Peoples: Colonialism, Ethnic Spaces, and Ecological Frontiers in Northwestern Mexico, 1700–1850*. Durham NC: Duke University Press, 1997.

Radin, M., and W. R. Benson. "The Stone and Kelsey 'Massacre' on the Shores of Clear Lake in 1849: The Indian Viewpoint." *California History* 11, no. 3 (September 1, 1932): 266–73. https://doi.org/10.2307/25178155.

Raibmon, Paige Sylvia. *Authentic Indians: Episodes of Encounter from the Late-Nineteenth-Century Northwest Coast.* Durham NC: Duke University Press, 2005.

Ramirez, Alex O., and Linda Yamane. *Tjatjakiymatchan (Coyote): A Legend from Carmel Valley.* Berkeley CA: Oyate, 1995.

Ramirez, Renya K. *Native Hubs: Culture, Community, and Belonging in Silicon Valley and Beyond.* Durham NC: Duke University Press, 2007.

Ramirez, Renya K., and Valentin Lopez. "Valentin Lopez, Healing, and Decolonization: Contesting Mission Bells, El Camino Real, and California Governor Newsom." *Latin American and Latinx Visual Culture* 2, no. 3 (July 1, 2020): 91–98. https://doi.org/10.1525/lavc.2020.2.3.91.

Rawls, James J. *Indians of California: The Changing Image.* Norman: University of Oklahoma Press, 1986.

Reader, Phil. "Branciforte History Chronology." *Santa Cruz History Journal* 3 (1997): 13–16.

———. *A Brief History of the Pajaro Property Protective Society: Vigilantism in the Pajaro Valley during the 19th Century.* Santa Cruz CA: Cliffside, 1995.

———. *"Charole"—The Life of Branciforte Bandido Faustino Lorenzana.* Santa Cruz CA: Cliffside, 1991.

———. *Harlots and Whorehouses: Stories of the World's Oldest Profession in 19th-Century Santa Cruz County.* Santa Cruz CA: Cliffside, 1991.

———. "History of Villa de Branciforte." *Santa Cruz History Journal* 3 (1997): 17–28.

———. "The 'Missing' Pioneers." *Santa Cruz County History Journal* 4 (1998): 12–19.

———. "Voices of the Heart: Memorial Poems from the Diphtheria Epidemic of 1876–78." Santa Cruz CA: Cliffside, 1993. https://history.santacruzpl.org/omeka/files/original/fdc762725dadde9d2a3f3f9c80cc29ee.pdf.

Reséndez, Andrés. *Changing National Identities at the Frontier: Texas and New Mexico, 1800–1850.* New York: Cambridge University Press, 2005.

———. "North American Peonage." *Journal of the Civil War Era* 7, no. 4 (2017): 597–619. https://doi.org/10.1353/cwe.2017.0084.

Rex Galindo, David. *To Sin No More: Franciscans and Conversion in the Hispanic World, 1683–1830.* Stanford CA: Stanford University Press, 2018.

Reyes, Bárbara O. *Private Women, Public Lives: Gender and the Missions of the Californias.* Austin: University of Texas Press, 2009.

Risling Baldy, Cutcha. *We Are Dancing for You: Native Feminisms and the Revitalization of Women's Coming-of-Age Ceremonies.* Seattle: University of Washington Press, 2018.

Rivera Andía, Juan Javier, ed. *Non-Humans in Amerindian South America: Ethnographies of Indigenous Cosmologies, Rituals and Songs.* EASA Series 37. New York: Berghahn, 2019.

Rizzo, Martin. "The Americanos Came like Hungry Wolves: Ethnogenesis and Land Loss in the Formation of Santa Cruz." Master's thesis, University of California, Santa Cruz, 2010.

———. "He Came from an Indian Kingdom: The Lorenzana Family, Race & Rights in a Changing Society." *Santa Cruz Museum of Art & History Journal* 8 (2016): 21–30.

———. "'If They Do Not Fulfill What They Have Promised, I Will Incriminate Them': Locating Indigenous Women and Their Influence in the California Missions." *Western Historical Quarterly* 51, no. 3 (Fall 2020): 291–313.

Rizzo, Martin, and Boyd Cothran. "The Many Lives of Justiniano Roxas: The Centenarian Fantasy in American History and Memory." *Native American and Indigenous Studies* 5, no. 1 (Spring 2018): 168–204.

Robin, Lois, and Patrick Orozco. "The Pajaro Valley Ohlone Indian Council." In *A Gathering of Voices: The Native Peoples of the Central California Coast*, edited by Linda Yamane, 216–17. Santa Cruz CA: Museum of Art & History, 2002.

Roediger, David R. *The Wages of Whiteness: Race and the Making of the American Working Class.* London: Verso, 2007.

Rosenthal, Jeffrey, and Jack Meyer. *Landscape Evolution and the Archaeological Record: A Geoarchaeological Study of the Southern Santa Clara Valley and Surrounding Regions.* Davis: Center for Archaeological Research, Department of Anthropology, University of California, 2004.

Rosenthal, Nicolas G. *Reimagining Indian Country: Native American Migration and Identity in Twentieth-Century Los Angeles.* Chapel Hill: University of North Carolina Press, 2012.

———. "Rewriting the Narrative: American Indian Artists in California, 1960s–1980s." *Western Historical Quarterly* 49, no. 4 (October 1, 2018): 409–36. https://doi.org/10.1093/whq/why109.

Ross Browne, J. *Report of the Debates in the Constitutional Convention of California, on the Formation of the State Constitution, in September and October, 1849.* Washington DC: J. T. Towers, 1850.

Roy, Aurelie. "The Tongva People." In *East of East: The Making of Greater El Monte*, edited by Romeo Guzmán, Caribbean Fragoza, Alex Sayf Cummings, and Ryan Reft, 17–25. New Brunswick NJ: Rutgers University Press, 2020.

Salomon, Carlos. "Secularization in California: Pío Pico at Mission San Luis Rey." *Southern California Quarterly* 89, no. 4 (2007): 349–71. https://doi.org/10.2307/41172390.

Sánchez, Rosaura. *Telling Identities: The Californio Testimonios.* Minneapolis: University of Minnesota Press, 1995.
Sandos, James A. "Between Crucifix and Land: Indian-White Relations in California, 1769–1848." In *Contested Eden: California before the Gold Rush*, edited by Ramón A. Gutiérrez and Richard J. Orsi, 196–229. Berkeley: University of California Press, 1998.
———. *Converting California: Indians and Franciscans in the Missions.* New Haven CT: Yale University Press, 2004.
———. "Identity through Music: Choristers at Missions San Jose and San Juan Bautista." In *Alta California: Peoples in Motion, Identities in Formation, 1769–1850*, edited by S. W. Hackel, 111–30. Berkeley: University of California Press, 2010.
———. "Levantamiento! The 1824 Chumash Uprising." *Californians* 5 (1987): 8–20.
———. "Levantamiento! The 1824 Chumash Uprising Reconsidered." *Southern California Quarterly* 67 (1985): 109–33.
Sandos, James A., and Patricia B. Sandos. "Early California Reconsidered: Mexicans, Anglos, and Indians at Mission San José." *Pacific Historical Review* 83, no. 4 (November 2014): 592–625. https://doi.org/10.1525/phr.2014.83.4.592.
San Francisco Archdiocese. SFAD.
Santa Barbara Mission Archive Library (SBMAL). California Mission Documents.
Santiago, Mark. *Massacre at the Yuma Crossing: Spanish Relations with the Quechans, 1779–1782.* Tucson: University of Arizona Press, 2016. https://www.jstor.org/stable/10.2307/j.cttlh64mm7.
Sarris, Greg. *Keeping Slug Woman Alive: A Holistic Approach to American Indian Texts.* Berkeley: University of California Press, 1993.
Saunt, Claudio. "'My Medicine Is Punishment': A Case of Torture in Early California, 1775–1776." *Ethnohistory* 57, no. 4 (October 1, 2010): 679–708. https://doi.org/10.1215/00141801-2010-041.
———. *West of the Revolution: An Uncommon History of 1776.* New York: W. W. Norton, 2014.
Schneider, Khal, Dale Allender, Margarita Berta-Ávila, Rose Borunda, Gregg Castro, Amy Murray, and Jenna Porter. "More than Missions: Native Californians and Allies Changing the Story of California History." *Journal of American Indian Education* 58, no. 3 (2019): 58–77. https://doi.org/10.5749/jamerindieduc.58.3.0058.
Schneider, Tsim D. "Heritage In-Between: Seeing Native Histories in Colonial California." *Public Historian* 41, no. 1 (February 2019): 51–63. https://doi.org/10.1525/tph.2019.41.1.51.

———. "Placing Refuge and the Archaeology of Indigenous Hinterlands in Colonial California." *American Antiquity* 80, no. 4 (October 2015): 695–713. https://doi.org/10.7183/0002-7316.80.4.695.

Schneider, Tsim D., Khal Schneider, and Lee M. Panich. "Scaling Invisible Walls: Reasserting Indigenous Persistence in Mission-Era California." *Public Historian* 42, no. 4 (2020): 97–120. https://doi.org/10.1525/tph.2020.42.4.97.

Schneider, Tsim D., and Lee M. Panich. "Landscapes of Refuge and Resiliency: Native Californian Persistence at Tomales Bay, California, 1770s–1870s." *Ethnohistory* 66, no. 1 (January 2019): 21–47. https://doi.org/10.1215/00141801-7217293.

Schuetz-Miller, Mardith K. *Building and Builders in Hispanic California, 1769–1850*. Tucson AZ: Southwestern Mission Research Center, 1994.

Scott, James C. *Domination and the Arts of Resistance: Hidden Transcripts*. New Haven CT: Yale University Press, 1990.

Secrest, William B. *When the Great Spirit Died: The Destruction of the California Indians, 1850–1860*. Fresno CA: Quill Driver, 2003.

Sepulveda, Charles A., and Mary Ann Irwin. "A Discussion of San Francisco's 'Early Days' Statue." *California History* 97, no. 1 (February 1, 2020): 55–59. https://doi.org/10.1525/ch.2020.97.1.55.

Sepulveda, Charles. "Our Sacred Waters: Theorizing Kuuyam as a Decolonial Possibility." *Decolonization: Indigeneity, Education & Society* 7, no. 1 (2018): 40–58

Shackley, M. Steven, Thomas Talbot Waterman, Leslie Spier, and Edward W. Gifford, eds. *The Early Ethnography of the Kumeyaay*. Classics in California Anthropology. Berkeley: Phoebe Hearst Museum of Anthropology, University of California, 2004.

Shaler, Andrew. "Mariposa and the Invasion of Ahwahnee: Indigenous Histories of Resistance, Resilience, and Migration in Gold Rush California." PhD diss., University of California, Riverside, 2019.

Shanks, Ralph C. *Indian Baskets of Central California: Art, Culture, and History: Native American Basketry from San Francisco Bay and Monterey Bay North to Mendocino and East to the Sierras*. Edited by Lisa Woo Shanks. Novato CA: Costaño Books in association with Miwok Archaeological Preserve of Marin, 2006.

Shoup, Laurence H., and Randall Milliken. *Inigo of Rancho Posolmi: The Life and Times of a Mission Indian*. No. 47. Menlo Park CA: Ballena, 1999.

Silliman, Stephen W. *Lost Laborers in Colonial California: Native Americans and the Archaeology of Rancho Petaluma*. Tucson: University of Arizona Press, 2004.

Silverman, David J. *This Land Is Their Land: The Wampanoag Indians, Plymouth Colony, and the Troubled History of Thanksgiving.* New York: Bloomsbury, 2019.

Simpson, George. *Narrative of a Voyage to California Ports in 1841–1842.* Fairfield WA: Ye Galleon, 1988.

Skowronek, Russel K. "Sifting the Evidence: Perceptions of Life at the Ohlone (Costanoan) Missions of Alta California." *Ethnohistory* 45, no. 4 (1998): 675–708. https://doi.org/10.2307/483300.

Sladeck, Jeremiah John. "Padres Descontentos: Spanish Imperial Policy, Franciscan Decline, and the California Mission System, 1784–1803." PhD diss., University of California, Los Angeles, 2020.

Sleeper-Smith, Susan, ed. *Rethinking the Fur Trade: Cultures of Exchange in an Atlantic World.* Lincoln: University of Nebraska Press, 2009.

Smith, Carolyn Ann. "Weaving *pikyav* (to-fix-it): Karuk Basket Weaving in-Relation-with the Everyday World." PhD diss., University of California, Berkeley, 2016.

Smith, Linda Tuhiwai. *Decolonizing Methodologies: Research and Indigenous Peoples.* London: Zed, 1999.

Smith, Norval S. H., and John R. Johnson. "Lengua de los Llanos: A Northern Valley Yokuts Catechism from Misión Santa Cruz, Alta California." *STUF: Language Typology and Universals* 66, no. 3 (2013): 299–313. https://doi.org/10.1524/stuf.2013.0015.

Smith, Paul Chaat, and Robert Allen Warrior. *Like a Hurricane: The Indian Movement from Alcatraz to Wounded Knee.* New York: New Press, 1996.

Smith, Stacey L. *Freedom's Frontier: California and the Struggle over Unfree Labor, Emancipation, and Reconstruction.* Chapel Hill: University of North Carolina Press, 2013.

Snell, Charles W. "New Almaden." *National Survey of Historic Sites and Buildings.* Washington DC: U.S. Department of the Interior, April 24, 1964. https://npgallery.nps.gov/NRHP/GetAsset/NHLS/66000236_text.

Spedding Calciano, Elizabeth. "Frank L. Blaisdell: Santa Cruz in the Early 1900s." Santa Cruz: Regional History Project. University Library, University of California, 1967.

Stewart, Omer C., Henry T. Lewis, and Kat Anderson. *Forgotten Fires: Native Americans and the Transient Wilderness.* Norman: University of Oklahoma Press, 2009.

St. John, Rachel. "The Unpredictable America of William Gwin: Expansion, Secession, and the Unstable Borders of Nineteenth-Century North America." *Journal of the Civil War Era* 6, no. 1 (2016): 56–84. https://doi.org/10.1353/cwe.2016.0000.

Stoll, Anne Q., John G. Douglass, and Richard Ciolek-Torrello. "Searching for Guaspet: A Mission Period Rancheria in West Los Angeles." *Society for California Archaeology Proceedings* 22 (2009): 1–9.

Stranger, Frank M., and Alan K. Brown. *Who Discovered the Golden Gate? The Explorers' Own Accounts, How They Discovered a Hidden Harbor and at Last Found Its Entrance.* San Mateo CA: San Mateo County Historical Association, 1969.

Street, Richard Steven. *Beasts of the Field: A Narrative History of California Farmworkers, 1769–1913.* Stanford CA: Stanford University Press, 2004.

Sullivan, Maurice, and Alexander Roderick McLeod. *The Travels of Jedediah Smith: A Documentary Outline Including the Journal of the Great American Pathfinder.* Santa Ana CA: Fine Arts Press, 1934.

Taber, Cornelia. *California and Her Indian Children.* San Jose: Northern California Indian Association, 1911.

Taylor, Alexander S. *The Indianology of California, or, Fragmentary Notes, Selected and Original, on the Indian Tribes of the Countries Formerly Called Alta and Baja California, in Four Series of 150 Separate Numbers.* Published in the *California Farmer*, San Francisco, 1860–63.

Tefertiller, Ruby. "Oral History from Ruby Tefertiller and Other Related Research from 1980s at the Lost Adobe, Santa Cruz, CA." Interview by Charr Simpson Smith, July 25, 1981. Unpublished manuscript, 2018.

Teixeira, Lauren S. *The Costanoan/Ohlone Indians of the San Francisco and Monterey Bay Area: A Research Guide.* Menlo Park CA: Ballena Press, 1997.

Thompson, Joseph A. *El Gran Capitan, José De la Guerra: A Historical Biographical Study.* Los Angeles: Cabrera & Sons, 1961.

Tibesar, Antonine, ed. and trans. *The Writings of Junípero Serra.* 4 vols. Publications of the Academy of American Franciscan History. Washington DC: Academy of American Franciscan History, 1955–66.

Trafzer, Clifford E., Jean A. Keller, and Lorene Sisquoc, eds. *Boarding School Blues: Revisiting American Indian Educational Experiences.* Lincoln: University of Nebraska Press, 2006.

Trafzer, Clifford E., and Joel R. Hyer, eds. *Exterminate Them: Written Accounts of the Murder, Rape, and Enslavement of Native Americans during the California Gold Rush.* East Lansing: Michigan State University Press, 1999.

Trouillot, Michel-Rolph. *Silencing the Past: Power and the Production of History.* Boston: Beacon, 2015.

Truesdell Kelly, Isabel, Mary E. T. Collier, Sylvia Barker Thalman, Tom Smith, and Maria Copa. *Interviews with Tom Smith and Maria Copa: Isabel Kelly's Ethnographic Notes on the Coast Miwok Indians of Marin and Southern Sonoma Counties, California.* San Rafael CA: Miwok Archaeological Preserve of Marin, 1991.

Turner, Sasha. "The Nameless and the Forgotten: Maternal Grief, Sacred Protection, and the Archive of Slavery." *Slavery & Abolition* 38, no. 2 (April 2017): 232–50. https://doi.org/10.1080/0144039X.2017.1316962.

Vancouver, George. *A Voyage of Discovery to the North Pacific Ocean, and Round the World: In Which the Coast of North-West America Has Been Carefully Examined and Accurately Surveyed . . . Performed in the Years 1790–1795 in the Discovery Sloop of War and Armed Tender Chatham, under the Command of Captain George Vancouver.* 3 vols. London: G. G. and J. Robinson, 1801.

Van der Kolk, Bessel. *The Body Keeps the Score: Brain, Mind, and Body in the Healing of Trauma.* New York: Viking, 2014.

Van Young, Eric. "The Cuautla Lazarus: Double Subjectives in Reading Texts on Popular Collective Action." *Colonial Latin American Review* 2, nos. 1–2 (1993): 3–26. https://doi.org/10.1080/10609169308569805.

Vaughn, Chelsea K. "Locating Absence: The Forgotten Presence of Monjeríos in Alta California Missions." *Southern California Quarterly* 93, no. 2 (Summer 2011): 141–74. https://doi.org/10.2307/41172570.

Veytia, Justo, and Cuauhtémoc Velasco Avila. *Viaje a la Alta California, 1849–1850.* Mexico DF: Instituto Nacional de Antropología e Historia, 2000.

Voorhies, Barbara, ed. *Prehistoric Games of North American Indians: Subarctic to Mesoamerica.* Salt Lake City: University of Utah Press, 2017.

Voss, Barbara L. *The Archaeology of Ethnogenesis: Race and Sexuality in Colonial San Francisco.* Berkeley: University of California Press, 2008.

———. "Domesticating Imperialism: Sexual Politics and the Archaeology of Empire." *American Anthropologist*, n.s., 110, no. 2 (2008): 191–203. http://www.jstor.org/stable/27563982.

Wallace, William J. "Northern Valley Yokuts." In *California*, edited by Robert F. Heizer, 462–70. Vol. 8 of *Handbook of North American Indians*. Washington DC: Smithsonian Institution, 1978.

Wagner, Henry R. "Spanish Voyages to the Northwest Coast of America in the Sixteenth Century." *California Historical Society Quarterly* 7, no. 1 (1928): 20–77.

Warner, Natasha, Lynnika Butler, and Quirina Luna Geary. *Mutsun-English, English-Mutsun Dictionary—Mutsun-InkiS, InkiS-Mutsun Riica Pappel.* Honolulu: University of Hawai'i Press, 2016.

Webb, Edith Buckland. *Indian Life at the Old Missions.* Lincoln: University of Nebraska Press, 1983.

Weber, David J. *The Spanish Frontier in North America.* New Haven CT: Yale University Press, 1992.

Whalen, Kevin. *Native Students at Work: American Indian Labor and Sherman Institute's Outing Program, 1900–1945*. Seattle: University of Washington Press, 2016.

Wiberg, R. S. "Archaeological Investigations: Skyport Plaza Phase I (CA-SCL-478), San Jose, Santa Clara County, CA." Submitted to Spieker Properties, San Jose. Holman and Associates Archaeological Consultants, San Francisco, 2002.

Williams, E. L. "Narrative of a Mission Indian, etc." In *History of Santa Cruz County*, edited by Edward S. Harrison. San Francisco: Pacific Press, 1892.

Williams, Samantha M. *Assimilation, Resilience, and Survival: A History of the Stewart Indian School, 1890–2020*. Lincoln: University of Nebraska Press, 2022.

Wolynn, Mark. *It Didn't Start with You: How Inherited Family Trauma Shapes Who We Are and How to End the Cycle*. New York: Viking, 2016.

Yamane, Linda, ed. "Profile: Isabel Meadows." In *A Gathering of Voices: The Native Peoples of the Central California Coast*, edited by Linda Yamane, 14. Santa Cruz CA: Museum of Art & History, 2002.

———. *The Snake That Lived in the Santa Cruz Mountains & Other Ohlone Stories*. Berkeley CA: Oyate, 1998.

———. *When the World Ended; How Hummingbird Got Fire; How People Were Made: Rumsien Ohlone Stories*. Berkeley CA: Oyate, 1995.

Yamane, Linda, and Dugan Aguilar. *Weaving a California Tradition: A Native American Basketmaker*. Minneapolis MN: Lerner Publications, 1996.

Zappia, Natale A. "California Indian Historiography from the Nadir to the Present." *California History* 91, no. 1 (2014): 28–34. https://doi.org/10.1525/CH.2014.91.1.28.

———. "Indigenous Borderlands: Livestock, Captivity, and Power in the Far West." *Pacific Historical Review* 81, no. 2 (May 2012): 193–220. https://doi.org/10.1525/phr.2012.81.2.193.

———. "The Original 'Farm-to-Table.'" *California History* 96, no. 4 (November 1, 2019): 88–92. https://doi.org/10.1525/ch.2019.96.4.88.

———. *Traders and Raiders: The Indigenous World of the Colorado Basin, 1540–1859*. Chapel Hill: University of North Carolina Press, 2014.

Index

abalone (red) shells, 25, 282n6; black abalone shells, 283; as currency, 27; gathering, 56, 241, 327n166; use in ceremony, 29; use in trade, 74, 316. *See also* Indigenous villages
abortion, 111, 303n179, 334n9
abuse, 7–8, 88, 191–92; of Indigenous peoples by mission clergy, 17–18, 53, 90, 115, 117, 121–23, 126, 133, 147, 163–69, 174; psychological, 6, 16, 24, 58, 62, 65–66, 90, 141, 144, 162–63, 174, 190–92, 266; sexual abuse of Indigenous peoples, 16, 49, 53, 122, 140, 162–66, 169, 220. *See also* punishment
Achachipe, 78, 80
Acjachemen, 8
Acogüen (Urbano), 105, 332nn217–18
acólito, 105. See also *pajes*
acorns, 1, 29; as food, 28, 42, 75; gathering, 97, 297; grinding, 160, 176, 197, 249
Adam, Joaquin, 192, 219, 221, 235
adobes, at Mission Santa Cruz, 233–34; construction, 93, 170, 193, 209, 412n43; Craig-Lorenzana Adobe, 215, 399n66; Don Jose Antonio Bolcoff Adobe, 416n75; as dwellings, 19, 176, 179, 185–86, 367nn122–23, 375n32, 379n56; handprints, 149; San Andrés Castro Adobe, 247, 385104, 421n119, 423n133
African slavery, 170, 334n7
Agueda, Maria, 237, 251
Águila, José Antonio, 150–51
Alameda (Santa Cruz CA), 93
alcaldes, 15, 52, 100–103, 127–28, 152, 157, 161–64, 172–74
alcaldes de mujere, 102, 305n203
Aleutians, 92
Almaden Air Force Station, 282n10
Alta California, 61, 66, 109, 129, 214, 329n194, 369n135; classification of Indigenous peoples, 92, 372n11; elections, 100; expeditions, 173; government, 170, 175, 177–78, 200, 202, 214–17, 371n4, 372n11; governor, 172, 175; missions, 195, 199; politics, 178; warfare, 353n7
Alvarado, Juan Bautista, 176
Alviso, Vicente, 377n47
Alviso CA, 45
Amador, José María, 140, 150, 194
Amador, Pedro, 61
Amah Mutsun Tribal Band, 2–3, 21, 261–62, 283n13–14; activism, 255, 266, 270n6, 282n10, 285n20, 316n34, 319n57, 413n51, 431n65, 426n157; formation, 26, 253; individuals, 128, 149, 251, 263, 284n16, 344n100, 378n51, 379n58; intermarriages, 259

Amaya, Antonio, 185
Amesti, José, 215, 400nn73–74
amulets, 33
animals, 18–20; antelope, 29; ants, 2; badgers, 29; bear-and-bull fights, 57–58; bears, 29, 32–35, 57–58, 74–75, 290n73, 307nn228–29, 362n78; birds, 29, 35, 47, 227, 237; burros, 21; cattle, 15, 20, 46–48, 55–57, 62, 75–76, 91, 151, 163, 174; chickens, 76, 159, 197; clams, 29, 241, 248; clan identities, 130, 290n76, 295n110; condor ceremony, 42, 296n123; condors, 35; coyotes, 25, 29, 32, 34–35, 77, 80, 154, 296n123; crows, 34; deer, 29, 34–35, 56–57, 62, 75, 159, 317n40; dogs, 29, 156, 240, 286n38, 418n92; doves, 29; ducks, 29; eagles, 25, 32, 34, 130; elk, 29, 56–57, 62, 75, 292n90; fish, 29, 56, 100, 227; fishing, 27, 29, 47, 243; hawks, 29, 35, 296n123; horses, 55, 57, 70, 75, 150–51, 174; hummingbirds, 25, 34, 282n10; Indigenous knowledge and relationship to, 20–21, 409n21, 415n69, 418n92; livestock, 56–57, 75, 162; mules, 20, 44, 55–57; mussels, 29, 74, 241; oxen, 306n221; pigs, 55, 75–76; quail, 29, 39; rabbits, 28–29, 34, 56; seals, 29; sheep, 19–20, 54–56, 75, 159, 197; snakes, 1–3, 29, 32–33, 35; spirits, 25, 32, 296n123; totems, 34–35; trade in, 48; wolves, 57, 75, 362n78. *See also* animism; Guacharron (Condor People); Unijaima (Fish People)
animism, 20–21, 31, 34–35, 56; bear medicine, 128–29, 135, 249–50, 262. *See also* doctors
Año Nuevo, 30, 42, 58, 97, 160, 241

anthropology, 5–8, 30, 149, 261, 263, 267
Antonio, Jose (Amonason), 167, 169, 183, 248
Antonio, Jose Miguel, 238
Antonio, Juan, 212
Antonio, Leto, 126, 342n80, 343n93
Antonio, Miguel, 124–25, 134
Antonio, Secundino, 126, 342n80, 343n93
Anza, Juan Bautista de, 76
Aptos (tribe), 11, 14, 26, 36–37, 50, 134, 259; *alcalde* elections, 101–2; baptismal records, 293n91; measles outbreak, 73–74
Aptos CA, 183, 210, 224, 230, 242, 248
Arana, Jose, 199–200, 387n121, 389n143, 392n164
Arana Gulch, 37, 219
archery, 36, 66
archives, 123, 137, 149, 267; colonial, 4, 6, 10, 298n141; erasure in, 115, 127, 167; Indigenous, 4, 154, 261, 289n57
Argüello, Luis Antonio, 156, 215
Armas, Antonia, 182, 220
Aror (Juan Francisco), 106
arrests. *See* Indigenous arrests
Arrillaga, José Joaquín de, 60–62
arrowheads, 40–41, 74, 97, 160
arrows, 23–24, 27, 30, 56, 61, 93, 143
Arroyo del Matadero, 195–96
Arroyo del Pajaro, 93
arson, 17, 227–29, 239–40, 243, 245, 257
artisans. *See* Indigenous artisans
Asisara, Lorenzo, 4, 38, 115, 120, 131–32, 139–41, 164–65; quotations, 17–18, 49, 54, 117–18, 122–24, 126–27, 136–37, 152, 161–62
Atauque (Paterno), 160

468 *Index*

Ausaima, 11, 14, 76–78, 80–83, 87
Awaswas language, 11, 14–16, 26, 73–74, 111–14, 144, 146
Ayaclo (Egidio), 155–57
Azebes, Jose, 49, 103
Aztecs, 95, 217

Baja California, 36, 49, 103
Baja Indigenous peoples, 41, 42, 54
baptisms, 63, 98; baptismal records, 4, 37–40, 52, 65, 77, 91, 110, 203, 219, 224, 232, 241; Catholic, 10, 13, 63, 103–6; of Indigenous peoples, 37, 43–55, 58–66, 76–77, 92–94, 103–6, 121, 125–38, 148, 245; at Mission San Carlos, 43; at Mission Santa Clara, 44–46, 48, 54–55, 80; at Mission Santa Cruz, 81, 85, 148, 153–55, 219
baskets, 1–2, 28–29, 147, 249, 263
beads, 27, 40, 42, 44–45, 56, 66–67, 98, 100
Bear Flag Revolt, 194
bear medicine. *See* animism
Ben Lomond Mountains, 39
births. *See* Indigenous births
blankets, 56, 67, 249–50
boarding schools, 256–57
boats, 92, 99, 262
Bolcoff, Jose Antonio, 145, 180, 185, 193, 196–97, 215, 237
Bonny Doon CA, 38
Borica, Diego de, 54, 84–87, 90, 93–95, 98, 106
Bouchard, Hippolyte, 143, 158, 360n65
bows, 2, 27, 56, 143, 264; Spanish prohibition of, 93
Branciforte, Marqués de, 92–93, 314n14

burials, 13, 59, 194; Indigenous, 35, 201, 249, 264–66; at Mission Santa Cruz, 110, 190, 219–21, 246, 249; records of, 4, 13, 77–78, 85, 87, 89, 162, 167, 234–35. *See also* Catholicism

Cabrillo, Juan Rodriguez, 36, 291n84
"Cache." *See* Lend, Jose "Cache"
Calenda-ruc, 37, 85, 137, 292n90, 306n218, 319n63, 320n73
Cañizares family, 121, 132
carpentry, 15, 95, 98–99, 159–60
Carranza, Domingo, 78, 94
Caste systems. *See sistema de castas*
castration, 122
Castro, Maria de los Angeles, 199, 231, 233, 237, 247
Castro, Rafael "Tahoe," 237, 239, 243, 390n148, 415n69; arrest, 245–46, 407n7, 408n16; background, 245–46, 421n123; fires, 227–30, 407n7, 421n125
Castro family of Soquel, 183–84, 237, 376n40, 377n47. *See also* San Andrés Castro Adobe
Catholicism, 88–89, 101–5, 121–22, 127, 140–41, 211; baptism categorization (*neofitos* and *gentils*), 10, 44, 63, 70, 84, 177, 208; baptisms and "conversion," 44–45, 65–67; Christian doctrine, 18, 88, 121; death and burials, 105, 129–30, 201, 234–35, 246; gender roles, 54, 97, 135; godparentage, 13, 15, 53, 59, 103–5, 119, 134, 181–82, 241–45; marriages and monogamy, 51–52, 58, 60, 88; mass, 49, 54, 163, 165; *monja*, 134–35; music, 188–89; renaming of Indigenous villages and tribes, 13

Index 469

ceremonies: Catholic, 51–52, 103, 105, 122; funeral, 35; Guacharron, 42; Indigenous, 20, 26, 102, 193, 235, 252–53, 256; Ohlone, 30–35, 262

Chachoix (Silvestre), 106, 360n68, 361n71

Chacualis (Toquato), 126

Chaitin (Agueda), 104

Chalelis (Roque Guerrero), 99

Chalognis (Vicencio Salvador), 351n115

Chalon, 35, 261, 266, 284n16, 317n41, 428n32

Chanech(e), 114, 149, 153, 155–56, 158, 159

Charquin (Mateo), 14, 58–63

Chauchilas, 83

Chesente (Maria Concepcion), 120, 138–39, 191

Chiemiit (Egidia), 157

Chitactac-Adams County Park, 79

Chitecsme (Mateo), 120

Chitemis (Rafaela Gazetas), 38

Chocheño, 109, 262

Cholmos (Acisclo), 51–52

Chomor (Daniel), 99

Chuchigite (Maria Francisca), 60–61

Chugiut (Geronimo Miguel Pacheco), 16, 99, 175, 194–96, 198, 200–201, 249; Barbara (wife), 175, 194–96

Chumash, 8–9, 251, 264, 288n49, 346n126; war for independence, 171, 280n73, 281n2, 353n9, 368n131, 371n8

Chuyuco/Chuyucu (Victoriano), 123, 169, 185–86, 234

cinnabar, 30, 40, 74, 221, 282n10, 295n115, 315n24

citizenship, 103, 177, 180, 211–12; Indigenous, 16, 94, 144, 171, 176, 205, 207, 259; Mexican, 145, 175, 178, 199, 206, 208–9, 216–17; Spanish, 92, 95; United States, 208–9

clans. *See* Indigenous kinship networks

class, 49, 214, 216, 245, 249, 260; in Spanish society, 63, 92

clothing, 18–19, 28, 52, 147, 160

Córdoba, Alberto de, 93, 135

corn, 55–56, 100, 160, 197, 247

Costanoan tribes, 26, 31, 222, 261–62; languages, 284nn16–17

Costansó, Miguel, 42–43

Cotegen, 41, 296n119

Cotoni, 99, 104, 115, 164, 188, 259; baptisms, 38, 49, 132; intermarriages, 37, 106; land, 26, 38–40, 92, 133

Coyulicsi, 354n15

Craig-Lorenzana Adobe, 215

Cuc chítí (Ninfa), 58

Cucufate, 120

Cueva, Pedro de la, 129–30

curanderas. See healers

dances, 17, 20, 30, 32–34, 129–30, 252; Ohlone spiritual practice, 122, 262; as resistance, 102, 193; Spanish prohibition, 66

Davenport CA, 38, 132

death, 252; within the missions, 6–9, 65, 85–86, 94, 110–12, 114, 130, 167

disease, 6–7, 36, 71, 156, 239; 1806 measles outbreak, 73–74; 1838 smallpox epidemic, 190; diphtheria, 12, 239; dysentery, 73; epidemics, 12, 72, 139, 144, 157, 173, 176, 181, 190–91, 193, 197, 239–40; European, 36, 52,; measles, 73; at missions, 73, 84, 107, 111, 144, 157,

181; pneumonia, 73; smallpox, 133, 139, 176, 187, 189–91, 193, 197, 221, 240; syphilis, 12, 144, 165, 169, 171, 240; venereal, 156, 165, 167
doctors, 32, 289n61; bear doctor, 34, 128, 249, 424n146; condor doctor, 42; corn doctor, 160; rattlesnake doctor, 33
dolls, 163
dormitories, 53–54, 102, 118, 133, 164, 330n199, 338n39, 368n131
Drake, Francis, 36, 291n83
dream helpers, 31, 34, 288n54

Echeandía, José de María, 172, 177–78, 372
education, 256–58; Catholic, 88; of Indigenous histories, 261; Ohlone, 47. *See also* boarding schools; Indigenous children and infants; Mission Santa Cruz
El Chivero, 155–56
elections, at California missions, 100–103, 304n191, 363n89
emancipation, 141, 190, 242; for baptized Indians, 172; Chumash war for independence, 171, 281, 368n129; Mexican, 144, 159, 170, 177–78, 208, 214–15; at Mission Santa Cruz, 171, 201, 226; after secularization, 16, 174, 176–80, 182–83, 187, 195–97
Enrríquez, Antonio Domingo, 331n206, 332n211
environment, 43, 53, 84, 141, 209; interrelationship with Indigenous peoples, 20, 27, 31, 100, 238; regulatory impacts on contemporary Indigenous groups, 266
Escude, Jayme, 143, 156, 158

Espi, José de la Cruz, 104
Estanislao, 145, 172–74
Étop (Antonio Alberto), 135–38
Euxexi (Ambrosio), 40, 131–32
evacuations, 42, 158–59
executions, 118, 122, 127, 211
exports, 27, 40, 74, 141
extortion, 48

Fages, Pedro, 56, 58, 286n42
Fernández, Manuel, 63–65, 77–78, 85, 88, 104, 148
fertility, 19, 79, 162
Figueroa, José, 178–80, 188, 373n15, 374n29
Filomena, Maria, 229, 233, 242–48, 266, 409n19, 10n133, 420n11, 421n119, 423n134
firearms, 56–57
Firebaugh CA, 148, 153, 230
fires, 33, 203, 214, 222, 232, 244–47; in Indigenous mythology, 282n10; as resistance, 24, 58, 61, 204, 227–30, 239, 408n16–17, 428n21; Roxas cabin fire, 393n1; Spanish prohibition, 24, 281n5; sweat lodges, 289n64. *See also* arson; Castro, Rafael "Tahoe"; Indigenous knowledge; Lend, Jose "Cache"
food, 32, 41, 56, 66, 75, 89, 97, 176; foraging, 28–29, 55; at missions, 18; as offerings, 31; shortages, 55, 67, 72, 84, 86; as trade, 42–43, 47, 98, 264; for visitors, 31. *See also* Indigenous diets
forests, 28, 37, 42, 46–47, 55, 65, 102, 138
Fort Ross, 190, 385n103; expeditions, 82

Franciscans, 9, 45, 70, 85, 94, 96, 106, 162, 167, 170; baptisms, 50, 52, 92–93, 103; challenges to authority, 143, 145, 155; colonial strategies, 24–25, 46, 83, 96, 103, 119, 257; conversion, 66–67; Indigenous violence towards clergy, 121–22, 129; intermarriage approval, 49; missionaries, 4, 10, 12–13, 18, 23; naming of Indigenous tribes, 292n87; records, 5, 77; rules and regulations, 88, 90, 101–2, 141, 174; sacristan, 105; sexual abuse, 340n67; views towards Indigenous beliefs, 130. *See also* abuse; Gil y Taboada, Luis; Quintana, Andrés
Frémont, John C., 207, 387n126, 391n157

Galindo, José Eusebio, 123, 339n43
games and gambling, 33, 35, 69–70, 96, 164; "gome," 35, 69–70
gardens, 176, 232, 237, 255
Gelelis (Gabriel Cañizares), 39, 51–52, 67
Gemos (Sebastion Aparicio), 99
genocide, 3, 8, 253, 267, 273n30; policies of, 203–4, 209, 222–26, 230
gente de razón/gente sin razón, 10, 92, 96, 103, 313n5, 376n38
gentiles. *See* Catholicism
Geturux (Canuto), 101, 329n196
Gilroy CA, 21, 79–80, 146, 220, 225, 249
Gilsic (Carlos), 153
Gil y Taboada, Luis, 165, 169–71, 355n20, 367n125, 369n134, 369n135, 376n38; sexual abuse of Indigenous women, 165, 220, 344n101, 364n99, 365n101
godparentage. *See* Catholicism
Gomez, Pedro, 178, 194

Gonzaga, Santos and Teodora, 247
Gonzales, Juan, 179–82
Gonzalez, Francisco, 104
Gonzalo Jose, 91, 324n127
graves, 157, 201, 222, 234, 264–66
grito de Dolores, 158
Guacharron (Condor People), 35, 44–42, 77, 130, 292n90, 296n123, 317n142, 319n63
Guadalajara, Mexico, 95, 274n39, 326n152
Guanajuato, Mexico, 95, 158, 274n39
Guejais (Josefa Antonio), 183, 248
Guerra y Noriega, Pablo de la, 207, 370n1
Guerro, Don Tiburcio, 22
Gustine CA, 114, 148

Hablitas, Mariano, 233, 411n34
healers, 30, 32, 52, 135
hegemony, 18, 58, 62, 66, 72
Henry W. Coe State Park, 114, 342n83, 404n108
herbs, 32–33, 311n280; herbalists, 135; herbal medicine, 66. *See also* healers
Hernandez, Jose Antonio, 95–96
Holy Cross Cemetery, 234, 239, 413n51, 422n130
Honoumne, 148, 152, 153
Huilgen (Juan Bautista), 106, 334n234
Humiliana, 123–24, 169, 344n101, 349n163

Indigenous arrests, 13, 210, 212–13; Quintana assassins, 15, 119, 121, 124, 132, 141, 143; Tahoe and Cache, 227–29, 239, 240, 243, 245
Indigenous artisans, 8, 95, 99, 103, 160; carpenters, 15, 95, 98–99,

159–60; masons, 15, 98–99, 159, 160, 176, 197–98; shoemakers, 15, 159–60; tailors, 15, 95

Indigenous births, 9, 11, 52–53, 110–11, 119–25; fertility, 162–67; midwives, 135

Indigenous chiefdom, 28, 30–31, 93, 101–3

Indigenous children and infants, 102, 134; abduction and servitude, 23–68, 146, 149, 204, 209, 212, 226; abuse at missions, 118; baptisms, 39–40, 44–46, 49–51, 58–59, 65, 78–80, 126, 220; conception and birth at missions, 162–66; education and roles at missions, 88, 103, 105, 119, 135, 188; fugitives from missions, 86, 88–89; mortality and survival at the missions, 11, 52–53, 73–74, 110–12, 169, 196, 230, 237, 239; orphans and separation from parents, 181–82, 226, 232, 247; rearing, 30, 47. *See also* boarding schools

Indigenous convicts, 95, 98, 119–20, 124–25, 131, 133, 135–36, 191. *See also* Indigenous escapees and fugitives

Indigenous diets, 28–29, 56, 74–75, 86, 176, 196–97

Indigenous economy, 9, 24, 34, 45, 114, 125, 195, 212; Amah Mutsun, 74; at Mission Santa Cruz, 100, 107, 176; in the mission system, 14–16, 52, 67, 71, 97, 100, 178, 249; Quiroste, 23, 59; Spanish disruption of, 75, 298n138

Indigenous erasure, 17, 115, 126–27, 253

Indigenous escapees and fugitives, 106–7, 143–46, 171–74; fleeing missions, 12–16, 23, 148, 152–53, 155–59; as forms of resistance, 71; harboring of, 81–89; Yaquenonsat, 128–29

Indigenous government, 100

Indigenous identity, 10, 267, 270n5, 290n73, 295n110, 354n15, 371n7; intermarriage formations of, 366n116; at Mission Santa Cruz, 77–78; and music, 384n95; racial, 216–17, 400n76; in relation to land, 288n51; after Spanish colonization, 92; tribal, 45, 78, 318n49; after U.S. control of California, 206. *See also* Indigenous music

Indigenous interrelations, 9, 20, 26, 36, 71, 87, 114, 125, 130

Indigenous kinship networks: clans, 3, 34, 52, 130, 139–40, 290n73, 295n110; intermarriages, 13, 30, 36–39, 49, 169–70, 187, 259–60, 293n97, 301n165, 331n207, 347n134, 366n116; moieties, 34–35, 130, 290n76; polities, 26, 78, 107, 126, 259

Indigenous knowledge, 5–6, 66, 11; land management and prescribed burns, 24, 28–29, 41–42, 297n124, 311n280; Traditional Ecological Knowledge (TEK), 5–6, 24, 28, 55, 237, 253, 255

Indigenous languages, 11, 26, 101, 182, 193, 222–26, 253, 257, 260–62; Algonquian, 423n135; Awaswas Ohlone, 11, 26, 124, 196, 263, 290n77; Iroquois, 423; Mutsun Ohlone, 11, 73, 255, 263, 282n11, 284n16, 299n151, 425; Tamyen Ohlone, 73, 262, 284n16, 398n60; Yokuts, 11, 106, 241

Index 473

Indigenous music, 7, 15, 188–89, 192, 252, 384nn95–96, 386n119
Indigenous villages: Acastaca, 78, 81; Achasta, 96, 301n167; Achila, 158; Achistaca, 38–40, 49, 87, 104–5, 133–34, 220; Asar, 38, 132, 347n139, 383n91; Atsnil, 149, 158, 247; Aulintak (place of the red abalone), 25, 37, 282n11; Auxentaca, 78, 80, 89, 358n51; Cajastaca, 37, 78, 45, 135, 137, 292n91; Chalahua, 348n142; Chalamü, 37; Chaloctaca, 26, 37–40, 45–46, 51–53, 120–21, 128, 259; Chalome, 383n89; Chanech, 357n41; Chieuta, 357n40; Chipletac, 41; Chipuctac, 77–78, 80, 88, 220, 225, 317n42, 320n69, 323n107, 425n149; Chitactac, 37, 77–80, 88–89, 102; Churistac, 80–81; Churmutcé, 41; Copcha, 149, 153, 355n23, 357n39; Cotoni, 132; Cutucho, 149, 152–53, 357n39; Hottrochtac, 37; Hualquemne, 149; Huocom, 351; Ippitak (Place of Rattlesnake), 35; Janalame, 158; Jasnil, 405n124; Jlli, 38, 132, 347n139; Juristac, 80–81, 252, 270n6, 318n54, 319n57, 426n157; Lamaytu, 79; Locobo, 358n50; Luchamme, 149, 155–56; Mallim, 148, 153–58, 357n39, 358n51, 360; Matamó, 332; Maynucsi, 80; Mitenne, 23, 41–42, 58–60; Muistac, 80; Murcuig, 80; Muyson, 79; Notualls, 149, 155–56, 158, 355n23; Nupchenches, 148, 152–53, 356n36, 357n39; Orestac (Place of Bear), 35, 74, 78, 87, 424n146; Orestimba, 35, 149–52, 355n22; Osocalis, 149, 299n151; Partacsi, 39, 77–79, 99; Piluri, 351; Pitac (Place of Tics), 37, 74, 77, 78–80, 88, 132, 315n106; Poitoquix, 77–78, 80, 317n42; Pornen, 79; Puchenta, 81; Quemate, 80; Ritocsi, 77, 78, 79, 318n49; Sitectac, 81; Sojues, 80; Solchequis, 79; Somontoc, 39–40, 45–46, 77, 131–32; Sorsecsi, 354; Suchesu, 52, 131, 346n127; Tamarox, 35, 87; Tape, 149, 153, 357n39; Taratac, 80; Taui, 80; Tejey, 154; Thithirii, 77; Tiuvta (Place of Tule Elk), 35, 41–42, 292n90; Tomoi, 78, 81, 89, 104, 114, 345; Uculi, 78, 81; Yeurata, 153, 336n18, 357n41

Indios, 92, 95–96
informants, 150, 154, 162, 223, 262
intermarriages. *See* Indigenous kinship networks

jails. *See* prisons
Jayme, Luís, 280n73, 334n1, 338n40
jayuntes. See dormitories

Kawachumne, 148, 153
Kelsey, Andrew, 150
Ketchum, Ed, 2–5, 35, 42, 44, 57, 130, 154, 251, 259, 266
kinship. *See* Indigenous kinship networks
Kotzubue, Otto von, 82
Kuksui religion (kuksu/kukui), 27, 32, 80, 193, 252
Kumeyaay, 8, 280n73, 334n1

Labarsec (Gabriel), 221, 404n112
labor, 7–9, 94, 172, 195, 204–6; at boarding schools, 257; forced labor, 90, 180–83, 191, 212, 232–33;

Indigenous labor at missions, 18–19, 47, 64, 71, 74, 86, 97–100, 107, 186–87; Indigenous maintenance of natural environment, 55; after mission secularization, 177, 371n4, 373n18; in Ohlone society, 31; in Spanish society, 71, 310n268; in U.S. California, 232–33, 237–39, 247–48; women and labor, 159–66, 303n180
Lacah (Julían Apodaca), 52, 101, 117
lands, 10, 16–17, 180, 202, 204, 218–19, 222; Amah Mutsun lands, 77, 80, 255, 266; Aptos lands, 37; Ausaima lands, 80–81; Cotoni lands, 38; distribution of mission lands after secularization, 175–80; "hinterlands," 9, 276n55; Indigenous landscapes, 5, 26, 28, 34–41, 55, 266, 271n11; Miwok lands, 356n36; Modoc lands, 396n37; Ohlone lands, 36, 264, 356n36; Partacsi lands, 79; Quiroste lands, 97, 241; ranchos, 179–82, 184, 187, 215; Tejey lands, 114, 159; Tomoi lands, 336n21, 424n146; U.S. lands, (Treaty of Guadalupe Hidalgo), 204, 206, 215–16; Uypi lands, 46–47, 50; Yokuts lands, 143–45, 148–49, 153–56, 172–73, 184–85
Langsdorff, Georg von, 129, 306, 316n33
languages, 367. *See also* Indigenous languages
Laquisamne, 173
Lasuén, Fermín Francisco de, 61, 65–66, 70, 83, 85, 88, 94, 99–100
Lend, Jose "Cache," 410n28, 413n52, 415n69, 417n84, 418n92, 421n123, 421n125; arrest, 245–46, 407n7, 408n16; background, 235–37, 239–40, 243; fires, 227–30
Lino, 18–20, 53,-342, 340n61, 344n101; life at Mission Santa Cruz, 131–41; as padrino, 105; Quintana assassination, 117–24, 169, 185–88, 338n35
Llaggen (Angela), 52
Lleguix (Angel), 133
Llencó (Venancio Asar), 132, 140, 179, 187–88, 190
Lluillin (Maria de la Purificacion de Landa), 39, 53, 120–21
Locobo, 78, 89, 104, 114, 155, 186
Lopez, Baldomero, 46, 59, 61, 63, 77
Lopez, Valentin, 3–4, 12, 149–50, 251, 263, 278n63
Los Banos CA, 148, 230
Los Capitancillos Creek, 40
Luchamme, 149, 155–56
Luecha, 129–30, 345n114
Luiseño, 8
lynchings, 16, 204, 213, 229
madrina. *See* Catholicism

Majors, Joseph Ladd, 145, 198–99, 231–34, 237, 256
Mak-Sah-Re-Jah, 25–31, 36, 45–46, 65, 77, 282n9, 291n82
malaria, 12, 144, 157, 173, 240
Malimin (Coleto), 16, 114, 143–45, 153–58, 160–62, 173; Guajsilii (son of Malimin), 154, 162, 164–65, 187
Mallim, 148, 153–58, 355n23, 357n39, 358n51, 360n62
Maria, Jesus, 236–39
marriage. *See* Catholicism; Indigenous kinship networks
Matalan, 35, 40
Maya, 340n67

mayordomos, 129, 179–81, 188. See also *alcaldes*
Mendota CA, 148, 153
Merced CA, 148, 151, 153–54, 224, 241
Meregildo, 235–39, 251, 412n39, 414nn61–63, 415n68, 416n75
mestizos, 91, 95–96, 214, 216–17
Mexican California. *See* Alta California
Mexico, 49, 70, 101, 166, 171, 216–17, 259–60; Mexico City, 46, 99, 119, 124, 130, 325; secularization, 177–78
middens. *See* shell mounds
migrations, 62, 394n6
Miguel, Jose, 213
Miscamis (Bonifacia Ubartondo), 60–61, 308
Mission Dolores, 45, 72, 74, 119; fugitives, 72, 84, 88
Mission La Purisima, 171
Mission San Carlos, 40, 43, 56–57, 72–73, 80–82, 103, 125; attacks upon, 306n218; baptisms, 106, 138; fugitives, 84–85, 89; Indigenous captives, 137
Mission San Diego, 300, 349, attacks upon, 24, 281n2; revolt, 334n1
Mission San Gabriel, 189, 242; punishment, 163; rebellion, 145
Mission San Juan Bautista, 72–73, 77–82, 91–92, 95, 231; abuse, 116, 149, 164, 260; baptismal records, 125, 251; fugitives, 85, 241, 249; Indigenous survivors, 255, 259, 263; labor, 183, 187; punishment, 91
Mission San Juan Capistrano, 158
Mission San Luis Obispo: arson, 281; attacks upon, 24, 281
Mission San Luis Rey, 13, 73, 183, 225

Mission Santa Barbara: attacks upon, 24
Mission Santa Clara, 62–63, 81–82, 120–21, 126, 151, 187, 214, 262; *alcaldes*, 173; attacks upon, 72; baptisms, 39–40, 78–80, 91–92, 131–32; deaths and burials, 234–39; establishment, 43–44, 297; fugitives, 370n141; kinship networks, 125–26, 138, 239; population, 13
Mission Santa Cruz, 4, 9–10, 258; abduction of children, 49; abuse of Indigenous peoples, 63, 90, 115–16, 122–23, 126, 133, 180–83; agriculture, 56, 75–76; *alcaldes*, 100–103; arson, 23–25, 229, 239–42; attacks upon, 10, 13–14, 23–25, 30, 58–64, 67, 76, 143, 229–30; baptisms and baptismal records, 11, 37–40, 59–65, 112–13, 120–21, 153, 203, 219; births, 11, 111, 224; captives, 60; death and burials, 7, 11, 73–74, 162, 165, 167–68, 190, 201, 219–21; disease, 73, 189–93; education, 45, 50; emancipation, 201, 353n5; environmental impact, 75–76; evacuation, 158–59; flooding, 300n161; founding, 13, 23, 37, 45–55; fugitives, 23, 82–89, 145, 156, 170–74, 184–85; games, 69–70; gender roles, 97–100, 111, 126–35, 159–70; Indigenous identity, 92–96; Indigenous resistance, 109, 116–18, 139–41, 177, 210; Indigenous rights and citizenship, 16; infant mortality rates, 55, 111; intermarriages, 49, 157, 124–26, 144, 166–70, 239; labor, 46, 90, 97–100, 159–66, 176, 180–83, 212; livestock, 57, 177, 197; marriages, 60, 96; music, 38n119; politics

at the mission, 143, 152, 154–55; population and demographics, 70–73, 109–10, 112–15, 143–74, 187–90, 205, 210, 260; Potrero del Carmen, 185–86; Rancheria de la Fuentes, 185–86; relocation into mission, 12–14, 52, 64, 76–82, 156–57, 204–5, 225–26; secularization, 178–80; social, racial, and geographic mobility, 187–95; spirituality and kinship connections, 103–7
Mission Soledad, 13, 183, 187, 213
Miwok, 36, 172–73, 196, 261–62, 283n13, 287n44, 344n99
Moctó (Agustin), 154, 161, 167, 187; Cachimtan (wife), 154
moieties. *See* Indigenous kinship networks
Molegnis (Baltasar Dieguez), 36, 50–51, 292n88, 293n93
money, 199; shell money, 66, 100
monjas, 127, 133–35
monjeríos. *See* dormitories
monogamy, 30, 51–52, 88, 287n48
Monterey Bay CA, 37, 158, 263
Monterey chert, 40, 74
Montrero, Clementina, 96, 132, 145
Moraga, Gabriel, 63, 82, 145, 152–53
Mount Umunhum, 25, 34, 39
mourning, 42, 110–11, 130, 140, 334n4, 346
Muñoz, Pedro, 153, 356n38
murder, 194, 213, 218, 229. *See also* Quintana, Andrés
Muwekma Ohlone Tribe, 261–62, 429nn33–6

Najam (Victoriana), 136
Native American diaspora, 70, 247
naturalization, 145

Nenoat (Maria Bibiana), 96, 237
neophytes. *See* Catholicism
New Almaden CA, 40, 221
Nicanor, Maria Petra, 123–24, 140, 169, 185–86, 192, 234, 366n116
Nisipen (Maria Guadalupe Cruz), 51–52, 411n34
nuns, 127, 134–35. See also *monjas*
Nuu-chah-nulth (Nootka), 49, 276n57, 301n166, 314n14, 327n158

Ochole, 14, 23, 61–63
Ohlone, 29–37, 44, 56, 112, 128, 149, 173, 175, 186–88, 221, 223, 229, 261; Awaswas speakers, 15–16, 73, 85, 111, 113–14; child rearing, 47; clothing, 28; cosmology, 31, 34; Costanoan Rumsen Ohlone Tribe, 20, 96, 261–63; egalitarianism, 31; funeral practices, 130; gender, 31; hunting, 29; intermarriages, 166–67, 169, 366; land, 28, 34, 77–78, 264; languages, 11, 14–15, 37, 70, 73, 106, 109, 263; medicine, 32; Mutsun speaking Ohlone, 76–82, 107, 112–14, 144, 146, 174; Ohlone Costanoan Esselen Nation, 31, 43, 91, 261–62; origin of name, 283n13; Rumsen speaking Ohlone, 20, 96, 261–63; social and kinship networks, 30–31, 130, 261–66; spiritual practices, 31–34, 122, 266
Ojoc (Feliciana Ormachea), 49
Olbera, Diego, 59
Olbés, Ramon, 54, 158, 162–65
Olivella shells, 27, 40, 74
Oljon, 41, 58–59, 92
Osocalis, 149, 299n151

Pablo, 44–45, 50, 298n144

Pacheco CA, 77, 81, 186, 250
padrinos. *See* Catholicism
Pagsin, 77, 87
Pajaro River, 37, 41, 76–77
Pajaro Valley CA, 26, 43
Pajaro Valley Ohlone Indian Council, 265
pajes, 15, 105, 119–21, 124, 126
Palóu, Francisco, 66, 288n53, 326n143
Pasen (Pagsim), 354n15
passports (*paseos*), 44, 83, 182, 321nn75–6
patriarchy, 30, 53, 97, 101, 110, 127, 159, 167, 196, 199
Perez, Cornelio, 184, 399n63
Pescadero CA, 40–41, 230, 243, 248
Pico, José Dolores, 153
pobladores, 146, 355n20, 373n19
poisonings, 10, 13, 29, 136, 139
polygamy, 30, 51, 58
Pomo, 150, 258
Pomponio, 145, 172
Portolá, Don Gaspar de, 41–43, 76
Portrero del Carmen, 185–87, 192
Posorou, 354n15
Potrero de la Huerta (reservation), 185–86, 230–34, 239
presidios, 90, 98–99, 136, 157, 191; Monterey, 91, 137, 179; San Diego, 62, 91; San Francisco, 119, 124, 139, 150, 155, 164, 169, 263; Santa Barbara, 62–63, 124, 131, 138, 189, 191
prisons, 54, 240; mass incarceration and mission system comparisons, 18–19. *See also* Indigenous escapees and fugitives; punishment
Puchute (Marina), 58–59
Punis (Bernardino), 199–200
punishment, 7, 124, 139–40, 180–83, 192; capital, 213; corporal, 19–20, 52, 66, 72, 84, 122, 191; interrogations, 227, 240, 247; lashings, 115–16, 206; for mission fugitives, 89; in the mission system, 90–91, 98, 101, 115–17, 162–64, 188; for Spanish soldiers, 48; vigilante justice, 209, 213, 218. *See also* abuse
Putiltec (Macario), 106

Quihueimen (Quirico), 120, 135–36, 138–40, 190–92, 236
Quintana, Andrés, 15, 17–18, 53, 94, 187; assassination, 109, 111, 115–50, 190, 194, 234, 236, 260, 349n161, 368n131, 419n106
Quiroste, 40–43, 72, 82, 138, 255, 259; attack on Mission Santa Cruz and rebellion, 14, 23–24, 58, 61–62, 67; baptisms, 59–60; early encounters with Spanish, 24, 41–43; intermarriages, 30; land management practices, 285n28; lands, 23, 26, 40, 92; resources, 30, 40, 97
Quisuam (Gregoria), 62
Quithrathre, 149, 187

rancherias, 32, 38, 93, 185–87, 247, 262
Rancho Corralitos, 95, 215
Rancho San Agustin, 256
Rancho San Andrés, 182–83, 215–16, 248
Real, Antonio Suárez del, 179, 188
rebellions 3–4, 7, 13–15, 19, 25, 115, 127, 145, 172, 253; at Mission Santa Clara, 62; Samecxi, 364n95; Toypurina, 280n73, 344n99; Yokuts, 145. *See also* Chumash; Quintana, Andrés; Quiroste
Rodrigues, Antonio, 195
Rodriguez, Maria de Alta Gracia, 179, 182

Roiesic (Pascual Antonio Arenaza), 38
Rosuem (Josefa), 37, 46, 50, 67, 120, 126
Roun, Carlos, 199–200
Roxas, Justiniano. *See* Yrachis (Justiniano Roxas)
Russian presence in California, 72, 82, 92–93, 129, 145, 171, 195, 215. *See also* Fort Ross
Rustico, 136, 138, 190–92, 224, 236, 249

Sagim, 149, 356n38
Sal, Hermenegildo, 46–48, 58, 60–64, 90, 95
Salazar, Isidro, 46, 63–64, 77
Salinan, 279n71, 288n54, 383n89, 425n149
salt, 74, 76, 81, 97, 116
Samecxi (Dámaso), 164, 364n95
Samórim (Fabiana Arraez), 104, 332n213, 365n102, 403n103
San Andrés Castro Adobe, 247, 385. *See also* Castro family of Soquel
San Bernardino CA, 79
Sánchez, María Antonia, 345n107
San Diego CA, 62–63, 91, 103; "*encargo de justiça*," 181
San Francisco CA, 26, 40, 43–44; cemeteries, 279n68; census, 387n123; Presidio, 124, 131, 155, 164, 169, 191, 263
San Joaquin River, 148, 151, 153–54, 224
San José CA, 63, 111, 213, 242, 256, 264; Pueblo San José, 63–64, 76, 98, 214, 216
San Pedro CA, 58–60
Santa Barbara CA, 9, 62–63, 131, 158, 171, 187, 189, 218

Santa Clara CA, 28, 56, 74, 224, 266
Santa Cruz Mountains. *See* Mak-Sah-Re-Jah
Santiago, Jose, 235–37, 239
Sauset (Isidro), 239
Sauten (Antonia Ynés), 133–34, 348
Sayanta, 11, 26, 45, 120–21, 146, 185, 256, 259, 354n13; individuals, 16, 39, 51, 99, 176, 182, 196–97; village site, 37–40, 175
scalp bounties, 204, 209
Scotts Valley CA, 39
secularization, 16, 170–71, 174–80, 187–89, 196, 231
Secundino Antonio, 126
Segejate, 164–65
Serra, Junipero, 20, 57, 66, 267, 273, 300n164, 308n247, 431n69
Seynte (Projecto): 165, 220
shell mounds, 39, 285n22
Shomam (Maria Tata), 123
Siberia, 49
Siboo (Canuto), 128, 197–98, 249–50
Sipieyesi, 149
Sirinte (Fulgencio), 121–22, 124, 138
sistema de castas, 10, 92, 170, 206, 325n138, 398n59, 400n76
slavery, 170, 181, 205–7
Solórsano, Barbara Sierra de, 32, 282
Solórsano, Maria Ascención, 2, 4, 128, 263; quotations, 20–21, 33, 69, 83, 86, 89–91, 115, 129, 146, 163, 166, 192, 249–53
Solue (Ana de la Relde), 50–51
Soquel (Hermenegildo), 37, 46–48, 50, 57, 343nn94–95; death, 67, 102; family members, 126, 302n174, 340n54; name change, 299n151, 300n162
Soquel CA, 17, 184, 210, 224, 247–48

Sostenes, 136–37
Spanish colonial empire, 158, 277; early encounters with Santa Cruz Mountain tribes, 36; explorers, 24–25, 31, 36, 41–42, 72, 180; Franciscan, 85; fugitive, 87; government, 54, 93–94, 98, 100, 115, 119; impact of environmental reorganization, 55–57, 65–67, 71, 74–75, 97, 107, 250, 272; Indigenous attacks upon Spanish settlements, 158, 260; Indigenous guides, 105–6; military, 113, 144, 173; notions of crime and punishment, 90–91, 95, 181, 229; Portolá, 41–43, 76; recruiting, 43; ships, 158; Spanish expeditions, 36, 60, 113, 129, 148, 151–53, 156
Stevens Creek CA, 78–79, 318
Sumus, 11, 89, 104, 114, 130; individuals, 105, 120, 129, 139, 191, 229, 239, 243; kinship networks, 15, 77, 81, 128
sweat lodges, 17, 33, 122, 193, 196, 230, 232, 238, 253

"Tahoe." *See* Castro, Rafael "Tahoe"
Tanca (Pantaleon), 52
Tapin, Estévan, 136, 139, 280
Tataviam, 8, 267
Taucha (Vicente Carlos), 169
Tayssen, 81
Tejey, 11, 114, 141; individuals, 143, 157, 169–70, 182, 185–87, 231, 234; at Mission Santa Cruz, 149, 153–55, 158–60
Tili, 354n15
Tipan (Maria del Carmen Hablitas), 51
Tomoi, 11, 81, 104, 124, 128, 186, 197–98, 221, 249, 345n112; lands, 77–78, 81, 106, 114

Tongva, 8, 276
Toypurina (Regina Josefa), 96, 145, 280n73, 344n99, 346n126, 353n11; descendants, 327nn159–60
Toyup, 88–89
transgenerational trauma, 6, 190, 210, 236, 246, 255
Treaty of Guadalupe Hidalgo, 202, 206–8
Tribal names, 34–35
tuberculosis, 73, 228, 304n194, 315n23
Tuicam (Margarita de Cortona), 38
Tuiguimemis (Manuela Yrien), 60–61
Tulareños, 106, 146, 148, 184
Tuliám (Prudencio), 138
Tuquion, 132
typhus, 84, 314n12

Uayas (Bartolome Lopez), 60
Uculi, 78, 81
Uégcém (Maria Bona), 41
Uiuhi (Pajaro), 354n15
Ulaximi (Coleta), 139, 154, 191
Ules (Andrés), 87, 120–22, 124, 294n106, 322n99; family members, 39, 53, 105, 117–18, 299n153, 346n127; Quintana assassination, 133, 136
Ullegen (Aciscla), 51
Ulsicsi, 354n15
Unijaima (Fish People), 35, 76–80
Unijunis (Catarina), 137, 139, 191
United States government, 226, 257, 266
Upejen (Serafina Josefa), 38
Uychilli (Columba), 103, 331n207
Uypi, 11, 14, 25–26, 50, 92, 259, 293n94; individuals, 49, 102–4, 106, 120, 138, 219, 299n151; kinship networks, 37–39, 45–46, 125–26

Vancouver Island, 49, 276n57
Velasquez, Ambrosio, 251–52
Velasquez, Antonio, 251
Velasquez, Maria Josefa, 251–52, 378–79, 389, 425–26
Villa de Branciforte, 69–70, 99, 170–71, 184, 192, 224; founding of, 72, 86, 91–93, 314n14, 405n116; relationship to Mission Santa Cruz, 95–96, 136, 145–46, 158, 164, 355n20, 361n70; residence, 194, 214–15, 217, 221, 395n23

Xuclan (José Ricardo), 191; family members, 385n113, 409n19, 419n106, 421n122; as homeowner, 200, 229, 231, 243–45, 375n32; as song leader, 139–40, 179, 189, 198, 229, 231, 243, 419n109

Yaccham (Emerenciana), 58–60, 307n233
Yachacxi (Donato), 117, 120, 123–24, 133–34, 160, 348nn148–51
Yaquenonsat (Fausta), 89, 139–41, 167, 344n103; family members, 339n48; as political leader, 133–35; Quintana assassination, 117–20, 127–31, 419n106. *See also* Quintana, Andrés
Yguichegel (Coleta), 154, 357n45

Yokuts, 15–16, 143–74, 225–26; abuse at missions, 143–44, 146–47, 150; baptisms, 182; early encounters with Spanish, 84–85, 152, 315; fugitives, 143–46, 148, 153, 155–59, 162, 167, 170–74; Huocom, 149, 186, 225–26; Hupnis, 149, 186; intermarriages, 139, 169, 191–92, 234; land and territories, 184–92, 198–200, 211, 230–31, 261–62; language, 11, 106, 114, 241; massacre at Orestimba, 150–52, at Mission Santa Cruz, 112–14, 141, 146, 148; as padrinos, 104; relocation and roles at missions, 143–76; resources, 74; spirituality, 154–55; village and tribal names, 148–49; women at missions, 159–69
Yozcolo, 145, 172–74, 280n173, 353n9, 370n143
Ypasin (Juana Eudovigis Pinedo), 39, 51, 294n104
Yrachis (Justiniano Roxas), 197, 203, 219–25
Ysabel, Maria, 239–40
Yuñan (Serafina), 120, 123, 160, 167, 174, 237; as godmother (*madrina*), 104, 133–35, 169, 237, 332n213; as *monja*, 127

Zayante, 17, 39, 146, 202, 255–58, 266
Zuem (Agapito de Albiz), 124

www.ingramcontent.com/pod-product-compliance
Lightning Source LLC
Chambersburg PA
CBHW021414300426
44114CB00010B/486